S0-AYD-914

Song Sheets to Software

A Guide to Print Music, Software, and
Web Sites for Musicians

Elizabeth C. Axford

The Scarecrow Press, Inc.
Lanham, Maryland, and London
2001

SCARECROW PRESS, INC.

Published in the United States of America
by Scarecrow Press, Inc.
4720 Boston Way, Lanham, Maryland 20706
www.scarecrowpress.com

4 Pleydell Gardens, Folkestone
Kent CT20 2DN, England

Copyright © 2001 by Elizabeth C. Axford

All rights reserved. No part of this publication may be reproduced, stored in a retrieval system, or transmitted in any form or by any means, electronic, mechanical, photocopying, recording, or otherwise, without the prior permission of the publisher.

British Library Cataloguing-in-Publication Information Available

Library of Congress Cataloging-in-Publication Data

Axford, Elizabeth C., 1958–
    Song sheets to software : a guide to print music, software, and web sites for musicians / Elizabeth C. Axford.
        p. cm.
    Includes bibliographical references
    ISBN 0-8108-4072-3 (pbk.: alk. paper)
    1. Music—Computer network resources. 2. Music—United States—History and criticism. I. Title.
    ML74.7 .A94 2001
    780.26—dc21   2001020867

♾™ The paper used in this publication meets the minimum requirements of American National Standard for Information Sciences—Permanence of Paper for Printed Library Materials, ANSI/NISO Z39.48-1992.
Manufactured in the United States of America.

1211 01252881 2

Contents

Introduction

The idea for this book came to me when I was working with the Opcode Vision sequencing program on my recording project *Merry Christmas Happy Hanukkah—A Multilingual Songbook and CD*.

As my producer and I were editing the keyboard/MIDI performances using the music notation-editing feature, I realized this program was picking up every little nuance of my playing. Every slight off-the-beat was notated as a sixteenth or thirty-second note. So, we quantized. I thought to myself, how could a person who does not read music use this editing feature? I suppose they just don't—they rely on their ear or the other editing features such as the piano roll. This is fine, I thought. Our ears are always the final musical judges anyhow.

Still this bothered me. I know many successful musicians and songwriters who would not know their own music if the score were set in front of them. They cannot read it. And how ironic—a software sequencing program with an editing feature that requires the ability to read music, used by musicians, many of whom do not read music! Perhaps I could help fix this situation, I thought.

Remembering not too far back, I was asked by someone who knew I read music if I ever "played by ear." I stopped and thought for a minute—what does she mean? When I am playing the piano, I suppose. Or does she mean, "Can I pick out a tune, add chords to it and improvise?"

My answer was "yes" to either question, whichever she had intended. But it felt like I was being tested, like I was being asked with a certain amount of suspicion, i.e., "you can read music, you must not play by ear." Which I interpreted to imply other inadequacies, of course.

My firm belief is that one ability, either reading music or playing by ear, does not have to exclude the other. Both are important skills for all musicians. And why should we deny ourselves any form of skill or knowledge—or discount that which we have?

In any case, this experience made me evaluate my own musical background, comparing it to those of other musicians I have known. I was fortunate to have piano lessons growing up, study music in college, and acquire a master's degree in music. One thing I know for certain is, in the United States, there is no singular, standard "music background."

Many of us took algebra and geometry in high school, U.S. history, world history, and all those college prep courses. Yet, we all come from such different experiences in our musical training. Can we pretty much vouch that we "don't know much about geography" only substitute the word "music" as Sam Cooke so aptly put it in his song *Wonderful World?*

And what in the world *do* we all know about music? Did we all take music courses x, y, and z in high school or college because they were *required?* No. Did we all take private lessons on an instrument? No. Did we all play in a marching band? No. Are there music flash cards or workbooks for sale in the children's toy section of the drugstore? No. So, where's the common ground? Simple . . . there isn't any.

Music has not been a priority in our American educational system. Budgets, academic priorities, all these "grown up" reasons have successfully helped us to fail to learn music in any standardized fashion.

So how do we learn it? Where do we go? Simple . . . we scavenge. We find coaches, private teachers, extension courses, junior college classes, songwriting workshops, books, computer software programs, the Internet, *anything* we can to learn music!

Because nobody made learning music a priority for us, we have had to make it a priority for ourselves. And then we wonder why some people bang guitars, make loud, unappealing noises, and call it "music"! Well, they are all "stray musical cats" in my opinion that never had a proper "musical home."

So what do we do? I know what I did. I spent countless hours gathering (scavenging) the information on these pages. It all looks so neat and pretty in its final form, like it was so easy. It was not, by any stretch.

I relentlessly sifted through piles of catalogs, magazines, brochures, whatever I could get my hands on, including pamphlets left on women's restroom sink countertops at trade conventions in Los Angeles. I spent hundreds (maybe thousands) of hours online combing (scavenging) the Internet for worthwhile Web sites.

This book is about learning and teaching music through new and stimulating (and hopefully accessible) means—computers and the Internet. It is intended for anyone who wants to know more about music. We can go to countless Web sites and use any number of music software programs to learn what this music stuff is all about. So, here they are . . . go for it!

And I truly hope this book helps you stray musical cats find a home.

P.S. I would like to extend a special "thank you" to all the people who helped me with this book and who offered their support and encouragement along the way. Thanks for your contributions to the "self-esteem fund." At the risk of leaving out someone's name, I'll just say, "You know who you are!"

1

Song Sheets Yesterday and Today

A Brief History of Printed Music

The musical content of *print music* or *sheet music* has changed along with the history of music itself. Printed music has evolved from the time of the early Catholic monks, the scribes and Gregorian Chant, to its present-day form. Sheet music is a generic term, covering many types of published music, including classical, popular, educational, instrumental, and vocal editions.

If not for the preservation of music through the print medium, centuries of music by the great composers and songwriters could not be performed and listened to today. We would not be able to recreate the great masterpieces of the Medieval, Renaissance, Baroque, Classical, and Romantic eras. We would not know the great songs of Stephen Foster and the Tin Pan Alley composers. We would know nothing of early vocal and keyboard music, symphonies and string quartets, operas and ballets. Before recordings, printed music was the only form of communication, documentation, and reproduction available to composers, musicians, musicologists, and consumers. Print music notation remains an important form of communication among musicians today for computer applications such as graphic music scoring, sequencer editing, and instrument instruction.

Gutenberg developed printing by movable type in the 1450s. Before this, handwritten music manuscripts sold throughout Europe, and did so well into the nineteenth century. During this time, more printed music sold than handwritten manuscripts. Music printing developed more slowly than that of literary works as it was more complicated, and involved more symbols than the letters of the alphabet.

In the fifteenth century, chant and one-line musical examples in texts were the only music printed by movable type. The staff lines were printed first, then the notes were added. Sometimes this process was done in reverse, with the staff lines being added last. Double impressions were done by first printing the lines and then the notes. A German gradual from around 1473 is the earliest known book of printed music.

Printing from blocks of wood or metal was used into the first half of the sixteenth century, and in some isolated cases, up to the nineteenth century. This system was used for the ninth edition of the *Bay Psalm Book* (1698), the earliest example of music printed in North America. The previous editions did not contain any music.

The first printed mensural music was Ottaviano Petrucci's *Odhecaton* (1501), in choir-book format, in Venice, Italy. The printing was done in three impressions, the first being the staves, next the text, and finally the notes. John Rastell was the first to use printing from one impression in London. Pierre Attaingnant, starting in 1527-28, later developed this process. This system, whereby the note head, stem, and staff lines were combined as a single type unit, was used for part books for the next 200 years by well-known printers in France, Italy, Germany, and Belgium.

In 1752, music from movable type was first printed in America. In the 1750s, J. G. I. Breitkopf further developed the process whereby the music was formed from a type font made up of note heads, stems, and flags, each attached to staff lines.

As music became more complex in florid melodies, keyboard chords, and opera scores, movable type was no longer a suitable process for printing music.

Engraving, where the music notation is drawn with a steel point on a copper plate, or punched onto a pewter plate, came to be the preferred system. Engraving was first used for music printing in the sixteenth century, gradually spreading over Europe in the seventeenth century. Venice was the main center for printed music in the sixteenth century.

Engraving was more common than typography by 1700, with the main music printing centers being Amsterdam, London, and Paris. Vienna became the main printing center later in the eighteenth century. The nineteenth century saw an increased market for printed music, leading to the establishment of music publishers and music stores.

Alois Senefelder invented *lithography* in 1796. It was fully developed by 1850. This chemical process made it possible for music to be written on paper as the preparation for plates. Engraving is still used for the preparation of camera-ready copy.

Most all of today's printing is done by the offset process, using photographic plates prepared from copy from engravings, music typewriters, transfers, composer's manuscripts, and more recently, music notation computer software. The use of computer scoring programs for preparing music notation for the printing process increased considerably during the 1980s and 1990s. The improved features of the programs and the quality of the graphics, along with the use of laser printers, have made it possible for smaller print music publishers to develop and produce their own line of products. Many of the larger print companies have greatly expanded their catalogs with the increased popularity and accessibility of electronic keyboards, multimedia teaching and learning aids, video, and audiocassettes, CDs and CD-ROMs.

The physical format of printed sheet music has more or less remained constant. This includes *single sheets* printed on one or both sides, *folios* with one sheet folded in half to form four pages, folios with a loose half-sheet inserted to form six pages, double-folios consisting of an inner folio inserted within the fold of an outer folio to make eight pages, and double-folios with a loose half-sheet inserted within the fold of an inner folio to produce ten pages. Print music formats and terms are defined further in chapter 2.

The term *song sheet* refers to popular songs, including words and music. Songwriters, musicians, scholars, collectors, dealers, and hobbyists alike are interested in the history of song sheets. Many collectors of print music do not read music, and are as interested in the artwork on the covers as they are in the music itself. Noted print music artists have often been overlooked except by collectors, many of whom frame and display sheet music with attractive covers. Collections may include song sheets with unique and artistic cover designs, or photographs of singers and entertainers, musicals, movies, images from World War I, World War II, pre-1900, and other categories of interest.

Early American Religious, Folk, and Popular Music in Print

Religious Music

The earliest examples of printed music in colonial America included books of psalms, hymns, and spiritual songs from England. These included *The Book of Psalmes: Englished Both in Prose and Metre* (1612) by Henry Ainsworth (1570-1623), the *Sternhold and Hopkins* Psalter (1549, 1553, over 600 different editions from 1562 to 1828), *The Whole Booke of Psalms* (1621, 1667), and *The Whole Booke of Psalms Faithfully Translated into English Metre*, later titled the *Bay Psalm Book* (seventy editions from 1638 to 1773), the first book of any kind to be printed in British North America, with the ninth edition being the first to include printed music.

Other early American publications of note included *An Introduction to the Singing of Psalm-Tunes* (1721) by the Rev. John Tufts (1689-1750), *The Grounds and Rules of Musick Explained* (1721) by Rev. Thomas Walter (1696-1725), *Youth's Entertaining Amusement* (1754) by William Dawson, *Urania* (1761) by James Lyon, *Collection of the Best Psalm Tunes* (1764) and *Sixteen Anthems* (1766) by Josiah Flagg, *Royal Melody Complete* (1767) by William Tans'ur (1706-1783), and the *Universal Psalmodist* (1769) by Aaron Williams (1731-1776). The publications of the 1760s added more than 300 tunes to those already printed in the colonies, quadrupling the tune repertory. Some of the new psalm tunes appeared in more complex musical styles than the three- and four-part harmonizations printed before the mid-1700s.

British publications of note were *New Versions of the Psalms of David, Fitted to the Tunes Used in Churches* ((1696-1828) by Nahum Tate (1652-1715) and Nicholas Brady (1659-1726), and *The Psalms of David Imitated* (1719) and *Hymns and Spiritual Songs* (1707) by Isaac Watts (1674-1748). The latter publication by Watts was the first collection of original, non-biblical devotional texts used in public worship in British and American Protestant churches, and was very well received. This led to the singing of more hymns and spiritual songs in both public and private worship into the eighteenth century. Watts believed that the texts sung for public worship should not be restricted to psalms and biblical canticles, as many did not have to do with the New Testament or the present circumstances of Christians.

Late in 1770, *The New-England Psalm-Singer: or, American Chorister,* the work of William Billings, was published by Benjamin Edes and John Gill in Boston. At this point in history, no more than a dozen musical compositions by native-born Americans had appeared in print. The Billings collection had 126 pieces, all composed by him, marking its place in the history of American music publication. The original composition of psalms, hymns, and anthems had taken root in America. Thousands of these pieces would be written in the coming decades, establishing the first native school of American composition.

Billings's second collection was the *Singing Master's Assistant*, published in Boston in 1778. It contained seventy-one pieces, and had four editions. *Music in Miniature* (1779) was his third book, and was a tune supplement for congregational singing. This collection contained seventy-four pieces, of which thirty-one were new tunes he had written, thirty-two were previously published, and eleven were from other composers. *The Psalm-Singer's Amusement* was published by Billings in Boston in 1781 for experienced choirs as opposed to congregational singing or singing-school instruction, with long, complex compositions. *The Suffolk Harmony* (1786) included thirty-two psalm and hymn texts in homophonic settings. Billings's last publication was the *Continental Harmony* in 1794, financially supported by anonymous friends and those who admired him. In early 1782, of the 264 musical compositions published by American-born writers, 226 of them were by Billings. Of the 200 anthems published in America by 1810, over a quarter were written by Billings.

Billings became widely known, and two of his pieces published in England, the first compositions by an American-born composer to be published abroad. Billings did not see any money from his pieces published in collections compiled by others due to the absence of effective copyright legislation. It was not until 1790 that the first comprehensive federal copyright bill came into place.

Other tune books of the period included *Gentleman and Lady's Musical Companion* (1774) by John Strickney (1744-1827) and *Select Harmony* (1779) by Andrew Law. In the 1780s, tune books abounded. Hundreds of them were published through the first decade of the nineteenth century. These included eclectic anthologies such as *Laus Deo, or the Worcester Collection of Sacred Harmony* published by Isaiah Thomas in 1786. This was the first collection to be printed in America from movable type rather than engraved plates. Similar books included the *Chorister's Companion* (1782) by Simeon Jocelyn and Amos Doolittle, *Select Harmony* (1783) by Timothy and Samuel Green, and the *Federal Harmony* (1784). Daniel Read (1757-1836) was the first American after Billings to publish a collection of entirely his own compositions titled the *American Singing Book* in 1785.

Other tune books from the time following the American Revolution that featured compositions by the compiler included *The New American Melody* by Jacob French (1789), *American Harmony* by Oliver Holden (1792), *Rural Harmony* by Jacob Kimball (1793), *The Psalmodist's Companion* by Jacob French (1793), *The Harmony of Maine* by Belcher (1794), *The Responsary* by Amos Bull (1795), *New England Harmonist* by Stephen Jenks (1800), *New England Harmony* by Timothy Swan (1801), *The Christian Harmony* by Jeremiah Ingalls (1805), and *Harmonia Americana* (1791) and *Columbian Repository of Sacred Harmony* (1803) by Samuel Holyoke (1762-1820).

The most successful American hymn writer of the nineteenth century was Lowell Mason (1792-1872). In 1821, his famous compilation the *Boston Handel and Haydn Society Collection of Church Music* was published. Even after his death, *The Hymnal of the Methodist Episcopal Church*, published in 1878, contained sixty-eight of his original hymns, along with twenty-two arrangements of tunes by other writers. *The Methodist Hymnal*, published in 1935, contained thirty-two of his original hymns.

Early American Music Education

Mason played an important role in American music education and believed that children should be taught to read music as they were taught how to read. His first book written for children was *Juvenile Psalmist; or, the Child's Introduction to Sacred Music* (1829). Mason was appointed the superintendent of music in the Boston public schools in September of 1838. Boston was the first town in America where music became part of the regular curriculum for children. Other music books for children by Mason included *Musical Exercises for Singing Schools* (1838) and *The Boston School Song Book* (1840).

Later publications by Mason included *The Boston Academy's Collection of Church Music* (1835-1863, twelve editions), *The Boston Academy's Collection of Choruses* (1836), *The Boston Glee Book* (1838), and *The Song-Garden* (1864), the first graded, progressively arranged series of school music books. The market was expanding for instructional music books due greatly to Mason's support of general music literacy. Between 1841 and 1860, *Carmina Sacra* sold over 500,000 copies, in thirteen editions. Mason had become very wealthy by the middle of the century, and was the first American to achieve a fortune from music.

William B. Bradury (1816-1868) followed in Mason's footsteps, publishing sixty books for the music education of young children and church choirs between 1841 and 1867.

These included *The Young Choir, The Sunday School Choir, The Shawn, The Jubilee,* and *The Devotional Hymn and Tune Book.* Like Mason, Bradbury combined adaptations of European pieces with his own compositions. Over two million copies of Bradbury's publications sold, including 250,000 copies of *The Jubilee.* Mason and Bradbury believed strongly that music should be a literate art, and that universal musical literacy was the way to improve the art in America.

Shape Notes

The first collection designed for singing schools used outside of New England was *The Easy Instructor* by William Little and William Smith in 1801. This book utilized a new system of notation called "shape" notes. Shape notes followed the four-syllable solmization system, where the octave was divided into two groups of three notes each, with the seventh note of the scale standing alone. This system was fixed visually by shape-note notation. This proved to be an effective teaching tool among the nonliterate, semiliterate, and newly literate people of the South and West. Many of these collections preserved the pieces sung in the camp meetings of the various populist religious movements of the late 1700s and early 1800s in America.

The Easy Instructor and other early shape-note books contained a New England repertory. By the 1820s, collections represented other parts of the country. These included *Repository of Sacred Music, Part Second* by John Wyeth (1813), *Patterson's Church Music* by Robert Patterson (1813), *Kentucky Harmony* by Ananias Davisson (1815), the *Kentucky Harmony* by Samuel L. Metcalf (1817), and *Missouri Harmony* by Allen D. Carden (1820). These collections came to be called folk hymns or white spirituals, frequently using pentatonic tunes and melodies similar to the ballads, songs, and fiddle and banjo pieces of the region. For pedagogical reasons, the composers drew on the indigenous melodic tradition of the people with whom they lived and worked, writing and arranging in a unique harmonic style. This included few triads, and many parallel fifths, unisons, and octaves, reflecting oral tradition polyphony, and was an American innovation.

Important shape-note collections in the Deep South included *The Southern Harmony* by William Walker (1935), which is said to have sold over 600,000 copies by the time of the Civil War. This collection was used in singing schools, church congregations, and social gatherings. It contained hymns, spiritual songs, and anthems by New England composers of the late 1700s and early 1800s, folk hymns found in early shape-note collections, and new pieces, many written or arranged by Walker, in the melodic tradition of Anglo-Celtic oral-tradition music.

The most successful shape-note book, and most widely dispersed of the 1800s, was *The Sacred Harp* by Benjamin Franklin White (1800-1879), published in 1844, with revised and expanded editions in 1850, 1859, and 1869. *Sacred Harp* singing continued into the twentieth century, with two new editions printed in 1911, one of which was called the *Original Sacred Harp.* Other such collections were *The Hesperian Harp,* compiled by William Hauser in 1848, and *The Social Harp,* compiled by John G. McCurry in 1855. Shape-note music continued with the melodic style of the tunes from oral tradition becoming fixed in musical notation. Still, many learned this music by rote.

Folk Music

Important collections of oral tradition folk songs and ballads printed in America included a five-volume set containing 305 ballads titled *The English and Scottish Popular Ballads* (1882-1898) by Francis James Child (1825-1896), *Folk Songs from Somerset* (five volumes, 1905-1909), and *English Folk Songs* (1920) and *English Folk Songs from the Southern Appalachians* (1917 with 323 tunes, 1932 with 968 tunes) by Cecil J. Sharp (1859-1924). Though brought to America in their original form by immigrants from the Old World, many of these British folk tunes and texts were altered in the course of their oral transmission. Child's collections did not include the British broadsides, which could be traced to the pen of an individual, versus the folk songs, which were transmitted by oral tradition, although more than likely conceived by an individual initially. American ballads and songs are those that originated in the United States, and are of completely American character both in text and music, and are sung by both adults and children.

Country dances brought over from England became popular in America. The first collection of dance figures published in the United States was by John Griffith, titled *A Collection of the Newest and Most Fashionable Country Dances and Cotillions* (1788). Thirty similar collections were published in America by 1800. Many publications of the nineteenth century contained both fiddle tunes and dance figures, including *Howe's Complete Ball-Room Hand-Book* (1858) and, also by Elias Howe, *The Musician's Omnibus* (1861).

Popular Music

Popular song was the first music to achieve a typically American character, representing a new style that combined several different national or ethnic styles. The first popular songs performed in America were from England. They were printed and sold as sheet music beginning in the 1780s, arranged for voice and keyboard accompaniment, and usually sung by amateurs for amusement in their parlors. At the turn of the century, Irish and Scottish songs became very popular, many of which were found in *The Irish Melodies* of Thomas Moore (1779-1852), published in Dublin and London from 1807 to 1834. These included *The Last Rose of Summer, Believe Me If All Those Endearing Young Charms* and *The Minstrel Boy*. A collection by Robert Burns (1759-1796) titled *Scots Musical Museum* appeared between 1787 and 1803, and included *Auld Lang Syne, Coming thru the Rye, John Anderson, My Jo,* and *Scots What Hae wi' Wallace Bled*.

Popular in the 1820s, 1830s, and 1840s were songs from operas such as *Away with Melancholy* by Mozart from *The Magic Flute*. Music publishers found a large market for songs based on Italian operatic airs and arias up to the middle part of the nineteenth century. Also popular in America was the German lied. Favorite sheet music items translated into English included songs by Franz Schubert, Franz Abt, and Friedrich Wilhelm Kücken.

Other British songwriters influenced the American market, including Sir Henry Bishop (1786-1855) who wrote *Home Sweet Home*. This was the most popular song of the nineteenth century in the English language, and sold over 100,000 copies in America a year after it was published in 1823, and several million copies before the end of the century. Many of his other songs were successful as well.

John Braham (1774-1856) wrote the most popular duet of the century, *All's Well*, from his opera *The English Fleet in 1342*. Samuel Lover (1797-1868) was the most successful Irish songwriter following Thomas Moore, and wrote *Rory O'More* and *The Low-back'd Car*. The son of a German musician, Charles Edward Horn (1786-1849) wrote hundreds of songs, including *Cherry Ripe* and *I've Been Roaming*. The best female songwriter of the century was Claribel-Charlotte Alington Barbard (1830-1869), who wrote *I Cannot Sing the Old Songs, Take Back the Heart,* and *Come Back to Erin*.

During the nineteenth century, living standards improved, and many homes could afford both a piano and sheet music, and had family members who could sing and play the piano. Many songs were written with the intention of being performed in the home, and were arranged with the limitations of amateurs in mind, using simpler vocal lines and piano accompaniments. Publishers also made simpler arrangements of pieces written for professional singers available.

The first person in America to write songs for voice and keyboard was Francis Hopkinson (1737-1791). His *Seven Songs for Harpsichord* was published in Philadelphia in 1788. In a letter to Thomas Jefferson, Hopkinson described himself as an author who composes from his heart rather than from his head. Benjamin Carr (1768-1831) came from London

to America in 1793, publishing sixty songs, including some he had written, as well as arrangements of traditional songs. His most successful song was *The Little Sailor Boy* (1798), which had the widest distribution of any song in America prior to 1800.

Other immigrant songwriters included James Hewitt, Alexander Reinagle, George K. Jackson, Raynor Taylor, and Charles Gilfert. *The Wounded Hussar* (1800) by Hewitt was one of the most popular sheet music items from 1800 to 1810, dealing with the tragedies of war.

Early American Songwriters

The first important songwriting movement in the United States was centered in New England. Musicians living in and around Massachusetts wrote songs for keyboard and voice following the American Revolution. Forty of these were published in *Massachusetts Magazine*, some were printed in periodicals, and others appeared as separate items of sheet music. Many of these songs were included in *The American Musical Miscellany* published in Northampton in 1798, and other anthologies. These songs were derived from English pleasure garden and comic opera pieces, and had limited distribution.

Oliver Shaw (1779-1848) was the first songwriter born in America to achieve national recognition, and spent most of his life in Providence, Rhode Island. Although he became blind early in life, he was a successful organist, singer, teacher, choirmaster, and composer. His most successful songs were *Mary's Tears* (1812), *All Things Bright and Fair Are Thine* (1817) and *There's Nothing True but Heav'n* (1816), which went through six editions in a decade, and earned Shaw $1,500 in royalties. Shaw was versed in classical music, and his pieces reflect the balanced, diatonic, symmetrical melodies and harmonies of the simpler works by the great composers of the 1700s.

Great commercial success was achieved by John Hill Hewitt (1801-1890) with the publication of his composition *The Minstrel's Return'd from the War* in 1825. A simple diatonic tune in strophic form, with a three-chord keyboard accompaniment, the song was very much in the style of the day. The song remained in print for over half a century, and sold all over the country. Its success was a surprise to Hewitt and his brother James, who published the first edition. Because they had failed to obtain a copyright, any publisher could print it without paying a fee or royalties, resulting in a loss of more than $10,000 to the Hewitts.

All of Hewitt's songs were well written, though some were more commercially successful than others. His songs showed the influence of several national schools imported to America. His greatest hit was *Farewell, Since We Must Part* in 1829, reflecting the English style. Other influences included the comic opera style, Italian opera, Swiss and Austrian mountain songs, and the black minstrel songs. Hewitt skillfully assimilated these different national elements into his songs, creating new sounding pieces and not imitations. His most popular songs included *Girls Beware* (1832), *Ah! Fondly I Remember* (1837), *The Alpine Horn* (1843), *Eulalie, Mary, Now the Seas Divide Us* (1840), and *All Quiet along the Potomac* (1862). Because the income from his songs was not enough to support his family, Hewitt made a living as a journalist and teacher. His style as a songwriter was distinctly American.

Another songwriter creating characteristically American songs was Henry Russell (1812-1901), the most important and successful songwriter before Stephen Foster. Russell performed his own songs, accompanied himself on the piano, and handled his own business affairs including advances and publicity. He strove for an emotional response from his audience. One of his most famous songs was *Woodman, Spare That Tree*. Tens of thousands of Americans attended his concerts and purchased copies of his songs. Russell helped to shape indigenous American song, and greatly influenced the next generation of American songwriters.

Early American Sheet Music Publishers

The publishing of sheet music in the United States was well established by the early nineteenth century. In 1800, there were several professional music publishers in Philadelphia. By 1820, there were publishers in southern cities as well. Most of the music produced during this time was of English and Irish origin. Not until the 1830s did American songwriters begin to achieve international success.

Engraved plates were used to print most music. Some music was published using *lithography* in the 1820s, but this was not very common until the 1840s. The development of *chromolithography* made it economically possible to do illustrated title pages. Both engraved and lithographed music continued to be issued during this period.

During the Civil War, Confederate imprints were lithographed. These processes required less equipment and materials, including metal, which was in high demand for the war, and in short supply for civilians. After the Civil War, there was a large increase in music publishing activity. The *stereotype process* made it possible for publishers to issue large numbers of music for consumption by the masses. This period in popular music history is known as the *Age of Parlor Music*.

Music publishers came to realize the commercial value of printing advertising on the blank pages of sheet music during the rise of parlor music in the 1860s. Entire catalogs of songs and music were printed on the back or inside front covers of publica-

tions. By the end of the nineteenth century, lists of songs with melodies or complete pages for the user to "try over on your piano" became standard. Manufacturing companies issued sheet music to advertise their products. During World War I, publishers promoted the war effort by using the margins of the music for slogans.

The *music publishing industry* in the United States was started by entrepreneurship. Before New York City became music publishing's headquarters in the late 1800s, many small music publishers sprang up around the country. For many, music publishing was not their only career. They may have been a local person who owned a printing press. This same printer who printed books, posters, stationery, and advertisements would be asked by local musicians to print sheet music copies of their songs and compositions.

The printer would often make an agreement with the composer whereby the composer and the publisher would share *royalties* based on the number of copies sold. This arrangement would later evolve into the *song contract*. The printer might sell copies of the sheet music in his printed goods store and at the local music store.

Traveling salesmen were hired to sell sheet music throughout a region on a commission basis, along with clothes and household goods. The salesmen would carry sheet music samples as part of his product line, and sell the sheet music to the local music store or five-and-ten-cent store. There were some salesmen who could actually play the songs they carried in their cases of sheet music on the piano.

Some of these salesmen became entrepreneurs and set up their own publishing companies. They wrote and published their own songs, or acquired new songs from songwriters whose sheet music they had sold previously. These new publishers might look for new songwriters to sign to publishing agreements. Some paid a printer to print their sheet music, and others acquired their own printing presses. In the mid-nineteenth century, publishers issued sacred and secular songs, lieder, opera excerpts, waltzes, marches, and études all from the same catalog.

As folk music has survived through oral tradition, popular music has been promoted as published sheet music, recordings, or performances. One of the main venues for popular song during the early to mid-nineteenth century was the *traveling minstrel show*. The *minstrel song* became the first American genre and was rooted in English comic opera. Created by white Americans, the characters portrayed were black Americans. The music was not related to that of African Americans at the time. Tunes were sung in broken English, and were simple, diatonic or pentatonic, with dancelike tempos, supposedly reflecting a primitive music. Music publishers issued many of the popular minstrel show songs in sheet music editions, including *Coal Black Rose*, *Jim along Josey*, and

Long Tail Blue. Many of the song texts portrayed black people as illiterate, comical, subhuman beings. Some tunes were borrowed or adapted from traditional Anglo-American pieces, with the accompanying instruments playing in a traditional, nonharmonic style. The most famous traveling minstrel troupes were the Virginia Minstrels and Christy's Minstrels, whose first performance was in the 1840s in Albany, New York, moving to New York City in 1846.

In the 1840s, Stephen Foster combined the European American and African American folk traditions. He composed hundreds of songs including *Oh! Susanna, Camptown Races,* and *The Old Folks at Home*. Stephen Foster is the father of American popular song, and was America's first internationally renowned songwriter.

Composer Profile: Stephen Foster

Stephen Collins Foster was born on July 4, 1826, in Lawrenceville, Pennsylvania, now part of Pittsburgh. That particular Fourth of July marked the fiftieth anniversary of the Declaration of Independence, as well as the deaths of the second and third presidents of the United States, John Adams and Thomas Jefferson. Stephen Foster was born the tenth of eleven children, but remained the youngest of the family when his younger brother died in infancy.

Foster's very American birth date coincides with his important role in creating songs very near to indigenous American folk songs. The songs brought by ancestors from all over the world were representative of the cultures of their native lands. Although they may have emerged differently, they were still recognizable, and not particularly American. The only race that developed a folk-song literature in America was the one which was brought here against its will and brutally exploited: the African American. The African American spirituals and Stephen Foster's songs have sometimes been confused as to authorship.

Active both politically and commercially, the Fosters were prominent people in western Pennsylvania. Stephen was different from the other members of his family. He was a dreamer and loved music. He could pick out tunes on the piano and learned to play the flute and violin. He began to compose as a teenager. Although his parents noticed his talent, they did little to train him in music. The other family members enjoyed music but felt it should not occupy too much of Stephen's time. They believed there was more important work to be done in their own pioneer community which was beginning to flourish. Stephen promised upon entering boarding school that he would limit his music to a pleasant pastime, not paying any attention to it until after eight o'clock in the evening. Stephen's father wrote in 1841 that his son's leisure hours were all devoted to music, for which he possessed a strange talent.

In 1841, the Foster family moved to Allegheny, Pennsylvania. During the five years that he lived there, Stephen wrote many of his first songs. Stephen's father, William Barclay Foster, became the mayor of Allegheny. During this time, Stephen visited his brother Morrison in Youngstown. Morrison went to New Orleans and visited the towns and cities along the Ohio and the Mississippi Rivers. He brought home with him many tales of Southern life. When the two brothers returned to Allegheny, they went many places together, often borrowing from each other and trading between themselves.

Stephen was becoming more and more absorbed in his music. Those who knew him recalled that he was beginning to write songs. His first song published was issued in December of 1844, when he was eighteen, probably written when he was sixteen. He wrote only the music to a poem by George P. Morris, *Open Thy Lattice, Love*. It appeared in a supplement to the *New Mirror* (1843-44), a Saturday paper edited in New York by Morris and Nathaniel P. Willis.

The song was issued by George Willig of Philadelphia as a two-page song, without a title page, with a heading on the first page listing Stephen's name as "L. C. Foster." The publisher had failed to print Stephen's name correctly on his very first song!

Starting in 1845, a club of young men met twice a week at the Fosters' home. They were known as "The Knights of the S. T. [Square Table]." The club meetings were secret and marked by formal, semiburlesque rituals. Each of the five members had a fraternal name, and was described in a poem written by Stephen, dated May 6, 1845, "The Five Nice Young Men." Along with the writing of personal poems, the most important outgrowth of these meetings was that the group practiced songs. When they had learned all the current popular pieces, Stephen would try writing songs for them himself.

Stephen first wrote *Lou'siana Belle* for the group. They liked it so well, he was encouraged to write *Old Uncle Ned* for another meeting. His sister, Ann Eliza, claimed later that *Oh! Susanna* was also composed for the club. This type of setting was an early model of the songwriting workshops and openmics popular around the United States today.

After trying to make Stephen conform to an accepted and conventional pattern, including trying to get him appointed to West Point, his family decided to send him to Cincinnati. His brother Dunning would teach him how to do the bookkeeping for his commission business. At the age of twenty, Stephen sailed down the Ohio River on one of the riverboats he would immortalize in song. He was much more interested in the singing of the black deckhands than adding columns of figures, which he proceeded to do for over three years.

Stephen lived in Cincinnati from the fall of 1846 until early 1850. He was a good bookkeeper and was left in the office with Dunning's partner when Dunning enlisted in the army during the Mexican War. He was primarily interested in writing music and verses, however, and spent much of his spare time getting acquainted with the minstrel performers who might perform his songs in public.

The type of songs Stephen wrote at this time are indicative of the prominent influence that affected his early creative efforts. He thought the songs of the current minstrel shows to be crude and vulgar but, nevertheless, representing something definitely American. While this was a medium that influenced and affected Foster profoundly, he himself completely reformed it.

Some of the minstrel singers Foster encountered were unscrupulous and took his manuscript copies (which he had given them to perform) to publishers who in no time issued pirated editions.

When he found a publisher to issue *Oh! Susanna* and *Old Uncle Ned*, other firms had already published these songs. It is still uncertain who first printed *Oh! Susanna* and *Old Uncle Ned* and where some of the manuscripts came from.

Because Foster was generous with manuscript copies and because common law copyright protecting the author of a manuscript until publication was apparently not established, the first to present a work at a district copyright office was allowed to take out a copyright.

Of the twenty editions printed of *Oh! Susanna*, some were printed from the manuscript copies Stephen had given to minstrel performers, and others were from transcriptions by those who had heard the song and written out their own versions. This can be seen in the musical and poetic differences between the many editions printed in southern New York, Massachusetts, Maryland, Kentucky, and eastern Pennsylvania.

Foster was credited for authorship on some of the editions of his early songs, but, on most of them, there was no mention of his name.

It is probable that the pirated editions show the variety of uses to which the song *Oh! Susanna* was immediately put: minstrel shows, in some collections of *Negro Songs* as the *Susanna Polka*, and in numerous arrangements with *Easy Variations for the Piano Forte*.

Oh! Susanna is an example of Foster's comic, Ethiopian songs. It was first performed in public at Andrews' Ice Cream Saloon in Pittsburgh on September 11, 1847.

While in Cincinnati, Stephen came in touch with W. C. Peters, a music publisher Stephen's family knew in Pittsburgh. He gave to Peters a number of songs, including *Oh! Susanna,* for either $100.00 or as an outright gift. Foster had no royalty interest, and Peters made a fortune from his early songs. Foster gained only the fame he needed to establish himself as a songwriter.

Oh! Susanna was an overnight hit and was sung by the forty-niners on their way to California. Most of the minstrel troupes sang it at every performance. From this success, two other publishers, Firth, Pond & Co. in New York and F. D. Benteen in Baltimore, offered royalty contracts to Stephen, agreeing to pay him two cents for every copy of his songs sold by them.

Stephen returned to his family in Allegheny, able to prove to them he could make a living as a songwriter. On July 22, 1850, Stephen married Jane McDowell, daughter of a Pittsburgh physician. They honeymooned in New York and Baltimore, then went to live with the Foster family in Allegheny.

Foster published eleven songs during the first six months of 1850, including *Camptown Races,* issued by Benteen. He composed his finest songs during the first six years of his married life. These included: *Old Folks at Home,* 1851; *Massa's in de Cold Ground,* 1852; *My Old Kentucky Home* and *Old Dog Tray,* 1853; *Jeanie with the Light Brown Hair,* 1854; *Come Where My Heart Lies Dreaming,* 1855; and *Gentle Annie,* 1856.

Jeanie with the Light Brown Hair was written for his wife during their separation in 1854. It is an example of Foster's poetic songs and ballads. Due to Stephen's temperament, and Mrs. Foster's possible lack of interest in his songwriting, hoping to make him more of a businessman, their marriage was often strained. They were separated several times, and in the later year, Jane left him when he could no longer support her. He loved his wife and daughter, Marion, dearly and never showed an interest in another woman. He very much wanted them to be happy and enjoy their lives.

In 1851, Foster began to establish transactions on a business basis with E. P. Christy of the famous Christy's Minstrels. He offered Christy the opportunity to be the first performing troupe to perform his songs prior to their being issued by the publisher for a fee of $10.00 on such songs as *Massa's in de Cold Ground* (July 7, 1852) and *Old Dog Tray* (1853) and $15.00 for *Old Folks at Home* (October 1, 1851) and *Farewell My Lilly Dear* (December 13, 1851). Once issued, these songs were announced on the cover as being sung by the Christy Minstrels. Christy had his name alone put on *Ellen Bayne*. These songs were issued by Firth, Pond & Co.

In the case of *Old Folks at Home,* entered for copyright by Firth, Pond & Co. on August 26, 1851, the title page deposited October 1, 1851, stated:

OLD FOLKS AT HOME
Ethiopian Melody
as sung by
Christy's Minstrels
Written and Composed by
E. P. Christy

There is no record of any reply from Christy to Stephen's letter of May 25, 1852, in which he asked to receive credit on the title page of his published songs. Future printings of *Old Folks at Home* continued to list Christy's name as author and composer. When the copyright was renewed by Stephen's widow and daughter, future editions bore his name, beginning in 1879. It is believed that the extra $5.00 Christy paid Foster for the privilege of first performing his songs and having his name appear as a performer of the songs further included being named as author and composer.

The money Foster received from Christy for the privilege of introducing his songs was all Stephen is known to have received for what today is called a performing right. Stephen's income would have been far greater than it was if the copyright laws of the 1850s provided that public performance of a song for profit was the exclusive right of the copyright owner. Had there been organizations such as ASCAP, BMI, or SESAC to assert this right and collect for him, Stephen would have made much more money from the public performance of his songs.

Though they were not supposed to advertise *Old Folks at Home* as being written by Foster, his publishers were quick to capitalize on his increasing fame. It finally came out that he was the actual composer of *Old Folks at Home* in the February 19, 1853, issue of the *Musical World,* under "Answers to Correspondence."

Foster had a comfortable income from the contracts signed with his publishers. In just over six years, he earned $9,596.96 from Firth, Pond & Co. and $461.85 from Benteen. An annual income just under $2,000.00 was adequate in the 1850s for living comfortably. It did not, however, constitute wealth or anything near what songwriters today would earn with works equal in popularity to those of Stephen Foster. The Fosters spent a little more than he earned every year, and his accounting books clearly show debts to his landlords and tailors and money borrowed from his brothers Morrison and William. He continued to draw advances from his publishers.

Financial matters reached a crisis level in 1857. Stephen drew a list of what each song had earned and what he estimated each one would bring him in the future. He calculated the thirty-six songs on royalty with Firth, Pond & Co. were worth $2,786.77. He negotiated with them to sell his future rights to those songs for the estimated amount. They settled with him for about two-thirds of the amount for which he asked. He received $1,500.00 in cash and notes and canceled the amount of $372.28 overdrawn on his previous royalty account. The total sum was $1,872.28. He sold to Benteen for $200.00 the future rights to sixteen songs which had previously earned $461.85.

The following year, a new contract was negotiated with Firth, Pond & Co. He was to compose exclusively for them for two-and-a-half years. He would receive a 10 percent royalty on the retail price of his songs and an advance of $100.00 on each song he wrote—up to twelve per year. This was a better contract than his previous one, but he had already passed his creative peak.

Foster published sixteen songs in the two-and-a-half years of the agreement, earning only $700.00 in royalties. He was again overdrawn at the publishers by nearly $1,400.00 by July of 1860. Once more he sold his future rights to Firth, Pond & Co. for $1,600.00. The overdraft was deducted, and Stephen was paid $203.36. With this money Stephen moved his family to New York to be in closer touch with publishers and minstrel performers. Firth, Pond & Co. offered him a salary of $800.00 for writing twelve songs a year. The Philadelphia publisher Lee & Walker offered him $400.00 for six songs. His income was guaranteed at $1,200.00 a year.

Upon arriving in New York, Stephen presented to Firth, Pond & Co. *Old Black Joe.* It proved to be only a momentary flash of his former genius. Though he turned out over a hundred songs during his last four years, they were not the quality of his previous work. He collaborated more often with lyric writers as he no longer wrote the words himself.

The salary contracts did not last long, and Stephen began selling songs to other publishers for cash. They were not especially particular about the material as they were glad to have songs bearing his name in their catalogue. Stephen spent the cash as soon as he was paid, much of it on liquor. He had become an incurable alcoholic. After trying to help cure him of his habit, and talk him into leaving the strain and tension of New York, Stephen's wife, Jane, finally left him and moved away to live with her sister. Stephen's brother Morrison spent time with him during the last few years and tried to help him. Stephen stayed in New York after being invited to move to Cleveland with Morrison. He stayed in New York with his friends who would not try to reform him.

Stephen had an accident while living alone in a lodging house in January of 1864. He was ill and suffering from a fever, possibly tuberculosis. He fell and cut his neck near the jugular vein. He was taken to Bellevue Hospital where he fainted on the third day, and never again regained consciousness. He died January 13, 1864, at 2:30 in the afternoon. His body was taken by Morrison and Jane back to Pittsburgh where it was placed in the family plot in the Allegheny Cemetery.

Vaudeville

The music industry flourished in the latter half of the nineteenth century, mostly through the sale of sheet music, pianos, and organs. Many of the most successful songs of this period were created for and performed in the minstrel shows. Publishers relied on performers to promote their songs, and even more so as the minstrel tradition evolved into American vaudeville.

Vaudeville was made up of variety shows featuring entertainers, singers, opera singers, soft-shoe dancers, comedians, comedy teams, contortionists, and animal acts. Vaudeville theaters appeared in cities all over the country. By mid-1869, the first American transcontinental railway was completed. Tens of thousands of miles of railroad tracks were put into place during the next two decades. Entertainers originating in New York City could now travel across the United States and perform in theaters and music halls in most of the country's major cities. This traveling variety show, vaudeville, gave music publishers a constant supply of performers needing new material.

New York City was a busy center for American vaudeville with many theaters, barrooms and dance halls, booking agents, and the industry trade paper the *New York Clipper* located in the district between West 14th and 30th Streets. By 1890, music publishers had also started to locate here, mainly on West 26th, 27th, and 28th Streets. Since this was where the entertainers were, and because they frequently traveled around the country performing songs before large audiences of prospective sheet music buyers, it made sense for the music publishers to be located in the same neighborhood. This area came to be known as Tin Pan Alley. As the theater district moved farther uptown to Broadway, the music publishers also moved to be near the performers and songwriters of the stage. The term Tin Pan Alley came to refer to the entire American music industry in the first part of the twentieth century.

Tin Pan Alley

Sheet music continued to be issued in large numbers in the twentieth century, centering on the area of Manhattan known as Tin Pan Alley. Tin Pan Alley refers to 28th Street between 5th and Broadway in New York City. The name comes from the sound made by many songs being played at the same time through open windows, in different keys on poorly tuned pianos. A newspaper reporter by the name of Monroe Rosenfeld is said to have been responsible for the name. Although he did not use the phrase "Tin Pan Alley" in his *New York Herald* article on the publishing houses in the district, he referred to the area as the "Alley," and the noise they collectively created as being "not unlike the sound of tin pans banging together."

Tin Pan Alley gained momentum with the coming of the American industrial revolution, and marked the golden age of the piano in the songwriting world. Musically uneducated tunesmiths fed the fledgling New York publishing houses. During this period, copyright laws were not enforced, and plagiarism was common. The American Society of Composers, Authors, and Publishers (ASCAP) would not be formed for another thirty years. Many songs were sold for very little money, and their success provided the finances needed for the small publishing companies to survive. Songwriters who were tired of selling their hit songs for such small fees eventually became their own publishers.

Tin Pan Alley's most important publishing companies included T. B. Harms, Irving Berlin, Shapiro & Bernstein, M. Witmark & Sons, F. A. Mills, Leo Feist, Inc., Harry Von Tilzer Music Publishing Company, and Jerome H. Remick & Company. Many hit songs came from these publishers, and sheet music became so popular it was issued as supplements to Sunday newspapers.

Some of these music publishing companies were started by the sheet music salesmen who had become publishers. Each of these companies had an office with one or more rooms and a piano. Songwriters were hired to sit in the rooms during the day and write new songs at the piano.

Songs were continually needed, and there was a lot of competition. Musicians and lyricists collaborated all along Tin Pan Alley to come up with new song material. When the Tin Pan Alley songwriter or songwriting team had finished a new song, the publisher would go out and try to convince an entertainer to perform it in his or her act. This process, originating in Tin Pan Alley, came to be known as *song plugging.*

In the early days of song plugging, there were no set rules. The song plugger could be either the publisher himself or a singer hired to persuade the entertainer, the more famous, the better, to perform the number. Once an agreement was reached between the publisher and the entertainer, the publisher would print sheet music of the song. The entertainer's picture would often appear on the cover of the sheet music. This was done both to flatter them, and to insure that the performer would continue using the song in his or her act.

The sheet music was distributed to wholesalers, also known as *jobbers,* throughout the country, with the expectation of orders from retailers. Performers would travel the vaudeville circuit on the train routes throughout the United States, having been booked by Tin Pan Alley booking agents. After performing in a city, the local music store and other stores that sold sheet music would receive requests for copies of the new song that had been performed the night before.

During the 1800s, pianos had become a primary source of entertainment in the home. Sheet music was in high demand. This is almost hard to imagine in today's world of recorded music, where virtually any genre of music can be purchased and listened to, involving no effort to read music or play an instrument on the part of the consumer. During the Tin Pan Alley era, it was the number of copies of sheet music sold that determined whether or not a song was a *hit*, not record sales or a song's position on the Billboard charts.

Sheet music sales rose considerably during this period, and the music publishers profited. Millions of copies of sheet music had been sold by 1910. The most popular songs sold as many as a million copies each *in sheet music!*

Charles K. Harris's *After the Ball* was the first popular song to sell a million sheet music copies in 1893. By 1903, it had sold over ten million copies. During the gay nineties and the early 1900s, sentimental Victorian ballads and clever novelty songs were in vogue. *In the Shade of the Old Apple Tree* and *Little Annie Rooney* were the biggest sellers of this period. Comic songs like George M. Cohan's *So Long Mary* from the musical play *Forty-Five Minutes from Broadway* were also popular.

The advent of the recording industry and the birth of commercial jazz and blues caused a decline in the popularity of the sentimental ballads. Tin Pan Alley came to draw on a variety of new sources, including African American artists and rural American yodelers. The main source of popular music in America from 1900 through the late 1940s was the Broadway stage. From the Broadway shows came many hit songs by such great songwriters as George and Ira Gershwin, Jerome Kern, Richard Rodgers, Oscar Hammerstein II, Lorenz Hart, and Harold Arlen.

The player piano, the phonograph, radio, and motion pictures gradually brought an end to Tin Pan Alley. As sound became synchronized with film in 1926, the demand for music to accompany the silent films was high. Publishing companies were bought out by the film tycoons and transplanted within the movie companies themselves. Tin Pan Alley came to serve the movie, record, and radio industries.

Tin Pan Alley Composers

Sheet music collectors often collect by composer, searching for representative works of an individual or team of composers. Tin Pan Alley composers who wrote both words and music included Paul Dresser, George M. Cohan, James Thornton, Charles K. Harris, Irving Berlin, Walter Donaldson, and Cole Porter. Irving Berlin occasionally collaborated with others. Walter Donaldson often worked with lyricists.

Early Tin Pan Alley composers included Henry Dacre, Paul Dresser, Ed Harrigan and David Braham, Charles K. Harris, Harry Kennedy, Ed Marks and Joe Stern, Kerry (F. A.) Mills, Monroe Rosenfeld, William J. Scanlan, Joseph P. Skelly, and Jim Thornton.

Middle Tin Pan Alley composers included Ernest R. Ball, Irving Berlin, Will J. Cobb and Gus Edwards, George M. Cohan, Raymond Egan and Richard Whiting, Victor Herbert, Ballard MacDonald and Harry Carroll, Edward Madden and Theodore Morse, Andrew Sterling and Harry Von Tilzer, Albert Von Tilzer, Harry Williams, and Egbert Van Alstyne. The late Tin Pan Alley composers included Irving Berlin, Buddy De Sylva, Lew Brown and Ray Henderson, Walter Donaldson, Al Dubin and Harry Warren, Dorothy Fields and Jimmy McHugh, Ira Gershwin and George Gershwin, Jerome Kern, Sam Lewis and Joe Young, Cole Porter, and Richard Rogers and Lorenz Hart.

Music was one of the first professions open to African Americans. *Oh, Dem Golden Slippers* (1870), *Carry Me Back to Old Virginny* (1878) and *In the Evening by the Moonlight* (1879) were written by James A. Bland, one of the first African American composers, and influenced by the works of Stephen Foster. Other African American composers include William C. Handy, father of the blues, and Scott Joplin, ragtime master.

Jazz great Duke Ellington wrote *It Don't Mean a Thing, If It Ain't Got That Swing* in 1932, along with many other standard popular jazz tunes. Edward Kennedy composed *Don't Get around Much Anymore* (lyric by Bob Russell) in 1942. The most active women composers of Tin Pan Alley prior to 1920 were Hattie Starr, the first successful woman composer, Charlotte Blake, Beth Slater Whitson and Carrie Jacobs-Bond. Dozens of women who occasionally wrote songs included Nora Bayes, May Irwin, Anita Owen, Clare Kummer, Minnie Iris, Dorothy Fields, Mabel Wayne, and Beth Slater Whitson.

Popular Song Sheets
without Lyrics

Popular song sheets without lyrics included cakewalks, rags, foxtrots, the hesitation waltz (Boston), Indian intermezzos or ballads, marches, and blues. Also included were dance styles such as the tango. Following are some examples of "music only" popular song sheets.

Cakewalks

Cakewalks were popular in the 1880s and 1890s. The best performing couple of this exaggerated strut received a cake as a prize, thus the name. Occasionally, lyrics were included. Examples of cakewalks include *After the Cakewalk* by Nathaniel Dett (1900), *At a Georgia Camp Meeting* by Kerry Mills

(1897), and *Golliwog's Cakewalk* by Claude Debussey (1908). The cakewalk was associated with
ragtime rhythm. Although ragtime rhythm was established prior to 1896, the cakewalks were the first music to be published in this rhythm.

Rags

From the cakewalk, ragtime developed into a
dance craze that captured the nation unlike any other,
reaching its peak in 1913. The ballroom idols of the
day were the Irene and Vernon Castle and Maurice
Mouret and Florence Walton dance teams. Ragtime
rhythm typically includes a syncopated melody played
alongside a steady bass beat. Begun in brothels and
honky-tonks, ragtime was not originally accepted by
the upper class. People came to love the syncopated
melodies with the compelling beat.

The most famous ragtime master is Scott Joplin,
who composed and performed ragtime piano tunes.
Other ragtime composers included James Scott, Joseph F. Lamb, Tom Turpin, Ben Harney, George
Botsford, Charles L. Johnson, and Eubie Blake. Hundreds and hundreds of rags were written by scores of
writers. Most rags did not have lyrics. The first rag to
be published was *Mississippi River* by William Krell
in 1897. Rags lead all other categories in song sheet
collecting. Some examples of ragtime titles include
*Fuss and Feathers, Chills and Fever, Barbed Wire,
Holy Moses,* and *Coal Smoke. Alexander's Ragtime
Band* by Irving Berlin is not a rag, although he contributed greatly to ragtime music.

Foxtrots

At the peak of the Tin Pan Alley era, the nation
was obsessed with new dance creations. Tin Pan Alley composers complied to the demand. The foxtrot
was the successor to the rags. Some examples of foxtrot titles are *Frisky, Dr. Brown, Tiddledy Winks,
Reuben, Cruel Papa,* and *Tickle Toes.* Foxtrot composers included Lucky Roberts, Chris Smith, Joe
Jordon, and Charles L. Johnson.

Hesitations (Boston)

The waltz was once considered to be suggestive
and indecent, but later earned a position of respectabil-
ity. By the late 1800s, many people had lost interest
in the 3/4 waltz time rhythm. With the coming of the
automobile, telephone, and telegraph was a new
American rhythm. The new century had little in
common with the old country-originated waltz, giving way to the foxtrots, one-steps and two-steps. To
keep the waltz from fading into obscurity, a modified
step called the *hesitation* or *Boston* was born. Hesita-
tions were written for the dance idols of the day. The
Lame Duck hesitation was written for Irene and
Vernon Castle. The *Maurice* hesitation was composed for Maurice Mouret of the Mouret and Florence
Walton dance team. Unlike the rags and foxtrots,

these waltzes were not given humorous titles. Examples of hesitation titles include *Waltz Elaine, Waltz
Brune, Old Fashioned Roses, Love Thoughts, Yes
and No Valse,* and *Valse June.* The covers were also
designed respectably, artistically, and occasionally
with a touch of humor.

Dances

To appeal to a variety of tastes in dance styles, it
was common among publishers to advertise a song as
being suitable for several different dance rhythms.
Tangomania is a typical example as it could be a one-
step, two-step, or tango. Usually the dance step
named in the title, regardless of any other dances mentioned, is considered the correct classification. The
dance mentioned first would take priority. Other
dances include the turkey trot, kangaroo dip, fish
walk, Texas Tommy, snake, crab step, grizzly bear,
airplane dip, and the waltzes, either syncopated or
hesitated. Some examples of one- or two-steps include *Cannon Ball* by Joseph C. Northrop (1905),
Captain Betty by Lionel Baxter (1914), *Cup Hunters*
by Julius Lenzberg (1915), *Fu* by George P. Howard
(1919), *Great Snakes!* by Ernest Reeves (1911),
Melody Maids by W. Leon Ames (1914), *Ole Virginny* by J. S. Zamecnik (1916), *Pepperpot* by Harold Iver (1913), *Pink Poodle* by Charles L. Johnson
(1914), *Silhouette One Step* by Harold Bien (1914),
Thanks for the Lobster by Clarence Jones (1914),
Tsin Tsin Ta Tao by D. Onivas (1914), and *Yo San*
by Al W. Brown (1914). Examples of tangos include
El Irrisistible by Egbert Van Alstyne (1914), *Every-
body Tango* by Paul Pratt (1914), *Pass the Pickles*
by Grace LeBoy (1913), *Tangomania* by Egbert Van
Alstyne (1914), and *Tom Tom* by Rosardios Furnari
(1914).

Indian Intermezzos and Ballads

In 1903 *Navajo* by Williams and Van Alstyne
received national attention. *Silver Heels, Red Wing,
Fawneyes, Morning Star, Red Man, Anona, Golden
Arrow, Iola, Moon Bird,* and others were published
as Indian intermezzos, or short, independent instrumental musical compositions. Lyrics were added to
the more popular ones, and the songs became ballads.
Because of their popularity, songwriters and publishers produced many Indian songs, calling them intermezzos. The Indian category is a popular field of collecting. The Indian song sheet covers are very attractive, especially the ones of Indian maidens. Other
examples of Indian intermezzos and ballads include
Hiawatha by Neil Moret (1902), *Indian Love Call* by
Harbach, Oscar Hammerstein II, and Rudolph Friml
(1924), *Kachina-Hopi Girl's Dance* by Albert Van
Sand and Arthur Green (1914), and *Oh! That Navajo
Rag* by Williams and Van Alstyne (1911).

Marches

Marches were written for every event, including inaugurals, expositions, political campaigns, and wars. John Philip Sousa, the "March King," composed over 150 marches, including the *Washington Post March, The Stars and Stripes Forever, Semper Fidelis,* and *Liberty Bell.* Many march composers were part of the Tin Pan Alley scene. E. T. Paull, Harry J. Lincoln, J. S. Jamecnik, Paul Lincke, and George Rosey (G. M. Rosenberg) are some of the better known march composers. After the turn of the century, march music was published with colorful covers encompassing a variety of subjects, including photographs of presidents and current events.

The Blues

W. C. Handy's 1911 publication of *The Memphis Blues* helped to credit him as the "Father of the Blues." Sorrows were expressed by singing the blues, a twelve-bar refrain with flatted thirds and sevenths. Duke Ellington, Jelly Roll Morton, and Fats Waller all contributed to the blues. Many non-blues songs had a blues title due to their popularity, and Tin Pan Alley profited. The blues remained popular well into the post-Tin Pan Alley era. Blues singers Gertrude "Ma" Rainey and Bessie Smith became famous for their singing of Tin Pan Alley blues songs. Several blues styles evolved from primitive blues. Tin Pan Alley blues songs numbered in the hundreds.

Composer Profile: Scott Joplin

The "Ragtime Master" Scott Joplin was born November 24, 1868, in Texarkana, Texas. His mother, Florence Givens Joplin, was from Kentucky and had been free from birth. His father, Giles Joplin, was an ex-slave from North Carolina. Slavery ended only five years before Scott Joplin was born. The Joplin family led a very musical home life. The father was a violin player, having performed as a dance musician while he was a slave, and the mother sang and played the banjo. Scott had three brothers and two sisters. The two younger brothers, Will and Robert, both sang. Will also played the guitar and Robert composed. The older brother, Monroe, and sisters Myrtle and Ossie were also musical.

Scott played the guitar and bugle when he was very young. He discovered a piano at a neighbor's house when he was seven, and loved playing it. His musical talents soon became obvious to both his father and the neighbors. Giles Joplin managed to scrape together enough money to buy a secondhand square piano. Scott was at the piano day and night.

The ten-year-old Joplin became known through the black community as a remarkable improviser, and rumors spread to the white community about his talent. A German music teacher who had heard him play offered him free piano lessons. The professor also taught him sight-reading, the principles of harmony, classical music and composers, and introduced him to the famous operas. Although his first benefactor's name is unknown, Joplin never forgot him, and in his later years he sent his old, poor, and ailing teacher money.

Scott Joplin's mother Florence died when he was a young adolescent. Friction developed between Scott and his father over learning a trade. This resulted in his leaving home in 1882 when he was about fourteen. His younger brothers Will and Robert followed him a little later. This move brought Scott into the subworld of the American honky-tonk and red-light districts where piano players, both black and white, were in demand. He traveled from Texas to Louisiana, and all over the Mississippi Valley states of Missouri, Arkansas, and Kansas.

This region was "the cradle of ragtime. He was now in a different school: adult education for a child. He met hundreds of mainly self-taught musicians and singers, and heard popular music, light classical music, and folk music, old and new, black and white, respectable and not-so-respectable. It would be a prime source of melodic inspiration for the rest of his life. . . . It was a hurrying, exciting world of music, wine, and contraband love, a terrain not cosmopolitan, but still frontier. Its real music was not Strauss nor Waldteufel nor, even, our own Gottschalk. Nor was it the lugubrious teary ballads of the New York Rialto. It was a heady new music called RAGTIME, a dance-song alembicated from the native air, an intoxicant bubbling with the spirit of a wholly American time and place. . . . For a young man marked out to become the greatest composer of this new music, this folk-conservatory was far more valuable than a real conservatory could have been at that moment. It was a world where for the very first time in America black and white musicians were meeting as equals, competing, trading, and borrowing from the musical traditions of their two different races."[1]

Ragtime composition was prominent during the first two decades of the twentieth century. The first ragtime publication was William Krell's *Mississippi Rag* in 1897. This was followed by Tom Turpin's *Harlem Rag* the same year. By 1899 to 1900, many published compositions with the title "rag" started to appear. The ragtime style was extremely simple and light the first five years. More serious or "high class" rags came out towards the end of the first decade. The leading composers of ragtime were Scott Joplin, James Scott, Joseph Lamb, Artie Matthews, and Tom Turpin. After 1910, ragtime became a national rage. The major ragtime composers published through the teens, with a few rags published in the early 1920s. By 1925, ragtime composition slowed down considerably due to the commercial exploitation of Tin Pan Alley, giving way to the Jazz Era. There are a limited number of rags recorded "straight." Ragtime was preserved primarily through the printed page and piano rolls, not through recordings.

Scott Joplin became ragtime's special master as it began to take shape in the early to mid-1890s. At the age of seventeen, he arrived in St. Louis just as it was all beginning in 1885. The Mississippi was still a great trade and travel river, and was heavy with traffic. The wealth on the river on St. Louis generated one of the most wide open "districts" in the country. The sound of syncopated pianos filled the saloons and cafes, pool halls and parlors of the ill-famed Chestnut and Market Streets. "Jig piano," as ragtime was first called, was everywhere. Ragtime would come of age during the next eight years, centering mainly in St. Louis and another Missouri city, Sedalia.

Scott Joplin lived in St. Louis from 1885 to 1893, supporting himself by playing in the local honky-tonks. He then moved to Chicago, seeking work there in the clubs, bars, and honky-tonks that sprang up around the 1893 World's Columbian Exposition. Following this, he settled in Sedalia, Missouri, for a brief period, where he played second cornet in the Queen City Concert Band. He spent the next two years touring with a vocal group he had formed called The Texas Medley Quartet, which included his two younger brothers Will and Robert. During this phase, Joplin began writing his own compositions. He published some of them, namely a pair of waltz songs and three piano pieces. In 1896, his vocal group dissolved and he returned to Sedalia.

This move marked a crucial turning point in Scott Joplin's career. He decided to attend an educational institution for blacks, George Smith College, sponsored by the Methodist Church. There he worked at translating the characteristic ragtime rhythms into musical notation, and continued to refine his creative imagination. He composed his first rag, *The Maple Leaf Rag*, and immortalized a club in Sedalia by that name. The Maple Leaf Club became a favorite in Sedalia due to Joplin's piece, attracting the best pianists from all over to play there. Despite this fame, Joplin had difficulty getting the piece published. Both a local firm and a St. Louis publishing house which had bought his original rags turned it down. A break finally came for him in 1899 when a local Sedalia music dealer named Joseph Stark heard *The Maple Leaf Rag* and decided to publish it. This produced instant nationwide success for both Joplin and Stark.

With his newly acquired fortune resulting from *The Maple Leaf Rag*, Stack moved to St. Louis and established an expanded publishing firm. Joplin, newly married, soon followed him there. The two men developed a close relationship despite their differences of age and color. Prosperous from his royalties, Joplin was able to retire from the ragtime world of piano playing, buy a large house, and focus on teaching and composing. He continued to compose rags, and in 1902 brought out *Rag Time Dance*, a folk

ballet based on material he had written three years earlier. Not long after this, his first ragtime opera, *A Guest of Honor*, appeared. Neither of these efforts met with much success, and the score to *A Guest of Honor* was subsequently lost and was never found.

Personal problems started to afflict Joplin. His baby daughter died a few months after birth, and strained relations with his wife led to a separation. She had no interest in music. After their breakup, Joplin moved back to Chicago briefly, then to St. Louis and on to New York, all within a year.

He again hit the entertainment circuit, performing in hotels and rooming houses, attempting to sell his new compositions. Joplin sold his pieces to many different publishers over the years, and published some himself as well. He remarried happily in 1909, after his first wife had died, and settled into a house on West 41st Street. He later moved uptown to Harlem. He began devoting most of his time to a new opera, *Treemonisha*.

The original production of *Treemonisha* received only one performance during Joplin's lifetime, in Harlem in 1915. Lacking in scenery, costumes, lighting, and orchestral backing, the production was unconvincing. The audience, including potential backers, walked out. This dealt a terrible blow to Joplin's spirit. His health began to fail, and in the fall of 1916, he was taken to Manhattan State Hospital. He still composed occasionally, but never recovered. He died in the hospital April 1, 1917, at the age of forty-nine from complications due to syphilis.

In Joplin's later years, from 1909 on, he was moving towards more varied and interesting structures, almost towards classical forms. This probably was not deliberate or conscious, but inevitable. For example, *Magnetic Rag* points towards the sonata form, and *Euphonic Sounds,* the rondo. In ragtime, form was the servant of substance. As stated by Gunther Schuller: "It has become increasingly clear that 'form' need not be a confining mold into which tonal materials are poured, but rather that the forming process can be directly related to the musical material employed in a specific instance. In other words, form evolved *out* of the material itself and is not imposed upon it. We must learn to think of form as a verb rather than a noun."[2]

Ragtime differs from jazz and other related music because it is a body of written compositions. Where jazz is improvised or arranged music, and in some cases recordings are the only permanent illustration, ragtime is printed music for the piano. This reflects a difference in the orientation of the music. In jazz, the creative process, whether written arrangements or improvisations, involves what is done with the melody and harmony. In ragtime, the creative process involves the writing of the whole piece in all its parts, both horizontal and vertical. In this sense, ragtime is more oriented towards concert music than jazz. Some ragtime is referred to as "early jazz," however.

Ragtime is formal music, originally composed for the piano. It consists of three or four sections, each with its own melody. Improvisation and variation were not often found in classic ragtime, although they did occur in some performances around the turn of the century. Many early jazz pieces, especially Dixieland with its several sections and themes, owe their structures to ragtime.

In ragtime form, the elements of scale, key, and harmony, as well as the instrument itself, came from the "white side." The essential catalytic polyrhythms came from the "black side," going back to earlier Afro-American music and its retentions from African music of the duple and triple polyrhythms. Ragtime added syncopations to the cakewalk rhythm. This was "ragged" time.

The late cakewalk = ONE two THREE four. Ragtime = ONE and a TWO and a THREE and FOUR. Rhythmically, ragtime is characterized by its right-hand rhythmic phrases. These typical rhythmic phrases are found in all published rags. Sixteenth-note runs stopping on a syncopated beat are common. The left hand is normally in a supporting role "oom-pah" pattern of alternating single notes and chords. The left hand rarely engaged in syncopation.

"James Scott's frequent left-hand syncopation always knows its place—that is, it is inserted in the eighth or sixteenth or perhaps seventh and eighth measures of a strain, where it will not interfere with the orthodox ragtime momentum. This rhythmic phrasing is virtually never more complicated. It is of the essence of ragtime style that it can be trusted not to throw in less regular rhythmic patterns. One of the surest giveaways of Jelly's (Morton) *jazz*, not ragtime, posture is his hitting the left hand a sixteenth note early. This can be seen in his 'transformation' of the *Maple Leaf Rag* and *Original Rags* by Scott Joplin. No rag written would dream of such a blatant New Orleans crudity. Many of the revivalists fail to get an appropriate rag sound because of left-hand syncopation alone."[3]

Ragtime's conventional form includes the organization of the whole strain, usually sixteen bars divided into four equal parts. Many strains are organized as ABAC—"B" being a semicadence and "C" a full cadence. This organization of tunes carried over into jazz. There are few exceptions to the rule in ragtime, and even fewer in jazz, once the early New Orleans stage was over, because of the requirements of improvisation.

Most ragtime compositions are organized on the basis of four strains, either ABCD or ABACD, and less often ABACDC. In most cases, a repeat will be indicated for all strains, except the return of a strain. Of the thirty-nine Joplin rags, including the collaborations, twenty-seven are ABACD. Joplin's rags are

considered the archetype of the music and are unusually fixed, until his later experimental period. In all of Joplin's literature, only two rags, *Euphonic Sounds* and *Palm Leaf Rag*, have less than four themes. Only his first and last rags have more.

Several approaches were used to develop the four-strain structure into a coherent whole. The "A" theme will usually be a straightforward statement, complete in itself, acting as a home base. The "A" theme gives the rag its individuality. The "B" theme is lighter, with a less filled-in treatment. It may begin with an unaccompanied right hand on the dominant. The "B" theme melodic line often has a tendency to soar, so that the effect of returning to "A" reinforces the home base feeling. This is further emphasized by leading off theme "A" with a tonic chord, and theme "B" with a dominant chord. In Scott Joplin's *Chrysanthemum*, the "B" strain modulates to the dominant key. In his *Strenuous Life*, he modulates to the dominant chord of the dominant key.

The final two strains function to extend the development of the rag. Where the "B" strain is lighter, strain "C" is slightly darker, often modulating down a fifth in the lower register of the treble. Rhythmically, the "C" strain may have a kind of subdued excitement, which is released in the "D" strain. The "D" strain sometimes returns to the original tonic, as in *Maple Leaf Rag*, but it usually remains in the new key, the subdominant. The "D" strain often has more of a riff quality than the other strains, and is generally more relaxed.

Ragtime harmony is based mostly on standard tonic-dominant changes. Extensive use of the common change tonic to submediant to supertonic to dominant back to tonic can be found. Tonic to subdominant is also used. Often, the final four bars will be IV - IV minor - I - VI - II - V - I. In the middle of a strain, the harmony will often move to the mediant minor, then to the dominant, returning to the second half of the strain. These harmonies are similar to those used in early jazz. Harmonically speaking, everything found in early jazz is found in ragtime, except early jazz placed far more emphasis on the standard blues chorus and internal harmonies appropriate to that series of chord changes. Jazz did not require more complex harmonic resources until well into the 1920s.

One of Joplin's most famous pieces is continually played today by piano players of all levels and ages, *The Entertainer*. It first appeared in 1902, and was dedicated to James Brown and His Mandolin Club. Wandering string groups called "serenaders" performed at this time. These groups included guitars, mandolins, fiddles, and string bass. They played ragtime, waltzes, and popular ballads in the streets, and would join with the piano player when invited indoors. *The Entertainer* was popular among these groups. A quote from his article "Notes on Boogie

Woogie" by William Russell in the *HRS Rag* could perhaps also describe the evolution of ragtime and other popular musical forms: "An amateur is not to be regarded however with condescension. A perusal of the history of music and other arts shows that many important creative innovations have been due to the amateur. Usually in art a new style has its inceptions with the people, and not with cultivated performers."[4]

And if you're considering playing some of Scott Joplin's rags, remember the composer's request: "Notice! Don't play this piece fast. It is never right to play 'ragtime' fast." (From the scores.)

Popular Song Sheets with Lyrics

Among the many popular song sheets which included lyrics, the following topics were found:

Alcohol and Prohibition

The subject of alcohol was popular among Tin Pan Alley songwriters and publishers, both pro and con. Many songs were associated with "the bottle."

Some examples include *Budweiser's a Friend of Mine* by Bryan and Furth (1907), *Glorious Beer, Beer, Glorious Beer* by Leggett and Goodwin (1895), *Ida, Sweet As Apple Cider* by Eddie Leonard (1903), *I'm on the Water Wagon Now* by West and Bratton (1903), *Little Brown Jug* by Eastburn, *Prohibition Blues* by Ring Lardner and Nora Bayes (1919), and *What'll We Do on a Saturday Night When the Town Goes Dry* by Bert Kalmar and Harry Ruby (1919).

Blackface

Blackface songs, a result of the presence of African Americans and slavery in the American South, developed from the minstrel shows into a respected musical style in the late Victorian period through the Tin Pan Alley songwriters. Although many of the song titles used the word "coon," which by today's standards is politically incorrect, and some of the caricatures on the covers appear as exaggerated stereotypes, these songs are a part of the American heritage.

Blackface songs were very popular from 1890 to 1910. Some examples include *Ain't Dat a Shame* by John Queen and Walter Wilson (1901), *All Coons Look Alike to Me* by Ernest Hogan (1896), *New Coon in Town* by Paul Allen (1883), *Rufus, Rastus, Johnson, Brown (What You Gonna Do When de Rent Comes Around?)* by Andrew Sterling and Harry Von Tilzer (1905), and *The Sound of Chicken Frying, Dat's Music to Me* by Chris Smith (1907).

Children

Although not many Tin Pan Alley songs were written about children, those that were had endearing melodies and tender lyrics. Both the song sheet covers and titles were beautiful. Mammy lullabies were very popular.

The most famous children's song was *School Days* by Edwards and Cobb (1907). Other examples include *Hush Little Baby, Don't You Cry* by Rosenfeld (1884), *Little Puff of Smoke, Goodnight* by White and Lardner (1909), *Baby Shoes* by Joe Goodwin and Ed Rose (1916), *Sonny Boy* by DeSylva, Brown, and Henderson (1928), *Ten Little Fingers and Ten Little Toes* by Ira Shuster and Ed G. Nelson (1921), *There's No More Buster Brown* by Harry Breen and James Conlin (1908), and *Toyland* by Glen MacDonough and Victor Herbert (1903).

Clothing

The most frequently referred to item of clothing in Tin Pan Alley songs was the "hat," fashioned after the popular Gibson girl hairdos of 1890 to 1910. Mention was also made of pinafores, sunbonnets, bustles, bloomers, peg-bottom trousers, derbies, and raccoon coats. In the field of fashion, Tin Pan Alley perpetuated whatever Paris dictated.

Examples of clothing songs include *Bandanna Days* by Noble Sissler and Eubie Blake (1921), *Bell Bottom Trousers* by Moe Joffe (1943), *Bloomer Girl* by Arlen and Harburg (1944), *Button up Your Overcoat* by DeSylva, Brown, and Henderson (1928), *Get on Your Sneak Shoes Children* by Gussie L. Davis (1898), *The Gingham Girl* by Fleeson and Albert Von Tilzer, *Keep Your Skirts Down, Maryanne* by King, Sterling, and Henderson (1925), *The Lady in Red* by Dixon and Wrubel (1935), *Let a Smile Be Your Umbrella* by Irving Kahal and Francis Wheeler (1927), *One, Two, Button Your Shoe* by John Burke and Arthur Johnson (1936), *Top Hat, White Tie and Tails* by Irving Berlin (1935), *Where Did You Get That Hat?* by Joseph J. Sullivan (1886), and *Who Threw the Overalls in Mrs. Murphy's Chowder?* by George L. Geifer (1899).

Current Events

Headlines fueled the songs of Tin Pan Alley, including political themes, campaigns, new laws, inaugurals, dedications to political figures or entertainers, expositions, festivals, fairs, roundups, catastrophes, and famous news celebrities.

The association of a hit song with a singing or movie star helped to advertise the song. When a photograph of the star appeared on the song sheet cover, it helped to promote the star. Dedication of songs by songwriters was a show of friendship, admiration, or appreciation. "This song is respectfully dedicated to" often appeared near the top border of the song sheet cover, elsewhere on the cover, or on the inside title page.

Examples include *Goodbye Teddy Roosevelt, Meet Me in St. Louis* (1904 World's Fair), *Lewis and Clark Exposition March* (1905, Portland, Oregon), *Panama Canal March and Two-Step* (1914), *The Wreck of the Titanic* (1912), and *Little Colonel*, dedicated to Shirley Temple (1935).

Dixie

"Dixie" geographically includes the entire area south of the Mason-Dixon Line. Hundreds of songs of the Southland, with or without the word "Dixie" in the title, were written during the Tin Pan Alley era. These include *I Want to Be in Dixie* by Berlin and Snyder (1912), *Rockabye Your Baby with a Dixie Melody* by Jerome and Schwartz (1918), and *There's a Lump of Sugar Down in Dixieland* by Bryan, Yellen, and Gumble (1918).

Feminine Names

During the Tin Pan Alley era, "Rose" was the most frequently used female name in a song title. It was a very fashionable name at the time, and was conducive to rhyming. Other female names such as "Edna" and "Gertrude" were also popular, but were much harder to rhyme. Songs with feminine names in the title were usually love songs written by men, and were sometimes humorous.

Female rebellion against Victorianism came with the 1920s. Women wore bobbed hair, shorter skirts, rolled-down stockings, and smoked cigarettes, all symbols of freedom. The "vamp" was a sex symbol capable of getting her wishes and leaving a trail of broken hearts. The lyrics of these songs give an interesting insight into this rebellious time.

Many girls' portraits were used on song sheet covers, and many were very beautifully done. Girls' names frequently used in Tin Pan Alley songs were Rose, Mary, Katie, Sue, Kitty, Maggie, Sally, and Marie. Various other female names included Hannah, Bessie, Lulu, Liza, Jane, Ida, Irene, Peggy, Polly, Lessie, Rebecca, Rosalie, Ruby, and Sandy.

Flowers, Nature, and Animals

The rose, symbolic of love, is found more often than any other flower in flower-related Tin Pan Alley songs. Daisies and violets are the next two most popular. Many song sheet covers show flowers, in particular, the linens. Many dance steps were associated with animals, as the song sheets suggest. These included the grizzly bear, fox trot, bunny hug, kangaroo hop, and tiger rag, among others.

Examples of flowers, nature, and animal songs include *And the Green Grass Grew All Around* by William Jerome and Henry Von Tilzer (1912), *Cherry Blossoms* by Emma I. Hart (1907), *Down among the Sugar Cane* by Cecil Mack and Chris Smith (1908), *Who's Afraid of the Big Bad Wolf?* by

Frank E. Churchill and Ann Ronell (1933), *Be My Little Baby Bumblebee* by Stanley Murphy and H. T. Marshall (1912), *When the Mocking Birds Are Singing in the Wildwood* by Lamb and Blake (1905), and *When the Red Red Robin Goes Bob Bob Bobbin' Along* by Harry Woods (1926).

Food and Beverages

Gratification from food was a subject of Tin Pan Alley songs. Examples include *Big Rock Candy Mountain, Blueberry Hill* by Stock, Lewis and V. Rose (1940), *A Cup of Coffee, a Sandwich, and You* by Billy Rose, Al Dubin, and Joe Meyer (1925), *I'm Putting All My Eggs in One Basket* by Irving Berlin (1935), *Life Is Just a Bowl of Cherries* by Brown and Henderson (1931), *On the Good Ship Lollipop* by Sydney Clare and Richard Whiting (1934), *Oyster, a Cloister, and You* by Richard Connels (1925), *Tea for Two* by Harback, Ceasar, and Youmans (1925), *Yes, We Have No Bananas* by F. Silver and Irving Cohen (1923).

Locations

Songs about locations include Ireland, Hawaii, states, cities, rivers (e.g., the Mississippi River), Broadway, the South, Heaven, and other miscellaneous locations. For almost every state and major city, there is a song title containing its name. Rivers, mountains, and streets were all sources of sentimentality.

Two well-known examples of location songs include Paul Dresser's *Banks of the Wabash* and James Bland's *Carry Me Back to Old Virginny,* which became Virginia's official state song in 1956. Other examples include *For Freedom and Ireland* by Woodward and Mack (1900), *Blue Hawaii* by Leo Robins and Ralph Rainger (1937), *California and You* by Leslie and Puck (1914), *Chicago* by Fred Fisher (1922), *Moonlight on the Colorado* by Billy Moll and Robert King, *Give My Regards to Broadway* by George M. Cohan (1904), and *Cheyenne* by Harry Williams and Egbert Van Alstyne (1906).

Mother

Sentimental feelings having to do with a mother dying or honoring her moral attributes while living were written about in hundreds of "Mother" songs throughout the Tin Pan Alley era. These songs were done so often it sometimes became necessary to remember that mother also divorced, smoked, drank, and even had a sense of humor.

Examples of "Mother" songs include *Always Keep a Smile for Mother* by Converse (1884), *Handful of Earth from Mother's Grave* by Joseph Murphy (1883), *I Want a Girl Just Like the Girl That Married Dear Old Dad* by Will Dillon and Harry Von

Tilzer (1911), *Ireland Must Be Heaven for My Mother Came from There* by McCarthy, H. Johnson, and Fisher (1916), *Mother's Prayer* by Arnstein and Gilbert (1932), *Stories Mother Told* by Frank J. Gurney (1895), *There's Nothing Will Forgive Like a Mother* by Cooper and Wege Farth (1891), and *You've Got Your Mother's Big Blue Eyes* by Irving Berlin (1913).

Novelty Songs

As sentimental songs were the mainstay of Tin Pan Alley, novelty and comical songs helped to break the monotony, developing in the twenties and thirties as signs of the times. Extra verses were added to many novelty songs such as *It Ain't Gonna Rain No Mo'*, with at least a dozen or two extra verses.

Novelty songs included *The Grass Is Always Greener* by Egan and Whiting (1924), *He Used to Be a Farmer but He's a Big Town Slicker Now* by Sterling and Harry Von Tilzer (1919), *Nobody Else Can Love Me Like My Old Tomato Can* by Downs and Baskette (1923), and *Yes, We Have No Bananas* by Silver and Cohn (1923).

Sports and Games

Although our society is very sports oriented, there were few sports-related Tin Pan Alley songs. Most had to do with horse racing and polo or college fight songs, and a few about games.

Examples include *Take Me Out to the Ball Game* by Jack Norworth and Albert Von Tilzer (1908), *The Gliders-Skating Waltz* by William Schroeder (1916), and *Checkers* by Edgar Allen and Leo Edwards (1919).

Tearjerkers

Tin Pan Alley songwriters and publishers composed many tragic stories set to music. Some examples include Paul Dresser's *The Convict and the Bird* (1888), *Don't Tell Her That You Saw Me* (1896), *I Wonder Where She Is Tonight* (1899), *Just Tell Them That You Saw Me* (1895), *The Letter That Never Came* (1886), *The Outcast Unknown* (1887), and *The Pardon That Came Too Late* (1891). Songs by Ed Marks and Joe Stern include *Break the News to Mother Gently* (1892), *Don't Wear Your Heart on Your Sleeve* (1901), *His Last Thoughts Were of You* (1894), *The Little Lost Child* (1894), *My Mother Was a Lady* (1896), and *The Old Postmaster* (1900). One more example is Charles K. Harris's *After the Ball* (1892).

Transportation and Communication

Tin Pan Alley made songs about transportation and communication legendary. These songs included the railroad, the automobile, the steamboat, the telephone and telegraph, the United States Postal Department, airborne transportation, walking, the bicycle, the covered wagon, sleigh rides, trolley rides, buggies, rolling chairs, and newspapers.

Railroad songs lent themselves to the hypnotic rhythm of the train's engine moving along the track, such as *Shuffle off to Buffalo, Wabash Cannonball,* and *Casey Jones.*

Any new invention became the subject of a song, such as *I'll Build a Subway to Your Heart,* coinciding with the building of the New York subway system. Many songs about the telephone were written at the time of its invention.

Songs about walking included *Walking My Baby Back Home, Let's Take an Old-Fashioned Walk,* and *Let's Take a Walk around the Block.*

The bicycle became a national pastime in the 1890s. Henry Dacre wrote *Daisy Belle,* also known as *A Bicycle Built for Two.* Postcards and the U.S. mail were other popular Tin Pan Alley song topics, reflected in songs such as *The Postcard Girl* (1908) and those dealing with letters or the United States Postal Department.

War Songs

Tin Pan Alley produced its share of war songs, some pro, some con. With World War I came many songs and emotions, including *Don't Take My Darling Boy Away* and *America, Here's My Boy,* depending on the current political view.

War songs were comical, tragic, and patriotic. During World War I, in order to save paper, the old large sized song sheets gave way to the present standard size. During the war, songs were printed in four sizes including large, standard, small, and miniature for the armed forces.

Of the hundreds of songs published during World War I, *Over There* by George M. Cohan (1918) was the most popular. Issued under three different covers, Norman Rockwell's portrayal of soldiers singing by a campfire is considered the most dramatic and unique.

Other examples of war songs include *Gee! What a Wonderful Time We'll Have When the Boys Come Home* by Mary Earl (1917), *Good-by Ma, Good-by Pa* by Herschell and Walker (1918), *Goodbye, Broadway, Hello, France* by Reisner, Davis, and Baskette (1917), *Hello, Central, Give Me No Man's Land* by Lewis, Young, and Schwartz (1918), *I'd Like to See the Kaiser with a Lily in His Hand* by Leslie, Johnson, and Frisch (1918), *Joan of Arc, They Are Calling You* by Bryan, Weston, and Wells (1917), *Just Like Washington Crossed the Delaware, General Pershing Will Cross the Rhine* by Johnson and Meyer (1918), and *Liberty Bell, It's Time to Ring Again* by Goodman and Mohr (1917).

Song Sheet Cover Art and Artists

Song sheets are collected as much for their covers as for the music itself. Those of Norman Rockwell are the most sought after, and not many were issued.

Over There, Little Grey Mother of Mine, Down Where the Lilies Grow, and the later *Lady Bird Cha Cha Cha* are the four known ones. The scarcity, along with Rockwell's popularity as the *Saturday Evening Post* artist, explains their high price.

Well-known illustrators Archie Gunn, Hamilton King, and James Montgomery Flagg also appeared as song sheet cover artists, and they too are rarities. Archie Gunn illustrated the cover of *The American Girl March* by Victor Herbert in the Sunday supplement to the *Examiner.* Hamilton King illustrated the cover of *Peggy O'Neil.* James Montgomery Flagg did the cover of George M. Cohan's *Father of the Land We Love.*

Almost half of all the song sheet covers were unsigned, and included many outstanding and artistic covers. The signatures of over 150 different artists are found on large and standard song sheets. These should not be confused with celebrity autographs. Other notable cover artists and photographers include Alpeda, Starmer, J. V. R., Albert Barbelle, Andre Petakacs, Pfeiffer, John Frew, Frederick S. Manning, R. S., Carter/Myers/Pryor, and Gene Buck. Starmer, Barbelle, and R. S. contributed the most on both large and standard size song sheets. A new breed of artists emerged in the 1920s with a strong feeling for Art Deco. J. V. R. contributed greatly to this style, creating and signing many striking covers. The signatures of Art Deco artists Wohlman, Perret, Griffith, Leff, Pud, and Lane varied little and can be found easily.

E. T. Paull, composer of marches, arranger, and later publisher, produced extremely popular and brilliant five-color lithographed song sheet covers, executed by the A. Hoen Lithograph Company. His songs were advertised on the back side of a standard 1922 reissue as "thirty-seven magnificently lithographed songs by E. T. Paull Publishing Company." All but six of the songs were marches. Almost all were solely Paull compositions, although he collaborated with others on twelve of them. In these cases, he was probably the arranger, as in *Midnight Fire Alarm,* where Harry J. Lincoln wrote the music and Paull the arrangement. Though his covers are more prevalent than Norman Rockwell's, they are considered in the scarce category, often found dirty and torn due to their popularity.

Art Deco (1910 to 1935)

The artistic elements of Art Deco included flower garlands, fruit baskets, popular trees, fountains, nudes, geometric designs, masked harlequins, jesters, clowns, long-legged beautiful women in billowy skirts, deer, flowers, greyhounds, streamlined human figures in exaggerated positions, Cubism, and Egyptian, American Indian, Mexican, and African influences. As Art Nouveau was a revolution against traditional art, Art Deco revolted against its predecessor, Art Nouveau.

Between 1910 and 1920, cover artists such as Starmer, Pfeiffer, R. S., DeTakacs, and Frew played an active role in the development of Art Deco. By the 1920s, new names appeared on Art Deco song sheet covers including C. E. Millard, Wohlman, G. Kraus, Perret, Politzer, and Griffith. Art Deco is well represented on song sheet covers, both large and standard size. Examples of Art Deco covers in large size include *Cabaret Rag* by Pfeiffer, *The Kangaroo Hop* by F. E. Looney and *Tiddle-de-Winks* by Starmer. Covers in standard size include *Let Me Call You Sweetheart* by Mary Kidder, *Secondhand Rose* by Wohlman, and *You Said Something When You Said Dixie* by Wohlman.

Cartoonists

Covers by prominent Art Deco era cartoonists such as Opper, Billy DeBeck, Clare Victor, Dwiggins, Swinnerton, Gaar Williams, Paul Fung, George McManus, and Harold Gray are rare. A few examples are *Barney Google* by DeBeck, *Little Orphan Annie* by Harold Gray, and *Seattle Town* by Paul Fung from the comic strip *Dumb Dora.*

Linens

Linens were issued in both large and standard size on a superior quality white, small pebbled surface with a matte finish, distinguishing them from other song sheets. Flowers and landscapes were often found on linen cover designs. Carrie Jacobs-Bond & Sons and Sam Fox Publishing Co. used linens to print sheet music. Linen cover samples include *Basket of Roses* by Fred G. Albers (1913) in the large size, and in the standard size, *Lazy River* by Carrie Jacobs-Bond (1923).

Sunday Supplements

From 1895 to 1908, before microphones, promoters tried to popularize a song by issuing supplemental song sheets in the Sunday newspaper. These Sunday supplements were issued on low quality paper.

Over the years, many became yellowed and brittle. The covers were often drawn by cartoonists on the staff of the newspaper with which they were issued. A popular Sunday supplement artist was H. B. Eddy. Sunday supplement songs were frequently composed for the newspapers as a good source for musical stars and musical shows. Sunday supplement song cover samples include *American Girl March* by Archie

Gunn and *I Caught You Making Eyes at M e* by H. B. Eddy.

Advertising Song Sheets

The Garland Stove Company was the first to use the song sheet as an advertising medium in 1889. The cover was a black-and-white lithograph. Soon to follow was the Bromo Seltzer Company, which used 171 song selections to promote their product, mostly standards and hymns. These were distributed to local pharmacies throughout the country. Anyone could submit a two-cent stamp and a Bromo Seltzer wrapper, and in return select and receive two songs.

A prime example of an advertising song sheet was a colored lithograph by Gugler Company, *Wait for the Wagon,* published by the Studebaker Brothers. Free copies were distributed in 1884 for the new year. The cover showed the four Studebaker Brothers, Adams County, Pennsylvania, where they were born, and a horse-drawn wagon of folks celebrating New Year's. On the back side was printed a four-verse parody of *Wait for the Wagon* titled *A Carol of the Studebaker Wagon,* with information promoting it. In 1941, a free song sheet titled *Honeymoon for Three* advertised the new Chevrolet, the third party being the new car.

Miss Samantha Johnson's Wedding Day was covered the most by advertisers. Every available border space was used by twenty different advertisers. In some instances, parts of the music were blocked. Advertising song sheets published by the companies themselves, or expressly for the companies, are hard to find. Using song sheets as a promotional scheme was quite successful, and continued throughout the Tin Pan Alley era, and even later.

More advertising song sheet samples include *Cable March and Two Step* by the Cable Piano Company (1903), *Song of the Great Big Baked Potato* by the Northern Pacific Railroad (before 1918), and *Way Down upon the Suwannee River* by the Southern Railway System (1921).

Cowboy and Action Westerns

The fascinating wild west was depicted in some song sheet covers, including the colorful action westerns reminiscent of Russell and Remington. Some examples of large sized western song sheet covers include *Cheyenne, In the Land of the Buffalo,* and *Santa Fe Song* by Starmer.

Songs in Musicals, Silent Films, Talkies, Radio, and Records

Musicals

The earliest form of American entertainment, the minstrel shows, originated in the 1840s. By the 1880s, variety shows took over, followed by operet-tas, vaudeville, the follies, revues, scandals, and others, evolving into Broadway musicals. These musical entertainment forms became interwoven with Tin Pan Alley. Each contributed to the continuation of the show and its songs.

Musicals were advertised on the covers of song sheets. Samples of musical shows advertised on pre-1920 song sheets include George M. Cohan's *Hello Broadway* and Victor Herbert operettas, including *Naughty Marietta.*

The Ziegfeld Follies, which ran from 1907 until 1943, was one of the most famous musical shows. Irving Berlin's *Music Box Revues* ran from 1921 to 1924. Other famous shows included George White's *Scandals,* the *Greenwich Village Follies,* Jack Norworth's *Odds and Ends,* the *Hippodrome Shows,* Earl Carroll's *Vanities,* Schubert's *Passing Shows,* the *Wintergarden Shows,* and the *Broadway Brevities.* Major producers of the period included Daniel Arthur, Richard Carle, Charles Dillingham, Lew Fields, Joe Hertig, Klaw and Erlander, George W. Lederer, Oliver Morosco, August Pitou, Henry Savage, Mort Singer, and Whitney.

Before radios and phonographs, minstrel shows, stage shows, and vaudeville were the only avenues of song plugging available to music publishers. Not unlike today, the association of a song with a star performer assured its success. Every publisher or song plugger used any means available to convince a star to include a song in his or her repertoire. This included anything from giving expensive gifts such as jewelry, to giving up a percentage of the song's royalties. This was "payola" in its early stages. Songs and singers were dependent on each other for survival. Songs were made successful by a star performer's rendition, and singers became successful by introducing great songs. "Sung with great success by," "prominently featured by," "introduced and sung by the phenomenal," "triumphantly featured by," and "sung with tremendous success by" were phrases used along with a star's photograph on many song sheet covers from the late 1800s through the early 1900s.

Blackface songs were the end result of the minstrel shows, and were very popular at this time. Blackface song entertainers overwhelmed audiences with the power of their throaty tenor voices. In the minstrel shows, a carry over from the Civil War, the entire cast consisted of male members who personified the popular caricature of the African American in song and dance. They frequently worked in pairs, such as Primrose and West. The culmination of this impersonation came in the early 1900s with the legendary performer Al Jolson. Stars who were successful prior to and after the age of movies, phonograph, and radio included Al Jolson (*Bring Along Your Dancing Shoes*) and Sophie Tucker (*Darktown Strutters' Ball*).

Songs of the Silent Films

In 1895, Ed Marks came up with the idea, with the help of an electrician, to photograph actors and actresses in subsequent portrayals of episodes from his tearjerker song *Little Lost Child*, cowritten with Joe Stern. These photographs were placed on slides and projected through a lantern onto a screen as the song was being sung. This was an instant success, and the lantern slide and *Little Lost Child* became synonymous. The silent movie and the theme song followed, as did the synchronization of musical score and film, and later, the *talkies*.

In 1926, Warner Brothers purchased a device called the *Vitaphone* which synchronized a wax sound recording with a film projector. That same year, Warner Brothers produced the movie *Don Juan* with a musical score. Al Jolson sang the songs in *The Jazz Singer* in 1927. The first all talking film, *Lights of New York*, was produced in 1928 by the Warner Brothers Vitaphone process. William Fox used a similar device called *Movietone*. Silent movie theme song covers advertised the movie from which they came. The film stars were normally shown on the cover, as well as the film company and the producer. These songs were often dedicated to the stars by the songwriters.

The first movie theme song to gain national popularity was *Mickey* from Mack Sennett's 1918 film of the same name, starring Mabel Normand. This song was issued in three different sizes, with the star Mabel Normand in three different cover poses. The large and small sized song sheets were published in 1918. The standard sized one was issued in 1919. A second standard sized publication with Mabel Normand in yet another pose was also published, making four total distinct song sheet covers.

Some song sheets were definitely designated as a theme song or introduced in a motion picture, and are collected as such. Other silent film song sheets are collected by the stars pictured on the covers. These covers often stated that the photograph was reproduced by permission of the film company with which the star was affiliated. Any song sheet marked *Vitaphone* or *Movietone* came from a movie that at least had partial sound. By 1930, there were no more silent films, however, Charlie Chaplin produced two such films at a later date.

Songs of the Talkies, Radio, and Records

In the post-silent screen era, radios and phonographs were becoming popular among the American people. The piano was almost completely ignored, and the player piano came to be considered out of style. Not only did pianos take up a lot of space, but a person had to work at learning how to play it. Turning a radio knob or phonograph crank was much easier, and could produce many sounds at once from all

over the world. "Successfully featured by" was still used on song sheet covers during the 1920s, in combination with a star and the song, but was soon replaced by "introduced by" or "as featured in."

Eventually, it was hard to distinguish if a song sheet cover star was associated with radio, film, or a record.

Some stars were popular in all three mediums, including Al Jolson, Eddie Cantor, and Sophie Tucker. The movie performers took over the song sheet covers, providing a gallery of collectible stars. Along with individual performers, famous band leaders or entire bands were being featured on the covers of song sheets.

Because they were instrumental in making so many popular hit songs, the most sought after covers are those featuring Al Jolson, Charlie Chaplin, Shirley Temple, and Eddie Cantor. There are many covers featuring Al Jolson, Rudy Vallee, Bing Crosby, Sophie Tucker, and Ruth Etting. Bing Crosby, Shirley Temple, and Kate Smith were part of the Tin Pan Alley era early in their careers, but their greatest popularity was achieved later. Individual songs were often issued with several different stars on the covers. For example, *Bye, Bye, Blackbird* was issued with four separate covers, all identical, except for the star photographs of Gus Edwards, Frank Richardson, Olive O'Niel, or the Angelus Sisters.

Tin Pan Alley's cut-off date is usually considered to be the early 1930s. Shirley Temple was born on April 23, 1928, and her first movie was produced in 1932. In 1928, Walt Disney produced his first animated cartoon, *Plane Crazy*, marking the beginning of the Disney dynasty. From the 1933 Walt Disney film *Three Little Pigs* came the first song written for an animated cartoon, *Who's Afraid of the Big Bad Wolf?*

Song sheets associated with Walt Disney and Shirley Temple are among the most sought after of those published in the post-Tin Pan Alley era, along with those issued during World War II. News, political, and exposition songs have also been popular with collectors. The post-Tin Pan Alley song sheet covers show many star celebrities from radio, records, and film.

Collecting Song Sheets

Song sheets are most valuable when they're in mint condition. If the sheet music has been damaged or reduced in size, the monetary value goes down. Sheet music is best kept in unsealed plastic bags, allowing it to breathe. The paper used for song sheets before 1900 and for the Sunday supplements was easily perishable, and requires extra care.

When determining the value of a song sheet, the following criteria are considered: age, composer's popularity, performer(s), scarcity, cover artist, category, early or late issue, condition, and identical songs with different covers or performed by different stars. Individual songs were sometimes issued under several different covers, and the same cover design may have been used for different performing artists. The best resource for current prices is *The Sheet Music Reference and Price Guide* by Anna Marie Guiheen and Marie-Reine A. Pafik. Songs are cross-referenced alphabetically, by cover artists, performers, composers, and by miscellaneous categories. Many pictures of actual sheet music covers are included.

Using mint condition as the standard from which to work, the following guidelines should be followed when determining the value of a song sheet. Mint condition means near music store condition, with an absence of names, smears, tears or frays, and is valued at 100 percent. If there is a music store stamp, but the condition is otherwise mint, the value is 90 percent of the mint condition value. If the owner's name appears in ink, but the condition is otherwise very good, the value is 75 percent. A sheet with carefully trimmed edges, but otherwise very good condition is valued at 65 percent. Sheets with a separated cover, but otherwise in very good condition are worth 55 percent. Dog-eared or slightly frayed sheets are worth 50 percent. Torn, somewhat smeared, or badly frayed sheets are worth 25 percent. Dirty, badly torn, or incomplete sheets are valued at 10 percent.

Song sheet covers show America's character and history. Those who collect song sheets do so both for the music and for the cover design. The collector may have an interest in certain composers, stage shows, theme music from the silent movies, Walt Disney, the various dances and rhythms of the era, locations, communications, political issues, news songs, sad songs, songs about mother, or novelty songs. Those who collect by cover may do so for the cover artists, Art Deco designs, advertising song sheets, or favorite categories. Song sheets are sometimes collected as a part of other antique collections.

Song sheets are seldom in mint condition as they were used frequently when the song was in vogue. The majority of music published prior to 1900 had covers decorated with black-and-white engravings. The pre-1900 black-and-white engravings consisted of fine lines. The name of the engraving or lithograph company was ordinarily placed somewhere near the bottom of the song sheet.

There are two basic sheet music sizes. Prior to 1917, with a few exceptions, all music was published in the large 13- x 10-inch size. From 1920 onward, all music was published in the standard 12- x 9-inch size. Dimensions in both instances could vary as much as an inch. The transition period from 1917 to 1919 was during World War I. As in any war, resources were needed for the war effort. This included paper. During this time, music was published in four different sizes, those being large, standard, small, and

miniature. The small 10- x 7-inch was to help further the war effort. A miniature version 4- x 5-inch was distributed free to those in the armed services.

Because all popular music was published in the standard size from 1920 on, it is possible to date a late or early issue of a song sheet by its size, especially if the first release was prior to 1917. The first issue of *In My Merry Oldsmobile* was in 1905 and was large sized. A revival of the song reissued after 1926 was in the standard size.

"Now try this over on your piano" was a stock phrase used extensively by publishers to advertise current song issues, which were printed on the back cover or on the inside of the front cover. These current song samples had their copyright dates listed just below a printed line of the song.

First release issues are often difficult to determine. Copyright transfers can be a clue. William C. Handy's *Memphis Blues* was first published by Handy, but the copyright was later transferred to Theron C. Bennett, and then again to Joe Morris Publishing Company. W. C. Handy's original publication is subsequently classified as a rare imprint.

First release songs or imprints, like first edition books, are highly valued. Whatever the reason for the copyright transfer, it is often the one and only clue to a first release. At the bottom of the title page, that being the first page of song, the copyright date of the song appears. This normally indicates the publication date of the song. If the copyright has been transferred, the original owner's date of copyright is listed first. Below this is listed the new copyright owner and date.

Successful marches, intermezzos, and waltzes prompted publishing companies to call in lyricists, changing the musical compositions into singable ballads, and thus requiring recopyrighting in the new form.

Occasionally, songs were sold to another company, which would supply the lyrics and publish the song as a ballad. This also required a copyright transfer. Songwriters would sometimes publish their own songs either because they were unable to interest a publisher, or because they wished to reap the profits. If a song achieved any degree of success, publishing companies eagerly sought a copyright transfer.

Identifying the date of a song sheet publication can be difficult. There has been more interest in the printing and publishing of music in the eighteenth and early nineteenth centuries than in the publications from 1825 to the Civil War. Copyright dates are not universal in the publications before the enactment of the first U.S. copyright law in 1871.

Because music was engraved on plates, publishers often kept the plates in storage for long periods of time, printing new copies as the stock ran low. They would sometimes sell plates to other publishers who may not have bothered changing the original copyright information on the plates. A plate number can sometimes be used to identify an approximate date of publication, but that depends on how much is known about the engravers or publishers.

Care and Repair

One of the difficulties of caring for sheet music collections is that music was intended to be used, and people did just that. The sheet music may have been stored on a music rack or in a piano bench, but it was usually played or sung, and therefore came to show signs of wear and tear. Some pieces survived better than others.

Much of the music printed from engraved plates in the nineteenth century is in fairly good condition because the paper was usually made of rags rather than wood pulp, and was a little thicker than paper used for other purposes. Music printed on cheap paper made of wood pulp becomes very brittle in a short period of time.

To preserve sheet music items, they are often placed in acid-free folders, in acid-free boxes with low light conditions, in climate-controlled stacks. Albums are a good place for storage and easy viewing of song sheets, consisting of plastic envelopes sized to fit the music. Before filing, framing, or inserting into an album, it is a good idea to go over a song sheet with a soft, dry cloth to remove dirt. Attempting to remove an ink signature by erasure or ink eradicator will only leave a white area. Watercolors can sometimes be used effectively to color the white worn or creased areas noticeable on the darker covers. A pencil signature can be carefully removed with a gum or rubber eraser. Tape carefully applied can be used to repair torn song sheets.

Many song sheets had an insert sheet. If this is missing, the value decreases, and the pages are no longer numbered consecutively. Missing inserts can be combined with incomplete copies. Before the 1920s, nearly all pianos came with a stool. Sheet music cabinets rather than benches were used for storing sheet music.

After the 1920s, pianos came with benches which could accommodate standard sized sheet music. If a new piano was purchased, the borders of large size song sheets were sometimes cut off with scissors, leaving the music intact. Cut down song sheets show cut-off designs and lettering on the covers, and were usually not cut straight.

The large size song sheets were generally considered more attractive than the standard size covers for several reasons. Pre-1920 era artists used the entire color spectrum, with no preference for any particular color.

The 1920 or 1930 era frequently used orange-blue, orange-green, orange-black, and orange-purple combinations. As the movie and record industries emerged, portraits of singers and movie stars were placed wherever they would gain exposure, including song sheet covers.

Song sheets came to serve the movie and record industry, and thus the decline in artistic covers. This was true somewhat in the pre-1920 era when vaudeville, minstrels, and stage shows were sometimes advertised on sheet music covers. But the trend became more common in the 1920s and 1930s. Simplicity of life in the 1930s was reflected in the sterile quality of interior design. This could also be seen in song sheet cover designs.

Framed song sheets compliment any room and decor, and the decorating possibilities are endless. Simple frames matching or coordinating with a color in the cover art itself work best. Song sheets can be framed in pairs or sets, and may thematically compliment a room.

Song sheets have sentimental as well as monetary value, and can hold a special meaning in the heart of the collector.

The Print Music Business Today

The music publishing industry was greatly affected by the new technology of the early twentieth century. Initially, the U.S. Copyright Act, on which publishing principles are based, was not keeping up with the rapid growth of technology, not unlike the situation today with Internet technology. Before the U.S. Copyright Act of 1909, there was confusion as to what should be owed to publishers by the piano roll manufacturers. The new law established that the publisher would receive two cents for each of his songs appearing on a piano roll or recording manufactured by these quickly growing American industries.

Beginning in the 1920s, recordings and radio had become important new forms of entertainment in the home. Many vaudeville entertainers had become radio stars. Publishers wanted the new radio stars to perform their songs on the radio, with the anticipation of greatly increased sheet music sales. Still more profits could be made from record sales of their songs sung by the stars.

Before the end of the 1920s, the addition of sound to film was another technological advancement creating major changes in the world of Tin Pan Alley. On October 6, 1927, the first movie musical, *The Jazz Singer*, starring Al Jolson, opened. This was the first film to use songs and moving pictures on the big screen, and it was a hit at the box office. This success caused Hollywood to turn to Broadway, and Broadway to Hollywood.

Many stars and songwriters, now in demand by Hollywood studios, headed for California. Motion picture companies began purchasing entire publishing companies from the original owners. Sheet music became a less important part of the music industry as sound recordings became prominent after World War II.

By the early 1950s, many publishers started to *job out* the printing portion of their business to companies that specialized in printing sheet music for many different publishers, including song folios, band, orchestra, and choral arrangements. This new practice led to today's *print publishers*.

Print publishers own few or no copyrights, with the exception of original material composed for teaching method books or choral productions, and the copyrights on their particular arrangements of popular or public domain songs. They print and distribute music on behalf of the publishers that hold the copyrights on the music material printed, and share in the income earned from the print sales. Very few music publishers today have their own print departments. The print business today is a much smaller part of the music industry than it was in earlier times, but it remains an important one.

By the time of Elvis Presley in the 1950s, the songwriters who had been an important part of Tin Pan Alley were writing primarily for Broadway and film, or had been replaced by younger songwriters whose songs were those with which newer audiences identified. Very few songwriters of Tin Pan Alley's heyday made the transition to rock music. Older songwriters who adapted to the new styles of popular music in the 1950s survived in the music industry. New York still had many music publishers, the new ones of which specialized in rock and pop music.

By the early 1960s, the music publishing industry followed the youthful dance crazes that were popular all over the country. The Hollywood film industry did so as well. Many publishers moved into the recording industry, signing acts to record songs composed by the publisher's staff writers. The new independent record/publishing companies achieved much success.

In 1964, the Beatles brought their songs to America, written by themselves. American publishers were not ready for this. Unlike Elvis Presley who needed songwriters, popular music acts of the middle 1960s began to write their own material.

Many publishers tried to convince the self-contained acts that it was still necessary to sign over their publishing rights to properly promote and administer their songs. Not knowing how they were going to get their songs recorded, publishers signed the artists who had recording contracts and got the publishing rights to all the songs on their albums. Many well-known acts signed away the publisher's share to publishers who did little more than profit from their work.

Many of the self-contained acts began to realize the importance of publishing. They set up in-house publishing companies with the help of entertainment attorneys and managers, consisting of song catalogs written and recorded by themselves. When recordings were sold, instead of paying the publishing royalties to an outside publisher, the record company paid them to the publishing company owned by the self-contained act.

Many of the jobs that used to be the publisher's now belonged to the record company. In the Tin Pan Alley era, it was the publishing company's job to print, distribute, and promote sheet music. When recordings came to dominate home entertainment after World War II, it became the record company's responsibility to press, distribute, and promote records. As a result of this, if a self-contained act wanted to sign a recording contract with a label, the act also had to sign a publishing agreement with the label's in-house publishing company. This is how many record companies became owners of the important popular music publishing catalogs of the 1950s through the 1970s. Similar deals are made less frequently today. Usually record labels will ask for only a percentage of the publishing as opposed to all of it.

The music publishing industry is very much alive today in New York City and Los Angeles. Publishers resembling those of Tin Pan Alley, with staff writers and song pluggers who take their songs to artists and producers on a daily basis in an effort to get them recorded, are found today on Music Row in Nashville, Tennessee. Other publishing and recording centers in the United States include Miami, Seattle, Minneapolis, Chicago, Memphis, Philadelphia, Boston, and Muscle Shoals, Alabama. There are other regions throughout the United States where publishers and print music publishers do business. For the songwriter who does not perform, there are still many performers who do not write and need new songs.

Music publishers today have started doing developmental deals with up and coming artists/songwriters who do perform. Rather than signing a songwriter to compose songs for others to record, many publishers look for singer/songwriters or self-contained acts that the publisher can take into the recording studio, walk away with a polished demo or master recording, and shop to a major record label. The publisher gets all or part of the publishing rights to the songs written by the artist in exchange for paying for the demo and production costs, and helping to secure the record deal. By becoming involved in producing self-contained artists, many music publishers have survived in an industry that is constantly changing.

In recent years, music publishers have begun buying in and selling out. At one point in time, music publishing was an industry of several dozen major companies, each of which owned thousands of copyrights, and hundreds of smaller companies, each of which owned one to several hundred copyrights. The Hollywood film industry started buying up publishing companies in the early part of the twentieth century because it was an easy way to acquire many readily available songs.

Since that time, the number of publishing companies has risen and fallen considerably. While new companies are constantly emerging, new and old companies are being bought and incorporated into larger ones. The 1980s and 1990s, and into the new millennium, saw an unprecedented amount of buying and selling among music publishers. Songwriters and their songs have become part of huge catalogs, often with little priority being given to their work amongst thousands of other copyrights.

While performing artists, with rare exceptions, tend to come and go, great songs stand the test of time. In earlier days, they were marketed as sheet music. Today, music publishers have many ways to market songs, resulting in many different sources of income. While copyright laws and technology continue to change, it is still the music publisher that owns, promotes, and administers songs. Chapter 2 will discuss the print music market today, including royalties, copyright laws, and legal issues, as well as print music formats and terms.

Notes

1. Rudi Blesh, "Scott Joplin: Black American Classicist," in *Scott Joplin Collected Piano Works* (Miami, FL: Warner Bros./CPP/Belwin, 1971), 15.

2. Gunther Schuller, "The Future of Form in Jazz" in *Saturday Review,* January 12, 1957, 62.

3. Guy Waterman, "Ragtime," in *Jazz,* ed. by Nat Hentoff and Albert McCarthy (New York: Rinehart, 1959), 47-48.

4. William Russell, "Notes on Boogie Woogie," in *Frontiers of Jazz,* ed. by Ralph de Toledano (New York: Ungar, 1962), 64.

2

Print Music Royalties, Copyright Laws, Formats, and Terms

Print Music Royalties

Before the invention of the phonograph, music publishers earned the majority of their income from the sale of printed music. Over one hundred songs sold over one million copies of *sheet music* from 1900 to 1910. Today, music publishers exploit songs in many different ways, including recordings, music videos, music for movies and television, music for the Internet and video games, music for the theatre, and commercials for radio and television.

The demand for sheet music fell substantially with the coming of these new media. Today, *music print publishers* deal only in printed music. Only a few major music print publishers are in operation, often acting as distributors for the smaller ones. A list of music print publisher Web sites can be found in chapter 4 under "Music, Print Music, and Music Book Publishers."

The print department of a publishing company will be in-house only if the publishing company is large. Very few publishers today have their own print departments. Instead, the copyright-owning publishing companies farm out their print work to print publishers who specialize in printing sheet music, folios, band and choral arrangements, and any other printed editions of songs. Whether the print department is in-house or not, it is the job of the copyright-owning publishing company to authorize the printing of music. It is the job of the print department or print publisher to account to the royalty department the amount of printed music that has been sold.

Print royalties are earned from the sale of printed editions of songs. This was the original source of income for music publishers and songwriters in the early days of music publishing. Although print royalties are not usually as great as mechanical, synchroni-

zation, and performance royalties, printed editions of songs are still an important part of music publishing.

Print publishers must acquire the rights to create printed editions of songs. They attempt to make exclusive deals with copyright-owning publishers. Exclusive deals give the print publisher the right to create printed editions of all the songs in the publisher's catalog for a given length of time. For song publishers, the major points of negotiation for agreements with print music companies include the advance, the royalties, and the term.

One print publisher may own the print rights of a large number of copyright-owning publishers at one time. The rights the print publisher acquires can include the rights to print sheet music, folios, and arrangements for bands, orchestras, and choirs. The print publisher usually pays an advance to the copyright-owning publisher in exchange for these rights. A percentage of royalties the print publisher earns from sales of the printed editions is then paid to the publisher.

It is the publisher's responsibility to see that, once a song has become successful, it is made available in printed editions and is properly distributed. This includes use of the song in sheet music, songbooks, folios, and marching band or choral arrangements. Of the different types of printed editions available, sheet music is the most frequently published.

Songwriters earn a percentage of the retail-selling price of each copy of sheet music sold, depending on the print royalty agreement in the songwriter contract. Payment for use of a song in songbooks and folios is either a one-time fixed sum or a percentage of the retail-selling price of editions sold containing the song. The royalties from print music are usually split between the music publisher and the songwriter fifty-fifty, but some deals may vary. It is possible for a songwriter to discuss with the print publisher directly appropriate uses for a song in various print formats, deriving more income from the song in its printed versions.

Copyright Laws

Copyright law moral rights are of European origin, historically Roman, and reflect an early appreciation of the fact that the work of an artist is inseparable from the artist's soul. The work is an extension and representation of the person who created it, reflecting their inner spirit and vision, and projecting the artist's personality. The *Statute of Anne* was a 1709 British law recognized as the first true copyright law anywhere in the world. Copyright is a form of protection provided by the laws of the United States to the authors of "original works of authorship" including literary, dramatic, musical, artistic, and certain other intellectual works. This protection is available for both published and unpublished works.

A copyright gives the owner the exclusive right to reproduce, distribute, perform, display, or license his or her work. The copyright owner also has the exclusive right to produce or license derivatives of his or her work. A work must be original and in a concrete "medium of expression" to be covered by copyright law. Under the current law, works are covered whether or not there is a copyright notice and whether or not the work is registered.

United States Copyright Law

The U.S. Copyright Act is federal legislation enacted by Congress to protect the writings of authors under its constitutional grant of authority. The federal agency in charge of administering the act is the Copyright Office of the Library of Congress. Evolving technology has led to many changes in the meaning and interpretation of the word "writings." The Copyright Act now includes architectural design, software, the graphic arts, motion pictures, sound recordings, and Internet technology. Copyrighted works on the Internet include music, news stories, software, novels, screenplays, graphics, pictures, and E-mail. Copyright law protects the majority of the items on the Internet.

The first United States copyright act was the Copyright Act of 1790, granting copyright protection for books, maps, and charts. The first United States copyright act to grant copyright protection for musical works was the Copyright Act of 1831. The Copyright Act of 1909 called for a general revision of copyright law in the United States. It was the first law to recognize the *mechanical right,* originally licensed by publishers for works used in *piano rolls,* the first widely accepted means of recording songs. The 1909 law also helped to strengthen the *performance right.*

To prevent any one manufacturer of piano rolls from monopolizing the industry with the only recording of a popular song, Congress enacted the Compulsory Mechanical License in the Copyright Act of 1909. This law stated that once a copyright owner had recorded a song for public distribution, or had given permission to someone else to record the song, anyone could record that song as long as they followed certain procedures, including paying a royalty of two cents per recording to the copyright owner. The copyright owner therefore controlled the first recording of a work, but anyone willing to pay the two-cent mechanical royalty to the copyright owner could record the song.

As the phonograph came to replace piano rolls in the first half of the twentieth century, and recordings started to sell in the millions, music publishers gladly accepted the two-cent per recording mechanical royalty, half of which went to the composer. Music publishers and songwriters made millions of dollars by the 1950s and 1960s at the fixed mechanical royalty rate of two cents per recording. The mechanical royalty rate remained the same until the new Copyright Act of 1976.

On October 19, 1976, President Gerald R. Ford signed into law a new and long overdue revision of United States copyright legislation. Copyright Revision Bill S.22 became Public Law 94-553 and was the first completely new copyright law since 1909. Congress took twenty-one years to approve the modern copyright law, which began revision in 1955. Provisions of the new statute became effective January 1, 1978, superseding the Copyright Act of 1909, which remained in force until the new enactment took effect.

Most of the elements of the Compulsory Mechanical License of the 1909 Act were retained in the Act of 1976, with "mechanicals" referring to all recorded media including vinyl records, tapes, CDs, music boxes, and MIDI disks played only in audio format. The mechanical royalty rate was raised from two cents to two and three-quarter cents or one-half cent per minute of playing time, whichever was greater. The Copyright Royalty Tribunal, a panel established to review royalty rates on compulsory licenses of all types, would periodically review the rate.

Although this panel no longer exists, increases in compulsory royalties have been revised under the jurisdiction of the Copyright Office, and continue to be subject to revision. This involves negotiation between copyright owners and users, and requires approval of the Copyright Office. The mechanical royalty rate from 2000 to 2002 is 7.55 cents per recording, and is the maximum rate allowed by statute.

Occasionally lower mechanical rates are negotiated between copyright owners and record companies, especially in the commercial music industry. MIDI disks with computer codes other than audio, for example those that can print scores, and CD-ROMs that contain visual images, are not covered by the Compulsory Mechanical License, and a separate fee must be negotiated between the copyright owner and the producer of the MIDI disk or CD-ROM.

The 1976 law established a single national system of statutory protection for all copyrightable works, whether published or unpublished. Common law, which gave a work protection under the common laws of the various states before it was published, was superseded by the single national system effective January 1, 1978.

Notice of Copyright

The new law does call for published copies of music to contain the notice of copyright; however, omission or errors in the notice of copyright do not immediately result in the copyright becoming public domain. The copyright notice on any tangible work, be it printed or recorded, should include (1) the symbol, either the letter "C" in a circle ©, the word "Copyright," or the abbreviation "Copy," (2) the first year of publication of the work, and (3) the name of the copyright owner of the work, or its abbreviation; in the case of compilations or derivative works using previously published material, the date of first publication may be used and/or the new date; examples: Copyright 2001 Elizabeth C. Axford; © 2001, 1992 Piano Press. A copyright notice should appear on all copies of a piece of music, even if it has not been registered with the U.S. Copyright Office.

Duration of Copyright

By the Copyright Act of 1976 and the subsequent Copyright Term Extension Act passed in 1998, the duration of copyright provides for the following terms: (1) works published before 1923 are in the public domain; (2) works published between 1923 and 1963 have an initial term of twenty-eight years and must be renewed for an additional sixty-seven-year term for a total of ninety-five years; (3) works published between 1964 and 1977 have an initial twenty-eight-year term plus an automatic sixty-seven-year second term for a total of ninety-five years; (4) works published after 1977 have a term of the life of the author plus seventy years, or in the case of works with multiple authors, seventy years after the death of the last surviving author.

Fair Use

There are limited exceptions to the exclusive rights of copyright owners for certain types of "Fair Use." These include such use by reproduction in copies or phonorecords or by any other means for purposes such as criticism, comment, news reporting, teaching, scholarship, or research, and are not considered an infringement of copyright.

There are four factors, which are used in determining a Fair Use. These include (1) the purpose and character of the use, including whether such use is of a commercial nature or is for nonprofit educational purposes; (2) the nature of the copyrighted work; (3) the amount and substantiality of the portion used in relation to the copyrighted work as a whole; and (4) the effect of the use upon the potential market for or value of the copyrighted work. The fact that a work is unpublished does not influence a finding of Fair Use if it is made by considering all the above factors.

This first factor takes into account the following three subfactors: (1) commercial nature or non-profit educational purposes; (2) preamble purposes including criticism, comment, news reporting, teaching, scholarship, or research; and (3) degree of transformation.

The second factor acknowledges the fact that some works are more deserving of copyright protection than others, and attempts to determine where the work is in the spectrum of worthiness of copyright protection.

The third factor looks at the amount and substantiality of the copying in relation to the copyrighted work as a whole. The critical determination is whether the quality and value of the materials used are reasonable in relation to the purpose of copying, and is not a pure ratio test. The quantity, as well as the quality and importance, of the copied material must be considered.

The fourth factor considers the extent of harm to the market or potential market of the original work caused by the infringement, taking into account harm to the original, as well as harm to derivative works.

Photocopying of Print Music

Regarding the photocopying of print music, the Fair Use guidelines include (1) emergency copying to replace purchased copies which for any reason are not available for an imminent performance, provided purchased replacement copies shall be substituted in due course and (2) for academic purposes other than performance, single or multiple copies of excerpts of works may be made, provided that the excerpts do not comprise a part of the whole which would constitute a performable unit such as a section, movement, or aria, but in no case more than 10 percent of the whole work; the number of copies shall not exceed one copy per pupil.

Under the Fair Use guidelines, the following are expressly prohibited: (1) copying to create or replace or substitute for anthologies, compilations or collective works; (2) copying of or from works intended to be "consumable" in the course of study or teaching such as workbooks, exercises, standardized tests and answer sheets, and like material; (3) copying for the purposes of performance except for emergency copying to replace purchased copies as outlined in (1) of the Fair Uses; (4) copying for the purpose of substituting for the purchase of music, except as in Fair Uses (1) and (2); and (5) copying without inclusion of the copyright notice which appears on the printed copy.

It is important to note that copyright protection is not related to the print status of a piece of music. Permission must be granted for copying a piece of out-of-print music. Photocopying a piece of out-of-print music is as much an infringement of copyright as copying one that is in print. Check the copyright notice for the date and subsequent duration of copyright on any piece of music that is out of print.

Other uses requiring permission from the publisher include photocopying works from collections, extra parts for bands, or choral or speaking parts for musicals. Most contests prohibit the use of photocopies, and require that an original copy of the music be provided to the judges.

Public Domain

Public domain is the repository of all works that for any reason are not protected by copyright, and are free for all to use without permission. Works in the public domain include items that by their very nature are not eligible for copyright protection such as ideas, facts, titles, names, short phrases, and blank forms.

The public domain contains all works which previously had copyright protection, but which subsequently lost that protection. An example includes all works published before January 1, 1978, that did not contain a valid copyright notice. Owners of works published between 1978 and March 1, 1989, that did not contain a valid copyright notice were given a five-year grace period in which to correct the problem before their work was placed into the public domain.

The public domain contains all works for which the statutory copyright period has expired. Any work published before 1964 in which the copyright owner failed to renew the copyright is considered public domain. Copyrightable works may enter the public domain if the copyright owner grants the work to the public domain.

Some aspects of a piece of music may be protected by copyright, while other parts are in the public domain. For example, although a piece of music and its lyrics may be in the public domain, a specific recording of the music may be protected by copyright. Anyone wishing to use that recording would be required to get a master recording license from the holder of the recording rights.

Furthermore, some parts of a piece of music, for example, the melody, may be in the public domain, while other parts, say the lyrics, may be protected by copyright. The rights to a specific recording may be held by someone different than the holder of the rights to the music, lyrics, or arrangements.

Performing Rights Organizations

ASCAP, BMI, and SESAC are licensing organizations that collect performance royalties (radio airplay, TV broadcasts, Web casts, etc.) through licensing fees, which are then distributed to the organizations' members, including artists, songwriters, lyricists, and composers. More detailed information on these organizations can be found at their respective Web sites.

ASCAP, BMI, and SESAC are excellent resources for identifying the copyright holder for any given piece of music, or of a particular recording of a piece of music. These organizations have Web sites with searchable databases, making it possible to find the rights holders to any piece of music in question. These Web sites, along with many others with information on copyrights and current copyright issues relating to the Internet, are listed in chapter 4 under "Copyright, Legal, and Tax Information-Performing and Mechanical Rights-Digital Watermarking-Privacy Rights."

Compulsory Mechanical License

Artists may record a *cover version* of any song through a compulsory mechanical license. A compulsory mechanical license is authorized by copyright law and issued by the Copyright Office. This license can be secured without the permission of the copyright owner, and allows the licensee certain use rights of copyrighted material. All compulsory licenses, however, have many conditions, restrictions, fee payment requirements, and liabilities inherent to their use that are defined by copyright law. Information on procedures that must be followed to obtain such a license may be received from the Copyright Office or its Web site.

Who Can Claim a Copyright

(1) The author of the work; (2) Anyone to whom the author has assigned his or her rights of ownership to the copyright; (3) In the cases of a work made for hire, the employer rather than the employee, or creator, is regarded as the author and can claim copyright. Only those authorized people are permitted to sign the copyright application form.

Copyright Registration and Forms

Copyright registration is a legal formality intended to make a public record of the basic facts of any given copyright. Although registration is not required for protection, the copyright law provides several advantages to encourage copyright owners to register their work.

Registration establishes a public record of the copyright claim. Before an infringement suit may be filed in court, registration is necessary. If made before or within five years of publication, registration will establish evidence in court of the validity of the copyright and of the facts stated in the certificate. If registration is made within three months after publication of the work or prior to an infringement of the work, statutory damages and attorney's fees will be available to the copyright owner in court actions.

Otherwise, only an award of actual damages and profits is available to the copyright owner. Copyright registration allows the owners of the copyright to record the registration with the U.S. Customs Service for protection against the importation of infringing copies.

The Copyright Office supplies various application forms for copyright registration. *Form PA* is for works in the performing arts, including published and unpublished musical works, any accompanying music, motion pictures, and other visual works. This form does not cover sound recordings. *Form SR* is for sound recordings and includes published songs. *Form TX* is for nondramatic literary works, including all types of published and unpublished works. The form covers lyric books and also poems that may be used as lyrics. *Form RE* is for renewal registrations. *Form CA* is for correction of an error in a copyright registration or to amplify the information given in a registration. Most applications for copyright will be made on Form PA, and are then issued a PA copyright number. These forms may be obtained for free by writing: Copyright Office, Library of Congress, Washington, D.C. 20559-6000 or call (202) 707-9100, or visit the Web site.

To register a work for copyright, send the following in the same package to the Register of Copyrights, Copyright Office, Library of Congress, Washington, D.C. 20559-6000: (1) a properly completed application form; (2) a nonrefundable filing fee for each application; (3) a complete recording (cassette, CD, etc.) of the work or a lead sheet or complete score; (4) a complete lyric sheet, if applicable.

Prior to 1978, songwriters had to submit lead sheets of their work for copyright registration. Because many songwriters could not notate music, this requirement was changed in the Copyright Act of 1976 to allow recordings such as demo tapes to be used instead. It is important to keep a copy of any submission, as the one submitted to the Copyright Office will not be returned.

For the copyright registration of musical works, the new law allows for one complete copy or phonorecord of an unpublished work to be submitted. For a published work, two complete copies or phonorecords of the best edition of the work must be submitted.

More than one song per application may be registered as a "collection" under a single title. This is an economical means to protect two or more songs under the same copyright registration number. If there is interest in a particular song by a publishing, produc-

tion, or recording company, it is best to register it separately.

Assignment of Copyright

This states that the writer assigns or transfers the copyright ownership of a musical composition to a publisher. Under copyright law, this may be done in full or in part. Exclusive rights, i.e., rights that may be exercised only by a single person or company in copyright are divisible.

Copyright Infringement of Musical Compositions

A copyright registration certificate does not guarantee originality of a song. It is evidence of the approximate date of a song's creation. This information and registration certificate is necessary in order to file a lawsuit against an alleged infringer of a composition in federal court. A lawsuit in federal court as opposed to state court provides for stipulated damages and in some circumstances for tripling those damages.

Before January 1, 1978, an original work that had not been published was protected under the common law without requiring the filing of a copyright claim. In the event an infringement occurred regarding an unregistered composition, one would bring a lawsuit in the state court under common law. To prove plagiarism or copyright infringement, one had to prove substantial similarity between the songs and that the alleged copier had access to the song.

Copyright infringement cases involving musical works deal initially with similarity. Substantial similarity between two compositions brings up the possibility of an infringement. Despite the popular misconception, there is no rigid standard for the exact number of duplicate bars that will constitute an infringement. If substantial similarity is found, then the element of "access" must be considered to determine if the alleged copier had access to the song. Access may include anything from hearing a song played on the radio to seeing a written lead sheet of the song.

The Audio Home Recording Act of 1992

This act allows for the digital copying of copyrighted music. It is generally acceptable to make one copy of copyrighted music, provided it is for personal use and not for distribution to others. Fees are built into the sales of all blank digital media and digital recorders, which are collected and distributed to copyright holders. The act requires a built-in fee of 3 percent to be added to all blank digital tapes and of 2 percent to be added to all digital recording devices. The fees are collected and distributed to copyright holders, including record companies, publishers, performers, and songwriters. Included in the act was the requirement of the inclusion of a Serial Copy Management System (SCMS) circuit to be included in all digital recorders. The circuit allows users to make copies of copyrighted works, but not to make second generation copies, or copies of copies.

The Digital Performance Rights in Sound Recording Act of 1995

This act gives copyright owners of sound recordings the exclusive right, with some limitations, to perform the recording publicly by means of a digital audio transmission. This act extends the provision for compulsory mechanical licenses to include downloadable music.

The Digital Millennium Copyright Act of 1998

This act states that without permission from a song's owner, it is illegal to make copyrighted music available online for unlimited distribution. This law also puts specific limitations on the length of public broadcasts, the types of song and artist announcements, and the frequency and sequence of songs played.

Print Music Formats

Print music publishers license the rights to print, package, and distribute music from the publisher, copyright owners, or administrators. Printed music falls into two main categories: *popular* and *educational*.

Popular Print Music

Popular music includes pop songs, rhythm and blues, dance, rock and roll, adult contemporary, alternative, country, new age, jazz standards, gospel, contemporary Christian, and other radio hits that appear on the charts. They are printed as single *song sheets* and collections of songs in *songbooks* or *folios*.

Popular print music includes *sheet music, mixed folios,* or collections of songs by a variety of artists around a theme such as *Hits of the Sixties*, or *Country Song Hits of the Nineties, matching folios,* those that match a specific record album, movie, TV show, or Broadway musical and have the same cover art or photo, and *personality folios,* which include collections of an artist's or group's songs or greatest hits.

Major publishers of popular music will not print sheet music for a song unless it has become a *hit single* as a recording, and has more than likely been on the *Billboard Hot 100 Chart* or is a *Top 100 Album.* Print publishers will often publish various *arrangements* of popular songs, in addition to a sheet music version that matches the key and style of the original recording.

Not all hit songs are considered marketable as sheet music. Because printing costs are high, print publishers will print only those songs that have made it to the top of the popular song charts, are well suited as piano/vocal/guitar arrangements, or those that have become standards over time. For example, a popular groove-oriented dance tune with two chords may never be released as sheet music as the arrangement would be "thin" and the demand would more than likely be minimal.

Sheet music buyers are often musicians who want to learn how to play songs for performances such as weddings, casuals, or piano bars, music teachers and students, or hobbyists on their instrument. The sheet music section of a local music store will usually include racks of current hits and many standards from all eras.

Current popular print music formats include *Piano/Vocal/Guitar, Easy Piano, Five-Finger Piano (Very Easy), Guitar Tablature, E-Z Play,* and *Fake Books.* Piano/Vocal/Guitar arrangements consist of three staves, with the top line including the melody line and song lyrics. Sometimes the song lyric is written all the way through on multiple pages. In some cases, only the first verse, chorus, and bridge are written out, with any additional lyrics typed on the last page, and direction signs instructing the player to repeat certain sections. Above the top line will appear guitar chord symbols either as alphabet letters or actual tablature.

The bottom two lines of a Piano/Vocal/Guitar arrangement will include a treble and bass clef with a piano accompaniment (indicated by a brace joining the two lower staves), that may or may not include the song melody. It is usually the Piano/Vocal/Guitar arrangement that most closely resembles the original recording. When these arrangements are written in the same key, as they often are, they can actually be practiced along with the original recording.

Easy piano arrangements consist of two staves, usually treble and bass clef, and include the song melody, a simple piano accompaniment, the song lyric, and chord symbols above the top staff. Because these are "easy" piano arrangements, they are sometimes not in the same key as the original recording, and are often in the "easy" keys of C, F, or G major, or a related relative minor key.

Five-finger piano arrangements are written on two staves, usually treble and bass clef, and include only the song melody as single notes played between the two hands, with a few accompaniment notes, and in easy keys. Song lyrics and simple chord symbols may be included.

Guitar tablature books are written for guitarists, and include the guitar chords, song lyrics, and occasionally guitar solo transcriptions. Fake books include only the melody line, lyrics, and chords of a song, and are usually used by professional performing musicians who can improvise around the tune at a glance. E-Z Play books are similar to fake books, but the print is usually larger and the actual note names are printed on the note heads. They are frequently used for playing the organ or electronic keyboards with one-finger chord accompaniment functions.

While some popular songs work well as piano arrangements, especially those which are "piano-based," meaning the piano was used substantially in the original recording, others do not. For example, a student will have a hard time playing a heavy metal guitar song on the piano, especially if there is no clearly defined melody line, and the original recording is comprised primarily of melodic fragments and guitar riffs. Similarly, a "piano-based" song might not lend itself well to guitar chord strumming or finger-picking patterns.

The popular songs that sell the most as sheet music editions are those that cross over into a variety of instrumental markets. A recent example of a major sheet music seller is the theme from the movie *Titanic* by James Horner, *My Heart Will Go On*. Melodically, this song adapted to many different instrumental arrangements. Other examples of extremely popular sheet music sellers include *Theme from Love Story*, *Theme from Ice Castles*, *The Rose*, *Music Box Dancer*, and any of the twentieth-century popular songs that have become standards.

Educational Print Music

Although many arrangements of popular songs can be found in educational print music, especially piano and guitar methods and those for school bands and orchestras, chart action is not a factor when considering original educational material.

Educational print publishers look for work that fits into their publishing program and is appropriate for those who use their music, such as private teaching studios, school and church choirs, and school bands or orchestras. Unlike popular song publishers, choral, religious, and educational print music publishers want a fully written arrangement included in a submission package. A print music publisher needs every note of the arrangement to be legible, clear, and complete. Composers and arrangers must be familiar with the capabilities of school age performers or church musicians.

Educational print music includes choral, band, orchestral and instrumental ensemble arrangements, and *instrumental method* or *how-to books*. There are companies who print both popular and educational music, those who produce just popular music, and those that fall into various areas of educational print music, such as piano methods or band and orchestra. There are also several religious print publishers who publish sheet music, books, and choral music, and distribute primarily to churches and religious bookstores.

Educational and religious print companies accept original songs suitable for choral arrangement, in some cases requesting 2-, 3-, or 4-part harmony. When submitting a choral piece to a print publisher, it is a good idea to also send a recording of the piece being performed by singers in the age group for which the arrangement is intended, such as elementary or high school students. This will show that the notes in the arrangement are within the singing range of the particular age group. Look for material similar to the composition and direct submissions to that publisher. Submissions should be made to someone on the choral publisher's editorial staff. It is a good idea to call before submitting to get a contact name.

Other educational print publishers look for original piano, jazz band, concert band, marching band, or instrumental ensemble pieces. Instrumental arrangements for high school marching and jazz bands and college or community orchestras make up a large market. Submissions of band and orchestra arrangements to potential print publishers are made in the same format as submissions of choral arrangements.

When submitting an arrangement for a marching band, the piece needs to be in 4/4, 2/4, or 6/8 time (march tempo) on a full score lead sheet. Do not send the individual parts that each musician reads. The publisher will want to hear a recorded performance of the arrangement by a high school band or community orchestra. The cover letter should be similar to the one used for a choral arrangement submission.

Arrangements

Many music educators have done some arranging for their students. The issue of copyright must be considered before making an arrangement. An arrangement of a copyrighted work done without permission from the copyright owner is considered an infringement of copyright.

One of the five exclusive rights granted to copyright owners is "the right to prepare derivative works based on the copyrighted work." A derivative work is defined as any adaptation of a copyrighted work. In music, derivative works include arrangements, transcriptions, simplified editions, adaptations, translations of texts, orchestrations, and instrumental accompaniments to vocal publications and parody lyrics. Permission must be granted before arranging, adapting, simplifying, editing, or translating a copyrighted work.

To obtain permission to make an arrangement, it is first necessary to identify the copyright owner. The copyright notice at the bottom of the first page of a printed sheet music edition provides this information, or the credits on a CD label or insert. This information can also be obtained from ASCAP, BMI, or SESAC, with the exact title and writer information. Always check the copyright date. If the work was published before 1923, it is in the public domain and permission is not necessary to make an arrangement.

After locating the copyright owner, it is necessary to write and request permission to make an arrangement of the work. It is important to be specific and provide as much information as possible, including the type of arrangement, the number of copies or parts, who will be performing the arrangement, who will actually be making the arrangement, and whether or not the arrangement will be sold and for how much.

It is also important to note if the arrangement is to be used for one occasion only, or if it will be performed regularly. The more information provided, the better the chance of getting a response from the publisher. This information is necessary for them to decide if permission should be granted to make the arrangement, and whether or not to charge a fee.

A copyright owner is not obligated to grant permission to make arrangements. For example, if the type of arrangement suggested has already been done, the publisher may deny the request. If the request is within reason, the copyright owner will grant permission to arrange and may or may not charge a fee.

The copyright owner will always require a copyright notice to be shown on an arrangement, and will specify how it should be stated. In the case of an instrumental arrangement, the copyright notice should appear on the score and all the accompanying parts.

If permission to arrange is denied, then an arrangement should not be done as the arranger could be sued for copyright infringement.

Publishers consider the sale of unauthorized arrangements a serious copyright infringement. Several popular music publishers have successfully sued jazz and marching band arrangers who have sold unauthorized arrangements, resulting in stiff fines and penalties from the courts.

One more important point: arrangements themselves are copyrightable, and may not be adapted or orchestrated without permission, even if the basic work is in the public domain.

Adaptations

An adaptation of a work can range anywhere from a complete orchestration to changing several notes in one part of a choral work. Permission must be obtained to adapt a musical work in any way.

Any adaptation which may result in lost sales for the publisher, or which changes the character of the work, requires permission from the copyright owner. This includes instrumental accompaniments to vocal or choral works.

One Fair Use that covers adaptations is the case of printed copies that have already been purchased. They may be edited or simplified, as long as the fundamental character of the work is not distorted or the lyrics changed, or lyrics added if there were none originally.

The general principle of Fair Use will help to determine whether or not permission should be requested to adapt a work.

Transcriptions

Prior to transcribing a copyrighted musical work or arrangement from one format to another, for example from a chamber ensemble to a piano duet, permission must be obtained from the copyright owner of the work. Parody lyrics, altered texts, and translations also require permission from the copyright owner.

Writing, Arranging, and Copying

Writing, arranging, and copying can be a good source of income for musicians skilled in these areas. This includes writing lead sheets, full arrangements, and scores. It is a good idea to network at recording studios, jingle agencies, music schools and conservatories, music stores, music trade conventions, and songwriter groups to meet the people who need these services. Transcribers, arrangers, and specialists on their instrument can have lucrative print music careers.

Lyric Sheets

A lyric sheet is a sheet of paper containing the typed lyrics or words to a song. The purpose of the lyric sheet is to make the lyrics of a song accessible to the listener and to avoid the possibility of misheard lyrics. When submitting songs to song publishers, it is essential that a lyric sheet be included with the song demo.

Lyric sheets should be typed or computer generated on standard sized paper (8.5- x 11-inch) with the title at the top. The song title should be in capital letters. The chorus should be in capital letters or indented, or both. It is also acceptable to type all the lyrics in capital letters, and type the title and chorus in bold face caps. In either case, the style should be consistent.

The lyric should be centered from top to bottom and symmetrically aligned with the margins. Set the lyrics up so that the parts of the song stand out. The way a lyric is set on the page should clearly indicate the sections of the song. Labeling the verse, chorus, and bridge is optional, but not necessary. It is also not necessary to retype a chorus that has identical wording. Typing "Chorus" or "Repeat Chorus" or "Chorus Repeats" is sufficient.

A lyric sheet should be as clean and uncluttered as possible. It is not necessary to insert chord changes over the lyrics, or the melody note names. Handwritten lyric sheets or a typed lyric sheet with handwritten chord notations look unprofessional. Never make ink or pencil corrections on a lyric sheet. If there are errors, retype the lyric sheet.

Besides the lyrics themselves, the only information the lyric sheet needs to contain is the copyright notice and the name, address, phone number, and E-mail address of the songwriter(s). If the lyric sheet is typed on plain paper, this information should appear at the bottom of the page, at least two spaces below the copyright notice.

Using letterhead stationery gives a more professional look to a lyric sheet, although lyrics typed neatly on plain white paper are perfectly acceptable. Most word processing programs can generate a letterhead each time a lyric sheet is printed. It is easy enough to purchase special paper, for example "gray marble" to add a letterhead to, with each separate printing of the lyric sheet. This can help the writer to avoid the cost of having stationery specially printed, and having leftover, unused, or shelf-worn paper.

Custom printed or typed cassette, J-card or CD labels, envelopes, and address labels also look much more professional than handwritten ones. The songwriter should be prepared with multiple copies of lyric sheets for demo and recording sessions as well as song pitching opportunities.

Lead Sheets

Lead sheets communicate the melody, chords, and lyrics of a song in written format. Before the Copyright Act of 1976, songwriters were required to submit a lead sheet with any song sent in for registration with the United States Copyright Office. As of the new law effective January 1, 1978, a cassette recording and lyric sheet are considered sufficient documentation for copyright registration.

Lead sheets are no longer required as part of the copyright registration process, nor are they appropriate or necessary to send as part of a song submission package to a song publisher. They may still be used for copyright purposes, however. It is not necessary to submit a complete piano arrangement of the song. The melody line, lyrics, and chords are sufficient. There is also the argument that a paper copy of a song may have a longer shelf life than a magnetic tape. CDs are also more durable than a cassette tape for the purpose of copyright registration.

A lead sheet is musical manuscript hand-written, engraved, or computer generated on five-line staff paper. Lead sheets made on ten-stave paper are easier to read than those done on twelve-stave paper. If the melody notes and rests are written in pencil, mistakes can be easily erased and corrected. There are many computer software notation programs available that can produce lead sheets as well as complete scores in a variety of formats. These are listed in chapter 3 under "Notation and Scoring Software."

A properly formatted lead sheet should include the following:

(1) The song's title and the author(s) of the words and music; (2) contact information including name, address, telephone number, E-mail address, and/or Web site; (3) copyright notice on the first page, even if the song has not been registered with the Copyright Office; (4) the style or tempo of the music should be placed above the first measure such as "waltz" or "moderately"; (5) a treble clef sign as all lead sheets are written in the treble clef; (6) the key signature indicated by accidentals after the treble clef sign; (7) the time signature directly after the key signature; (8) vertical bar lines separating the measures; (9) notes below the third line should have stems going up and on the right side; notes on or above the third line should have stems going down and on the left side; (10) even spacing; (11) complete measures; each measure must contain the exact combination of note and/or rest values as indicated by the top number of the time signature; (12) the lyric typed below the musical staff with each word or syllable placed directly under the note it corresponds to; for a sustained note such as a tie or whole note, insert the word or syllable directly under the note and draw a straight line from the bottom of the last letter of the word or syllable to the beginning of the next note or rest; (13) chord symbols should be written in their proper places above the musical staff, above a particular note, rest, or beat; (14) measure or rehearsal numbers; (15) section breaks.

It is important to keep a master copy of a lead sheet, sending out only duplicate copies. The three basic techniques for reproducing lead sheets and other music manuscripts include the diazo process white-print reproduction, photocopying, or photo-offset reproduction.

The diazo process white-print reproduction is the most flexible method of manuscript reproduction. Copies come in many sizes, they can be printed on one or both sides, and they may be bound in many ways. Paper with a special diazo chemical coating is used for this process. The transparent master copy of a work, preferably dense, black engrossing ink printed on a special kind of onion skin paper referred to as deschon or vellum, is placed in contact with the paper and is then exposed to ultraviolet light, then developed in ammonia fumes. The copies come out as black print on white paper.

Photocopying is the reproduction of copies by photocopying machines. It is a convenient method to use because of the availability of photocopying machines and the most economical when only small quantities are needed. Two-sided prints can be punched and bound with a plastic binding. Photocopying machines can reproduce 8.5- x 11-inch and 11- x 17-inch copies, as well as color copies for covers.

Photo-offset reproduction or offset printing is the most economical process to use when over five hundred copies of a work are needed. In this process, the manuscript is photographed and a printing plate is made from the photographic negative. This plate is then mounted on a rotary press, inked, and the image is printed onto a rubber blanket on the press. The resulting copies are clear and professional.

For more information and prices on reproduction techniques, consult a music copyist or printer listed in the yellow pages under *Music Copyist, Music Manuscript Reproductions,* or *Music Printers and Engravers,* in advertisements in trade magazines or online.

Those unable to write or generate on a computer a lead sheet, can seek the help of someone who knows how to notate music. They can sing, present on cassette tape, or play the song on an instrument to a music copyist or stenographer, arranger, musician, music teacher, or friend who is able to write a lead sheet. A fee will be charged for the transcription of the melody onto paper and the notation of the chord symbols and lyrics. Professionals can be found in the yellow pages under *Music Copyists, Music Arrangers, Music Teachers,* or in the trade magazines or online.

Many arrangers will use a lead sheet when writing out the musical parts of a song. While some parts are worked out intuitively or by ear, other songs are recorded by groups of musicians who read off charts. In writing out the charts, the arranger works from the original lead sheet of the song. It is best if the lead sheet is written as uncomplicated as possible so that a vocalist or musician can interpret the song without becoming confused.

A lead sheet can be helpful in the demo-making process of a song, especially when hiring musicians who do not know the song. However, experienced musicians will usually make a spontaneous *head arrangement,* using only a chart showing the chord changes written over the lyrics on the lyric sheet.

In Nashville, charts using the Nashville Number System are used with session players. These charts include the chords written as Arabic numerals that can easily be transposed to any key. A work-tape of a song demonstrating the suggested style and groove is helpful for a demo-recording session. A great song demo is useful for communicating the song's intended interpretation to a publisher or producer. Despite all the technological advancements in computer generated lead sheet production, in today's market, it is still the recorded demo that sells the song.

If a song is going to be recorded by an artist for commercial release, it is a good idea to supply the producer with a full lead sheet, showing melody, chords, rhythms, and lyrics, in addition to a quality song demo. The degree to which the songwriter's ideas are adapted in the final recording can vary considerably. Having strong ideas initially, such as a strong intro lick or groove pattern, will best help to influence the final outcome of the production.

Only if a popular song is a hit will sheet music be printed. At this stage, it is very important that the music publisher be supplied with an accurate lead sheet to use as a reference. Most music publishers want the sheet music to be like the final recording, reflecting the creative changes that took place in the studio.

The most important quality of a professional-looking lead sheet is legibility. The musical notation must be accurate. The notes must add up to the correct number of beats per measure, and the stems must face the right direction. The lyrics should be clearly written and accurately placed under the appropriate notes.

Many successful singer/songwriters do not play an instrument or know how to write songs down. Many of the great jazz and blues artists did not use writing to communicate their songs and arrangements to others. They learned by listening and played by ear. This method is used by many pop and rock musicians today. It is not necessary to know how to notate music in order to create it. Writing down music is simply another form of communication and documentation, another skill. A good natural ear can create great music with or without this skill.

Lead sheets may be used to teach songs to others, especially for songwriters who can't sing on key. Lead sheets are a convenient reference on the songwriter's piano or shelf. Having a lead sheet makes it possible to play a song on the spot, be it for pleasure, to share with others, or to rework the song. Tunes or parts of a tune may be written out then returned to later when the writer is inspired to improve or finish it.

A tape recorder is a powerful songwriting tool, and can be used as an auditory notebook. Using a tape recorder gives the songwriter an opportunity to review his or her ideas, as well as a way to communicate ideas to a collaborator or other musicians working on a song. Synthesizers, drum machines, sequencers, MIDI devices, and music software have created many new possibilities for musical experimentation and home recording for the songwriter. Chapters 3 and 4 list many of the options available.

Chord Charts

The standard lead sheet format is not always necessary. Many instrumentalists find a chord chart to be sufficient, even preferable. A chord chart must clearly show the chords and when they change. Typing out the complete lyric of the song and placing each chord symbol directly above the word or syllable where the change occurs accomplishes this.

Some chord charts are written out using rhythm-figure notation or slash marks. These marks use the same system of open and filled-in noteheads and stems, flags, and beams as standard notation, except that the quarter-note slash mark is usually drawn without a stem. When the rhythm is consistent, only quarter-note slashes are used. Important riffs or musical hooks can be indicated in standard notation. Stops, pushes, or anticipated rhythms can be written in, as well as chords that change off the beat. This type of chord chart can be used by any instrumentalist and by singers when the lyric is added.

The Nashville Number System

Most Nashville musicians substitute Arabic numerals in place of chords or note symbols when making musical notations. This quick and effective system has become standard. Using this method, musicians can hear a song one time, write out the numbers, and then play it. If the key of the song is too low or too high for the singer, the musicians can easily transpose or change key while using the same number chart.

Tablature

When tablature is used, musical notes are represented on a staff in which the staff lines depict the strings of the instrument played, usually the guitar. This is in contrast to a normal staff where the lines represent musical tones. Bends, slides, pops, hammers, and strums are represented by different symbols, and are displayed according to the position and sequence in which they are performed.

Reading and Writing Music

There is no mystery to reading and writing music, and it is not a difficult task to become musically literate. It is simply a matter of practice. Usually a person who plays an instrument is familiar with notes, chords, and their names. Those who play or sing entirely by ear will need some help writing down music. In either case, it is a good idea to become familiar with the accepted formats. There are many useful Web sites and music software programs available for learning basic music theory and notation skills. Many of these are listed in chapters 3 and 4 under "Music Theory Fundamentals Software," "Aural Skills and Ear Training Software," "Rhythm Skills Software," and "Music Theory and Composition-Notation-Ear Training Web Sites."

Sample Templates

A demo with sample templates from the notation software program *Finale*, used by publishers, composers, arrangers, and songwriters for preparing scores, can be downloaded at www.codamusic.com.

Print Music and Copyright Terms

Abridgment of Music Removing or changing parts of a song to create a new arrangement.

Administration When a songwriter retains ownership of the copyright and assigns a portion of the publisher's share of rights to a publisher in exchange for its services in administering the copyright.

American Society of Composers, Authors, and Publishers (ASCAP) Founded in 1914; the first performing rights organization in the United States; offices in New York, Los Angeles, and Nashville.

Arrangement A new and different version or adaptation of the lyrics, melody, instrumental, or vocal parts of a song; a new orchestration of an instrumental; an orchestration to which new ideas are added; an enhancement of the performance of a song.

Arranger One who orchestrates or adapts a musical composition by scoring for voices or instruments other than those for which it was originally written.

Author One who creates or originally writes the lyrics and/or music to a musical composition; the author's name.

Blanket Performing License A license purchased from a performing rights organization; licensee obtains the performance right for all works written and/or published by all the members of the organization.

Broadcast Music, Inc. (BMI) U.S. performing rights organization; founded in 1939.

Broadcast/Public Performance License The right to broadcast a copyright on radio, television, Internet streaming, or to perform it in concert; issued to broadcasters, arenas, and clubs; issued by performing rights organizations (ASCAP, BMI, SESAC); rate varies by usage.

Catalog A collection of all the songs owned by a music publisher.

Chromolithography Lithography adapted to use multicolored inks.

Collaborator Cowriter; person(s) with whom musical works are written.

Compose To write a musical work.

Composer A person who composes.

Composition An intellectual and artistic creation of music; a musical work.

Contractor Anyone who is under contract or works for another under contract; an independent contractor; a music contractor.

Contracts Written legal agreement between two or more parties.

Copublishing When a songwriter transfers part of the copyright and assigns all or a part of the publisher's share of the rights to a publisher for an advance.

Copy Reproduction of an original work; to reproduce an original work; work ready to be set up for printing.

Copyist Person who copies music from a lead sheet or score in written or computer manuscript form.

Copyright Infringement A violation of any of the exclusive rights granted by law to a copyright owner.

Copyright Owner Owner(s) of any or all exclusive rights granted under copyright law.

Cowriter Collaborator.

Derivative Works A work based on one or more preexisting works; an arrangement, dramatization, transcription, orchestration, or simplified edition; a derivative or sample license issued by the publisher is required.

Distortion Any changing of the fundamental character or melody of a copyrighted work.

Dramatic Work Performing arts work such as a play, musical play, opera, or ballet, which is primarily dramatic in nature.

Electrical Transcription The right to use a copyright as background music on an airplane, electronic game, Karaoke system, or jukebox; an electrical transcription license issued by the publisher is required.

Engraving The production of music notes, letters, or illustrations by means of incised lines on a metal plate.

Exclusive Rights The specific rights granted under copyright law to a copyright owner, or his licensee.

Exempt Performance A public performance covered by one or more of the limitations placed upon the performance right by the Copyright Act of 1976.

Fair Use A limitation placed on an exclusive right of a copyright owner.

First Sale Doctrine A portion of the U.S. Copyright Act stating that anyone who purchases a recording may then sell or otherwise dispose of that recording; the seller may not keep, sell, or give away any other copies.

First Use The right to record and commercially release a copyright for the first time; a first use license issued by the publisher to a company or individual commercially releasing the copyright is required; fee is negotiable.

Fixed The way in which music is fixed is legally separated into two classes: (1) sound recordings including records, CDs and tapes; (2) all others, including material copies such as printed copies, and audiovisual copies such as video, and motion picture synchronizations; a work's physical existence where it is embodied in a tangible medium of expression; the fixation must be done by, or under the authority of, the author; the embodiment must be sufficiently permanent or stable to permit it to be perceived, reproduced, or otherwise communicated for a period of more than transitory duration; a fixed work is in contrast with a "non-fixed" work as a piece that is memorized or a work that is performed or played from memory.

Folio A collection of songs of printed sheet music; the songs may be by a particular artist or group, or by a number of different artists.

Full Publishing When a writer transfers the copyright and assigns all of the publisher's share of the right to a publisher, usually in exchange for an advance.

Grand Rights Another name for performance rights in dramatic works.

Harry Fox Agency, Inc., The Used by many copyright owners for the licensing of recordings of their musical works.

Head Arrangement A spontaneous arrangement of a musical work where a musician plays from memory, experience, and habit.

Independent Contractor A person or business who performs a service for another under verbal or written contract, as opposed to a person who works for wages or salary or an employee; contractor retains control of the means, method, and manner of production or execution concerning the work or service contracted; neither the contractor nor the contractee may independently terminate the contract before completion of the work by the contractor; an independent contractor is not, by tax law, considered to be an employee.

Instrumental A composition written for a musical instrument; a musical performance involving only musical instruments; a recorded performance of a musical instrument.

License A contractual permission to act; given by written agreement granted by an authority that is legally authorized to grant such permission; a grant of one or more of the exclusive rights of copyright owners by the owner of that right to another party.

Literary Work A nondramatic work of prose or poetry.

Lithography The process of printing from a flat surface such as stone or a metal plate; the surface on which the image is printed is ink-receptive and the blank area is ink-repellant.

Lyric License License to print lyrics.

Lyric Sheet A page with only the lyrics or words to a song.

Lyricist A person who writes the words to a song.

Lyrics The words of a song.

Mechanical Reproduction License The right to mechanically reproduce a copyright on a CD or tape, or to digitally download it to a hard drive; a mechanical license is issued to record companies by a publisher or license clearance agency such as the Harry Fox Agency.

Mechanical Right One of the exclusive rights granted to copyright owners; the right to record the copyrighted work.

Music Manuscript A set of symbols used to fix a musical composition in written manuscript form; the music notation symbols are placed on a five-line staff and convey the meter, key, notes, rests, etc., of a musical composition.

Music Publishers Association of the U.S. An association of publishers of primarily serious and/or educational music.

Musical Play A dramatic work, such as a musical, musical comedy, or operetta, incorporating music as an integral part of the work.

Musical Work A term used in copyright law that refers to the actual notes and lyrics used in a song.

National Music Publishers Association An association of publishers of primarily popular music.

No Electronic Theft Act The No Electronic Theft Act of 1997 amends the U.S. Copyright Act to define "financial gain" to include the receipt of anything of value, including the receipt of other copyrighted works.

Nondramatic Work A work of the performing arts, such as a musical work, which is not dramatic in nature.

Nonexempt Performance A public performance which falls under the purview of the performance right.

Orchestra Large group of musicians performing on brass, woodwind, string, and percussion instruments; may include the piano or unique instruments not usually associated with the western European orchestra; genre specific orchestras include the klezmer and tango orchestras, consisting of traditional and ethnic instruments.

Orchestral Sketch Linear form of writing music; harmonic content shown with symbols.

Orchestration Written music for orchestra separated into performance parts for specific instruments.

Orchestrator A person who transcribes a musical composition for orchestra with performance specifications.

Original Material Song, lyrics, or music written or composed by an individual or group of individuals.

Original Work Independently created work of authorship.

Out-of-Print Music A music publication which is no longer available for sale; the copyright on a musical work does not expire when the work is placed out of print.

Parody Lyrics Any lyric which replaces the original lyric of a vocal work.

Performance Right One of the exclusive rights granted to copyright owners; the right to publicly perform the work.

Performing Rights Organization An organization which administers the performance rights in musical works for its publisher and writer members; in the United States, these are ASCAP, BMI, and SESAC.

Print To make a copy by use of a machine that prints or transfers print from an inked or carbon surface, or applies ink, carbon, or other printing material to paper.

Print License Defines the agreement to assign the print rights of a copyrighted work; the assignment is made by the legal owner of the print right, or his representative (licensor), to another (licensee); usually assigned to, and administered by, the music publisher.

Print License Fee The monetary compensation paid to a print right licensor to obtain a print license; the payment is a negotiated rate.

Print Publisher One who issues a printed edition of a work; may or may not be the copyright owner of the work.

Print Right The right, authorized by copyright law, to reproduce a copyrighted work in printed form; one of the exclusive rights granted to copyright owners, that being the right to print copies of the work.

Print Royalties The standard royalty paid on all printed sheet music collected and distributed by publishers; the compensation paid to a copyright owner for the printed use of his work in, for example, song folios and sheet music; if the work has been assigned to a music publisher by the songwriter(s) who created the work, the royalty is paid by the music publisher to the songwriter(s); the amount paid is proportionate to the license fees received by the publisher from its print publisher licensees or from the sales gross if the publisher is printing and publishing in-house; the royalty rate paid is defined by the songwriter/publisher contract.

Public Domain The absence of copyright; a work is in the public domain if no copyright is claimed on the work or if the copyright on the work has expired; arrangements of works in the public domain are copyrightable.

Public Performance To perform or display a work at a public place live or by any device or process capable of transmitting or recording an image of a performance or display.

Published Work A work which has been distributed to the public in copies or recordings by sale, rental, lease, or lending.

Publishing License Defines the agreement to assign the publishing rights of a copyrighted work; assignment is made by the legal owner or licensor of the publishing; publishing licenses include the print license, mechanical license, compulsory license, purchase license, transcription license, and synchronization license.

Publishing Rights Publishing is the administration of a copyright and is divided into two parts: the writer's share and the publisher's share: 100 percent of the Writer's Share + 100 percent of the Publisher's Share = 200 percent of the total publishing rights; publishing rights can be assigned without transferring ownership of the copyright; ownership of a copyright can be transferred without assigning publishing rights.

Register of Copyrights The director of the United States Copyright Office.

Rental Music Music which is distributed through the rental of scores and/or parts rather than through the sale of copies; a rental work is considered a published work, and is granted the same copyright protection.

Reproduction Right The exclusive right, granted by copyright law, to reproduce a copyrighted work in copies of phonorecords, piano copies, CDs, cassette tapes, and all fixed material objects that can be perceived, reproduced, or otherwise communicated.

Reversion Clause A statement requiring the publisher to provide a release of a commercial recording on the national level within a specified period of time; if this requirement is not met, the contract terminates and all rights revert to the songwriter.

Right of Attribution Concerns the right of the creator to be known as the author of his/her work, the right to prevent others from being named as the author of his/her work and the right to prevent others from falsely attributing to him/her the authorship of work which the author has not written.

Right of Integrity The right of integrity concerns the right to prevent others from making deforming changes in the author's work, the right to withdraw a published work from distribution if it no longer represents the views of the author, and the right to prevent others from using the work or the author's name in such a way as to damage his/her professional standing.

Role of the Publisher The primary publisher functions are authorizing the use of a copyright, collecting income generated by the copyright, protecting the copyright against illegal use, and promoting the copyright.

Royalties Royalties are payment made to a composer by an assignee or copyright holder for each unit or copy sold of the composer's work; royalty income sources, according to the contractually agreed-upon amount, include mechanical, which covers CD, tape, and album sales; sheet music sales; sync licenses for synchronization of music to film, movie videos, etc.; background music for elevators and similar uses; special licenses such as commercial, merchandising, etc.

Royalty Rates In the royalty rates section of a song contract, the percentage rate of royalty payment for various uses of the song.

Royalty Statement An accounting statement made by the user licensee to the licensor or by the copyright assignee; statement shows the dates and sources of income, itemized deductions and costs, total sales, royalty rates, and royalties owed and paid out; sent out quarterly by registered mail.

Self-Publishing The act of carrying on the duties of a music publisher by oneself.

SESAC The smallest of the three performing rights organizations in the U.S.

Sheet Music Printed music that is sold to the public.

Single-Song Contract Where a publisher signs one song; term is typically for the duration of copyright; common with new writers.

Small Rights Performance rights in non-dramatic works.

Software Publishers Association Publishers of computer software.

Song Dex Index system that lists the writer, publisher, copyright proprietor, lyrics, and melody line of various songs.

Song File A publisher's checklist and data sheet for an individual song that is part of its catalog; file contains various information including the song name, the songwriter(s) name(s), the date of the songwriter/publisher contract, royalty income distribution dates, when and to whom mechanical licenses were granted, when and to whom compulsory licenses were granted, when and to what performance rights society a publisher registration card was sent, the date of copyright, the copyright registration number, and the song's status as published or unpublished.

Song Registration The act of establishing a written record to substantiate the ownership and date of ownership of a song.

Song Rights All the legal rights in a musical composition that may be sold or assigned.

Song Royalties Royalties received from the sale of the rights to a song from performance, publishing, compulsory, jukebox, or derivative work licenses.

Song Shark Any person who charges a fee to publish a song; anyone who profits by exploiting the ignorance of a novice songwriter.

Songwriter's Biography Form A form kept by a music publisher with information concerning one of their contracted or affiliated songwriters; includes the songwriter's name, professional name, address, address of a close relative, birth date, birthplace, citizenship, driver's license (state and number), social security number, music organization affiliates, union membership, spouse's name, children's names, published songs, and other publishers of the songwriter's music.

Stereotype Process A solid metal duplicate of a relief printing surface that is made by pressing a molding material such as wet paper pulp against it to make a matrix; molten metal is then poured into the matrix to make a casting which may then be faced with a harder metal to increase durability.

Subpublishing When a publisher licenses the copyright and the publishing rights associated with the copyright to a third party to administer; used most often when dealing with foreign territories; subpublisher receives a percentage of the publishing share.

Synchronization Right The right to affix, or synchronize, a musical work in an audiovisual work such as a film or video; the right to use a copyright by "syncing" it up with a visual picture, such as in film or television; a synchronization or sync license is issued to a film or TV production company by the publisher or license clearing agency.

Union Contractor Union musician that performs supervisory functions for a recording session; contractor that employs union labor.

Universal Copyright Convention An organization of nations, all of which agree to provide copyright protection in their countries to copyright works from all member nations; the United States is a member.

Unpublished Work A work which has not been distributed to the public in copies or recordings by sale, rental, lease, or lending; unpublished works may be protected by copyright.

WIPO The World Intellectual Property Organization; negotiates treaties that help make copyright laws more consistent between nations; the WIPO treaties, negotiated in 1996 by more than one hundred countries, make it possible to fight piracy worldwide, regardless of the location of the copyright holder or the infringer.

Work for Hire When a writer is hired or contracted to write for a company or other second party; often utilized in jingles, corporate themes, and some TV and film uses; the employer is the copyright owner; by law, the writer always retains the writer's percentage of income from the publishing except in the case of a work for hire.

3

Software for Musicians

The purpose of this chapter is to help sift through the maze of music software brochures and catalogs currently available, providing an easy-to-use sample listing of products. Over six hundred music software titles are organized by category, then alphabetically. The manufacturer name appears in parentheses immediately following the product title. The annotations list product features, as well as system specifications (SYSTEM SPECS). It is important to check these before purchasing to make sure the product is compatible with the computer setup available. A "Hybrid" works on both Macintosh and Windows platforms. Version numbers and years, which may be included in the software title, are not included here. Please consult the manufacturer's Web site as listed in chapter 4 under "Computer and Electronic Music-MIDI-Software" for the latest version of a program and any available upgrades. No product endorsements are intended, and any choice of purchase is left to the discretion of the consumer.

The programs listed here include those for scoring and notation, composition and songwriting, professional or home studio recording, sequencing applications, digital audio recording and editing, CD burning, multimedia, MIDI file libraries, sample sounds and loops, software synthesizers, plug-ins, and MP3-related software. Many of these programs overlap in function. There are also many programs listed for computer assisted instruction (CAI), including children's music software, music theory fundamentals, aural skills, rhythm skills, music appreciation, history and composers, piano, guitar and vocal instruction, jazz, and band, choir, and studio management.

Music software products for musicians and music educators are available from the manufacturers directly either online or offline, in music or school libraries, in multimedia labs, at computer software trade shows, through computer software retailers and catalogs, or on the Internet. Not surprisingly, new titles will appear as this book is being printed, and some may go out of print. To stay current on new music software products, it is a good idea to consult music trade and recording magazines, attend music industry conferences, and to browse the Internet.

By searching on the Internet under "music software" at any of the major search engine sites, thousands of related Web sites can be accessed. Many titles are available as downloadable freeware, shareware, or demoware. The best way to stay current on new titles, new versions, and upgrades is to visit software company Web sites often, as listed in chapter 4 under "Computer and Electronic Music-MIDI-Software."

Company E-mail addresses, phone numbers, and street addresses can be accessed from their respective Web sites. In most cases, products can be ordered and/or downloaded from the software company's Web site. Please note that individual products not listed in this chapter may instead be listed under "Computer and Electronic Music-MIDI-Software" in chapter 4, especially if they have their own Web page or site, and/or if the product is downloadable. In a few instances, software company Web sites do not exist, especially if the program is no longer in print and/or the company no longer exists. These programs may still be found in site-licensed multimedia labs, however.

Some music software retailers offer discounts when purchasing several titles at once, or "bundles," which may or may not include related hardware items such as keyboards or MIDI interfaces. Discounts are frequently given to teachers, and to educational and religious institutions. It is a good idea to inquire about these. When purchasing a single software title as an individual for private use, one will usually pay the list price, possibly at a discount, depending on the retailer. Many of the music instruction software programs available are intended for both individual and group use.

Working with music software programs is a creative and effective way to improve musicianship skills and general knowledge about music. Many music instructors use software programs in their private studios, as well as in teaching labs and multimedia centers. Some students own their own copies for home use. There is no reason why any individual couldn't obtain those titles which interest him or her, and begin learning music on their own, consulting an instructor when necessary.

Children's Music Software

3 2 1 Music Match CD-ROM (Clearvue/eav): Interactive matching games; enhance listening skills; humorous characters; wide variety of keys, tonalities, and meters; essential listening and theory skills. SYSTEM SPECS: Macintosh: PowerPC processor or better, 8 MB RAM, System 7.1 or later; Windows: 486/66MHz processor or better, 8 MB RAM, Windows 95 or later.

A Little Kidmusic (Ars Nova): Introduction to music notation using traditional songs; with "play" button, can play song by tapping computer keys; pitches come out correctly; harmonic accompaniment follows; includes practice in playing a rhythm; voice sings solfege syllables in appropriate key; for teaching melody and harmony; concentrates on understanding music notation; for beginners, ages three-thirteen. SYSTEM SPECS: Macintosh.

Adventures in Music with the Recorder CD-ROM (Ubisoft): Sixty interactive lessons for teaching students the recorder; covers reading music, rhythm, harmony, and other important musical concepts; students can download songs from the Internet and upload songs they have written; encourages creativity; free recorder included; for ages seven and up. SYSTEM SPECS: Windows.

Adventures in Musicland (ECS): Animations; colorful graphics; general music program; listening skills; music notation; White Rabbit serves as a guide; Music Match tests identification of musical symbols, notes, rests, and instruments; Sound Concentration tests aural memory skills, including various sounds, single notes, intervals, triads, and scales; in Melody Mix-Up students duplicate a melody with pitches from a major triad, pentatonic scale, or the major scale; in Picture Perfect students identify instruments, musical signs, or composers; can save scores in the Hall of Records; features characters from Lewis Carroll's *Alice in Wonderland;* for beginners, grades K-6. SYSTEM SPECS: Hybrid; Macintosh: System 6.0.7 or greater, 2MB free RAM, 8MB hard disk space, Mac-256 color monitor; Windows: Windows 3.1/95/98, VGA monitor, 4MB RAM, sound card, 8MB hard disk space; CD-ROM version requires CD-ROM drive.

Allie's Playhouse CD-ROM (Opcode): Interactive multimedia-rich environment; encourages children to explore, interact, and create; covers important subjects including math, music, spelling, geography, the solar system, and more; begins with a choice of six different friends who serve as child's companion; Allie, a little green alien friend, is the coach and tour guide; hours of exciting educational activities; for beginners, ages three-eight. SYSTEM SPECS: Macintosh; Windows.

Children's Songbook CD-ROM (Voyager): Fifteen traditional songs from around the world; each recording is accompanied by an animated illustration, lyrics, notation, and background information; instrumental version of each song so children can sing along; games teach children to recognize music and lyrics; historical and cultural information about each song; for beginners, ages six-twelve. SYSTEM SPECS: Hybrid.

Dr. T's Sing-Along (Dr. T's Music Software): Classic children's songs, animation, song lyrics, and music notation; an animated sequence that correlates with the song appears as it is played; simultaneously, the song lyrics and the melody in music notation appear in other windows on the screen; four easy-to-use graphic buttons control program operation: Play, Stop, Rewind, New Song; by clicking on the Turtle and the Rabbit, the computer says "slower" and "faster"; in Little Kid's Mode the entire screen fills with graphics and hides the Windows program and the menu bars; in Jukebox can customize a list of songs from the song list; can print the melody and words of song selected; can set up a Kid's Karaoke using a microphone plugged into the microphone jack of a computer sound card and an audiocassette recorder connected by cables to the sound card; for younger musicians; reading skills. SYSTEM SPECS: Macintosh; Windows: 3.1/95/386, SoundBlaster/compatible sound card, VGA color monitor, printer, CD-ROM.

Fortune Cookie (Maestro Music): CD-ROM; basic skill development for piano, vocal, and instrumental students; nine learning modules; tutorial explanations; drill and practice sequences; optional speech for pre-reading and special needs users; *Fortune Cookie* for grades K-2; *Fortune Cookie 2* for grades 1-3. SYSTEM SPECS: Hybrid.

Games for Young Friends (Maestro Music): Drills and practice of theory fundamentals in game format; each contest may be played by two students; if only one person is playing, computer will provide an opponent; format for each game is suitable for a second-grade student who knows the musical concepts presented; includes nine different games with three levels of play. SYSTEM SPECS: Macintosh; Windows.

Jump Start Music CD-ROM (Music in Motion): Instrument sounds; compose tunes; recognize rhythms; melody; harmony; K-elementary. SYSTEM SPECS: Macintosh; Windows.

Lamb Chop Loves Music CD-ROM (WB): Shari Lewis and Lamb Chop introduce kids to the world of music; animated storybook based on the children's classic *The Musicians of Brement;* learn the shapes and sounds of more than fifty instruments; fun musical activities; disc features a video of Shari Lewis and Lamb Chop; comes packaged with a Lamb Chop finger puppet; for beginners, ages three-seven. SYSTEM SPECS: Hybrid.

Lenny's Music Toons (Paramount Interactive): To familiarize children with music; approachable and fun; penguin character Lenny helps children explore music by participating in five different high-tech games and other activities; in "Lenny's Theater" students practice creating musical arrangements, choosing the star of the show, band members, rhythm, setting, props, tempo, and volume; students then hear the performance; in "Pitch Attack" players develop and use pitch recognition and sight-reading skills; in "Lenny's Puzzle Book" players learn to read written music by hearing short pieces, then recreating them by placing puzzle pieces containing sections of the music in place; in "Penguin Television" students produce a music video, either rock and roll, hip-hop, techno, or pop, as well as chose the star, costars, and visual effects; "Lenny's Matching Game" helps players develop memory skills; when the matching is complete, a picture is shown and Lenny's band plays a tune; clicking on most things in Lenny's living room results in a surprise; students are encouraged to explore and discover everything in Lenny's penthouse pad; creative program; fun to use; superb sound effects and graphics; available on floppy disk or CD-ROM; for all musicians ages six-fourteen; reading and listening skills. SYSTEM SPECS: Windows: 4 MB RAM, super VGA color monitor, 20 MB hard disk space, CD-ROM recommended.

Making More Music CD-ROM (Forest Technologies): Follow-up to Making Music CD-ROM; introduces standard music notation; children act as composer, performer, and audience; includes drawing notes on an animated screen, experimenting with different instruments, and putting together sections of a score; games; music making tools; covers musical heritage of Western culture. SYSTEM SPECS: Hybrid.

Making Music CD-ROM (Forest Technologies): By author/composer Morton Subotnick; "to allow children to experience what composing music is like before they are training on a musical instrument"; uses a graphic approach; no manual, other than installation instructions; overview to learn about all of the program's capabilities; all instructions are available through spoken online help; five work areas; students manipulate sounds with the mouse, choosing from the instrument palette in the main composition space; other creative areas include Building Blocks, Flip Book, and Melody and Rhythm Maker; students learn about repetition, sequence, inversion, retrograde, and sectional forms as composition tools; scales screen where the composer may select from major, minor, pentatonic, chromatic, whole tone, or "your own" scales; scales are shown as a series of stair steps; game area where users compare short tunes to determine if they are same-different, higher-lower, faster-slower, forward-backward, upside-down, etc.; sharpens aural skills; students may save, retrieve, modify, or play back their work; no score or grade, except in the games section; aims to foster creativity, even before the student learns to play or read music; takes thought and listening; can learn a great deal about the basic elements of composition—rhythm, melody, combining sounds, timbre, and form—using only auditory skills as a guide; ability to manipulate sounds and pitch sets extends beyond that of traditional instruments; a true composing space for children; presents the components of music visually and aurally; for children of any age; for all musicians, ages six-ten (possibly preschool students). SYSTEM SPECS: Hybrid; Macintosh: 680/25 MHz, CD-ROM, System 7, 8 MB RAM, color monitor; Windows: 486SX/33 MHz, Windows 3.1, DOS 5.0, 8 MB RAM, CD-ROM, VGA color monitor, sound card with speakers or headphones.

Merry Christmas Happy Hanukkah: A Multilingual Songbook and CD (Piano Press): Thirty-two traditional favorites; sixteen Christmas and sixteen Hanukkah songs; five-finger, easy-piano, and duet piano accompaniments; 112-page songbook; complete verses; multilingual texts include English, Hebrew, Spanish, German, French, and Latin; guitar chords; full MIDI orchestrations on play-along, sing-along audio CD; CD-ROM version prints scores. SYSTEM SPECS: Hybrid.

Midisaurus (Musicware): Award-winning edutainment; musical dinosaur introduces music with animation, games, and songs to play and sing; onscreen keyboard; MIDI keyboard optional; user friendly; eight-volume CD-ROM series; 510 activities; read, play, compose, and appreciate music; from simple to basic to advanced concepts; relates graphics or animated sequences with sound; instructions on screen and read aloud; thorough grounding in music fundamentals; for private teacher and schools; accounts for up to 250 students; four companion CD-ROMs include *Notation, Rhythm, Instruments,* and *Composers;* for ages four-eleven. SYSTEM SPECS: Hybrid.

Mrs. G's Music Room (Creative): Fundamentals of music theory; interactive learning activities; songs; games; five rooms with corresponding game or exercise; covers the musical staff, clef signs, notes in the music alphabet and on the staff, time values, bar lines, measures, time signatures (2/4, 3/4, and 4/4), rhythm patterns, and exercises. SYSTEM SPECS: Hybrid.

Music Maker CD-ROM (Music Sales): Play fifteen popular songs; five options include: One Key Play, JamTrax, Drum Along, Quiz, and Melody Play. SYSTEM SPECS: Windows, 486DX33, 8 MB RAM, sound card, CD-ROM drive.

Peter and the Wolf CD-ROM (Clearvue-eav): Narrated by Jack Lemmon; story; classic piece performed in its entirety by the Prague Festival Orchestra; animation; select stories, pictures, or sound. SYSTEM SPECS: Macintosh: 60830 processor or better, 4 MB RAM, System 6.0.7 or later; Windows: 386 processor or better, 4 MB RAM, Windows 3.1 or later, SVGA monitor.

Ricky Recorder (Gvox): Learn about the recorder; covers parts; playing posture and instrument care; twelve interactive lessons; thirty-two exercises; instant feedback; for ages six-eleven. SYSTEM SPECS: Windows.

Smack-a-Note (ECS): Music games covering staff note reading, solfege, and piano key names; can set skill levels; works in keys of C, F, G, D, and B-flat; Solfege game; Note Names game in treble, bass, or grand staff; Keyboard Names game with or without accidentals; for beginners, ages one-six. SYSTEM SPECS: Windows 95/98, Pentium 100mhz processor or Cyrix 166mhz processor, 32MB RAM, SVGA Display, 8MB free hard drive space, 16-bit color, sound card, CD-ROM drive.

Sophia's Dreams CD-ROM (Clearvue/eav): Listening skills; Sophia is a cat character; match melodies that are the same; over fifty characters; over 150 melodies; music appreciation; scorekeeping. SYSTEM SPECS: Macintosh: PowerPC processor or better, 8 MB RAM, System 7.1 or later; Windows: 486/66MHz processor or better, 8 MB RAM, Windows 95 or later.

Sound Toy (Forest Technologies): Improvise blues music by gliding the mouse over colored squares; hear a set of musical sounds; harmonica, guitar, and an African bell; clicking the center orb activates one of three bass and rhythm tracks; for ages three and up. SYSTEM SPECS: Macintosh.

Thinking Things 1 (Edmark): Auditory discrimination; visual relationships and patterns; melodic and rhythmic dictation; audio and visual memory; for Pre-K-3. SYSTEM SPECS: Hybrid.

Thinking Things 2 (Edmark): Strengthen listening skills and auditory memory; jamming machine; audio and visual memory; for grades 2-5. SYSTEM SPECS: Hybrid.

Music Theory Fundamentals Software

Clef Notes (ECS): In a drill, students use the mouse or arrow keys to move the note to match the indicated note name; student must successfully complete ten tries in a row to place a designated note on the treble, bass, tenor, or alto staff; student is prompted to try again if a mistake is made until the correct answer is given; help menu shows the name for all notes on a particular staff; timed games encourage students to improve the speed at which they accurately identify notes on the staff; students choose note names by selecting from a musical alphabet displayed at the bottom of the screen; at the end of each game a screen displays the percent of correct answers and the time in seconds; program automatically makes a record for each student tracking the time and score for the first and last game and an average for all games played; Hall of Fame displays top ten scores; student may choose one clef or all clefs; instructor may view or print the roster or individual records; program is copy protected; a backup copy cannot be made; for all music students ages six-fourteen; reading skills. SYSTEM SPECS: Macintosh: System 6.04; Windows: 386, 3.1, 4 MB RAM, VGA monitor; MIDI soundboard or MIDI keyboard recommended; can be used with headphones or speakers; Apple (non-MIDI); PC-DOS (non-MIDI).

Computer Activities (PBJ): Prep-2 and Levels 3-4 on two separate disks; note identification; half and whole steps; intervals; major/minor five-finger positions; triads; scales in C, F, G, D, and B-flat major and A minor; 2/4, 3/4, 4/4, and 6/8 meters; eighth notes; cadences; major key signatures; scales; key signatures in A, E, D, G, C, and B-natural and harmonic minor; major and minor intervals; major and minor triads and inversions; diminished triads; primary and secondary triads; dominant seventh chords; rhythm including 2/2, triplets, sixteenth notes; analysis of repetition, sequence, and imitation in music. SYSTEM SPECS: Hybrid.

Discovering Rudiments I and II (Musicware Canada): Tutorial and drill program; teaches music theory fundamentals in four volumes including pitch, time values, and keyboard recognition; scales and key signatures; simple and compound time; intervals, chords, seventh chords, and inversions; teachers can design and determine lesson sequences to fit the needs of the individual student; automatic record keeping available for up to 500 students; ages seven-adult. SYSTEM SPECS: PC, MIDI interface, MIDI keyboard.

Dolphin Don's Music School (A Class All Your Own): Nine games, each with ten skill levels that can be set up for treble, alto, tenor, or bass clef; in Read Notes students identify notes on the staff; in Hear Notes two notes are played and student identifies the second; a one-measure rhythm is shown with one hidden note in Rhythm Read; in Hear Rhythm a short rhythm is played and student selects the correct written version from the three displayed; in Read Keys students identify the correct key for the key signature shown; Interval and Chord games are similar; games may be paused; examples may be replayed or wrong answers tried again, but timer continues to run; final score and the highest recorded score are displayed; games begin by clicking on the Start button; computer counts backward from ten; points are scored equal to the amount of time left when the player enters a correct answer; answers are selected from a multiple choice list or group of possible notes; a large *Yes* appears for correct answers, along with a rippling chime sound; in hearing drills, the correct response is played again as reinforcement; for wrong answers, a visual *No, Try Again* appears; each game advances to the next level upon achieving a score of ninety or more points; progress tallied by giving a rank which has both a number and an ocean-related name such as Seaweed or Octopus; highest rank is Dolphin; students can view their scores any time; teacher can view or print all students' scores by entering a password; maximum of fifteen players is recorded; a well-sequenced program; complete set of theory and ear-training skills for the young student; for music students ages six-ten; reading skills; rhythm skills; video resolution is restricted to 640x480 pixels; most all multimedia computers default to higher resolutions, requiring users to reset the video and restart Windows. SYSTEM SPECS: Windows: 386SX, 4 MB RAM, 6 MB hard drive, MIDI soundboard, can be used with headphones or speakers.

Dynamics and Tone (Clearvue/eav): Elements of dynamics and tone; keynote; scale; chords; piano; forte; tone color; changing use of these elements in different style periods shown with examples. SYSTEM SPECS: Macintosh; Windows.

Early Music Skills (ECS): Introduces beginning students to four basic musical concepts: line and space recognition, numbering lines and spaces on the staff, direction of melodic patterns, and steps and skips; multiple-choice answers; if a MIDI keyboard is used, answers are played on the keyboard; for beginners, grades K-3. SYSTEM SPECS: Macintosh (MIDI optional); Windows (MIDI optional); Apple (MIDI or non-MIDI); PC-DOS (MIDI optional); color monitor (Windows and PC only).

Echos (ECS): Sight-reading skills, rhythm and note reading; students echo musical examples of notes from bass C to treble C on the staff, and rhythms up to eighth notes at the keyboard; dotted quarter notes in

Level II; ability to identify key signatures up to five flats and sharps is assumed; six sharps and flats for Level II; sight-reading/ear-training combination; students hear each example before they play it; wrong notes are highlighted; student is given three tries to play correctly; when played correctly, the program gives a praise word; if played incorrectly three times, program states, *No, but let's go on;* holds up to fifty names and passwords; keeps a record of the last time the student used the program only; gives the percentage of correct responses for each section; Music Reading, Sight-Reading Boxes, and Mystery Boxes; repetition of musical examples; for students ages ten-eighteen. SYSTEM SPECS: Macintosh, not Mac System 7.5-8.x compatible, (MIDI); Windows (MIDI); PC-DOS (MIDI).

Elements of Music (ECS): Beginning music program for children or adults; random drills; includes naming major and minor key signatures and naming notes on the staff or keyboard; progress tests and reports for each drill; instructor file for access to student records; for beginners, grades K-adult. SYSTEM SPECS: Macintosh (MIDI optional); Windows (MIDI optional); Apple (non-MIDI); PC-DOS (non-MIDI).

Essentials of Music Theory Levels 1-3 (Alfred): Interactive way to learn music; for classroom or individual instruction; CD-ROM; exercises reinforce concepts; narration, musical examples, and animations; ear-training exercises with acoustic instruments and scored reviews; Glossary of Terms; spoken pronunciations; audio and visual examples of each term; scorekeeping; record keeping; custom tests; separate Vocal, Piano, and Gold editions available; for ages eight-adult. SYSTEM SPECS: Hybrid.

Explorations (Mayfield Publishing Company): Music fundamentals course with textbook and computer software; intended for students with no previous knowledge of music or computers; covers note recognition, intervals, diatonic melody, rhythm and meter, triads, voice leading, key signatures, seventh chords, scales (major, three forms of minor, and modal), and chord function; textbook provides written explanations, suggested activities for exploring musical elements on the computer, creative exercises, written exercises, and a step-by-step guide on using the software program and MIDI keyboard; software explores each musical subject; practice sessions and tests separated into written theory skills and ear-training skills; students enter musical information using the computer by writing notation with the mouse, entering answers by clicking on interval names, solfege and so on, and playing music on a MIDI instrument or the on-screen keyboard; practice session mode includes detailed feedback; in test mode, students respond to a series of questions and are told how many have been attempted and how many were correct; Music Editor for music writing assignments and compositions; can collect test scores; automatic record keeping; easy-to-use comprehensive music fundamentals program; adult beginners may use the software and textbook for self-instruction; tool bar for entering music notation; choice of solfege or musical alphabet for identifying melodies; exploration mode for learning each subject; for music students, ages ten-adult; listening skills; rhythm skills; music notation. SYSTEM SPECS: Macintosh: Macintosh Plus, 8 MB RAM, 8 MB hard disk space, can be used with MIDI keyboard; Apple II.

Functional Harmony (ECS): Drill packages; displays grand staves with four-voice chords; key signatures provided; select answers by moving cursor through boxes identifying chord types; covers borrowed and altered chords, diatonic sevenths, and secondary dominants; cannot hear sound on a single-voice Apple II computer; MIDI keyboard required to hear sound; in Section 1, the user practices analyzing basic chords in major or minor keys and in root position or inversions; Section 2 presents diatonic seventh chords; Section 3 presents secondary dominants; Section 4 covers borrowed and altered chords; instructor may select the number of problems in each quiz; when using the MIDI option, the chord displayed on the screen will play through the audio device to aid in chord identification; for high school students and above. SYSTEMS SPECS: Macintosh (MIDI optional); Windows (MIDI optional); Apple (non-MIDI); PC-DOS (MIDI optional).

Harmonic Progressions (ECS): Designed to help the user in analysis of functional harmony; includes root position chords, inverted chords and the V7, embellishing sixth chords and the V7, diatonic sevenths, and cadence patterns; over 200 chord sets; practice analyzing chords, harmonic dictation, and aural identification; user must detect the quality of a chord sounded harmonically, as well as the position and voicing of the chord; correct answer given at the end of the example; for advanced students, high school-college. SYSTEM SPECS: Macintosh (MIDI optional); Windows (MIDI optional); Apple (MIDI); PC-DOS (MIDI optional).

Juilliard Music Adventure (Theatrix Interactive): CD-ROM game; developed by the Juilliard School; in the Queendom, students solve musical puzzles, learn music fundamentals, and experiment with composition; students work through puzzles in five rooms in the Queen's castle on three levels of difficulty; player solves specific musical problems by using the Rhythm and Melody Tools; player earns instrument keys by solving each puzzle correctly; no other scores are given; at the end of each level, player's listening skills are tested by matching the instrument keys to a series of musical locks; player is guided throughout the game by the Queen who has been imprisoned in an amulet; Queen describes the problem, refers the player to her magic scroll, then

corrects the player's work; players may leave the castle and experiment with composition on the musical tools; players may even have compositions performed by the program, accompanied by animation; the game portion of the program is somewhat repetitive; Rhythm and Melody Tools use tiles as measures and rectangles of different sizes and colors to determine duration and accent; pitch is determined by the position of rectangles on each tile; high quality sound and graphics help to sustain the student's interest; helpful in introducing musical concepts and introducing students to the composition process; print materials accompany the CD-ROM; 68-page Teacher's Guide; for beginners, age nine and up. SYSTEM SPECS: Macintosh: System 7.0 and 8 MB RAM, double-speed CD-ROM, LCIII with color monitor; Windows: Windows 3.1, MS-DOS 5.0 and 8 MB RAM, CD-ROM, 486/25 MHz, MPC2 video card and sound card.

MacGamut (MacGamut Software International): Drill and practice in both aural identification and notation skills; includes Intervals, Scales, Chords, Melodic and Harmonic Dictation; easy to use; all interaction with the computer is done with the mouse; can control the number of times a student may hear a particular example; printout of student statistics; for high school to college music students. SYSTEM SPECS: Macintosh: Apple QuickTime, System 6.02.

Maestroscope Drills (Maestro Music): Groups of drill-and-practice programs to supplement Maestro Music's tutorial series; includes Music Literacy Series, Rhythm Series, and Generic Drills. SYSTEM SPECS: Macintosh; Windows.

Maestroscope Music Theory Series (Maestro Music): Four sequential levels designed to develop students understanding of music fundamentals; each level includes eighteen lessons, grouped into modules of six lessons; tutorial lessons contain six to nine paragraphs in a variety of formats; the sixth lesson is a graded examination; students may complete a lesson in twenty to thirty minutes working by themselves at a computer. SYSTEM SPECS: Macintosh; Windows.

Maestroscope Theory Readiness Series (Maestro Music): Drills designed for the young student; can be done with minimal reading skills and ability on the computer keyboard; organized in developmental order; drills are not tutorial so some explanation is required; Theory Readiness A is for students who want to learn to read and understand music; Theory Readiness B introduces students to symbols useful in learning to read music. SYSTEM SPECS: Macintosh; Windows.

Maximum Learning in Key Signatures (WBW Software): Three games, Accidental Squares, Sigtrek, and Mr. Fixit drill key signatures; students play against the computer or another student; Accidental Squares uses a standard tic-tac-toe format for identification of major or minor keys; Sigtrek's meteor field is an identification game for all key signatures; in Mr. Fixit the student corrects given key signatures; for elementary to junior high students; music theory. SYSTEM SPECS: PC, 512 K RAM.

Maximum Learning in Note Naming (Notendo) (WBW Software): Three games, Noteblitz, Pink Panda, and Note-in-a-Box drill note names in timed and untimed formats; treble and bass staves are used; advanced levels add ledger lines; in Noteblitz student correctly identifies notes to complete words; in Pink Panda students place notes in correct positions as part of a detective game; Note-in-a-Box uses note identification as a means to earn balloons for a party; utility module keeps scoring records; for elementary to middle school students. SYSTEM SPECS: PC, 512 K RAM.

MiBac Music Lessons (MiBac Music Software): Comprehensive music theory and ear-training program; eleven drill types: Note Names, Circle of Fifths, Key Signatures, Major/Minor Scales, Modes, Jazz Scales, Scale Degrees, Intervals, Note-Rest Durations, Intervals Ear-Training, and Scales Ear-Training; each drill has five to eight levels of difficulty; user can choose to work with treble, bass, alto, or random choice of clefs; in some drills, students enter answers by clicking on a note on the on-screen keyboard or by playing a key on a MIDI keyboard; in other drills, students enter answers by clicking an answer button with the mouse; students may select any of the eleven drills as well as the level of difficulty by clicking one of eleven buttons at the top of the screen; correct answers are displayed in several ways; for example, a black diamond shape appears above an answer box for a correct answer and the number of correct responses, the number of tries, and a percentage score are shown on the screen throughout the exercise; incomplete drills show a zero percent; complete drills show a score for each level and an average score for all of the levels for that drill type; requires no previous musical background. SYSTEM SPECS: Macintosh: System 7 or better, MIDI is optional; Windows: Windows 3.1/95, NT4 compatible, VGA or SVGA video, SoundBlaster or MIDI interface.

Multimedia Music Games CD-ROM (Voyetra): Three games that build musical skills; Music Quiz tests general knowledge of music; in Note Blaster the student reads musical notes and shoots them off the screen with the on-screen keyboard or an external keyboard; in Rhythm Master the player matches rhythms heard with what appears on the screen; for beginner-intermediate, all ages. SYSTEM SPECS: Windows.

Multimedia Music Theory CD-ROM (Voyetra): Self-paced course; interactivity; animation; audio examples; covers the fundamentals of music in eight lessons: Nature of Sound, Melody, Harmony, Tonality, Notation, Rhythm, Harmony and Texture, and Form and Style; Music Glossary; click on a term to hear pronunciation and see definition; for beginner-advanced, all ages. SYSTEM SPECS: Windows.

Music Ace 2 CD-ROM (Harmonic Vision): Second title in series; introduces standard notation, rhythm, melody, key signatures, harmony, intervals, and more; features Maestro Max and choir of Singing Notes; over 2,000 musical examples; new instruments; introduction to music fundamentals and theory; twenty-four comprehensive lessons; games; composition tool; tracks progress through lessons and games; Music Doodle Pad. SYSTEM SPECS: Macintosh: 68040 @ 35 MHz or higher, System 7.5 or better, 12 MB RAM, 640x480 256-color monitor, 8 MB free hard disk space, CD-ROM drive, MIDI keyboard optional; Windows 3.1: 486 33 Mhz or better, 8 MB RAM, 640x480 256-color Super VGA, 8 MB free hard disk space, CD-ROM drive, MPC compatible sound card or general MIDI required; MIDI keyboard optional; Windows 95/98: 16 MB RAM.

Music Ace CD-ROM (Harmonic Vision): Includes Music Ace and the Music Doodle Pad; colorful graphics; animated conductor named Maestro Max teaches music fundamentals from the staff through key signatures and scales; six students may be enrolled at one time; students select their name, then one of the twenty-four lessons or twenty-four correlating games; instruments may be presented in treble and bass, treble only, or bass only; lesson control buttons include: skip forward, skip backward, volume control, pause/resume, and a game button; each lesson and game has several sections to complete to win the game; games include "The ABC's of the Piano Keyboard," "The ABC's of the Treble Staff," "Half Steps and Whole Steps," and "Introduction to Major Scales"; "Lesson Progress Tracking" shows how many times a user has completed each lesson section; "Game Progress" screen shows if a game was won, as well as the total score; "High Scores" section allows users to see who has the highest score on each of the twenty-four games; with the "Music Doodle Pad" users can listen to and change sample melodies or create and hear their own; sample songs are selected and played by clicking the "Jukebox" button; new melody can be created by dragging a "face"; melodies can be heard on six different instruments: piano, guitar, oboe, trumpet, marimba, and synthesizer; each "face" sings as it is played; introduction to music fundamentals; for beginning music students ages eight-adult. SYSTEM SPECS: Macintosh: 68030 @ 25 MHz or better, 5 MB RAM, 256 color monitor, System 7.0.1 or better, CD-ROM drive, 16 MB hard disk space; Windows: 386 25 MHz or better, 4 MB RAM, 20 MB hard disk space, MPC compatible sound card or general MIDI required, keyboard is optional; Windows 95 requires 8 MB RAM; PC: 386, VGA color monitor, SoundBlaster/compatible sound card, MIDI adapter, or MPU 401/compatible MIDI interface, MIDI instrument.

Music Achievement Series (Alfred): Book and three disks; companion to "Practical Theory"; three levels of tests; scores for up to fifty students can be stored on disk and printed out; for beginner-advanced, all ages. SYSTEM SPECS: Macintosh: Macintosh System 6 to 6.0.7 and 512K RAM, MIDI keyboard optional; PC-DOS: PC compatible, PC-DOS 3.2 or higher, 640K RAM, MIDI keyboard optional, MPU-401 compatible MIDI interface required.

Music Flash Cards (ECS): Important music material in a drill-and-practice format; nine lessons; Section 1 includes names of notes, rhythm values, and rhythm value equivalents; Section 2 includes major scales, minor scales, modal scales, and key signatures; Section 3 includes intervals and basic chords; user evaluation displayed at the end of each lesson; for beginner-early advanced, grades K-9. SYSTEM SPECS: Macintosh (MIDI optional); Windows (non-MIDI); Apple (non-MIDI); PC-DOS (non-MIDI).

Music Game (Microforum): Interactive multimedia program; video appearances by Oscar Peterson, Liona Boyd, and the Canadian Brass; covers fundamentals of music theory; four users can play at the same time or users can challenge the computer; includes Musical Notes, Musical Words, Musical Math, Musical Signs, Musical Rhythm, and Music Makers; multimedia board game; for beginners, ages eight and up. SYSTEM SPECS: Windows 3.1, CD-ROM.

Music Lab Harmony CD-ROM (Clearvue-eav): Recognize, read, and transcribe chords; hear harmony; eight interrelated units; quiz mode; record-keeping functions; monitors student work; offers remedial help; directions; explanations; theory facts and examples. SYSTEM SPECS: Windows: 486 processor or better, Windows 3.1 or later.

Music Reading CD-ROM (Clearvue-eav): Evaluation and teaching tool; match sounds with symbols; check answers and save scores; five levels of difficulty. SYSTEM SPECS: Macintosh; Windows.

Music Terminology (ECS): Five programs for improving student's knowledge of music terminology; includes: Glossary of Terms, Categories of Terms, True/False Test, Multiple-Choice Test, and Fill-In Questions; programs randomly select questions from a pool of over one hundred terms; summary of terms to be reviewed is displayed at the end of each program; for beginner-intermediate, grades 5-12. SYSTEM SPECS: Macintosh; Windows.

Musica Analytica Advanced Music Theory Software (ERTechnologies): Integration of music notation, multimedia elements, auto grading, and help for students; create multimedia documents with tool palettes; convert documents into assignments, tests, or tutorials; covers fundamentals to part writing, voice leading, and chord progression treatment; class

management; MIDI playback. SYSTEM SPECS: Macintosh; Windows.

Musical Stairs (ECS): Introduction to interval reading; screen displays an interval in the treble or bass clef; student reproduces the interval at the MIDI keyboard; ten problems in each session; scoring is based on the number correct out of ten; Hall of Fame for the top ten scores; covers intervals within one octave on the white keys; for beginners, grades K-3. SYSTEM SPECS: Macintosh (MIDI optional); Windows (MIDI optional); Apple (MIDI or non-MIDI): PC-DOS (MIDI optional).

Musique (ECS): Self-paced exercises for theory instruction; ear-training and theory drills present immediate feedback; maintain achievement scores for student and instructor; includes interval and chord analysis, harmonic dictation, aural identification of chord function within a chord series, keyboard topography, note placement, scales and modes, and over one hundred basic music terms; for advanced, high school-college. SYSTEM SPECS: Macintosh (MIDI optional); Windows (MIDI optional); Apple (MIDI); PC-DOS (MIDI optional).

Musition (Rising Software): Educational music theory package; drill-based teaching; covers Scales, Intervals, Instrument Range, Note Reading, Advanced Clefs, Key Signatures, Scale Degrees, Symbols, Terms, Musical Concepts, Chord Recognition, Meter Recognition, Rhythm Notation, and Transposition; customize to needs; set up tests; define contents of test; extensive reporting features; twenty built-in reports. SYSTEM SPECS: 486 100 MHz or Pentium processor, hard disk with 10 MB free space, Windows 95/NT, mouse, SoundBlaster/compatible sound card.

Note Speller (ECS): Players identify words created by on-screen staff notation; each game has a ten-example quiz; clef options include treble, bass, grand staff, and alto, and upper or lower ledger lines; game speed options are adagio, moderato, or allegro; word length can be short (three to four letters) or long (up to seven letters); user clicks the on-screen Answer button, the example disappears and the user types the correct spelling of the notational word with the computer keyboard or plays the alphabetical spelling of the word on a MIDI keyboard; Continue button is clicked when finished; if word is spelled correctly, points are awarded based on the time it takes to answer; negative points are given if an incorrect answer is given; higher points for using faster game speeds, but not for using longer words or ledger lines; if the user runs out of time on an example but gives a correct answer, no points are awarded; no second rides for incorrect answers; up to ten student names can be listed in the Hall of Fame; four Halls of Fame include Treble, Bass, Treble and Bass (grand staff), and Alto; help menu includes the sayings *Every Good Boy Does Fine, Great Big Dogs Fight Animals,* and *All Cows Eat Grass* for identifying grand staff lines and spaces; alphabetical spelling also appears to the right side of the staves; alphabetical note identification; easy to use; on-screen graphics; for beginners, grades K-6. SYSTEM SPECS: Macintosh (MIDI optional); Windows (MIDI optional); Apple (non-MIDI); PC-DOS (non-MIDI).

Patterns in Pitch (ECS): Companion program for Patterns in Rhythm; two-part aural-visual program; Part 1, The Composer, allows user to create pitch patterns in treble or bass clef; Part 2, The Dictator, plays pitch patterns based on the key and number of pitches selected by the user; Level I uses C, G, and F with up to eight notes in the series; Level II adds D, A, B-flat, and E-flat and plays up to twelve pitches; in Level III, the user may choose any major or minor key and up to twelve pitches to be played; for beginner-advanced, all age groups. SYSTEM SPECS: Apple (non-MIDI); PC-DOS (non-MIDI).

Practica Musica 4 (Ars Nova): Comprehensive music-literacy training for middle-school through adult students; includes textbook, *Exploring Theory with Practica Musica,* with tutorial and references to specific activities; to reinforce classroom and studio learning or to be used as an independent study package; each learning activity has four levels of difficulty; includes Pitch Matching, Reading and Dictation; Rhythm Matching, Reading and Dictation; Pitch and Rhythm Reading and Dictation; Scales and Key Signatures; Interval Playing, Spelling, and Ear Training; Chord Playing, Spelling, and Ear Training; Chord Progression Ear Training; Melody Writing and Listening; students can select the musical elements they wish to practice in one of several clefs; answers are entered with a MIDI keyboard, an on-screen keyboard, or guitar fretboard or computer keyboard; assumes a certain level of musical skill for students at Level One of each activity; difficulty of exercises presented changes with the student's success; students earn points toward a mastery goal; shows student progress toward goal during each practice session; points are displayed in a colored box that matches a chart on the title page of the program when student masters an activity; instructors can create custom exercises using the Melody Writing activity or by using Songworks; Student Files can be used if multiple students use the program on one computer; Student Disks and site licenses, which include additional Instructor Options, are available for multiple computers with or without a network; complete music theory and ear-training package; interactive as it responds to and corrects input and it is customizable; supports QuickTime Musical Instruments (Mac) and Sound-Blaster compatible sound cards (PC); OMS and USB MIDI are supported; for beginner–advanced, middle or high school and college theory courses. SYSTEM SPECS: Macintosh: 68040 or PowerMac, System 7/8, 32 MB RAM, 16 MB hard drive space; Windows: Pentium or equivalent, sound card, Windows 95/98, 32 MB RAM, 16 MB hard drive space.

Practical Theory (Alfred): Drill and practice approach to learning music theory; covers the beginning basics through chord inversions and voice leading; well-paced method; presents concepts clearly; eighty-five comprehensive lessons; Practical Theory Volume One, Lessons 1-28: for beginners, middle school and up; covers basics of the musical staff, treble and bass clefs, notes, rests, accidentals, ties, slurs, and ledger lines; Practical Theory Volume Two, Lessons 29-56: intermediate, middle school and up; covers major and chromatic scales, key signatures and the circle of fifths, dynamics and tempo markings, intervals, triplets, and syncopation; Practical Theory Volume Three, Lessons 57-85: intermediate-advanced, middle school and up; covers major triads and chords, chord progressions, relative, harmonic, and melodic minor key signatures, harmonizing and composing melodies, passing and neighboring tones. SYSTEM SPECS: Macintosh: Macintosh System 6 to 6.07, 512K RAM, MIDI keyboard optional; PC-DOS: 3.2 or higher; 640K RAM, MIDI keyboard optional, MPU-401 compatible MIDI interface required.

Rhythm and Melody (Clearvue/eav): Science of sound; rhythm; theme and variation in melody; developments in instruments and musical styles from all periods with examples. SYSTEM SPECS: Macintosh; Windows.

Symbol Simon (ECS): Teaches music symbols and terms; game-based drill format; sound effects and graphics use a nautical metaphor; two games, each divided into two levels; drills symbols, terms, rhythm values, time signatures, and note names; "Invention Island" presents multiple-choice lists to show a series of symbols; in "Hatch Match," cabin windows and portholes match symbols with their definitions; installation instructions and trouble-shooting procedures for sound and MIDI cards; online help; Reference displays definitions and examples of all terms and symbols used in the program; students sign in with their name and a password; program functions involve using a mouse or other pointing device; video-game format; Hall of Fame records highest scores; when sound option is activated, a pirate voice is heard; for elementary music students, beginners, grades 3-6. SYSTEM SPECS: PC/Windows 386, 3.1 or 95, 4 MB minimum RAM, 8 MB RAM recommended, 2MB hard disk space, VGA monitor, sound card optional but recommended.

Symbols and Terms (WBW Software): Two games designed to teach standard musical symbols and terminology to music students ages eight-fifteen; players rescue "Sigmoid the Android" from a shower of symbols by correctly identifying them; "Green Submarine" drills recognition and understanding of dynamics, pitch and rhythm, phrasing and tempo, and expression; record utility provides teachers with scores for every game played; advanced levels of the games use some obscure terms; for elementary to junior high students. SYSTEM SPECS: PC, 512 K RAM.

Theory Games (Alfred): Helps students learn important music theory concepts; each game covers a different topic, from note names and intervals to musical terms and rhythms; to be used with Alfred's Basic Piano Library Levels 1A - 5; may also be used with other methods; games include: Name That Key, Note Names Race, Chord Name Race, Cross the Road, Melodic Intervals, Counting Game, Scale Game, Carnival Fun, Invader, and Composer Game; for beginners, all ages. SYSTEM SPECS: Macintosh: MAC II or higher (68020 or higher), System 7.0 or higher, 6 MB RAM, 5 MB hard disk space, 13" color monitor, MIDI keyboard optional; Windows: 386DX or better, Windows 3.1 or better, 4 MB RAM, 6 MB hard disk space, Windows compatible sound card or MIDI interface, MIDI keyboard optional.

Aural Skills and Ear-Training Software

Aural Skills Trainer (ECS): Intervals; basic chords; seventh chords; student records; diagnostic information; progress reports; completion scores; advanced. SYSTEM SPECS: Macintosh: System 6.0.7-8.x, 2MB RAM, MIDI optional; Windows: 3.1/95/98, 4MB RAM, VGA/SVGA display, sound card or MIDI; Apple (non-MIDI); PC-DOS (non-MIDI).

Auralia (Rising Software): Aural training course; includes Cadences, Chords, Chord Progression, Cluster Chords, Interval Recognition, Interval Singing, Jazz Chords, Meter, Pitch, Rhythm Dictation, Rhythm Elements, and Scales; each subject area has several levels of difficulty; lower levels for beginners; testing features; give test a name, save, and use again; for beginner-advanced, ages twelve and up. SYSTEM SPECS: 486 or better, 16 MB RAM, hard drive with 8MB free, Windows NT or 95, SoundBlaster or compatible sound card or any MIDI device, mouse.

Ear Challenger (ECS): Listening skills, hand-eye coordination; pitches are played by the computer, each represented by a different color key; student plays back pitches on the MIDI keyboard; correct answer is shown in response to right or wrong answers; helps student develop good listening habits; students visualize the notes and hear the intervallic movement among the pitches; seven levels of difficulty based on the number of pitches presented; students advance at their own pace; one or two players may play at the same time; Hall of Fame records student scores; self-explanatory; quick and easy installation; aural-visual music game designed to increase player's ability to remember a series of pitches as they are played by the

computer; for beginners, all ages. SYSTEM SPECS: Windows: MIDI soundboard, VGA color monitor (recommended), MIDI keyboard optional; Apple (non-MIDI).

Ear Training Expedition (Trail Creek): Tutorial introductions; practice drills; listening skills games; high and low pitch recognition; ascending and descending note patterns; recognizing major and minor triads and scales; identifying intervals; general theory concepts. SYSTEM SPECS: Windows.

Earmaster Pro (Miditac): Ear-training tutor; graded exercises; design own course; covers intervals, scales, chords, rhythm, and melody. SYSTEM SPECS: Windows.

Earmaster School (Miditac): Premium edition of Earmaster Pro; extra features for classroom use; customized reports; overview results. SYSTEM SPECS: Windows.

ECS Music Suite (ECS): Includes a metronome and tuner; automatic note sensing in real time; broad chromatic range; transpose function to shift entire scale to match instruments not in the key of "C"; Music Metronome helps users play more accurately in tempo. SYSTEM SPECS: Windows 95/98, MPC2, 8MB RAM, SVGA display, microphone, SoundBlaster sound card (no compatibles), 4MB free hard drive space, full duplex SoundBlaster drivers.

Euterpe (Hohner Media): Helps students develop an ear for music by distinguishing musical tones from one another; includes intervals, chords, scales, rhythms, melodies, counting measures, etc.; can test a student while using coding to prevent cheating; multiple choice testing method; ideal for musicians wishing to develop a stronger ear for music; classroom music tool; for beginner-advanced, ages twelve and up. SYSTEM SPECS: Windows 3.1 or higher, 386 or higher, 4 MB RAM, sound card or MIDI interface/keyboard for playback.

Harmonic Hearing (Ibis): Extensive harmonic ear training for development of chord recognition; through a series of chord progressions, students listen and modify until notes appearing on-screen match what is heard; on-screen visual and aural feedback to identify where corrections are needed; standard harmonic dictation method of identifying the bass note and then the chord quality; user hears a chord progression (usually eight measures) and mutes melody or chords at his or her option to isolate the bass, then moves bass notes to their proper positions to match the progressions; the student then listens to the chords combined with the bass; lists dozens of chord qualities, grouped into traditional categories of triads, seventh chords, dominants, and suspended chords; includes a variety of seventh, minor seventh and half-diminished chords, and every type of upper chord extension commonly used in modern music; trains users from the simplest triads to highly advanced jazz chords containing altered ninths, elevenths and thirteenths; Unit 1 for beginning-intermediate; Unit 2 for intermediate-advanced; grades 9-college. SYSTEM SPECS: Macintosh: MacPlus or newer, 4 MB RAM, hard drive, MIDI playback device.

Hear Today . . . Play Tomorrow (ECS): Includes disks on descending and ascending intervals, ear training, and melodic identification; requires a reasonable understanding of key signatures and scales; automatic scorekeeping; able to print rosters and scores; aural-visual exercises designed to improve ear training and music reading skills; Find That Tune shows three melody lines and plays one of the excerpts for the user to identify; in Ear Training Skills the user identifies and notates intervals or simple melodies; in the Beginning Level of Melodic Dictation the user completes a simple melody by filling in the missing notes; in the Intermediate Level, more complex melodies are used; in Descending/Ascending Intervals the user identifies and notates intervals; Keyboard Melody Task Cards teach music reading by numbers for learning interval relationships and melodic contour, and correlating sight and sound; Keyboard Rhythm Task Cards teach rhythm counting by answering questions on a worksheet and playing the melodies on the cards; Teacher's Manual covers implementation of the task cards and integration with classroom lessons; for beginner-intermediate students, grades 4-8. SYSTEM SPECS: Apple (non-MIDI); PC-DOS (non-MIDI).

Hearmaster (Emagic): Music theory program and ear-training program; graphic interface; covers music theory, including intervals, chords, and melodies; exercises for hearing and playing randomly generated rhythmic patterns; statistical record of learning progress; can fit individual needs such as degree of difficulty and musical style; for beginner-advanced, middle school to college. SYSTEM SPECS: Macintosh; Windows 95.

Inner Hearing (Ibis): Interactive melodic ear-training program; uses MIDI as a sound source; includes dictations of familiar folk melodies with notation on the screen; students adjust the notation to match what was played; good progression of learning steps from simple to difficult; flexible record keeping; student is awarded points for successful completions; teacher can view, sort, and print student work reports; for beginner-advanced students, ages ten to adult. SYSTEM SPECS: Macintosh; Windows.

Listen! A Music Skills Program (ECS): A condensed version of *Aural Skills Trainer* designed for home users; no record keeping. SYSTEM SPECS: Apple (non-MIDI); PC-DOS (non-MIDI).

Music Lab Harmony (Musicware): Recognize, read, and transcribe chords; master aural and symbolic techniques of harmonization; learning activities are interactive with immediate feedback; remedial help; each level consists of eight game-like tutorials called modules; Name: aural recognition; Analyze: visual

recognition and naming; Sing: vocal harmonic and reading skills; Echo: builds keyboard ability to mimic music; Play: keyboard performance from music symbols; Notate: traditional harmonic systems; final two modules, Read and Write, summarize all skills. SYSTEM SPECS: Macintosh; Windows.

Music Lab Melody (Musicware): Tutoring sight-reading, singing, and writing music; complete skill development system paced according to student's capability; through microphone, software reads student's singing voice to develop pitch matching and sight-reading skills; practice with immediate feedback; covers rhythm, ear training, writing, and performance skills interactively; includes eight units: Sing (pitch), Notes (solfege), Names (pitch recognition), Echo (rhythm reading), Notate (rhythm writing), Read & Write (combine all skills into sight-singing and melodic dictation); beginner-advanced, ages seven and up. SYSTEM SPECS: Macintosh: Quadra, Centris, PowerMac, and most Performa models with a microphone; PC-DOS: 286 or better, sound card, microphone, hard disk, VGA.

Play It By Ear (Ibis): Emphasizes learning to recognize, identify, and play single notes, melodies, scales, chords, and intervals; six predefined levels; may customize to fit specific needs; visual feedback; tracks progress; ear-training/dictation program appropriate for beginning theory classes through advanced college classes. SYSTEM SPECS: Windows.

Super Ear Challenger (ECS): Aural-visual game designed to increase a student's memory of a series of pitches played by the computer; based on a twelve-note chromatic scale, a major scale, and a minor scale; each pitch is represented visually by a color on the on-screen keyboard; for beginner-intermediate, all age groups. SYSTEM SPECS: Macintosh (MIDI optional); Apple (MIDI or non-MIDI); PC-DOS (MIDI optional).

The Art of Listening CD-ROM (Clearvue/eav): Develop active listening skills; interactive CD-ROM; numerous types of music and sound; explanations of terms such as melody, harmony, timbre, and rhythm; many examples from numerous forms; for beginners, grades 4-9. SYSTEM SPECS: Hybrid.

Toon Up (ECS): Covers intonation; users choose between a carnival game or a more traditional instrument, for example, the violin, to try to get pitches in tune; for beginner-intermediate, grades K-6. SYSTEM SPECS: Windows (MIDI optional).

Tune-It II (ECS): Practice in matching pitches; graphic-representation of a stringed instrument fingerboard; two pitches are played, with the second one sounding out of tune with the first one; student adjusts the second pitch until it matches the first one; pitch differences are finer for the more difficult exercises; student score record keeping; for beginner-advanced, grades K-6. SYSTEM SPECS: Macintosh; Apple (non-MIDI); PC-DOS (non-MIDI).

Rhythm Skills Software

Advanced Rhythmaticity (Musicware): Sequel to *Basic Rhythmaticity*; uses same format; thirty additional levels of real-time rhythm-reading and performance skill-building; includes 6/8 meter, triplets, sixteenth notes in all patterns, syncopation, and duplet/triplet combinations; video-game format for one or two players; rhythm pattern is notated on screen, then student clicks Begin and the metronome starts ticking; then student taps the exercise on any computer key or MIDI keyboard; lesson controls accessed by pull-down menus; includes a Tap Practice section in which the student taps along with the metronome; students achieve a numerical score for each rhythm exercise tapped correctly; optional Hall of Fame records the top ten scores as an improvement incentive; students can click on Analysis at the end of any performance to see whether each note was early or late; exercises are presented as melodies rather than a one-pitch rhythm pattern; can be installed in English or Spanish. SYSTEM SPECS: PC, VGA color monitor, sound card, MIDI interface, MIDI keyboard optional.

Challenge Musicus (ECS): Next title in series; rests are introduced; 9/8, 12/8, 7/8, and 7/4 meters; understanding of the relative lengths of notes and rests as well as combinations of tied notes; move note blocks of rhythms to complete lines of music; hear completed lines played at end of game. SYSTEM SPECS: Windows.

Musicus (ECS): Students complete measures in a given meter with music blocks; student completes as many lines within a given time frame as possible; five levels of difficulty; players are not required to understand the rhythmic notation, only to fit the blocks of notes into a given space; falling note blocks of rhythm must be put into measures of specific meters; student selects the space for the note block to fall by pressing a button; another note appears at the top of the screen for placement; each game is timed and the speed that notes fall can be adjusted at the beginning of each session; total points are accumulated by completing lines of rhythms with the note blocks; each note offers a different point value that is added to the total score; user has the option to hear their completed rhythmic lines at the end of the game; for elementary to middle-school students; rhythm game. SYSTEM SPECS: Macintosh (MIDI optional); Windows (MIDI optional), color monitor, sound card; PC-DOS (non-MIDI).

Patterns in Rhythm (ECS): Aural-visual program designed to increase rhythmic memory; students compose simple and compound meters; The Composer section plays melodies based on rhythms designed by the user; The Dictator is a quiz section which plays rhythmic examples the user must identify; in Level I, the user selects from 2/4, 3/4, and 4/4; Level II adds 6/8; Level III uses all meters, simple and complex; student records; for beginners-advanced, all age groups. SYSTEM SPECS: Apple (non-MIDI); PC-DOS (non-MIDI).

Rhythm Ace (Ibis): Comprehensive rhythm-training program; jazz or classical library; create and save rhythmic patterns; three exercise types: reading, dictation, or custom; twelve predefined levels; notation includes: whole notes and rests to sixteenth notes and rests, quarter and eight-note triplets, dotted notes and ties, simple and compound meter; for beginners-advanced, ages twelve and up. SYSTEM SPECS: Windows.

Rhythm Factory (ECS): Rhythmic notation; audio voice explanations; keywords; Time and Notation sections; Beat Machine; Beat Splitter; Tempo Warehouse; Paint Shop; Part Shop; Inventory Time; Pattern Shop; evaluation and feedback; learning activities; time tests; quizzes; puzzles; for ages eight-fourteen. SYSTEM SPECS: Macintosh: 2MB free RAM, System 8 or higher, CD-ROM drive, 4MB free hard drive space; Windows: Windows 98/2000, 300 MHz min, 8MB free RAM, SVGA Display, CD-ROM drive, 4 MB free hard drive space, sound card.

Super Musicus (ECS): To help learn time values of notes; whole, half, quarter, eighth, sixteenth, and triplets; combinations of tied notes of equal values and tied notes of unequal value or dotted notes; how these note values relate to different musical meters including 6/8 and 5/4; follow-up to *Musicus*. SYSTEM SPECS: Macintosh; Windows.

Tap-It II (ECS): Sequel to *Tap-It* program; includes more difficult rhythm patterns; syncopation, eighth, and sixteenth note values; actual note heads are introduced; online help menu; each of three levels includes new rhythms; Tutorial; Listening & Tapping; Reading & Tapping; each level has a quiz of twenty measures; seven different tempo settings from 54-144 for practice; full record keeping; for intermediate-early advanced. SYSTEM SPECS: Windows (MIDI optional).

Tap-It (ECS): Aural and visual rhythmic examples at four levels; each level includes three levels of difficulty and seven tempo choices; students play rhythms at the computer keyboard; quiz and percentage scores are given at the end of each level; automatic score-keeping is available; final quiz is considered the "All-Pro" level; ear training and sight-reading; for beginners, all age groups. SYSTEM SPECS: Macintosh (MIDI optional); Windows (MIDI optional); Apple (non-MIDI): PC-DOS (non-MIDI); color monitor (PC and Windows only).

Tap-It II Lite (ECS): Sequel to *Tap-It* program; includes more difficult rhythm patterns; syncopation, eighth, and sixteenth note values; records student achievement for three students; functions with one preselected tempo for quiz playback; one level of skill development. SYSTEM SPECS: Windows.

The Rhythm Performance Test-Revised (ECS): Computer-based test instrument for tapping a steady beat and rhythm patterns; standardized for children ages four-twelve; screening tool; research and assessment. SYSTEM SPECS: Windows.

Composition, Creative, and Songwriting Software

12-Bar Tunesmith (ECS): To help students compose and play simple melodies; eight pitches used are based on the C major scale; four different pitch durations; tunes can be played at different tempos; iconic notation is used on a graphic screen to help the user understand pitch and duration; for beginner-advanced, grades K-4. SYSTEM SPECS: Apple (non-MIDI); PC-DOS (non-MIDI).

21st-Century Music Series: Playing, Reading, and Composing Music (ECS): Student is taught how to play, read, and compose music using a MIDI-compatible electronic piano keyboard; Disk I covers white key names and the treble clef; Disk II introduces rhythm along with time signatures, barlines, and measures; Disk III introduces rests, the bass clef, dotted notes and ties, and the grand staff; Disk IV introduces the playing of melodies using both treble and bass staves; in Disk V students compose musical compositions and print them out; for beginner-intermediate, grades 6-8. SYSTEM SPECS: Apple (MIDI); PC-DOS (MIDI).

All My Hummingbirds Have Alibis (Forest Technologies): CD-ROM; American composer Morton Subotnick presents two musical and visual compositions; shares the creative and technical processes; textual explanations and musical examples explain how and why he composes; commentary from the programmer and recording engineer explains the technology behind the music; *Hummingbirds* (1992) is performed on flute, cello, MIDI grand piano and MIDI mallets; music is accompanied by the surrealistic images and text of Max Ernst; experience a great performance of the composition, view Ernst's images and text, hear narrative from the composer, and follow the full score; second composition is *Five Scenes from an Imaginary Ballet;* first piece composed for CD-ROM; each scene can be heard and viewed with or without Subotnick's remarks; "Program Notes" tell how the works were created and inspired, as well as a biography, a discography, and a catalog of works; brief biographies of the performers on the recording; "About the Music" describes the musical structure, the use of text from the collage novel, and how the works were composed and recorded; "About the Technology" describes the technology used in the composition and recording the works; for all musicians, ages ten-adult; composition, music technology, chamber music. SYSTEM SPECS: Macintosh: CD-ROM,

System 6.7, 5 MB RAM recommended, 13" color monitor, speakers or headphones.

Band-In-A-Box (PG Music): Select a song from the MIDI fake book, or type in chord changes; select from one of many styles included with program; automatically generates a five instrument accompaniment; with Automatic Soloing can select a virtual soloist from over one hundred available; will create and play a solo; save songs in standard MIDI file format; full featured digital audio track; add live vocals or guitar playing; intelligent style selection wizard which shows what styles work best for song; highlights all styles with similar tempo, genre, and feel; guitar enhancements; tablature display; automatic feature creates pro quality guitar chord solo to any melody; displays on guitar fretboard; Big Lyrics Window with selectable font and size; Big Piano Window displays a piano with large size keys and optional note names; record a track of CD quality with audio features; can overdub audio parts to add in harmonies; MIDI and audio tracks are compatible with other sequencers and sound programs like PowerTracks, Sound Forge, Cubase, or Cakewalk; automatic guitar chord solos; standard, advanced, or embellished chords; view in notation or guitar tab; print out; save song as MIDI or WAVE file (.WAV); render file from MIDI to audio; send it to others or put on the Internet; use CD-burning software to save .WAV file onto a conventional audio CD; save song in compressed Internet formats; accurate placement of lyrics under each note; lyrics can be saved with MIDI file; Big Lyrics (Karaoke) Window; Style Selection Wizard; "Jazz Up" Chords, "Jazz Down" Chords; convert harmony part to notation track; notation enhancements; Keystroke Note Editing; notation range; enhanced event list editing; harmony enhancements; solo around the melody option; add chord shortcuts; StyleMaker enhancements; larger style limit; pattern trim routine; event list; enhanced song list window; song endings option; new lyric functions; enhanced volume control; stereo/mono panning menu items; total time for song in minutes and seconds displayed at top; polyphonic adjustment of melody tracks; omit lead-in option; quick-copy option. SYSTEM SPECS: Macintosh; Windows.

Band-In-A-Box Melodist Disk Sets (PG Music): Melodist Disk Set #2, Country, Pop, and EZ-Listening; compose songs in these styles complete with intro, chords, melody, arrangement, and improvisation; auto-generate any part of composition; have *Band-in-a-Box* create a new Pop, Country, or EZ-Listening song from scratch; requires *Band-in-a-Box* version 8.0. SYSTEM SPECS: Macintosh: System 6, 7, or 8, 8MB RAM, MIDI interface and synthesizer/module; Windows: Windows 3.1, 95/98, NT, 8MB RAM, sound card or MIDI Interface.

Band-In-A-Box Soloist Disk Sets (PG Music): Soloist Disk Set #2, Killer Jazz Soloing; #3,

Specialty Jazz Soloing; #4, Rock Soloing; #5, Blue-grass; #6, Killer Pop and Older Jazz; #7, Blues, Pop, Funk, and More; #8, Killer Jazz Waltz and Jazz Fusion; #9, Blues Guitar, Country Piano, Pop Eighths, and Pop Swing Sixteenths. SYSTEM SPECS: Macintosh; Windows.

Band-In-A-Box Styles Disk Sets (PG Music): Styles Disk Set #4, Jazz, Country, Pop, and More; #5, Jazz, Ethnic, and More; #6, Latin and Jazz; #7, Country and Pop; #8, Jazz, Ethnic, and More; #9, Latin and Salsa; #10, Pop and Rock; #11, Classical and Classical MIDI Fakebook; #12, Country, Swing, Rock, Waltz, Boogie; #13, Euro-Techno; #14, Jazz, Fusion; #15, Nashville Country; #16, All Blues; #17, Unplugged; #18, Praise and Worship; #19, Most Requested; #20, Southern Gospel; #21, Top 40; #22, 60s British Invasion; #23, Contemporary Country. SYSTEM SPECS: Macintosh; Windows.

CD Looper (Replay): Learn to play any song directly from computer's CD player; can slow down any audio CD two, three, or four times without changing pitch; can learn songs note for note; set loop points anywhere within a track; can set a loop point for every two-bar phrase; loop options can play each loop once, twice, or continuously, pausing between each loop or user-settable amount of time; highlight multiple loops and loop an entire section. SYSTEM SPECS: Windows 95, 100 percent compatible SoundBlaster sound card, 8 MB RAM.

CD Looper Pro (Replay): Upgrades CD Looper with select sampling resolution; 8 bit or 16 bit; select either mono or stereo recording; improved slow-down algorithms; improved speed-up by percentage algorithms; visually see the WAVE file for the note grabber. SYSTEM SPECS: Windows 95, 100 percent compatible SoundBlaster sound card, 8 MB RAM.

Decomposer (Replay): Advanced filtering program; filter out a single instrument or sections of instruments from any digital audio file. SYSTEM SPECS: Windows.

Jam-Boree (Jump! Software): Play music without any musical training; turn on, press play, and watch the LEDs move to the beat; choose a groove; add an effect; hit the drums; automatically generates music in perfect harmony; for kids ages six and up. SYSTEM SPECS: Windows 486 or MPC level 1, Windows 3.1, CD-ROM, VGA monitor, Sound-Blaster sound card; MIDI keyboard optional.

Jammer Songmaker (Passport): Creates music; enter the chords to a favorite song; pick from 200 band styles including rock, jazz, pop, bluegrass, polka, classical, and many more; use styles to build a song; arrange and mix tracks using the multi-track MIDI studio. SYSTEM SPECS: Windows.

Jammin' Keys (Voyetra): Creates original MIDI music; wide variety of styles including rock, jazz, Latin, and more; 128 general MIDI instruments; virtual five-part band adds backups and riffs; compose music by clicking the "Jam Grid," the on-screen music keyboard, or use an external keyboard; professional-sounding fills and endings; more than thirty-five sound effects files to use with the drum pads; record song as a MIDI file and load it into a sequencing program; includes a video tutorial and media check diagnostic utility. SYSTEM SPECS: Windows.

Lyricist (Virtual Studio Systems): Word processor designed for lyricists, musicians, songwriters, and poets; includes rhyming dictionary, spell checker, thesaurus, album categorization, and more. SYSTEM SPECS: Hybrid.

Music Doodle Pad (Harmonic Vision): Compose music using a variety of instrument sounds; compositions can be saved and played back, showing knowledge and skills acquired from the lessons and games; can also listen to and modify popular music selections from the Jukebox section of the Music Doodle Pad; The Doodle Pad is contained in the Music Ace CD-ROM; for beginners, ages eight-adult. SYSTEM SPECS: Hybrid.

Music-Maker CD-ROM (Music Sales): Play fifteen pop hits; five options include One Key Play, Jamtraz, Drum Along, Quiz, Melody Play; for beginners, all ages. SYSTEM SPECS: Windows, 486 DX33, 8 MB RAM, Windows compatible sound card, CD-ROM drive.

Novinotes (Novinotes): CD-ROM; curriculum-based composition and instrumentation resource for teachers and students; multipurpose tool; electronic book; multimedia; worksheets; over 500 professional recordings in all genres; on-screen scores; includes separate audio CD. SYSTEM SPECS: Hybrid.

Number Chart Pro (Haines): Custom font enables users to create any sized professional Nashville Number System song charts; computer-generated charts can be archived, updated, E-mailed. SYSTEM SPECS: Macintosh; Windows.

Reality (Seer Systems): Professional software-based Synthesizer for Pentium PC; create and play multiple synthesis types simultaneously and at different sample rates; multilayer Patchworks; multiple patches and synthesis types; up to four oscillators, four filters, four LFs, and four envelopes on analog, FM and PCM/sample patches; access any library of sounds and samples by loading as WAV files. SYSTEM SPECS: PC with Intel Pentium Pro or Pentium Processor with MMX, 133 MHz or faster, Windows 95, 24 MB RAM, L2 Cache, any Creative Labs 16-bit Audio Card, AWE64 Gold Preferred.

Retro AS-1 (Mark of the Unicorn): Professional, fully programmable, polyphonic, software synthesizer; multi-timbral, 16-bit 44.1KHz quality; arpeggiator; effects; splits and layers; OMS and FreeMIDI integration for use with MIDI applications; professional analog synthesizer. SYSTEM SPECS: Macintosh OS compatible computer system with 120 MHz PowerPC processor or faster, 32 megs of RAM, 40 megs hard disk space, compatible CD-ROM drive.

Rock Rap 'n Roll CD-ROM (Clearvue-eav): Original music combined with a unique interactive interface; user can produce professional quality music; music in program was recorded using professional vocalists and musicians; ten separate genre/sound studios; students can modify and manipulate sounds and record vocals or sound effects to add to the mix. SYSTEM SPECS: Macintosh; Windows.

Slowgold (Voyetra): Slows down, loops, and transposes musical segments as short as a single note or chord; learn anything by ear; slowdown algorithm; direct digital recording; hear musical choices, techniques, and phrasing in detail; work out chords, melodies, and hooks to any song; expand musical vocabulary; play and sing along with any recording; transcribe any piece of music; digitally record any CD track to hard disk with perfect fidelity; record music from any tape, LP, or other source to hard disk with built-in recorder; export chords and lyrics to a text file to print out and give to band; study ornamentation in classical music; play along with orchestral accompaniment at tempo of choice; master details of any style of music. SYSTEM SPECS: Windows.

Soft Concert (Hal Leonard/Tune 1000): Add lyrics to MIDI files; make sets for a live show; play standard MIDI files with lyrics; add lyrics syllable by syllable to the melody track and indicate with special chord editor the chords to play; chords line up to the right beat on the screen; altered accordingly if key changes; program the sequence of songs to play on stage; supports all standard MIDI file formats including general MIDI, GS, and standard MIDI with lyrics. SYSTEM SPECS: Windows.

Song Factory CD-ROM (Jump! Software): Sing tunes into the included microphone, play on a MIDI keyboard, click in notes with a mouse, or use auto mode; automatically adds accompaniment to melody with drum fills, piano licks, and other musical enhancements; creates intros, fills, and endings; songs sound professionally arranged; save as a standard MIDI file; thirty-six styles of music; SYSTEM SPECS: Windows 486 or MPC level 1, Windows 3.1, CD-ROM, VGA monitor, SoundBlaster sound card, MIDI keyboard optional.

Songster Software (Songster): Songwriting and lyric writing software; pitch list; song profile; lyrics; contacts track sheet; import sound files; schedules; royalty statements; copyright forms and more. SYSTEM SPECS: Macintosh; Windows.

Songworks (Ars Nova): Produce and print lead sheets; experiment with melody and harmony; produce a melodic or harmonic idea, and change it into something completely different. SYSTEM SPECS: Macintosh Plus or better.

Songworks II (Ars Nova): Notate compositions on multiple staves with up to eight voices per staff; invents tune ideas and suggests chord progressions; with Active Listening, can perform one part of a composition while computer plays the others; explore polyphony; learn a part in a choral piece; experience being part of a music ensemble; can export music to an AIFF, MIDI, or PICT file for use on multimedia projects; MIDI compatible; MIDI not required; Macintosh 16-bit sound. SYSTEM SPECS: 68040 Macintosh or PowerMac, System 7 or 8, 10 MB RAM.

Sound Toys (Voyager): Composition software; CD-ROM; musical instruments and synthesized sounds; compose, record, and save creations; over 300 original samples; prerecorded background loops; no reading required. SYSTEM SPECS: Hybrid.

Studio 6 Studio Recording Session CD-ROM (Midisoft): Record lead vocals, harmony, live solos, or entire band; unlimited tracks; event tool to work with MIDI controllers; MIDI editing; print out music including lyrics, guitar chords, percussion notation, and dynamics. SYSTEM SPECS: Windows.

Techno–Do It (Hohner): Arrange and produce Techno music; MIDI basics; digital audio; recording techniques; music theory; arrange the provided Techno samples with the included MIDI sequencer and hard disk recording software; for beginners, ages twelve and up. SYSTEM SPECS: Windows 3/1 or higher, 486/33 or higher, 4 MB RAM, sound card or MIDI interface, CD-ROM drive.

The Jammer Professional (Soundtrek): Virtual studio musicians ready to improvise, harmonize, exchange ideas, and lay down original tracks; control the style of each musician on each track; over 200 band styles; complete control over player styles, note ranges, velocities, and transitions; blend multiple styles together; 25-track MIDI studio located in the PC; six-part harmony; load and save individual drum styles; automatic fades and crescendos. SYSTEM SPECS: Windows.

The MIDI Fakebook (PG Music): Hundreds of favorite tunes; load songs into *Band-in-a-Box* and play along; create own arrangements on computer; learn traditional jazz and improvisational skills with Soloist feature; includes 300 songs in a variety of styles; Traditional/Original Jazz and Pop, fifty songs; Classical, 200 songs; Bluegrass, fifty songs. SYSTEM SPECS: Macintosh; Windows.

Transkriber (Reed Cotler): Play music to learn on computer CD player or on an external CD or tape player hooked up to the sound card; record music using the recording panel; play music back at 3/4, 2/3, 1/2, 1/3, 1/4, or 1/26 of the original speed without changing the pitch; phrase selection to focus on one part of the music at a time; slow down algorithms, tuning, and smoothing filters; reinforce or remove certain frequency bands from the music to better focus on the part being transcribed; adjust the pitch to match the recording exactly; transpose the sound up or down as much as an octave; pitch generator identifies which note is being played on the recording; for beginning to advanced transcribers. SYSTEM SPECS: Macintosh: 60 MHz Power PC or better, 20 MB RAM; Windows: Windows 95/98/NT, 8 MB RAM, Pentium 100 or better.

Visual Arranger (Yamaha): Creative sequencing program; user combines and edits pre-recorded options; during playback, icons are highlighted showing which section of piece is being played; includes eight styles of music, various options for musical form, a set of two-to-four-bar chord progressions, rhythms, additional instrumentation, and arranger options; user combines all of the elements to create a piece; prerecorded riffs and suggested chord progressions allow user to mix creatively; melody and rhythm may be added afterwards; helps develop improvisation skills; help screen; for all ages ten-adult. SYSTEM SPECS: PC; Windows, 8 MB RAM hard disk space, MIDI soundboard, can be used with headphones, speakers, or MIDI keyboard.

Zillion Kajillion Rhymes (Eccentric): Thesaurus for rhymes; for songwriting, poetry, parodies, plays on words, jingles, product names, and more; enter word and will produce a list of rhyming words. SYSTEM SPECS: Macintosh; Windows.

Piano and Keyboards Software

Alfred's Basic Adult Piano Course (Alfred): Learn to play the piano using a computer; sequential, easy-to-use approach for adult students of all ages; learn sight-reading, ear training and fundamentals of music theory; correlates with Alfred's Basic Adult Piano Course and Alfred's Adult All-in-One Course (Levels I and II); for beginners, ages twelve and up. SYSTEM SPECS: PC 386DX or better, Windows 3.1 or better, 4 MB RAM, 6 MB hard disk space, Windows compatible sound card or MIDI interface, four 8va or more MIDI keyboard.

Blues Piano CD-ROM (MGI Interactive): Includes diagrams, notation, and video clips; go through videos frame by frame or set loops to separate difficult parts; includes tracks with full rhythm section; topics covered include: standard blues progressions, blues scales, improvisations and licks, music theory, chords, scales and endings, walking blues techniques, daily exercises, and more; for intermediate level, all ages. SYSTEM SPECS: Windows 486 DX, 66 MHz or better, 2X CD-ROM, 4-8 MB RAM, Windows compatible sound card, speakers.

Century of Jazz Piano (Hal Leonard): Dick Hyman; history of jazz piano; CD-ROM; recreates styles of sixty-three pianists; 103 tunes; over five hours of music; twenty-one rare historical videos; over one hundred historical photographs; more than 500 pages of documentation by Joel Simpson, Dick Hyman, and others; biographies; stylistic analyses; discographies; complete bibliography. SYSTEM SPECS: Hybrid.

Clavisoft (Yamaha): Book/disk collections; "You are the Artist;" educator collections; disk orchestra collection; complete instrumental accompaniments. SYSTEM SPECS: MIDI compatible keyboard or computer.

Contemporary Keyboardist Stylistic Etudes (WB): Includes eighty-six studies covering many of the contemporary popular keyboard styles: jazz, rock, funk, Latin, country, stride, blues, pop, gospel, and more; short etudes of moderate difficulty; demonstrate key music fundamentals; compact disk and general MIDI computer disk provided with stylistically appropriate versions of all eighty-six etudes; for intermediate-advanced, all ages. SYSTEM SPECS: Macintosh; PC; requires a sequencer.

Cuetime Smartkey (Yamaha): Control tempo of prerecorded instrumental background by how fast or slow user plays at the keyboard; mixed genre song selections. SYSTEM SPECS: Yamaha Clavinova digital pianos; Smartkey equipped Disklavier pianos.

Discovering Keyboards (Voyetra): Introductory keyboard training course; history of keyboard instruments; an overview of MIDI and synthesizers; songbook for storing MIDI song fields which can also be printed; multimedia: full-motion videos, colorful computer graphics, digital audio, and MIDI sound; interactive system; explore the history of keyboard instruments in text, photographs, video, and sound with Keyboard Tour; Understanding MIDI and Synthesis shows how to make music with the computer; Keyboard Lessons introduces basic music notation, theory, and playing techniques with video clips and exercises; On-Screen Songbook includes classics, folk tunes, and holiday and patriotic songs, sorted by title, style, composer, or level of difficulty; Game Room gives three video games that build musical skill; for beginners-intermediate, all ages. SYSTEM SPECS: Windows 486SX/25 MHz or higher, Windows 3.1/95, 4 MB RAM, CD-ROM drive, 16-bit Windows compatible sound card, MIDI-compatible keyboard required to record.

Fast Fingers, Vols. I-IV (Fast Fingers Software): Instruction in note learning and keyboard fingering of scales, arpeggios, and triads in major and minor scales, as well as jazz modes and chords; exercises and visual playback of the exercises for the student; triad inversion section; teachers should check fingering as the computer is unable to monitor correct fingering; helps students attain fluency of aural, tactile, visual, and mental mastery of scales and chords; for third-grade to adult keyboard students. SYSTEM SPECS: PC, MIDI interface, Roland MPU-r01 or equivalent, color monitor, mouse.

In Concert (Cakewalk): Student's accompanist; practice and perform classical music together with a symphony orchestra; work through difficult sections of music; practice left-hand or right-hand parts only; stop, pause, or skip to a new section; to use, open any standard MIDI file, choose the part to play, and start playing; performs all other parts automatically; change tempo or volume; jump from place to place in the song; listens and responds; on-screen displays of tempo, location, and volume; adjust the volume of every instrument in the backup band; mute instruments; transpose piece; record and play back performance; built-in pauses. SYSTEM SPECS: Hybrid; Macintosh: System 7.1 or greater or Power Mac with System 7.1.2 or greater, 1.5 MB RAM, CD-ROM drive, MIDI interface, MIDI keyboard or other MIDI instrument; Windows: Windows 95, 486 DX-2 66 MHz, 16 MB RAM, CD-ROM drive, MIDI interface or sound card with MIDI adapter, MIDI keyboard, or other MIDI instrument.

Instant Keyboard Fun (ECS): Twenty-six songs the user plays on a synthesizer keyboard; user does not have to read music—just the note names shown on the screen; at the end of each song, the percentage of correctly played notes is given; words to popular tunes are displayed with the corresponding note names. For beginners, grades K-3. SYSTEM SPECS: Apple (MIDI).

Isong CD-ROMs (iSong/Hal Leonard): Teaching tool; animated score and tab; synced instructor video; arrangements in varying levels of difficulty; virtual keyboard; tempo control; looping with exact cueing; Classical piano; artists. SYSTEM SPECS: Hybrid.

Jazz Piano Masterclass (PG Music): Interactive piano lessons; illustrates basic skills to the beginning pianist; enhances skills of more advanced pianists; includes over sixty topics such as Roots and Shells, Block Chords, Stride Piano, Playing the Blues, Scales, Common Progressions, Improvisation, and more; practice exercises; backing tracks; eleven tunes included in the program; over five hours of verbal instruction; nearly one hundred exercises; practice tip for each exercise; multimedia features. SYSTEM SPECS: Windows.

Keyboard Arpeggios (ECS): Covers key signatures, notes, and fingerings in major and minor two-octave arpeggios; designed to review arpeggio performance and fingerings; students enter correct fingering, then play the requested arpeggio on the MIDI keyboard; program is presented in five parts: Instructions, Hand-over-Hand Triads (major and minor), Major Triads (two octaves), Minor Triads (two octaves), and a Final Quiz; two-octave triads are presented to the user for both right-hand and left-hand fingerings; final exams record percentage scores; top ten scores are listed; evaluation is stored in student records for the instructor; for beginners to intermediate, grades 3-7. SYSTEM SPECS: Macintosh (MIDI); Windows (MIDI); Apple (MIDI); PC-DOS (MIDI), color monitor.

Keyboard Blues (ECS): Presents simple blues chords; twelve-bar blues; practice playing and hearing chord changes, first with the music, then without; drill-and-practice section scores student's knowledge of simple blues chords; student creates an original solo with a computer accompaniment; student evaluation and record keeping; requires MIDI; for beginners, grades 4-8. SYSTEM SPECS: Macintosh (MIDI); Windows (MIDI); Apple (MIDI); PC-DOS (MIDI).

Keyboard Chords (ECS): Tests students' knowledge of major and minor triads in all positions; one note of a triad is provided and student answers by spelling the triad or playing the triad on the keyboard; percentage scores are recorded; presents qualities of simple chords; composed of a tutorial on major, minor, diminished, and augmented chords; chord spelling drill; keyboard drill; test; drill-and-practice programs allow user to select the inversion (root, first, or second) and the clef (treble or bass) for the drill; score is displayed after student correctly answers ten consecutive items; test randomly selects the inversion and clef for each item, and the student's score is displayed; student evaluation and record keeping; for intermediate to advanced pianists, all age groups. SYSTEM SPECS: Macintosh (MIDI optional); Windows (MIDI optional); Apple (MIDI); PC-DOS (MIDI).

Keyboard Extended Jazz Harmonies (ECS): Sequel to *Keyboard Jazz Harmonies;* designed to teach students to identify and build ninth, eleventh, and thirteenth chords; tutorial presents option to hear each chord played through MIDI synthesizer keyboard; four sections are included in the lesson: Visual Chord Recognition, Aural Chord Recognition, Chord Symbol Drill, and Chord Spelling Drill; final quiz included; student record keeping allows instructor to monitor progress; for advanced, all age groups. SYSTEM SPECS: Macintosh (MIDI); Windows (MIDI optional); Apple (MIDI); PC-DOS (MIDI).

Keyboard Fingerings (ECS): Drill program; combines scale construction reviews with fingering practice; major, natural, and harmonic minor scales presented in standard and special fingerings for student review and practice; for both the right and left hands; single staves are used, with treble for the right-hand exercises and bass for the left hand; students enter scale fingerings, then play the same scales correctly at the MIDI keyboard; help is available; automatic scorekeeping; student roster and scores are available for printout; Hall of Fame provides top scores; computer judges the accuracy of the scale performance in each section and on the final test; for beginners-intermediate. SYSTEM SPECS: Macintosh (MIDI); Windows (MIDI); Apple (MIDI); PC-DOS (MIDI).

Keyboard Intervals (ECS): Designed to help music students learn to play major, minor, diminished, and augmented intervals; must be able to read music and play notes on a keyboard; student evaluation and record keeping; for intermediate students, all ages.

SYSTEM SPECS: Macintosh (MIDI optional); Windows (MIDI optional); Apple (MIDI); PC-DOS (MIDI).

Keyboard Introductory Development Series (KIDS) (ECS): Four disk series for very young beginners; Zoo Puppet Theater introduces learning correct finger numbers for playing the piano; Race Car Keys teaches the lay-out of the keyboard by recognizing solfege syllables or note names; Dinosaurs Lunch teaches notes on the treble staff; Follow Me asks the student to play notes after hearing them; computer graphics; designed to correlate with Yamaha Music Education System Primary One Course; for grades K-3. SYSTEM SPECS: Macintosh (MIDI); Windows CD-ROM (MIDI); Apple (MIDI); PC-DOS (MIDI).

Keyboard Jazz Harmonies (ECS): Designed to teach chord symbols, seventh chord recognition and chord spelling; basic knowledge of traditional harmonies and musical intervals required; tutorial; four drills; four quizzes; final quiz uses MIDI equipment to provide aural chord examples; for advanced, all age groups. SYSTEM SPECS: Macintosh (MIDI); Windows (MIDI optional); Apple (MIDI); PC-DOS (MIDI).

Keyboard Kapers (ECS): Provides staff-to-keyboard drills for pitch identification, melodic dictation and sight-reading; scores are kept for correct answers per clef; no automatic record keeping; consists of three challenging piano keyboard games: Keyboard Clues plots a note on the grand staff and requires that the note be played on the keyboard; ?Mystery? Notes presents one note visually and aurally, then asks the student to identify other notes(s) played by the computer; Kwik Keys is a timed game requiring the student to play back notes presented on the screen as quickly as possible; two levels of difficulty and Halls of Fame; scores are displayed; for beginner to intermediate, all age groups. SYSTEM SPECS: Macintosh (MIDI); Windows (MIDI optional); Apple (MIDI); PC-DOS (MIDI).

Keyboard Namegame (ECS): A drill-and-practice game designed to teach note position in the treble and bass clef; drills note recognition through a word game; a melodic fragment is flashed on the screen; student is given a verbal clue; the answer to the clue is entered on the MIDI keyboard; scoring is based on the time it takes to play the words presented; Hall of Fame records high scores; for beginning keyboard students, grades K-4. SYSTEM SPECS: Macintosh (MIDI); Apple (MIDI); PC-DOS (MIDI).

Keyboard Note Drill (ECS): Designed to increase speed in identifying notes randomly placed on the bass and treble staves; musical keyboard used to allow for selection of correct answers; twenty notes must be identified to complete each session; summary score presented at the end of each session; response time can be adjusted to the level of difficulty; for beginners, all age groups. SYSTEM SPECS: Macintosh

(MIDI optional); Windows (MIDI optional); Apple (MIDI); PC-DOS (MIDI).

Keyboard Speed-Reading (ECS): Sight-reading program flashes groups of notes on a monitor; students then play notes on a MIDI keyboard and are graded for speed and accuracy; completion time can be set by the user; Hall of Fame records top ten scores; for beginner-intermediate keyboard students, all age groups. SYSTEM SPECS: Macintosh (MIDI optional); Windows (MIDI optional); Apple (MIDI); PC-DOS (MIDI).

Keyboard Tutor (ECS): Provides tutorial and drill for students beginning to learn note location on the grand staff; presents exercises for learning elementary keyboard skills including knowledge of names of the keys, piano keys matched to notes, notes matched to piano keys, and whole steps and half steps; each lesson allows unlimited practice of the skills; for beginning keyboard students, all age groups. SYSTEM SPECS: Macintosh (MIDI optional); Windows (MIDI optional); Apple (MIDI); PC-DOS (MIDI optional).

Kids Piano (Jump! Music): Designed for younger children; teaches piano keyboard and music basics in a fun, easy, and educational way; includes keyboard overlay; works with any standard MIDI keyboard; covers correct posture and hand position; how to find notes on the piano; sharps and flats; playing piano with both hands; treble and bass clef; playing along with a metronome; pitch and rhythm; playing along with an accompaniment and much more; for beginners, ages six-twelve; SYSTEM SPECS: Macintosh; Windows: Windows 3.1 or better, 486/33 or better, CD-ROM drive, SoundBlaster compatible sound card, 10 MB disk space, 25 recommended, MIDI compatible keyboard or controller.

Magic Player (Jump! Music): Includes seventy-five favorite songs to sing along, play along, or listen; to play any song, tap the song rhythm on the computer keyboard or MIDI piano; as each key is tapped, the song advances, playing the right notes and chords; sing along with the lyrics or change the instrument sounds. SYSTEM SPECS: Macintosh: System 7.1, MIDI keyboard optional; Windows: 486 or MPC Level 1, Windows 3.1, CD-ROM, VGA monitor, SoundBlaster sound card.

Masters Collection: Piano Masterpieces CD-ROMs (Clearvue-eav): Nine CD-ROMs: Bach, Beethoven, Chopin, Debussey, Joplin, Mendelssohn, Mozart, Schubert, and Schumann; Piano Masterpieces; over 500 total compositions; listen while following score; study hand and finger position; virtual keyboard; change tempo and MIDI instrumentation; export files and graphics; complete anthology available on one CD-ROM; available in five languages. SYSTEM SPECS: Windows: 486 processor or better, 16 MB RAM, Windows 95, 98, NT, or later.

Multimedia History of Music Keyboards CD-ROM (With an Introduction to MIDI) (Voyetra): Color photographs; videos; sound and text; history of keyboard instruments from the earliest spinets to sophisticated electronic synthesizers; fundamentals of computer-generated music; sample MIDI and WAV files; glossary of important terms; included with *Discovering Keyboards;* for beginners-intermediate, all ages. SYSTEM SPECS: Windows.

Music Cartridge Songbook Series (Yamaha): Play along without melody line; easy piano; E-Z Play Today; style cartridges. SYSTEM SPECS: Yamaha PSR230, 320, 330, 420, 520, 530, and 620 models.

Music Dynamics Sight-Reading Software (Paul Renard): Learn to read and play standard piano sheet music; designed for those who have never been able to sight-read; for the beginning sight-reader; includes a foundation in music theory; see music as a series of interval patterns; transmit musical patterns to hands; will catch mistakes and correct through entire course; tracks progress of multiple users; musical glossary; interval training section. SYSTEM SPECS: Hybrid; Macintosh: PowerPC processor, CD-ROM drive, 32 MB RAM, MIDI interface; Windows: Windows 95/98, Pentium or compatible processor, CD-ROM, 32 MB RAM, SoundBlaster or compatible sound card; MIDI keyboard with 61, 76, or 88 keys.

Note Detective (ECS): Helps beginning students in locating notes on the grand staff and the keyboard; graphic tutorial and game series that is designed to help students develop keyboard skills; Section 1 introduces beginners to basic concepts such as high and low sounds, the musical alphabet, and staff note reading; Section 2 helps students develop fluent music reading skills; practice in note reading on the grand staff, ledger line recognition, interval recognition, and reading sharps and flats; letter name answers are entered at the computer keyboard and notes at the computer MIDI keyboard; *Sherlock* provides guidance and instructions throughout the program; automatic scorekeeping for up to fifty student records; records provide information only on levels completed; for beginning keyboard students of reading age and above, grades K-5. SYSTEM SPECS: Macintosh (MIDI); Windows (MIDI optional); Apple (MIDI); PC-DOS (MIDI).

Noteplay (Piano Lesson in a Box) (Ibis): Multimedia program; game context; assumes no previous experience; thirty-six skill levels; supplement to any piano curriculum; for beginners to advanced, ages ten and up. SYSTEM SPECS: Windows.

Oscar Peterson Multimedia CD-ROM (PG Music): Fourteen complete audio/video performances by Oscar Peterson; ten MIDI transcriptions of his famous blues performances; signature CD-ROM; integrates interactive audio/visual performances with on-screen piano display and notation; see and study exactly what the master is playing; musical journey through his life and career; comprehensive multimedia autobiography with audio and video clips; exclusive photographs from Oscar Peterson's private collection. SYSTEM SPECS: Windows.

Oscar Peterson Note for Note (PG Music): Transcriptions of Oscar Peterson's jazz piano performances; authorized volume of eighteen full-length transcriptions all taken directly from original recordings; selected and approved by Oscar Peterson. SYSTEM SPECS: Windows.

Piano Courses One, Two, Three, and Four (Musicware): Each course consists of over 250 lessons and assignments; correlating Songbook; wide variety of presentation, content, and feedback; balance of visual, aural, and tactile activities; large words and notes; colors; Play Pointer arrow trains eye to look ahead to the next note as each note is played; variety of presentations; incorrect notes are highlighted; opportunities to try again; immediate feedback; keyboard practice tips appear throughout the program; emphasizes inner hearing; vocabulary of common-practice musical terms; on-screen pronunciation guides; Glossary of Musical Terms in User's Guide; student responses and most lesson controls are done on a MIDI keyboard; students can see which lessons have been completed; scores for individual exercises appear in a separate window on the screen; hands-on program; interactive lessons; reads lesson text out loud; works by itself or as a supplement to a piano teacher; for keyboard students, ages seven-adult. SYSTEM SPECS: Windows: 386/25 MHz, Windows 3.1, 4 MB RAM, Windows 95, 8 MB RAM, VGA or SVGA monitor, SoundBlaster compatible sound card, MIDI keyboard, MIDI adapter cable, CD-ROM drive.

Piano Discovering System Package (Jump! Music): Piano lessons for kids and adults; endorsed by jazz legend Herbie Hancock; teaches piano and music basics; includes MIDI keyboard and cable; full year of lessons; over fifty songs; shows how to read music and play piano with both hands; interactive instruction; practice performance; recording; games; jammin' fun; music tutors teach through live narrations; for beginners; more difficult lessons for advanced students; can record and save songs to MIDI files; over 600 lessons; thirty chapters; fifty-one songs; animations and graphics; includes four-octave, forty-nine key, MIDI piano keyboard and connecting computer cable; CD-ROM-based software includes over 200 lessons, songs, and exercises, and other musical activities; the six musical activity areas are: The Schoolhouse, The Bungalow, The Arcade, The Performance Hall, The Jam Stage, and The Recording Studio; for beginners, ages six-adult. SYSTEM SPECS: Macintosh: 68040 or higher (25 MHz), 12 MB RAM, 2x CD-ROM drive, MIDI interface, MIDI keyboard; Windows: 486/33 MHz, 8 MB RAM, CD-

ROM, SVGA color display, Windows 3.1, Windows 95 compatible, 10 MB hard drive space, 25 recommended, 16-bit SoundBlaster compatible sound card.

Piano Mouse (Piano Mouse): CD-ROM; basic foundation for beginning music students; theory lessons; games; introduction to keyboard basics. SYSTEM SPECS: Windows.

Piano Partners Music Learning (Piano Partners): Recommended for use in group keyboard classes; tutorial; interactive games; drills and improvisation programs; four disks; graphics; animation; for beginning keyboard students. SYSTEM SPECS: PC, MIDI interface, color monitor, MIDI keyboard.

Piano Suite Basic (Adventus): Customizable and expandable tools; interactive voice tutor; continuous feedback; in-depth interactive theory lessons; large musical repertoire; personal and musical biographies of over 150 composers and performers; compositions can be exported to MIDI format and made available on the Internet; contains one hundred musical pieces covering Classical, Jazz/Blues, Country, Pop/Rock, Children's, Folk/Traditional, and more. SYSTEM SPECS: Windows 95, 16MB RAM, 486 100Mhz or better, CD-ROM drive, SoundBlaster 100 percent compatible sound card, standard MIDI keyboard is optional but recommended.

Piano Suite Premier Edition (Adventus): Customizable and expandable tools; record music; display and print musical notation; add own composition with a photo to Learning Library repertoire; includes Piano Player: supervised piano practice with audio/visual feedback; Library: over 400 pieces from Pop/Rock, Classical, Folk, and Jazz/Blues; sixty-five licensed songs; animation, lyrics, and voice recordings; Theory Thinker: hundreds of narrated, step-by-step theory lessons with practice exercises to teach notation, sight-reading, and playing skills; Composers Corner: compose, edit, and print music; pieces can be saved to a custom library and learned by others; Personal Profile: individual performance records to review progress; tracks results of every piece practiced or game played for any number of users; History Happens: biographies of famous composers and performers. SYSTEM SPECS: Windows.

Pianosoft Solo Collections and Pianosoft Plus Ensemble Collections (Yamaha): Artists; Broadway; children's; Christmas; classical; contemporary; country; international; jazz; movie and TV themes; pop; sacred; standards; accompanist; educational. SYSTEM SPECS: Yamaha or compatible keyboard with disk player.

Play Piano (Midisoft): Multimedia; nine levels of difficulty; three modules: demo, learn or practice; optional theory lessons; videos of professional pianists performing some of the forty classical and rock/pop selections; best used as a practice aid under a teacher's direction; for keyboard students, ages eight-

adult. SYSTEM SPECS: Windows, CD-ROM, 8 MB RAM, 18 MB hard disk space, MIDI soundboard, MIDI keyboard, VGA color monitor, headphones or speakers.

Play-a-Piece First Steps (Passport): Practice Companion for beginning-level piano or keyboard students; reinforces skills learned during first two years of study; interactive methods of instruction; audiovisual practice sessions; software offers feedback; can watch each song as the notes are displayed; can isolate any section of song to work on; correct fingering instruction; fifty classic pieces at five practice levels; built-in metronome; scoring and a Hall of Fame; for beginners, all age levels. SYSTEM SPECS: Windows: 486 or better, Windows 3.1 or 95, 8 MB RAM, sound card, MIDI keyboard, and PC MIDI interface recommended.

Ricochet (ECS): Innovative music game; in Ricochet Random, play highlighted keys after random balls ricochet off piano keys on computer screen; number of balls and movement speed will increase at higher level of difficulty; in Ricochet Melody, choose a melody from a play list and try to play the notes before the ball leaves the screen; tempo can be changed. SYSTEM SPECS: Pentium 90 or faster computer, Windows 3.1/95/98, 16MB RAM, SVGA display, 2MB free hard drive space, Windows compatible sound card or MIDI interface, MIDI keyboard is optional.

Sample Disks (Yamaha): Professionally edited high quality samples. SYSTEM SPECS: Yamaha PSR7000 and PSR2700.

Style Disks (Yamaha): Auto-accompaniments. SYSTEM SPECS: File-compatible Yamaha Clavinova keyboards.

Teach Me Piano (Voyetra): Over 150 lessons and more than one hundred exercises; beginners learn basic techniques; advanced players reinforce musical skills; Keyboard Lessons include note reading in treble and bass clefs, rhythm and timing, finger numbering and finger positions, key signatures, time signatures, scales and chords; keeps records; Songbook organizes songs; Trainer Screen for practice; Performance Screen to play with full accompaniment; Musician's Reference for commonly used musical terms; includes MediaCheck; for beginner-intermediate, ages ten-adult. SYSTEM SPECS: Windows.

Technics Music Disk Collection (Technics): Comprehensive music education system; popular and electronic musical instruments. SYSTEM SPECS: Technics compatible keyboards.

The Blues Pianist (PG Music): Large library of original blues tunes performed by top studio musicians; wide variety of styles: Boogie Woogie, Slow/Fast Boogies, Jazz Blues, New Orleans Style, Chicago Blues, and more; styles made famous by Pete Johnson, Albert Ammons, Jelly Roll Morton, Jerry Lee Lewis, etc.; Trivia and Guess the Song games; notes; biographies; all levels can use the games and biographies; advanced, all ages. SYSTEM SPECS: Macintosh; Windows.

The Children's Pianist (PG Music): Over seventy outstanding piano performances of the world's favorite children's songs for listening or singalong; large Karaoke-style display for singing along; great for sight-reading practice or learning to play by ear; on-screen piano keyboard shows exactly what notes are being played; can slow down songs or step through them chord by chord; can print out the music (Windows version); over four hours of music; includes words and music for seventy songs including *London Bridges, Camptown Races, Home on the Range*, and many more; great for teaching piano, and as a classroom tool; for beginners-intermediate, all ages. SYSTEM SPECS: Macintosh; Windows.

The Christmas Pianist (PG Music): Library of over fifty traditional Christmas favorites; see lyrics on screen and sing along (Windows version only); on-screen piano keyboard. SYSTEM SPECS: Macintosh; Windows.

The Gospel Pianist (PG Music): Over fifty Gospel-style piano standards played on MIDI keyboard by top gospel pianists; includes *Amazing Grace, By and By, At the Cross, Go Tell It on the Mountain, Sweet Chariot, Wade in the Water, Old Time Religion*, and many more; Music Trivia questions; Guess the Song game; program notes; pianist biographies and more; for advanced (all levels can use the games and biographies), all ages. SYSTEM SPECS: Macintosh; Windows.

The Latin Pianist (PG Music): Over fifty tunes played on MIDI keyboard by Latin pianist Rebecca Mauleon-Santana; includes authentic Latin and Salsa piano songs and styles: Conga, Cumbia, Merengue, Son, Mambo, Cha-Cha-Cha, Guaracha, Samba, Partido Alto, and more; on-screen piano keyboard shows what pianist is playing; slow down piece or step through chord by chord; learn music note for note watching notes on screen; load MIDI files for further study; advanced. SYSTEM SPECS: Macintosh; Windows.

The Modern Jazz Pianist (PG Music): Top jazz/studio pianists play over fifty jazz standards in a wide variety of styles; on-screen piano keyboard shows exactly what is being played; slow down piece or step through chord by chord; learn the music note for note by watching the piano notes on the screen; load MIDI files into programs for further study; Music Trivia and Guess the Song games; program notes; biographies; music dictionary and more; all levels can use the games and biographies; advanced. SYSTEM SPECS: Macintosh; Windows.

The New Age Pianist (PG Music): Collection of solo piano compositions inspired by the natural world; covers New Age piano music; full range of piano techniques presented; over four hours of music; song memory, biographies, and information on important New Age musicians; advanced, all ages; all levels can use the games and biographies. SYSTEM SPECS: Macintosh; Windows.

The New Orleans Pianist (PG Music): Over sixty New Orleans Style piano music standards; wide variety of New Orleans, R & B, Blues, and Ragtime piano music; on-screen piano keyboard shows what the pianist is playing; slow down the piece, or step through chord by chord; learn the music note for note by watching the notation on screen; Music Trivia and Guess the Song games; program notes; biographies; music dictionary and more; all levels can use the games and biographies; advanced, all ages. SYSTEM SPECS: Macintosh; Windows.

The Pianist Volumes 1-5 (PG Music): Educational music program; large collection of over 200 popular classical piano pieces; performed by world-renowned concert pianists; includes *Moonlight Sonata, Sonata Pathetique, Claire de Lune, Liebestraume, Minute Waltz, Hungarian Rhapsody, Military Polonaise*, and much more; includes music trivia Guess That Song game; program notes; biographies of famous musicians; music dictionary; for intermediate-advanced, all ages. SYSTEM SPECS: Macintosh: System 6 or 7, 2 MB RAM, 3 MB hard disk space, MIDI interface and synthesizer or sound module with piano sound; Windows: 2 MB RAM, 3 MB hard disk space, sound card, or MIDI system with piano sound.

The Ragtime Pianist (PG Music): Over ninety great ragtime performances by Eubie Blake, Joseph Lamb, and Daniels; every Scott Joplin rag; includes *The Entertainer, Maple Leaf Rag, Chevy Chase, Easy Winners, Elite Syncopations, Fig Leaf Rag, Pineapple Rag*, and more; Music Trivia and Guess the Song games; program notes; biographies; music dictionary; for advanced (all levels can use the games and biographies), all ages. SYSTEM SPECS: Macintosh; Windows.

Virtuoso (Virtuoso): Artist-oriented recordings for reproducing pianos, digital keyboards, and multimedia computers. SYSTEM SPECS: Yamaha Disklavier, Yamaha Clavinova, PianoDisc, Roland KR and HP Series, Baldwin Concert Master, and Kurzwel Mark Series.

You're the Star! (Turbo Music): General MIDI performances and print; book/disk series; MIDI accompaniments; change tempo and keys; create own orchestration and mix; improvise solos; for computers and instruments with disk drives; some with E-Z play notation. SYSTEM SPECS: General MIDI compatible.

Guitar Software

A History of Santana (Graphix Zone): History and artistry of one of the greatest guitarists of all time; CD-ROM; journey into the mind and spirit behind the music of the Grammy Award winning artist; for all levels, all ages. SYSTEM SPECS: Hybrid.

Acoustic Guitar Volume 1 CD-ROM (MGI Interactive): For beginners, all ages; how to buy a guitar; how to use the capo; chords, harmony, and rhythm; typical accompaniments; vocal playbacks; picking and fingerstyle techniques; basic exercises. SYSTEM SPECS: Windows.

Blues Guitar Volume 1 CD-ROM (MGI Interactive): Standard blues progressions; blues scales; improvisations and licks; music theory, chords and scales; endings; walking blues technique; daily exercises; intermediate; for all ages. SYSTEM SPECS: Windows.

Classic Rock Guitar (Ubisoft): Over eighty lessons and 180 exercises for eight acoustic song arrangements; full-screen zooming and lesson looping; two digital tuners; digital metronome; songs include: *Hey Joe, Blackbird, No Woman, No Cry, Sweet Home Alabama, Dust in the Wind, Wild World, Life by the Drop,* and *Blowin' in the Wind.* SYSTEM SPECS: Windows 3.1 or 95, 486 DX 66 MHz or better, 4 MB RAM or better, 256 color SVGA, MPC compatible sound card, 2X CD-ROM driver or better, mouse.

Guitar 101 (Lyrrus): Thirty self-contained lessons for the beginning guitarist; learn the parts of the guitar; how to sit when playing; Fender Method of playing. SYSTEM SPECS: Windows.

Guitar Method (eMedia): CD-ROM; more than thirty videos demonstrating techniques and tips and comments from instructor; includes over seventy songs; major and minor chords; chords needed to play most pop songs; private on-screen instructor; step-by-step lesson content; over eighty comprehensive lessons, including twenty-five new lessons on reading music; automatic tuner to visually tune up guitar to computer; 250-chord chart; built-in recorder, metronome and chord dictionary. SYSTEM SPECS: Windows: 68020 or better, Power PC; Macintosh: System 7 or greater; CD-ROM drive (1x or faster); 5MB of free RAM.

Guitar Workshop (Heritage Music Press): Platform for a series of song-packs and interactive lesson modules in a variety of skill levels and styles; guitar tutorial; fretboard finger positions; music window with score, tablature, chord frames, and performance notes; piano keyboard; lesson window; adjustable tempo/metronome; alternate tunings; user song entry. SYSTEM SPECS: Windows 3.1, 16-bit sound card, VGA color monitor, 486/33 MHz recommended; supports MIDI synthesizers.

Guitropolis CD-ROM (Alfred): Teaches guitar; humor; musical game play; award-winning game design; live video; solid guitar techniques for the beginning guitarist; licks; chords; popular melodies. SYSTEM SPECS: Macintosh; Windows.

G-Vox Basics (Lyrrus): For beginning guitar students; interactive CD-ROM contains the Riffs Lite software program, five song libraries, and an introduction to guitar; interactive video and graphics; how to hold the guitar and pick; how to play notes, chords, fingerpicking, and more; five song libraries cover different musical styles such as blues, rock, jazz, and folk; over sixty full motion videos. SYSTEM SPECS: Windows 386, Windows 3.1, sound card recommended.

G-Vox Blender (Lyrrus): Collection of software designed to help improve guitar playing; includes Riffs Lite, Riffs Collection Library, Steve Morse Prime Cuts, and Duquesne University Starter Set; Riffs Lite program helps improve skills, technique, and understanding of music theory; step through the riff note by note, at any tempo without changing the pitch; riffs are displayed in both staff and tablature notations, and on the graphic fretboard; shows where to place fingers and which fingers to use; Duquesne University Starter Set demonstrates examples of finger exercises, scales, and arpeggios; in Prime Cuts, Steve Morse concentrates on areas that are most important to proficient guitar playing; Riffs Collection Library contains Riffs from G-VOX titles currently available. SYSTEM SPECS: Macintosh: Mac Plus, System 6.0.5; PC-286, DOS 3.3, sound card.

G-Vox Guitar Libraries (Lyrrus): Learn songs by famous artists; separate programs/songbooks for B. B. King, The Police, Eric Clapton, and Santana. SYSTEM SPECS: Windows.

Isong CD-ROMs (iSong/Hal Leonard): Teaching tool; animated score and tab; synced instructor video; arrangements in varying levels of difficulty; virtual fretboard; tempo control; looping with exact cueing; Classical guitar; artists. SYSTEM SPECS: Hybrid.

Jazz Guitar CD-ROM (MGI Interactive): Standard chord progressions; improvisational techniques; harmony theory; chords and scales; blues scales; daily exercises; for intermediate, all ages. SYSTEM SPECS: Windows.

Jazz Guitar Masterclass (PG Music): Interactive guitar lessons; illustrates basic skills to the beginning guitarist; enhances skills of more advanced guitarists; sixty lessons including Chord Voicings, Inversions, Right-Hand Techniques, Comping, Scales, Modes, Arpeggios, Common Progressions, Improvisation, Chord Melodies, and more; each lesson has an accompanying exercise and a practice tip; ten program tunes feature common chord progressions in a variety of styles and tempos; reference sheets and practice backing tracks; integrates interactive audio lessons with on-screen guitar display and notation. SYSTEM SPECS: Windows.

Memphis (Passport): For songwriters, guitarists, and combos; includes a spell checker, Thesaurus, and Rhyming Dictionary; create and print Charts with lyrics, chords, and more; choose from over 700 fret diagrams; does not use MIDI; see song on the screen; change the key; watch it transpose fret diagrams. SYSTEM SPECS: Windows.

MGI Interactive (MGI Interactive): Interactive CD-ROMs; diagrams, notation, and video clips; set loops to isolate difficult parts; backing tracks with full rhythm section; real guitar sounds; Guitar Library. SYSTEM SPECS: Windows 486 DX 66, MHz or better, 2X CD-ROM, 4-8 MB RAM, Windows compatible sound card, speakers.

MIDI Bass Works (ECS): Create bass lines and practice along with them; different tuning standards may be selected; bass lines may be printed; for all musicians; requires MIDI; for beginners-intermediate. SYSTEM SPECS: PC-DOS.

PIXymbols Guitarteach (Page Studio Graphics): Fonts and drawings designed specifically for preparing guitar playing instructions; features GuitarNotes, a font designed to create simple music notation references, and GuitarChords, a font that allows the user to create modular fingering and chord diagrams in vertical and horizontal formats; illustrations in the package include a generic guitar, guitar head, and two tuning charts in either PostScript or TIFF format; PostScript or True Type fonts are available; requires the use of a layout program. SYSTEM SPECS: Macintosh; Windows.

Play Blues Guitar (Play Music): Instruction by master blues guitarist Keith Wyatt; easy-to-use CD-ROM; includes four songs and lessons for playing the solo and rhythm guitar parts of each; multitrack music video of a band playing the songs; instruction in four classic blues styles: the 12-bar medium shuffle, the slow blues, the minor-key blues, and the 8-bar blues; over one hundred minutes of video and animation; forty interactive MIDI practice sessions and more; for intermediate-advanced, all age groups. SYSTEM SPECS: Windows 3.1, 66 MHz 486, MPC compatible sound card, MIDI synthesizer, 8 MB RAM, CD-ROM drive.

Play Guitar CD-ROM (Play Music): Intensive one-on-one guitar instruction; lessons proceed step by step; play basic chords and scales; play original songs that follow each lesson; music theory; for beginners, all ages. SYSTEM SPECS: Windows 95, 66 MHz 486, 8-bit sound card or better, 8 MB RAM, CD-ROM drive.

Play Rock Guitar (Play Music): Videos, songbooks, and MIDI; intensive one-on-one guitar instruction; features four classic rock songs: *Crossroads, Little Wing, Freeway Jam,* and *Black Magic Woman;* interactive multimedia links rock guitar technique lessons to the songs; play great rock riffs note for note; watch a demo and take a lesson at the same time; features Keith Wyatt; learn scale patterns, phrasing techniques, and musical concepts; for intermediate-advanced, all age groups. SYSTEM SPECS:

Windows 95, 66 MHz 486, 8-bit sound card or better, 8 MB RAM, CD-ROM drive.

Plugged-In Volume 1: The Next Generation in Guitar Instruction (Ubisoft): Interactive guitar tutorial; songs by some of rock's all-time greats and the licks that made them famous; intermediate guitarists go step by step through eight guitar classics; songs chosen for style and stature; arrangements presented in a challenging acoustic format; over 180 exercises in over seventy lessons; digital tuner; scrolling music; tablature and lyrics; customize each lesson through looping riffs, rewind and fast forward features, and zooming in full screen to see strumming and fingering up close. SYSTEM SPECS: Macintosh; Windows.

Richie Sambora Interactive Guitar CD-ROM (Enteractive): Features Richie Sambora, lead guitarist of Bon Jovi; teaches different riffs and techniques; play lead with the band; rock star shares his photo collection, popular music videos, personal interviews, and more; includes tuner, scale charts, chord dictionary, and over forty rock guitar techniques; interactive multimedia; user-friendly. SYSTEM SPECS: Macintosh: Mac LC II o better, 8 MB RAM, color monitor, 2X CD-ROM or better, System 7.1 or later; Windows: 3.1 or 95, 486 DX 33 MHz or better, 2X CD-ROM or better, Windows compatible sound card, 8 MB RAM.

Teach Me Blues Guitar (Voyetra): Method; video clips; animation; voice-overs; classic blues riffs, solos, and songs; comes with picks, chord dictionary, and software-based tuning system; for beginners and advanced players. SYSTEM SPECS: Windows.

Teach Me Guitar (Voyetra): Shows how to play chords and songs with videos, intuitive charts, and diagrams; online instructor demonstrates techniques; talks user through lesson; animated fretboard shows neck fingerings in real time; control tempos or loop sections to learn songs at own pace; play with virtual backup band; comes with picks, a chord dictionary, and software-based tuning system; for beginners and advanced players. SYSTEM SPECS: Windows.

Teach Me Rock Guitar (Voyetra): by Method; videos, charts, and diagrams; animated fretboard shows fingerings on the guitar neck in real time; control tempos or loop sections; learn songs at own pace; jam and play along with band; comes with picks, chord dictionary, and software-based tuning system; for beginners and advanced players. SYSTEM SPECS: Windows.

The Bluegrass Band (PG Music): Over fifty performances of bluegrass standards; MIDI equipped bluegrass instruments include banjo, fiddle, bass, guitar, and mandolin; pictures; biographies; trivia. SYSTEM SPECS: Windows.

The Blues Guitarist (PG Music): Music programs containing studio recordings of performances; listen to session players perform blues music; learn riffs, licks, and tricks; each instrument (guitar, piano, bass, and drums) recorded on a separate track; listen to each part independently; multimedia features; study arrangements; hear music; play along with top studio musicians. SYSTEM SPECS: Windows.

The Master Flatpick Guitar Solos (PG Music): Interactive music program with professional flatpick arrangements of fifty songs by top studio musician Marty Cutler; includes accompanying piano (comping), bass, drums, and strings; almost three hours of flatpick guitar soloing; on-screen guitar fretboard shows exactly which notes and chords are being played; note names are given to help learn the fret/string positions; guide notes display scale tones in the correct key; large library of flatpick solos; all solos are mainstream playing, based on typical chord progressions; most use eighth notes or triplets; each song has three or more full choruses; can hear the solos, slow down, or step through one note at a time; solos may be printed out; notation also contains TAB; advanced looping features; can loop a number of bars, what is on the screen, or entire song; includes *Band-in-a-Box* files. SYSTEM SPECS: Windows 3.1, 95/98, NT, 16 MB RAM, PC sound card or MIDI module, CD-ROM drive; Macintosh: MacOS 7.6 or later, 4 MB RAM, 6 MB available hard drive, MIDI module or QuickTime, CD-ROM drive.

The Master Jazz Guitar Solos (PG Music): Interactive music program with professional jazz quartet/quintet arrangements of fifty songs; each song features a jazz guitar solo played by a top studio musician; accompanying piano (comping), bass, drums, and strings; almost five hours of jazz guitar soloing; on-screen guitar fretboard shows exactly which notes and chords are being played; guide notes for typical positions for the key; note names to help learn the fret/string positions; large library of jazz solos; all solos are mainstream playing based on typical chord progressions; most use eighth notes or triplets; each song contains six full choruses; hear solos, slow them down, or step through one note at a time; solos may be printed out; notation also contains TAB; advanced looping features; loop a number of bars, what is on screen, or entire song; adjust tempo or key. SYSTEM SPECS: Windows 3.1, 95/98, NT, 16 MB RAM, PC sound card or MIDI module, CD-ROM drive; Macintosh: MacOS 7.6 or later, 4 MB RAM, 6MB available hard drive, MIDI module or Quick-Time, CD-ROM drive.

The Rock Guitarist (PG Music): Music programs containing studio recordings of performances; listen to session players perform rock music; learn riffs, licks, and tricks; each instrument recorded on a separate track; listen to each part independently; multimedia features; study arrangements; hear music; play along with top studio musicians. SYSTEM SPECS: Windows.

The Sor Studies (PG Music): Classical guitar performances of 121 of Fernando Sor's studies for guitar; music notation and chord symbols on-screen; audio performance; on-screen guitar, fretboard, and fingering; print a high-resolution copy; three CD-ROMs; biography of Sor; historical time line; multimedia features. SYSTEM SPECS: Windows.

Vocal-Choral-Singing Software

Audio Mirror (ECS): Practice singing and matching pitches using the latest in technology; listens to notes in real time and determines the note being sung and how sharp or flat the note is in cents; set the sensitivity of the program to compensate for various mic level inputs and impedances; record keeping is included so progress can be tracked and performance evaluated; for all ages. SYSTEM SPECS: Windows 95/98, MPC2, 8MB RAM, 4 MB free hard drive space, SVGA display, microphone, SoundBlaster sound card, full duplex SoundBlaster drivers.

Auto-Tune and Microphone Modeler Plug-In (Antares): Pitch correcting software; available in RTAS format for Digidesign Digi 001 users. SYSTEM SPECS: Macintosh; Windows.

Claire—The Personal Music Coach (Opcode): Objective is to develop ear training through singing; progressively difficult melodic patterns for students to sing; as notes are sung, computer evaluates pitch and provides visual feedback; up arrow means "sing higher," down arrow means "sing lower," black dot indicates "way off"; includes "practice mode" or "test mode" where a score is given; summary of scores given in session log; each exercise can be sung in four ways; several customizable features: "auto-curriculum" can be switched to "user-guided" mode to allow user to manually select exercises; notation can be displayed by scale degrees, "moveable do," "fixed do," or letter names; tempo and sensitivity range can be user-determined; "echo-singing" can determine an appropriate key for the user's voice range; extra instrument modules for violin, cello, and recorder use a sampled sound of the instrument; features real-time vocal (singing) input and evaluation; for vocalists ages ten-adult; reading and listening skills. SYSTEM SPECS: Macintosh: Macintosh LC with built-in microphone or compatible digitizer, digitizing software, and System 7.0, math-coprocessor recommended.

ECS Music Tuner (ECS): Software tool designed to help student play or sing in tune; sing or play any note; program shows if playing is sharp or flat in real time; range is +/- 50 cents; if pitch is outside of this range, program displays the next musical half step; for musicians of any skill or age. SYSTEM SPECS: Windows-MPC2, Windows 95, 8 MB RAM, SVGA display, 3.5-inch disk drive, 4MB free hard drive space, Windows compatible sound card, microphone, full duplex SoundBlaster drivers recommended.

Global Voices in Song (Global Voices): Aural and visual model of vocal music from different cultures; interactive CD-ROM with music and cultural information; resource guide; supplementary audio CD and videotape; for multicultural and choral studies; all ages. SYSTEM SPECS: Macintosh; Windows.

Interactive Songbook (Ibis): Learn to sing and play some of the greatest songs of all time; interactive songbook; teaches note by note to sing and play ten legendary tunes; voice captured on-screen; instant feedback on every note; learn the rhythm and melody of each tune; free Songbook complete with music lyrics; easy setup with any sound card and inexpensive microphone or MIDI keyboard; songs include: *Hey Jude, Let It Be, All My Loving, When I'm 64, Norwegian Wood, The Fool on the Hill, And I Love Her, Yesterday, Penny Lane,* and *Michelle;* for beginners, ages seven-adult. SYSTEM SPECS: Windows 3.1 or 95, 486DX=50MHz or better, 8 MB RAM, 15 MB hard disk space, 2X CD-ROM or better, SoundBlaster compatible sound card, microphone, MIDI adapter, and keyboard (optional).

JamRam (JamRam/Hal Leonard): CD-ROM Songbook Series; eight fully orchestrated MIDI song files; Roland Sound Canvas soft-synth tone generator driver with over 300 instrument sounds; 16-track recorder/sequencer; songbook with melody, guitar chord frames, and lyrics. SYSTEM SPECS: Windows 95/98, Pentium-based processor, 16 MB RAM, 7 MB hard drive space, 640 x 480 or higher display, 16-bit stereo; double-speed CD-ROM drive, 8-bit sound card, mouse.

Kool Karaoke (Vorton Technologies): CD-ROM; adjustable tempo and pitch, melody and volume control; changeable lyrics display; over fifty popular songs; download songs; for all ages. SYSTEM SPECS: IBM PC or compatible 486; Windows 95/98; 8 MB RAM; CD-ROM drive; sound card.

Sight Singing Made Simple CD (Hal Leonard): Solfege method; hear sounds music symbols represent; for home or school; over sixty exercises; for vocal and choral studies; audio CD. SYSTEM SPECS: Hybrid.

Sing! (Musicware): Complete beginning vocal course on CD-ROM; advanced software "reads" voice; ear training; control voice and breath easy; applies proven voice training methods; match pitches, hold notes, match rhythms, sight-read music, and sing along with dozens of musical accompaniments; learn to read notes, hear correct notes, and sing simple tunes; for beginners to intermediate, ages seven-adult. SYSTEM SPECS: Pentium 75 MHz or better, Windows 95, 8 MB RAM, 10 MB free hard disk space, double speed CD-ROM drive, SoundBlaster card or compatible, microphone.

Soloist (Ibis): Learn to play and practice virtually any acoustic and electric instrument, including the voice; select the instrument from the instrument panel and the skill level; follow along as Soloist composes exercises and gives immediate feedback on playing accuracy; use Soloist to tune instrument; for beginner to advanced, ages ten and up. SYSTEM SPECS: Windows.

The Bach Chorales (PG Music): Performance of Bach's four-part Chorales; professional choral ensemble; detailed mutimedia history; each voice (soprano, alto, tenor, and bass) recorded on a separate track; listen to independently; interactive program; vocal music; history of Bach; time line. SYSTEM SPECS: Windows.

The Barbershop Quartet (PG Music): Music program; favorite barbershop songs; interactive multimedia history of barbershop singing in America; each voice (tenor, lead, baritone, and bass) recorded on a separate track; listen to each part independently; study arrangements; hear music; sing along; made with the assistance of SPEBSQSA (Society for the Preservation and Encouragement of Barbershop Quartet Singing in America), the leading authority in America. SYSTEM SPECS: Windows.

Voice-Tradition and Technology: A State-of-the-Art Studio (Clearvue-eav): Voice pedagogy, voice and science; findings of medical and scientific researchers to enhance traditional voice training in the studio; interactive CD-ROM and book; techniques; feedback; special challenges. SYSTEM SPECS: Hybrid.

Worship Pro (Servant PC Resources): Song management system for church choirs. SYSTEM SPECS: Windows.

Worship Studio (Midisoft): Create music for hymns and choir; lead sheets; orchestral scores; record and play back; comes with 1,000 hymns; add notes, symbols, lyrics, and instrumentation; print out music; MIDI keyboard required. SYSTEM SPECS: Windows.

Jazz and Blues Software

Elements of the Jazz Language for the Developing Improvisor (WB): Comprehensive book on jazz analysis and improvisation; elements used in jazz improvisation are examined in recorded solos; suggestions are made for using each element in the jazz language; specific exercises are provided for practicing the element; ideal environment for developing fluency with the jazz language; for intermediate-advanced, ninth grade and up; contains five 3.5-inch disks. SYSTEM SPECS: Macintosh: Mac plus or greater with a least 2 MB RAM and a synthesizer for MIDI playback; Windows.

Herbie Hancock Presents Living Jazz CD-ROM (Graphix Zone): Interactive odyssey back to the eras of places where jazz evolved: the streets of New Orleans, Chicago, New York, Los Angeles, and into the New Jazz Horizon; music, poetry, history, art, and dance are combined to expose students to the jazz evolution; seven original songs composed and performed by Herbie Hancock and Joe Manolakakis; hundreds of photos, interviews, exclusive footage, and performances from dozens of jazz legends; for beginner-advanced, all ages. SYSTEM SPECS: Hybrid; Macintosh: Color Mac, 68040 processor or better, 5 MB available RAM, 10 MB disk space, double speed CD-ROM or better, System 7.01 or better; Windows: 486 DX2 66 MHz or better, 8 MB RAM, CD-ROM, Windows compatible sound card.

Jazz Tutor CD-ROM Volume 1 (Masterclass Productions): Learn to play jazz in a sophisticated and innovative way; five original tunes created especially for the CD-ROM title featuring the Phil Woods Quintet; includes jazz music theory interactive textbook; MIDI transcription with over 2,000 variations and over 2,000 chords and scales in all keys; for advanced, upper high school to college. SYSTEM SPECS: Windows.

Joy of Improv (Hal Leonard): Twelve to twenty-four-month foundation course for music improvisation on all instruments; fifty-two lessons; emphasize practice rather than theory; strengthens all aspects of playing, including technique, theory, and ear training; organized for beginning and intermediate players having some basic music reading skills and at least a year of experience playing any musical style; experience real-time synthesis of feeling, hearing, and playing. SYSTEM SPECS: Hybrid.

MiBac Jazz (MiBac Music Software): MiBac (Music Instruction By A Computer) breaks jazz into four main styles; each of these main styles has three different tempo subgroups that can be mixed and matched with any of the other styles or groups; many playing options; manual includes a tutorial that covers all twelve styles; how to type in chord progressions; printing charts; tempos and transposition; based on the basic blues progressions; user can experiment with the rhythm section, intros, voicings, and chord alternations; section on printing and setup; last section is a complete reference for all of the commands used; detailed discussions on the twenty-eight possible chord combinations; tool for developing jazz improvisational skills; practice examples; play with a jazz combo on any tune; can play in any key, at any tempo; comes with twenty-three jazz styles including 4/4 and Ballad, Swing, Bebop, Rock Shuffle, Bossa Nova, Samba, Slow 12/8, and Two Beat; for all music students, intermediate-advanced, ages fifteen-adult. SYSTEM SPECS: Macintosh: System 6 or 7, MIDI and multitimbral synthesizer or sound module required.

MIDI Jazz Improvisation Volumes I and II (ECS): Provides instruction and practice in jazz improvisation for all instruments; jazz ensemble is played through the MIDI synthesizer and records the student's solo keyboard improvisation; each exercise is organized into eight separate tracks: Bass Line, Chords, Melody, Riff or Counter Melody, Scale Study, Sample Improvised Line, Drums (Vol. II only), and User Solo; Volume I covers ii-V-I progressions and twelve-bar blues; Volume II covers advanced materials and assumes student knowledge of scales and basic improvisation techniques such as harmonic substitution and complex ii-V-I progressions; knowledge of MIDI operation is essential; detailed learning sequence is provided to give students guidance and goal-oriented practice; for middle-school through adult keyboard students. SYSTEM SPECS: Macintosh (MIDI); Windows (MIDI); PC-DOS (MIDI).

Saxophone Lessons with Alan Neveu (Parakeet): Twenty multimedia saxophone lessons; finger technique, embouchure, articulation, reeds, vibrato, intonation, time, repertoire, and more; lessons on soprano, alto, tenor, and baritone sax playing specifics; multimedia experience; movie clips; CD-quality sounds; color photos; music notation; rich text. SYSTEM SPECS: Macintosh; Windows.

The History of Jazz CD-ROM (Clearvue/eav): History of jazz; performers; jazz from different cities; 1900s to present; interactive; shows how jazz was created by the descendants of the slaves brought from Africa; preserves the spirit and beat of African drum music; includes jazz music legends Louis Armstrong, Dizzy Gillespie, Scott Joplin, Duke Ellington, Benny Goodman, and others; for beginner-intermediate, grades 4-college. SYSTEM SPECS: Hybrid.

The Instrumental History of Jazz CD-ROM Set (Clearvue/eav): History of jazz; audio CD and CD-ROM; ragtime; Dixieland; swing through twentieth century; roots of instrumental jazz; twenty-two audio tracks; archival photos; video clips; different types of jazz; virtual time line; fifty-six page book with text and photos. SYSTEM SPECS: Macintosh; Windows.

The Jazz Saxophonist (PG Music): Music program with studio recordings of great jazz saxophone music; learn riffs and tricks; each instrument (sax, piano, bass, and drums) recorded on a separate track; listen to each part independently; multimedia features; study arrangements; hear music; play along with top studio musicians; hot jazz; tips and techniques; integrates multitrack audio, MIDI, chord symbols, and music notation. SYSTEM SPECS: Windows.

The Jazz Soloist (PG Music): Professional jazz quartet arrangements of fifty songs per volume; each song features a jazz solo played by jazz musicians, piano comping, bass, and drums; over three hours of jazz soloing on each volume; MIDI files; for intermediate-advanced, high school and up. SYSTEM SPECS: Macintosh: 4 MB RAM, System 6 or 7,

MIDI interface and synthesizer/module with guitar, bass, and drum sounds, 2 MB hard disk space; Windows: 4 MB RAM, sound card or MIDI system with guitar, bass, and drum sounds, 2 MB hard disk space.

The Rock Saxophonist (PG Music): Music program with studio recordings of great rock and roll saxophone music; learn riffs and tricks; each instrument recorded on a separate track; listen to each part independently; multimedia features; study arrangements; hear music; play along with top studio musicians; tips and techniques; integrates multitrack audio, MIDI, chord symbols, music notation, and chord progressions. SYSTEM SPECS: Windows.

Music Appreciation, Music History, and Composers Software

Alfred Enhanced CDs (Alfred): Can be played in a conventional audio CD player; can also be used in computer CD-ROM drive; follow along with the musical notation and record while playing along. SYSTEM SPECS: Windows.

Apple Pie Music: The History of American Music (Lintronics Software Publishing): CD-ROM multimedia reference and anthology; contains over 400 songs, over 300 pictures, fifty-four chapters of interactive text; covers the Colonial Era, the Expansion Era, and the Industrial Era; divided into Folk Music, Popular Music, and Religious Music; cursor appears over any text that can be copied; set of hierarchical menus for navigation; Hotwords are used to indicate titles of songs that can be played, reference to related areas, names of instruments, or names of composers or lyricists; Music Alley is a special search and indexing system that allows songs to be located based on specific criteria and then played; includes a selected bibliography and discography; for all musicians, ages ten-adult. SYSTEM SPECS: Windows Multimedia PC or Windows 3.1, super VGA, CD-ROM, sound card, 4 MB RAM.

Appreciating the Orchestra CD-ROM (Clearvue/eav): Includes Britten's *Young Person's Guide to the Orchestra;* colorful visual presentations; detailed narrations; easy-to-use multimedia format; self-directed study; instruments and basic structure of the orchestra; diverse musical styles and eras; also includes Prokofiev's *Peter and the Wolf,* Copland's *Billy the Kid Suite,* and Tchaikovsky's *1812 Overture;* beginner-advanced, grades 4-9. SYSTEM SPECS: Hybrid.

Art and Music CD-ROMS (Clearvue/eav): Interactive series; exploration through history from the medieval era through surrealism; shows parallels between art and architecture and music; humanities in a new light; series of eight includes the following titles: THE MEDIEVAL ERA: the art, architecture, and music of the era were created for and governed by the Church; evolution of art and music during Medieval times; THE RENAISSANCE: Renaissance artists and composers, influenced and inspired by the new humanistic philosophy, developed new forms and techniques from painting with oils to four-part polyphony; THE BAROQUE: examples of the dramatic effect of art from Caravaggio to Rembrandt; the energetic, expressive style of music from Frescobaldi to Handel; the drama of opera; THE EIGHTEENTH CENTURY: developments in painting and sculpture parallel music's changing styles; comic opera, Viennese classical style, emerging Romanticism; art and music of the French Revolution; comparison between the works of David and Beethoven; THE ROMANTIC ERA: Berlioz's *Requiem* and Delacroix's *Liberty Leading the People;* numerous works of music and art that are related; IMPRESSIONISM: Impressionist art and music; parallels between the artist's use of color and light and the composer's use of instrumentation; THE TWENTIETH CENTURY: significant artistic developments; abstraction in art and atonality in music emerge, followed by Fauvism and Cubism; SURREALISM: parallels between the artistic methods of Ernst, Magritte, and Dali and the musical works of Satie, Bartok, and Cage; all titles are in hybrid format; for intermediate-advanced, grades 7-college. SYSTEM SPECS: Hybrid; Macintosh: 68030 or better, 256 colors recommended, 8 MB RAM, System 7.0 or later, 2X speed CD-ROM or better; Windows: 486 DX/25 or better, 8 MB RAM, VGA or better, sound card, 2X speed CD-ROM or better, Windows 95.

Bach and Before CD-ROM (Voyager): Overview of 2,000 years of music from ancient Greek rituals to Bach and Handel in the mid-eighteenth century; for beginner–advanced, eighth grade and up. SYSTEM SPECS: Macintosh.

Beethoven and Beyond (Voyager): Covers the music of Beethoven and the Romantic movement through the compositions of Schubert, Chopin, and Brahms; for beginner–advanced, eighth grade and up. SYSTEM SPECS: Macintosh.

Beethoven Lives Upstairs (Classical Kids): Interactive CD-ROM; learn and create music; paint pictures; play musical games; based on the audio recording of the same name; CD-quality audio, sound effects, and video; Beethoven goes through each exercise and provides suggestions and directions; adventure begins in the main room; click on the bell tower outside the window and choose any of ten prerecorded tunes to play on the bells each hour (in real time), or record; Christoph's journal is the entrance to many activities; from each page, enter an interactive space to explore and play games; watch video clips from the movie *Beethoven Lives Upstairs*; games include Notes Afloat, Name That Musical Square Game Show, Town Square and Instrument Fling, The Great Pen Chase, Beethoven's Room, and Beethoven's Rehearsal; drills previously taught basics; easy installation; Read-Me file contains detailed information on installation and trouble shooting; learn all aspects of music, from composition to interpretation; can record every stage in a full-color journal; wide variety of goal-oriented and creative activities; choose a piece of music, select the instruments, and hear a version of Beethoven's music; for beginners, ages eight and up. SYSTEM SPECS: Windows 486 SX/33 MHz, Windows 3.1, CD-ROM, MIDI soundboard, VGA color monitor, 4 MB RAM, 8 MB RAM recommended; can be used with headphones and speakers.

CD Time Sketch (ECS): To facilitate listening and analyzing CD music; create listening lessons with any audio CD; for fundamentals and appreciation courses, or music history courses at any level; annotated listening format can be applied to classes and activities and the music performance curriculum; glossary of terms includes dynamics, tempo markings, stylistic expression markings, music symbols, and standard musical terms. SYSTEM SPECS: Windows.

Classical Music Notes (Voyager): Reference for concert goers, music students, and classical music fans; nearly 2,000 program notes, 500 composers, 500 audio examples; musical term glossary; audio lectures; charts; music examples; suggested classical music library lists; great orchestras of the world; photos; video; comprehensive test covering music directors, history, discography, special programs, ticket and seating information; learn about instruments; picture library and text. SYSTEM SPECS: Windows 3.1 or better, CD-ROM drive, sound card.

Classical Music Series (Voyager): Includes Pocket Guide: single screen overview of the symphony; play any major section instantly; A Close Reading: running commentary across the whole composition, measure by measure play through, or search and browse; A Composer's World: sets music in a historical and cultural context; Games: test expertise; A Comprehensive Glossary: terms and definitions; includes Beethoven: *Symphony #9*; Mozart: *The Dissonant Quartet*; Stravinsky: *The Rite of Spring*; Dvorak: *From the New World*; Franz Schubert: *The "Trout" Quintet*; Richard Strauss: *Three Tone Poems*; for beginner-advanced, eighth grade and up. SYSTEM SPECS: Macintosh.

Classical Orchestra Notes (Hopkins Technology): Almost 2,000 program notes, many with complete vocal text in their original language with English translations; 500 text-audio links; read about a piece and hear music examples of timeless masterpieces; CD-ROM; full-text search; portraits of over 500 composers; picture library and text covering scores of instruments; hypertext classical glossary with hundreds of music terms; information on the world's greatest conductors and music directors.

SYSTEM SPECS: Windows 3.1, VGA monitor, CD-ROM drive, sound card.

Composer Quest (Opcode): Music history tour through time; covers music, history, arts, and sociological change from the year 1600 into the twentieth century; over sixty musical performances of the masters; great paintings by Rembrandt, Monet, Turner, and others; important developments in the world of art. SYSTEM SPECS: Windows 386/3.1, CD-ROM, super VGA monitor, soundboard.

Computer Music: An Interactive Documentary (Digital Studios): Educational CD-ROM; covers computer music for middle-school through college-age students; palette of sounds created by digital instruments; over two hours of movies and animation that demonstrate key concepts in digital audio, MIDI sampling, sequencing, editing and composition; pioneers in computer music; career advice from professionals; Lab Annex allows students to make their own instruments, experiment with WAVEforms, and edit a composition. SYSTEM SPECS: Hybrid.

Discovering Music (Voyetra Technologies): Provides a foundation of theory and an overview of music; experimentation with different sounds; create music, edit it on screen, and print it out; five programs including Music Conservatory, Music Writer, JamminimumKeys, Recording Station, and SoundCheck; Music Conservatory is subdivided into five modules: Great Composers, History of Music, Music Theory, Musical Instruments, and Music Glossary, and includes more than sixty high quality symphonic recordings and fifty AVI video clips; in the JamminimumKeys mode, choose from among 128 general MIDI instruments, select a musical style and start playing; five-part band accompanies lead with backups and riffs; built-in recorder saves performances to transfer them into Recording Station for editing; in Recording can add, overdub, mix, and modify MIDI tracks, change instrumentation and tempo, and add harmony vocals or acoustic instruments; includes two digital audio tracks, ten MIDI tracks, and 129 general MIDI instruments; Music Writer creates sheet music and prints it out; place musical notes and symbols on the staff with the mouse, as well as combine notes to create chords, change notes by dragging them to a new location, and add lyrics and dynamics; easy to use; requires no musical background; includes SoundCheck, a multimedia diagnostic tool essential for troubleshooting; each feature is available as a separate program. SYSTEM SPECS: Windows 486 SX/25 MHz, Windows 3.1 or 95, CD-ROM, sound card, MIDI keyboard recommended.

Enhanced CDs (Intersound): Works as an audio CD and as a CD-ROM in a Macintosh or Windows computer; combines the mastery of great composers with the newest musical format in Audio Plus Enhanced CDs; the histories of composers, an introduction to notation, musical scores, and interactive staves for composing original melodies; complete album is audible; includes *Beethoven, The Man and His Music*; *Bach, The Man and His Music*; *The Best of Baroque*; *Chopin, The Man and His Music*; *Piano Masterpieces: The Definitive Collection*; *Tchaikovsky, The Man and His Music*; *Mozart, The Man and His Music*; *Puccini, The Man and His Music*; *R. Strauss, The Man and His Music*. SYSTEM SPECS: Hybrid.

Great Composers: Their Lives and Music CD-ROMs (Clearvue/eav): Six-volume multimedia presentation about the lives of composers; to supplement music education of grade-school through high-school students; text, images, audio, animation, and video; hear composers' works behind the script; users highlight multiple-choice answers; tally of user answers; multiple-choice answers test the student on the time period in which the composer lived; includes a dictionary and encyclopedia; click on blue or green words in the text for explanations of terms; score-keeping feature; for a group studio or study at home; Volume 1: Johann Sebastian Bach, Robert Schumann, Sergei Rachmaninoff; Volume 2: George Frideric Handel, Frideric Chopin, Claude Debussy; Volume 3: Wolfgang Amadeus Mozart, Felix Mendelssohn, Antonin Dvorak; Volume 4: Ludwig van Beethoven, Edvard Grieg, Howard Hanson; Volume 5: Franz Joseph Haydn, Pyotr Ilich Tchaikovsky, Maurice Ravel; Volume 6: Franz Schubert, Johannes Brahms, Johann Strauss; traces the lives and music of the great composers; interactive multimedia programs; tells composers' life stories from their first musical training to their greatest achievements; highlights musical selections; chronicles the events that influenced their music; explains characteristics that identify their work; for all music students, ages six-eighteen. SYSTEM SPECS: Hybrid; Macintosh: 68030 or better processor, 8 MB RAM, System 7 or later, 2X speed CD-ROM or better; Windows: 486 DX/25 or better, 8 MB RAM, VGA or better, sound card, 2X speed CD-ROM or better, Windows 95.

Instruments of the Symphony Orchestra CD-ROM (Clearvue/eav): Instruments in the symphony orchestra; select an instrument and view a summary of its history and development; identify instruments by appearance, sound, and musical capability; how to hold and play each instrument; music; colorful photography; detailed narration; for beginners, grades 7-12. SYSTEM SPECS: Macintosh; Windows.

Intermuse CD-ROM (Clearvue-eav): Create listening guides for any piece of music; design assignments in music appreciation; multimedia presentations on music history and fundamentals; self-testing; coordinates with *The World of Music* textbook. SYSTEM SPECS: Macintosh: 68040 processor or better, 8 MB RAM, System 7 or later, 37 MB free

hard disk space; Windows: 486/66 MHz processor or better, 8 MB RAM, 37 MB free hard disk space.

Laserlight Digital CD-ROM series (Music Pen): Seventy classical music CDs that include CD-ROM information; can listen to the performance, browse the complete musical score, read program notes and biographical information; use as audio CD with stereo; view and print scores; for multimedia presentations; CD-ROM booklet; multi-part orchestra scores are synchronized with the music; zoom in and out for different views; colorful video footage of the composers' native homeland; includes Mozart: *Symphony #40*; *Symphony #41 (Jupiter)*; *Eine Kleine Nachtmusik*; Beethoven: *Symphony #1*; *Symphony #2*; *Symphony #3*; *Symphony #4*; *Symphony #5*; *Symphony #6 (Pastorale)*; *Symphony #7*; *Symphony #8*; *Symphony #9 (Choral)*; Vivaldi: *Four Seasons*; Bach: *Brandenburg Concertos #1-3*; *Brandenburg Concertos #4-6*; *Orchestral Suites*; Dvorak: *New World Symphony*; Chopin: *Piano Concerto #1*; *Piano Concerto #2*; Tchaikovsky: *Symphony #5*; *Ballet Suites*; *The Nutcracker*; Liszt: *Piano Concerto*; Prokofiev: *Peter and The Wolf*. SYSTEM SPECS: 486 PC or better; Windows 3.1, sound card, CD-ROM drive, 4 MB RAM, 7 MB hard disk space.

Maestroscope "Music History" Series (Maestro Music): Covers the high points of the development of Western Civilization; contains nine lessons; each lesson contains six events to explore; designed for sixth grade students and above and take twenty to thirty minutes to complete; placemark allows student to stop at any point in a program and continue later; content of each program is based on the historical events that occurred during that specific time in history. SYSTEM SPECS: Macintosh; Windows.

Making Music: The Symphony Orchestra CD-ROM (Clearvue/eav): Denver Young Artist Orchestra; interviews with conductor and orchestra members; footage of orchestra's rehearsals, seating auditions, dress rehearsal, and final performance; structure and organization of the symphony orchestra; different sections of a typical orchestra; instruments in each section; full motion video clips; grade book feature to save student quiz scores; for beginners, grades 4-12. SYSTEM SPECS: Hybrid.

Maximum Learning Skills: Composers (WBW Software): Tests knowledge of composers; biographical, musical, and historical clues; select the correct composer from a list of ten; clues present repertoire, biographical, and historical information; covers Bach through Kabalevsky; includes Menu, Sign-in and Instructions, Game, Composer Portrait, and Hall of Fame; student types a menu number, signs in, reads the instruction screen, then plays the single-screen game; master list of composers and first of five clues appears on the screen; students type in the number of the composer to which the clue refers;

three composer identifications make up one game; if the correct answer is entered, a screen with the composer's portrait appears, then a musical excerpt by the composer; after an incorrect response, the computer beeps and the next clue is presented; five clues in all; after the fifth clue, the correct composer's name is given; points are earned when the composer is identified and decrease with each additional clue; Hall of Fame records the fifteen highest-scoring games; uses the computer's internal speaker for sound; a sound card or MIDI option is preferred; concise game-based format; for music students, ages ten-eighteen. SYSTEM SPECS: Windows; PC; VGA monitor.

Multimedia Composers/CD Companions (Forest Technologies): Series of CD-ROMs; features musical pieces by the composer, as well as information about life and times, sources of inspiration, and theories about music; includes text, color photographs, sketches, and diagrams; CD-quality audio; includes: *Pocket Audio Guide,* an overview of the composers music; *A Close Reading,* commentary throughout the composition, synchronized to the music; *The Composer's World,* historical and cultural information, detailed bibliographies, color art, and photographs; *Game,* tests knowledge of the information presented; many of the questions are based on passages from the composers' works; glossary and help are available online; for all musicians, ages fifteen-adult. SYSTEM SPECS: Macintosh; Windows; CD-ROM.

Multimedia History of Music CD-ROM (Voyetra): Covers eras in musical history, including background music from each era; links for word definitions; lives and works of prominent composers are set against the history, arts, science, culture, and politics of their times; includes the Renaissance, Baroque, Classical, and Romantic eras; for beginner-advanced, all ages. SYSTEM SPECS: Windows.

Multimedia Musical Instruments CD-ROM (Voyetra): Learn about the instruments of a symphony orchestra; includes instruments from other cultures and traditions; how instruments were invented; how they developed through history; how they produce sounds; full-screen color images identify the parts of each instrument; videos demonstrate playing technique of more than fifty instruments; for beginners, all ages. SYSTEM SPECS: Windows.

Music and Culture CD-ROM (Clearvue/eav): Covers the music and traditions of Polynesian, African, and North American Indian peoples; instruments, vocal music, and dance; authentic recordings and graphics; audiovisual presentation with text linked to an encyclopedia and glossary; multiple-choice questions for quizzes; identifies the four major instrument groups classified by ethnomusicologists; for beginners-intermediate, grades 7-college. SYSTEM SPECS: Hybrid; Macintosh: CD-ROM, 68030/25 MHz, color monitor, System 7.0, 8 MB RAM; Win-

dows: 386/33 MHz, Windows 3.1, 8 MB RAM, VGA color monitor.

Music Appreciation Course-Intermediate Level CD-ROMs (Clearvue/eav): Two interactive CD-ROMs; periods of music; composers; instruments; hands-on activities; video clips; archival images; quizzes; encyclopedia; dictionary; teachers guide; Presentation Manager. SYSTEM SPECS: Macintosh; Windows.

Music Appreciation: A Study Guide (ECS): Music terminology and history emphasized in music appreciation courses using the book *Exploring Music through Experience;* review and quiz on music terminology; review of Western music history from Greek times to contemporary music and quiz; for advanced, grades 9-college. SYSTEM SPECS: Apple (non-MIDI); PC-DOS (non-MIDI).

Music Composer Quiz (ECS): Twenty questions randomly selected from a pool; users have three chances to answer a question correctly before the answer is displayed; instructor may edit or print any of the one hundred quiz questions; feedback is given at the end of each quiz session; student records are retained; for grades 6-college. SYSTEM SPECS: Macintosh; Windows; Apple; PC-DOS.

Music Conservatory (Voyetra): Covers music history, theory, instruments, and composers; listening examples; learn about lives and works of composers; Baroque through twentieth century; notation, rhythm, tonality, and harmony; audio and video demonstrations of over seventy-five orchestral instruments; glossary of 250 musical terms and concepts; for beginners, all ages. SYSTEM SPECS: Windows.

Music History Review: Composers (ECS): Test knowledge of composers; Renaissance to twentieth century; select quiz from ten categories; multiple-choice format; feedback; coordinated with *A History of Western Music,* 4th ed., by Grout and Palisca (published by W.W. Norton); student records; for beginners, grades 6-college. SYSTEM SPECS: Macintosh; Windows; Apple; PC-DOS.

Music History: A Study Guide (ECS): Three disk series; quick reference outline; Disk I reviews Western music history form early influences through the late Renaissance; Disk 2 covers early Baroque (ca.1600) through late Beethoven (ca. 1825); Disk 3 reviews material from early Romantic through contemporary music; coordinates with *A History of Western Music* by Grout and Palisca (W.W. Norton, 1988); for beginners-intermediate, grades 9-college. SYSTEM SPECS: PC-DOS.

Music Mentor (Midisoft): Covers fundamental elements of music: melody, rhythm, harmony, timbre, texture, and form; covers how composers combined these elements; easy-to-use interface; on-screen buttons; integrates history, composers, and creativity; covers thirteen centuries of musical style; learn how different instruments sound; complete multitrack studio (sequencer) to make, record, edit, and print music; for beginners-advanced, ages twelve and up. SYSTEM SPECS: PC; Windows; MIDI interface, MIDI keyboard or soundboard, color monitor, mouse.

Perspectives in Music History (ECS): Covers composers, countries, dates, style periods, and compositions; examines events and connections that have occurred between 1400 and 1987; graph of style periods and four quizzes; for beginners-intermediate, grades five-twelve. SYSTEM SPECS: Apple; PC-DOS.

Piano Mouse Meets Great Composers (Piano Mouse): CD-ROM; introduction to the lives and music of eight great composers from the Baroque, Classical, and Romantic periods; biographies; games. SYSTEM SPECS: Windows.

PIXymbols Musics (Page Studio Graphics): Package of fonts featuring musical instruments; more than sixty detailed drawings of musical instruments; simplified forms for small-scale reproduction; PostScript or True Type; includes piano key symbols and characters representing diagrams of traditional orchestra seating. SYSTEM SPECS: Macintosh; Windows.

Soundtree General Music Curriculum (SoundTree): Covers musical concepts; eleven multi-lesson units, including lesson plans, print materials, scores, charts, and general MIDI sequence files; evaluation criteria, outcomes, and suggested extension activities. SYSTEM SPECS: MIDI keyboard or sound module; computer sequencer or music workstation recommended.

The Anatomy of Music (Tom Snyder Productions): Includes three CDs, a Hypercard stack, and accompanying guidebook and lesson plan; OK to photocopy twenty-six pages of the tutorial for classroom use; "a learning tool to help students with no previous musical knowledge develop specific comprehension skills in classical music"; for undergraduate college students in a typical music appreciation course; six chapters: Minuet, Rondo, Theme and Variations, Sonata and Concerto forms, and a complete performance of *Beethoven's Symphony No. 3* "Eroica"; each chapter is titled "Anatomy of" the form under study; each is highlighted as the music plays; first five chapters include listening exercises and self tests; in the listening exercises, the composition is performed, then the user clicks on the tile corresponding to each formal unit as it is played; in self-test mode, three selected formal segments are highlighted from the full set of tiles; the composition is performed, and the user clicks on the tile corresponding to the formal section as it is reached; points are given for correct answers and subtracted for incorrect answers; students can enter their names; scores are not saved; no record-keeping function; scores can be printed; for all music students, ages fifteen-adult. SYSTEM SPECS: Macintosh; Windows.

The Classical Ideal (Voyager): Covers the Classical era and the emergence of Haydn and Mozart; eighteenth-century music; performances. SYSTEM SPECS: Macintosh.

The History of Country Music CD-ROM (Clearvue/eav): Multimedia survey; history and development from roots in the rural South to mainstream modern music; song examples; index. SYSTEM SPECS: Hybrid.

The History of Folk Music CD-ROM (Clearvue/eav): Information about the European and African influences on the development of American folk music; five sections: Roots of American Folk Music, Country Music, Black Folk Music, Folk Music in History, and Folk Music in History, Part II; tracks the roots of American folk music from early Native American music, to the music of new settlers, to country music, and to African American music; in-depth surveys; includes aural examples of folk instruments, singing, and chanting; spoken text between the examples; color pictures showing costumed groups singing, playing different instruments, and dancing; main program runs through the musical examples and spoken text; click on different icons to access extra information and references, question and answer sections, and quizzes; Intro to Power CD answers questions about how to access other areas of the program such as references, printing, and quizzes; Question and Answer icon takes user through several multiple-choice questions; when an incorrect choice is made, the correct answer is shown, and the reasons why; preparation for the seven timed quizzes; score and the correct answers are given at the end of each timed quiz; quiz topics include Ethnic and Cultural Aspects, Important People, and Styles of Music; quiz scores are automatically recorded; information can be printed; references given for more in-depth research; clicking the Magnifying Glass icon enlarges the picture on the screen; helps users see instrument and costume details; CD is installed each time it is used; addition to any American music history curriculum; offers technical support; for all music students, ages ten-adult. SYSTEM SPECS: Hybrid; Macintosh: 68030/25 MHz, System 7, color quickdraw, 4 MB RAM; Windows: 386/20 MHz, Windows 3.1, 4 MB RAM, VGA color monitor.

The History of Music CD-ROM (Clearvue/eav): Two volumes; four hours of material; overview of the evolution of music from ancient Greece and Egypt through the avant-garde compositions of John Cage and Philip Glass; includes composers such as Palestrina, Bach, Mozart, Beethoven, Wagner, Mahler, Gershwin, Stravinsky, and others; Part One: Origins of Music into the Classical Period, the Middle Ages, Renaissance, Baroque, and Classical periods; Part Two: Romanticism into the 1980s, Early Romanticism, Later Romanticism, Early Twentieth Century, and Into the 1980s; an important theory principle is explained at the end of each chapter; this includes tonality, sonata-allegro form, rhythms, styles, textures, consonant and dissonant sounds, serialism, and new systems of notation; explains concepts and terms such as motet, polyphony, counterpoint, toccata, oratorio, and pianoforte; focuses on factors and events that influenced music, such as nationalism, Freud, and electronic music; brightly colored diagrams; users can test themselves, choose the number of questions, and establish a time limit; self-paced review of music history or for an instructor and class; material is broad in scope; test questions are detailed; no record keeping except for scoring each test; many possibilities for organizing test questions; large amount of material presented; extensive indexing and search capabilities; certain words are highlighted in blue or green; clicking on them brings up a definition or glossary; full-color images can be enlarged, clipped, saved, and copied; ideal for a general music course, a music appreciation class, an independent music studio, or home library; concerts, art galleries, and lectures from all parts of the world and from all eras of history; narration is printed on the screen and read; because of the visual, audio, and interactive capabilities, this CD-ROM accommodates many learning styles; combination of history, music, art, drama, and philosophy; teaching tool for all ages; for music students, ages ten-adult. SYSTEM SPECS: Hybrid; Macintosh: 68030/25 MHz, System 7, color quickdraw, 4 MN RAM; Windows: 386/20 MHz, Windows 3.1/95, 4 MB RAM, VGA color monitor.

The Musical World of Professor Piccolo (Opcode): Interactive, educational CD-ROM; introduces various genres of music; foundation for understanding the elements of music; covers music theory, music notation, musical styles, history, and instruments; includes form, instrumentation, structure, and more; in *Piccolo's Music Town*, every building contains musical experiences; CD-quality musical performances; graphics and animation; for beginners, grades three and up. SYSTEM SPECS: Macintosh: System 7.0, 256-color monitor, CD-ROM; Windows: 386, Windows 3.1, MPC compatible sound board, super VGA monitor.

The Norton Masterworks CD-ROM: Student Edition (Clearvue/eav): Interactive; explores twelve pieces or movements in depth; information about the composer, era, music, genre, author of literary text, and more; examine form, melody, rhythm, harmony; animated real-time listening guides; scores and text illustrations; watch music play; major works; encourages in-depth music study; facilitates further research; customize to all ability levels; interactive quizzes test aural perception and factual knowledge at different levels of difficulty. SYSTEM SPECS: Macintosh: 68030 processor or better, 2 MB RAM, System 7.1 or later, 1 MB free hard disk space.

Timesketch Series (ECS): Each sketch includes a CD recording and a form analysis of the piece; for use in music fundamentals, music appreciation, and music history courses; listening lab or private studio; for all grade levels. Includes *Portrait of Bach, Toccata and Fugue in D Minor*; *Portrait of Beethoven, Symphony #5*; *Portrait of Brahms, Symphony #3*; *Portrait of Mozart, Symphony 40*; *Portrait of Schubert, Unfinished Symphony*; *Portrait of Dvorak, New World Symphony*; *Pathetique Sonata, Beethoven*; *Piano Concerto, Beethoven*; *Brubeck Sketches #1, Jazz Series*; *Miles Davis Sketches #1, Jazz Series*; *Grainger Sketches #1, Lincolnshire Posey*. SYSTEM SPECS: Macintosh: Mac-System 7.0 or greater, color monitor recommended, CD-ROM drive with audio extensions required, 1 MB free RAM, 1 MB hard drive space; Windows: PC-MPC2 compliant computer, Windows 3.1/95, VGA monitor minimum, 4 MB RAM, 1 MB hard disk.

Willie: The Life and Music of Willie Nelson (Graphix Zone): Interactive CD-ROM; six previously unreleased songs; rare early recordings; interview with Willie Nelson and Chet Atkins, Paul Englis, Waylon Jennings, and Kris Kristofferson; Willie Trivia Game; for all levels, all ages. SYSTEM SPECS: Hybrid; Macintosh: Color Macintosh, 68040 processor or better, 5 MB available RAM, 10 MB hard disk space, double speed CD-ROM or better, System 7.01 or better; Windows: 486DX 2 66 MHz or better, 8 MB RAM, CD-ROM, Windows compatible sound card.

Studio, Choir, and Band Management Software

3D Dynamic Drill Design (Pyware): Drill design software used by high schools, colleges, universities, and corps around the world; fast drawing and animating drill program; count-to-count technology; view, edit, or print any count of the drill at any time; with Morph feature can create transitions by morphing existing formation instead of recreating formations from scratch; Time Track process removes the limitation that requires all transitions to begin and end at the same time; Follow-the-Leader function; with Rewrite can rewrite drill in seconds; on-screen help; Stride Zone; unlimited drawing tools; reduced editing of symmetrical shapes; resize a drill any time to reflect current band size; animated color with music; position numbers or labels; flexible instructional printouts include drill book; cast sheet; design props; hash marks; measuring tape and compass; measurement tool (Mac only); coordinates printed by performer; animation tempos. SYSTEM SPECS: Macintosh: 16MB RAM, System 7 or 8, 14-inch color monitor; Windows.

3D Java Drill Design (Pyware): New innovative features with highly requested features contained in earlier versions; upgrade; cross compatibility; can operate on any computer that supports Java including Windows, NT, Unix, and Macintosh; 3D Java data files are not downward compatible to Original 3D and Virtual 3D; complete control of grid design; grid designs can be saved as .GRD files and used in any 3D Java drill file; specialized drawing and editing tools are implemented as 3D Java Plug-Ins; plug-in sets include Military Style Editing Tools, Pageantry Tools, Showband Style Editing Tools, and many more; animated drills can synchronize to MIDI files and to CD recordings of live performances; labels or position numbers can be automatically positioned along the curvature of shapes or places manually; design a drill backwards; Charting Aid program; with Static Charts drills can be designed without animation capabilities for idea books where each page is an unrelated chart and for creating a library of standard charts used by a performing group such as a school name or logo; Static Chart can be copied and pasted into a drill file that has animation capabilities; improved Drill Rewrite; special Internet distribution features for professional drill designers; drill files can be locked internally to read only, not print, view first eighty counts, and display the designer information such as name and phone number; customer can download from the Internet and review a drill for purchase; drill can be unlocked by the customer with a password provided by the drill designer. SYSTEM SPECS: Macintosh: System 8 or greater, 400 MHz machine or greater, 64 MB RAM; Windows: Windows 95/98/NT, 400 MHz machine or greater, 64 MB RAM.

3D Virtual Dynamic Drill Design (Pyware): Analyze every aspect of drill; view every count of drill for collisions, excessive strides, and visual voicing including phasing and balance of actual music through MIDI capabilities; for use in marching techniques class; students can turn in projects on disk; grade and return with built-in multimedia report for review; NCAA hashes; perspective view; changing of performer colors and symbols during animation; measurement tool; unlimited drawing tools; props; flexible instructional printouts; new features added in Version Two include largest stride indicator, fixed intervals, mixed intervals, additional rewrite features, additional print layout options, additional labeling features, show/hide shapes. SYSTEM SPECS: Macintosh: System 7 or 8, 16MB RAM, 14-inch color monitor; Windows.

Amadeus Al Fine (Pyware): Pitch-to-MIDI device; use wind instruments for input with notation software or instructional courseware; hardware box that converts microphone input of any wind instrument into standard MIDI data; compatible with any software that normally uses a MIDI keyboard as a way of input; any notation program will operate with Amadeus for transcribing a performed passage into notation on the computer. SYSTEM SPECS: Macintosh; Windows.

Amadeus Tutor (Pyware): Assessment and evaluation software; works with *Amadeus Al Fine*; develop a curriculum for students; Graphic Tuner: graphically displays, assesses, and compares the intonation perception and performance of students individually or in groups; Scale Drills: practice and assessment application for developing and testing student's knowledge and performance of any scale type; Finger Module: contains fingering and alternate fingerings for most instruments; Pitch Pong: game for ear training and pitch detection; Practice Monitor: practice a solo as Amadeus plays the accompaniment; listens and assesses, showing an accuracy grade for rhythm and pitch on each measure. SYSTEM SPECS: Macintosh; Windows; requires *Amadeus Al Fine* to work.

Audio File (Doubleware Productions): Record records, CDs, and cassettes; recall any recording or song in the collection; information about each recording includes title, performer, music type, recording media, record label, and more. SYSTEM SPECS: Windows 3.1 or 95, 386 or better, 4 MB RAM, 2 MB hard disk space.

Brass Instrument Tutor (ECS): To teach students fingerings for trumpet, horn, euphonium, and tuba; scale patterns and random drills; three-button mouse required to reinforce actual valve interaction. SYSTEM SPECS: PC-DOS (non-MIDI).

B-Sharp (Tuc Software): Financial management program for music studios; tracks income, expenses, billing statements, student lesson schedules, and instrument rentals; automated billing; automated payment recording; teacher/program overviews; student lists; mailing labels; year-end financial reports; for individuals or multiteacher studios. SYSTEM SPECS: PC; MS-DOS 3.1.

Choirs, Claviers, and Computers (Doubleware Productions): Designed for the church music director; glossary of over 1,200 religious and musical terms; charts of transposing instruments; useful data. SYSTEM SPECS: Windows.

Digital Music Mentor (ECS): For classroom or private instruction; teacher records exercises or tunes for study; student can study away from the lesson time by hearing how the piece is supposed to sound and then record their version of the piece; teacher can review and discuss with the student; all ages. SYSTEM SPECS: Windows (non-MIDI).

Director's Communication Kit (Hal Leonard): Text-only computer disk includes over thirty-five letters, brochures, and guidelines for parents and administrators; recruitment retention; advocacy and more; for all band programs. SYSTEM SPECS: Macintosh; Windows.

Double Reed Fingerings (ECS): Musical examples review Forked F, Left Hand E-Flat, Half-Hole, or the Octave Keys (oboe) and the Whisper Key, Half-Hole, Alternate A-Sharp, or Alternate G-Sharp (bassoon) fingerings; may select fingering problem to review and number of problems; feedback; records retained for instructor. SYSTEM SPECS: Apple (non-MIDI); PC DOS (non-MIDI).

Drill Quest (Edugraphics): Automatic matching and animation; easy-to-read charts; unlimited number of symbols; perspective view; free site license; multimedia; stand-alone drill player; extensive editing capabilities; charting assistants; customize symbol colors; pit area; toll-free phone support; SYSTEM SPECS: Macintosh; Windows.

ECS Music Metronome (ECS): To help play more accurately in tempo; can set tempo from 40-220 beats per minute (bpm); musical tempo references include largo to presto. SYSTEM SPECS: Windows 95/98 (MIDI optional).

Expressive Conducting (Weins): Interactive, multimedia presentation of the conductor's skills and gestural grammar; video clips; moving animations; begins with the most basic gestures; progresses to complications faced by professionals; fourteen chapters; program coordinated with textbook; for the classroom or independent study; approximately 500 video clips; 200 animations; author is an experienced teacher of counducting and a choral/orchestral conductor at Wheaton Conservatory of Music; two CDs; program will AutoRun (AutoStart) from CD or may be installed to hard drive; installer checks for adequate space and provides required version of QuickTime as necessary. SYSTEM SPECS: Hybrid; for best results, computers should run above 100 MHz, minimum 16MB RAM, 4X CD player, 1195 MB space required for installation to hard drive (optional).

Intonation Trainer (Coda): Teaches students how to listen for and eliminate intonation beats; learn which notes on instrument are flat and which are sharp; learn to anticipate pitch problems and how to solve them. SYSTEM SPECS: Hybrid; Macintosh: Power PC 180 MHz, System 7.6.1 or higher, 16MB RAM, CD-ROM drive, audio speakers; Windows: Pentium 166 MHz or higher, Windows 95/98, CD-ROM drive, SoundBlaster 16-compatible sound set with record/playback capability, audio speakers; for slower PCs add SoundBlaster AWE32 or AWE64 sound card.

Master Music Manager (Manager Software): Music library; membership files; personnel directory; inventory/uniform manager; recordings library; for all choral and instrumental educators; access commands by pulling down menu bar or clicking on buttons; datafile capacity limited only by the amount of hard disk space. SYSTEM SPECS: Macintosh; Windows.

Microband (ECS): Two-part program designed to help band director in creating drills for marching bands; Charting Calculations used to determine parameters of various drill configurations; Drill As-

signment Editor compiles and prints drill assignments for designated groups or sections in the band; store and edit drills for future use; Apple IIe and II+ versions require an 80-column extension card. SYSTEM SPECS: Apple; Commodore; PC DOS.

MS2 (Music Software Solutions): Complete business program; contact management; designed exclusively for the music industry; to aid musicians, record labels, managers, booking agents, studios, and consulting firms. SYSTEM SPECS: Hybrid.

Music Administrator (Pyware): Modifiable database including student files, music library, equipment and uniform inventory, general ledger; predesigned file templates. SYSTEM SPECS: Macintosh version 7 or 8, 2 MB RAM.

Music Directors Assistant (Midisoft): Management tool for all types of music directors; organize music program; event calendar; record keeping for instrument inventory, recordings, and literature; plan rehearsals; manage room schedules, equipment, and more. SYSTEM SPECS: Macintosh.

Music Ministry Manager (Manager Software): Data management system for church musicians; includes modules for music library, recordings, personal directory, music inventory, and personnel; generates customized memo forms and letterhead; will dial phone numbers with a mouse and modem. SYSTEM SPECS: Windows.

Music Office (Pyware): For record keeping including student grades, student addresses, music in music library, fund-raising, or uniform and equipment inventories; maintainance and accounting; export data function in file menu; copy to/from floppy feature so files can be easily transferred between computers; added font options allowing better control of fonts during printing; added restore function to revert a data file easily to a backup; additional backup security to protect work. SYSTEM SPECS: Windows 3.1/95/98, 16 MB RAM.

Music Terminology for Bands, Orchestra, and Choirs (ECS): Covers fundamental music terminology; includes dynamics, tempo markings, stylistic expression markings, music symbols, key signatures, scales, and string terminology; final test of fifty questions and record keeping included; for beginner-intermediate, grades 5-12. SYSTEM SPECS: Macintosh; Windows.

Musical Performance Art Collection: Volume 1 (J Graphics): CD-ROM collection of musicians, instruments, musical symbols, humorous musical characters and instruments, musical borders and themes on music; for music teachers and computer graphic artists; includes Concert, Jazz, Marching Band, Musical Borders, General Music, and Just Instruments; 1" illustrations; over 250 line art illustrations; import, place, or insert into page layout and word processing applications that support TIFF graphic formats for both Mac and PC/Windows platforms; images are sharp, black-and-white line art drawings that can be colorized; all MPAC illustrations are copyrighted and may not be duplicated or copied for unauthorized distribution in any form; can be used freely only by the original registered user for the purpose of publication in non-commercial use on a single computer; licensing is required for commercial use purposes. SYSTEM SPECS: Macintosh; Windows.

Omnipak for Macintosh (PG Music): Includes every PG Music program for Macintosh; twenty-three popular music software titles. SYSTEM SPECS: Macintosh.

Omnipak for Windows (PG Music): Includes every PG Music program for Windows; thirty-eight popular music software titles. SYSTEM SPECS: Windows.

Power On Software (Power On): Trio for total network control; OnGuard: desktop and work group security; LAN Commander: software distribution and centralized control; Screen to Screen: screen sharing and remote control. SYSTEM SPECS: Macintosh.

RCI Music Library CD-ROM (RCI Software): Organize and track performances; create program notes; catalog composers; keep track of music and instrument loans; access music library by title, composer, arranger, or accompaniment; keep track of concert and recital dates; order music from publishers; keep track of robes and uniforms; print customized reports. SYSTEM SPECS: Macintosh; Windows.

Scorekeeper (Doubleware Productions): Index and cross-reference sheet music; for use by instrumentalists, singers, music teachers, choruses, bands, and orchestras; store any information about each piece of music; find any music by genre, composer, title, subject matter, key signature, and more; plan recitals or programs; keep a history of previous recitals along with performance notes for each. SYSTEM SPECS: Windows 3.1 or 95, 386 or better, 4 MB RAM, 2 MB hard disk space.

SlowBlast! (PG Music): Help students practice difficult musical passages; slows music down; play along or transcribe riffs and tunes at own speed instead of at full pace; master difficult phrases. SYSTEM SPECS: Macintosh; Windows.

SmartMusic Studio CD-ROM (Coda): Practice program for woodwinds, brass players, and vocalists; improvement in the ability to perform solo repertoire comes from working with accompaniment; provides accompaniment and follows player; metronome; practice loops; vocal warm-ups; vocal and instrument microphones included; foot pedal. SYSTEM SPECS: Hybrid.

Standard of Excellence Software Books 1-3 (Pyware): Student enters name into computer and picks lesson assigned by teacher; all exercises in that lesson are loaded for the student; student plays; program records student's performance objectively by evaluating pitch and rhythmic precision; grade and target goals are logged. SYSTEM SPECS: Macintosh: System 7 or higher, 8 MB RAM, tone generator or synthesizer; Windows: Windows 95, 16 MB RAM, MIDI-compatible sound card, tone generator, or synthesizer; requires *Amadeus Al Fine*.

Stormware Command Center (Stormware): Music Administration software; true 32-bit technology; powerful reporting; full text searching within reports; data drill-downs; summary charts and graphs; ability to export data to over forty file formats including Crystal Reports, CSV, DIF, Excel, HTML, Lotus 1-2-3, ODBC Database, Rich Text, Tab-Delim. Text, and Word for Windows; can be exported to organization's Intranet site or to the Internet; student profiles; multiple class administration; picture file; instruments of focus; parent employer info; medical history and info; parent conference log; student portfolio; drag-and-drop to attach documents to student portfolio; student profiles reused across classes; view all class enrollment and assignments from one screen; adding multiple classes does not require student data duplication; music library inventory; equipment inventory; custom categories; track individual parts: parts check-out, comprehensive search tool, performance history, track purchase information, composer, arranger, publisher, and more; custom equipment types: track purchase information, serial number, model, and more; repair history: check-out facility, comprehensive search tool; uniform inventory; student financial account management; define custom uniform types; "find match" search utility; check-in/out; create unlimited number and type of accounts; create special accounts for specific students; drag-and-drop to transfer funds between accounts; detailed transaction log for each account; activity planner; personal phone/address book; plan all meetings and events; create student, staff, director, and parent calendars, and more; print group activity calendars; store personal and professional contacts; record phone, pager, address, E-mail, Web address, and more for both business and personal; create custom contact types; search tool interactive; video library; seating chart visualizer; Lotus Screen Cam video. SYSTEM SPECS: Windows: Intel Pentium 120 MHz, Windows 95, 98, NT Workstation, Win2000, 40 MB free disk space, 32 MB RAM, monitor and video card supporting 800x600 256 color, mouse.

Stormware Seating Chart Visualizer (Stormware): Integrates with Stormware Command Center; can also be used as a stand alone seating chart and attendance tool; create database-driven seating charts; drag-and-drop objects onto the drawing area and assign a student to each seat; save designs as templates for reuse; record daily attendance records for each class; display each student's name next to his/her assigned seat; completely customizable; use included objects to design seating charts, or use other graphics; can import standard icon files and add them to a custom library; add text, circles, lines, and more to label and enhance design; use a custom background image; export seating chart as a standard graphic file. SYSTEM SPECS: Windows: Intel Pentium 120 MHz, Windows 95, 98, NT Workstation, Win2000, 40 MB free disk space, 32 MB RAM, monitor and video card supporting 800x600 256 color, mouse.

Student's Roadmap to the Internet CD-ROM (Forest Technologies): Guide to academic resources on the Internet; interactive and collaborative projects for the classroom; includes a diskette full of all the links needed; for beginners, grades three and up. SYSTEM SPECS: Hybrid.

Teacher's Roadmap to the Internet CD-ROM (Forest Technologies): Guide to the Internet written for teachers; book/CD-ROM; lesson plans; information; databases; new events; other teachers; send E-mail; for adult beginners. SYSTEM SPECS: Hybrid.

The Music Maid (Signature Music Software): Tool for creating music worksheets, exams, and answer keys; for use in individual lessons or classrooms, with or without an instrument; focus is primarily on keyboard skills, but can be adapted for use with any instrument; topics include: note names, interval or chord qualities, seventh chords, scales, key signatures, rhythmic exercises, and harmonic progressions; can create specific worksheets; exercises can be written on a grand staff, single staff, or single line for rhythmic exercises; single-line staffs default to treble clef; can be changed to bass, tenor, or alto clef; text can be edited and displayed in any font size or style; worksheets can be created for ear training, sight-reading, harmonization, and composition; remedial exercises in note reading, interval or chord identification, and harmonic analysis; can save custom exercises; harmonic progressions are voice-leading and analysis exercises in choral style; can create an answer key on command for any worksheets; exercise menu displays frequently used exercises; manual is easy to read; begins with four tutorials that create sample worksheets; provides installation directions; user support is available from the publisher through E-mail or toll-free number; for music teachers. SYSTEM SPECS: Macintosh, System 6 or higher.

The Teacher's Apprentice for Music Theory (Creative Software): Create question and answer sessions for interactive testing; create printed music tests; keep student records of progress; two different work areas, one for the teacher and one for the student; customize the program by adding, editing, or deleting questions; add custom graphics and basic aural capabilities to the questions; can create written tests and computer online interactive tests; can use the questions that come with the program or create them; database to keep records on students' progress; multiple levels of questions; can review or print any

questions that were missed during the testing session; students can monitor scores and view a graph that shows progress made; last twenty scores are saved for future reference. SYSTEM SPECS: Macintosh: 68020 or better, 4 MB RAM free, 8 MB recommended, System 7.0 or higher, 13-inch monitor recommended; Windows: 386SX or better, Windows 3/1 or better, 6 MB RAM.

Time Signature (Casa de le Musica): Studio-management program; allows teachers to keep track of lesson schedules and other lesson information; generate billing statements; maintain financial records; keep track of special events such as performances or contests; data can be saved as a text file and exported to spreadsheets. SYSTEM SPECS: PC.

Timesketch Editor (ECS): To facilitate listening to and analyzing CD music with CD-ROM and computer; create teacher-developed listening lessons with any audio CD; for fundamentals courses, appreciation courses, or music history courses at any level; annotated listening format can be applied to classes, activities, and music performance. SYSTEM SPECS: Windows (non-MIDI).

Winband and Winchoir (Music Data Management Software): Complete student, parent, and booster records; individual fund-raising accounts with automatic tab and project totals; grade tabulations; complete music library information; equipment and uniform inventory; easy to use; shortcut keys. SYSTEM SPECS: Macintosh: minimum of 68040 with 4 MB or better, 8 MB hard disk space, System 7 or better, 14-inch monitor; Windows: 486 with 4 MB RAM or better, 6 MB hard disk space, Windows 3.1 or better.

Winensemble (Music Data Management Software): For scheduling solo and ensemble festivals; make complete schedules and reports; automatic scheduling of events; flexible start, break, and event interval times; random or specific time scheduling; automatic matching of event type to judge; labels for comment sheets; mailing labels for participating schools and judges; imports data from WinBand, WinChoir, or WinEnsemble. SYSTEM SPECS: Macintosh: minimum of 68040 with 4 MB or better, 8 MB hard disk space, System 7 or better, 14-inch monitor; Windows: 486 with 4 MB RAM or better, 6 MB hard disk space, Windows 3.1 or better.

Notation and Scoring Software

Amadeus Opus Lite (Sincrosoft): Entry level program; up to sixteen staves; eight parts per staff; cross-staff beaming; easy to use; automatic or manual functions including spacing of notes, staves, systems, and bar lines; dialog windows; playback includes dynamics, tempos, and articulations. SYSTEM SPECS: Macintosh; Windows.

Autoscore Deluxe Version (Wildcat Canyon): Same as Autoscore Professional, but does not have pitch bend tracking, volume tracking, customizable instrument filters, or direct connection with popular music programs. SYSTEM SPECS: Macintosh; Windows.

Autoscore Professional (Wildcat Canyon): Pitch-to MIDI converter; converts sound into written music, ready to edit, play back, or print; tracks pitch bend and volume; MIDI transcriptions of instrumental solos; records vibrato; comes with microphone. SYSTEM SPECS: Macintosh: 68040 or better, 8 MB RAM, Mac compatible microphone and notation/sequencing program; Windows: 486 or better, 8 MB RAM, sound card, microphone included.

Autoscore SE (Wildcat Canyon): Same as Autoscore Deluxe, but only step time entry, singing one note at a time; free mic not included. SYSTEM SPECS: Hybrid.

Composer's Mosaic (Mark of the Unicorn): Unlimited voices per staff; real-time, step-record and mouse/keyboard MIDI input; click-and-drag placement of over 160 musical symbols; multiple views feature; same music formatted differently in separate windows; flexible page formatting; adjust slurs, ties, dynamics, and more; word-processing-style lyric entry; engraver spacing; cross-staff beaming; all forms of musical transposition; rhythm and range commands; complex meters. SYSTEM SPECS: Macintosh.

Cubase Score (Steinberg): Integrated MIDI recording and score printing; thirty-two parts per system; four-voice polyphony per part; full page digital editing; drum notation; scalable view; free-form layouts; full orchestral scores; many symbols and articulations; can move any element of the score. SYSTEM SPECS: Macintosh; Windows: 8486 or better, 4 MB RAM, Windows 3.1 or better, MIDI instrument and interface.

Desktop Sheet Music (Midisoft): Real-time input; drum notation; embed graphic images in score; lead sheets; scores; parts; add clip art and photos to sheet music; add lyrics; for every instrument. SYSTEM SPECS: Windows.

Encore (Passport): Transcribe and edit print music; used for motion picture scores, orchestral arrangements, choir songbooks, and teaching music in schools; includes guitar tablature with fret position for up to eight strings in any tuning; customizable toolbar; percussion staff for notating complex percussion parts; zoom in and out; tempo window, color, bank select, and on-screen keyboard. SYSTEM SPECS: Macintosh: Mac Classic II, System 7, 4 MB RAM, hard disk, optional True Type compatible printer, MIDI interface and keyboard; Windows 3.1, 3.11 or 95, sound card, 80486 CPU or greater, 8 MB of RAM, SVGA Video, MIDI keyboard and PC MIDI interface; printer.

Fermata (Opcode): Notation software; step entry to quickly enter or delete notes, rests, rhythmic slashes, and chord symbols via MIDI or the computer keyboard; functions are active without switching modes; comprehensive MIDI sequencing features; editing functions; EPS file capture; MIDI playback of all dynamics; flexible lyric handling; guitar tablature; graphic edit window; part extraction and transposition; jazz articulation palette. SYSTEM SPECS: Macintosh 68020 (or better) or PowerMac, System 7.0 or later, 2 MB application RAM on 68k, 4 MB application RAM on Power Macs, 3 MB HD Space.

Finale (Coda): Seven ways to enter music; online help; lyrics line up to the notes; chords and guitar notation; up to four layers per staff; unlimited number of staves; move any part of score; open any number of scores at once; transfer pieces of one score to another; view a whole page of music while working on one magnified measure; create page sizes up to 9' x 9'; charts; lead sheets; used by professional musicians, composers, arrangers, copyists, and publishers; range checking automatic dynamic placement based on performance; easy repeats/easy measure numbers check region for durations; with Set-Up Wizard select instruments needed and instantly set up score; staff names, transpositions, and clefs are automatic; dozens of templates such as Lead Sheet, Chamber Orchestra, Jazz Band, Guitar Tablature, or SATB with piano; click notes into place with Simple Entry Palette; play MIDI keyboard and watch HyperScribe notate; use the computer keyboard with or without a MIDI keyboard for Speedy Note Entry; open scanned music directly from Musitek products such as MIDIScan and PianoScan; import Encore files, MIDI files off the Internet or from popular sequencers; translates MIDI into notation; plays music so you can easily hear wrong notes or decide how to rearrange a passage. SYSTEM SPECS: Macintosh: System 7.0 or higher, 8MB RAM (12MB recommended), 10MB available hard drive space, 10MB of free working space, 20MB additional hard drive space required to load online documentation, MIDI devices are optional, works with PostScript and Non-Postscript printers; Windows: IBM compatible 486 processor, hard drive, Windows 3.1 or 95 operating system, VGA monitor, 4 MB RAM, MIDI interface, MIDI keyboard or controller, and MIDI playback device or MIDI-compatible sound card optional.

Finale Allegro (Coda): QuickStart interface; online video tips; five different ways to enter music; features selected from Finale; creates simple lead sheets or fully orchestrated scores; print professional looking parts; automatic multimeasure rests, music spacing and formatting of any layout style; export TIFF (Windows) and PICT (Macintosh) files; reads Standard MIDI, Finale, Allegro, Encore (3.0 or higher), and Rhapsody files from either Windows or Macintosh platforms. SYSTEM SPECS: Hybrid.

Finale Notepad (Coda): Set-up Wizard; Web publishing; hear and see music as it plays; simple note entry; free download; CD-ROM. SYSTEM SPECS: Macintosh; Windows 95/98/2000/ME/NT.

Finale Plug-In Tools (TGTools): Provides over forty powerful extensions to Finale; tools menu; easier music entry; lyrics enhancements; faster spacing corrections; layout tools; detailed feature list "Music" menu; "Spacing" menu; "Layout" menu; align/move dynamics; print multiple files for Windows; new spacing; "Lyrics" menu; "Miscellaneous" menu. SYSTEM SPECS: Hybrid.

Midiscan (Musitek): Converts sheet music into multitrack MIDI files; processes any score type, up to twenty-four pages at a time; recognizes note and rest time values, pitches, chords, ties, accidentals, bar lines, clef signs, and time and key signatures with 90-98 percent accuracy; TWAIN compatible; works with all MIDI sequencing and notation software; easy editing; processing time varies from thirty seconds to three minutes per page; supports Notation Interchange File Format (NIFF); LIME NIFF notation software included allowing for transposition, part separation, and reprinting in same page layout. SYSTEM SPECS: Windows 3.1 or 95, 4 MB RAM, grey scale or color digital scanner or 200 dpi fax machine with fax modem/software, MIDI compatible sound card or MIDI synthesizer with MPU401 compatible interface.

Music Manuscriptor (Erato Software): For notating music by computer; uses MIDI interface, digitizing tablet, high-resolution video, and laser printer. SYSTEM SPECS: PC, MIDI interface, MIDI synthesizer or instrument.

Music Mastery (AABACA): For playing, learning, teaching, and composing music; print music on a variety of printers; control titles, lyric blocks, footers, and fonts. SYSTEM SPECS: Macintosh: 68030/25 MHz, System 7; Windows: 80286, Windows 3.1.

Music Write (Voyetra): Use mouse to place notes and musical symbols on the staff; play MIDI keyboard and see notation; play back on-screen music using sound card or external MIDI synthesizer; print music with title and lyrics; create songs; includes many classical pieces; up to ten staves or parts per system. SYSTEM SPECS: 486 or better running Windows 3.1 or better, 8 MB RAM, SoundBlaster-compatible sound card or MIDI interface.

Music Write Plus (Voyetra): Record music from MIDI keyboard to convert to music notation; use mouse or MIDI compatible keyboard; on-screen video tutorial; cut, copy, and paste music; insert notes, chords, and ties; add lyrics and copyright information; insert dynamic symbols. SYSTEM SPECS: Windows.

Music Write Professional Edition (Voyetra): Advanced notation program with MIDI; MIDI capabilities for sequencing and playback; up to forty-eight parts; all clefs and transpositions; for choirs, concert bands, orchestras, jazz ensembles, rock groups, and singer/songwriters; guitar tablature; chord generation; lyric features; MIDI keyboard or mouse entry; sixteen MIDI channels; record digital audio tracks and synchronize them to notated parts; MIDI time code; SMPTE for video and film scoring. SYSTEM SPECS: Windows.

Music Write Standard Edition (Voyetra): Music notation, orchestration, and MIDI recording; can do full ensemble scores; enter parts with mouse or record in real time using a MIDI keyboard; automatically notates what is entered; set up clef signs, key signatures, and transpositions for each instrument; notate lyrics, melody, chord symbols, drum parts, or guitar chords. SYSTEM SPECS: Windows.

Music@Passport (Passport): Identical to Musictime Deluxe, except can input music vocally with microphone (included). SYSTEM SPECS: Windows 3.1 or Windows 95, sound card, MIDI keyboard, and MIDI interface recommended.

Musicscan (Hohner): Can enter sheet music into computer in minutes; place a page of music on scanner; in a few moments will see page on screen; play back through sound card; built-in sequencer to transpose or arrange music; reprint the reprocessed score; up to twenty-four pages of music can be processed simultaneously including solo, two-part, and piano scores. SYSTEM SPECS: 386 or higher, 4 MB or RAM, Windows 3.1 or higher, scanner (300 dpi minimum).

Musictime Deluxe (Passport): Tools for creating and printing music with lyrics, text, and notation; transposition; real-time and step-time entry; part extraction; repeat endings; improved notation engine; up to sixteen staves with as many as eight instruments per staff; editing features include letting users place notes and rests anywhere on scores; ideal for smaller ensembles and choirs. SYSTEM SPECS: Windows 3.1 or Windows 95, sound card, MIDI keyboard, and MIDI interface recommended.

Nightingale (Musicware): Produce scores; control the size, appearance, and placement of every symbol; one to sixty-four staves and a total of one hundred voices; score appears on screen as it will look printed; input music from any MIDI instrument using Real-Time Recording or Step-Time Recording; input music using only the Mac keyboard and mouse; import standard MIDI files and automatically notate them; scan music directly into; edit music and insert text, dynamics, tempos, articulations, or any performance information; control over appearance and placement of symbols; playback all or part of score through MIDI; automatically transpose entire lines of music; print individual parts or a whole score; customize over one hundred default settings; automatic transpositions and extraction of parts; ten magnifications from 25 percent to 600 percent; imports Finale Files; with

NoteView, can publish work on the Internet; supports OMS; printable-online User's Guide. SYSTEM SPECS: Macintosh Plus or higher, 4 MB RAM, hard drive, System 6.05 or higher, printer, optional MIDI Interface and MIDI Keyboard.

Notation (Magix): Jazz symbols; guitar tab; drum notation; automatic alignment of lyrics with notes; unlimited staves per system; up to sixteen multitimbral voices per staff. SYSTEM SPECS: Windows.

Opus (Sincrosoft): Professional music notation software; mouse input from palette or keyboard; MIDI keyboard input; real-time or step-time entry; hundreds of symbols used in music, jazz, and twentieth-century music; unlimited number of staves per document; insertion of multiple lyrics; custom settings of fonts, sizes, and styles; preview score; modify default settings and specify dimensions and margins for every page; scores of any dimension, in any configuration; extracts single or multiple individual parts; compresses bar rests into multimeasure rests with appropriate breaks; supports any type of printer. SYSTEM SPECS: Macintosh; Windows.

Overture (Cakewalk): Sixty-four staves or parts per system; eight voices per staff; EPS and PICT file capture; part extraction; control all elements with the mouse or computer keyboard; can nudge notes; hide or show, zoom in and out, or scale any portion of the score; fine-tune work in detail; complete MIDI playback of all dynamics, repeats, and endings; piano-roll view allows graphic editing of performance; Strip Chart for editing controllers, velocity, and more; play drum kit onto a five-line percussion staff; instrument libraries organize part transpositions and MIDI playback; compresses multiple empty measures into composite rests; automatically prints composing instruments into the correct key. SYSTEM SPECS: Hybrid; Macintosh: 68020 Processor, System 7, 8 MB RAM; Windows: Pentium 100 or higher, 16 MB RAM or more.

Personal Composer (Hohner): Real time or mouse entry; zoom 25 percent to 200 percent; shaped note heads; text and symbols; notation sequencing and publishing program for composers, arrangers, performers, educators, or multimedia enthusiasts. SYSTEM SPECS: Windows.

Photoscore (Neuratron): Scans and reads printed music into *Sibelius*; requires *Sibelius*; edit or transpose score; play back score; transpose parts; print. SYSTEM SPECS: Macintosh; Windows.

Pianoscan (Musitek): Same as Midiscan, but creates MIDI files with one or two MIDI tracks from scores containing up to two staves per system. SYSTEM SPECS: Windows.

Print Music! (Coda): Create, play, and print music; QuickStart video tips; comes with over one hundred free pieces of music to arrange and print; can use to download and print free MIDI files from the Internet; playback feature; can open Finale and Allegro files. SYSTEM SPECS: Hybrid; Macintosh; Windows: Windows 95/NT or higher, 16 MB RAM, 20 MB hard drive space; MIDI interface and MIDI keyboard optional.

Quickscore Copyist (Sion): Notation software; works with existing QuickScore files; fine-tune any score created in QuickScore. SYSTEM SPECS: Windows

Quickscore Elite (Sion): Score, piano roll, controller, event list, and song views; score templates; easy note entry; up to sixteen staves or parts per system. SYSTEM SPECS: Windows 3.1 or 95, 4 MB RAM, 4 MB of hard disk space, Windows-compatible sound card or MIDI interface.

Quickscore Elite Level II (Sion): Forty-eight parts per system; six-string guitar tablature notation with adjustable string tuning; automatic spacing for lyrics; automatic quantization of real-time recording; print scaling on any printer; editing features; adjust height of beams and position accidentals; repeats and first and second endings play automatically. SYSTEM SPECS: Windows 3.1/95, 4 MB RAM, 4 MB hard disk space, Windows compatible sound card or MIDI interface.

Score Writer (Cakewalk): Transcribe music from MIDI keyboard or enter notes with mouse; notation for piano, band, orchestra, or choral groups; includes educational music files; loads and saves standard MIDI files. SYSTEM SPECS: Windows.

Sibelius (Sibelius): Professional quality notation program; notate, edit, play back, and publish every kind of music; fast and easy to use; clear, instant graphics; Flexi-time MIDI input; Expressive and SoundStage playback; PhotoScore Lite music scanning plug-in included; write other plug-in features with ManuScript language; search and edit score using filters; includes guitar tab, nested tuplets, drum kit notation, figured bass, and other specific notations; export graphics in a variety of standard file formats; add music to posters, covers and exams, papers, books and magazines; plays back score through sound card or MIDI equipment; reads and plays all standard markings; score reformatting and part extraction; add scores to Web site; concise manual; Platinum Edition plug-ins check for redundant dynamics, suspect mutes, pedaling, and errors in the full score. SYSTEM SPECS: Macintosh: G3/iMac/PowerMac, Mac OS 7.1 or later, 6 MB+ free RAM, 12 MB+ recommended, CD-ROM drive any speed, 10MB free hard disk space; Windows: 486DX-100 or faster PC, Pentium 166MHz or faster recommended, Windows 95/98/NT 4 or later, 16 MB+ RAM, CD-ROM drive any speed, 10 MB free hard disk space; some features require a printer, MIDI keyboard, Internet access, Web site or scanner.

Sibelius Teaching Tools (Sibelius): Educational resources to help teach music in the classroom; covers all levels, K-12; ready-to-use exercises and worksheets; covers notation, composing, and more; dozens of music files on CD-ROM; includes guides for teachers and students. SYSTEM SPECS: Macintosh; Windows.

Smart Score (Musitek): Integrated music scanning, scoring, and MIDI sequencing; advanced recognition intelligence; plays back repeats, dynamics, and articulation; displays contrapuntal voices with direct voice-to-MIDI channel linking; automatic instrument assignments according to number of staves; playback continuity; intelligent control of instrumental parts; creates scores using mouse, keyboard, MIDI instrument, MIDI file, or scanner input; control over page layout, spacing, and irregular systems; part and voice separation; notation-to-MIDI-to-notation implementation; import standard MIDI files to display, transpose, or print out scores. SYSTEM SPECS: Hybrid.

Smart Score Piano Edition (Musitek): Same as orchestral version, but limited to processing sheet music with one, or two staves per system; import one- or two-track MIDI files and convert into sheet music; MIDI sequencing and MIDI recording not included; scan, transpose, and print out music; instant playback; simple editing; Quick Select keys and Unify Key and Time functions. SYSTEM SPECS: Hybrid.

Sequencing Software

Cakewalk Home Studio (Cakewalk): Sequencing program; record, edit, play back, and print music; create music with any instrument; record eight tracks of stereo along with MIDI; combine and edit loops, grooves, and CD samples; mix audio and MIDI tracks in real time; create music for CDs, home movies, and the Internet; support for MP3, RealMedia G2, and Windows Media Audio formats for delivering audio on the Internet; online tutorials; multitrack piano roll editing of MIDI; audio and MIDI drum loops; enhanced console for real-time mixing of audio and MIDI; style enhancer MIDI plug-in for applying different performance styles to MIDI tracks; use Virtual Piano to play and record music; edit notes with mouse click; music can be entered with mouse or from MIDI keyboard; build music layer by layer using different sounds; record each part or instrument separately; uses general MIDI patch names; screen divided into several sections; tutorials are helpful for learning the basic operations of the program; control bar at top of screen resembles an audiocassette deck, with buttons for rewind, play and record, help, step record, tempo, meter, and key signature; track/measure view, event list view, piano roll view, velocity view, and staff view; shows note durations and velocities; piano-roll view displays notes graphically in a grid format; notes are represented by horizontal bars; the longer the bar, the longer the note duration; the higher the bar on the screen, the higher

its pitch; velocity view graphically displays the dynamics of the recorded performance; new velocities and tempos can be added with the mouse; can record accompaniments for duets, ensembles, and technical exercises; performances can be recorded for aural and visual analysis; record melodies, rhythms, chords, and intervals for ear-training exercises. SYSTEM SPECS: Windows 286, Windows 3.1, MIDI interface or soundboard, optional MIDI keyboard.

Cakewalk Metro (Cakewalk): Integrated MIDI and digital audio; supports up to sixty-four tracks of simultaneous digital audio; Real-Time audio effects including two-band parametric EQ, stereo delay, stereo chorus, stereo reverb, stereo flange composition, and editing features; groove quantize and quantize to selected notes; transpose, reverse, harmonize, human feel, quantize, compress/expand; rhythm explorer allows experimentation of rhythm and arpeggiation in real time; professional sync and automation capabilities; extensive automated mixing, with assignable faders, knobs, fader grouping, cross fading, and master volume; QuickTime Movie sync for multimedia; edit and print notation; creative songwriting tools; fast, powerful MIDI sequencer and digital audio authoring tool for the MAC. SYSTEM SPECS: Macintosh Power PC based system, OS System 7.0, 0.5 MB RAM free per track, Sound Manager 3.2, QuickTime 2.5 and OMS and Quick Time musical instrument, Macintosh-compatible MIDI interface.

Cakewalk Pro Audio (Cakewalk): Digital audio and MIDI software; WAVEPipe technology for faster audio effects processing, mixing, and track playback on Windows audio cards; export audio to MP3, RealSystem G2, and Windows Media Advanced Streaming Format for delivering music and sound on the Internet; includes the patented Fraunhofer MP3 Encoder technology; advanced support for professional audio cards using AudioX technology; AudioX-compatible cards include the Yamaha DSP Factory, Sonorous STUDI/O, Digital Audio Labs CardDeluxe, and others; analog-tape style audio scrubbing for smooth, accurate queuing and auditioning of audio tracks; enhanced mixdown options for bouncing audio tracks and mastering to stereo, mono, and dual mono WAVE file formats at variable bit depths; guitar tablature editing and printing with synchronized, real-time fretboard display; AmpSim Lite audio plug-in for adding vintage amp simulation to digital audio tracks; Chromatic Tuner display for tuning guitars or other instruments through a PC audio card; system meters provide real-time visual feedback over CPU and disk activity to monitor system capabilities; over thirty usability enhancements, including global mute/solo/record, enhanced MIDI patch browsing and organizing, drag-and-drop enhancements, MIDI and audio effects presets, and others; record 16-, 18-, 20-, 22-, and 24-bit audio at variable sampling rates of 11.025, 22.050, 44.1, 48, and 96 kHz; add DirectX audio plug-ins; apply real-time plug-ins to MIDI tracks in Console view; MIDI Session Drummer and Style Enhancer plug-ins, along with Quantize, Delay/Echo, MIDI Filter, Transpose, Velocity, and Chord Analyzer; with StudioWare can control studio hardware from within using a virtual control panel that emulates the hardware; panels for popular studio gear; multitrack Piano Roll view; recording and mixing console; add up to 256 real-time effects to tracks with included MIDI effects, 32-bit audio effects; enhanced Mixdown options; arrange and edit multitrack sections of music using flexible clips; ideal for loop-based recordings and remixes; video playback window display; frame-accurate sync of video to audio tracks; audio/video scrubbing; exporting of video and audio back to AVI; context-sensitive, searchable online help system. SYSTEM SPECS: Windows 95/98, Pentium 200 MHz or higher, 64 MB RAM, Pentium 300 MHz or higher, 128 MB RAM, Windows NT 4.0 SP5, Pentium 300 MHz or higher, 128 MB RAM, Windows-compatible MIDI interface and/or sound card required for digital audio record/playback.

Cakewalk Pro Audio Deluxe (Cakewalk): Cakewalk Pro Audio 9 plus the Musician's Toolbox III: two-CD-ROM collection of MIDI and audio files, tools, digital video clips, and interactive tutorials; over a gigabyte of multimedia data; toolbox search engine; Drumtrax features 6,000 measures of realistic MIDI drum grooves, fills, intros, and endings in fourteen styles ranging from alternative to hip-hop; Sonic Implants transforms SoundBlaster card into a professional sampler using SoundFont technology; load industrial, electronica, ambient, and live band sound banks; Big Fish Audio sample libraries; ninety-nine WAV files; extensive selection of loops and grooves from around the world; sound effects, breakbeats, salsa, and funk samples; Archeological Sound Engineering; electro-acoustic drone tones from rhythmic to atmospheric; drones follow the changes in timbre of natural sounds and/or sound effects; Western and Eastern timbres, mechanical and industrial based tones; Oddball Film and Video stock; clips to support project; CanvasMan32 CE editor/librarian for Sound Canvas and GS synthesizers; Cakewalk Audio Browser; organized audio disk; Cakewalk TECHniques; twelve screen tutorials, covering advanced Cakewalk editing techniques, MIDI plug-ins, vector automation, Cakewalk StudioWare, digital video, and more. SYSTEM SPECS: Windows.

Cakewalk Pro Suite (Cakewalk): Professional multitrack recording, effects processing, and digital sampling; complete software workstation for multitrack recording, real-time mixing, and hard-disk based sampling; create professional music and sound projects entirely in the digital domain; arsenal of software tools; integrated studio solution; Cakewalk Pro Audio 9; MemmeSys GigaSampler LE and GigaPiano; Cakewalk Audio FX 1 dynamics processing;

Cakewalk Audio FX 2 analog tape and amp simulation; Cakewalk Audio FX 3 SoundState Design for custom reverb; Musician's Toolbox III. SYSTEM SPECS: Windows 95/98, Pentium II 300 MHz or faster (or Cyrix MII 300 MHz or faster, or AMD K6 III or faster), 128 MB of RAM or more, 6.4 GB disk space available, Ultra DMA, Ultra IDE, or Ultra/Ultra Wide SCSI hard disk with 512 KB hard drive cache (9.5 millisecond or less access time), CD-ROM or DVD drive, SVGA display (1027x768), Windows sound card with either a GIGA-compatible or Microsoft DirectSound-compatible driver.

Computer Music Starter Kit (Voyetra): Turns multimedia PC and MIDI keyboard into a desktop music system; connect MIDI cable to sound card's joystick port, plug in MIDI keyboard, and load CD-ROM; ready to play; includes *MIDI Orchestrator Plus* sequencer program; record, edit, and play MIDI music; print sheet music; *Jam Grid* interactive music utility; multimedia course on MIDI and music synthesis; variety of songs. SYSTEM SPECS: Windows.

Cubase VST (Steinberg): Up to sixty-four tracks of digital audio; unlimited MIDI tracks; plug-in interface for optional Steinberg and third party plug-ins; up to 128 real-time EQs; ASIO compatible audio card support; 16,360 PPQ (per quarter note resolution); integration of audio and MIDI recording; with MIDI interface, any combination of MIDI keyboards and MIDI sound modules can be connected; prints MIDI parts as notes with text and titles; auto-layout functions for score printouts; no additional DSP hardware is required; suggest small mixer and good monitoring system; add multiple inputs and outputs with PCI audio cards; audio effects are included and can be extended with plug-ins; Cubase VST 4 adds sixty-four audio channels; four equalizers per channel; four insert effects per channel; eight auxiliary sends; eight global effects; full automation; audio hardware expandability; high definition MIDI recording; superb MIDI real-time editing; notation editing; automatic layout and printing; up to 128 real-time EQs. SYSTEM SPECS: Macintosh: 601/120MHz processor, 32 MB RAM, 256K second level cache, MacOS System 7.6.1 or later; Windows: Pentium Processor 166 MHz, 64 MB RAM.

Cubase VST Score (Steinberg): Adds professional notation editing, layout, and printing. SYSTEM SPECS: Macintosh; Windows.

Cubase VST/24 (Steinberg): Adds ninety-six audio channels; support for 24 bit/96 kHz operation; extended audio hardware options; professional notation editing, layout, and printing. SYSTEM SPECS: Macintosh; Windows.

Cubasis AV (Steinberg): Record both MIDI and digital audio; arrange and edit recordings; every MIDI note can be edited in detail; pitch, length, volume, attack, and instrument sounds can all be altered while the music is playing; up to eight stereo digital audio tracks available; mixing deck to stage sound at exactly the right moment; set videos to music. SYSTEM SPECS: Macintosh: Apple PowerPC or compatible computer, 6100/66 MHz minimum, 16 MB RAM minimum, 24 MB RAM recommended, CD-ROM drive, second level cache, MacOS System 7.5 or higher; Windows: 386SX with 25MHz or higher, VGA graphics, Windows 3.1, multimedia extensions, MME supported, MIDI instrument, GM/GS recommended.

Cubasis VST PC (Steinberg): Entry level MIDI sequencing and digital audio software; up to thirty-two tracks of digital audio; automated mixing; two bands of EQ; two effects sends; one insert effect on each channel; rout audio to eight separate outputs depending on the ASIO supported sound card used; virtual studio instruments; CD burning; real VST features. SYSTEM SPECS: Windows.

Digital Music Starter Kit (Voyetra): Digital Audio and MIDI sequencing software; *Digital Sound Gallery II* library of digital music samples; drag and drop; MIDI adapter cable connects PC to any MIDI-compatible digital musical instrument. SYSTEM SPECS: Windows.

Digital Orchestrator (Voyetra): Turns PC into a complete desktop recording studio; unlimited tracks of MIDI; four tracks of digital audio; editing features and ability to print sheet music; on-screen video tutorials; intuitive interface; record, copy, paste, and mix MIDI and digital audio tracks; add digital FX; integration of MIDI and digital audio. SYSTEM SPECS: Windows.

Digital Orchestrator Plus (Voyetra): Create music enhanced with vocals and other acoustic sounds; MIDI and digital audio technology; MIDI sequencer; multitrack digital audio; digital audio effects; music notation; video tutorials; demo files; digital sound clips; MIDI drum tracks; multitrack MIDI and digital audio recorder/editor; control up to 256 MIDI Channels; extensive help; MIDI/WAV Sync; digital sound effects processing; drag-and-drop user interface displays MIDI and digital audio tracks together; record, zoom edit, move, mix, or copy MIDI and digital audio tracks. SYSTEM SPECS: Windows 486 DX2/66 MHz, Windows 3.1 or Windows 95, 8 MB RAM, 10 MB hard disk, sound card with 16-bit digital audio record/playback capability, onboard MIDI synthesizer, double speed CD-ROM or faster.

Digital Orchestrator Pro (Voyetra): More than 1,000 tracks of MIDI and digital audio; works with PC and sound cards; prints sheet music; desktop music production; multitrack digital audio recording and feature-rich MIDI sequencing; zoom, edit, move, mix, or copy sections of the song with a few simple mouse movements; merge tacks by dragging one on top of the other; add digital sound effects processing;

transcribe and print professional quality sheet music from MIDI tracks. SYSTEM SPECS: Windows.

Digital Performer (Mark of the Unicorn): Transpose a voice by a fifth or more; scale the tempo of audio and MIDI tracks; transpose and change the tempos of audio and MIDI tracks together; transpositions without converting to MIDI information; integration between MIDI and audio; work with both at the same time; with PureDSP can transpose a third, fourth, or fifth or more and maintain sonic integrity; add octave doublings above and below; create harmony parts; change tempo; Performer with digital audio capabilities; unlimited virtual tracks; automated mixing environment; pitch shifting, time stretching, and sample rate conversion for digital audio; plays Quicktime Movies, allowing random access video scoring; track, mix, and master without an external mixing board or rack of effects; widely used for postproduction work; integration of MIDI and audio combined with superior quality, comprehensive editing, and ease of use. SYSTEM SPECS: Macintosh.

Freestyle (Mark of the Unicorn): MIDI sequencing and notation software; trackless approach; instant notation display and printing; built-in support for general MIDI sound modules and other popular devices; select sounds from instrument categories rather than patch numbers; graphic editing displays music for all players in full color; tape recorder style composing; 960 PPZ timing resolution; real-time notation transcription; create music using ensembles, players, takes, and arrangements; dozens of drum riffs; create own riffs; notate performances while playing; composition, orchestration, arrangement, and notation transcription; does not have tracks; uses an ensemble of players with unlimited takes; premade ensembles and groove templates; create custom templates; piano-roll view; works in either linear or loop record and playback; arrangement window provided for easy drop and drag assembly of songs; multiple versions of takes and songs can be stored within a file or shared with other files; any font can be used for text; no staff limit for score views; part extraction and transposition is automatic. SYSTEM SPECS: Macintosh 68020, System 7.01.

Logic Audio Gold (EMagic): Complete MIDI, audio, and score section; integrated stereo sample editor; many editing options including Event, Hyper, Score, Matrix, Arrange, and Environment; up to sixty-four audio tracks; supports Korg 1212, EMagic's Audiowerk8, and Digidesign's Audiomedia II and Audiomedia III; systems can be used simultaneously with built-in AV/MME capabilities; variety of real-time DSP Effects; size and functionality good for mobile laptop studios; supported hardware includes Audiowerk8, DAE, CBX, 1212 I/O, and AV. SYSTEM SPECS: Macintosh: Power Macintosh 603e/132 MHz, G3 CPU recommended, System 7.6.1 or higher, 64 MB RAM, 96 recommended;

Windows: Pentium 200, Pentium II recommended, Windows 98, 64 MB RAM, 96 recommended, MME-compatible sound card.

Logic Audio Platinum (EMagic): Synthesis of digital audio recording, digital signal processing, MIDI sequencing, and notation; flexible window architecture, allowing music to be viewed appropriately for task; user interface can be configured to suit any working style; menus can be set to display in many languages; uses the same core code for both the Mac and Windows versions; attention to detail; unique feature set; flexibility; potential for expansion with MIDI interfaces and digital audio hardware; audio; effects; sample editing; arrange; editors; multiple hardware support allows the simultaneous use of different types of audio hardware in one computer, e.g., a combination of two Audiowerk8 and a Sonorus Stud I/O; the following digital audio hardware is supported: Mac and Windows, Audiowerk2, Audiowerk8 (max. 3), ASIO (e.g., Lexicon Studio, MotU 2408), Yamaha DSP Factory Mac only, TDM (Digidesign ProTools II, III, 24, and 24 MIX including all TDM-Plug-Ins), DAE (Digidesign AudioMedia II/III, Session8, ProTools Project), Direct I/O (Digidesign hardware), Yamaha CBX-Serie, AV (Sound Manager), Korg 1212 I/O, Sonorus Stud I/O (direct hardware support, ASIO-driver not required), AKAI DR8/16 (no sample editing, only graphic editing of audio regions in the Arrange window); Windows only: AV (multichannel and stereo-MME-sound cards), LA Platinum. SYSTEM SPECS: Macintosh: Power Macintosh, 20 MHz or better, System 7.6.1 or newer, 64 MB RAM recommended, G3 processor, 128 MB RAM, hard disk for audio files only, digital audio card; Windows: Pentium 200, Windows 98, 4 MB RAM, MME compatible sound card recommended, Pentium II, 128 MB RAM, hard disk for audio files only, digital audio card, MIDI interface.

Logic Audio Silver (EMagic): Up to twenty-four audio tracks in stereo or mono; twenty different audio plug-ins; support of audio hardware with up to eight individual outputs; localized user interface; detailed manual; feature set virtually identical regardless of which version; platform specific benefits included; under Windows a polyphonic WAVEPlayer can be played simultaneously with the audio tracks in real time, provided a DirectSound driver is used; audio hardware support on the Mac includes ASIO drivers and Direct I/O for Digidesign cards; upgrade options from Silver to Logic Audio Gold or Platinum; arrange; audio; effects; Adaptive Track Mixer; Screen Sets and Key Commands; Environment; Editors; copy-protected via floppy disk; a 3.5-inch floppy disk drive is required for installation under Windows and Mac; supported hardware: Audiowerk2, Audiowerk8, ASIO; Mac only: AV, Direct I/O, DAE (eight mono tracks); Windows only: MME (stereo, multistereo or multichannel), DirectSound. SYSTEM SPECS: Mac-

intosh: PowerPC processor 120 MHz, System 7.6.1 or higher, 64 MB RAM, 3.5-inch floppy disk drive, G3 processor or higher, 128 MB RAM or more, System 8.6, dedicated hard disk for audio data only, digital audio card, MIDI interface; Windows: Pentium 200, Windows 98, 64 MB RAM, MME compatible sound card, 3.5-inch floppy disk drive recommended, Pentium II or III, 128 MB RAM or more, dedicated hard disk for audio data only, digital audio card, MIDI interface.

Master Tracks Pro (Passport): Sixty-four tracks with track looping; step entry and real-time entry; automated punch-in; OMS support; easy to use; graphic user interface offers several views of a musical piece; any section can be deleted, moved, or copied with cut and paste edits; supports SMPTE; synchronize music to film, video, multimedia presentations, or multitrack audiotape; automatically adjust tempo to fit a specific length of time or precisely match a visual event; graphic note editor; event list editor; support for Quicktime 2.0 internal synthesizer; looped overdub and record for drum machine-style recording. SYSTEM SPECS: Macintosh: Macintosh Classic II, LC, Performa or greater, 4 MB RAM; System 7, hard disk, MIDI keyboard, Internal Synth playback requires QuickTime 2.0 (included) and 68020 processor or higher; Windows: Windows 3.1 or better, 386 SX or better, 4 MB of RAM, mouse, SoundBlaster sound card or Windows 3.1, MIDI Interface.

Master Tracks Pro Audio (Passport): Four stereo or mono tracks of digital audio; complete MIDI sequencing; full nondestructive editing; accurate synchronization; modular approach; combines SAW digital audio recording technology. SYSTEM SPECS: Windows 3.1 or better, 486 DX66 or better, Pentium 120 recommended, 16 MB RAM, sound card.

Micrologic AV (EMagic): Multifunctional entry-level program; up to sixteen audio tracks; easy real-time effects; integrated stereo sample editor; virtual general MIDI mixing consoles; desktop studio technology; simple sound card is sufficient; for creating soundtracks, any Quicktime or AVI movie can be played in perfect synchronization; interactive real-time windows; system resolution. SYSTEM SPECS: Macintosh: Power Macintosh 603e/132 MHz, System 7.6.1 (or higher), 48 MB RAM, recommended: 604e CPU, 64 MB RAM; Windows: Pentium 133, Windows 98, 48 MB RAM, MME-compatible sound card, recommended: Pentium 200, 64 MB RAM.

MIDI Composer (QuickShot): Includes forty-nine note keyboard, cables, and Cakewalk Home Studio music software. SYSTEM SPECS: Windows.

MIDI Connections Classic (Hohner): All the functions of Multimedia; Stylemaker; sixty-four track sequencer; drum grid and event editor; notation editor; step recording; scalable printing and music symbols. SYSTEM SPECS: Windows.

MIDI Connections Multimedia (Hohner): Sequencer, arranger, and publisher; compose, arrange, and print music; enter chords in the arranger part and select a style; eighteen-track MIDI-sequencer to record, edit, and play back tracks; print out sheet music for assigning instruments; "Song Text" function allows for placing lyrics below the corresponding musical notes. SYSTEM SPECS: Windows.

MIDI Connections Pro (Hohner): All the functions of Classic plus WAVE Tracks; twenty-four staff score; arranger; advanced printing facilities; drum track printing; print to clipboard; part extraction; MIDI Controller Library; SysEX Message Library and WAVE Family Library. SYSTEM SPECS: Windows.

MIDI Kit CD-ROM (Midisoft): Multitrack digital audio recording; MIDI sequencer; print entire score or selected tracks; connect keyboard, drum machine, or other MIDI instrument with included cable; unlimited tracks; free MIDI set-up video; real-time notation; virtual music sheet highlights notes during playback. SYSTEM SPECS: Windows.

MIDI Orchestrator Plus (Voyetra): Audio Mixer control panel shows activity in sixteen MIDI channels; print music; up to 1,000 tracks of MIDI data; change, view, and edit MIDI music in several different ways; Quick View buttons switch instantly between Piano Roll view (pitch and durations on a graphical time line), Notation view and Event List (detailed data for very MIDI event); multiple-level undo/redo; includes a wide variety of MIDI music files, drum tracks, video demos, and more. SYSTEM SPECS: Windows 3.1 or higher, 486 DX266 or higher, 8 MB of RAM, 10 MB of hard disk space, Windows-compatible sound card or MIDI interface and MIDI synthesizer, double speed CD-ROM or faster.

Music Master VS (Datasonics): Control the power of the Roland VS-880 digital workstation from a computer; on-screen control; record and edit audio and MIDI in one integrated environment; cut and paste; full editing; completely automated mix; control of effects; interface via MIDI; simple connections without SCSI; infinite undo/redo on all MIDI and audio functions; synchronizes with the VS-880 via MTC and MMC; full control of EQ and Mix parameters; each VS-880 track shows the virtual track selected; automated mixdown of mixer parameters including faders, mutes, sends, EQ, and Master controls; use of faders and pans on Music Master or VS-880. SYSTEM SPECS: Windows.

Music Shop (Opcode): Sequencing and notation printing; high resolution; real-time editing; supports Quick Time Musical Instruments; virtual software music recording studio when used with a MIDI interface and MIDI keyboard; on-screen display uses familiar tape deck style controls; recording, playback, and MIDI editing; standard music notation and graphic piano roll editing; multichannel recording and thirty-

two mixing channels. SYSTEM SPECS: Macintosh: Macintosh Plus, System 6.07, 2 MB RAM, hard disk; Windows: Windows 3.1 or later, 8 MB of RAM, CD-ROM drive, MIDI interface, or sound card.

Music Station (Steinberg): Recording sequencer; score printing; used with an MME-compatible sound card; included WAVE Player software adds digital audio recording and playback; add vocals, voice-overs, or sound effects to MIDI sequences; ten sample songs provided on disk; records and displays up to sixty-four tracks; additional track for time signature and tempo controls; one of the music tracks can contain digital audio; entry methods are real time, step time, mouse entry, and standard MIDI file import; primary display is the Arrange window; placement and length of all tracks is graphically displayed; edit one track or several with scissors, paste, eraser, and zoom tools; editing may be done while music is playing; Style Tracks feature plays a chord progression in different styles or variations; can create accompaniments; KeyEdit window is a graphic events editor which controls velocity, pitch, duration, pitch bend, pan, and more; editing can be done in real time during playback, including quantizing and undoing quantize; Score Editor displays selected tracks in standard notation; staves are vertically aligned in the order of the tracks in the Arrange windows; editing toolbox adds a chord symbol tool and a text tool; Auto quantize real-time entry into the most readable notation. SYSTEM SPECS: Windows, 4 MB RAM, MIDI soundboard, optional MIDI keyboard, can be used with headphones or speakers.

Musicator Audio (Musicator): Sixteen tracks hard disk recording; thirty-two parts per system; general MIDI compatible; supports multiple sound cards; mixdown audio parts to single track; create song sheets and large scores; record, view, edit, and mix audio and MIDI data; enter notes with a MIDI keyboard; quantize notation without affecting underlying MIDI data; sync to SMPTE/MTC; use multiple MIDI devices; export notation to PageMaker and other DTP programs; automatically inserts rests, ties, and beams whenever notes are entered, moved, or deleted; prepare scores; extract parts. SYSTEM SPECS: Windows.

Musicator Intro (Musicator): Sixteen staves per system; single score setup; single track of digital audio; entry-level program; contains the core features found in Musicator Win; fundamental set of sequencing, scoring, and digital audio recording tools; requires any 16-bit sound card and a MIDI keyboard to record, edit, play, and print music. SYSTEM SPECS: Windows.

Musicator Win (Musicator): Digital audio; sequencing and scoring; thirty-two staves per system; flexible page layout; part extraction; one track of digital audio recording; can control all aspects of performance; edit music the way it sounds versus the way it looks; song sheets to giant orchestrations. SYSTEM SPECS: Windows 486 or better, 8 MB of RAM, any 16-bit sound card or MIDI device compatible with Windows 3.1 or later.

Performer (Mark of the Unicorn): QuickTime video playback; instantly switch sequences; multiple takes per track; automated visual phrasing; virtual automated mixing; intuitive graphic interface; tape deck style transport controls; QuickScribe music notation display; notation editing and printing; high-resolution print font included; graphic piano-roll style editing; animated faders with grouping; graphic sequence chaining; real-time editing; unlimited tracks; Groove Quantize; Swing Quantize; chromatic, diatonic, and modal transposing; generate and scale tempos; unlimited meters; automatic pop up sound lists; over one hundred popular synths and sound modules; SMPTE synchronization; MII Machine Control; markers with SMPTE/lock; direct Sample Cell support; supports QuickTime Musical Instruments, Apple's built-in software synthesizer; play sequences using the Macintosh's built-in, 8-bit General MIDI sounds played back from the computer's internal speaker. SYSTEM SPECS: 68030, 68040 Quandra, or Power Macintosh, 8 MB RAM required with System 7.1, 12 MB RAM required with System 7.5 on a 680x0 Macintosh, minimum of 16 MB RAM required with Power Macintosh.

Power Tracks (PG Music): Entry level sequencer; event list editing; real-time and step-time entry; punch in/punch out; forty-eight tracks. SYSTEM SPECS: Windows.

Powertracks Pro Audio (PG Music): Digital audio and MIDI workstation; integrated digital audio/MIDI recording; music notation; video training CD; three multitrack CD-ROM play alongs; forty-eight tracks; real-time effects and audio plug-ins. SYSTEM SPECS: Windows 95, 98, NT, or 3.1, 8 MB RAM, digital audio features require 486 or Pentium, 16-bit sound card, 20 MB free hard drive space.

Q-Tracks (Hohner): A 256-track sequencer; full professional editing facilities; chord track with auto accompaniment; audio track enables simultaneous playback of WAVE files; cut, copy, paste, quantize features; piano roll/event/score and drum-editor; conductor window allows control over tempo, time and key signatures; sixteen-channel MIDI mixer gives onscreen control of MIDI instruments with real-time record and playback. SYSTEM SPECS: Windows 486 or higher, 4 MB RAM or higher, sound card or MIDI Interface.

Q-Tracks Professional (Hohner): All the features of Q-Tracks plus punch in/out, MTC/MC sync, programmable patch list, merge song, multitrack record, extended mixer options, multiple staff printing, multiple windows editing, and global track split function. SYSTEM SPECS: Windows.

Recording Station (Voyetra): Create songs with MIDI and digital audio; two digital audio tracks; ten MIDI tracks; video tutorial; includes MIDI drum tracks and songs; load and play; scrolling lyrics display; MIDI portion of song played by sound card's synthesizer or an external MIDI synthesizer; digital audio is played by the sound card's WAV audio hardware. SYSTEM SPECS: Windows.

Soundscore (Hohner): Plug the microphone provided into the sound card; start the included sequencer program and sing or play a melody; analyzes the tone length and pitch; assigns notes accordingly; play back part using any sound from sound card; multitrack several parts; save work as a MIDI file; experiment with other arrangements; works with acoustic solo instruments as the sound source; does not do pitch bend or velocity. SYSTEM SPECS: 386 or higher, 4 MB RAM, Windows 3.1 or higher, sound card.

Studio (Midisoft): Record, edit, and compose music with MIDI; record and edit WAVEform audio, including vocals; print sheet music; MIDI tracks limited only by computer memory; add lyrics synced to music; highlight notes during playback. SYSTEM SPECS: Windows.

Studio Vision Pro (Opcode): Digital audio and MIDI sequencing; audio MORF DSP for futuristic resynthesis; accepts Adobe plug-ins; support up to forty-eight audio channels; Sequence Events and nested looping for more flexible arranging options; consolidated Select and Modify Dialog handles a wide array of editing functions; true stereo file DSP processing, all new comprehensive cross-fade functionality; Bounce-to-Disk functions; total Pro Tools 24 compatibility; choose a track, choose an instrument, hit record, and start playing; with loop-based recording mode can experiment and construct an entire multi-instrumental groove without ever stopping the music; all applicable editing functions work the same way with digital audio and MIDI; bring in digital audio tracks from AIFF, SDII, WAV files, Quicktime movies, or even normal audio CDs; integrate drum loops, synth hits, ethnic percussion, or vocal snippets from sample CDs, textures and ambience from sound effect CDs, audio files from the internet or Windows PCs. SYSTEM SPECS: Macintosh 6820 or better, System 7.0.1 or later, 8 MB RAM (12 MB for digital audio), compatible hardware for digital audio, any Power Mac, Quandra 660AV, 840AV, PowerBook 520, 540, 5300.

Unisyn (Mark of the Unicorn): Organizes a MIDI system of multiple sound modules, keyboards, and other hardware components which can be accessed from a single software application; editor/librarian, along with MIDI interface, acts like system software and a CPU; all MIDI modules are configured in the software, and accessed through the interface; track assignments and configurations are saved for each project; well-organized, integrated system; command center is Modules window; create multiple system setups; configure MIDI cable routing; add new MIDI modules; supports over 200 popular MIDI devices; move patches or sounds; various modules that support subordinate patches; transfer operation similar to cut and paste or download sounds to a sampler with CD-ROM; try any sound with an on-screen virtual keyboard; select any module and patch, then click on a key to hear it; micro-edit patches with a sophisticated editing window environment including fundamental sound-generation parameters such as envelopes and filters; creation of banks and libraries; requires various MIDI equipment. SYSTEM SPECS: Macintosh; Windows.

Vision DSP (Opcode): Digital audio recording and editing; unique multimedia features; mixing consoles; new DSP features borrowed from Studio Vision; record, edit, and view 24-bit audio in the same window with MIDI music tracks; import and export all multimedia file types; support for Adobe Premiere plug-ins; Deluxe CD Edition includes virtual rack full of effects like Reverb, EQ, Compression, and more; QuickTime support; directly read and write Quick-Time audio and music (MIDI) files; save MIDI and audio tracks as a QuickTime movie; reads and writes all major audio file types including WAV, AU, AIFF, and Sound Designer II; use like a batch processor to compress and export multiple audio events; uses Sound Manager and SmartSync technology to achieve tighter track synchronization, while doubling the number of audio tracks; fastest Power Macs can support up to twenty tracks of audio without any additional hardware; Verticle Zoom buttons to see more tracks; add Digidesign Audiomedia card for high quality Analog and Digital I/O; Power Mac Native and DSP Additions; Power Mac native code makes screen redraws and DSP functions up to twenty times faster; effects from the new DSP Menu: Normalize, Reverse, Invert Phase, Convert Sample Rate, EQ or Fade In/Out; use Adobe Premiere-style plugs, such as Arboretum Hyperprism or WAVE Audio Track; Galaxy and digital audio recording are not available on the Windows version. SYSTEM SPECS: Macintosh: Power Macintosh, Level II Cache, MacOS 7 or higher, 12 MB RAM partition for application, large hard disk (2 gig, 7200 RPM preferable), defragmentation utility, CD-ROM drive, speed doubler, Audio-media II/III use Digidesign DA, MIDI keyboard, MIDI interface.

Vision for Windows (Opcode): Professional system for recording, editing, and playing music; extensive editing with notation, graphic, and list windows; Open Music System (OMS) for seamless interfacing to PC sound cards, MIDI hardware, and multitrack recorders. SYSTEM SPECS: 486/66 MHz or faster PC compatible, Windows 3.1, Win95, Win98, minimum 12 MB RAM (16 recommended), hard disk

with 8 MB free, Windows compatible MIDI interface and/or sound card.

Digital Audio Recording and Editing—CD Burning—Multimedia—MIDI File Libraries—Sample Sounds and Loops—Software Synthesizers—MP3 Software

A2B Player (A2B Music): MP3 player; streaming audio. SYSTEM SPECS: Macintosh; Windows.

Acid (Sonic Foundry): Loop-arranging and editing; gives musicians unprecedented creative flexibility; hundreds of cutting-edge loops; bring your own audio samples to create custom music in minutes; preview any loop before adding it to mix; automatically matches the tempo and key in real time; click-and-drag to easily add or delete loops; allows real-time changes to pitch and tempo to unlimited tracks, based on system RAM; control the volume, pan and effect envelopes for each track to create a perfect mix between loops; add finishing touches by applying multiple real-time effects with DirectX Audio Plug-Ins; MP3 encoding; loops in many different instruments and musical styles: Techno, Rock Rave, Break Beat, Funk, Country, Hip-Hop, Disco, Alternative, House, Industrial, Guitar, Bass, Synthesizer, Drums, Vocal, Brass, Turntable Sound Effects, Ambient, and more. SYSTEM SPECS: Windows.

Acid Loops (Sonic Foundry): High quality sound files for use with Acid; store special data to optimize time stretching/compressing and pitch change features; standard .WAV or AIF sound files with extra data; includes *Essential Sounds Vol. 2, Funky Extremes 1, Street Beats, Voices of Native America, Cyclotonic Resonator, Pandoras Toolbox, Rads Drum Construction Kit, Vortexual Amplitude, Funky Extremes 2, Sytonic Generator*. SYSTEM SPECS: Windows.

Acid Music (Sonic Foundry): Same features as Acid, without effects and synchronization features; does not accept plug-ins. SYSTEM SPECS: Windows.

Acid Pro (Sonic Foundry): Loop-recording/mixing software; bundled with Sound Forge XP 4.5 for audio editing and file conversion; includes DirectX audio plug-in pack that provides real-time reverb, delay, chorus, and other effects; ships with hundreds of loops in various styles, syncs to MIDI Time Code and does CD burning. SYSTEM SPECS: Windows 95/98/NT4.

Audioactive Player (Audioactive): MP3 player and encoder software. SYSTEM SPECS: Windows.

Audiocaster (Sek'd): Radio broadcasting automation program; noncommercial radio stations, local stations, schools, universities, hospitals, health resorts, and military institutions are potential users. SYSTEM SPECS: Windows.

Audiocatalyst (Xing Technologies): MP3 player and encoder software. SYSTEM SPECS: Macintosh; Windows.

Audiostation (Voyetra): Run multimedia PC like a home stereo system; intuitive, hardware-style interface unites MIDI, WAV, and CD functions; edit MIDI and digital audio WAV files; group files into playlists for automated playback; play audio CDs with CD-ROM drive and create custom playlists of songs; includes dozens of MIDI music and digital audio files; diagnostic program to help fix common multimedia setup problems. SYSTEM SPECS: Windows.

B. Box Sampling Groove Machine (Steinberg): Groove sampler in software form; build groove patterns with simple step-by-step input technique; wide variety of drum sounds representing a variety of musical genres; single drum sounds and entire loops can be integrated. SYSTEM SPECS: Windows.

Big Fish Audio Sample CDs and CD-ROMs (Big Fish Audio): Quality sample libraries since 1986; can find extensive selection of sample library and sound effects products from around the world; all products are license free; no clearance forms or additional licenses are required; Big Fish sounds are featured in hundreds of charting songs and top film scores; products contain Loops/Performances and/or Sounds; formats include: Akai, Audio E-mu, GigaSampler, Kurzweil, Mac (AIFF)/SampleCell, MPC 2000, Roland, SoundFont, Soundscan, TC, and WAV; Big Fish Audio Listening Centers at music stores nationwide, including Guitar Center, Sam Ash Music, Mars Music, Manny's Music, West L. A. Music, Bananas at Large, Veneman Music, and many others; feature an extensive selection of discs so can audition before buying. SYSTEM SPECS: Macintosh; Windows.

Bill Bruford Drum Samples and Loops (AKAI S1000 Format) (BitHeadz): Seventy minutes of acoustic and electronic drum samples and loops in Akai S1000 format; for importing into Unity DS-1 with complete multisamples and programs. SYSTEM SPECS: Macintosh; Windows.

Bill Bruford Drum Samples and Loops (CD Audio) (BitHeadz): Seventy minutes of acoustic and electronic drum samples and loops in CD audio format; import into Unity DS-1 and other digital audio applications, or play in CD player. SYSTEM SPECS: Macintosh; Windows.

Black & Whites Professional Acoustic and Electric Pianos (BitHeadz): First piano module on CD; no other software or hardware needed; turns computer into a nine-foot Steinway grand, or a classic Rhodes electric piano, or a seven-foot Steinway. SYSTEM SPECS: Macintosh; Windows.

Cakewalk Pyro (Cakewalk): Turn CDs into MP3s; burn CDs from MP3 and WAV files; record from LPs and cassettes; record, play, and organize digital music; tutorials. SYSTEM SPECS: Windows 95/98; Pentium class 200 MHz PC or higher, minimum 32 MB RAM, CD-ROM drive, CD-R drive for creating audio CDs.

Camps V 4 (Microworks): Generates new melodies, bass lines, drum patterns, chord patterns, and chord progressions from scratch; loads standard MIDI files and reharmonizes existing melodies. SYSTEM SPECS: Windows 95/98/NT and Macintosh.

CD Architect (Sonic Foundry): Burn Red Book audio CDs with speed and precision; read audio from compact discs; record from DAT or digitize material through sound card; includes dozens of professional effects and tools to process sound files; can be used as a Sound Forge plug-in; PQ editing, including track times, subindices, ISRC codes, and printed cue sheets; includes Sound Forge XP for WAVE editing. SYSTEM SPECS: Windows.

CD Recorder (Steinberg): Make music CDs from CDs, records, tapes, MIDI or MP3 files; can record sound files from a CD or stereo; separate tracks; clean up songs; organize tunes into a play list; write an audio CD to play in any CD player; make music CDs from MIDI or MP3 music files. SYSTEM SPECS: Pentium CPU, Windows 95/98 or NT, 16-bit sound card, CD-R or CD-RW for CD recording.

Clean (Steinberg): Restore old records and cassettes; take out noise, clicks and cracks; burn CDs; record music into computer from a variety of sound sources; process recording to CD quality audio; CD can have up to ninety-nine tracks. SYSTEM SPECS: Pentium MMX 200 MHz, 16-bit MME-compatible sound card, 32 MB RAM, 20 MB free hard disk space per minute of audio processing, CD-ROM drive, SCSI CDR burner, Windows 95/98/NT.

Concertware (Jump! Software): Music composition, sequencing, recording, editing, and printing in one program; creates, imports, and exports standard MIDI files; can be used as a player when searching the Internet for music shareware and public domain MIDI files; download any standard MIDI file and the music is transposed into notation; press Play to hear how it sounds; change the instrument arrangement or key; upgradable to a thirty-two stave version; includes over one hundred popular songs in MIDI format; multimedia tutorial. SYSTEM SPECS: Macintosh: 68040, System 7.1, 8 MB RAM, CD-ROM, MIDI keyboard optional; Windows: 486 or MPC level 1, Windows 3.1, 8 MB RAM, CD-ROM, SoundBlaster sound card, VGA monitor.

Cool Edit Pro (Syntrillium): Supports ActiveMovie/DirectX Plug Ins; top-quality digital effects modules; mix up to sixty-four tracks using any sound card; more than thirty DSP effects; processing power. SYSTEM SPECS: Windows 95 or NT, 486 or better, 16 MB RAM, 4 MB free hard disk space, stereo sound card.

Dart (Dartech): CD-Recorder software; complete audio toolkit for PC; record audio, apply restoration processing; make music CDs in computer's CD-R or CD-RW drive; record from a compact disc or stereo; clean up digital recordings using DeHiss and DeClick DirectX plug-ins; enhance audio using nine-band equalizer; Volume Control and Fade In/Fade Out features; organize tunes into playlists; write an audio CD that can be played in any CD player; *SureThing Lite CD Labeler* included; batch file conversion; converts WAV or MP3 to CD audio format; connect to the Internet and add artist, title, and other CD track information to the online CDDB music database; erase CD-RW disks for reuse; free updates from Dartech via the Internet. SYSTEM SPECS: Windows, CD-R, or CD-RW drive required for burning audio CDs.

Deck (Bias): Multitrack recording application; provides up to sixty-four tracks and supports Adobe Premiere plug-ins and ASIO; owned and distributed by BIAS; upgraded for OS 9 compatibility. SYSTEM SPECS: Macintosh.

Deck II (Macromedia): Hard disk recording software; record and edit up to 999 16-bit digital audio tracks; play back up to thirty-two tracks in real time on Power Mac. SYSTEM SPECS: Macintosh.

Deck II/Sound Edit (Macromedia): Sixteen bundle hard disk recording and sound design software; complete software-only recording studio; create audio for multimedia or music on the Internet. SYSTEM SPECS: Macintosh.

Digital Sound Gallery Volume 1 (Voyetra): More than 475 WAV files to enhance narration and multimedia presentations or to experiment with digital audio; twelve high-quality production songs in stereo; news theme, corporate anthem, urban funk, jazz, ballads, and more; includes eight piano classics and more than 400 sound effects grouped by category. SYSTEM SPECS: Windows.

Digital Sound Gallery Volume 2 (Voyetra): Composer's toolkit; custom groove variations; intros; fills; real drum patterns; music samples to enhance compositions; drag-and-drop; enhance MIDI music compositions with musical sound effects; assemble rhythm grooves using digital audio drum tracks; requires *Digital Orchestrator*. SYSTEM SPECS: Windows.

Digitranslator (Digidesign): Interchange application; conversion of OMF files to and from Pro Tools; file interchange is made simple and dependable; OMF Interchange standard developed by Avid to facilitate seamless exchange of sound and picture elements; allows bidirectional conversion of OMF files to Pro Tools files and Pro Tools files to OMF files; developed in collaboration with working postproduction audio engineers; sophisticated conversion options; allows translation of clip-based volume data; choice between rendered audio effects or untreated sources;

options for media copying and consolidation; online tool tips provide constant feedback at every step of the conversion process; for postproduction professionals who require seamless OMF-to-Pro Tools and Pro Tools-to-OMF session interchange. SYSTEM SPECS: Macintosh 8 or higher, 128 MB RAM, floppy drive (check Compatibility Documents for Digidesign approved diskette drives for Blue and White G3 and G4 configurations; additional required components include AVoption or AVoption|XL for import and playback of AVID video media.

Drumatix (Hohner): MIDI drummer; comprehensive drum sequencer; recreates human feel; create drum parts. SYSTEM SPECS: Windows.

Drumatix + (Hohner): All the features of Drumatix plus the possibility to add a complete band with bass, rhythm, and fills to drum grooves. SYSTEM SPECS: Windows.

Easy CD Creator (Adaptec): Select music from LPs, cassettes, and other sources, digitally filter unwanted noise, then record to CD; make jewel case inserts, complete with titles and artwork; includes CD Spin Doctor to turn LPs into clear CDs; store photographs and video; design jewel case inserts and labels; copy from one CD to another; create any type of CD: ISO 9660 (Data) Audio, Mixed Mode, Video CD, and CD Extra; Deluxe version is MP3 and WAV compatible. SYSTEM SPECS: Windows 95 or NT 4.0, CD recorder of rewritable drive, recordable CDs, 16 MB free hard disk space.

Echoview Pro (Mirage): Integrated suite of interactive music calculating tools for musicians, sound engineers, and producers; 32-bit package; freeware; download from the Internet; delay time calculator; delay time grid; metronome; tap tempo utility; chord cue; song length calculator; stopwatch; sample calculator; synthesisers; printing features. SYSTEM SPECS: Windows 95, 98, or NT.

ES1 (EMagic): Comprehensive range of virtual instruments for the Logic Series; software synthesizer; flexible tone generation; entire palette of analog sounds; basses, rich pads, and textures, screaming leads, ultrasharp percussion and exotic effects; depending on computer's performance, can use up to eight ES1 instruments simultaneously in Logic Audio program (MicroLogic AV, Silver, Gold, and Platinum), each with up to sixteen voices; sample-accurate timing superior to MIDI hardware; every parameter can be automated; includes all the effect plug-ins of Logic's internal digital mixer; with Logic Audio Gold and Platinum, audio recordings can be routed into the ES1 and used as modulation sources; ergonomic user-interface for experimenting with sound creation; clear layout; unique control elements. SYSTEM SPECS: Macintosh minimum: Logic Audio/MicroLogic AV 4.0 or higher, 604e processor or fast 603e, System 8.5, 64 MB RAM, 128 MB RAM for MacOS 8.6 or newer, USB requires System 8.6 or newer, CD-ROM drive, does not run together with the Digidesign DAE/TDM systems, the Yamaha CBX Series, the Yamaha DSP Factory, or the AKAI DR8; Macintosh recommended: G3 or G4 Processor, 128 MB RAM, digital audio card, MIDI interface. Windows minimum: Logic Audio/MicroLogic AV 4.0 or higher, Pentium 200, Windows 98, 64 MB RAM, multimedia compatible sound card, CD-ROM drive, more than 256 colors, does not run together with Logic's native support for the Yamaha DSP Factory; Windows recommended: Pentium II or III, 128 MB RAM, digital audio card, MIDI interface.

EXS24 (Logic Audio) (Emagic): Up to thirty-two voices of sample-playback synthesis with low-pass filtering; like the ES1 requires Logic as a host application; dual LFOs and dual ADSRs included; 24-bit samples are supported; output can be processed by other plug-ins; parameter changes can be automated by Logic. SYSTEM SPECS: Macintosh; Windows.

Freeamp Player (Open Source): MP3 player software. SYSTEM SPECS: Windows; Linux.

Galaxy Plus Editors (Opcode): Supports over 150 of the most popular MIDI instruments; integrates easily with sequencers such as Opcode's Vision and Studio Vision; stores synth patches; automatically shows names in the sequencer; edit sounds while the music plays; instantly compare any voice edit with the original; keep track of all files and create custom banks; nongeneric editors; see all parameters on-screen; graphic editing of all envelopes; eight synthesizer effects; copy and paste parameters and envelopes. SYSTEM SPECS: Macintosh 680X0 or Power Mac, 4 MB RAM, hard disk, MIDI Interface, System 7.01 or higher.

Get It On CD (Steinberg): Record, edit, and compile customized CD; record material from line or microphone inputs on sound card or copy digitally from another CD; drag-and-drop audio files into CD program; split a large file into separate sections with markers; insert pauses between tracks; listen to final result before burning; extensive editing functions; real-time effects; unlimited UNDO; SYSTEM SPECS: Windows 95/98/NT.

Gigastudio 160 (NemeSys): Offshoot of GigaSampler; redesigned user interface; real-time effects; support for sixty-four MIDI channels; bundled audio editing software; up to 160 streaming disk-based voices depending on processor and hard drive speed; comes with a 1GB grand piano multisample; compatible with GigaSampler-format sounds, and the Akai S1000/S3000 library, E-mu SoundFonts, and WAV files; timing latency is in the 3-8ms range. SYSTEM SPECS: Windows 95/98.

Hip-Hop Ejay (Voyetra): Create and mix hip-hop tracks; CD-ROM; drag audio loops, samples, and sound effects into eight-track sequencer; sounds color-coded by category; bass loops; drum beats; raps; scratches; keyboards; effects; create a WAVE or MP3 file; burn to a CD. SYSTEM SPECS: Windows.

Hip-Hop Ejay 2 (Voyetra): Over 3,500 professionally recorded audio samples; slammin' drum beats, bass lines, keyboard parts, raps, vocal hooks, sound effects, and more; record own voice or samples and drop into songs; utilities; robotize, echo, overdrive, and filter in Effects Studio; cut and scratch audio clips in Scratch Generator II; blend songs in 16-Track Mixer; make any audio sample compatible with Time Stretch utility. SYSTEM SPECS: Windows.

Hip-Hop Ejay Sample Kit (Voyetra): Includes *Breakdances* and *Unplugged* CDs. SYSTEM SPECS: Windows.

Hum (Utopiasoft): MP3 player software. SYSTEM SPECS: Windows CE.

Hypercard (Apple): Development tool for multimedia presentations and computer-based classroom materials; automatically integrates text, graphics, video, sound, spoken text, and links. SYSTEM SPECS: Macintosh.

Internet Music Kit Deluxe (Wildcat Canyon): Add music to Web page in three easy steps; create music with hundreds of professional quality musical phrases; combine phrases into a song in a variety of music styles; convert music with Webtracks technology to play music immediately when Web page is accessed; embed music by streamlining the process of placing music on Web page with an automated embed wizard; includes a multitrack sequencer and professional layout features for Web page design. SYSTEM SPECS: Windows.

Jam CD Recording Software (Adaptec): Creates 100 percent Red Book compliant, audio CD image files; edit PQ subcodes, create cross fades between track, or set the gain for each channel of each track; use Sound Designer II Playlist and regions; each region becomes a separate track; drag-and-drop SDII, AIFF, or WAV files, then record CD; supports most SCSI CD-R and CD-RW drives; set the volume track by track, independent for each channel; create CD extra discs (requires Adaptec Jam and Toast); edit sound with included Peak LE software; writes in Disc-at-Once mode. SYSTEM SPECS: Macintosh.

Jinglecaster Virtual Cart Machine (Sek'd): Tool used for playing back songs, audio clips, and jingles; all common audio file formats (MP3, MS Audio) are supported; for theatres, radio stations, public halls, discos, and all situations requiring fast and interactive access to audio files; can be used in a network; beta tested by well-known broadcast and theatre audio engineers. SYSTEM SPECS: Windows 95/98/NT/2000.

Kyma (Symbolic Sound): Integration with Sentech motor mix; features motorized faders; high-level user interface includes library of useful factory settings, time line for performance automation and new effects and synthesis algorithms; includes Capybara hardware system with 96MB of RAM and four channels of 24-bit, 100kHz I/O. SYSTEM SPECS: Macintosh; Windows.

Liquid Audio Player (Liquid Audio): Streaming audio; MP3 and WAV compatible; CD burning. SYSTEM SPECS: Macintosh; Windows.

Macamp/Macamp Lite Player (@soft): MP3 player and encoder software. SYSTEM SPECS: Macintosh.

Mastering House (Sonic Foundry): Includes *Sound Forge* digital audio editor, *CD Architect* for burning audio CDs to Red Book spec, XFX1 and XFX2 real-time DirectX Audio Plug-in effects and processors. SYSTEM SPECS: Windows.

Masterlist CD (Digidesign): Creates Red Book standard CD masters; used as direct source for glass mastering by many duplication facilities worldwide, or as one-off reference discs playable on any commercial CD player; supports full-feature set of many SCSI-based CD recorders; full support of all PQ subcodes; imports Sound Designer II format files, regions, and playlists, including split stereo files and regions directly from Pro Tools; individual track level cut and boost; definable cross fades among MasterList items. SYSTEM SPECS: Macintosh; Windows.

Max Multimedia Programming Environment (Opcode): Interactive real-time graphic programming environment for multimedia; object-oriented language; create custom applications; write programs by graphically connecting objects from an on-screen object palette; with the real-time environment, can run multiple events simultaneously; see the results of programming changes immediately; accurate timing services; includes everything needed to write and distribute applications; over 150 onboard objects, each with an extensive help window; distribute finished product without paying any licensing fees; unifies diverse disciplines. SYSTEM SPECS: Macintosh.

MCAPS (GIISi): Matrix Cells Audio Processor Synthesizer (MCAPS) uses neural network processing called Neuronal Synthesis, implemented on PCI card; virtual analog, additive, sample playback, and custom synthesis possible; card will do multichannel recording and multichannel effects; additive synthesis processes allow up to 1,024 oscillators with amplitude, frequency, and phase envelopes. SYSTEM SPECS: Windows 95/98.

Media Tools (Apple): Set of add-ons for Hyper-Card; play audio from CDs; record and play back digital audio and QuickTime movies; play standard MIDI files. SYSTEM SPECS: Macintosh.

Metasynth 2.5 (U&I): Waveshaping tool; spectrum synthesis; custom scales; preset tuning tables; displacement mapping for time acceleration; filter processes including motion blur, trace edges, and color remap; advanced graphics-based sound editing; unlimited oscillators for non-real-time synthesis; can preview up to 400 oscillators in real time on fast computers. SYSTEM SPECS: Macintosh.

MIDI Music Gallery (Voyetra): More than 400 MIDI files to transform multimedia PC into an orchestra; use songs for education, multimedia presentation, parties, sing-alongs, or listening enjoyment; use MIDI sequencer to alter instruments, tempos, and notes or add parts; requires a MIDI sequencer. SYSTEM SPECS: Windows.

MIDI Screen Saver (ECS): Screen saver protects computer from having images burned into the screen; will play music through MIDI keyboard coordinated with images displayed; MIDI tunes can be selected from a list; new tunes can be added. SYSTEM SPECS: Macintosh: MIDI, requires After Dark, not available for Macintosh 7.5-8.0; PC DOS: MIDI, requires EGA.

Midiquest (Sound Quest): Editor/librarian; easy to use; supports over 250 instruments; fast tips online help; comprehensive sound auditioning tools; all functions are active while playing; extensive sound sorting capabilities; sophisticated patch organization and editing for banks; store sound and banks from different MIDI devices together; "Sound Checker" has complete graphic MIDI systems analysis; uses advanced graphic editing. SYSTEM SPECS: Macintosh: MIDI interface, 2 MB RAM, hard drive; Windows: MIDI interface, 386 or better, 4 MB RAM.

Miroslav Mini Symphonic Orchestra Samples (BitHeadz): Collection of world class symphonic orchestral samples in native Unity DS-1 format; comes complete with twenty-five individual instruments including banks of cellos, violins, oboes, bassoons, and more. SYSTEM SPECS: Macintosh; Windows.

Mixtreme Digital Powerpak (Soundscape): All-in-one music bundle; audio card with sixteen channels of 24-bit TDIF digital I/O; stereo 20-bit analog I/O; software: NemeSys GigaSampler 1E sampler, Seer Systems SurReal synthesizer, Emagic Micrologic AV thirty-two-track sequencer/recorder, and Sonic Foundry Sound Forge XP audio editor; mixing by Soundscape 2.0, which includes a Wave Mechanics reverb and other real-time effects. SYSTEM SPECS: Windows 95/98.

MP3 Export (Digidesign): Allows Pro Tools and Pro Tools LE users to export and/or bounce audio to MP3 file format in the Pro Tools operating environment; based on compression technology of Germany's Fraunhofer Institute; implemented into Pro Tools v5.0 and Pro Tools LE v5.0 (WinNT & 98 in v5.0.1) as a user-friendly export option; post musical compositions on the Internet; improvements in processing speed, enhanced processing quality, and support of constant bit rate (CBR) and variable bit rate (VBR); encoding at bit rates of up to 320 kbps. SYSTEM SPECS: Macintosh-based Pro Tools or Pro Tools LE system running version 5.0 or higher software; Windows NT Pro Tools or Windows 98 Pro Tools LE system running version 5.0.1 or higher software.

MP3 Producer Professional (Opticom): MP3 encoder software. SYSTEM SPECS: Windows.

Multimedia Audio Accessories (Voyetra): Includes audio calendar; MIDI screen saver; Windat! to record, play, and edit digital audio files; embed sound files into other documents; Say It! to embed voice annotations into documents; sound script to create presentations with MIDI, WAV, and CD; image station to select, view, catalog, and manage image files; media check, a multimedia diagnostic utility. SYSTEM SPECS: Windows.

Multi-MPU-401 Driver (PG Music): Allows ten programs to use the MPU-401 at the same time; allows interprogram MIDI communication; requires MPU-401. SYSTEM SPECS: Windows 3.1/95.

Music Passport (Passport): Expands directly into Web site; music files; online training; search features gives access to an expanding music library of files from musicians; guide to music places on the Web; PitchWrite technology captures sound with a microphone (included); play an instrument, plug a guitar into the sound card, or hum or sing in a part. SYSTEM SPECS: Windows 95, Windows-compatible sound card, Web access, modem and service provider, MIDI keyboard and PC MIDI interface optional.

MusicMatch (MusicMatch): MP3 player and encoder software; MP3 and WAV compatible; CD burning. SYSTEM SPECS: Windows.

MxTrax Native (Minnetonka): Compatible with Yamaha DSP Factory; run with any Windows sound card using a WAV or ASIO driver; surround mixing on any multichannel Windows sound card available via Minnetonka MX51 software. SYSTEM SPECS: Windows.

My MP3 (Steinberg) All-in-one MP3 and CD burner software; play back, convert, organize, and burn music onto CD; audition music, copy tracks from CDs, record MP3s, add effects, and mix in real time; drag-and-drop to create best-of collections; compile albums; record music directly in MP3 and WAVE format. SYSTEM SPECS: Windows.

Neato CD Labeler Kit (Neato): Design on any computer; print on any laser or ink-jet; apply with precision; includes assortment of CD/DVD labels, jewel case inserts, media labels, and inserts; Neato applicator; MediaFace media labeling design software for MAC and PC; templates for most major design software; digital background art for labels; jewel cases and other media labeling needs in black and white or color; all copyright free. SYSTEM SPECS: Hybrid.

Nuendo (Steinberg): Surround mixing; video track; 24-bit/96kHz recording; ASIO and VST 2.0 compatibility; postproduction system; compatible hardware audio interfaces, including Nuendo 8 I/O (eight-channel A/D and D/A conversion) plus ADAT and TDIF connectors, and PCI 96 52 (three ADAT connectors) available. SYSTEM SPECS: Windows 98/NT/2000.

Osmosis Sample Conversion Utility (BitHeadz): Reads Akai S-1000/3000 and Roland S-760/770 formatted CDs and converts them to Unity DS-1, Sample Cell II, AIFF, WAV, and SDII formats. SYSTEM SPECS: Macintosh; Windows.

Peak (Peak): Digidesign DAE support; TDM and Audiosuite plug-in support; real-time Adobe Premiere plug-ins; support for 24- and 32-bit files; playlist-direct CD-R burning; QuickTime movie window; SMPTE synchronization; expanded sampler support; two-track digital audio editing program; take audio from conception to final mix, CD, video, film, or the Web; use with any Mac audio program, multitrack workstation, integrated MIDI sequencing software, sound card, multimedia authoring program, or nonlinear video editing system; support for AIFF, SDII, WAV, QuickTime; Pro Tools-style dual-mono files; RealAudio 2.0, 3.0, and 5.0 Internet sound files; multiple compression formats including QDesign, IMA, and others; support for files up to 32-bits; Loop Tuner; Loop Surfer creates real-time, tempo-based loops from audio clips; advanced batch file processing; click repair; custom blend and fade envelopes; DSP tools; import multiple audio tracks from CD; support for MIDI samplers, including AKAI, E-mu, Ensoniq, Kurzweil, Peavey, Yamaha, and others; customizable tool bar; floating palette; left and right channels can be independently processed; pencil tool for precise, sample-level editing simply by drawing a line; QuickTime support; import digital video movies; synchronize audio to video; multimedia production; support for 8-, 16-, 24-, and 32-bit audio files; Digidesign DAE recording and playback support; real-time Adobe Premiere audio plug-ins; SMPTE/EBU timecode synchronization. SYSTEM SPECS: Windows Power PC, System 7.1 or later, Quicktime 3.0 or later, 32MB RAM minimum, 5MB available hard disk space for program and online help, 18ms average seek time recommended for SCSI hard drive, 640 x 480 minimum screen resolution, color monitor recommended, Apple Sound Manager 3.3 or later, recording and playback of sounds at higher bit depths (e.g., 16-, 24-, 32-bits) may require compatible hardware or third party audio card and drivers; DAE support requires an additional 10MB RAM and supported Digidesign audio hardware.

Phrazer (BitHeadz): Digital audio loop sequencer; instantly change tempo and pitch; add FX; connectivity with Pro Tools, Logic, Digital Performer, Cubase, and all MIDI gear. SYSTEM SPECS: Macintosh.

Phrazer Real Time Audio Loop Sequencer (BitHeadz): Real-time audio loop sequencer; pitch and tempo-matching algorithms; built-in sample editing;

onboard digital effects; multitrack digital audio and MIDI combined for comprehensive loop-based production. SYSTEM SPECS: Macintosh.

Postconform (Digidesign): EDL (Edit Decision Lists) import/auto-conform software application; enables automatic capture and spotting of audio elements to picture; increases productivity by automatically loading and conforming production sound and other audio elements according to industry-standard CMX EDL files; EDLs specify where to place specific sound elements within a program; PostConform automates process of assembling an EDL into a Pro Tools session file; can record 24-bit audio and export 24-bit Pro Tools sessions; supports USD for positional and clock reference (as well as MTC); supports USB MIDI interfaces for MTC; supports Keyspan USB-to-serial adapters for machine control; supports Blue&White G3 and G4 computers; supports the option to store unique identifier strings in sound file names; for postproduction professionals who require integrated EDL auto-conform for Pro Tools. SYSTEM SPECS: Digidesign approved Pro Tools|24 or Pro Tools|24 MIX system running Macintosh 8.6 or higher; additional required components for machine control include 9-pin serial Machine Control cable; requires Digidesign Universal Slave Driver or LTC-to-MTC converter.

Powertracks Pro Audio (PG Music): Professional, fully featured digital audio and MIDI workstation; for musicians, students, and songwriters; integrated digital audio/MIDI recording; built-in music notation; offers support for multiple sound cards and professional multiline recording cards; simultaneously record and play back up to sixteen digital audio inputs and outputs; JukeBox feature includes next song, previous song, stop and start buttons, stop between songs, and play on command for live performances; sixteen-track Mixer Window allows simultaneous precision control of up to sixteen Audio, MIDI, or a combination of MIDI and Audio tracks; MIDI to Audio Sync adjustments allow accurate recording playback sessions; with Markers View can insert song position markers displayed at top of Bars Overview Window; virtual guitar fretboard; Fill Blank Track Names with Patches; shows exact track names in a dedicated column on the left side of the Bars window; saves any individual track that is contained in a project to its own file outside of the project; auto-transpose MIDI data of a song to new key; includes PowerGuide CD-ROM Video Tutorials; nineteen professional-quality audio plug-ins: Compressor, Gate, Distortion, Reverb, Echo, Chorus, Flanger, Ring Mod, Tremolo, Tone Control, Graphic EQ, Parametric EQ, Gain Change, Pitch-Shift, De-Ess, AutoWah, Exciter, Enhancer, Hum Filter; MultiTracks Volume 1 and MultiTracks Volume 2 have full-length songs recorded by top studio musicians; each MultiTracks volume comes with three CD-ROMs with jazz,

blues, and rock songs provided in MultiTracks format. SYSTEM SPECS: Windows 95, 98, NT or 3.1, 8 MB RAM, Digital Audio features require fast 486 or Pentium, any Windows-compatible 16-bit sound card (e.g., SoundBlaster 16, AWE32, AWE64, Ensoniq, Yamaha, etc.), 20 MB free hard drive space, MIDI and other features requires 386, MIDI interface or sound card, CD-ROM drive and printer (optional).

Pro 5 (VST) (Native Instruments): Dual oscillators with cross-modulation; resonant filters; ADSR envelopes included; runs only as a VST plug-in not freestanding. SYSTEM SPECS: Hybrid.

Pro Tools Avoption (Digidesign): Supports capture, import, and playback; Avid-compatible video media directly within Pro Tools; delivers "plug and play" video media compatibility with the roughly 25,000 Avid Media Composer, Film Composer, and Xpress/Mac systems currently in use worldwide; two-card solution based on the ABVB hardware subsystem; "Janus" Advanced JPEG Compression PCI Card, ABVB (Avid Broadcast Video Board) PCI Card for Video I/O, AVoption Software and Documentation, Video I/O Breakout Cable. SYSTEM SPECS: Mac OS-based, Digidesign-approved Pro Tools|24, Pro Tools|24 MIX, or Pro Tools|24 MIXplus system.

Pro Tools Avoption|XL (Digidesign): Supports capture, import, and playback of Avid-compatible video media directly within Pro Tools; based on Avid's newer Meridien hardware; adds a breakout box for component, composite, and S-video (SDI optional) I/O; captures and plays back JFIF media from 15:1 compression up to uncompressed (1:1) video; finest quality resolution available on any audio workstation; compatible with all Avid systems based on the Meridien video subsystem, including Avid Symphony, Media Composer|XL, and Xpress NT; Meridien PCI Interface Card, Break Out Box (with interface cable) for video I/O, AVoption software and documentation. SYSTEM SPECS: Mac OS- or Windows NT-based, Digidesign-approved Pro Tools|24, Pro Tools|24 MIX, or Pro Tools|24 MIXplus system.

Pro Tools DIGI 001 (Digidesign): Complete audio/MIDI, hardware/software solution; eight analog inputs; eight analog outputs; eight channels of ADAT optical I/O and two S/PDIF I/O channels, all at 24-bit resolution; one-in, one-out MIDI interface built in; footswitch input for QuickPunch control; pair of analog monitor outputs; headphone output with separate volume control; two of the eight analog inputs include high-quality microphone pre-amplifiers with gain control and phantom power, reducing the need to incorporate a separate mixer; self-contained, fully featured hardware interface for all aspects of home studio recording; with Pro Tools LE software; cross-platform package; integrated system featuring hardware and software, both by Digidesign; complete unit in one location. SYSTEM SPECS: Macintosh; Windows.

Pro Tools DIGI Toolbox XP (Digidesign): Audiomedia III interface card; PCI card for better than CD-quality audio into and out of computer; 18-bit analog stereo I/O and 24-bit S/PDIF digital I/O; interface with a small mixer or transfer DAT recordings; Digidesign's simplest cross-platform solution for music, sound design, and multimedia production; with Pro Tools LE; access to all the real-time processing and mixing power and high track count of Pro Tools LE; two analog inputs: -10dBV, unbalanced RCA connections; two analog outputs: -10dBV, unbalanced RCA connections; Analog Converter Resolution: 18-bit, 1-bit Delta-Sigma; 128x oversampling; stereo digital input and output: S/PDIF, RCA connections; maximum digital resolution: 24-bit; used together, the analog and digital inputs or outputs function as four simultaneous inputs or outputs with Pro Tools LE; THD: 0.008 percent @ 1 kHz; signal-to-noise ratio: 88 dB, 22 Hz - 22 kHz band-limited, input-to-output; frequency response: 20 Hz to 20 kHz. SYSTEM SPECS: Macintosh; Windows 98.

Pro Tools LE Software (Digidesign): Powerful MIDI sequencing; real-time digital mixing; twenty-four playback tracks of 16- or 24-bit audio; DigiRack bundle of Real-Time AudioSuite (RTAS) and file-based AudioSuite plug-ins; access to many additional Digidesign and third party development partners' plug-ins; 128 MIDI tracks; real-time digital mixing; five effects inserts and sends per track with sixteen internal busses; sample-accurate editing of audio and MIDI simultaneously; MP3 and RealAudio G2 support (Mac only). SYSTEM SPECS: Macintosh; Windows.

Pro Tools Plug-Ins (Digidesign): Power and flexibility of Pro Tools platform comes from its open architecture; supports a wide variety of software products, both from Digidesign and its Development Partners; plug-ins are add-on software that add capabilities to Pro Tools; they provide real-time effects like EQ and dynamics, and file-based processes like time compression and normalization; more economical than hardware-based signal processors; every Pro Tools system comes with a standard set of plug-ins; check out the online Plug-In Finder for more information on the different types of plug-ins; Digidesign environment also supports many standalone programs, including audio editors, mastering programs, and backup utilities; Pro Tools can also share information with audio software programs like synthesizers, sample players, and loop generators; online Development Partner Catalog lists many compatible programs and options.

Pro Tools/24 (Digidesign): Industry's leading digital audio workstations; power and performance with ease of use; true 24-bit, integrated digital recording, editing, processing, mixing, and mastering system; integrated MIDI sequencing; advanced editing functions for professional music and postproduction; advanced audio/MIDI editing and mixing interface; cross-platform for Macintosh and Windows NT operating systems; high-end music production, postproduction, and multimedia; d24 audio card, DSP Farm card, DigiRack TDM and AudioSuite plug-ins, Pro Tools software; requires at least one Digidesign audio interface: the 888|24 I/O, 882|20 I/O, 1622 I/O, or ADAT Bridge I/O. SYSTEM SPECS: Macintosh; Windows NT.

Pro Tools/24 Mix (Digidesign): Up to three times the DSP power of Pro Tools|24 system; single PCI card; up to sixty-four tracks of audio with MIX system; opens up computer slot availability for other cards, such as a SampleCell II Plus or a video card; true 24-bit, integrated digital recording, editing, processing, mixing, mastering, and MIDI sequencing system; advanced audio editing and mixing interface; cross-platform for Macintosh and Windows NT operating systems; ultra high-end audio production, postproduction, sound design, and multimedia; MIX Core card, DigiRack TDM and AudioSuite plug-ins, Pro Tools software; requires at least one Digidesign audio interface: the 888|24 I/O, 882|20 I/O, 1622 I/O, or ADAT Bridge I/O. SYSTEM SPECS: Macintosh; Windows NT.

Pro Tools/24 Mix Plus (Digidesign): System for digital audio production; more than doubles the mixing and DSP power of Pro Tools|24 MIX system by adding an additional MIX Farm Card; exceptionally powerful system; create an entire album from start to finish; score a complete film project; run thirty-two audio tracks with pristine 4-band EQ, dynamics, five sends on every track, ten delay-based effects, plus reverb effects simultaneously; industry's leading digital audio workstations; true 24-bit, integrated digital recording, editing, processing, mixing, and mastering system; most advanced audio editing and mixing interface and is cross-platform for Macintosh and Windows NT operating systems; for any professional recording, postproduction, sound design, or multimedia project; MIX Core Card, MIX Farm Card, DigiRack TDM and AudioSuite plug-ins, the latest version of Pro Tools software; requires at least one Digidesign audio interface: the 888|24 I/O, 882|20 I/O, or ADAT Bridge I/O. SYSTEM SPECS: Macintosh; Windows NT.

Professional CD Factory (Sonic Foundry): For burning CDs on a Pentium PC; includes Play Write 4080; Panasonic 4x8 External CDR Recorder; Advansys SCSI Card to connect CDR Recorder to PC; Sonic Foundry CD Architect software to burn CDs; Sound Forge XP software to input recordings into PC; two pieces of blank media. SYSTEM SPECS: Windows.

Quicktime Player (Quicktime): Streaming audio and video; MP3 and WAV compatible. SYSTEM SPECS: Macintosh; Windows.

RealJukebox (Real Networks): Streaming audio and video; MP3 and WAV compatible; recording. SYSTEM SPECS: Windows.

RealPlayer (Real Networks): Streaming audio and video; MP3 and WAV compatible. SYSTEM SPECS: Macintosh; Windows.

Reason (Steinberg): Stand-alone music station software; comes in the shape of a classic studio rack; samplers; analog synths; mixers; step-time drum machines; effects; real-time multitrack sequencer; full automation of all fader and control movements; patching and routing possibilities; full synchronization with other MIDI equipment; total recall; setup and sounds are saved with song; self contained song format; AIFF and WAV file export; ASIO; MME; DirectX and Soundmanager support; 500 MB of high quality samples; REX files; kits and patches. SYSTEM SPECS: Macintosh; Windows.

Rebirth RB-338 (Steinberg): Total integration with Steinberg Cubase VST 2.0; up to eighteen individual audio channels direct to VST; alternative drum machines available; virtual software instrument; includes two synthesizers and two drum machines; inspired by the legendary TR-808, TB-303, and TR-909, originally created by Roland Corp.; unique sounds and visual images reborn through digital simulation by Propellerhead software; distortion units, PCF, compressor, shuffle, and digital delay; quirks and subtle qualities of analog synths, coupled with convenience of modern computers; minimum of cables; integration with sequencer software; complete front panel automation; real-time audio streaming; no external samplers or special cards required; mixer section with panning, level, effect, and distortion; audio quality: 16-bit, 44.1kHz output stereo export of stereo AIFF or Wave audio files; MIDI clock synchronization to external hardware. SYSTEM SPECS: Macintosh; Windows.

Recycle! (Steinberg): Audio processing tool for drum loops and grooves; uses a technique called slicing to "atomize" loops; once a loop has been sliced, it is transmitted to user sampler and mapped to keyboard; can also be sent to Steinberg Cubase VST as an audio part; from there the final audio is played back; automatically slaves tempo of any drum groove to sequencer tempo; layers grooves originally recorded in different tempi; groove quantizes loops as fast and simple as with any MIDI recording; sends different sounds in the groove to different sampler outputs; removes and/or replaces sounds without altering the feel; transmits and receives samples from most popular samplers; Windows and Macintosh specific features. SYSTEM SPECS: Macintosh; Windows.

Red Roaster 16-Bit (Hohner): Mastering and writing program for audio CDs; record mix on the hard disk of PC; mastering of CD. SYSTEM SPECS: 486/66 or higher, Windows 3.1 or higher, 8

MB of RAM, SCSI-Controller, CD-Writer that supports the "Disc-at-Once" Mode.

Red Roaster 24-Bit (Hohner): Converts audio material into a 24-bit float format and stores it on hard drive; audio-editing and processing is done in 24-bit format; difference in the sound quality. SYSTEM SPECS: Windows 95.

Retro AS-1 Soundburst Collection (BitHeadz): Set of 384 high quality synth presets for the Retro AS-1 software synthesizer; wide variety of sounds programmed by Sound Burst Italian sound design company; Soundburst Collection included with Retro AS-1 version 2.0. SYSTEM SPECS: Macintosh; Windows.

Retro AS-1 Virtual Analog Synthesizer (BitHeadz): Classic Analog sounds; mind warping effects; wicked filters; unlimited lfo's; up to sixty-four notes of polyphony. SYSTEM SPECS: Macintosh; Windows.

Retro AS-1 VST Virtual Analog Synthesizer Plug-In (BitHeadz): All the features of Retro AS-1 packaged into Steinberg's VST 2.0 plug-in format; offers Cubase users the convenience of using Retro's synthesis engine as a plug-in within the VST sequencing environment. SYSTEM SPECS: Windows 95/98.

Retro Lite Virtual Analog Synthesizer (BitHeadz): Entry-level softsynth package; based on the Retro AS-1 Virtual Analog Synthesizer; affordable solution for generating classic analog synth sounds from computer. SYSTEM SPECS: Macintosh; Windows.

Roland Virtual Sound Canvas VSC-88H3 (Roland): Turn MIDI files into stereo WAVE files; MIDI player and software synthesizer; over 900 high quality sounds; twenty-six drum sets built-in reverb, chorus, delay, and TVF. SYSTEM SPECS: Hybrid.

SampleHeads (SampleHeads): Real sound sample libraries; 100 percent copyright free; www.sampleheads.com; AUDIO CD or CD-ROMs for AKAI, E-MU (EOS), Gigasampler, Roland 700 series, SampleCell (AIFF files/Mac), and WAV files (ACID compatible). SYSTEM SPECS: Macintosh; Windows.

Samplitude 2496 v.5.5 (Sek'd): Search for audio that contains energy in various frequency bands; effects can be applied to individual audio clips, not just tracks; MIDI sequence editing and enhanced track count; all the same features as Samplitude 2496 but lacks multiband dynamics processing and 96 kHz support. SYSTEM SPECS: Windows 95/98/NT, 2000.

Samplitude Multimedia (Hohner): Real hard disk recording and playback; supports mono and stereo projects; four tracks: four mono or two stereo; undo function with up to one hundred levels; non-destructive editing; automatic loop optimization; edit audio material; record mono or stereo tracks directly onto the hard disk; sample editing options include cut, copy, paste, loop optimization, sound effects, equalizer, and sample rate converters. SYSTEM SPECS: 486 or better, will work with 386, Windows 3.1 or better, 4 MB RAM, 16-bit Windows-compatible sound card.

Samplitude Pro (Hohner): All the features of Samplitude Multimedia version plus more; eight tracks: eight mono or four stereo; MIDI sample drum support for transferring samples with MIDI samplers; high quality resampling, time stretching, pitch-shifting functions; sample rate conversion; track bouncing for converting virtual projects into a physical file; combine up to eight tracks; real-time surround effect for virtual projects; for audio to video; record while playing; requires support of the mode by the sound card. SYSTEM SPECS: Windows.

Samplitude Studio (Hohner): All the features of the Pro Versions; can have up to sixteen tracks: sixteen mono or eight stereo; runs multitasking with MIDI sequencers; high quality digital filters; external synchronization via SMPTE/MTC/MIDI clock; dynamics compressor, expander, limiter, noisegate with real-time preview; time display and transport bar; real-time scrubbing, varipitch with sound card. SYSTEM SPECS: Windows.

SC-Pro Editor (Roland): Provides mixing, editing, and storage of every feature on the Sound Canvas and other Roland GS and GM modules, including SCC1, SC-55, SC-155, CM-300, JV-30, SC-7, E-70, etc.; edit and design new sounds, new scales, and tunings; plays MIDI files so can hear changes while being made. SYSTEM SPECS: Macintosh; Windows.

Sequoia (Sek'd): High-end digital audio workstation system; for sophisticated stereo and multitrack editing; HD recording tools; cut and cross fade features for precise audio editing; report/interview edits, complex assembling of classical music productions or editing of dialogue for film, video, and radio plays; developed in cooperation with distinguished audio engineers and music producers. SYSTEM SPECS: Windows.

Siren Jukebox (Sonic Foundry): Music management engine; allows users to customize the viewing of music collections by applying filters, groupings, and sort functions normally found in advanced database applications; playlists can be imported and exported; song files can be accessed from a hard drive, removable media, or network directory; updated interface including a compact mode that reduces the application into one of many user-selected skins; 16-band equalizer; advanced reverb effects; ability to slow down or speed up songs; plays and encodes both MP3 and Windows Media files and transfers music to popular MP3 portable devices; supports Microsoft's Internet Keyboard Pro with Intellitype software. SYSTEM SPECS: Windows 98, Windows NT, and Windows 2000 operating systems.

Sonar (Cakewalk): MIDI Sequencing; digital recording; audio loop editing; integrated multitrack recording, editing, mixing, and delivery of audio and MIDI. SYSTEM SPECS: Windows.

Sonique (Mediascience): MP3 player and encoder software; MP3 and WAV compatible. SYSTEM SPECS: Windows.

Sound Driver (Emagic): Sound management and editing; over 300 dedicated modules or adaptations for popular MIDI devices; universal module for creating adaptations; context sensitive online help system; intelligent dependency management; automatic MIDI patchbay support; automatic device scanning; computer-based patch editing; create and recall backup of sound and effects at any time. SYSTEM SPECS: Macintosh; Windows.

Sound Forge (Sonic Foundry): Hard disk-based digital sound editor for Windows; record, edit, and play mono or stereo files using any Windows-compatible sound card; resolutions of 8- or 16-bit with sample rates ranging from 2,000 to 60,000 Hz are fully supported; choose SMPTE, time, samples, frames, measures, and beats for position entry or display; open more than fifty windows simultaneously; accommodate rapid construction of complex sound files using extensive drag-and-drop support; customizable workspace with docking toolbars; context sensitive online help; expandable plug-in architecture; preview and clear operations prior to removing data; open dialog displays internal sound file information, permits multiple files selection, and auditions Microsoft WAV files. SYSTEM SPECS: Windows 95, all Windows NT platforms, and Windows 3.1 on a single CD-ROM.

Sound Forge XP (Sonic Foundry): Record and play 8- or 16-bit audio; works with any Windows-compatible sound card; edit with multilevel undo/redo; powerful audio processing tools and effects; copy, cut, and paste to more striking media files; output RealAudio, RealMedia, Active Streaming format, Java AU and Microsoft AVI files; upgrade patch from Sound Forge XP to the full-featured Sound Forge. SYSTEM SPECS: Windows.

Sound Jam MP Plus (Sound Jam): MP3 player and encoder software; MP3 and WAV compatible. SYSTEM SPECS: Macintosh.

Soundsuite (Voyetra): Audio Power Pack for Multimedia PC; AudioStation; VideoStation; ImageStation; AudioView; MIDI Orchestrator; Jukebox; MIDI Screen Saver; Audio Calendar; Say It; Sound Events; SoundScript; VoiceNet; Level Controller; MIDI Orchestrator Plus; Music Gallery; Additional Files and Utilities. SYSTEM SPECS: Windows 3x or 9x.

Steve Reid's G.P. Software Percussion Module (BitHeadz): Exotic percussion; trigger sounds in real time from any MIDI keyboard; incorporate instruments into MIDI sequencer running on same computer; comes in Unity DS-1 and Voodoo format. SYSTEM SPECS: Macintosh; Windows.

Stream Anywhere (Sonic Foundry): Software solution for developing high-impact streaming media for the Internet; develop dynamic multimedia presentations that integrate easily into any Web site or export directly into Microsoft FrontPage projects; import or capture video files; use the visual time line interface to trim clip and add fade-ins and fade-outs to audio and video; commands and markers that synchronize other Web events as streaming media plays back; overlay logo as an image watermark; encode project to multiple Web streaming formats and bit rates in a single operation to maximize audience's viewing potential. SYSTEM SPECS: Windows 9x, NT, 4.0, or 2000, 233 MHz processor (400 MHz recommended), Windows-compatible sound card, 32 MB RAM, 5 MB hard disk space for program installation, DirectX Media 6.0 Run Time or later; Internet Explorer 4.0 or later to view online.

Surreal (Seer Systems): Brings audio quality of professional music synthesizers and samplers to the personal computer; add piano, brass, percussion, guitar, bass, classic synth, techno, ambient, and other musical instruments and sounds; makes sound card sound better; sixty-four-note polyphony; up to sixteen channels; control panel for each channel; five forms of synthesis include sample playback, FM, physical modeling, analog, and modal; built-in sequence player; wide variety of sounds; full GM patch set; eight GS drum kits. SYSTEM SPECS: Windows.

TDM (Digidesign): Available on Pro Tools|24, Pro Tools|24 MIX, and Pro Tools|24 MIXplus; foundation of Digidesign's professional mixing environment; 24-bit, 256-channel data highway delivers full-featured mixing and real-time digital signal processing (DSP) capabilities; exceeds performance of real-time host-based alternatives; offers power on demand for easy expandability; can add another DSP Farm or MIX Farm card; immune to latency and trade-offs between plug-in count, edit density, automation, and track count often necessary on host-based systems; for digital mixing and processing. SYSTEM SPECS: Macintosh; Windows NT.

Techno Ejay (Voyetra): Create songs in techno, drum 'n bass, trance, and acid jazz; more than 3,000 samples; sixteen tracks per song. SYSTEM SPECS: Windows 95/98/ME or NT 4.0.

Tempo Tantrum Drum Loops (BitHeadz): Collection of drum loops and breakbeats specially treated for Unity DS-1's Oscillator Stretch feature; change loop tempo without changing pitch; compatible with Phrazer. SYSTEM SPECS: Macintosh; Windows.

Tempo Tantrum Virtual Breakbeats (BitHeadz): CD-ROM; over 200 megabytes of stereo drum loops; instantly adjust the tempo and feel of each breakbeat! SYSTEM SPECS: Macintosh; Windows.

Toast CD Recording Software (Adaptec): Create data, audio, or multimedia CDs with mouse clicks; compile audio tracks from different sources; store and distribute data files, graphics, images, and video on CDs quickly and easily; select what to record then drag-and-drop tracks or directories into the Toast window or icon for one touch CD recording; standard CD formats including Mac HFS, IOS, 9660, Mac/IOS Hybrid with or without shared data, Audio CD, Video CD, CD-1, CD Extra (Blue Book), Mixed Mode (data+audio); supports AppleScript; SCSI CD-recorders; supports almost all CD-recorders; Auto-loader supports for automatic recording. SYSTEM SPECS: Macintosh, SE30 or newer, 68040 or PowerMacintosh recommended, Macintosh OS 7.5.1 or later, 8 MB of RAM, 24 recommended, 4 MB on hard disk.

Tubes, Tines, and Transistors Virtual Keyboard Library (BitHeadz): Features Hammond organs, vintage synthesizers, and other keyboard instruments; Unity sample engine included for instant access to all instruments and total integration with MIDI sequencer. SYSTEM SPECS: Macintosh; Windows.

Tune 1000 (Hal Leonard): General MIDI files; sound-alike arrangements; songs of top artists; lyrics display; backup vocal parts; 157 titles in catalog. SYSTEM SPECS: General MIDI-compatible keyboard.

Twiddly Bits MIDI Files (Keyfax): Standard MIDI files; real musicians playing real instruments; hundreds of riffs, runs, patterns, grooves, and licks; sequences can be cut and pasted; drums, keyboard, guitar, horn section, and more. SYSTEM SPECS: Macintosh; Windows.

Unisyn Editor/Librarian (Mark of the Unicorn): Manages synthesizers and MIDI effects; morph gradually from one sound to another; sort by name and date; support of 215 MIDI devices; create unlimited libraries of banks of sounds; recall any sound without ROM cartridges or floppy disks; use full screen to create new sounds using virtual faders and graphic envelopes; create unlimited new patches or generate randomly with user selectable parameters. SYSTEM SPECS: Macintosh; Windows.

Unity DS-1 (BitHeadz): Real-time time-stretching within oscillators; up to 128-note polyphony; three new filter types; multitap chorus; support for Digidesign DirectConnect; support for automated OMS and FreeMIDI sound names. SYSTEM SPECS: Macintosh.

Unity DS-1 Real Time Digital Sampler (BitHeadz): Software sampler; editing; compatibility; award winning. SYSTEM SPECS: Macintosh; Windows.

Unity Player Real Time Digital Sample Player (BitHeadz): All the features of Unity DS-1 in a package designed for sample playback; geared towards musicians and producers not requiring advanced editing features; professional quality sample playback. SYSTEM SPECS: Macintosh; Windows.

VAZ Modular (Software Technology): Can run sixteen separate synths at once, each with up to sixteen-note polyphony and up to 255 modules; includes sample-playback module, several types of filters, support for DirectX, VST, and ASIO, and arpeggiator, pattern sequencer, MIDI control of on-screen sliders and delay, chorus, phaser, flanger, and reverb effects. SYSTEM SPECS: Windows 95/98.

Vegas Pro (Sonic Foundry): Multitrack recorder and editor; audio production; tools for video and Internet authoring; efficient and versatile audio production environment; simple drag-and-drop operations; visually align, cut, paste, move, and cross fade audio events between tracks or on the same track with sample-level precision; synchronize video and audio frame by frame; streaming media productions and presentations; music composition, multitrack remixing; film scoring; broadcast editing and Internet content creation; add time line metadata; automatically synchronize Web pages with media files; support for many popular digital audio and video formats and hardware inputs and outputs; create and manipulate several audio files at once; play back audio while recording or overdub new audio; unlimited number of tracks without limits or restrictions; nondestructive editing of multiple tracks with visual alignment; import multiple file formats (AIF, AVI, MOV, MP3, MPG, WAV) into the same project or on the same track without having to convert them; DirectX Audio plug-in support; Undo/Redo history; professional recording tool for live performances and in-studio productions; save projects in Windows Media Technologies 4.0 and RealNetworks RealSystem G2 formats; add time line metadata to audio and video files, such as URL captions and markers. SYSTEM SPECS: Windows Processor 200 MHz Operating System, Microsoft Windows 9x, NT 4.0, or 2000, at least 32 MB RAM, at least 20 MB free disk space, Windows-compatible sound card, CD-ROM drive for installation from a CD, VGA display, DirectX Media Runtime 6.0, and Internet Explorer 5.0 (both included on CD-ROM).

Virtuosa Gold (Virtuosa Gold): MP3 player and encoder software. SYSTEM SPECS: Windows.

Voodoo (BitHeadz): Programmable beatbox for triggering drum samples and loops from computer keyboard, MIDI or sequencer; up to four samples can be layered on each of the fourteen performance pads for velocity switching; piano-roll and event-list editing supported; filtering and effects; hundreds of drum samples. SYSTEM SPECS: Macintosh.

Wave Burner (EMagic): CD mastering program with cross fade options for perfect transitions; real-time 44.1 kHz conversion; CDTEXT support; full PQ editing; cross fades; used with an Audiowerk2 card, includes WAVEBurner, or an Audiowerk8 card,

can record DAT tapes, or other sources, directly to hard disk; CD document automatically grows in the background; converts 48 kHz DAT output to the Red Book required 44.1 kHz in real time during recording; create master CD for glassmaster, archive, or Red Book master for final duplication writing; speed 1x-8x; recording function; digital or analog sources; interactive WAVEform display; nondestructive editing; nondestructive normalizing; full PQ editing; tracks, pauses and indexes; audio in track pauses; tracks with multiple audio files; multiple tracks from one audio file; supported data formats; SDII and AIFF; SDII regions; mono, interleaved stereo, split stereo; import of 20/24-bit files with dithering; import of files with 32 or 48 kHz; disc image export/import; text export (track list). SYSTEM SPECS: Macintosh: Power Macintosh, 32 MB RAM, SCSI CD recorder or other supported recorders.

Wavelab (Steinberg): Sound editor; professional audio processing; time stretching; pitch shifting; dynamic processing; frequency analysis; batch processing; integrated audio database; supports WAV, AU, RQW, and AIFF files (8-, 16-, 20-, 24-bit); load sounds from a sampler into a computer; handle multimedia material; everything in one program with a single interface; recording and editing; correcting mistakes; detailed analysis; final cut; CD mastering; 24-bit, 96 kHz resolution with an appropriate audio card; true 32-bit program; no delay when scrolling; no waiting when zooming in or out; true 24-bit audio support; cut, copy, paste between different formats; real-time processing; six slots for real-time dsp processors; fourteen plug-ins supplied; complete stereo editing; extended stereo/dual mono mode; vst plug-in compatible; full Red Book compatible CD burning. SYSTEM SPECS: Windows 95/NT, 16 MB RAM, 486 DX, Pentium 120 MHz or faster.

Winamp (Nullsoft): MP3 player software; MP3 and WAV compatible; plug-ins. SYSTEM SPECS: Windows.

Windows Media Player (Microsoft): Streaming audio and video; MP3 and WAV compatible; supports RealAudio and RealVideo formats. SYSTEM SPECS: Macintosh; Windows.

XAudio MP3 Player (Xaudio): MP3 player software. SYSTEM SPECS: Unix.

Xing MP3 Encoder (Xing Technologies): MP3 encoder software. SYSTEM SPECS: Windows.

Xmms (Xmms Project): MP3 player software. SYSTEM SPECS: Linux; Unix.

X-pose Visual Sampler (Steinberg): No dedicated video hardware required; combine music and visuals; easy to use; turn PowerMac into a digital video tool; displays visuals triggered from Mac or MIDI keyboard on monitor in full screen resolution (640 x 480); apply video FX in real time; assign any visuals to a key, add an effect on top, activate the engine, and hit a key; includes a variety of powerful video FX: twirls to zooming and plasma to morphing, all in real time. SYSTEM SPECS: Macintosh OS PowerPC, 16 MB RAM minimum, System 7.5.3 or higher, double speed CD-ROM, 256 color monitor or better.

Xx (U&I): Uses algorithmic composition tools to generate harmonic, melodic, and rhythmic variations on MIDI data; pattern-based tools can create complex arrangements from simple source melodies; PICT files can be used as source material; included in the U&I Studio Bundle, which also includes MetaSynth and graphic-oriented mixing application called Meta-Track. SYSTEM SPECS: Macintosh.

Zap (EMagic): Loss-free compression of audio files for archiving and transmission of high quality audio data via the Internet; zero-loss audio packer; stand-alone application; archive digital audio recordings via digital audio compacting; digital audio can be compressed up to 90 percent without any loss of information; when expanded from compressed files, original audio is restored with bit accuracy; typical reduction between 20 percent and 60 percent; supports SDII, AIFF, and WAV; mono, split, and interleaved stereo files; creates .zap or .sea archives; Drag&Drop of folders and volumes; background processing; pre-listen function of zapped audio files; multiprocessor support. SYSTEM SPECS: Macintosh; Windows.

Plug-Ins

A8 (Seasound): PCI card/breakout box audio interface equipped with eight channels of 24-bit/96kHz A/D and D/A conversion, plus stereo monitor outs—all .25 inch; input/output switch lets user monitor input or output signals; two volume knobs give user separate control over monitoring levels; can also be used as an expansion module for Seasound's Solo two-channel mic preamp/audio interface. SYSTEM SPECS: Macintosh; Windows 95/98.

AD8 Pro (Swissonic): Combination eight-channel mic preamp and AD converter with word clock I/O; variety of sources (microphones, guitars, keyboards, etc.) can be connected to XLR/phone jack inputs; two channels feature an insert jack; all channels support 44.1/48/88/96kHz sampling rates; using the 88.2/96kHz mode, two ADAT lightpipe outs will transmit audio in S/MUX, a format that uses two 44.1/48kHz channels to transmit one 88.2/96kHz signal allowing user to record 24-bit/96kHz audio into ADAT. SYSTEM SPECS: Windows.

Ambisone (Steinberg): Mix VST tracks in full 3D stereo; includes placing sound sources outside or above the speakers to provide mix with width and depth. SYSTEM SPECS: Macintosh; VST.

Apogee UV22 Encoder (Steinberg Mastertools): Available for Soundscape SSHDR1, Mixtreme, and R.Ed digital audio workstations. SYSTEM SPECS: Windows 95/98/NT.

AudioFX (Cakewalk): DirectX audio plug-ins for digital audio; add real-time, 32-bit, audio processing to Windows music applications; AudioFX1 includes a compressor/gate, limiter, expander/gate, and dynamics processor; with AudioFX2, can simulate amplifiers and tape simulation to add to tone; with AudioFX3, can create custom reverb in any environment. SYSTEM SPECS: Windows 95/98.

Audiosuite (Digidesign): Available on all Pro Tools systems; AudioSuite plug-ins provide file-based processing; process or alter sound file and create new file with processed sound; resulting effect is uniform across the entire file; for conserving DSP power and certain types of processing where there is no real-time benefit or application, such as normalization and noise reduction. SYSTEM SPECS: Macintosh; Windows 98/NT.

Audiosystem EWS88 D (TerraTec): 24-bit/96kHz EWS-series PCI digital audio interface cards; provides optical I/O for either eight channels of ADAT in and out, or stereo S/PDIF signals, coaxial S/PDIF I/O, and a stereo analog out minijack; can serve as sample-rate converter by routing signals from optical to coaxial connectors and vice versa. SYSTEM SPECS: Windows 95/98/NT.

Batch Converter Plug-In (Sonic Foundry): Time-saving utility for converting tens, hundreds, or thousands of sound files to a different format; for a multimedia developer needing to support different computer platforms and compression formats, or a sound engineer requiring a specific sample rate; reduces the process to a few simple mouse clicks; installs within Sound Forge. SYSTEM SPECS: Windows.

Compressor X (Sonic Timeworks): Available for Soundscape SSHDR1, Mixtreme, and R.Ed digital audio workstations. SYSTEM SPECS: Windows 95/98/NT.

D Pole Filter Module (Steinberg): Offers experimental capabilities; filter voice with five filter types; morph a simple acoustic drum loop into a dance rhythm using the LFO; add overdrive to a lead guitar; create new audio material for sound FX purposes. SYSTEM SPECS: Hybrid; VST.

Declicker (Steinberg): High-performance DSP plug-in for real-time restoration of audio material; restore vinyl or gramophone records; removal of static discharge cracks; removal of digital clicks; for any remastering suite. SYSTEM SPECS: Windows; VST; DIR X; TDM.

Denoiser (Steinberg): Removes broadband noise from any source of audio material in real time; reduce noise by up to 20dB without creating any artifacts; denoise of single takes or complete recordings; remastering of historical recordings; denoising of speech in post-pro or broadcast. SYSTEM SPECS: Macintosh; Windows; VST, DIR X, TDM.

Direct X Acoustics Mirror (Sonic Foundry): Imparts the acoustics of real environments, signal processors, and microphones onto sound files; can simulate responses from large concert halls to the sound of an old microphone. SYSTEM SPECS: Windows; DIR X.

Direct X Noise Reduction (Sonic Foundry): Analyzes and removes background noise such as tape hiss, electrical hum and machinery rumble from sound recordings; separate click removal and vinyl restoration tools for specific conditions are also included. SYSTEM SPECS: Windows; DIR X.

Direct X XFX 1 Plug-In (Sonic Foundry): Six plug-in effects: Simple Delay, Multitap Delay, Reverb, Chorus, Pitch Shift (maintaining the correct tempo or speed), and Time Compression (maintaining the correct pitch); create multi-effects within Sound Forge; with real time previewing. SYSTEM SPECS: Windows; DIR X.

Direct X XFX 2 Plug-In (Sonic Foundry): Six plug-in effects: Graphic Equalizer (ten-band), Parametric Equalizer (four Filter Modes), Paragraphic Equalizer, Graphic Compressor, Multiband Limiter, and Noise Gate; hear the results as screen setting change; for mastering and CD prep. SYSTEM SPECS: Windows; DIR X.

Direct X XFX 3 Plug-In (Sonic Foundry): Six plug-ins: Amplitude Modulation, Gapper-Snipper, Flange-Wah-Wah, Vibrato, Distortion, and Smooth-Enhance; optimizes editing time by allowing real-time previews; as parameters for an effect are modified, the result is heard immediately; can be used with any Windows audio editor that fully supports DirectX Audio plug-ins, including Sound Forge. SYSTEM SPECS: Windows; DIR X.

DSP•FX (Power Technology): Gives PC-Digital Audio Workstation users access to real-time effects processing with pro studio quality; every one of the DSP•FX plug-ins has received excellent reviews in the leading audio magazines; works in real time with Cakewalk Pro Audio, Cubase VST, Sound Forge, WAVElab, Samplitude, Cool Edit Pro, and other high-end pro-quality programs. SYSTEM SPECS: Windows; DIR X.

Dynamics (TDM) (Drawmer): Plug-in for Pro Tools; includes gating, compression, and limiting; increases the number of instantiations per DSP chip, doubled from two to four; expander/compressor/limiter plug-in based on Drawmer's DL241 Auto Compressor and DL251 Limiter. SYSTEM SPECS: Windows.

Easy Waves Audio Track and EZVerb Hybrid Plug-In (Waves): Easy-to-use reverb; loads, previews, and processes twenty-one different reverb "dry" and "wet" setups including concert halls, plates, rooms, cathedrals, tight drum rooms, and more; provides the four most frequently used audio processing tools in one application; features a four-band True

Parametric Equalizer, Compressor/Expander, and Gate. SYSTEM SPECS: Hybrid.

ED UA-30 (Roland): Part mixer, part digital audio interface; equipped with two faders and two types of digital I/O connectors: S/PDIF coax and optical; UA-30 can shuttle digital audio into and out of PC via USB; stereo line ins and outs (RCA), .25-inch mono ic/guitar input, and minijack stereo headphone out; Syntrillium Cool Edit pro multitrack recording software for Windows is included. SYSTEM SPECS: Windows.

EMagic Plug-Ins (EMagic): Native audio editing under Macintosh and Windows; new proprietary plug-ins; 32-bit floating point precision for audio formats up to 24-bit/96 kHz; underlying algorithms; design goal for plug-in series was to take the best circuit design concepts known and model them digitally; audio processing tools with added options; plug-in Overview: Fat EQ, Compressor, Expander, Noise Gate, Enveloper, Overdrive and Distortion, Bit-Crusher, AutoFilter, Spectral Gate, Tape Delay, Stereo Delay, Modulation Delay, Phaser, Ensemble, Pitch Shifter, PlatinumVerb, GoldVerb, SilverVerb, EnVerb; detailed information regarding which program version contains which plug-ins can be found in the Comparison Charts at the EMagic Web site. SYSTEM SPECS: Macintosh; Windows.

Free-D (Steinberg): 3D audio simulation; gives space that audio needs in the mix; position material anywhere; place the lead vocal a little bit further to the right or left, or to the rear a few inches away. SYSTEM SPECS: Macintosh; VST.

Free-Filter (Steinberg): Linear phase real-time 1/3 octave equalizer tool; up to thirty bands; offers fine adjustment for all sensitive frequency regions; accurate analyzing ability of Free-Filter; with the morph function, can morph between the source and processed file at any time. SYSTEM SPECS: Hybrid; VST; DIR X.

Fusion:Filter (Opcode): Audio filter technology; control any of the independent filter modules with tempo-programmable LFOs, envelopes, or the sequence modulator. SYSTEM SPECS: Macintosh; Windows; Audio Suite; DIR X; TDM; Adobe Premier; Digital Performer.

Fusion:Vinyl (Opcode): Add worn record sound into audio files; make mixes sound like an old 45 record; complete control over the pops, scratches, warp, RPM, and more. SYSTEM SPECS: Macintosh; Windows; Audio Suite; DIR X; TDM; Adobe Premier; Digital Performer.

Fusion:Vocode (Opcode): Creates unusual sounds; emulate retro and modern vocoder effects; clear interface; fuse sounds with one another. SYSTEM SPECS: Macintosh; Windows; TDM Version works with Digidesign Products; Audio Suite; DIR X; TDM; Adobe Premier; Digital Performer.

IBOX 8 XLR24 and IBOX XLR Fibre
(Soundscape): 240-bit A/D and D/A converter with
eight balanced XLR inputs and outputs; word
clock/super clock I/O and eight channels of TDIF and
ADAT I/O; iBox XLR Fibre is a 20-bit A/D and D/A
converter that also features eight balanced XLR ins
and outs, along with eight channels of TDIF and
ADAT I/O; XLR Fibre lacks word clock/super clock
IO of the XLR24; both units can be connected to
Soundscape's R.Ed, SSHDR1-Plus, and Mixtreme
systems via TDIF cable. SYSTEM SPECS: Windows 95/98/NT.

12 Ultramaximizer (Waves): 2U stand-alone limiter and 24-bit/96kHz A/D and D/A converter; includes IDR technology; allows for 24-bit dithering
down to 16-bit; equipped with balanced stereo analog
(XLR), S/PDIF (coaxial), and AES/EBU (XLR) I/O.
SYSTEM SPECS: Windows.

Loudness Maximizer (Steinberg): Dynamics
processor; algorithms specifically optimized for lift-
ing the effective loudness of audio material; zero-
overshot limiting/guaranteed clip-free loudness
maximization; loudness maximization for mastering;
zero-headroom optimization; SYSTEM SPECS:
Macintosh; Windows; VST; DIR X; TDM.

**Magneto Analog Tape Sound for Digital
Audio Workstations** (Steinberg): Brings the positive qualities of analog recording to digital system;
recreates the sound of analog tape saturation; for almost any musical instrument: drums, bass, vocals,
synth, and the final mix. SYSTEM SPECS: Hybrid;
VST; DIR X; TDM.

Maxxbass Hybrid Plug-In (Waves): Extends
bass response to include frequencies that are two octaves below the original limit; takes bass to the
maximum regardless of speaker size or audio source;
allows the perception of low frequencies to be increased; actual energy associated with low frequencies
is reduced; makes the speaker more efficient and extends the bass response; natural reproduction of the
signal over small speakers; effect of a subwoofer over
full range speakers. SYSTEM SPECS: Hybrid.

Native EQ Works Package (t. c. electronic):
Includes two plug-ins: TC Native EQ-P and TC
NATIVE EQ-G; Native EQ-P features seven fully
configurable bands and three additional bands, controlled by a joystick and preset for fast treble and
loudness control; the seven bands can be assigned to
work as parametric, hi shelf, lo shelf, or notch filters,
or any combination; Native EQ-G is a twenty-eight
band graphic equalizer with a graphic interface for
access to the band gain controls; draw the desired frequency response onto the display with the mouse, and
the EQ is set; user can operate with full twenty-eight,
fourteen, or seven bands; bands can be grouped for
easier settings. SYSTEM SPECS: Windows; DIR X.

Native Essentials Package (t. c. electronic):
Line of digital signal processing plug-ins for Direct X

compatible audio applications such as Cakewalk,
SoundForge, WAVELab, Cool Edit Pro, and Cubase
VST PC; entry-level, three-function software plug-in
bundle including TC quality reverb, equalization, and
dynamics processing. SYSTEM SPECS: Windows;
DIR X.

Native Power Pack Plug-Ins (Waves): Uses the
CPU of computer to give quality sound for recording,
mixing, or multimedia; complete system of software
processors that plug into many audio editing pro-
grams, including Cubase VST, Pro Tools 4, Sound
Forge, Deck II, WAVELab, Cakewalk, and Studio
Vision; includes the following plug-ins: TrueVerb
Virtual Room/Reverb Processor, Q10 Parametric EQ,
C1 Compressor/Gate, WAVEConvert (Multimedia
Batch File Processor), L1 Ultramaximizer, and S1
Stereo Imager. SYSTEM SPECS: Macintosh; Win-
dows.

Native Reverb (t. c. electronic): Intuitive user interface; includes Color, Diffuse, and Shape; integrate
all aspects of reverb tail sound design into a highly
graphical interface; permanent ROM presets within
the plug-in provide the important basic kinds of reverbs; can be quickly and simply edited and saved into
custom user presets. SYSTEM SPECS: Windows;
DIR X.

Nuendo 8 I/O (Steinberg): Eight-channel A/D and
D/A 24-bit/48kHz converter; provides eight channels
of ADAT I/O (via lightpipe) and eight channels of
TASCAM TDIF I/O; will perform bit-splitting
whereby 24-bit audio data can be recorded onto 20-
and 16-bit machines; Sync Align and Sync Check
functions guarantee data alignment throughout a digital system and allow user to monitor clock sync
status for errors. SYSTEM SPECS: Windows
98/NT.

Nuendo PCI 96 52 (Steinberg): I/O card provides
twenty-six ins and outs via three ADAT lightpipe
connectors, one S/PDIF optical I/O and one S/PDIF
coaxial I/O; supports recording and playback of 24-bit
audio with variable sample rates (32, 44.1, 48, 88.2,
and 96kHz); S/MUX format is supported for recording
24-bit/96kHz audio onto ADAT; word clock is available with included expansion card. SYSTEM SPECS:
Windows 98/NT.

Pro-FX Plus (Waves): Bundle adds Doppler and
Enigma processors, for a total of six plug-ins in the
Pro-FX bundle; Doppler plug-in's effect can be triggered manually or automatically based on signal
level; can control start/stop points, air damping, reverb tail and path curve; intended to create complex
filtering, the Enigma plug-in combines a notch filter,
short delay feedback loops, and a modulator.
SYSTEM SPECS: Macintosh; Windows 95/98/NT.

QTools/AX Plug-In (QSound Labs): Audio processing technologies; transform music and sound effects into realistic, multidimensional audio; set of
three plug-in tools providing mono-to-wide-3D, ste-

reo-to-3D and mono-to-positional 3D effects; extends the capability of standard stereo systems; optimized for Cakewalk Pro Audio. SYSTEM SPECS: Windows; DIR X.

Ray Gun (The Noise Zapper) (Arboretum Systems): Restore the sound quality of vinyl and tape recordings; removes pops, clicks, hum, hiss, and other noise automatically. SYSTEM SPECS: Macintosh; Windows.

Real-Time Audiosuite (Digidesign): RTAS available on Digi ToolBox and Digi 001 or any system with Pro Tools LE; plug-ins similar to regular AudioSuite; both rely on computer's CPU or host-based processing to do processing; functionally, are more like TDM Plug-Ins, where effect parameters can change in real time and are not permanently written as part of audio file; other real-time benefits such as automation; limited by available CPU processing power. SYSTEM SPECS: Macintosh; Windows 98.

RealVerb (Kind of Loud): Stereo version plug-in that includes most of the parameters found in Real-Verb 5.1; ability to morph between room shapes and wall materials. SYSTEM SPECS: Macintosh.

RealVerb 5.1 (Kind of Loud): Plug-in for Pro Tools; map reverberations spatially with four location controls; specify and morph between two room shapes and wall materials. SYSTEM SPECS: Macintosh.

Red Valve-It (The Tube Preamp Plug-In) (Steinberg): Includes a preamp with different tube sound characteristics and speaker emulations; deliverers any sound. SYSTEM SPECS: Macintosh; VST; TDM.

Renaissance Compressor Plug-In (Waves): Factory presets serve as starting points; from vocal to master program to supercrunch settings; produces fat, punch, smooth, or pumping qualities. SYSTEM SPECS: Macintosh.

Restoration-NR (Arboretum): High-resolution hiss removal plug-in for Windows sound editors; uses up to 4,000 separate filter bands for noise reduction; automatic adaptive filtering; Learn mode; high-end preservation features; artifact reduction technology; 24-bit/96kHz compatible; works with any Windows audio card. SYSTEM SPECS: Windows.

Roomulator (Steinberg): For different size ambiences; provides highly flexible, natural sound reverb; dense hall reverbs with canyon-like decay times; simulated narrow spaces or close-up situations; all-in-one five plug-in reverb effects kit. SYSTEM SPECS: Macintosh; VST.

SFX Machine (Peak): Combines power and flexibility of modular synthesis with convenience of a multi-effects unit; includes sophisticated DSP algorithms; edit screen offers easy access to all controls; create effects such as tremolo, vibrato, am, fm, chorus, delay, echo, flanging, ring mod, echofeedback, multivox, pitch tracked panning, sitar drone, crystal

glissando, and more. SYSTEM SPECS: Bias Peak, Deck II 2.5, Vision 3.5 or later, and Premiere; Power PC Macintosh, System 7.1 or later, 16 MB RAM, 3 MB available hard drive space.

Sound Bridge (Alesis): Latest version for Alesis QS-series synths; enables user to map individual sounds into a single multisampled instrument; can download software from Alesis Web site. SYSTEM SPECS: Windows.

Sounds and Cycles (Steinberg): Professional sound library with REX files for Cubase VST; professional sampling/sound libraries produced for Steinberg by Sounds Good; each title presents 300-400 MB (500-1,000 Sounds) of audio material presented in four different formats on each title; formats are WAV, AIFF, Audio, and REX; compatible with everything that does sampling and hard disk recording; six different volumes available for each style of music; triple disk set; original and license free samples; loop connector; titles in series work interactively as one library of interchangeable loops. SYSTEM SPECS: Macintosh; Windows.

Spark (TC Works): TDM version of Spark mastering software; includes restoration tools de-noising and de-clicking; Pro Tools users can run up to four TDM plug-ins with native processing plug-ins simultaneously inside Spark. SYSTEM SPECS: Windows.

Spectralizer (Steinberg): Enables spectral enhancements of digital audio recordings without artifacts or noise caused by the analog device itself; does not affect the phase. SYSTEM SPECS: Windows; VST; DIR X; TDM.

Spectrum Analysis Plug-In (Sonic Foundry): Offers Sound Forge users a powerful method of analyzing vital frequency content in digital recordings; powerful analysis capability of the two graphic formats: Spectrum Graph and the Sonogram display; installs within Sound Forge. SYSTEM SPECS: Windows.

Steinberg Plug-Ins (Steinberg): Software modules which add more functionality (effects, synths) to host applications like Cubase VST, WaveLab, or Nuendo; Q-Metric HiEnd seven-band parametric equalizer plug-in; SPL DeEsser HiEnd DeEsser plug-in; EQ-1 classic valve equalizer plug-in; Free-D Realtime 3D simulation plug-in; GRM Tools sound manipulation plug-in collection for VST; GRM Tools Vol. 2 sound manipulation plug-in collection for VST; Quadrafuzz Multiband distortion plug-in; D-Pole Waldorf filter module; Voice Designer Real-time voice pitch transformer Plug-In; Free Filter Linear phase 1/3 octave equalizer plug-in; Loudness Maximizer real-time loudness optimizer; Magneto Analog tape sound; Mastering Edition complete mastering solution; Spectralizer real-time sonic optimizer; Model-E Virtual analog synthesizer for VST Platforms; LM-4 VST drum module; Pro-52; Waldorf

PPG; Wave 2.V classic wavetable synthesizer for VST. SYSTEM SPECS: Macintosh; Windows.

Surround Bundle for Nuendo (Steinberg): Comprises six plug-ins designed for 5.1 surround-sound mixing; can be linked for up to eight-channel operation without losing balance of the surround mix; octocomp compressor, octoMaxx loudness maximizer, OctoQ seven-band parametric EQ, and OctoVerb reverb; two tools included specifically for low-frequency emitter; LFE Splitter generates bottom-end signal based on frequencies it extracts from specific channels; LFE Combiner feeds extracted signal back to specified channels. SYSTEM SPECS: Windows 98/NT.

Systems Hyperprism (Arboretum): Available for soundscape SSHDR1, Mixtreme, and R.Ed digital audio workstations; Soundscape version of Hyperprism includes Bass Maximizer, Tube-Tape Saturation, Sonic Decimator, Quasi Stereo, Filter 1, Filter 2, Ring Modulator, Flanger, and Phaser plug-ins found in the Macintosh version. SYSTEM SPECS: Windows 95/98/NT.

Systems Hyperprism 2.5 (Arboretum): Includes three new plug-ins: Granulator, Formant Pitch Shift, and HyperPhaser; Granulator allows user to chop up audio files into small pieces and rearrange them; Formant Pitch Shift lets user change size of singer's head and throat; HyperPhaser has eight separate resonant filters, configurable as either bandpass or band-reject, all under LFO control. SYSTEM SPECS: Macintosh.

TC Tools 3.0 (TC Works): TDM plug-in bundle for Pro Tools; includes reverb, EQ, and chorus; replaces or updates previous TC Works TDM plug-ins; MegaReverb plug-in replaces original TC Reverb; user interfaces of TC EQSat and TC Chorus/Delay updated to same look as MasterX and MegaReverb. SYSTEM SPECS: Windows.

Voice Tools (TC Works): Plug-in bundle for Pro Tools 24/Mix; includes Intonator, used for pitch correction and Voice Strip virtual channel strip with compressor, de-esser, EQ, low-cut filter/gate, and SoftSat; can be used to emulate sound of analog gear. SYSTEM SPECS: Windows.

WD8 (Swissonic): For digitally equipped studios such as Digidesign; word-clock generator/distributor; for connection with non-synchronizable devices such as DAT and multitrack recorders. SYSTEM SPECS: Windows.

4

Web Sites for Musicians

The Web sites listed in this chapter are all music related, or are in some way of practical use to musicians. They are organized by category, then alphabetically. Most of the **URLs** *(Uniform Resource Locators)* or *Web addresses* begin with **http://**, meaning *hypertext transfer protocol*. This is the protocol by which computers exchange information on the *World Wide Web,* or **www.** A Web address also includes the host's name, that being the name of the server location or computer from which the information is being received, a two- to three-letter designation for the type of server it is on, the directory path, sometimes followed by one or more subpaths, and a file name. There are six three-letter codes used in the U.S. to indicate the type of server or domain: **.com** = commercial, **.edu** = educational, **.gov** = government, **.net** = network, **.org** = nonprofit organization, and **.mil** = military. Addresses outside the U.S. may have a two-letter code at the end of the server location, such as **.uk** (United Kingdom) or **.au** (Australia).

A *home page* is the starting point on a Web site, which is often composed of many Web pages. A home page usually includes a table of contents, logos, photos, and links to other pages on the Web site. Most of the Web sites included in this chapter have information about the company, product, or organization, bios, a description of services, goals, or projects, answers to frequently asked questions or *FAQs,* images, graphics, sound, contact information, and links to related Web sites on the Internet.

Search engines, also known as *Web searchers* and *search directories*, are a great help in finding information on the Web. By choosing a category or subject heading, or submitting a word or descriptive phrase, one can locate any type of information. The search engine retrieves lists of related hypertext links.

Because these lists can often be very long, it is important to sift through them, deleting unwanted, outdated, or unnecessary links. Some search engines help to narrow or refine a search, and some will eliminate duplicate site listings. Setting *bookmarks* or *favorites* saves the trouble of typing in the URL each time a Web site is accessed, making it possible to quickly find and click on to frequently visited sites. An extensive list of search engines can be found in this chapter (see "Search Engines").

In trying to locate music-related Web sites of interest and of value, a lot of "sifting" was done before choosing those listed in the forty-eight categories that follow. Although some Web sites could be listed under more than one category, each one is listed only once, under what was believed to be the most appropriate category. As with music software programs, URLs are subject to change and discontinuation. As this book is being printed, new Web sites will appear, and some will expire. If any topic of interest, such as a particular artist or composer, is not listed here, simply do a search. It is important to regularly use a search engine to find the most current information available. Happy surfing!

Artists A-Z

10,000 Maniacs **www.maniacs.com**
Abba **www.abbasite.com**
Aerosmith **www.aerosmith.com**
Aimee Mann **www.aimeemann.com**
Al Jarreau **www.jarreau.com**
Alanis Morissette **www.alanismorissette.com**
Alice Cooper **www.alicecoopershow.com**
Amy Grant **www.amygrant.com**
Arlo Guthrie **www.arlo.net**

Average White Band
    www.averagewhiteband.com
*B*witched* **www.b-witched.com**
Backstreet Boys **www.backstreetboys.com**
Bad Company **www.bad-company.com**
Bad Religion **www.bad religion.com**
Badfinger **www.badfinger.com**
Barenaked Ladies **www.barenakedladies.com**
Beach Boys **www.beachboysfanclub.com**
Beastie Boys **www.beastieboys.com**
Beck **www.beck.com**
Bee Gees **www.columbia.edu/-
    brennan/beegees**
Bela Fleck and the Flecktones
    www.flecktones.com
Bellamy Brothers **www.bellamybros.com**
Bill Anderson **www.billanderson.com**
Bjork **www.bjork.co.uk**
Black Crowes **www.blackcrowes.com**
Black Sabbath **www.blacksabbath.com**
Blink 182 **www.blink182.com**
Blondie **www.blondie.net**
Blues Traveler **www.bluestraveler.com**
Bob Dylan **www.bobdylan.com**
Bob Marley **www.bobmarley.com**
Bon Jovi **www.bonjovi.com**
Bonnie Raitt **www.bonnieraitt.com**
Boston **www.boston.org**
Boyzone **www.boyzone.co.uk**
Brian Ferry/Roxy Music
    www.dlc.fi/~hope/main.htm
Brian Wilson **www.cabinessence.com/brian**
Britney Spears **www.britneyspears.com**
Brooks and Dunn **www.brooks-dunn.com**
Bryan Adams **www.bryanadams.com**
Bush **www.bushonline.com**
B-Witched **www.b-witched.com**
Captain Beefheart **www.beefheart.com**
Cat Stevens **www.catstevens.com**
Charles Mingus **mingusmingusmingus.com**
Charlie Daniels **www.charliedaniels.com**
Cheap Trick **www.cheaptrick.com**
Chely Wright **www.chely.com**
Cher **www.cher.com**
Chet Atkins **www.chetatkins.com**
Christina Aguilera **www.christina-a.com**
Clint Black **www.clintblack.com**
Cocteau Twins **www.cocteautwins.com**
Commander Cody **www.commandercody.com**
Country Joe **www.countryjoe.com**
Cranberries **www.cranberries.com**
Crosby, Stills, Nash, & Young **www.csny.net**
Crystal Gayle **www.crystalgayle.com**

D'Angelo
    **www.okayplayer.com/dangelo/interface.
    htm**
Dave Matthews Band
    www.davematthewsband.com
David Bowie **www.david.bowie.com**
David Lee Roth **www.davidleeroth.com**
Dean Martin **www.deanmartinfancenter.com**
Deborah Harry
    www.primenet.com/~lab/deborahharry
Deep Purple **www.deep-purple.com**
Def Leppard **www.defleppard.com**
Depeche Mode **www.depechemode.com**
Diamond Rio **www.diamondrio.com**
Dixie Chicks **www.dixiechicks.com**
Don Henley **www.donhenley.com**
Doobie Brothers **www.doobiebros.com**
Dr. Dre **www.dre2001.com**
Dwight Yoakam **www.dwightyoakam.com**
Eagle-Eye Cherry **www.eagleeyecherry.com**
Earth, Wind, and Fire
    www.earthwindandfire.com
Eddie Money **www.eddiemoney.com**
Ellis Paul **www.ellispaul.com**
Elton John **www.eltonjohn.org**
Elvis Costello **www.elvis-costello.com**
Elvis Presley **www.elvis-presley.com**
Emerson, Lake, and Palmer
    www.emersonlakepalmer.com
Eminem **www.eminem.com**
Enrique Iglesias **www.enriqueig.com**
Eric Burdon **www.ericburdon.com**
Everclear **www.everclearonline.com**
Fabulous Thunderbirds
    www.fabulousthunderbirds.com
Faith Hill **www.faith-hill.com**
Fatboy Slim
    www.skint.net/artists/fbs/index.html
Fisher **www.fishertheband.com**
Foreigner **www.foreigneronline.com**
Frank Sinatra
    www.nj.com/sinatra/gif/upperleft.gif
Frank Zappa **www.zappa.com**
Fresh **www.mdvdnetwork.com**
Fugees
    www.sony.com/music/artistinfo/fugees
Garbage **www.garbage.com**
Garth Brooks **www.planetgarth.com**
Gary Puckett and the Union Gap
    www.puckettgap.com
Gene Clark **www.geneclark.com**
Genesis **www.genesis-web.com**
George Michael **www.planetgeorge.org**
George Strait **www.georgestrait.com**
Goo Goo Dolls **www.googoodolls.com**

Grand Funk Railroad
    www.grandfunkrailroad.com
Grateful Dead **www.dead.net**
Hal Ketchum
        www.curbrecords.com/home.html
Hanson **www.hansonline.com**
Herbie Hancock **www.herbie-hancock.com**
Hole **www.holeonline.com**
Hootie & The Blowfish **www.hootie.com**
Hot Tuna **www.hottuna.com**
Innosense **www.innosense.com**
Iron Butterfly **www.ironbutterfly.com**
Iron Maiden **www.ironmaiden.com**
J. Geils Band **www.jgeils.com**
J. J. Cale **www.jjcale.com**
James Brown **www.funky-stuff.com**
Jamiroquai **www.jamiroquai.co.uk**
Jennifer Lopez **www.jenniferlopez.com**
Jerry Lee Lewis **www.jerryleelewis.net**
Jessica Andrews **www.jessicaandrews.com**
Jessica Simpson **www.jessicasimpson.com**
Jethro Tull **www.j-tull.com**
Jimi Hendrix **www.jimi-hendrix.com**
Joan Jett **www.joanjett.com**
Joe Cocker **www.cocker.com**
Joe Satriani **www.satriani.com**
Joe Walsh **www.joewalsh.net**
John Fogerty **www.johnfogerty.com**
John Mellencamp **www.mellencamp.com**
John Michael Montgomery
    www.johnmichael.com
Johnny Cash **www.johnnycash.com**
Joni Mitchell **www.jonimitchell.com**
Journey **www.journeytheband.com** or
    www.journeycontinues.com
k. d. lang **www.kdlang.com**
Kate Bush **www.gaffa.org**
Keith Emerson **www.keithemerson.com**
Kenney Chesney **www.kchesney.com**
Kid Rock **www.kidrock.com**
Kiss **www.kissonline.com**
Korn **www.korn.com**
Kraftwerk **www.kraftwerk.com**
Kylie **www.kylie.com/kylieultra.html**
Lauren Hill **www.laurynhill.com**
Led Zeppelin **www.led-zeppelin.com**
Lee Ann Womack **www.leeannwomack.com**
Leonard Cohen **www.serve.com/cpage/LCohen**
Lynyrd Skynyrd **www.skynyrd.com**
Li'l Kim **www.lilkim.com**
Lila Mccann **www.lilamccann.com**
Limp Bizkit **www.limp-bizkit.com**
Little Feat **www.littlefeat.net**
Lonestar **www.lonestar-band.com**

Lorrie Morgan **www.lorrie.com**
Lou Reed **www.loureed.org**
Lovin' Spoonful **www.lovinspoonful.com**
Machinehead **www.machinehead1.com**
Macy Gray **www.macygray.com**
Madonna **www.madonnanet.com/mland**
Marc Anthony **www.marcanthonyonline.com**
Maria Muldaur **www.maria.muldaur.com**
Mariah Carey **www.mcarey.com**
Marilyn Manson **www.marilynmanson.net**
Mark Lindsay **www.marklindsay.com**
Marshall Tucker **www.marshalltucker.com**
Martina McBride **www.martina-mcbride.com**
Matchbox Twenty **www.matchboxtwenty.com**
Meatloaf **www.meatloaf-oifc.com**
Megadeth **www.megadeth.com**
Mel Tillis **www.meltillis.com**
Melissa Manchester **www.melissa-manchester.com**
Meredith Brooks **www.meredithbrooks.com**
Metallica **www.metallica.com**
Michael Jackson **www.neverland.dk3.com**
Michael Penn
    **www.epiccenter.com/EpicCenter/
    MichaelPenn**
Michael Peterson **www.michaelpeterson.com**
Molly Hatchet **www.mollyhatchet.com**
Moody Blues **www.moodyblueworld.org**
Morrissey **www.morrissey-solo.com**
Muddy Waters **www.muddywaters.com**
N'Sync **www.nsync.com**
Nanci Griffith **www.gbla.com/nancigriffith**
Natalie Imbruglia **www.natalieimbruglia.com**
Neil Young **www.neilyoung.com**
Neville Brothers **www.nevilles.com**
Nine Inch Nails **www.9inchnails.com**
No Doubt **www.nodoubt.com**
Oasis **www.oasisnet.com**
Ozark Mountain Daredevils
    www.ozarkdaredevils.com
Ozzy Osborne **www.ozzynet.com**
Pat Benatar **www.benatar.com**
Paul Revere and the Raiders
    www.paulrevereraiders.com
Pavarotti **www.deccaclassics.com**
Pearl Jam
    www.sonymusic.com/artists/pearljam
Pete Townshend **www.petetownshend.com**
Peter and Gordon **www.peterandgordon.com**
Peter Frampton **www.frampton.com**
Peter Gabriel **www.petergabriel.com**
Phish **www.phish.com**
Pink Floyd **www.pinkfloyd.com**
Prince **www.npgonlineltd.com**

Public Enemy **www.public-enemy.com**
Puff Daddy **www.puffdaddy.com**
Queen **www.queen-fip.com**
Radiohead **www.radiohead.com**
Rage Against the Machine **www.ratm.com**
Raspberries **www.raspberries.net**
Reba McIntire **www.reba.com**
Red Hot Chili Peppers
      www.redhotchilipeppers.com
REM **www.remhq.com**
REO Speedwagon **www.speedwagon.com**
Ricky Martin
      www.rickymartinmanagement.com
Robbie Williams **www.robbiewilliams.co.uk**
Rod Stewart **www.rodstewartlive.com**
Roger McGuinn **www.mcguinn.com**
Roger Whittaker **www.rogerwhittaker.com**
Rolling Stones **www.the-rolling-stones.com** or
      www.stonesworld.com
Ronnie Milsap **www.ronniemilsap.com**
Rush **www.rush.net**
Santana **www.santana.com**
Sarah Brightman **www.sarahbrightman.co.uk**
Sarah McLachlan **www.sarahmclachlan.com**
Savage Garden **www.savagegarden.com**
Savoy Brown **www.savoybrown.com**
Sepultura **www.sepultura.com.br**
Shania Twain **www.shania-twain.com**
Sheena Easton **www.sheenaeaston.com**
Shelby Lynne **www.shelbylynne.com**
Sherrie Austin **www.sherrieaustin.com**
Sheryl Crow **www.sherylcrow.com**
Simply Red **www.simplyred.co.uk**
Sisqo **www.sisqo.com**
Slipknot **www.slipknot1.com**
Sly and the Family Stone **www.slyfamstone.com**
Smashing Pumpkins **www.smashing-**
      pumpkins.net
Sound Garden **www.imusic.com/soundgarden**
Spencer Davis Group **www.spencer-davis-**
      group.com
Spice Girls **c3.vmg.co.uk/spicegirls**
Statler Brothers **www.statlerbrothers.com**
Steely Dan **www.steelydan.com**
Steppenwolf **www.steppenwolf.com**
Steve Miller Band **www.stevemillerband.com**
Steve Vai **www.vai.com**
Steve Winwood **www.stevewinwood.com**
Sting **www.stingchronicity.co.uk**
Super Tramp **www.supertramp.com**
Suzanne Vega **www.vega.net**
Taj Mahal **www.taj-mo-roots.com**
The Artist **www.npgonlineltd.com**
The B-52s **www.theb52s.com**

The Buckinghams **www.thebuckinghams.com**
The Cure **thecure.com**
The Doors **www.thedoors.com**
The Guess Who **www.theguesswho.com**
The Mavericks **www.themavericks.com**
The Red Hot Chili Peppers
      www.redhotchilipeppers.com
The Rolling Stones **www.the-rolling-**
      stones.com
The The **www.thethe.com**
The Turtles **www.theturtles.com**
The Verve **the-raft.com/theverve**
The Who **www.thewho.net**
They Might Be Giants **www.tmbg.com**
Tim McGraw **www.timmcgraw.com**
TLC **www.peeps.com/tlc**
Todd Rundgren **www.tr-i.com**
Tom Jones **www.tomjones.com**
Tom Petty **www.tompetty.com**
Tommy James **www.tommyjames.com**
Tori Amos **www.toriamos.com**
Trace Adkins **www.traceadkins.com**
Travis Tritt **www.travis-tritt.com**
Trisha Yearwood **www.trishayearwood.com**
Tupac Shakur **www.tupacshakur.com**
U2 **www.u2one.com**
Van Halen **www.van-halen.com**
Van Morrison **www.harbour.sfu.ca/-**
      hayward/van/van.html
Vertical Horizon **www.verticalhorizon.com**
Victoria Shaw **www.victoriashaw.com**
Vince Gill **www.vincegill.com**
Violent Femmes **www.vfemmes.com**
Whitney Houston **www.whitneyhouston.com**
Will Smith **www.willsmith.net**
Yes **www.yesworld.com**
Yoko Ono **www.yoko.com**
Z Z Top **www.zztop.com**

Ballet—Ballroom and Modern Dance—Ice Skating Music

American Ballet Theatre
      www.abt.org/home.html Home page.
Ballet Alert! **www.balletalert.com** Ballet in
      America and around the world; information on
      ballets, companies and dancers; ballet talk for
      fans; dancer of the week; weekly quiz; photos;
      interviews; articles about ballet.
Ballet and Dance Art **www.danceart.com** E-zine
      for dancers; feature articles; chat and message
      boards; interviews with famous dancers; advice
      from teachers.
Ballet Dance Home Page
      balletdance.miningco.com or

**balletdance.about.com/arts/balletdance/
mbody.htm** One of over 700 sites.

Ballet Dancers' Injuries
   services.worldnet.net/aguierre Ballet-
   related injuries.

Ballet Dictionary **www.abt.org/dictionary**
   Ballet words and terms.

Ballet **www.Ballet.co.uk** UK dance Web site and
   discussion group.

Ballet News
   **www.vicnet.net.au/vicnet/ballet/ballet.
   html** The Australian Ballet.

Ballet Shop **ballet.net-shop.net** Ballet books,
   music, and video.

Ballet: The Classical Method Instructional Video
   www.amproductions.com/ballet.html
   Ballet exercises; tone body; improve posture;
   video with classical music.

Ballet-DANS Library Listings
   **www.chebucto.ns.ca/Culture/DANS/
   Library/ballet.html** Ballet-related books,
   videos, CDs, and cassette tapes.

BalletWeb Index **www.novia.net/~jlw** Classical
   ballet site; photo essays; commentary;
   QuickTime animations; reader-submitted ballet
   jokes.

Ballroom Dance Music Resource-Dance Plus
   www.danceplus.com Ballroom dance supply
   company; strict-time ballroom dance CDs from
   all over the world.

Ballroom Standard and Latin Dance Music
   **www.palominorecords.com/dancelisten/
   catalogue.htm** UK strict tempo ballroom
   dance music producers specializing in
   standard/modern and Latin music.

Critical Dance **www.criticaldance.com**
   Moderated bulletin board; news articles;
   interviews with dance celebrities; performance
   reviews; links to popular dance sites.

Dance and Music World
   **www.expage.com/page/danceandmusicw
   orld** Free monthly E-mail E-zine.

Dance Books Online **www.dancebooks.co.uk**
   Publish and sell books, CDs, videos, and DVDs
   on dance and human movement.

Dance Links **www.dancer.com/dance-links** One
   of the largest collections of dance-related links.

Dance Magazine **www.dancemagazine.com**
   Magazine on dance music.

DanceWeb **www.danceWeb.co.uk** Interactive
   directory; searchable database for all sorts of
   dance related information.

English National Ballet **www.ballet.org.uk** UK's
   premier touring ballet company; highest quality
   classical ballet at prices everyone can afford;
   news; performances; resources.

Lotus **www.lotusarts.com** Music and dance
   multicultural studio.

New York City Ballet **www.nycballet.com** E-
   mail list; season details; tickets.

Nutcracker Ballet **www.nutcrackerballet.net**
   History of the Nutcracker Ballet; music; links;
   movies; information on performances.

On the Ice-Music History
   **members.xoom.com/C_A_M_3/
   MusicHistory.htm** Links to each ice skater's
   performing music history.

Russian Classical Ballet **www.aha.ru/~vladmo**
   History; outstanding choreographers; ballet
   teachers; ballet dancers; musicians; education;
   photo gallery.

San Francisco Ballet **www.sfballet.org** Repertory
   season; casting information.

The Art of Ballet
   **www.geocities.com/Vienna/Choir/6862/
   classics.html** Ballet; dance information;
   photos; clip art; ballet class; performing arts;
   adult beginners; instructional; classics; MIDI;
   famous ballets; steps; exercises; stretching tips;
   recommended books and videos; links.

The Bolshoi Theater Ballet and Opera
   www.alincom.com/bolshoi The great
   Russian composers; classic performers; modern
   performers; noteworthy performances; history of
   the Bolshoi Theater; meet Vladimir Vassiliev.

The Joffrey Ballet of Chicago **www.joffrey.com**
   Leading ballet company; performs the finest
   ballets from the great choreographers of the
   twentieth century.

The Kirov Ballet and the Kirov Academy
   www.kirovballet.com or **www.kirov.com**
   or **www.Webcom.com/shownet/kirov**
   Based in St. Petersburg, Russia; dates back 250
   years; Kirov Academy in Washington, D.C.
   upholds the tradition.

The National Ballet of Canada
   www.national.ballet.ca/home.html
   Repertoire; tickets; artists.

The National Ballet School
   www.nationalballetschool.org School of
   ballet.

The Royal Ballet School **www.hubcom.com/rbs**
   School of ballet.

USA International Ballet Competition
   www.usaibc.com Official International Ballet
   Competition site in the USA.

Booking—Touring—Gigging—
Clubs and Venues

Air Travel Manager **www.airtm.com** Airline
   reservation system.

Air Traveler's Handbook
   www.cs.cmu.edu/afs/cs/user/mkant/

Public/Travel/airfare.html Travel
information.

American Bed & Breakfast Association
www.abba.com Regional directory of bed and
breakfasts.

Amtrak **www.amtrak.com** Train schedules and
reservations.

Atlanta Night Clubs
**www.atlantaentertainment.com/
ATLANTA/clubs.htm** Nightclub guide for
Atlanta.

Atlas of the World
cliffie.nosc.mil/~NATLAS/atlas Maps of
cities and countries.

AutoPilot **www.freetrip.com** Maps and driving
directions.

Barnes & Noble **www.barnesandnoble.com**
Chain store venue; list of stores nationwide;
contact the community relations coordinator.

Billboard International Talent & Touring Directory
www.billboard.com *International Buyer's
Guide:* labels, publishers, wholesalers,
distributors, manufacturers; *Record Retailing
Directory:* independent record retail stores,
chains, contacts, specialty; *Country Music
Sourcebook:* Country labels, publishers, radio
stations.

Borders Books and Music
www.borders.com/stores/index.html
Chain store venue; list of stores nationwide by
state, including contact information, phone,
address, directions; contact the community
relations coordinator at each store.

Boston Night Guide
www.bostonnightguide.com Guide to
Boston nightlife; bars, clubs; restaurants;
dancing; date spot; events and more.

Chicagoland Night Clubs **chicagoclubs.8m.com**
Dance clubs in the Chicagoland area; all types of
nightclubs; information about each one.

City Guide **cityguide.lycos.com** Information on
world cities.

Club Connexion **www.clubconnexion.com**
Guide to UK clubs.

Club New York **www.clubnyc.com** Club resource
online.

ClubPlanet.com **www.clubnyc.com** New York
music clubs.

Clubs by Night **www.phx.com/listings/music/
CLUBS_BY_NIGHT_INDEX.html** Club
calendar listings.

Clubs Index **www.clubsindex.com** Online
nightclub database.

CNN Airport **cnn.com/airport** Flight information;
travel news; weather.

CNN Weather **cnn.com/WEATHER** Four-day
forecasts for towns in the United States and many
cities around the world.

CNN: Travel Guide **www.cnn.com/TRAVEL**
Travel journalism and multimedia.

Cowboys.com: Night Clubs
www.cowboys.com/nightclubs.htm
Information on horses, cattle, tack, guest
ranches, rodeos, country music, dancing,
Southwestern art, Western wear, collectibles,
food, events, classified ads, and more.

Digital City: Austin-Bars & Clubs
home.digitalcity.com/austin/bars Inside
bars and clubs; event planner; features.

DIY Tour Guide **deterrent.bc.ca/tour.html**
General information; venue size; genre; hints on
how to get a gig.

EF Performing Arts Tours **www.efperform.com**
Bring performers on tour.

EventsLINK **www.eventslink.com** Festivals,
seminars, gatherings, etc. listed by location and
theme.

Expedia **www.expedia.com** Booking and issuing
of airline tickets.

Fact 42 Online **www.fact42.com** Concert touring
industry; news; opportunites.

Factor **www.factor.ca** Touring; showcase; album
production.

Flifo Cyberagent **www.flifo.com** Travel
reservation system.

Foreign Languages for Travelers
www.travlang.com/languages Online
multilingual phrase book.

Gig Connection **www.deepblueblack.com/gig_
connection** For the touring musician.

Gig Magazine **www.gigmag.com** Webzine.

Gig Mania **www.gigmania.com** Indie music
company; music scene.

Gig Masters **www.gigmasters.com** Indie music
company.

Gig.com **www.gig.com** Home page.

GigMan **www.dedocsoft.com** Database designed
for freelance musicians, band leaders, and agents.

GigMaster **www.shubb.com/gigm.html** From
Schubb; lists, organizes, and makes easy every
aspect of gigging.

Gig-O-Rama **www.giglogic.com** Software for
working musicians.

Internet Travel Network **www.itn.net** Airline and
other reservations.

Jack's Sugar Shack **www.jackssugarshack.com**
Los Angeles club.

Las Vegas Bars, Pubs, and Night Clubs
www.lvindex.com/vegas/nite.htm
LasVegas bars and night clubs; bars with live
music; dance clubs.

Las Vegas Leisure Guide
www.best.com/~lvnv/lvnight.htm Las Vegas nightlife.

Lastminute.com **www.lastminute.com** UK live music resource; tickets to London shows.

Licensed Clubs Directory
www.afb.com.au/lcndclbs/lcndclbs.html International Licensed Clubs Directory; sporting, recreational, or nightclubs around the world.

Local Music.com **www.localmusic.com/splash** Local music scene for major U.S. cities; artists; bands; venues; events.

London Clubs
www.londonnet.co.uk/ln/out/ent/clubs. html Regularly updated guide to London's best clubs from dance music to retro; club listings; venues; reviews; previews; free tickets.

Los Angeles Bars and Dance Clubs
weekendevents.com/LOSANGEL/ lamusic.html Club guide.

Los Angeles Clubs
www.whatshotin.com/nite/la/nitela. shtml LA clubs.

Los Angeles Music Scene
www.losangeles.music.com Music in LA.

Map Blast **www.mapblast.com** Road maps online.

Map Quest **www.mapquest.com** Road maps online.

Maps On Us **www.mapsonus.com** Interactive maps.

Microsoft Expedia **expedia.msn.com** Magazine, travel agent, and resource guide.

Ministry of Sound **www.ministryofsound.com** Dance Webzine; MP3s; news; reviews; club listings.

Mr. Roadie **www.mroadie.com** Mr. Amp carts; weightless flight and instrument cases.

Musi-Cal **www.musi-cal.com** or **www.concerts.calendar.com** Free concert calendar listing dates for many musicians and venues; lists all genres, including blues, folk music, country music, classical music, and more.

Music and Gigs Link
www.musiciansgiglink.com Contacts; gigs.

National Weather Service **www.nws.noaa.gov** Weather disaster warnings.

Night Clubs In San Diego
www.insandiego.com/nightclubs.html The San Diego County Internet Directory and City Guide of over thirty clubs in San Diego County.

Night Clubs London
www.studios92.com/clubs.html Complete list of all the nightclubs in London; addresses and phone numbers.

Night Clubs USA **www.nightclubsusa.com/** Databases of nightclubs in the U.S.

Night Life and Night Clubs on the Gold Coast Australia
www.goldcoastaustralia.net/night_life/ clubs.html Guide to businesses.

Night-Out **www.night-out.co.uk** UK guide to theme bars, nightclubs, and venues.

NY Clubs **soho.ios.com/~nynet/clubs.html** New York area nightclubs.

NYCE Clubs **nyceclubs.com/clubs** Club guide.

Peak Performance Tours
www.peakperformancetours.com Touring Web site.

Performance Magazine-International Touring Talent Weekly Newspaper
www.performanceclassified.com or **www.performancemag.com** Subscription includes fifty-one weekly magazines and ten yearly directories; artist tour itineraries, news features, box office reports, international news and market reports, information about personnel and companies in the touring industry; Performance Series of Directories includes *Talent/Personal Managers; Clubs/Theatres/Colleges; Concert Productions; Facilities; Booking Agencies; International; Country Talent; The Black Book* phone and fax guide; *Manufacturers/Production Personnel;* individual directories available separately.

Pollstar **www.pollstar.com** Subscription includes weekly magazine plus five biannual directories; weekly magazine has tour itineraries, music industry news, box office summaries, *Concert Pulse Charts* for album sales and radio airplay in nine formats; directories include *Talent Buyers & Clubs, Concert Venues, Concert Support Services, Agency Rosters, Record Company Rosters;* individual directories available separately; mailing labels available for an additional fee.

Polly Esther's Night Clubs Dance Clubs Discos
www.pollyesthers.com Nightclubs, dance clubs, bars, and discos in New York City, Boca Raton, Philadelphia, Chicago, Miami, Washington, D.C., and more.

Power Gig **www.powergig.com** Book gigs.

Preview Travel **www.previewtravel.com** Airline reservation system.

Pubs & Clubs
www.cuisinescene.com/pubs/publist. htm Pubs and clubs; piano bars; breweries; wineries; distilleries; nightclubs; private clubs.

Rand McNally **www.randmcnally.com** Get directions anywhere.

Raveworld.net
> **www.raveworld.net/portal/Night_Clubs/**
> Live and on-demand audio and video streams;
> MP3 downloads; live DJ performances from top
> DJs, online record store; DJ equipment; event
> calendars, etc.

Roadie.net **www.roadie.net** True stories from the
> road.

Roadsideamerica.com
> **www.roadsideamerica.com** Unusual tourist
> attractions.

Sdam.com **www.sdam.com** San Diego bands; local
> music scene.

SFX.com **www.sfx.com** Live entertainment; all
> genres; buy tickets online.

South Florida NightLife
> **www.floridagoldcoast.com/nightlife/**
> **index.htm** Nightclubs; bars; dancing; clubs;
> pubs; listings of nightclubs organized first by
> region and then by format.

Stayfree Holiday Club **www.stayfree.org**
> Clearinghouse for home-exchange agreements.

Storm Watch **www.fema.gov/fema/trop.htm**
> Storm warnings.

Talent & Booking **www.talentandbooking.com**
> Talent and booking directories; record labels; A
> & R contact/artist roster; public relations firms.

Teen Night Spots in LA
> **home.inreach.com/chucky/rockwell/**
> **clubs.html** Clubs.

The John F. Kennedy Center for the Performing Arts
> **www.kennedy-center.org** Information on
> the performing arts center.

The Musician's Guide to Touring and Promotion
> **www.musicianmag.com** or
> **www.musiciansguide.com** Lists agents,
> bands, clubs, labels, lawyers, press, fan
> magazines, radio stations, music stores, and
> more.

The Palace **www.hollywoodpalace.com**
> Famous Hollywood venue.

The Rough Guide **www.travel.roughguides.com**
> Budget travel advice.

The Trip.com **www.thetrip.com** Online travel-
> booking site.

The Universal Currency Converter
> **www.xe.net/currency** Count in foreign
> denominations.

The Weather Underground
> **www.wunderground.com** Weather updates.

The Whiskey **www.whiskeyagogo.com** Famous
> LA club.

This Is London **www.thisislondon.co.uk** Guide
> to the city; clubs.

Time Out **www.timeout.com** Clubbing.

Total Travel Network **www.totaltravel.net**
> Planning trips.

Tour Dates **www.tourdates.com** Place to list
> bands.

Translating Dictionaries
> **dictionaries.travlang.com** Translations of
> foreign words.

TravelASSIST Magazine **travelassist.com** Online
> magazine; bed and breakfast directory.

Travelocity **www.travelocity.com** Full-service
> online travel agent.

U.S. Chambers of Commerce
> **www.uschamber.org/mall** Information on
> U.S. cities and locals.

U.S. Gazetteer **www.census.gov/**
> **cgi-bin/gazetteer** Maps of the United States.

UK Night Clubs **www.clubsuk.com** International
> UK dance night club.

Universal Currency Exchange **www.xe.net/ucc**
> Exchange money.

USA Today Weather
> **www.usatoday.com/weather/wfront.**
> **htm** U.S. weather map.

USA Today: Travel
> **www.usatoday.com/life/travel/ltfront.**
> **htm** Travel news.

Washington, D.C. City Pages: Entertainment: Clubs
> **www.dcpages.com/Entertainment/Clubs**
> / Washington, D.C. clubs.

Web of Online Dictionaries
> **www.facstaff.bucknell.edu/rbeard/**
> **diction.html** Directory of foreign-language
> dictionaries on the Internet.

Web-Chart Category: Night Clubs **www.Web-**
> **chart.com/ent/club** Regional directories of
> nightclubs; rave venues; etc.

Wholesale Travel Centre **www.trax.com/wtc/**
> Discount travel tickets.

WILMA: The Internet Guide to Live Music
> **www.wilma.com** Concert and touring
> information.

World Clubs Net **www.worldclubs.net** Guide to
> clubs around the world.

World Stage Concerts and Tours, Inc.
> **www.worldstageconcerts.com** Tours.

Worldwide Brochures **www.wwb.com** Travel
> brochures.

Worldwide Guide to Hostelling
> **www.hostels.com** Travel cheap.

Worldwide Internet Live Music Archive
> **www.wilma.com** Live music and tours in the
> U.S.; artist interviews; live chats; biographies.

Brass and Woodwind Instruments

A Physical Approach to Playing the Trumpet
> **www.trumpetbook.com** New method book
> for trumpet by Lynn K. Asper; use the body's
> reflexes to enhance trumpet performance.

A Tutorial on the Fife **beafifer.freeshell.org** Tutorial book and CD with seventy-five lessons keyed to CD tracks; forty-nine tunes of varying difficulty; tips on how to buy a new fife or recondition an old one.

AAIIRR Power AcoustiCoils for Brass and Woodwinds **www.dmamusic.org/acousticoils** Produces enhanced response for all brass and woodwind musical instruments.

Alamo Trade Woodwind & Brass Instrument Stores **www.music.teo.ie/wind.html** or **www.1source.com/alamo/wind.html** Sydney, Australia flute page; flute-in; Japanese bone flute; old wooden flute; 'Ryuteki' flute; Japanese flute; clarinet FAQ; clarinet jokes; the oboe edition.

All Woodwind & Brass **www.sydneymetro.com/allwind** Sales and service of new and secondhand woodwind and brass instruments; Sydney, Australia.

Altissimo **www.pathcom.com/-ydparish/altissimo** Technique tips, fingering charts, and articles about the saxophone.

Amazing Music World **www.amazingmusicworld.com/h_trombone.asp** Special page for trombonists.

America's Shrine to Music Museum Frequently Asked Questions **www.usd.edu/smm/FAQ.html** Serial numbers for many brass and woodwind instrument makers.

Anaheim Band Instruments **www.abimusic.com/** Brass and woodwind specialists.

Associated International Music **www.custommusiccorp.com** Educational series; tubas; euphoniums; trumpets; trombones; saxophones; bassoons; woodwinds and brass; oboes; flutes; piccolos; marimbas; xylophones; string instruments.

ASW Guide to Historical Brass Instruments **www.capecod.net/aswltd/guidebr.htm** Cornets and more.

Band & Orchestra **www.performancemusic.com/brass.html** Authorized dealers.

Band & Orchestra Product News **www.testacommunictions.com** Home page.

Band Instruments **www.encoremusicinc.com/band.html** Canadian music store.

Best Band Instruments **www.bcity.com/bbi_ireland** Musical instruments; brass and woodwind for amateur and professional musicians and music groups.

Blas-Basen **www.blas-basen.se** Brass; woodwind; big band music; Sweden.

Borodi Music **www.borodimusic.com** Brass and woodwind instruments.

Brass Band Instruments **www.fred-rhodes-courtois.com/index.htm** Brass band and woodwind instruments; northwest UK.

Brass Band World **www.brassbandworld.com** Webzine.

Brass **www.bymt.org.uk/brass.htm** Opportunities for brass players.

Calicchio Brass Musical Instruments **www.calicchio.com** Trumpets; trombones.

Charles Double Reed Company **www.charlesmusic.com** Reeds.

Chartier **www.chartierreeds.com** Reeds.

Clarinet Embouchure **clarinet-embouchure.com** Learn to make perfect embouchure; single-lip and double-lip.

Clarinet Music **www.sneezy.org/clarinet/music/index.html** Printable and MIDI files.

Cornetto **members.home.net/mieczko/cornetto.htm** The Renaissance Cornetto is a wind instrument that is a cross between a woodwind and a brass instrument.

Custom Music Co. **www.custommusiccorp.com** Tubas; euphoniums; trumpets; trombones; bassoons; oboes; brass winds.

Dean Pelling Woodwind & Brass **www.dpelling.cjb.net** Supplies and repairs.

E. M. Winston Band Instruments **www.emwinston.com** Band instruments; orchestra instruments; stands; sax straps; recorders; percussion; educational toys; mouthpieces.

Emerson Musical Instruments **www.emersonflutes.com** Emerson flutes.

Empire Brass Sheet Music **www.empirebrass.com/sheet.html** Brass arrangements.

Flute World **www.fluteworld.com** Flutes; piccolos; sheet music; accessories.

Flute.net Publications **www.flute.net/publications** Works for flute choir.

Flutes are Fun **www.releport.com/-fluter/index.html** Informative and fun links dealing with the flute.

French Horn Home Page **www.jump.net/-rboerget/Hornfaq.html** Answers to commonly asked questions about the French horn.

Gemeinhardt **www.gemeinhardt.com** Flutes and piccolos.

Giardinelli **www.giardinelli.com/** Band and orchestral instruments and accessories.

Globeclubs **globelists.theglobe.com/lists/ amati_band_instrumen/** Reviews.

Hall Crystal Flutes Inc. **www.halcyon.com/hall** Crystal Flutes; Crystal Piccolos; Panpipes; Didgeridoos.

Horn Place **www.hornplace.com** Online catalogue of music instruction books, CDs, videos, and software for tenor saxophone, alto saxophone, baritone saxophone, soprano saxophone, flute, trombone, and trumpet.

How Woodwind Instruments Work **tqd.advanced.org/3656/html/wood.htm** Like brass instruments, woodwind instruments require being blown; however, they differ from brass instruments in that they rely on a wooden reed to vibrate instead of the player's lips.

International Saxophone Home Page **www.saxophone.org** Information; resources; links.

Jazz Trombone Workshop **idt.net/ -phone/links.html** Links for the trombone enthusiast.

Jones Double Reed Products **www.jonesdoublereed.com** Jones; Meason; Pisoni; Daniel's.

Jupiter Band Instruments Inc. **www.jupitermusic.com** Jupiter Brass & Woodwinds; Ross Mallet Instruments.

Kirkland Concert Band: Instruments **alcor.concordia.ca/~smw/kcb/english/ instruments.html** Concert bands generally include woodwind, brass, and percussion instruments, but not strings.

Leblanc **www.gleblanc.com** Wind instrument manufacturer and distributor.

Let's Play the Recorder **www.frontdsk.com/lptr** Designed for classroom instruction as well as for individual use; Macintosh; Windows.

Lighthouse Media Group **www.lighthousemediagroup.com** Tips and Techniques videos for repairing band instruments, string, and percussion.

Maggio System for Brass **www.maggiomusic.com** A book for trumpet, trombone, French horn, and tuba; available in five languages.

Maintenance Tips and Repair FAQ **www.ssemusic.com/repfaq.html** Common problems, especially with beginning brass players.

Matthew's Music **www.matthewsmusic.nl** Vintage saxophones.

Mouthpiece Express.com **www.mouthpieceexpress.com** Mouthpieces and accessories for brass and woodwind instruments.

Mr. Music . . . Brass and Woodwind **www.mrmusic.co.nz/wind/brass_woodw ind.html** Services to all wind instruments; new corks or rubbers; replacement mouthpiece; oil and grease, etc.

Music Accompaniments for Woodwind, Brass, and Stringed Instruments **pages.infinit.net/daxmusic/ accompaniments** Free music accompaniments for woodwinds, brass, and strings on CD or cassette; sheet music for the solo instrument.

National Flute Association **www.nfa.flute.org** Information; resources; links.

Nine-Note Recorder Method **members.aol.com/PG9Note** Book and CD to teach children to read music and play the recorder; duets and trios for classroom instruction.

Northwest Music **www.northwest- music.com/nw-band.html** Band instruments.

Oberloh Woodwind and Brass Works **www.oberloh.com** Repairing and rebuilding.

Osmun Music **www.osmun.com** Brass and woodwind instruments; accessories.

Play the Recorder **www.frontdsk.com/lptr** Interactive format; for classroom instruction as well as individual use.

Podium Music **www.podiummusic.com** Chamber music for brass and woodwind instruments; music for hundreds of traditional and unusual instrumentations.

Rayburn Musical Instrument Company **www.rayburn.com** Brass, woodwind, and string instruments; new and used; accessories.

Recorder Music Publishers **www.iinet.net.au/~nickl/music.html** Comprehensive directory of publishers and retailers of music for the recorder.

Recorder Teacher **www.theshops.co.uk/childsplay** Software program for learning to write and read music, and to play the recorder; Windows.

Rico International **www.ricoreeds.com** Reeds; mouthpieces.

Samuel King Music Publishers **demo.clickandbuild.com/cnb/shop/ samuelkingmusic** Music publisher; specialist in music for wind instruments; concert band; woodwind ensembles; solo woodwind; brass ensembles; solo brass saxophone.

Sawday's Horn Repair and Restoration **www.sawdays.com** Repair and restoration of all brass and woodwind instruments.

Secondwind **www.secondwind.co.uk** New and used brass and woodwind instruments.

Selmer **www.selmer.com** Saxophone makers.

Sheet Music for Baritone Horn
www.trombonepuppy.com/cat68.html
List of items in the category.

Sheet Music for Baritone Saxophone
www.saxpuppy.com/cat46.html or
www.saxspot.com/cat46.htm List of items
in the category.

Sheet Music for Bassoon
www.bassoonspot.com/cat28.htm List of
items in the category.

Sheet Music for Soprano Saxophone
www.saxpuppy.com/cat71.html or
www.saxspot.com/cat71.htm List of items
in the category.

Sheet Music for Tenor Saxophone
www.saxpuppy.com/cat43.html or
www.saxspot.com/cat43.htm List of items
in the category.

Sheet Music for Tuba
www.trombonepuppy.com/cat61.html or
www.trombonespot.com/cat61.htm List
of items in the category.

Softwind Instruments **www.softwind.com**
Synthophone MIDI Sax.

SR Mouthpieces **www.srtechnologies.com** SR
Technologies; SR Mouthpieces.

Sugal Mouthpieces **users.ids.net/mouthpcs**
Saxophone mouthpieces.

Tap Music Sales **www.tapmusic.com** Woodwind
and brass instrument recordings on compact
discs, tapes, records, and videocassettes; imported
and artist produced; publishes sheet music.

Tech Tips for Horn & Woodwind Players
www.idsi.net/dmmusic/tips.htm or
www.dandmmusic.com/tips.htm
Technical tips; forum for discussion.

The Bandstand Ltd. **www.bandstand.ab.ca** Wind
instrument specialists.

The Bate Collection of Musical Instruments
www.ashmol.ox.ac.uk/bat/visinf.html
Collection of historical woodwind, brass, and
percussion instruments.

The Clarinet Pages **www.sneezy.org/clarinet** or
www.sneezy.mika.com/clarinet Clarinet
pedagogy; equipment; hints; tips and techniques.

The Horn Guy **www.hornguy.com** Band
instruments; trumpet; trombone; flute; clarinet;
saxophone; sales and repair.

The L.A. Sax Co. **www.lasax.com** Saxophones;
horns.

The Music House **www.musichouse.com** Band
and orchestra rental program.

The Woodwind and the Brasswind
www.wwandbw.com Music store; large
selection of musical instruments and accessories.

Tone Music
www.tonemusic.com/accessories.html

New and used band instruments; accessories;
instrument service.

Trombone USA **www.trombone-usa.com** Home
page.

Trumpet Players International Network
www.dana.edu:80/~trumpet For trumpet
players of all ages and levels from around the
world.

Vandoren **www.daddario.com** Mouth pieces.

Verne Q. Powell Flutes Inc.
www.powellflutes.com Handmade metal
flutes; handmade wooden flutes and piccolos;
clarinet reeds; alto sax reeds; tenor saxophone
reeds; pads.

Web of Art Makers of Musical Instruments
www.netspace.net.au/~aflutist/
MANU.html Instruments; historical flutes.

Wind Player **www.windplayer.com** Webzine.

Wind Shop
www.angelfire.com/biz/thewindshop/
prices.html Repair services.

Windband **www.yell.co.uk/sites/windband-**
instruments or **www.windband.co.uk**
Specialists in woodwind, brass, folk, and early
musical instruments including bagpipes, banjos,
bassoons, clarinets, concertinas, flutes, folk
instruments, mandolins, and saxophones.

Windcraft Limited & Dawkes Music Limited
www.windcraft.co.uk or
www.dawkes.co.uk Woodwind and brass
instruments; accessories; mouthpieces; spares;
repair materials and tools.

Woodsy's Brass, Woodwind, and String Instruments
www.woodsys.com/winds.htm Band and
orchestra department.

Woodwind & Brass Instrument Stores
www.daviestrek.com/music/wind.htm
Tuba; trumpet; French horn; double reeds;
woodwind and brass instruments.

Woodwind Instruments **www.minstrels-**
music.co.uk/woodwind.htm Learning the
recorder in school.

*Woodwind, Brass, and Percussion Instruments of the
Orchestra*
www.music.indiana.edu/~l631/skei.
html William and Gayle Cook Music Library,
Indiana University School of Music;
bibliographic guide.

Zachary Music **www.zacharymusic.com**
Clarinet, trumpet, trombone, flute, and
saxophone.

Zine **www.yamaha.com/band/INSTRMNT/**
index.htm Yamaha brass; woodwind;
percussion; related accessories and brass
mouthpieces.

Children's Music

Bear Children's Choir **www.bearcanada.com**
Children's music; RealAudio and RealVideo
stream and downloads; children's playground;
games and music.

Best Children's Music.com
www.bestchildrensmusic.com Children's
music for parents and teachers.

Canadian Children's Songwriters Network
**www.geocities.com/enchantedforest/
cottage/5207/ccsn.html** For writers of
children's songs.

CBC4Kids **www.cbc4kids.ca** Canadian Web site
for children.

Child Guide Music Company
www.childguidemusic.com Children's
music; Christian resources.

Children's Group **www.childrensgroup.com**
Children's music, videos, and media.

Children's Music **www.childrensmusic.co.uk**
UK-based Web site for children's music.

Children's Defense Fund
www.childrensdefense.org Information
about the organization.

Children's Television Workshop **www.ctw.org**
Children's educational programming; includes
Sesame Street.

Children's Music House
www.childrensmusichouse.com Recorded
music, videos, audiobooks, and read-alongs.

Children's Music Web
www.childrensmusic.org Non-profit
organization dedicated to music for kids;
resources; information; links; guide to children's
music online; children's concert calendar;
database of musicians; children's radio list;
RealAudio children's music programming; music
education.

Children's Music Network **www.cmnonline.org**
Music for children; information; resources; links.

Children's Pre-School Music Programs by Mr. Pete
www.mrpete.com Original theme songs;
teaching, learning, and sing-along songs; for two
to eight year olds.

Children's Songs and Rhymes
**www.wuziegames.com/childrensmusic.h
tml** Children's music and rhyme resources on
the Internet; CDs and books of songs, rhymes,
stories, games, and poems.

Coloring.com **www.coloring.com** Coloring book
online.

Crafts for Kids
**www.craftsforkids.miningco.com.
mbody.htm** Fun projects.

Daniel's French Children's Music
www.abcdaniel.com Children's songs
performed in French and English.

Discover Learning
www.bc.sympatico.ca/learning Learning
site for children, parents, and teachers.

Disney **www.disney.go.com** All things Disney;
music; graphics.

Disney Magic Music Days
www.magicmusicdays.disney.com Disney
Web site.

Dr. Toy **www.drtoy.com** Guide to children's
products; links; awards.

Educational Web Adventures
www.eduWeb.com/adventrue.html Games
for learning.

Family PC for Kids
www.yahooligans.com/content/fpc Web
site for kids.

Family Planet Music
www.familyplanetmusic.com Quality
children's music.

Family.Com **www.family.com** Online family
magazine; part of Disney.com; search box at top
of page to find children's music reviews.

Four Fish Fly Free **www.4fishkids.com** Videos
for children five to ten.

Free Children's Music by David Jack
www.davidjack.com Popular children's
music site; kid's singing star David Jack; free
MP3s, audio samples and cassette giveaways for
parents and teachers.

Free Zone **freezone.com/home** E-zine for kids.

Funnies **www.scheffer.com/funnies** Archive of
funnies and jokes.

Girl Tech **www.girltech.com/index.html**
Resources for girls on the Internet.

Go-Go-Diggity **www.go-go-diggity.com** Music
and books for children ages zero to six.

Heather's Happy Holidaze Page
www.heathersholidaze.com Music and
holiday material; links.

Horace Hopper's Musical Adventures
preschoolmusic.com Teaches the preschooler
how to play twenty-three simple songs and
phrases on the keyboard; used in an imaginary
TV show with Diana the Dinosaur and Smith the
Penguin.

Hunk-ta-Bunk-ta Music
www.hunktabunkta.com Music for children
by platinum-selling and award-winning
singer/songwriter Katherine Dines; CDs;
songbooks; performances; workshops.

In the Land of Staff **www.landofstaff.com**
Children's book series that teaches music theory
with a new method employing audiovisual
concepts with CDs and painted four-color
illustrations appropriate for primary grades.

JazzKids Music Program **www.jazzkids.com**
Useful information about jazz.

Kid Zone **www.newyorkphilharmonic.org**
Child-focused information on composers, the
orchestra, and instruments.

Kids Entertainment
www.kidsentertainment.com Children's
entertainment; music; links.

Kid's Space **www.ks-connection.org**
International Web site.

KIDiddles **www.kididdles.com** Children's music
Web site.

*KIDiddles Mojo's Musical Museum: Complete Song
List*
**www.kididdles.com/mouseum/allsongs.
html** Lyrics to hundreds of children's songs and
lullabies; stories; games; contests; search for a
song by title.

Kids Domain **www.kidsdomain.com** Web site for
kids and parents.

Kids' Camps **www.kidscamps.com** Directory of
camps.

KidsCom **www.kidscom.com** Web site for kids.

Kindermusic **www.kindermusic.com** Early
childhood music instruction.

Knowledge Adventure
www.knowledgeadventrue.com Learning
and fun for kids of all ages.

Lori Diefenbacher Music for Children
www.diefenbacher.com/lori Music for
children's education in nature, intercultural, and
early childhood; lesson plans.

Lucerito's Music **www.thegrid.net/lucerito**
Children's music in Spanish.

Mister Rogers' Neighborhood
www.pbs.org/rogers Online version of the
TV series; popular children's program.

Moscow Children's Theater of Musical Art
**moscow.lvl.ru/culture/theater/detestr/
edetestr** Profile of the famous theatre and
school.

Music and Movement
**www.perpetualpreschool.com/music.
html** More than 200 hands-on songs and music
activities for young children.

Music for Young Children **www.myc.com** Music
education program for children.

Music Together **www.musictogether.com** Early
childhood music workshops.

Musicopoly **www.musicopoly.com/cgi/disps**
or **www.musicopoly.com/cgi/dispscat.
cgi?Children%60s** Musical version of
Monopoly.

Musik Garten **www.musikgarten.org** Early
childhood music education workshops.

NNCC Music and Movement Activities
**www.nncc.org/Curriculum/cc21_music.
movement.html** Music and rhythm activities
for young children.

Only Kids Music **www.onlykidsmusic.com**
Online retailer specializing in children's music.

PEP: Parents, Educators, and Publishers
www.microWeb.com/pepsite Informational
resource on children's software and computers.

Play Music **www.playmusic.org** Introduces kids
aged seven to eleven to the instruments of the
orchestra using games, animations, audio, and
more.

San Jose Children's Musical Theater Online
www.sjcmt.com Musical theater that's young
at heart.

SchoolHouse Rock **gentxtvland.simplenet.com/
SchoolHouseRock/index-hi.shtml** Online
version of the TV series.

Seussville Games
**www.randomhouse.com/seussville/
games** Dr. Seuss books online.

Singing Stories **www.singingstories.com** Home
page.

Studio Brio **studiobrio.com** Children's musical
instruments; drums; Celtic instruments and
more.

Synergy Music **www.synergykids.com**
Children's music production company; creative
movement CD designed to help teach children the
art of dance and fitness.

The Kids **www.thekids.com** Storytelling.

The Review Corner
**www.geocities.com/~reviewcorner/
parents.html** Detailed reviews of children's
software with ratings; family software reviews;
educational product reviews; reviews of
Playstation games for kids; articles about kids
and computers; software news; software
shopper's guide.

Toys to Grow On **www.ttgo.com** Musical
instruments for kids.

Turtle Frog Music **www.turtlefrog.com** Music;
magic; stories; puppets; games; balloons;
kazoos; kid's disco; children's family
entertainment and educational music programs;
audience participation.

Twin Sisters Productions Inc.
www.twinsisters.com Educational products
for children.

Young Composers **www.youngcomposers.com**
Web site for publishing musical compositions of
kids, teens, and young adults.

Young Voices **store.yahoo.com/youngvoices**
Offers a music enrichment program for children
preschool through 2nd grade; includes games,
hands-on activities, songs, and art projects; for
parents, home schools, educators, nursery and day
care workers, and volunteers who have little
training or background in music.

Youngheart Music
> **www.youngheartmusic.com/season.html**
> Entertainment company that distributes musical
> audio and video product for the children's, family,
> and educational markets; recordings and videos of
> top children's performers.

Classical Music and Composers

All Classical Guide **www.allclassical.com**
> Classical music and CD database.

American Composers Forum Index
> **www.composersforum.org/noframe/
> acf.html** Arts service organization which
> provides grants, fellowships, recordings, and
> other services for composers of contemporary
> music.

Arioso **www.arioso.com** Concert music's online
> business directory; over 5,800 contact listings for
> performing arts groups, music schools,
> competitions, festivals, radio stations, concert
> management companies; foundation and grant
> providers.

Arsis Press: Music by Women Composers
> **www.instantWeb.com/~arsis** Publisher of
> concert and sacred music by women composers;
> music for chorus, solo voice, keyboards, and
> chamber ensembles.

Artek Recordings-Classical
> **www.artekrecordings.com** Range of
> classical music that spans traditional and well-
> known repertoire and rarely heard masterpieces
> from little-known composers.

Awadagin Pratt-Classical Music Links
> **www.awadagin.com/prattlnk.htm** General
> classical music links.

Bach MIDI Page **student-
> www.uchicago.edu/users/mao2/bach.
> html** Brief introductory information about
> Bach's organ, clavier (string keyboard), and
> orchestral music; canons, fugues, and vocal
> works.

Bach Organ Works
> **www.mhrobinson.demon.co.uk/bach.
> htm** Bach's early career was devoted to the
> organ; 250 Bach organ works have survived;
> MIDI versions of some of the most significant.

BBC Music Magazine
> **www.bbcmusicmagazine.com** Classical
> music reviews; reviews by subject; search by
> composer; search by type of music: orchestral,
> opera, choral and song, chamber instrumental.

BMG Classical Music World
> **www.classicalmus.com** Home page.

BMGClassics **www.bmgclassics.com** Classical
> music and artists.

Cadenza **www.cadenza.org** Resources and
> information for classical and contemporary music
> and musicians.

Central Links Resource for Research on Composers
> **www.lib.duke.edu/music/resources/
> classical_index.html** Information on
> composers.

Chamber Music Society of Lincoln Center
> **www.chamberlinc.org** Chamber music;
> links.

Clásica **www.clasica.com** Online guide to
> classical music performance and recordings;
> news; reviews; links to classical music-related
> sites.

Classic Online **www.klassik.com/eindex.htm**
> Comprehensive index of information about
> classical music on the Internet; links to hundreds
> of music-related Websites; free classified ads;
> television music programs.

Classical Composers Database
> **users.knoware.nl/users/jsmeets** Ever-
> growing list of composers; over 1,100 entries;
> links and contributions accepted.

Classical Insite-Competitions
> **www.classicalinsites.com/live/
> conserva/connect/fs_competit.html** Lists
> worldwide classical music competitions.

Classical Insites
> **www.classicalinsites.com/live/
> hallfame.masters/mahlbio.html**
> Collection of classical music resources; town
> square performing arts complex.

Classical Insites: Conservatory
> **www.classicalinsites.com/live/
> conserva/fundamen/** Provides viewers with
> tools for active listening; separates music into
> six fundamental parts: melody, harmony,
> rhythm, texture, color, and form.

Classical is Cool **www.classicaliscool.com**
> Classical music information and fun; list of
> classical music radio stations, program listings,
> concert schedules, and more.

Classical Links around the Web
> **www.demon.co.uk/creative/fairfiel/
> classics.html** Links to classical music Web
> sites.

Classical MIDI Archives
> **www.prs.net/midi.html** Thousands of
> classical music files to listen to or download;
> works by over 350 composers; arranged
> alphabetically by composer; public domain files.

Classical MIDI Collection **www.dtx.net/-raborn**
> Collection of MIDI files.

Classical MIDI
> **www.ndirect.co.uk/~regr/page7.htm**
> Great pieces to download; crafted by dedicated
> people who have given there time so that all can
> enjoy listening to great classical music.

Classical Music Archives **ftp.sunet.se/cma**
Thousands of classical music files; listen to at the click of a mouse; most composers are represented; search engine included.

Classical Music Bloopers
www.hubcap.clemson.edu/ -alevin/Bloopers.html Humorous collection of unintentional spelling and grammatical errors from college students in a music appreciation class.

Classical Music Cube . . . The Music Beat
www.search-beat.com/classic.htm Classical music-related links; Web directory including composers, conductors, opera, early music, and the history of classical music; beginning a classical music collection; record companies.

Classical Music Hall of Fame
www.classicalhall.org Dedicated to honoring and celebrating the many facets of classical music in the United States; seeks to recognize those who have made significant contributions to classical music.

Classical Music History Timelines on the Web . . . The History Beat **www.search-beat.com/composer.htm** Classical music history timelines; composer history resources on the Web and more.

Classical Music **w3.rz-berlin.mpg.de/cmp/musical_history.html** Music in the Western culture as the result of various influences; formalization of improvised traditions; the growth of notation; the development of tuning systems.

Classical Music **www.classical-music.net** Over 2,100 recordings from Baroque to Contemporary.

Classical Music
www.cs.cmu.edu/afs/cs.cmu.edu/user/pscheng/www/music.html Classical music FAQ; individual composers; bibliography database.

Classical Music
www.iag.net/~akoustic/classical.html Chronology of 180 classical music composers.

Classical Music **www.igc.apc.org/ddickerson/ -music.html** Classical music links; streamed audio.

Classical Music
www.scs.unt.edu/labs/music/Muslink.html Classical music sources; locate music, CDs, references, etc.

Classical Music Jukebox **www.bmcc.org/music** Listen to selections of classical music.

Classical Music Links
www.tdware.com/links/classical.htm Classical music links; features; testimonials; downloads; period instruments; performing ensembles; early music vocal ensembles.

Classical Music MIDI Page
www.odyssey.net/subscribers/scior/music.html Classical Music MIDI.

Classical Music Newsgroups
www.classicalmusic.co.uk/newsgroups.html Guide to classical music Web sites in the UK; concerts; videos; CDs; jobs; site reviews; links.

Classical Music on the Net
www.musdoc.com/classical Source for classical music on the Internet.

Classical Music on the Web (UK)
www.musicWeb.uk.net Classical and film music composer and CD review site.

Classical Music on the Web **www.Unc.edu/ -baker/music.html** Links to music resources on the Internet including high-fi music, video reproduction, and film.

Classical Music on the Web USA
classicalusa.com Resources; search engine; reviews; links.

Classical Music Online
www.scapecast.com/onworld/CMO Online resource dedicated exclusively to classical music.

Classical Music Shop
www.classicalmusicshop.com Classical music retailer.

Classical Music Suite 101
www.suite101.com/welcome.cfm/classical_music Information on classical music.

Classical Music UK
www.classicalmusic.co.uk Links, videos, CDs, concerts, and jobs; guide to classical music Web sites in the UK.

Classical Music Web Ring
www.orchestranet.co.uk/ring.html Chain of classical music Web sites; add site to the largest classical music Web ring on the Internet.

Classical Net Home Page
www.classical.net/music Comprehensive collection of information and news on classical music subjects; articles and CD reviews; composers and their music; repertoire; recommended classical music recordings; CD buying guide.

Classical Net **www.futurenet.com/classicalnet** Links to classical music resources on the Internet; includes repertoire, classical CD buying guide, recommended classical CDs, and composer data.

Classical Search **www.classicalsearch.com** Classical music search engine.

Classical USA-Classical Music on the Web
classicalusa.com Music resources on the Internet; video and film links.

ClassicWeb **www.classicWeb.com** Classical music.

Composers Biographies and Their Works **www.hnh.com/qcomp.htm** Information on composers and their works.

Composers Club **www.composers-club.de** For composers.

Composers **www.daviestrek.com/music/composer. htm** Composer links.

Composers Page **www.composers.net** Devoted to composers of all the centuries, past and present; information; snippets of music; opinions; recommendations of pieces.

Concert Finder UK **www.concertfinder.co.uk** Find classical music concerts in the UK; searchable database of events; choirs, orchestras, and recitals.

Conductors Home Page **www.hubcap.clemson.edu/-alevin** Advice on pursuing a career in conducting; information about conductors of choral and wind ensembles.

Dimension Music Connect **www.dmconnect.com/Band_Websites/ Classical** Homepages of classical music composers on the Internet.

Directories at Classical Music UK **www.classicalmusic.co.uk** Concerts; videos; CDs; jobs; site reviews and links.

Early Music News **www.earlymusic.org.uk** Events listings, concerts and festivals for Baroque, choral, Renaissance, and early music.

Early Music on the Web . . . The Classical Music Beat **www.search-beat.com/earlymusic.htm** Classical music history Internet links; timelines; composer history resources on the Web and more.

Early Women Composers/Artists/Poetry **music.acu.edu/www/iawm/pages** Annotated CD discography of music by women composers born before 1760 with bibliographic sources; MIDI sound files; notes on music publishers; illustrated by historical women artists.

Essentials of Music **www.essentialsofmusic.com** Music facts and information.

Essentials of Music **www.essentialsofmusic.com** From Sony Classical and W.W. Norton; basic information about classical music; eras; terms; composers; audio examples.

Gershwinfan.com **www.gershwinfan.com/boards/ sheet_music/** Gershwin Web site.

Get Music Classical **www.rcavictor.com** Source for classical musical enthusiasts.

Global Music Network **www.gmn.com** Classical music; downloads; streaming audio.

GMN.com **www.gmn.com** Classical, opera, and jazz; exclusive live events; buy CDs; listen to complete pieces of music; video interviews with artists; GMN radio.

Gramophone **www.gramophone.co.uk** Classical music magazine.

Grove Music-The New Grove Dictionary of Women Composers **www.macmillan-reference.co.uk/GroveMusic/TNGWC. htm** Presents information on 875 women composers who have made a significant contribution to the history of Western music.

Heitor Villa-Lobos **www.ibase.org.br/ -mvillalobos** Information on the composer.

HyperMusic History of Classical Music **www.crosswinds.net/~musichistory/ index.html** Exploration of classical music history from the Middle Ages to the twentieth century; includes the main periods, subtopics, forms, and composers important to classical music.

Impulse Classical Music Website **www.impulse-music.co.uk** or **www.cdj.co.uk/impulse** Pages on contemporary classical composers and performers; photographs; biographies; reviews; down-loadable musical tracks.

International Alliance for Women in Music (IAWM) **music.acu.edu/www/iawm/home.html** A community archive for women composers and women in music topics.

Internet Classical Music Almanac **www.u.arizona.edu/ -rcampbel/caloct.html** Interesting music-related events that took place on "this day in history."

Internet Classical Music Pages **www.u.arizona.edu/-rcambel** Music and the media, performing artists, and more; interesting links.

Internet Resources for Composers **kahless.isca.uiowa.edu/ -kcorey/sci/resources.html** Web sites of interest to composers.

Kalvos and Damian's New Music Bazaar **www.goddard.edu/wgdr/kalvos/kalvos. html** New music composers from around the world.

Klassik Online **www.klassik.com** Classical music on the Internet; resource center for classical music.

Leonard Bernstein Page **www.leonardbernstein.com/splash/ index.html** Information about the composer/conductor.

Meet the Composer **www.meetthecomposer.org** Information on composers.

MIDIWorld.com Classical
midiworld.com/classic.htm Classical music MIDI files listed by composer.

MIDIWorld.com Composers
midiworld.com/composers.htm Alphabetical listing of links to composer Web sites.

Morton Subotnick
newalbion.com/artists/subotnickm American composer of electronic music; innovator in compositions using instruments, media, and interactive computer music systems.

Mozart **www.classical.net/music/compt.lst/ mozartwa.html** Composer resource.

Multimedia Beethoven Encyclopaedia
www.geocities.com/Vienna/1636 Information on Beethoven.

Music on the Web (UK)
www.musicWeb.f9.co.uk/music/ music.htm Classical and film music composer and CD review site.

Music Resources on the Internet
www.skdesigns.com/internet/music Free music graphics; links to regional symphony orchestras and music organizations.

Music Web UK **www.musicWeb.uk.net** Search engine; UK classical news and releases.

Musical Online-Classical Music Directory
www.musicalonline.com or **www.musicalonline.net** Classical music directory; music education; music instruction; virtual concert hall; online music directory listing service and Web page design source for artists, musicians, and performers; resource for locating professional musicians and companies; listings of opera singers and instrumentalists as well as composers and conductors; opera companies and orchestras are indexed.

New Music in Classical Styles-MIDI Audio
www.Webster.sk.ca/greenwich/ musicmid.htm New music compositions in MIDI audio format written in the styles of classical, Baroque, or other traditional styles, with emphasis on counterpoint.

New Zealand Symphony Orchestra Amusements
www.nzso.co.nz/fun/index.html Entertaining anecdotes.

OrchestraNET **www.orchestranet.co.uk** UK classical music Web site.

Orchestras and Ensembles on Classical Net
www.classical.net/music/links/ musicgrp.html Guide to orchestral and ensemble groups.

Pachelbel, Johann
www.hnh.com/composer/pachelbe.htm (1653-1706) German composer of Protestant church music; *Canon in D.*

Paul Geffen's Mostly Classical Music Index
www.richter.simplenet.com/music.html Good source for classical music in general and classical record collecting; comprehensive listing of discographies.

Paul James's Modern Music Review
www.meteo.physik. uni-muenchen.de/~paul/music.htm Guide to twentieth-century century classical music; links.

Play Music **www.playmusic.org** American Symphony Orchestra League; Meet the Composer; Meet the Musician; new items.

Purcell Page **www.voicenet.com/ -hohmann/purcell/index.html** Information about the composer.

REC Music Foundation **www.recmusic.org** Promotes new classical music composers, primarily through the development of new computer tools.

Robert Finley's Classical MIDI Page
www.ultranet.com/-rfinley Classical MIDI sequences of piano and concerto works in real time; sequencing techniques; concert reviews; links to famous musician and composer sites.

Selected Classical Music Resources
www.medieval.org/emfaq/misc/ res_class.html Selected classical music resources; academic and grass-roots material link collections; music resource list; Indiana University Music Library; music resources.

Sibelius Academy
www.siba.fi/Kulttuuripalvelut/music. html Extensive list of music; instrument and art resources; based in Helsinki.

Society of Composers, Inc.
www.societyofcomposers.org Home page.

Some Classical Music Web Sites
www.maths.tcd.ie/~dwilkins/Links/ Music.html Virtual library.

Sony Classical **www.sonyclassical.com** Artists and new releases; sound clips; tour schedules; upcoming releases.

Sony Music
www.music.sony.com/Music/Classical Home of Columbia, Epic, Legacy, and associated labels; music; news; chat; videos; tour updates; information on artists; tours, Webcasts; contests.

Soundout
www.tmn.com/Oh/Community/juechi/ soundout.html Webzine for classical music; articles; interviews; new releases; reviews; links; contemporary music.

Symphonic Orchestra Samples **www.marcati.com** CD-ROMs; string ensembles, wood and brass, solos, percussion and harp, mini library, violin ensembles.

Symphony Orchestra Schedules
www.hoptechno.com/symphony.htm
Links to major symphony orchestra home pages.

The Art Music Web Ring
**classicalmus.hispeed.com/artmusic/
index.html** Classical music starting point for
composers, history, genres, forms, theory,
musicology, education, instruments, and classical
musical media .

The Cleveland Institute of Music
**www.cim.edu/library/Internet/resources.
htm** Selective list of Internet resources relevant
to classical musicians and scholars.

The George and Ira Gershwin Archive
**www.sju.edu/_bs065903/gershwin/
homepage.htm** Home page.

The J.S. Bach Home Page **www.jsbach.org**
Extensive biography; tour of Bach's life in
Germany; catalog of complete works;
bibliography; recommended recordings; other
Bach resources on the Web; Bach discussion list.

The Mozart Project
www.frontiernet.net/~sboerner/mozart
The life, times, and music of Wolfgang Amadeus
Mozart; complete Köchel listing; bibliography;
biography; links to related sites and commentary
on individual compositions.

The Picture Gallery of Composers
**www.spight.physics.univ.edu/picgair2.
html** Pictures of composers; biographies.

The Woman Composer Question
**www.interlog.com/~hartl/Kapralova/
BIBLIOGRAPHY** Comprehensive
bibliography on women in music.

Vox Music Group **www.voxcd.com** Catalog of
classical compact discs and recordings.

Yahoo Classical Music
**www.dir.yahoo.com/Entertainment/
Music/Genres/Classical** Major search
engine with an excellent list of classical music-
related links.

Young Concert Artists, Inc. **www.yca.org** Home
page.

Computer and Electronic Music—MIDI—Software

AABACA **www.aabaca.com** *Music Mastery;
Clip Creator* CD needle drop; music software
distributor; educational bundles; workshops.

ABC2Win **www.c7r.com/abc** Integrated program;
supports writing and editing of tunes, file
management, and playback; view tunes as
publication-quality music; registration enables
printing.

Acon AS Acoustica **www.aconas.de** Audio editor
for Windows 9x/NT.

Adaptec **www.adaptec.com/easycd/key** CD
burner manufacturer; *Easy CD Creator.*

Advanced Digital Audio **wwwcip.informatik.
uni-erlangen.de/~hovolk/ada** New
technology for lossless compression of high
quality audio files in real time on PC.

Adventus **www.adventus.com** Music instruction
software for Windows.

Akai **www.akai.com** Developer of the sampler;
produces digital equipment including digital
recorders, postproduction equipment, sound
modules, and support software; news; reviews;
FAQs; manual and samples to download;
software to update equipment; discussion forum.

AKG Acoustics **www.akg-acoustics.com**
Microphones; headphones; sound processing
equipment; mixers; news; distributors; links.

AKoff Sound Labs **www.akoff.com** *Music
Composer;* music recognition software; WAV to
MIDI conversion.

Alabama Music Inc.
**www.alabamamusic.com/Main/
education.htm** Sells products from a
collection of music software for learning,
producing, writing, recording, printing, and
scanning music.

Alesis **www.alesis.com** ADAT digital audio
recorder; ADAT interface a standard for
connecting digital equipment; synthesizers; synth
modules; speakers; signal processors; mixers;
drum machines; keyboards.

Alesis Semiconductor Inc. **www.alesis-
semi.com** Alesis Semiconductor.

Algorithmic Arts
geneticmusic.com/software/#softstep
Win9x modular step sequencer.

Algorithmix **www.algorithmix.com**
SoundLaundry software for cleaning and
mastering old recordings; download demos.

Alien Disko Systems 3000 **inneraktive.
e-zone.com/ladd.html** Win9X pattern based
sequencer; MIDI macros for creating fill and
overlay patterns that you can trigger on the fly.

AmazindMIDI **www.pluto.dti.ne.jp/~araki/
amazingmidi** WAV to MIDI converter for
music transcription, chord analysis, and making
MIDI files.

AMG **www.amguk.co.uk** Electronics.

Amsaro Electronics **www.amsaro.com**
Electronics.

Analog Synths **www.analogsynths.com** Home
page.

Analogue Samples **www.analoguesamples.com**
Samples online.

Antares **www.antares-systems.com** or
www.antarestech.com Digital signal
processing software; *Auto-Tune* automatic and

graphical intonation correction for voices and solo instruments; *Infinity* sample looping program for Macintosh; *Multiband Dynamics Tool* five-band dynamics controller; *JVP Voice Processor* de-esser, compressor, three-band EQ and Delay FX processor for vocals; details of software; demos to download; technical support; news; links.

Antex Electronics **www.antex.com** High- end sound cards.

Anvil Studio **www.anvilstudio.com** Win9x/NT freeware to multitrack record, compose and edit with audio and MIDI.

Aphex **www.aphex.com** Electronics.

Apogee Electronics Corp.
www.apogeedigital.com Apogee; Wyde-Eye; Session Tools; developer of digital audio software and hardware; product information; download manuals; updates; links; news.

Apple Computer Inc. **www.apple.com** News; information; updates; software downloads.

Applied Research and Technology
www.artroch.com Pre-amps; compressors; equalizers.

Arabesque Software **www.arasoft.com** Developer of *Rental* and *Production Manager,* a full-featured software package for theatrical lighting, sound, and gear rental and sales companies.

Arboretum Systems Inc. **www.aboretum.com** Developer of digital audio software for Macintosh and PC; access and download manuals; new products; download demos and plug-ins; newsgroup; mailing list; links; *Hyperprism; Ray Gun; Ionizer; Restoration-NR; Arboretum Harmony; Arboretum Realizer.*

Armadillo **www.clavia.com** Nord modular.

Ars Nova Music Software **www.ars-nova.com** Educational music software.

Arturia **www.arturia.com** *Storm;* virtual home studio for music composition, both modular and real time; virtual instruments, sequencers, synthesizers, and effects.

ASM Audio **www.voyce.com/asm/index.html** Audio company Web site.

AtmosFear's Major Sample Site
www.servtech.com/staff/spetry/ samples.html Synthesizer samples; drum machines; MIDI software.

Audio Compositor
home.att.net/~audiocompositor MIDI file player for GM files; software wavetable synthesizer; Windows 95/NT; edit instrument samples and patches.

Audio Ease **www.audioease.com** Web audio batch processors.

Audio Effects Software
www.cl.spb.ru/asm104/snt_alon.htm

Power multi-effects studio; guitar effects processor.

Audio Shareware **www.partnersinrhyme.com** Music software; sound utilities; MIDI sequencers; audio editors and convertors; sound tutorials; shareware request board; Macintosh; Windows.

Audiograbber
musicglobalnetwork.com/audiograbber. html Software that grabs digital audio from CDs or from a sound card using the Line In sampling function; make perfect copies of originals.

Audioworks **www.audioworks.com** Developer of Sound2MIDI PC software; converts audio data onto MIDI data; information; reviews; links.

Audition **www.bowrad.ndirect.co.uk** MIDI sequencer for Windows written exclusively for Roland GS and Yamaha XG Synthesizers; demo available.

Audix **www.audixusa.com** Electronics.

AuReality
midiworld.com/AuReality/index.htm Multifunctional MIDI application/modular sequencer; build custom controller remapping, LFOs, arpeggiators, autochords, drum and note sequences and echoes.

BBE Sound **www.bbesound.com** BBE Sonic Maximizer.

Be, Inc. BeOS **www.be.com** Software synthesis.

BeOS **www.lebuzz.com** BeOS operating system.

Beotel.yu **www.beotel.yu/~leon/index.html** Links; over 600 on Techno-related topics; virtual synthesizer sites.

Berklee Media **www.berklee.edu** Home page.

Bias Inc. (Berkley Integrated Audio Software Inc.)
www.bias-inc.com Macintosh digital audio software; *Peak*; plug-ins such as *SFX Machine*; product information; news; updates; demos to download.

Big Fish Audio **www.bigfishaudio.com** Large selection of sample CDs; sample libraries.

BitHeadz **www.bitheadz.com** Software synthesizers.

Boardwatch Magazine **www.boardwatch.com** Coverage of online services and the Internet.

Bomb Factory **www.bombfactory.com** Analog sounds in digital form.

Bose **www.bose.com** Speaker manufacturer; sound technologies; product information; sound reproduction; car audio systems; new developments.

BuyDirect.com **www.buydirect.com** Download Web site; commercial software and hardware.

Byte **www.byte.com** Online magazine about hardware and computer technology.

Cakewalk **www.cakewalk.com** Developer of *Cakewalk* sequencer software; plug-ins; hardware; accessories; download free trials.

Cakewalk Links **www.cakewalk.com/Partners/links.html** Music hardware and software companies; publications; Web browser software.

Calmus **rvik.ismennt.is/~kjol** Sequentially calculates values of musical objects in a composition; constructs melodies for each object; concepts used in the program are musical objects, polyphony, melody, MIDI, harmony, and graphical representation.

Capella Music Software **www.users.bigpond.com/kdeane** Score scanning and editing; MIDI entry.

Cappella **www.cappella.net** Software to dub audio to movies.

Casa de la Musica **www.casamusica.com** Music education software.

CD Recording Software **www.CDRecordingSoftware.com** Multitrack digital audio recording software; MIDI software; sound modules; effects plug-ins; music software for quality audio production from home recording studio; browse by brand or category.

CD-ROM Shop **www.cdromshop.com/cdshop** Online CD-ROM store.

CDS Inc. **www.cds-ny.com** Developers of industry standard and custom scheduling and picture management in the fashion industry.

CD-Tools by NovaStor **www.cd-tools.com** Professional level CD-R, CD-RW, and DVD mastering system; powerful CD duplication capability; audio editing including sound samples, loops, and more.

Celemony Software GMBH 1.GR. **www.celemony.com** Home page.

CERL Sound Group **datura.cerl.uiuc.edu** Analysis/Synthesis and notation software; downloadable trial version available.

Chezmark.com **www.chezmark.com** New Macintosh software reviewed.

Chonwoo Corp. **www.chonwoo.co.kr** *Chonwoo; MuSac; Bamboo Country; Cover the World;* Korean.

Chord Arranger Pro **ourworld.compuserve.com/homepages/MichaelBrick** Chord arranger for Win9x; creates styles from any MIDI file; identifies chords to convert song measures into style parts.

Cinram **www.cinram.com** Media duplicator; design templates.

Circuit City **www.circuitcity.com** Electronics retailer.

Classical Kids **www.unidial.com/~fflaxman/ClassicalKids.html** Music software.

CLEARVUE/eav Inc. **www.clearvue.com** Maker and distributor of educational music software products.

Clixsounds **www.clixsounds.com** Developer of shareware program *Agent Audio*; sounds and sample CDs for Macintosh; demos to download; news; information.

Clockwork **ourworld.compuserve.com/homepages/clockworkmusic** Music and studio related software; tutor for CAL.

Club Cubase **www.cix.co.uk/~gal/ccd/index.html** Club membership; magazine; discounts on most Steinberg products.

CNET **www.news.com** Technology news Web site.

CNet Shareware.Com **www.shareware.com** Source of shareware for all computer platforms; not music specific.

CNMAT Home Page Center **www.cnmat.berkeley.edu** At the University of California, Berkeley; showcases creative interaction between music and technology.

Coda Music Technology **www.codamusic.com** Developer of music software programs, including *Finale*, *Allegro* and *SmartMusic Studio*; pro-end notation and printing package used by professional music typesetters; current and new products; technical support; FAQ; demos to download; related sites; forum; mailing list.

Computer Game Developers Association **www.cgda.org** Demos; resources.

Computer Generated Music **www.prospernet.com/surfing/music/computergenerated.html** Music generated by computer.

Computer Music Consulting **www.computer-music.com** Produces music and sound effects for games; information about making music with computers; articles.

Computer Music Journal **www.mitpress.mit.edu/e-journals/Computer-Music-Journal** Quarterly journal; topics relating to digital audio signal processing and electro-acoustic music; software and hardware; aesthetics of contemporary music.

Computer Music Programs for the Macintosh **shoko.calarts.edu/~tre/CompMusMac/** Includes links for downloading.

Computer News Daily **www.computernewsdaily.com** Commentary on high-tech news.

Computer Shopper **www.zdnet.com/computershopper** Information on buying computers.

Computers and Music
www.computersandmusic.com Retailer of audio interfaces and more.

Creamware GMBH **www.creamware.com** *Scope; Pulsar; Powersampler; Elektra; Luna; Triple Dat.*

Creative Labs and Seer Systems NetSynth **www.ctlsg.creaf.com/club/connect/ music/music.html** Software synthesis; Windows.

Creative Labs **www.creativelabs.com** *Sound Blaster* sound cards.

Creative Labs WaveSynth; WaveSynth/WG **www.soundblaster.com** Software synthesis; Windows.

Creative Synth **www.creativesynth.com** Reviews; technical tips.

Crescit Software Incorporated **www.crescit.com** Software tools for lighting plots and paperwork; PC-based DMX control, show control, and sound playback; meeting both professional and educational needs.

Crown International **www.crownaudio.com** Amplifiers; microphones.

CrusherX-Live **www.crusher-x.de** Vapor algorithm enables creating very complex waves; can be used as a synthesizer or as a versatile effect unit; creates unusual sounds with oscillators, WAV files, and real-time inputs.

Crystal River Engineering **www.cre.com** Developer of *AudioReality 3D* processing technology; simulators; *Proton* plug-in for *Pro Tools.*

Cubase for Windows Users **www.instanet.com/~thedusk** Independent support site for users of *Cubase* under Windows.

Cybercorder **skyhawktech.com** Provides VCR-like recording for radio shows or any audio input.

Cycling '74 **www.cycling74.com** *Pluggo; Max; MSP; M.*

Datasonics **www.datasonics.com.au** VSPro; Win95 sequencing and notation package; full graphic interface for Roland VS880 control and integration.

Dave Central **www.davecentral.com** Internet freeware; shareware; commercial demos.

David Karla rack747 **www.be.com/beware/Audio.html** Software synthesis; BeOS.

Dbx **www.dbxpro.com** *Dbx* noise reductions systems; compression/limiters; EQ; preamplifiers; technical information.

Declick 2000 **pWeb.de.uu.net/mpaar** Sound editor that works with Cool Edit 2000 and Cool Edit 96; gallery of 3D pictures.

Deepsound sample calculators **deepsound.net/calculation.html** Sample calculators to help sampler users deal with time-stretching, pitch-shifting, delay times, etc.

Denon **www.denon.com** Speakers and car stereo systems; CD and DVD players; pro audio products; news items; links; FAQs; dealer lists; Denon Active Media includes CD replication and MPEG services.

Depopper New! **www.droidinfo.com/software/depopper** Software to get near CD quality from vinyl disks; minimizes clicks, scratches, and noise without removing treble sounds.

Digalo TTS **www.digalo.com/developer.htm** Designed for developers and end users; empowers all SAPI and Microsoft Agent compliant applications; TTS mode ID, source code samples, and technical support provided to speech enable application.

Digidesign **www.digidesign.com/index1.html** Developer of *Pro Tools* direct-to-disk recording system/workstation; first specialized in high quality digital audio hardware and software for Macintosh; now includes PC; product information; downloads.

Digigram **www.digigram.com** *Vxpocket*-equipped laptop or PowerBook.

Digimusic.Net **www.digimusic.net** Digital music Web site.

Digital Music Corp. **www.voodoolab.com** *Voodoo Lab; Ground Control System; Pedal Power.Aardvark* **www.aardvark-pro.com** *Direct Pro 24/96* integrated recording system; hardware and software.

Digital Music Nation **www.digitalmusicnation.com** Digital music Web site.

Digital Sound Page **www.xs4all.nl/~rexbo/pc_synth.htm** Software synthesis.

Digitech **www.digitech.com** Guitar and studio effects; upgrades; online documents; new products; downloads; user group information.

Dimension Arc **www.dimensionarc.com** Revolve 100m pattern based step sequencer for Win95; analog sequencing interface, Rebirth file conversion and other features; full MIDI control of sequencing functions.

Discovery **www.discoveryfirm.com** Sample CDs and CD-ROMs.

Dissidents **www.dissidents.com** Develops software for audio, music, and multimedia applications for Windows and Amiga computers; Web audio batch processors.

D-lusion Rubber Duck **www.neurotix.303dim.com/tools.htm# RubDuck086** Software synthesis.

Dod **www.dod.com** Catalog; technical support; effects manufacturer.

Dolby Laboratories **www.dolby.com** Invented noise reduction; site includes new information, press releases, Dolby news, statistics, cassettes, technical information, movies and cinema, home theatre, multimedia, cinema products, professional products, literature, Dolby digital, DVD, company information, people, career opportunities, and trademark information.

Doubleware Productions **www.doubleware.com** Music software.

Download **www.download.cnet.com** MIDI files; karaoke; freeware; shareware.

Download.com **www.download.com** Shareware.

Dr. T's Music Software **www.foryourhead.com/DrTs.htm** FAQ.

DUY **www.duy.es** Developer of digital audio plug-ins for Macintosh; information; feature lists; demos.

DVCPRO Errorchecker **www.errorchecker.de** Software tool to report the OnTape error rate of DVCPRO and DV tapes.

East West Sounds **www.soundsonline.com** Sample sounds superstore; over 500 CDs.

Easy Mix **perso.wanadoo.fr/easymix/info1.htm** For mixing with a turntable.

Easy Music Composer **www3.justnet.ne.jp/~miyawakims** MIDI sequencer for Windows.

Eccentric **www.eccentricsoftware.com** *A Zillion Kajillion Rhymes*.

Echo Corp. **www.echoaudio.com** Home page.

Echoview **www.mirage1.u-net.com/echoview.htm** Pro music calculating tools for musicians, composers, producers, and sound engineers.

Edge City Sound Vault **www.novia.net/~ejanders/sndvault.html** Synthesizer and percussion samples.

Edirol, inc. Virtual Sound Canvas **www.edirol.com** Software synthesis; Windows.

Ego Systems **www.egosys.net** Home page.

Electrix **www.electrixpro.com** Rackmount and tabletop effects.

Electronic Arts Research **autoinfo.smartlink.net/ray** GSMP or Genetic Spectrum Modelling Program; Fractal Melody Generator; MIDI files and Wave files; download software.

Electronic Courseware Systems (ECS) **www.ecsmedia.com** Educational music software company based in Champaign, IL;

downloadable demos; developers of music instructional, multimedia, and MIDI software.

Electronic Instruments **www.ief.u-psud.fr/~thierry/history/history.html** Brief history of electronic instruments.

Electronic Music Foundation (EMF) **www.emf.org** Materials and information for understanding the history and development of music technology.

Electronic Musical Instruments 1870-1990 **www.obsolete.com/120_years** Vintage electronic music instruments.

Electronisounds.com **www.Electronisounds.com** Sounds; samples.

Electrophile-Substitution-Recordings **home.balcab.ch/m-electric-rec** Information about music machines, links, and live Webcam.

Emagic Germany **www.emagic.de** Original German site; English version.

Emagic **www.emagicusa.com** U.S. site; links to German site; *Logic* sequencer and *Logic Audio* hard-disc recording software for Macintosh and PC; *SoundDiver* librarian/editing program; technical support; tutorials.

EMIS **dspace.dial.pipex.com/emis/museum/museum.htm** Synthesizer Museum; collection of instruments based in Bristol; information on 400 instruments.

Emu Systems **www.emu.com** Synthesizers, samplers, and sound modules; SoundFonts technology used in Creative Labs sound cards; sampled sounds.

EMusic on the Net **alt-www.uia.ac.be/u/esger/emusic/emusic.html** Links to many electronic music sites.

Enport **www.en-port.com** Home page.

Ensign Systems **www.ensign.com** Home page.

Ensoniq **www.ensoniq.com** Electronic musical instrument manufacturer; keyboards, synthesizers, samplers, drum machines, effects, and more; multimedia soundcards; digital systems; semiconductors; information on products; technical support; press releases; company information; download section.

Ensoniq Resources on the Internet **www.op.net/~mikeh/ensoniq.html** Web pages; company sites; FTP sites and files; patches; software; mailing lists.

Epinoisis Software Corporation **digitalear.iwarp.com** Makers of the audio to MIDI conversion software Digital Ear.

ER Technologies **www.ERTECHSOFT.com** Educational music software.

ETantrum.com **www.freetantrum.org** Songprint SDK for eTantrum Music ID Service; free library; automatically identifies any piece of music; identifies songs through unique audio fingerprint based on analog signal, independent of codec used and bitrate of the compressed file; independent of ID3 tags or other information stored in file.

Etcetera **www.etcetera.co.uk** PC software for musicians.

European Imaging and Sound Association **eisa.techlink.gr** European editorial multimedia organization; annual EISA awards.

EveryMac **www.everymac.com** Lists every Macintosh computer ever made by manufacturer and processor; clones included.

Evolution Electronics **www.evolution-uk.com** Developer and distributor of *Sound Studio Gold* sequencer; direct-to-disk recording; other software programs and MIDI keyboards; product information; demos; patches; help files.

Evolution **www.evolution.co.uk** Music software and hardware for the PC with free demos; UK keyboard controller manufacturer.

ExtremeGroove **www.extremegroove.com** Home page.

Fap7 Shareware/Freeware Links **www.realtime.com/~fap7/synthesis/ synshare.htm** Links to Macintosh and PC sites; browser plug-ins; audio applications.

File Mine **www.filemine.com** Games and other shareware downloads.

FilePile **www.filepile.com/nc/start** Computer files for downloading; largest indexed collection of files in the world; over 1.2 million files.

Finale: IWBNI **www.greschak.com/notation/finale/ iwbni** "It Would Be Nice If"; comprehensive list of suggestions for improving the music notation software program *Finale;* visitors submit suggestions and votes; voting results are published.

Forest Technologies **www.foresttech.com** Instructional software.

Fostex **www.fostex.com** Hard disk recording systems; DATs; mixers and multitrack recorders; product information; FAQ on recording techniques; links.

Free On-Line Dictionary of Computing **wombat.doc.ic.ac.uk/foldoc/index.html** Dictionary of computer terms.

Frontier Design Group **www.frontierdesign.com** Dakota; Wave Center PCI; Zulu; Tango 24; Montana; Sierra.

Frontier Design Group **www.frontierdesign.com** *Wave Center PCI; Dakota; Tango 24; Montana; Sierra.*

Fruityloops **www.fruityloops.net** Loop creating tool; started as a drumloop creator; evolved into a complete loop and song creating package; can

hold an unlimited number of samples and channels; play stand-alone or by triggering MIDI equipment.

Galileo Designs **www.galileodesigns.com** Streaming media control libraries; development tools for MIDI and digital audio and video.

Gallery Software **www.demon.co.uk/gallery** Digidesign software partner; hardware utilities; accessories for Digidesign products; information; software updates and demo versions.

Giebler **www.giebler.com** Disk management and sequencer conversion software for musical keyboards and sequencers; convert MIDI files to load directly into keyboards and sequencers; supported products include Alesis, Ensoniq, Korg, Kawai, Roland, and Yamaha; disk recovery service for many keyboards.

Glowing Coast Technology **www.glowingcoast.demon.co.uk/index. htm** *Audio Suite*; multitrack digital audio workstation; integrated group of audio waveform editing tools.

Glyph Technologies Inc. **www.glyphtech.com** Home page.

GoldWave **www.goldwave.com** Digital audio editor for Windows; Multiple Document Interface for editing dozens of files in one session; large file editing, up to 1GB in size; configurable RAM; Realtime oscilloscopes.

Greytsounds **www.greytsounds.com** CD-ROMs, floppy disks, synth patches, and audio CDs; electronic delivery for some synth patches with Internet orders.

Groovestyle Sarl **www.groovestyle.com** Authentic Sound Systems; Techno Sound Bank Factory.

Groovy Loops **www.GroovyLoops.com** Loops.

GT Electronics **www.gtelectronics.com** Electronics.

Guillemot **www.guillemot.com** Maxi Studio ISIS; Maxi Sound Fortissimo.

Hands-on-MIDI **www.hands-on-midi.com** MIDI software; catalog.

Hardware Web **homepage.cistron.nl/~nctnico** MIDI hardware; interfaces; testers; switchers; mergers; keyboards; instructions; schematic diagrams; links; FAQ.

Harmonic Vision **www.harmonicvision.com** Educational music software; *Music Ace; Music Doodle Pad.*

Heavenly Music **www.ortiz.demon.co.uk** Programmers of MIDI files; developer of MIDI building block files; AWE SoundFonts.

Heritage Music Press **www.lorenz.com** MIDI accompaniment disks; methods.

Hinton Instrument Links
www.hinton.demon.co.uk/#links List of synthesizer and MIDI links.

Hiro's Page winGroove
www.cc.rim.or.jp/~hiroki/english Software synthesis; Windows.

Hitsquad.com
www.hitsquad.com/startup.html?nl21 Home page; Web site for active musicians; music software resources and information; links.

Hitsquad.com Software Titles
www.hitsquad.com/smm/alphabetic/a Large list of music software titles listed alphabetically; links.

Hohner Midia **www.sekd.com** Music software.

Hollywood Edge
www.hollywoodedge.com/samples.html Sampling.

Hopkins Technology **www.hoptechno.com** Music software; *Classical Notes*.

Hosa Technology Inc. **www.hosatech.com** *Hosa; Zaolla*.

Howling Dog Systems **www.howlingdog.com** Mod files.

Hubert Winkler Hubi's Loopback Device
www.hitsquad.com/smm/programs/ Hubis_LoopBack_device Software synthesis.

Hudson Music LLC **www.hudsonmusic.com** Home page.

I/O MUG **www.iomug.org** Macintosh group; links to Macintosh Web sites, companies, and software.

Ibis **www.ibis-research.com/Products.htm** Music software.

ICMA Computer Music Links
music.dartmouth.edu/~icma/links.html Links from the International Computer Music Association.

IDG.Net **www.idg.net** International technology news.

IK Multimedia Production
www.groovemaker.com Groovemaker; T-Racks.

IK Multimedia Production SRL
www.groovemaker.com Home page.

ILIO Entertainments **www.ilio.com** Sound sample libraries; audio CDs and CD-ROMs; 100 percent copyright clean and royalty free.

Imaja **www.imaja.com** Publishes animation, multimedia, graphics, music, and educational software for the Apple Macintosh.

Innovative Quality Software **www.iqsoft.com** Developer of *Software Audio Workshop*; multitrack direct-to-disk recording software for PC; plug-ins.

Innovative Trek Technology NovaStation MMX
www.ittrek.com/novastn.html Software synthesis; Windows.

IntelliScore **www.intelliscore.net** IntelliScore Polyphonic WAV to MIDI software; listens to polyphonic WAV files and helps figure out the notes, chord names, and key.

International Computer Music Association
music.dartmouth.edu/~icma Members home pages; links; algorithmic composition; MIDI; analysis; multitrack recording; notation; synthesis.

International Game Developers Network
www.igdn.org Resources.

International Print Edition **www.ipe-music.com** *Piano Passion; Masters Collection; IPE Scores; Multimedia Converter; Print Converter*.

International Standards Organization **www.iso.ch** Creates and publishes standards in technical areas; criteria; catalog.

Intersound
vestinternett.no/~fb/impsound.html Music software.

InVision Interactive CyberSound VS
www.cybersound.com Software synthesis; Macintosh/Windows.

Iomega **www.iomega.com** Zip drives.

ISong **www.isong.com** MIDI.

ITunes **www.apple.com/itunes** Free download; play audio CDs on Macintosh; convert files on CDs to MP3 format; manage songs collected; create playlists; download favorites to an MP3 player; tune in to Internet radio stations; create music CDs to play in car, stereo system, or portable CD player; unlimited encoding at maximum quality MP3 allows; unlimited burning at maximum speed.

J Graphics **www.j-graphics.com** Graphics.

J.Takeda **jesustakeda.virtualave.net** Freeware and shareware of multimedia and audio tools.

Jamie O'Connell MIDI Yoke
www.channel1.com/users/jamieo/jsoft. html Software synthesis.

JBL **www.jbl.com** Speaker manufacturer.

Jeorg Stelkin PHYMOD **www.harmony-central.com/Software/Windows/phymod 20.html** Software synthesis; Windows.

Jumbo **www.jumbo.com** Shareware supermarket; over 250,000 programs.

Jump! Software, Inc.
www.software.jumpmusic.com/HTML/ AboutJump *Piano Discovery*.

Justonic Tuning **www.justonic.com** *Justonic Pitch Palette;* software which makes tuning adjustments to pitch tables of synthesizer; pianos and guitars with a MIDI interface can play and modulate in just, or any other intonation, in real time.

Kable Keepers **www.kablekeepers.com** *Wrap-All.*

Karnataka **www.audioarchitect.com** Developer of *Audio Architect* software-based modular synthesizer; program information; reviews; tutorials; links.

Key Trax **www.keytrax.com** Audio library; musician's community; music portal.

Keyfax Software **www.keyfax.com** *Twiddly.Bits;* Master Series; *Phat Boy;* Keyfax Books; CVM Video; downloads.

Kid Nepro **www.kidnepro.com** Developer of sounds for many instruments; catalog; soundlists.

Kind of Loud Technologies **www.kindofloud.com** *SmartPan Pro; Tweetie; Woofie.*

Kurzweil K2000/K2500 Samples **www.sweetwater.com/k2000/sounds. html** Public domain sounds for the Kurzweil synthesizers; links.

K-v-R **www.k-v-r.freeserve.co.uk** For users of Cubase VST instruments; free instrument banks for download; submit; links.

Lexicon **www.lexicon.com** Digital effects; multiprocessor effects; MIDI reverberators; power amps; demos; downloads; upgrades; technical support.

Lintronics Software Publishing, Inc. **www.lintronics.de** Music software.

Linux Artist **www.linuxartist.org/audio** Site for Linux users.

LiveUpdate Crescendo **www.liveupdate.com/crescendo.html** Software synthesis.

Logic Users **www.logicuser.net/group** Mailing list.

Loopasonic **www.Loopasonic** Bass and drum loops.

Looper's Delight **annihilist.com/loop/loop.html** Information on making and using loops.

Lucid **www.lucidtechnology.com** Technology.

Lynx Studio Technology Inc. **www.lynxstudio.com** Lynx ONE; Lynx TWO.

Lyrrus **www.lyrrus.com** Developer of *G-Vox*; for guitar and computer.

M Audio **www.m-audio.com** Audio.

Mac Music **www.macmusic.org** Music on the Macintosh; large set of links; freeware; shareware; downloads; resources.

Macdownload.com **www.zdnet.com/mac/download.html** Software selections for Macintosh.

MacGAMUT Software **www.macgamut.com** Music software; ear training.

Macintosh MIDI User's Internet Guide **www.aitech.ac.jp/~ckelly/mmuig.html** Collection of information and links for the Macintosh musician; updates and new products; Getting Started information.

Mackie **www.mackie.com** Manufacturer of mixing consoles.

Macromedia **www.macromedia.com** Music software company; *SoundEdit.*

Macware **macware.erehwon.org/Audio-Midi.html** Downloadable shareware and freeware.

Macworld/MacWeek **macworld.zdnet.com** Information for Macintosh users.

Maestro Music **www.musicmart.com/maestro** Educational music software.

Magix Entertainment Corp. **www.magix.net** *Magix Music Maker; Artist Pools; MP3 Maker; Audio Video Composer; Magix Music Studio; Sound Pools; Notation; Music Maker Videojam; Magix Dance Maker; Guitar Workshop; PlayR; Live Act.*

Magma **www.magma.com** Home page.

Making Waves **www.pslnet.demon.co.uk** Shareware sample sequencer.

ManyMIDI **www.manymidi.com** Synthesizer sound libraries.

Marietta Design, Inc. **mariettadesign.com** Developers of *AccuPrompt* and *QuickPrompt* teleprompting software for Macintosh.

Mark of the Unicorn **www.motu.com** Developer of *Performer* sequencer software; one of the first high-end MIDI sequencers for Macintosh.

Martin Fay VAZ **www.cp.umist.ac.uk/users/martin/vaz. html** Software synthesis.

Master Bits **www.masterbits.com** CD-ROMS; sample data; *Monsterpack.*

Masterclass Productions **www.masterclass.com** Music software.

Maxim **www.abel.co.uk/~maxim** Digital audio freeware; collection of programs and utilities; one enables a PC to write and format Akai S-Series sampler floppy disks; list of Cubase VST plug-ins; free downloads.

Mayfield Publishing Company **www.mayfieldpub.com** Music software.

Maz Sound Tools **www.maz-sound.com** Large collection of MOD/S3M/XM/IT tracking software; *Mazzive Injection* sample CDs; free samples in .WAV format; downloads; links; software synthesizers; MP3 players and encoders.

MbooM **www.mboom.com** Sequencer/sampler; trial version.

McAfee **www.mcafee.com** Virus protection software; *VirusScan*; *Virex*.

Mediamation Inc. **www.mediamat.com** Home page.

MediaTech Innovations **www.midibrainz.com** Developer of *Drumz Wizard* and *Muzical Wizard* PC programs; drum tracks and patterns; information; FAQs; MIDI files; demos to download.

Melody Assistant **www.myriad-online.com** Music notation program; can use with a MIDI synthesizer; comes with bank of internal sounds.

MetaSynth **www.uisoftware.com** Synthesis and sound design software; downloads; Macintosh.

MGI Interactive **www.midi-classics.com/p4665.htm** Music software.

MiBAC Music Software **www.mibac.com** Home page; products; theory reference; Music instructional software; *MiBAC Jazz* and *Music Lessons*.

Microboards Technology **www.microboards.com** *Startrec; Jam Session; Inferno; CD Factory; Taiyo Yuden; Audio Write Pro; Multiwriter; Print Write*.

Microboards Technology LLC **www.microboards.com** Home page.

Microforum **www.microforum.com** Music software.

Microsoft, Inc. Microsoft Synthesizer **www.microsoft.com/music/home.htm** Software synthesis; Windows.

MIDI at Warp Speed **www.dinosoft.it/~midistation** MIDI Station Sequencer for OS/2.

MIDI Auto-Accompaniment Section **ourworld.compuserve.com/homepages/michaelbrick** MAAS auto-accompaniment software; virtual keyboard; song arranger; realtime chord recognition; up to sixteen fingered and ten two-finger chord types; MIDI controls; about thirty demo styles.

MIDI City **www.berkshire.net/~malancar/midicity.htm** MIDI files; all genres; links to other MIDI sites; technical information.

MIDI Editor **perso.magic.fr/llebot** MIDI manager; works with any MIDI device; design editor windows; two help files; English and French versions; presets for Alesis, Casio, Emu, Kawai, Korg, Roland, Sequential, Yamaha; information; demo to download.

MIDI Farm **www.midifarm.com** Major MIDI and music site; news; audio recording; press releases; free MIDI files; music software; FTP site; connection to MIDI and digital audio sites on the Internet; product updates; demos.

MIDI Farm Software Links **www.midifarm.com/midifarm/software.asp** Links to software developer sites.

MIDI Hits **www.midi-hits.com** Over 6,000 sequences; all genres; catalog.

MIDI Home Page **www.eeb.ele.tue.nl:80/midi** or **www.eeb.ele.tue.nl/MIDI/index.html** Information about MIDI; links to music sites and newsgroups.

MIDI HQ **www.midihq.com** Synthesizer sound libraries.

MIDI Karaoke **www.teleport.com/~labrat/karplayers.shtml** Lists programs that play karaoke files; MIDI file players; programs for Windows, DOS, Macintosh, and Amiga.

MIDI Link **www.xnet.com/~midilink** MIDI; synthesizer patches; samplers; PC and Macintosh files.

MIDI Links **www.wattyco.com/midi2.htm** Links to music and MIDI file-related sites.

MIDI Loops **www.midiloops.com/copyrite.htm** Site licensing MIDI files for use on the Internet; information about copyright and MIDI music; use of MIDI music under copyright; permission to use files, MIDI files, and shareware.

MIDI Manufacturers Association (MMA) **www.midi.org** Source for information on MIDI technology.

MIDI Mark **www.midimark.com** Sounds and samples.

MIDI Music **http//:midimusic.miningco.com/index** Information; MIDI files; book lists; newsgroup lists; discussions; links.

MIDI Music Web Site **www.quicknet.se/ftp/dialup/q-112005** Information, links, software, MIDI files, and samples; programs are for Macintosh, Atari, and PC; list of music links in different categories.

MIDI Solutions **www.midisolutions.com** Pedal Controller; MIDI-powered products.

MIDI Users Group **www.nowopen.com/mug** User group on the Internet with a subscription fee; lists of MIDI files; software; shareware; freeware; subscribe to a free newsletter; software lists; links.

MIDI Web **www.midiWeb.com/index2.html** Information on MIDI; DIY projects; demo software; shareware; freeware; MIDI and sound files to download.

MIDI Web Links **www.midiWeb.com/links/index.shtml** Links to MIDI on the Internet.

MIDI Workshop **www.midiworkshop.com** Music technology; training; college credit.

MIDI World **midiworld.com** Collection of MIDI and music-related information; basics; synthesizers; software; sounds; links; files; lab; marketplace; PC and Macintosh; downloads; archive of MIDI files; links to music software and hardware companies.

MidiFitz **www.midifitz.com** Real-time MIDI accompaniment system; plays bass and drum notes responding to chords.

MidiMan **www.midiman.net** Manufacturer of MIDI interfaces for Macintosh and PC; digital and audio patch-bays; digital-to-analogue converters; synchronizers; line mixers; MIDI accessories; product information; FAQs; drivers and utilities to download.

Midiman Inc./M-Audio **www.midiman.com** Home page.

MidiNotate by Notation Software, Inc. **www.notation.com/midinotate.htm** Free software; converts MIDI files to printable sheet music; can be viewed on screen while highlighted notes play.

MIDI-OX **ourworld.compuserve.com/homepages/ JamieOConnell/midiox.html** or **members.xoom.com/MIDIOX/midiox. htm** or **MidiOx.com** MIDI utility; Windows 95/NT 32-bit program; diagnostic tool; System Exclusive librarian; filtering and mapping of MIDI data streams; displays incoming MIDI streams; passes data to MIDI output driver or MIDI Mapper; generate MIDI data using computer keyboard or built-in control panel; record and log MIDI data and convert to a Standard MIDI File for playback by a sequencer; freeware.

MidiSoft **www.midisoft.com/html/newrel.htm** Sequencing and notation music software; Internet audio products; *Studio; Desktop Sheet Music; Internet Media Player; Internet Audio Postcard.*

MidiSyn - MIDI to WAVE File Converter **planeta.clix.pt/acesteves/MidiSyn/ MSynMain.htm** *MidiSyn;* Windows 95/98/NT program; convert MIDI to WAVE files; listen to generated WAV files directly; convert to MP3; burn into audio CDs.

MidiTec **www.earnmaster.com** Music software company; product information.

MikMak **www.stack.nl/~mikmak** Win95/NT port of IT-player; also available for Linux + Mac; plays IT, XM, S3M, and MOD.

Millennium Music Software **www.millennium- music.co.uk** Specialist in PC-based audiovisual technology; supplies all sizes of digital A/V production systems for the home or professional setup.

MiniDisc.org **www.MiniDisc.org** Home page.

Minimusic **www.5thwall.com/minimusic** Home page.

Mining Company MIDI Music **midimusic.miningco.com/index.htm** Features; information; hints; tips; music files; MIDI hardware and software; newsgroups; MIDI files.

Minnetonka Audio Software **www.minnetonkaaudio.com** Software.

Mixman **www.mixman.com** Triple-format sample CDs: audio, Mixman TRK, and WAV; maker of *Soundisc; StudioPro*; song construction kit; information; tips; links.

MixViews **www.ccmrc.ucsb.edu/~doug/htmls/ MiXViews.html** Unix digital audio editing/processing program; designed to allow users to edit and process digital sound and other forms of on-disk data.

MMF MIDI Links **www.geocities.com/~miditastic/ midilink.html** Links to free MIDI sites, MIDI directories and search engines.

Monolith Media **www.monomedia.com** Audio and video system design; proposal generation software package.

Moog Music **www.moogmusic.com** Robert Moog is one of the original synthesizer developers; information on current products including the Minimoog and modular synths; archive of older, classic instruments; news section; technical support; FAQs; patch sheets; online store.

Morph City **www.morphcity.com** Home page.

MOTU-MAC Mailing List **www.unicornation.com** Mailing list for users.

Multi-Media Music **www.wavenet.com/~axgrindr/Midi.html** MIDI software; Macintosh sound utilities; downloads; shareware; freeware.

Muscle Fish LLC **www.musclefish.com** Software provider and consulting company providing a variety of technologies for audio and music analysis and retrieval.

Music and Computers **www.music-and- computers.com** Information; extracts from issues; links.

Music Data Management. Software **www.winband.com** Software.

Music Loops **www.MusicLoops.com** Loops.

Music Machines **www.hyperreal.com/machines** Musical electronica on the Web; images; software; schematics; samples; MIDI files; sythesizers; effects; drum machines; recording equipment;

links to manufacturer sites; for electronic musicians.

Music Pen **www.musicpen.com** Music software.

Music Shoppe **www.musicshoppe.com/inside.htm** MIDI sites.

Music Software at Indie-Music.com **www.indie-music.com/software.htm** Resources; links; product information.

Music Software at Harmony-Central **www.harmony-central.com/Software** Online listing of music software products by platform.

Music Study **www.musicstudy.com** Music instruction software.

Music Technology **musictech.miningco.com** Information about instruments, software, synthesizers, artists, manufacturers; links.

Music World **members.aol.com/bobyang/music.htm** A collection of MIDI variety.

Musical Software **www.musicalsoftware.com** Online retailer of music software and hardware.

Musicator **www.musicator.com** Developer of the *Musicator* sequencer for Windows; program information; new features; demo to download; utilities.

MusicEase Software **www.musicease.com** Music notation software.

Musician Software **www.musiciansoftware.com** Software for musicians.

MusicTech.com **www.musictech.com** Home page.

Musicware **www.musicware.com** *Christmas Carols; Music Lab; La Songbook; Nightingale; MIDIsaurus; Piano Course 1-4.*

Musicware, Inc. **www.musicwareinc.com** Music education software; dedicated to the belief that all people can benefit from participating in music; software to help people of all ages and abilities develop music skills.

Musitek **musitek.com** Developer of *MIDIScan* software for the PC; scans printed music; converts to MIDI data; information; technical support; upgrades; demo.

MVP Home Entertainment Inc. **www.musicvideoproducts.com** Home page.

Myriad/Guillion Bros. **www.myriad-online.com** *Harmony Assistant* and *Melody Assistant;* software programs for computer-assisted tune writing and composition; Macintosh; Windows.

Mzone **www.mzone.dk** Danish company; *WaveIt Synth* CD-ROM; SoundFont editor.

Native Instruments **www.native-instruments.com/** Developer of *Generator* real-time synthesizer; create synthesized sounds on computer which can be played in real time; information; demo to download; plug-ins; *Reaktor; Generator; Transformator; Dynamo; 4Control.*

Navigator Systems **www.hiretrack.com** Developer of software for use by entertainment industry equipment rental companies.

Neato **www.neato.com** Media labeling products; CD labels, jewel case inserts, DAT tape j-cards and labels, audiocassette j-cards and labels, zip disk inserts and labels.

Needle Doctor **www.needledoctor.com** Large selection of needles cartridges, turntables, and phono accesories.

Nemesys Music Technology Inc. **www.nemesysmusic.com** Gigasamler; NCS44; Gigastudio; Nemesys Soundware.

Neurodancer's Home Page **www.sylaba.poznan.pl/~neurod** Digital audio editor; works in both time and frequency domains.

NewsPage **www.newspage.com** Directory of technology news.

Newtronic **www.newtronic.com** High-end tools for MIDI programmers; dance and electronic music; MIDI files; sample CDs; MIDI programming books, software, and synthesizer sounds.

NiceTracker **nicetracker.Webjump.com** Music editor that allows user to create complete songs, music, and vocals, using only Wave Sound Card; CD-quality.

Noise Music **www.noisemusic.org/it** Impulse tracker Web site.

Northstar Productions **www.northstarsamples.com** Sample CD-ROMs or floppies.

Norton AntiVirus **www.norton.com** Virus protection program.

Notation Software **www.notation.com** *MidiNotate;* MIDI player that will convert any MIDI file to sheet music.

Notation Technologies **www.notationtechnologies.com** Home page; *It's Music Time.*

Noteheads AB **www.noteheads.com** Notation software; Sweden.

NoteWorthy ArtWare **www.noteworthysoftware.com** Shareware Annotation; MIDI editor for MS-Windows-3.1 and MS-Windows-9x; functional downloadable demo; user forum.

NoteWorthy Composer **www.ntworthy.com/composer** Music

notation editor/player/printer program; reads and writes MIDI files; downloadable shareware demo version; free player.

Novation **www.novationusa.com** or **www.novationuk.com** Music technology.

Ntonyx **www.ntonyx.com** Style enhancer processes MIDI files to add human performance characteristics; stand-alone version of performance modeling software and a Cakewalk MIDI plugin.

n-Track Studio **www.alberts.com/authorpages/ 00013881/prod_291** or **fasoft.com** Multitrack recording program with support for real-time effects through DirectX plug-ins; Reverb, Chorus, Delay, and Autovol effects are included; audio and MIDI tracks, 24-bit sound cards and more.

Nullsoft **www.nullsoft.com** *WinAmp.*

Objekt ObjektSynth **www.objektsynth.com** Software synthesis; BeOS.

Omnirax **www.omnirax.com** Home page.

Opcode **www.opcode.com** Developer of *Vision* and *Studio Vision* sequencers and integrated digital recording software; *Fusion* plug-ins; MIDI interfaces; *OMS; Galaxy;* originally for Macintosh, now for PC also; news; events; product updates; downloads; technical support; owned by Gibson.

Paladin Enterprises **www.paladin-enterprises.com** Home page.

Palm Pilot **www.palmpilot.com** Personal digital assistant handheld computer.

Parakeet Publications **www.parapubs.net** Make and sell *E-Studio* teaching studio management software and *College Prep,* saxophone lessons on CD-ROM.

Passport Designs **www.passportdesigns.com** Developer of *Master Tracks* and *Master Tracks Pro* MIDI sequencers for the Mac and PC.

Patchman Music **www.patchmanmusic.com** Patch collection company.

PBJ **www.pbjmuisc.com** Music software.

PBJ Music **www.pbjmusic.com/activities.html** *Computer Activities* software by music teachers for music students; Windows.

Peak Limiter **www.sf-soft.de/peaklimit.html** Compresses 16-bit PCM sound files; raise the main volume of the sound file without causing clipping or distortion.

Peavey Electronics **www.peavey.com** Musical instruments manufacturer; guitars, amps, drums, and keyboards; product information; download instrument presets and WAVE files.

Perceptive Solutions, Ltd. Making Waves **www.psinet.demon.co.uk** Software synthesis; Windows.

Personal Composer **www.pcomposer.com/index.htm** Music notation, MIDI sequencing, and publishing program.

Peter Solley Productions **www.petersolleyproductions.com** MIDI sequences.

PG Music **www.pgmusic.com** Developer of *Band-In-A-Box* accompaniment software; software for pianists and guitar players; news; updates; demos; information; technical support; reviews; press releases; links.

PlayPro Software Inc. **www.playprosoft.com** PlayPro Interactive Guitar, Interactive Bass, and Interactive Keyboard.

Pocket Fuel **www.pocketfuel.com** Download free loops.

Polyhedric Software **www.polyhedric.com/software** Maker of the Acid WAV sound editor and synthesizer; WAVmaker, MIDI to WAV renderer.

Power On **www.poweronsoftware.com** Music software.

Power Technology **www.dspfx.com** Developer of *DSP/FX* digital audio DirectX plug-ins for PC; information about effects; magazine reviews; user comments; press releases; download a demo.

Power Tracks **www.powertracks.com** Sequencer for Windows; up to forty-eight tracks of digital audio with effects, EQ, and panning; third party plug-in support.

Practical Music Theory **www.teoria.com** Music software company.

Preview Systems **www.previewsystems.com** Home page.

Pro Music **www.promusicfind.com** Home page.

Proaudio.net **www.proaudio.net** Equipment and production.

Professional Sound Projects **www.psp.l.pl** VST plug-ins.

Propellerhead **www.propellerheads.se** Developer of Steinberg's *ReBirth RB-338,* bass and drum machines; songs; drum loops; software; products; press releases.

Propellerhead Software **www.propellerheads.se** Home page.

Pro-Rec **members.aol.com/prorec** Synthesizer sounds; sample CDs; MIDI files.

Prosoniq **www.prosoniq.com** Developer of *Sonic Worx* software for Macintosh and digital audio plug-ins for *Cubase VST.*

Purple Audio **www.purpleaudio.com** Music technology.

Pyware **www.pyware.com** Music software.

Q Up Arts **www.quparts.com** *Holy Grail Piano; Latin Groove Factory; Voices of Native America; The World; Streetbeats; Psychic Horns; Heavy Guitars; Denny Jarger Private Collection; Kodish; Dream Experience; Toner Textures; Pandora's Toolbox; Ambient.*

Q Up Arts **www.quparts.com** Home page.

Q-Sound Labs **www.qsound.com** Music software.

Quack: Sound Effects .WAV Editor **www.alberts.com/authorpages/ 00014768/prod_589** Create original sound effects.

Quadratic **www.quadratic.com** Develops shareware for Macintosh and Power Macintosh systems; freeware.

Quickscore Links **www.infoserve.net/quickscore/ related.html** Music Web sites; newsgroups; hardware; software; music software dealers.

QuickShot **www.quickshot.com** Music software.

Radikal Technologies **www.radikaltechnologies.com** Home page.

Radix Services **www.radix.co.uk/radsamp** PC Sample Player; supports vari-speed, looping, and volume for each channel and more; demo for download.

Redshift **users.iafrica.com/r/re/redshift** Collection of editors and patches for synths; software for Macintosh, PC, Atari, Amiga, and Unix; links.

Reed Kotler Music **www.reedkotler.com** *Transkriber.*

Replay **www.replaymedia.com/software.html** Music software.

RetroActive Audio Sampler **www.flytools.com** Records audio that has already happened.

Rising Software Music Education **www.risingsoftware.com** Australian software house of music education products; makers of *Auralia* ear-training software.

Ritter Outdoor Ltd. **www.ritter-bags.com** Home page.

RMCA Pro **ourworld.compuserve.com/homepages/ michaelbrick** *Realtime MIDI Chord Arranger* auto accompaniment software; major features of a high quality MIDI keyboard; ability to create accompaniment styles from MIDI files.

Rocket Network Inc. **www.rocketnetwork.com** Home page.

Roland **www.rolandus.com** or **www.rolandgroove.com** Electronics manufacturer; keyboards, digital pianos, synthesizers, studio work stations, sound modules, and more; the *VS-2480 Digital Studio*

Workstation is a self-contained hard disk recorder with 24-track/24-bit digital recording, onboard effects processing, CD recording, 64-channel digital mixer, seventeen motorized faders, VGA monitor output, mouse and ASCII keyboard inputs and 96kHz; *V-Producer* software for the *VP-9000 VariPhrase Processor; Dr. Sample SP-303.*

Roni Music **www.ronimusic.com** *Musician's CD Player* and *Slow Speed CD Transcriber* software; both products are intended for musicians wanting to slow down music without changing the pitch.

Rubber Chicken Software Co. **www.chickensys.com** Home page.

Sample Net **www.SampleNet.com** Sounds and samples.

SampleHeads **www.sampleheads.com** Real sound sample libraries; copyright free.

Samplelibrary.net **www.samplelibrary.net** Archive of samples in A3K, MP3, and other formats.

Samplenet **www.samplenet.co.uk** Sampling resource; free samples to download.

SampleTank **www.sampletank.com** Software sound module; combines sophisticated sampler/synth engine with high quality multisampled sounds into a VST instrument; for Cubase, Logic, or any VST compatible MIDI sequencer; browse highest quality natural and synthesized sounds with one click; select; hundreds of professional high-quality sounds.

Samson **www.samsontech.com** Music technology.

Seasound **www.seasound.com** Home page.

Seer Systems **www.seersystems.com** Developer of real-time software synthesizer for the PC, *Reality*; play from a MIDI keyboard.

SEK'D **www.sekd.com** *Samplitude* multitrack direct-to-disk recording software; digital audio cards for PC; product information; new releases; files, demos, and updated drivers to download.

Sekaku Electron Industry Co. Ltd. **www.sekaku.com.tw** Radioshack.

Sennheiser Electronic Corp. **www.sennheiserusa.com** Sennheiser; Neumann; Chevin; D.A.S. Audio.

Sennheiser **www.sennheiser.com** Manufacturer of microphones and headphones.

Seventh String Software **www.seventhstring.demon.co.uk** Software to help transcribe recorded music; ability to slow down the music without changing its pitch; shareware for Windows.

Shadow Elektroakustik Josip Marinic **www.shadow-pickups.com** Pickups; preamps; MIDI.

Shareware **shareware.cnet.com** Search for more than 250,000 shareware files.

Shareware Music Machine

www.SharewareMusicMachine.com or **www.hitsquad.com/smm** World's biggest music software site; over 2,500 music software titles currently available to download; software categories include: audio editors, audio players, audio recording, audio restoration, business application, SCD burner, SCD player, SCD rippers, collecting and cataloging, computer aided music, CSound drums and percussion, ear training, effects, format converters, guitar, jukebox and multiformat karaoke, label printing, metronomes, MIDI players and utilities, MIDI sequencers, miscellaneous, mod trackers and players, MP3, MPEG, multitrack recording, music calculators, music tuition, notation, oscilloscopes, patch editors and librarians, plug-ins, radio production, remixing and DJ software, samplers, software synthesizers, sound cards, device drivers, sound fonts, spectrum analyzers, streaming audio, media, tuners, video and multimedia, wavetable emulators.

Shockzone

www.macromedia.com/shockzone/ssod Find Web sites with Shockwave.

Signature Music Software **www.signature5.com** *Music Maid.*

Simtel.Net **www.simtel.net/simtel.net** Collection of shareware, freeware, and public domain software for Macintosh, Windows 3.1, and Windows 95; list of alternate servers in other countries.

Sincrosoft SRL **www.sincrosoft.com** Music software company.

Singing Electrons, Inc.

www.singingelectrons.com Wave Creator provides full editing and transformation capabilities; can add different effects to audio including 10-band equalization, echo, chorus, flange, normalize, reverse, and amplify.

Sion Software **www.infoserve.net/quickscore** *QuickScore Elite* and *Copyist;* award-winning music composition, arranging, notation, MIDI sequencing, and recording software; links.

Softlab **www.softlab-nsk.com** Multimedia and computer graphics; *DDClip* real-time audio and video multitrack editor; demos to download.

Softseek.com **softseek.com** Software for Windows only.

Software & Information Industry Association **www.siia.net** Software Publishers Association (SPA) and the Information Industry Association Web site.

Software Publishers Association **www.spa.org** Home page.

Software Synthesis

www.xs4all.nl/~rexbo/pc_synth.htm Software synthesizers; hardware-accelerated synths; MIDI-to-digital-audio real-time generators and non-real-time generators; links to sites and software.

Software Synths and Samplers

shop.store.yahoo.com/computers andmusic/sofsynandsam1.html Links.

Software Technology **www.software-technology.com/** Retailer and online supplier of computer-related products; lists products available.

Songlab

www.snafu.de/~rubo/songlab/midi2cs *Csound* and *Midi2Cs* sound synthesis and audio processing software; links.

Songplayer **www.songplayer.com** Musical instrument tutor to use with CD collection; uses simple graphics to illustrate, beat by beat, each chord in the song.

Songxpress **www.wbpdealers.com** Home page.

Sonic Control **www.soniccontrol.com** Over 600 sample CDs and CD-ROMS; free classified ads; discussion forums; Gigasampler users; network; newsletter.

Sonic Emulations **www.sonicemulations.com** Music technology.

Sonic Foundry **www.sonicfoundry.com** Canadian developer of *Sound Forge* wave edit software for PC; *Acid; Acid Loops; Vegas; CD Architect* audio CD burner; digital audio plug-ins and utilities; news; product information; FAQ; technical support; updates; demos to download; online store.

Sonic Implants or *Sonic Network Inc.* **www.sonicimplants.com** Home page.

Sonic Reality **sonicreality.com** Sample libraries on CD-ROM and audio CD

Sonic State **www.sonicstate.com** News; views; events; links to synthesizer sites; Macintosh and PC software to download; chat.

Sonic Timeworks **www.sonictimeworks.com** Music technology.

Sonomic **www.sonomic.com** Home page.

Sonorus Inc. **www.sonorus.com** STUDI/O; STUDI/O-Sync Backplate; MEDI/0; AUDI/O AES-8; AUDI/O 24; Audi/O Modular/8.

Sony Electronics Inc. **www.sony.com/proaudio** Home page.

Sound Central **www.soundcentral.com** Computer audio samples; MIDI files; freeware; shareware.

Sound Chaser **www.soundchaser.com** Music software; MIDI; audio; interfaces.

Sound FX Page **www.vionline.com/sound.html**
 Source for sound effects; .WAV files; free sound
 files.
Sound Jam **www.soundjam.com** Music software.
Sound Quest Inc. **www.squest.com** *MIDI Quest;
 Infinity; SQ MIDI Tools; Solo Quest.*
Sound Solutions **www.soundsol.com** Large range
 of musical equipment; sound cards; software;
 sound modules; MIDI interfaces; keyboards;
 speakers; MIDI cables and more.
Sound Tree **www.soundtree.com** Music software.
SoundApp **www-cs-
 students.stamford.edu/~franke/
 SoundApp/** Macintosh shareware; play or
 convert files to a variety of formats; supports
 Play Lists sound files; can be saved for later use
 or converted as a group or individually; supports
 random shuffle playback mode and repeated
 playback of Play Lists; useful for converting
 files; free to download.
Soundcards
 www.iqsoft.com/Links/soundcards.htm
 Links to sound card and MIDI interface
 manufacturers.
Sounder **www.sounder.com** Software for creating
 interactive music; Windows; free demo.
Soundprobe **www.soundprobe.co.uk** Sound
 editing, processing, analysis, and effects
 processor suite.
Sounds Factory **perso.magic.fr/j.p.glomot**
 MIDI Editor; universal MIDI sounds editor;
 MIDI shareware and sounds download.
Sounds Logical **www.soundslogical.com**
 WaveWarp.
Soundtrek **www.soundtrek.com** Developer of
 Jammer and *Jammer Pro*; product information;
 demos; MIDI files to download.
Soundwave's Sample Collection
 tilt.largo.fl.us/contents.html or
 **www.Webcom.com/cgould/samples.
 html** Digital samples from a variety of
 keyboards.
Spin Audio Software **www.spinaudio.com**
 Researches, designs, develops, and delivers audio
 plug-ins for using in computer-based Digital
 Audio Workstations.
Spinning Sound **www.spinning-
 sound.com/Tips/tip003.htm** For PC users
 in the studio.
Staccato Systems SynthBuilder
 www.staccatosys.com Software synthesis.
Stage Research, Inc. **www.stageresearch.com**
 Developer of SFX for Windows 98/NT; to aid
 the sound designer and the sound technician in
 creating, maintaining, and executing sound
 effects, music, and show control for a live
 entertainment environment.

Standard MIDI Files on the Net
 www.aitech.ac.jp/~ckelly/SMF.html or
 **www.cs.ruu.nl/pub/MIDI/MIRRORS/
 SMF** Lists of links for MIDI files.
Starland **www.starland.co.uk** Mail order; MIDI;
 UK-based.
Starlite Systems Technology Ltd.
 www.starlite.co.uk Manufacturer of moving
 lights and Windows software for sound and
 lighting.
Steinberg **www.steinberg.de** or
 www.steinberg-us.com or
 www.steinberg.net/products German home
 site and others; *Cubase*; *Rebirth RB-338*;
 information on products; demos; software
 updates; drivers; free plug-ins; dealer lists;
 information on compatible equipment; hints and
 tips; sound card information.
Steinberg North America **www.us.steinberg.net**
 Leading music software manufacturer.
Steinberg ReBirth RB-338
 **www.propellerheads.se/products/
 rebirth15.html** Software synthesis;
 Macintosh/Windows.
Storecase Technology Inc.
 http://www.storecase.com *Data Express;
 Data Silo; Rhino Jr.; Data Stacker; Infostation.*
Stormware **www.stormware.cz** Music software.
Studio Electronics **www.studioelectronics.com**
 Music technology.
Subnet-Audio **www.subnet-
 audio.co.uk/index.shtml** *Digital Sound
 Cabinet*; .WAV and MP3 sound files; some free
 patches.
Summit Audio **www.summitaudio.com** Music
 technology.
Super Loops **www.SuperLoops.com** Loops.
Super Tracks **www.supertracks.com** Home page.
SuperConductor **www.superconductor.com**
 Create instrument samples; aquire from other
 samplers; use advanced MIDI importing and
 exporting features; create streaming Internet
 music files on Web page.
Sweetwater Sound **www.sweetwater.com** Music
 technology supplier.
Swiftkick Productions **www.swiftkick.com**
 Developer of the *Environment Toolkit* book and
 disk; tools for customizing Logic Environment
 to MIDI studio; descriptions of advanced features;
 ET4 quarterly electronic journal.
Swissonic America **www.swissonic.com** AD24;
 DA24; AD96; AD8; AD8 Pro; USB Studio;
 USB Studio D; AD8 Fire Wire.
Symbolic Sound **www.symbolicsound.com**
 Music technology.

Synchro Arts **www.SynchroArts.co.uk**
Digidesign development partner; *ProTools* plug-ins; information; downloadable demos.

Synoptic **www.synoptic.net** Computer-based digital audio software; *Virtual Waves* program for sound synthesis, processing, and analysis; *Virtual Waves Light; Voice FX* is for voice processing with forty effects including reverberation, echoes, alien voices, robot voices, resonant filters, flanger, underwater, and more; *Easy Synth* virtual real-time analog synthesizer; downloads and demos.

Synth & MIDI Museum
www.synthony.com/museum.html
Database of electronic synthesizers and MIDI equipment; hundreds of old instruments; photographs.

Synth Museum **www.synthmuseum.com** Home page.

Synth Zone **www.synthzone.com** Synthesizer resources on the Internet; links to manufacturer and user group sites; music and audio software; MIDI, synthesizer, and electronic music; electronic keyboards and effects.

Synthfood **www.btinternet.com/~synthfood** British company; sound patches.

Syntrillium Software Corporation
www.syntrillium.com Developer of *Cool Edit* and *Cool Edit Pro*; information; technical FAQ; news; program demos; updates; manuals and utilities to download.

Tardis **www.tardis.ed.ac.uk/~psyche/cdda** List of MP3 compatible CD-ROM drives.

Tascam **www.tascam.com** Multitrack reel-to-reel recorders; data storage products; consumer audio equipment; mixers; DATs; product information; FAQs; technical support; list of repair centers; *Ministudio; Portastudio;* pro audio division of TEAC Corporation.

TC Electronic **www.tcelectronic.com** High-end signal processors for the studio, PA, and broadcast industries; product information; software updates; distributor lists; manuals to download; news; press releases; employment opportunities.

TC Works **www.tcworks.de** Digital audio plug-ins based on TC Electronic hardware designs; *TC Native Reverb, Native EQ,* and *Native Essentials;* information; news; demo downloads.

TC-SoftWorks **www.tc-softworks.com** MindExplorer SW, an AudioStrobe, and Turbosonix compatible software; audiovisual stimulation tool that allows user to create, edit, and perform light and sound sessions on a PC.

Tech Week Live **www.techweek.com** The technical community.

Techno Toys **www.technotoys.com** Software for electronic music; download programs; freebies; sounds and MIDI files; links for computer-based musicians; virtual synths; digital audio editors; plug-ins.

Terran **www.terran.com** Web audio batch processors.

Terzoid **www.terzoid.com** *NoiZe* for Windows universal MIDI patch editor/librarian; *WaveShop* DirectX plug-in for *Cakewalk;* download demos.

The "Really Easy" Synthesizer Course
www.really-ez.com Multimedia: videotapes, computer generated audio tapes that play the songs and the exercises in the course; over 300 pages of detailed instruction; support services; special learning aids and much more; Roland synthesizer is furnished with the course.

The ABC Musical Notation Language
www.gre.ac.uk/~c.walshaw/abc Software packages; tune collections; language description.

The Center for Computer Research in Music and Acoustics (CCRMA) **ccrma-www.stanford.edu** Home page.

The Complete MIDI File Directory
www.flexfx.com Archive of MIDI files organized by category.

The History of Electronic Music
www.sci.fi/~phinnWeb/history History of electronic music; important avantgarde/electronic music composers and producers.

The Melodious MIDI
www.fortunecity.com/tinpan/lennon/351 Classical, rock, folk, religious, and other MIDI music.

The MIDI File Organizer
www.midiorganizer.com Store MIDI files and lyrics in one location; store thousands of songs; accessed instantly.

The MIDI Archive
ftp://ftp.cs.ruu.nl/pub/MIDI/index.html Lists of links.

The Online Directory of Electronic Music
members.tripod.com/~emusic/index.html Links to electronic music sites.

The Sonic Spot **www.sonicspot.com** Music and audio software library for the PC; reviews; detailed descriptions; screen shots; links; downloads for shareware, freeware, and commercial software.

The Virtual Music Vault
www.tvmv.com/artists_new_age.html Music industry and technology news.

The World Wide Logic Users Group
www.mcc.ac.uk/~emagic Information; hints; tips; hardware guide; tutorials; PC soundcard survey; FAQs; mailing list; links.

Theatrix Interactive, Inc. **www.theatrix.com** Software.

Thinkware **www.thinkware.com** Software Web site.

Third Wave Media **www.thirdwavemedia.com** Home page.

TidBITS Guide to MIDI and the Macintosh **www.leeds.ac.uk/music/Info/MacMIDI/ Contents.html** Information about MIDI and the Macintosh.

Time and Space **www.timespace.com** Detailed online catalogue of the sample CD producers; details of their music software.

Tom Snyder Productions **www.tomsnyder.com** Instructional software.

Total Recorder **www.highcriteria.com/products.htm** Universal sound recording tool; captures sound being played by other sound players, either from a file or from the Internet; records audio from CD, microphone, line-in; converts any sound formats to WAVE.

T-RackS 24 **www.t-racks.com** IK Multimedia; analog modeled, stand-alone software dedicated to audio mastering; built with actual physical models of tube circuitry; updated to support 24-bit file processing; complete workstation made of four discrete processors; state-of-the-art six band parametric EQ; classic stereo tube compressor/leveler; multiband master stereo limiter; soft-clipping adjustable output stage.

Trail Creek Systems **www.trailcreeksystems.com** Makers of *Ear Training Expedition* software.

Tran Tracks **www.trantracks.com** MIDI files; rhythm, groove, and style disks.

Tray Transpose Tool **www.simusic.com/traytranspose.html** Program that will work with any Windows application to transpose chords into any key.

Trycho Tunes **www.trycho.com** Performance sequences; all genres.

Tune 1000 **www.midi-classics.com/tune1000.htm** MIDI.

Turbo Guide **cd-rom-guide.com/index.html** Links to software and CD-ROM companies.

Turtle Beach **www.turtlebeach.com** Division of Voyetra; digital audio cards.

Tyler Systems Inc. **www.tylerretail.com** Home page.

U&I Software **www.uisoftware.com** Software.

Ubi Soft Entertainment **www.ubisoft.com** Software.

Ueberschall **www.ueberschall.com** Sample service of Germany.

Unitec Products Corp. **www.unitecproducts.com** *Unitec; Mini Monster; Ritter Bags; Cruise Audio Systems.*

Universal Concept Inc. **www.prosoundWeb.com** Home page.

VB's Home Page **Webperso.alma-net.net/burel** Digital audio software for PC; effects based on plug-in architecture.

Velvet Development **hem.passagen.se/vicious** Supports SB (PRO;16); GUS (GUS PnP planned); MIDI input for GUS; enhanced volume; panning and vibrato envelope definitions; sample editor with effects-like flanger; chorus; crossfade; time compression; fix loop.

Vergence **www.vergenceaudio.com** Music technology.

Vestax **www.vestax.co.uk** Mixers; turntables; merchandise.

Vintage Synth **www.vintagesynth.com** Vintage synthesizers; pictures.

Vinyl to CDR Processing Software **www.ganymede.hemscott.net/ wavecor.htm** Support site for Wave Corrector; application for removing vinyl clicks, ticks, and plops from wave recordings of vinyl records prior to transfer to CD.

Virtual Synth Page **www.users.zetnet.co.uk/*white*/vsp** Software synthesis.

Virtuoso **www.Webcom.com/virtvirt** Music software.

V-Mix **macinsearch.com/infomac/gst/midi/ v-mix-191.html** or **www.hancock.net/~neosync** Shareware mix automation software; Macintosh.

Voicecrystal **www.voicecrystal.com** Developer of sounds and voices for synthesizers on floppy disk, CD, and RAM cards; sample CDs and music software; product information; sound clips to download; mailing list.

Voodoo Lab **www.voodoolab.com** Home page.

Vorton Technologies **www.vorton.com** Music software.

Voyager **www.voyager.learntech.com/cdrom** Music software company.

Voyetra Turtle Beach Inc. **www.voyetra-turtle-beach.com** Educational music software and games for all ages and levels; sound cards.

Wave Digital System **www.wavedigital.com** Studio PC; MP3 PC; Music PC; custom DAWS.

Wave Distribution **www.wavedistribution.com** Distressor; StudioPC; NoteMix.

Wave Mechanics Inc. **www.wavemechanics.com** *UltraTools; Sound Blender; Speed; Pitch Doctor; Pure Pitch.*

Waveform **www.Waveform.dk**

Waves **www.waves.com** Digital audio software and plug-ins for Macintosh and PC; *Native Power Pack; TDM Bundle;* list of products and platforms supported; new products; demos to download; free software updates; tips on using the software; FAQ; links.

Waves Links **www.waves.com/htmls/about/links. html** Sites of companies which support Waves software; MIDI links; links to audio and multimedia magazines.

Wavestation Patch Archive **www.city.ac.uk/~cb170/ws_subs.html** Swap patches.

Wavestation Users Mailing List **www.magic.ca/~lost/ws.html** FAQ; software.

WAVmaker **www.polyhedric.com/software/ wavmaker** MIDI to WAV renderer.

Weazle World **www.august.com/copular/ww/index.htm** or **www.weazle.demon.co.uk/images/front/ drum.htm** Techno sound samples in .WAV format.

Wildcat Canyon Software **www.wildcat.com** Software developer; *Autoscore; Internet Music Kit* for adding music to Web site; free downloads; technical support.

Windows 95 Music Shareware and Freeware **www.hitsquad.com/smm/edit/ win95.html** Software synthesis.

WinFiles.com **www.winfiles.com** Shareware for Windows 95, 98, CE, and NT.

Wired News **www.wired.com/news** High-tech news.

Wizoo **www.wizoo.com** Samples.

World Village **www.worldvillage.com** Software reviews; directories of downloads.

World Wide Woodshed **www.worldwidewoodshed.com** *Slow Gold; Slow Blast!*

WOW Thing **www.wowthing.com** Improves the quality of audio; produces deep rich bass from any speakers or headphones on the personal computer.

Yamaha Corporation of America **www.yamaha.com** Music manufacturer of keyboards, drums, guitars, Clavinovas, Disklaviers, receivers, stereos, tuners, pro-audio, mixers, brass, woodwind, recorders, and software.

Yamaha Corporation Yamaha S-YXG50 **www.yamaha.co.uk/xg/html** Software synthesis; Windows.

Yamaha UK **www.yamaha.co.uk/eurohome/ library.htm** Collection of product manuals.

Yan Terrien and Hameau de Peymian Synthia **www.hitsquad.com/smm/programs/ Synthia** Software synthesis.

ZDNET.com **www.ZDNET.com** Information on computer products; reviews.

Zero-G **www.timespace.com** Sample CDs and CD-ROMs.

Conferences and Showcases—Festivals and Fairs

AES Conference **www.aes.org** Held in NYC.

Aloud **www.aloud.com/festival.shtml** Festivals Web page; links; updates.

America's Music Festival **www.americasmusicfestival.com** Talent competitions; showcases.

American Music Conference **www.amc-music.com** American Music Conference.

Appel Farm Festival **www.appelfarm.org** Held the first Saturday in June in Elmer, NJ.

Arts Northwest **concertsource.com/artsnw** Annual conference held in October-November; trade show; showcases for theater, performing arts, music, children; arts council presenters in Washington, Idaho, and Oregon; membership required.

Association for Independent Music (AFIM-formerly NAIRD) **www.afim.com** Annual independent record conference held in late May; awards; showcase independent recording artists; membership required.

Association for the Promotion of Campus Activities (APCA) **www.apca.com** Annual conference in February-early March; trade show; showcase; all performance types interested in the college market.

Association of Performing Arts Presenters (APAP) **www.artspresenters.org** Annual conference in mid-January in NYC; regional conferences include (1) early September: Western Arts Alliance Association, (2) mid-September: Midwest Arts Conference, (3) late September: Southern Arts Exchange.

Atlantis Music Conference **www.atlantismusic.com** Held in Atlanta, GA.

Augusta Heritage Center Music Camp **www.augustaheritage.com** Held in August in Elkins, WV; Vocal Week; Festival.

Billboard Music Conferences **www.billboard.com/events** Billboard events.

Bluestock Festival **www.bluestock.org** Held in October in Memphis, TN.

Calgary Folk Music Festival
www.calgaryfolkfest.com Held in July in Calgary, Alberta, Canada.

Canadian Arts Presenting Association/L'Association Canadienne des Organismes Artistiques (CAPACOA)
www.culturenet.ca/capacoa Annual arts presenters conference; music, theater, dance showcases.

Canadian Folk Festivals www.interlog.com/-ufojoe Folk festivals in Canada.

Canadian Music Events-Festivals & Concerts
www.canadian.com/events.html Comprehensive guide to Canadian music events; concerts and festivals from British Columbia to Newfoundland.

Canadian Music Week www.cmw.net Annual music conference in early March; trade show; showcase; all genres.

Canmore Heritage Days
www.banff.net/users/canmorefolkfest Held in August in Canmore, Alberta, Canada.

Chamber Music Holidays and Festivals
www.chamber.music.holidays.mcmail.com Holiday events; chamber music.

Chamber Music Northwest www.cmnw.org One of the leading festivals of chamber music in North America; festival musicians have international solo and ensemble careers.

City Stages www.citystages.org Held in June.

CMJ Music Marathon & Music Fest
www.cmj.com Four days and nights in early September; conference and showcase in NYC clubs and at the Lincoln Center; all genres of music; subscription available to journal; college radio chart reports.

Comdex www.zdevents.com/comdex International electronics shows.

Consumer Electronics Show www.cesWeb.org January in Las Vegas.

Common Ground on the Hill
www.commongroundonthehill.com Held in July at Western Maryland College, Westminster, MD; workshop; festival.

Country Music Association (CMA) www.cma.org SRO country music conference late September; showcase new, signed, country artists.

Country Music Showcase International, Inc.
www.cmshowcase.org Home page.

Country Stampede Music Festival
www.countrystampede.com Four days of country music in June in Kansas.

Crossroads Music Expo www.bluestock.org Annual event held in Memphis.

Cutting Edge Music Business Conference
www.satchmo.com Annual music business conference, trade show, and showcase in early September; showcase all genres.

Dawson City Music Festival www.dcmf.com Held in July in Dawson City, Yukon, Canada.

EAT'M www.eat-m.com Emerging Artists and Talent in Music; annual conference and festival held in May.

Edmonton Folk Music Festival www.efmf.ab.ca Held in August in Edmonton, Alberta, Canada.

Falcon Ridge Folk Festival
www.falconridgefolk.com Held in July in Sharon, CT.

Fan Fair www.fanfair.com Home page; in Nashville in June.

Festival Finder www.festivalfinder.com Comprehensive guide to music festivals in North America; search by date, location, performer, or festival name.

FestivalFinder: Classical Music Festivals of North America
www.festivalfinder.com/classical Extensive guide to classical music festivals in the United States and Canada; search by genre, performer, location, date, festival name, and more.

Festivals of Music www.festivalsofmusic.com Home page.

Festivals.com www.festivals.com Information on music festivals.

Folk Festivals in the United States and Canada
oeonline.com/folk_fests Tracks folk festivals by state and province; glance at all the festivals of an entire state at once.

Gavin www.gavin.com Main annual conference and showcase in mid-February; annual Gavin Country conference and showcase in May; Strategy Summit conference and showcase in August; annual Americana Retreat conference and showcase in September; showcase signed independent and major label artists reflected in Gavin's radio charts; membership required; subscription available; includes news reports, radio chart reports.

Glastonbury Festival www.glastonbury-festival.co.uk/2000 UK festival; dates.

GrassRoots Festival www.grassrootsfest.org Home page; held in July; Cajun, Zydeco, stringband, African music, and more.

Heritage Festivals/Bowl Games of America
www.heritagefestivals.com Home page.

High Sierra Music Festival www.hsmusic.net Held in June and July in California.

Indie Music Forum
www.IndieMusicForum.com Annual conferences for independent artists; information; testimonials; past speakers; sponsorship; mailing list; conferences in San Francisco, Philadelphia, San Diego, Miami, and New York.

Intel New York Music Festival **www.thegig.com** Annual Music and the Internet conference in mid-July; trade show; showcase; online music festival; all genres of music in clubs; linked online.

Interactive Music XPO (IMX) **www.imusicxpo.com** LA conference and exposition; music industry; new media; Web radio; recording; technology.

International Association of African American Music (IAAAM) **www.IAAAM.com** Annual conference, awards, Emerging Arts Showcase in June; presents series of educational seminars; conference tour sponsorship; concert production.

International Bluegrass Music Association (IBMA) **www.ibma.org** Annual week-long trade show, showcase, and festival in mid-October; regional annual conferences on the West Coast and in the Southeast; showcase new and established bluegrass acts; membership required.

International Fairs Association **iafenet.org** Directory listing county, state, and international fairs and events in the U.S., Canada, and the world; associate membership available for performers and agents; directory free with membership, $85 for nonmembers; annual conference, trade show Las Vegas, early December.

KanawhaPalooza **listen.to/kanawhapalooza** Held in West Virginia.

Kerrville Folk Festival **www.kerrville-music.com** Annual folk event held in late May-early June (through Memorial Day weekend) in Kerrville, TX; songwriting; networking; performances.

Kerrville Wine Festival **www.kerrville-music.com** Held in September on Labor Day weekend in Kerrville, TX.

KRCL Performing Songwriter Showcase **www.krcl.org** Utah.

Lamb's Fall Retreat **www.springfed.org** Held in November in Michigan.

Lamb's Spring Retreat **www.springfed.org** Held in April in Michigan.

Llangollen International Music Eisteddfod **www.lime.uk.com** Wales welcomes the world to Llangollen every year at the International Music Eisteddfod.

Lotus World Music and Arts Festival **www.lotusfest.org** Series of events that offer opportunities to experience, celebrate, and learn about the diversity of the world's cultures; named after folk musician Lotus Dickey.

Louisiana Music-New Orleans Pride **www.offbeat.com/lmnop** Annual event held in April in New Orleans.

MerleFest **www.merlefest.org** Held in Wilkesboro, NC.

MIAC (Music Industries Association of Canada) **www.miac.net** MIAC Trade Show.

Mid-America Composers Festival **www.grinnell.edu/macf** Joint meeting of the Iowa Composers Forum and Region V of the Society of Composers.

MIDEM **www.midem.com** Premier international music market; MIDEM Europe in Cannes, France in mid-January; MIDEM Asia in mid-May; MIDEM Latin America and Caribbean Music in mid-September; international music licensing trade show with music showcases.

Mob Fest **www.mobfest.com** Held in Chicago.

Music Midtown **musicmidtown.com** Held in April in Atlanta, GA.

Music Planet **www.musicplanet.com/fest.htm** Music festival listings.

Music West **www.musicwest.com** Annual Vancouver-based music seminar; music festival; film festival; trade show in mid-May; showcase new, unsigned Indie bands in all genres.

NAMM (National Association of Music Merchants) **www.namm.com** Annual conferences; trade shows; concerts; late winter, LA; summer, Nashville; International Music Products Association; thousands of exhibitors; all types of music products and services displayed; online program book.

Napa Valley Music & Wine Festival **www.napafest.com** Annual event held in Napa Valley, CA.

Nashville Entertainment Association eX-travaganza **www.estravaganza.org** Annual music conference, showcase in mid-February; unsigned acts, all genres.

National Academy of Recording Arts & Sciences (NARAS) **www.grammy.com** Check for future showcase opportunities; sponsor showcases for unsigned and independent label rock bands.

National Association for Campus Activities (NACA) **www.naca.org** Annual conference, showcase, and exhibit hall in mid-February; regional conferences throughout the U.S. include the Southeast, South Central, Upper Midwest, East Coast, Great Lakes, Pacific Northwest, Heart of America, New England, Far West, Illiana, Wisconsin; showcase music of all genres, comedy, theater, and performance art; membership required.

National Association of Record Merchandisers (NARM) **www.narm.com** Annual conference, trade show, and showcase held in mid-March; presented by member labels.

NEMO Music Showcase & Conference **www.nemo99.com** Annual music conference, showcase, trade show; Kahlua Boston Music

Awards; rock, jazz, blues, hip-hop, bluegrass, country, rap, R&B, reggae, etc.

New Orleans Jazz & Heritage Festival
www.nojazzfest.com Annual event held in late April and early May in New Orleans.

New York Music & Internet Expo
www.newyorkexpo.com/home.htm Internet conference held in New York.

Newport Folk Festival **www.newportfolk.com** Held in August in Newport, RI.

Next Fest **www.nextfest.com** Held in Nashville.

North American Music Festivals
www.greatfestivals.com Home page.

North By North East (NXNE) **www.nxne.com** Annual music conference held in June in Toronto, Ontario, Canada.

North By North West (NXNW) **www.nxnw.com** Annual music conference, trade show, showcase held in Portland, Oregon; all music genres.

Northeast Regional Folk Alliance Conference
www.nefolk.org Held in November in Philadelphia, PA.

Northern California Songwriters Association
www.ncsasong.org Annual Songwriters Conference held in September; networking; seminars; workshops; song critiques; panel discussions.

Ottawa Folk Festival **www.ottawafolk.org** Held in August in Ottawa, Ontario, Canada.

Philadelphia Folk Festival **www.folkfest.org** or **www.pfs.org** Held in August in Philadelphia, PA; always before Labor Day.

Philadelphia Music Conference
www.gopmc.com Conference; trade show; showcases; all styles of commercial music.

ROCKRGRL Magazine Music Conference
www.rockrgrl.com Conducting a national search for over 200 female-inclusive artists in all musical genres to perform at the ROCKRGRL Music Conference; partnership between the bimonthly publication and founder of the South By Southwest Music Conference.

Rocky Mountain Folks Festival
www.bluegrass.com Held in August in Lyons, CO; Planet Bluegrass.

Sierra Nevada World Music Festival
www.snwmf.com Three-day Reggae and World Music festival held in Marysville, CA in June.

Sierra Songwriters **www.sierrasongwriters.com** California showcase.

South By Southwest Music and Media Conference (SXSW) **www.sxsw.com** Annual conference and showcase held in mid-March in Austin, TX; international talent; all genres.

Strawberry Music Festival
www.strawberrymusic.com Held in May on Memorial Day weekend and in September on Labor Day weekend in Sonora, CA.

Taxi Road Ralley **www.taxi.com** Free annual convention held in the LA area; music industry panels; song and demo critiques; networking.

Telluride Bluegrass Festival
www.bluegrass.com Held in June in Telluride, CO.

Telluride Festivals and Events **www.telluride-events.com** Calendar of festivals and events for Telluride.

Telluride Troubadour Contest
www.bluegrass.com Held in Telluride, CO.

The Aspen Music Festival
www.aspen.com/musicfestival/fsfest.htm Annual event in Aspen, CO.

The Association for Recorded Sound Collections (ARSC) **www.arsc-audio.org** Annual conferences in different parts of the U.S.

The Caribbean Music Expo **www.cme.com.jm** Web site; held in the Caribbean.

The Folk Alliance **www.folk.org** Annual international folk music and dance conference held in mid-February; rotate regional locations; Northwest and Midwest annual conferences; showcase folk, acoustic, world, ethnic music, and dance; membership required.

The Great River Folk Festival
www.viterbo.edu/personalpages/faculty/rruppel/fest.html Held in August at the University of Wisconsin, La Crosse, WI.

The Harvest Showcase
www.harvestshowcase.com Presentation of USA Harvest, a network of thousands of volunteers who have collected and distributed more than 3.8 billion pounds of food; event happens in September in Louisville, KY.

The Hillside Festival **www.hillside.on.ca** Held in July in Guelph, Ontario, Canada.

The Independent Music Festival
www.independentmusicfest.com See what's been missing from most commercial music circles; showcases rock, blues, folk, anti-folk, rap, avant garde, electronica, and more; over eighty-five bands and solo artists; April in New Brunswick, NJ.

The International Music Conference Alliance (IMCA) **www.rockrgrl.com** Held in November in Austin, TX.

The Rhythms of the World
www.harbourfront.on.ca Includes the JVC Jazz Festival; mid-June through September in Toronto, Ontario, Canada.

The South Florida Folk Festival
www.southfloridafolkfest.com Annual event; folk festivities; songwriting competition; held in January in Ft. Lauderdale.

The Swannanoa Gathering
www.swangathering.org Held in late July and early August in Ashville, NC; Guitar and Folkweek.

Tin Pan South **www.nashvillesongwriters.com** NSAI annual week-long event held in April in Nashville; club showcases of songwriters from everywhere; Legendary Songwriters Concert at the Ryman Auditorium.

True Value/Jimmy Dean Country Showdown **www.countryshowdown.com** Judged country music artist showcases; annual local, state, regional, and national winners compete for cash and a recording contract.

U.S. Mid-West Folk, Dance, and Storytelling Festivals **www.mcs.com/ -hammerd/fvfs/festlst.html** For folk dancers and storytellers.

Undercurrents **www.undercurrents.com** Annual music trade show and showcase held in mid-May; showcase acoustic, rock, blues, jazz, and pop.

Urban Focus **www.urbanfocus.org** Annual music conference and festival in Los Angeles in June; R&B, hip-hop, gospel, jazz, and reggae; new talent auditions.

Urban Music Festival **www.urbanmusicfestival.com** Urban Music Festival Web site.

Vancouver Folk Festival **www.thefestival.bc.ca** Annual event held in July in Vancouver, BC, Canada.

Walnut Valley Festival **www.wvfest.com** Held in September in Winfield, KS.

Webnoize Events **events.Webnoize.com** Conferences.

Western Fairs Association **www.fairnet.org** Listing of fairs and expositions in the Western states and Canada; membership available.

WestFest **www.westfest.net** Held in Vail, CO in September on Labor Day weekend.

Wildflower Arts & Music **www.cor.net/wildflower** or **www.wildflowerfestival.com** Held in April in Richardson, TX.

Winnipeg Folk Festival **www.wpgfolkfest.mb.ca** Held in July in Winnipeg, Manitoba, Canada.

Winter Music Conference **www.wintermusicconference.com** Miami Beach, FL; network with industry professionals; DJs; radio forums; exhibition area; technology.

Winterhawk Bluegrass Festival **www.winterhawkbluegrass.com** Held in July in Utica, New York.

Woody Guthrie Free Folk Festival **www.woodyguthrie.com** Annual event held in July in Midwest City, OK.

World Beat Music Festival **www.worldbeattnt.com** Annual music event bringing together worldbeat musicians from around the world to Port of Spain, Trinidad.

Copyright, Legal, and Tax Information—Performing and Mechanical Rights—Digital Watermarking—Privacy Rights

1-800-Tax-Laws **www.1-800-taxlaws.com/service.html** Tax information.

AFM (American Federation of Musicians) **www.afm.org** Musicians union; New York headquarters; how to hire musicians; member groups; booking agents; member benefits; history of the organization founded in the 1890s.

AFTRA (American Federation of Television and Radio Artists) **www.aftra.com** Union.

AKM (Staatlich Genehmigte Gesellschaft Der Autoren Komponisten Und Musikverlager) **www.akm.co.at** Performing rights organization of Austria.

APRA (Australasian Performing Right Association) **www.apra.com.au** Australasia.

ARIS Technologies, Inc. **www.musicode.com** Information on digital watermarking.

Artists Against Piracy **www.artistsagainstpiracy.com** Anti-audio piracy campaign.

ASCAP (American Society of Composers, Authors, and Publishers) **www.ascap.com** Performing rights organization; collects performance royalties; active members are composers, lyricists, songwriters, and music publishers; award-winning Web site; music database; legislative; licensing; insurance; music business; catalogs; links; created in 1914 to provide the essential link between the creators of music and the users of music; only performing rights organization in the United States whose board of directors is made up entirely of writers and music publishers elected by and from its membership.

ASCAP Capitol Connect **www.capitolconnect.com/ascap/howtouse.asp** Contact senators; E-mail legislators; suggested items to include in letter to senator; do not have to be an ASCAP member.

Band Radio Contracts **www.bandradio.com/law/samples.html** Links to many different sample music business contracts; recording, publishing, etc.

BayTSP **www.baytsp.com** San Jose, CA based corporation; developer, patent holder, and provider of effective means of branding and tracking online content over the Internet; software products and services are aimed to deter theft of online content as well as aid in the prosecution of those who engage in copyright infringement.

Better Business Bureau **www.bbb.org** Online site.

Blue Spike, Inc. **www.bluespike.com** Information on digital watermarking.

BMI (Broadcast Music Incorporated) **www.bmi.com** Performing rights organization; music-related links; writer and publisher member catalogs; licensing information; instrument insurance.

Bookkeeping, Income Tax and Small Business Help **www.geocities.com/wallstreet/2924** Tax information.

BUMA (Het Bureau voor Muziek-Auteursrecht) **www.buma.nl** Performing rights organization of the Netherlands.

Center for Financial & Tax Planning **www.taxplanning.com** Tax information.

Central Research Laboratories **www.crl.co.uk** Information on digital watermarking.

CMRRA (Canadian Musical Reproduction Rights Agency Ltd.) **www.cmrra.ca** Home page; reproduction rights in Canada.

Cognicity, Inc. **www.cognicity.com** Information on digital watermarking.

Copyright and Intellectual Property Resources **www.nlc-bnc.ca/ifla/ll/cpyright.htm** Comprehensive listing of sources on copyright.

Copyright Clearance Center **www.copyright.com** Information on obtaining licenses for copying text.

Copyright Imprints **host.mpa.org/agency.html** Listing of copyright imprints of publishers, both domestic and foreign; based on information submitted by the membership of Music Publishers Association, National Music Publishers Association, and the Church Music Publishers.

Copyright Office U. S. **www.lcWeb.loc.gov/copyright** Copyright information; copyright law; forms; pending legislation.

Copyright.Net **www.copyright.net** Announces content development division; helps Napster "get legit"; business-to-business Internet portal; *Copyrightagent;* fully automated Web-based software tool for the community of copyright owners, ISPs, and consumers to process Digital Millennium Copyright Act (DMCA) legal procedures via the Internet.

Digital Future Coalition **www.dfc.org** Group formed to help balance the protection of intellectual property and public access to it.

EAU (Eesti Autorite Uhing) **www.eauthors.ee** Performing rights organization of Estonia.

Electronic Frontier Foundation **www.eff.org** Civil-rights organization for the online community; general information on copyright; links; articles on issues of debate; freedom of speech rights.

Electronic Policy Network **epn.org** Public policy resources.

Entertainment Publisher **www.entertainmentpublisher.com** Automated contracts for a fee; music industry; film and television; labor.

Essential Links to Taxes **www.el.com/elinks/taxes** Tax information.

Federal Government Information **www.firstgov.com** Federal laws and more.

Federal Web Locater **www.law.vill.edu/Fed-Agency/fedWebloc.html** List of government Web sites.

FedWorld **www.fedworld.gov** Tax information.

GEMA (Gesellschaft Fur Musikalische Auffuhrungs Und Mechanische) **www.gema.de** Performing rights organization of Germany.

Government of Canada **www.nlc-bnc.ca/window/windowe.htm** Copyright; for book, music, periodical, electronic, and multimedia publishers; support programs; ultimate resource for music and entertainment professionals and consumers; phone, fax, Internet, toll-free numbers, trade shows, and more.

GPO Gate **www.gpo.ucop.edu** Directory of government databases.

IMRO (Irish Music Rights Organization) **www.imro.ie** Performing rights organization of Ireland.

Incorporated Society of Musicians **www.ism.org** Classical.

Independent Musicians Guild **www.scimg.com/img** Guide.

Indie-Music.com Sample Contracts **www.indie-music.com/contract.shtml** Links to many sample music industry contracts.

International Trademark Association (formerly the US Trademark Association) **www.inta.org** Home page.

KODA (Selskabet til Forvaltning af Internationale Komponistrettighederi Danmark) **ww.koda.dk** Performing rights organization of Denmark.

Kohn Music **www.kohnmusic.com** Copyright law and music licensing on the Internet; links to copyright and music rights clearance organizations; industry resources.

Library of Congress Home Page **www.loc.gov** Information resources and tools.

MARIA (Manitoba Audio Recording Industry Association) **www.manaudio.mb.ca** Canadian organization.

MCPS (Mechanical Copyright Protection Society)
www.mcps.co.uk UK collection agency.

Media Enforcer **www.mediaenforcer.com**
Fighting online piracy.

Mr. Smith E-mails Washington
www.mrsmith.com E-mail addresses of
members of Congress.

Multimedia and Entertainment Law Online News
www.degrees.com/melon Latest
developments in entertainment law.

Music and Recording Contracts Site
members.idnsi.com/dregar For recording
artists, music managers, music producers, music
publishers, musicians, and entertainment
attorneys searching for recording contracts,
copyrighting, etc.

*Music Law, Publishers, Copyright and Trademark
Search Services (Rain Music)*
**www.rainmusic.com/promotion/law.
htm** Information on music law, music
publishers, or copyright and trademark services.

*Music Library Association Guide to Copyright for
Music Librarians*
**www.musiclibraryassoc.org/Copyright/
copyhome.htm** FAQ; information.

Music Publishers' Association-Copyright Resources
www.mpa.org/crc.html Copyright Search
Center provides a step-by-step guide to
researching the copyright holder or publisher of a
piece of music.

Musician's Intellectual Law and Resources Links
www.aracnet.com/~schornj/index.shtml
Notes on copyright: new legislation; copyright
in compositions; copyright in sound recordings;
collection of royalties; mechanical royalties;
trademarks and servicemarks; miscellaneous
intellectual law links; thoughts on contracts;
analysis of recording contract clauses; musician
resources; my favorite musician related links;
jazz and music magazines; record company links;
booking agents, managers, and music publishers;
international venues; American venues;
musicians' Web pages.

Musician's Law **www.musicianslaw.com** Legal
issues concerning musicians.

Musician's Union UK
www.musiciansunion.org.uk Information
on local offices; press releases; FAQs; links;
members; gig list; copyright section.

Music-Law.com **www.music-law.com** Legal
issues concerning musicians.

NUS **www.nus.org.uk** Students' Union; contacts;
gig guide.

Pacific Music Industry Association
www.pmia.org Official Web site.

PrivacyPlace **www.privacyplace.com** Devoted
to furthering online privacy.

PRS (Performing Right Society) **www.prs.co.uk**
UK association of composers, songwriters, and
music publishers; administers performing rights.

Public Domain Music **www.pdinfo.com** Music in
the public domain.

Public Domain Report Music Bible
www.pubdomain.com Volumes I & II;
comprehensive, up-to-date listings of PD music
available; listings and reviews of more than
7,000 select PD songs; more than 2,000 songs
available in authenticated PD sheet music;
custom copyright search.

Quicken Financial Services **www.quicken.com**
Budget and tax planning.

RAO (Russian Authors Society) **www.rao.ru**
Performing rights organization of Russia.

Recording Industry Association of America (RIAA)
www.riaa.com Official Web site; digital
watermarking; copyrights; legislation;
technology; Web licensing; censorship; parental
advisory; Gold and Platinum awards; links.

Revenue Canada **www.rc.gc.ca** Tax information.

Rock Out Censorship **www.theroc.org** Grassroots
anticensorship organization; First Amendment
rights.

*SABAM (Societe Belge Des Auteurs Compositeurs
Et Editeurs)* **www.sabam.be** Performing
rights organization of Belgium.

*SACEM (Societe Des Auteurs Compositeurs Et
Editeurs De Musique)* **www.sacem.fr**
Performing rights organization of France.

*SCALA (Australia Songwriters, Composers, and
Lyricists Association)*
www.senet.com.au/~scala/more.htm
Home page.

Secure Digital Music Initiative **www.sdmi.org**
Piracy fighter; secure delivery of digital music
across all platforms; press releases; membership
requirements; schedule.

SESAC **www.sesac.com** Performing rights
organization; privately owned.

SGAE (Sociedad General De Autores De Espana)
www.sgae.es Performing rights organization
of Spain.

SIAE (Societa Italiana Degli Autori Ed Editori)
www.siae.it Performing rights organization of
Italy.

Small Business Administration **www.sba.gov**
Government office.

Small Business Taxes and Management
www.smbiz.com Tax information.

*SOCAN (Society of Composers Authors & Music
Publishers Of Canada)* **www.socan.ca**
Performing rights organization of Canada.

SODRAC Inc. **www.sodrac.com** Canadian
performing rights organization (French).

SoundExchange **www.soundexchange.com**
Collection agency by RIAA to procure royalties from sites that play music in streaming radio format.

Stanford University Libraries Comprehensive Copyright Site **fairuse.stanford.edu**
Copyright history; statutes; regulations; treaties; articles; links.

STIM (Svenska Tonsattares Internationella Musikbyra) **www.stim.se** Performing rights organization of Sweden.

TEOSTO (Bureau International Du Droit D'Auteur Des Compositeurs Finlandais) **www.teosto.fi** Performing rights organization of Finland.

The British Phonographic Industry **www.bpi.co.uk** British music industry; statistics; links.

The Copyright Website **www.benedict.com** Copyright information; all forms and subjects.

The Electronic Frontier Foundation **www.eff.org** Devoted to furthering online privacy.

The Electronic Privacy Information Center **www.epic.org** Devoted to furthering online privacy.

The Harry Fox Agency **nmpa.org/hfa.html** or **www.harryfox.com** Mechanical royalties and licenses; searchable database of songs and publishers; current statutory mechanical rate.

The Privacy Rights Clearinghouse **www.privacyrights.org** Devoted to furthering online privacy.

The United States Senate **www.senate.gov** Information on the Senate.

TONO (Norsk selskap for forvaltning av fremføringsrettigheter til musikkverk) **www.tono.no** Performing rights organization of Norway.

UBC (Uniao Brasilera de Compositores) **www.ubc.org.br** Performing rights organization of Brazil.

Uniform Code Council **www.uc-council.org** Bar codes for CDs and cassettes.

United Nations **www.un.org** Information about the U.N.

Webnoize **inside.Webnoize.com/specialreports/98-5/** Information on digital watermarking.

World Intellectual Property Organization **www.wipo.org** Song rights Web site.

Yahoo! Full Coverage-Digital Copyright Law **headlines.yahoo.com/Full_Coverage/Tech/Digital_Copyright_Law** Copyright issues related to digital music.

Country Music—Line Dancing

2Steppin.com **www.2steppin.com** Country music Web site.

About Country **countrymusic.miningco.com/entertainment/countrymusic** Country music Web site.

Arist/Fan Club Information List **www.tier.net/whwk/fan/fclubs.htm** Country artists and fan club addresses.

Artist-On-Line **www.nashville-sites.com/artiston.htm** Artists, singers, songwriters, and musicians; each artist's page includes a picture and a short biographical sketch.

Birthplace of Country Music Alliance **www.bcmamuseum.com** Site of the historic "Bristol Sessions" recordings in 1927; dedicated to calling attention to the crucial role played by artists from the southern Appalachian region in country and bluegrass music.

British Country Music Artists **www.mamcountry.freeserve.co.uk** Biographies, press reviews, and CD details for UK country music artists.

Canadian Country Music **www.canehdian.com/genre/country.html** Information on country music in Canada.

CMA Awards **www.cmaawards.com** Country Music Association Awards.

Country and Western Song Generator **www.outofservice.com/country** Country music Web site.

Country Band **www.countryband.net** Country music Web site.

Country Chatter **www.countrychatter.com** Music reviews; news; information; mailing list; message board and more.

Country Comfort MIDI Music **members.xoom.com/ctrycomfort** 250+ vintage and contemporary country and bluegrass MIDI files; links to country artists homepages.

Country Connection **www.maderaonline.com/country** Webzine; country music news; reviews; interviews.

Country Countdown **www.top40countdown.com** Country music Web site.

Country Fan Club Addresses **www.albany.net/~coollz/countryfanclub.htm** List of addresses for various country music artists.

Country Legends Association **www.clabranson.org** Help save classic country music; Country Legends Family Shows.

Country Music and Book Reviews **www.pbc-country-books.com** Nashville news.

Country Music Association (CMA) **www.countrymusic.org** Home site of the Country Music Association located in Nashville.

Country Music Association of Australia
www.countrymusic.asn.au Information on country music in Australia.

Country Music Association-CMA World
www.cmaworld.com Country Music Association; membership; artist member pages; CMA Awards; Fan Fair; E-news; resources; country music links.

Country Music Classics
www.countrymusicclassics.com Free weekly newsletter; classic country music.

Country Music Dance Network **www.cmdn.net** Step sheets; music; artists; new artists; chat and more.

Country Music Directories
www.tpoint.net/~wallen/country/ directories.html Country music sources.

Country Music Gazette
www.jdenterprises.co.uk/cmg/index. html Country music newspaper in the United Kingdom.

Country Music Hall of Fame
www.country.com/hof/members Information on Hall of Fame members.

Country Music History
www.thanksforthemusic.com/history "Thanks for the Music" provides information on favorite Country music stars.

Country Music **www.countrymusic.tsx.org** Country music Web site.

Country Music Ireland
www.countrymusicireland.com Ireland's leading country music site; artist profiles; contacts; albums; updated weekly.

Country Music Links
www.geocities.com/~tammys_escape/ countrylinks.html Links to official sites; magazines/cyberzines; radio; record labels.

Country Music Links **www.music.indiana.edu/ music_resources/country.html** William and Gayle Cook Music Library, Indiana University School of Music; worldwide Internet music resources; country music connection.

Country Music Lovers
www.angelfire.com/oh/ladycowboy Links to artists, Roughstock, Nashville Entertainment Association, Country.com, a site to learn line dances and a site to learn the lyrics to a song.

Country Music Lyrics
www.geocities.com/Nashville/5921 Collection of lyrics to many of today's most popular country songs.

Country Music Media Guide
www.talentandbooking.com Country music magazines, radio, TV stations, and shows.

Country Music Message Board
www.canehdian.com/country/country. html Open discussion on country music.

Country Music MIDI Files and Backing Tracks
www.seafieldmusic.co.uk Professional quality country MIDI files and backing tracks.

Country Music News & Events Magazine
www.country-music-club.com/country- events.htm Country, bluegrass, and independent artists; CD reviews; back issues archived.

Country Music News
www.angelfire.com/tn/nna/index.html Updated every Sunday evening for the past week's news; from Backstage at the Grand Ole Opry and news that does not make country magazines, newslines, or radio.

Country Music Round-Up **www.cmru.co.uk** UK country music magazine online.

Country Music Search Engine **www.country- music-club.com** Independent artists and clubs; directories; links; bluegrass news; hillbilly; folk; buy CDs; free MP3 downloads; MIDI and WAV; sheet music; lyrics; chat.

Country Music Store **www.cmstore.co.uk** Over 6,000 CDs available from stock.

Country Music Television (CMT)
www.country.com/cmt/cmt-f.html Music videos.

Country Music Trivia Tidbytes
www.countryfan.com/newpage/tidbytes Daily country music trivia questions; test knowledge of past and present country music artists.

Country Music USA **www.countrymusic- usa.com** Country music Web site.

Country Now **www.countrynow.com** Country music Web site.

Country Review **www.CountryReview.com** Country music reviews of all types; album, artist, and concert reviews.

Country Sheet Music
songmart.com/ca/country.htm Songbooks and single sheets.

Country Stars **www.countrystars.com** Links to stars of country music.

Country Weekly **www.countryweekly.com** Online magazine; artist tour dates by state; country notes; star stats; history; crossword.

Country.com **www.country.com** Internet home for The Nashville Network (TNN) and Country Music Television (CMT); country music; the outdoors; motor sports.

Countryman **www.countryman.com** Country music Web site.

CountryOnAir **countryonair.com** Free country radio show; industry news; promo; marketing tips.

Countrysong **countrysong.com** Country music Web site.

Country-Time **www.country-time.com** Over 2,400 line dances online; country dance music CDs for sale; homepages for well-known choreographers; cruises.

Ear 1 Country Music **www.ear1.com/ cgi-bin/WebObjects/WMCountryGenre** Source for country music; CDs; videos; interviews; contests; tour dates; over 1,000 official artist sites.

Elephant Country **www.elephantcountry.com** Country music Web site.

Essential Contemporary Country Music CDs **www.drjohnholleman.com/mu/ contcoun.html** Sample audio clips; reviews; listener comments.

Free MP3 Music Files of Country Music **www.amp3.net/country.html** Country guitar and vocals; free MP3 downloads.

Going to Graceland **www.goingtograceland.com** Home of Elvis Presley.

Goodwin Country Music **www.geocities.com/Nashville/1283** Country music artists; music; lyrics; sheet music; guitar reference; country links.

Grand Ole Opry: Country Music Showplace **www.letsfindout.com/subjects/art/opry. html** The Grand Ole Opry.

Greatest Films-Nashville (1975) **www.filmsite.org/nash.html** Detailed review, synopsis, and discussion of the film.

Honky Tonkin' **www.honkytonkin.com** Download site; MP3.

Honkytonk Jukebox **www.westerndance.co.uk** Music for linedancers.

iMusic Country Showcase **imusic.com/showcase2/country/music** Country music Web site; showcase.

International Country Music Association **www.radiocountry.org** Promotes country songwriters and artists worldwide.

Jam! Country Music **www.caldercup.com/JamMusicCountry/ home.html** Canadian country music news and reviews.

Jim Beam Country Band Search **www.jimbeam.com** Nationwide talent search; winner is awarded a private showcase in front of industry heavyweights on Music Row.

Las Vegas Country Music and Cowboys **www.2steppin.com/vegas.htm** Country music Las Vegas-style.

Let's Dance! Country & Western Web Links and Information **www.interlog.com/~rfielder/CWLinks. html** Events lists; links; FAQ.

Line Dance **www.linedance.co.uk** Line dance albums from the US and UK; compilations.

Made In America-Alternative Country Music **www.geocities.com/Nashville/Rodeo/ 7847** Radio show clips; news and comments on the alternative country music scene.

MIDI Country **www.midihq.com** Standard MIDI files; hottest country hits.

Music City News **www.mcnonline.com** or **www.nashvillemusicguide.com** Country music news; features; reviews.

Music.Com Country Charts **music.com/showcase/country** Country charts ranked by Top-20 major label artists weekly.

Nashville CitySearch **nashville.citysearch.com** City guide, clubs, music, etc.

Nashville Country **www.nashvillecountry.com** Country music Web site.

Nashville Music Link-Artists/Groups **www.nashville.net/~troppo/artg.htm** Directory of Web sites relating to or of interest to the Nashville Music Industry.

New Country **www.bowiemd.com/country** The best of the new generation.

New Country Magazine **www.newcountrymag.com** Country music magazine.

New Country Magazine: Links: Assorted **www.newcountrymag.com/members/ nclinks/other.html** Country links.

North America Country Music Associations, Int'l **www.nacmai.org** Nonprofit international country music association to promote aspiring artists, musicians, and songwriters through education and international competition.

Roughstock's History of Country Music **www.roughstock.com/history** Country music history site on the Internet; artists from Gene Autry, Roy Acuff, Bob Wills, Hank Williams to Patsy Cline, Lefty Frizzell, Willie Nelson, Garth Brooks, and many others; cowboy music.

Sicota's Country Music Jumpstation **www.geocities.com/Nashville/1345/ lyrics.html** Lyrics of country music songs; links to country related pages.

Sinfully Heart **www.sinfullyheart.com** Country music Web site.

Suite 101 Country and Western **www.suite101.com/welcome.cfm/ country_and_western** Country music Web site; links; genre guide.

Tennessee Country Music Association **www.geocities.com/Nashville/Opry/ 9920** Promotes country artists, musicians, and songwriters; showcases and seminars.

The Canadian Country Music Association **www.ccma.org** Canadian country music industry; events; CCMA Awards archives; Hall of Fame; links to artists; radio stations; magazines; record labels; organizations.

The Dancing Cow Page **www.cowdance.com** Dancing cows; MIDI music.

The Information Super Dance Floor **www.apci.net/~drdeyne** Country western dance instruction, choreography, and music.

The Lyrics Library-Country Music **www.futureone.com/~kander6/country. html** Country song lyrics.

The Roughstock Network **www.roughstock.com** Contemporary country music; audio files: COWPIE archives; chords; sheet music; Country Countdown; charts.

The Story of the Country Music Hall of Fame **www.countrymusic.org/awards/hof.html** Hall of Fame members; founded in 1961 by the Country Music Association; devoted to the recognition of noteworthy individuals for their outstanding contributions to country music.

Today's Hottest Women of Country **www.merimage.com/womenofcountry** Up-to-date women of country links.

Top Country Music and Life Magazine **www.topcountrymusic.com** Web site and industry magazine; artist news; lifestyle features.

Twang This: Exclusive Country Music News **www.twangthis.com** Interviews; photos; music/video downloads; contests; fan clubs; tour dates; new releases.

Twangin' Country Music **www.well.com/user/cline/twangin.html** E-zine about country and roots music.

Drums and Percussion

A. M. Percussion Publications **www.ampercussion.com** Repertoire for percussion recitals and ensembles.

American Drum **www.americandrum.com** Percussion.

American Drum School **www.americandrumschool.com** Drums; instructional drum videos; accessories; free drum lessons.

Audix **www.audixusa.com** Drum microphones.

Avedis Zildjian Co. **www.zildjian.com** A. Zildjian; A. Custom; K. Zildjian; K. Custom; Z. Custom; Oriental; Azuka; Zil-Bel; Earth Plates; Edge; ZBT-Plus; ZBT Cymal Safe; Zildjian Drumsticks.

B. J.'s Dare to Drum **www.daretodrum.com** Drum lesson program for kids and beginners; music education links and information.

Ballistic Drums **www.ballisticdrums.com** Play feet exactly like hands, combining singles, doubles, rests, and flams; free pounding audiotape and report.

Bear Percussion **www.bearpercussion.com** Bear Drumheads.

Beatboy **www.beatboy.com** Drum pattern programmers; product info; demos.

Cappella **www.cappelladrumsticks.com** Drumsticks; practice pads; percussion accessories; timpani sticks; bass drumsticks; tenor sticks; claves; slap sticks; toner boxes.

CB Educational Percussion **www.kamanmusic.com** Percussion for educational settings.

Clearsonic **www.clearsonic.com** Drum manufacturer.

CyberDrum **www.cyberdrum.com** Webzine for drummers.

Ddrum Electronic Percussion **www.clavia.com** Ddrum.

Drum-A-Long **www.drumalong.com** Home page.

Drum Bum **www.drumbum.com** Drums and accessories.

Drum Corps World **www.drumcorpsworld.com** Home page.

Drum Grooves Publications **www.drumgrooves.com** Seventy-two page book with CD; fifty play-along songs in many styles with accompanying scores; for beginning through intermediate drummers.

Drum Machine Museum **www.drummachine.com** Drum machine Web site; *Technosaurus*.

Drum Network **DrumNetwork.com** Home page.

Drum Tech **www.drumtech.com** Drum technology.

Drum Trax **www.drumtrax.com** Drum tracks.

Drum Workshop Inc. **www.dwdrums.com** Drums and percussion.

Drum! Magazine **www.drumlink.com** Publication for drummers.

Drumlicks Publications **www.drumlicks.com** *Advanced Drum Ideas* book and CD package; over forty pages of mini lessons; world rhythms; interesting patterns; solos; fills.

Drummer Jokes **www.cse.ogi.edu/Drum/jokes.html** Funny stuff.

Drumspan **www.drumspan.com** Drumsticks.

Drumstuff.com **www.drumstuff.com** For drummers.

Drumtech Drum and Percussion School **www.drum-tech.co.uk** Drum school in Europe; for every kind of drummer, beginner to advanced; private lessons; three month full-time course; one-year diploma; three-year Music degree.

Emmite Drumsticks **www.emmitedrumsticks.com** Home page.

Empire Music **www.empire-music.com** Bongos;
  congas; Latin percussion; recorders; kazoos;
  tambourines; rhythm.
Everyone's Drumming Co.
  www.everyonesdrumming.com Home
  page.
Fat Congas **www.fatcongas.com** Conga drums.
Georg Voros **www.big-drum.mcmail.com**
  Information for drummers of all levels;
  educational books.
Global Groove **www.globalgroove.org** Live
  drums and percussion over ISDN lines; kits set
  up and ready to go; custom loops.
GrooveMaker **www.groovemaker.com** IK
  Multimedia; combination of remixing software
  and sounds for creating hypnotic, non-stop dance
  tracks in real time with professional results;
  groove combinations in every dance style; ready-
  to-use loops; professional drum grooves; synth
  pads; sound effects; ambient loops; add-on loop
  libraries.
Innovative Percussion Inc.
  www.innovativepercussion.com
  Percussion.
Johnnyrabb Drumstick Co.
  www.johnnyrabb.com Drumsticks;
  publications.
Kat Electronic Percussion
  www.emu.com/KAT/KAT.html Electronic
  percussion maker.
Little Drummer Boy (LDB) **www.Master-
  Zap.com/ldb** Loop creation software
  shareware; composes Stomper and WAV drum
  sounds into a loop, adding velocity-morphable
  effects.
LP Music Group **www.lpmusic.com**
  Manufacturer of percussion instruments for
  thirty-four years; congas, bongos, udu drums,
  cowbells, tambourines, maracas, etc.
Ludwig Drums **www.ludwig-drums.com** Drum
  set equipment.
Merchandisers International
  www.merchandisers.com.pk Bagpipe;
  Practice Chanter; Tambourines; Bongo Drum;
  Conga Drum; Dumbek; Ceramic Dumbek; Drum
  Heads; Percussion Instruments; Folk
  Instruments.
Modern Drummer **www.moderndrummer.com**
  Modern Drummer; Drum Business.
Mountain Rythym **www.mountainrythym.com**
  Drums; Ashiko; Djembe; Conga; Simple Twist
  Tuning System.
Musser Mallet Percussion **www.ludwig-
  drums.com** Percussion.
Neztech Software **www.neztech.com** *SequBeat
  PRO* drum sample sequencing packaging for PC.

Not So Modern Drummer
  www.notsomoderndrummer.com Drum
  magazine.
Pearl **www.pearldrum.com** Drum manufacturer.
Percussive Arts Society **www.pas.org** Forums,
  databases, and downloadable files.
Porks Pie Percussion **www.porkpiedrums.com**
  Drums; hardware.
Pro-Mark Corp. **www.promark-stix.com** Drums
  and accessories.
Pure Sound Percussion
  www.puresoundpercussion.com
  Percussion Web site.
Quiet Tone Inc. **www.cp.digiWeb.com** Drum
  mutes; electronic drum system.
Regal Tip **www.regaltip.com** Drums and
  accessories.
Remixer Drum Loop Archive **www.remixer.com**
  Downloadable drum loops in MP3 and
  RealAudio format; can convert files to .WAV
  format.
Remo World Percussion **www.remousa.com**
  Modern world percussion; variety of drums.
Rhythm Band Instruments Inc.
  www.rhythmband.com Aulos Recorders;
  Kidsplay; Charlie Horse Music Pizza Rhythm
  Band Set; Sweet Pipes Recorder Music;
  Belleplates; Chromaharp.
Rhythm Fusion Inc. **www.rhythmfusion.com**
  Percussion.
Rhythm Tech **www.rhythmtech.com** Home page.
Rhythms Exotic Afro Percussion LLC
  www.afrorhythms.com Udu-Iqba; Oji.
Rocket Network Inc. **www.rocketnetwork.com**
  Rocket Shells drums.
Roots Jam: Collected Hand Drum Rhythms
  **www.alternativeculture.com/music/
  roots.htm** Music instruction book for African
  drumming, djembe, and percussion; hand drum
  lessons, drum rhythms, and drumming tips; easy
  notation for beginners or advanced drum groups;
  free samples.
RunRobot.com **www.runrobot.com** Techno and
  electronica loops in .WAV format; links to other
  electronic music sites and sample archives.
Sabian **www.sabian.com** Drums and accessories.
Secrets of Subdivision
  **home.earthlink.net/~dapandabear/Music/
  SOS.html** Drums and Percussive Arts
  publications with links to hints, tips, updates,
  and drum-related sites.
Sheet Music for Keyboard Percussion
  www.drumspot.com/cat121.htm List of
  items available.
Sheet Music for Percussion
  www.drumspot.com/cat62.htm Percussion
  sheet music.

Smith Custom Drums
www.smithcustomdrums.com Custom
drums; snares.
Sol Percussion **www.haight.ashbury.com/sol**
Percussion.
Sonor Drums
valley.interact.nl/av/musWeb/drumWeb/
sonor/home.htm Drum set equipment maker.
Spirit Drums of Australia
www.spiritdrums.com.au Drums; snare
drums and full kit.
The Drum Club **www.thedrumclub.com** Online
lessons teach students of all ages how to play the
drums; each lesson includes RealAudio
explanations, video, and play-along MIDI files.
The Drummer's Web
www.valley.interact.nl/AV/MUSWEB/
DRUMWEB Information; resources; links.
The Overseas Connection
www.overseasconnection.com
Rhythmkids; Agogo Gongs; Realafrica;
Shekeres; Djembes; Djun Djuns; Udu Drums.
Trip Toys **www.triptoys.com** BioDrummer
software drum machine; sixty-two built-in
percussion instruments; eighteen different time
signatures; ability to import WAV files as
percussion instruments.
Trueline Drumsticks **www.trueline.com** Original
T6 Trueline Grip; Natural Diamond Grip; Classic
Drumsticks.
Virtual Drummer **www.virtualdrummer.com**
Macintosh drum machine; uses QuickTime; no
external hardware required.
WojoWorks **www.WojoWorks.com** A virtual
session containing rock and blues tracks; seven
tracks with and without drums; loops and click
tracks provided to play drums along with the
tracks; performance tips included.
Zero-X PC **www.audiosoftware.com** Set up
seamless loops and create/edit breakbeats.
Zildjian **www.zildjian.com** Cymbals; percussion
accessories; instructional tips; QuickTime video
clips.

Film, Television, and Video Music

007 **www.mcs.net/~klast/www/bond.html**
James Bond Web site; famous movie theme
songs.
99 Lives
www.99lives.com/filmogs/index.htm
Film industry.
A Guide to 1980s Music Video Directors
members.aol.com/MG4273/musvideo.
htm Videographies for directors.

About Music Videos
www.musicvideo.about.com Guide to
watching and creating videos.
Academy of Motion Picture Arts and Sciences
www.oscars.org Academy Awards; resources.
Aidan's Soundtrack Archives
www2.dynamite.com.au/milner/
soundind.htm Resource for collectible scores
on the Web.
Ain't It Cool News **www.aint-it-cool-news.com**
Industry news.
Alfred Hitchcock
nextdch.mty.itesm.mx/~plopezg/
Kaplan/Hitchcock.html Famous movies and
movie theme songs.
All Movie Guide **www.allmovie.com** Guide to
films.
Alliance On-line **alliance.idirect.com** Company
behind many movies and TV shows.
American Film Institute **www.afionline.org**
News and events; activities around the country;
membership.
American Movie Classics **www.amctv.com**
Cable channel.
AngelCiti International Film and Music Festival
www.angelciti.com Online application;
independent films.
Arista Records **www.aristarec.com/aristaWeb/**
Soundtracks/artist_index.html
Soundtracks.
Art, Film, and Music
www.learner.org/collections/
multimedia/artfilm/ Learn about some of the
world's most impressive paintings, sculptures,
and works of architecture from ancient Greece to
contemporary New York; new art appreciation.
BMG Classics and RCA Victor
www.bmgclassics.com or
www.racvictor.com Information about scores
released.
BollywoodMusic.com
www.bollywoodmusic.com Hindi, Punjabi,
Pakistani, Ghazals, Pop, Filmi, and Bhangra
songs in RealAudio and MP3 format; over 1,000
songs; complete Indian music site.
Box Office Guru **www.boxofficeguru.com**
Comprehensive box office information.
Box Office Report **www.boxofficereport.com**
Film Web site.
Boxoffice Online **www.boxoff.com** Reviews;
articles.
Bright Lights Film Journal: Words and Music
www.brightlightsfilm.com/23/
wordsmusic.html Rodgers and Hart biopic;
first-rate production numbers.
C.A.M. Original Soundtracks **www.cam-ost.it**
Dedicated to Italian and French composers.

Cannes Film Festival **www.festival-cannes.com**
French film event.

CD Cellar.com **www.cdcellar.com** Soundtracks;
stocks score promos.

Celebrities **search.cnet.com/celebs** Celebrities
Web site.

Cinecon.com **www.cinecon.com** Film industry.

Cinema-sites.com **www.cinema-sites.com** Film
industry.

Cinematic Sound Home Page
www.geocities.com/Vienna/7070 Hosted
by Erik Woods; broadcasted from Hamilton,
Ontario.

CineMedia **afi.cinemedia.org** Web directory to
film sites.

Cinemusic **www.cinemusic.de** German language
score site; reviews.

Cinemusic Online **www.cinemusic.net** Reviews;
wide variety of scores; audio clip library.

Classical Film and Music
www.filmandmusic.com Home page.

Classical Music and Film Music CD Reviews
www.musicWeb.f9.co.uk Online classical
and film music composer and CD review site.

Classical Music Used in Film
www.hnh.com/cmuif.htm Pieces heard in
films.

Columbia TriStar Home Video **www.CTHV.com**
New releases.

Compass III Records **www.compassiii.com** New
score label.

CueSheet.net **www.cuesheet.net** Film and TV
music tip sheet; confidential service, detailing the
music licensing requirements of TV/Film
companies, advertising agencies, etc.

Cyber Film School Filmmaking
www.cyberfilmschool.com Web site with
instruction, tips, advice, techniques on how to
make, produce, direct, shoot, light, and edit TV,
films, movies, and videos.

Danny Elfman
members.tripod.com/~ELFMAN
Composer Web site.

Dawsons Creek Music
www.dawsonscreekmusic.com Music and
artists from the TV show; featured artists, bands,
and songs directory.

Digibid **www.digibid.com** Auction liquidation
music gear, audio, dj, lighting, audio, video,
synth, broadcast equipment, mics, effects,
guitars, keyboard, DAT, recording, MIDI.

Digital Audio Worldwide Network (D. A. W. N.)
www.dawnmusic.com Download CD quality
music.

Disney Pictures
**www.disney.com/DisneyPictures/index.
html** Film industry; studio.

Early Motion Pictures 1897-1916
lcWeb2.loc.gov/papr/mpixhome.html
Early films made in North America.

E-Links: Film, Music & TV
www.songnet.com/elinks List of
entertainment, film, music, TV, and related links
for professionals and fans.

Field of Dreams: Film Music on the Internet
www.fod-online.com Reviews and
commentary on recent film score issues.

Film Capital Corporation-Film Financing
www.filmcapitalcorporation.com
International film and TV investors and finance;
consultation company managed by professionals
with experience in finances and film productions.

Film Connection **www.film-connection.com**
On-the-job training in major film/video studios
and television stations; video clips; news;
articles; film and television resources; tips from
hit directors, editors, and producers; view other
helpful film-related sites; link site.

Film Festival **www.filmfestival.be** Home page.

Film Festival Information **www.on.tc/festivals**
Links for film festivals organized by category.

Film Music **www.filmmusic.com** Full listings of
all film music related sites.

Film Music Institute
www.filmmusicinstitute.com Classes and
seminars; schedule.

Film Music Magazine **www.filmmusicmag.com**
Trade publication for the film and television
music industry; comprehensive coverage of
industry news; feature articles; investigative
reporting; event calendar.

Film Music on the Web UK
www.filmmusic.uk.net Composer profiles;
reviews.

Film Music Online **www.filmmusiconline.com**
Pro List; NewsWire; JobWire.

Film Music Review
members.aol.com/MusBuff/page2.htm or
users.aol.com/MusBuff/page2.htm Film
scores and songs; CD reviews.

Film Score Magic
www.tufts.edu/~ylui/soundtrk.html
Collection of reviews; weekly audio clips;
marketplace.

Film Score Monthly
www.filmscoremonthly.com Online
magazine of motion picture and television music
appreciation.

Film Scouts **www.filmscouts.com** Independent
site featuring original multimedia programming;
movie trailers and stills; festival coverage;
celebrity interviews; useful information; humor;
reviews; commentary.

Film Site **www.filmsite.org/genres.html** Film
industry.

Film Sound Design-Film Sound Theory
filmsound.studienet.org Theoretical and practical aspects on narrative sound effects in film and TV; over one hundred Web pages on film sound design; over fifty linked online articles.

Film.com **www.film.com** Movies on the Web; movie reviews; trailers; interviews; streaming short films; video clips; news; box office reports; show times; film festivals; Soundtrack Cinema; multimedia.

FilmFestivals.com **www.filmfestivals.com** Portal into the universe of cinema via its actors, directors, and films being shown at film festivals all over the world; over 6,000 pages and hundreds of links.

FilmFests.com **www.filmfests.com.au** Film festivals.

Filmtracks Modern Soundtrack Reviews **www.filmtracks.com** Reviews of recent motion picture soundtracks; tributes to modern composers; information about film music CD collectibles.

FilmZone **www.filmzone.com** Previews and facts about movies; library full of links to homepages; large film database.

Flf.com **www.flf.com** Film industry.

Fujifilm.com **www.fujifilm.com** Information on products and services.

Gene Autry Oklahoma Film & Music Festival **www.cow-boy.com/festival.htm** Annual event in September at the Gene Autry Oklahoma Museum.

George Eastman House International Museum of Photography and Film **www.eastman.org** Collects and interprets images, films, and equipment in the disciplines of photography and motion picture.

GNP Crescendo Records **www.gnpcrescendo.com** Sci-fi soundtracks.

Greatest Films: The Sound of Music (1965) **www.filmsite.org/soun.html** Detailed review, synopsis, and discussion of the film.

Groovy Yak's Page O' Funk **www.msu.edu/user/perrinet** Emphasizes scores by Williams, Elfman, Arnold, and Goldenthal.

Guild of Canadian Film Composers **www.gcfc.ca** National association of professional composers and music producers for film, television, and new media. *Hindi Film Music* **www.cs.wisc.edu/~navin/india/ hindifilm.html** Archive of Hindi film music; newsgroup.

Hans Zimmer **apscore.freeservers.com** Zimmer resource.

Hindi Movie Songs **www.cs.wisc.edu/~navin/india/songs** Hindi movie songs.

Hollywood Creative Directory **www.hcdonline.com** Online data; specials; E-mail names; mailing labels; lists on disc; site licenses; industry links; resources; festivals; awards; guilds; organizations; unions; studios; business; actors; casting; celebrities; assistants; media; press; services; music; education; seminars.

Hollywood Network **www.hollywoodnetwork.com/innercircle** Hollywood news.

Hollywood Online **www.hollywood.com** Movie information; soundtracks.

Hollywood Records **hollywoodrecords.go.com** Features pages for score releases; audio clips.

Hollywood Reporter **www.hollywoodreporter.com** Inside information on film and TV upcoming projects.

Hollywood Stock Exchange **www.hsx.com** Virtual trading in the movie industry.

Hollywood.com **www.hollywood.com** Hollywood news.

In Hollywood **www.inhollywood.com** Online link to the motion picture industry; broad range of professional research databases covering film development, production, releasing, contacts, box office, and news; track thousands of detailed future film listings; retrieve the industry's most extensive production and release schedule; instantly access contact information for over 20,000 executives, agents, and managers in the film and TV industries, including major studios, networks, and talent agencies; obtain instant E-mail notifications when projects change; research over 300,000 historical film credit listings; find projects using shooting location and estimated budget; for industry professionals, producers, writers, directors, distributors, film commissions, international filmmakers, journalists, and more.

Independent Film Channel **www.ifctv.com** The Independent Film Channel (IFC) is the first channel dedicated to independent film presented twenty-four hours a day, uncut and commercial-free; reaches 31 million homes on a full-time basis.

Inside Film **www.insidefilm.com** Film festivals by month; links; articles.

Internet Film and Music Festival **www.cmj.com/events/atlanta.html** Hosted by Streamsearch.com.

Internet Movie Database **us.imdb.com** Movie trivia quiz; large movie database.

Intrada Records **www.intrada.com** Well-established score label; store features a "one of a kind" section and large catalog.

Jeff Rona **www.jeffrona.com** Store; chat room; biography.

Jerry Goldsmith
www.lipsia.de/~locutus/lcars25.htm
Reviews and interviews.

John Williams **www.classicalrecordings.com/johnwilliams** Resource for Williams information.

Kaleidospace Screening Room
www.kspace.com/screen Area of Kspace Internet artists featuring independent filmmakers, animators, relaxation video, art video, music video, and performance video.

Kilima **www.kilima.com/welcome.html** Intriguing films from a diverse selection of nations; films are listed by country and subject matter; comprehensive information on the films and filmmakers; includes art, music, and literature.

Kiraly Music Network **www.kiralymusic.com** Orchestral recordings for film.

L.A. Times Laugh Lines
http:www.latimes.com/HOME/NEWS/LIFE/LAUGHS Hollywood humor.

Learner **www.learner.org** American Cinema Film Studies video curriculum.

Lee Holdridge **www.leeholdridge.com** Official site; audio clips.

License Music **www.licensemusic.com** Original, pre-cleared songs from over seventy record labels and music publishers; search; listen; price; license; download.

Listen to Music from the Movies
www.listen.to/music-from-the-movies E-zine; reviews; interviews; composer information; news.

Los Angeles Film & Music Magazine
www.lafm.com Hollywood resource.

Mandy's International Film and Television Production Directory **www.mandy.com** Database of television film producers, facilities, and technicians worldwide; current film/tv jobs.

Mark Mancina
www.student.io.tudelft.nl/~io487099/mancina.html Pictures; interviews; reviews.

Mark Snow **www.marksnow.cjb.net** Articles; interviews; news and more.

MCA/Universal **www.mca.com** Clips of movies.

Megatrax **www.megatrax.com** Production music for film, TV, ads, multimedia.

MGM **www.mgmua.com** Studio site.

Michael Kamen **www.michaelkamen.com** News; interviews; articles; press releases.

Milan Records **www.milanrecords.com** Current score releases; audio clips from all recent releases.

Mining Co. Guide to Classic Movies **Classicfilm.about.com** Classic films.

Miramax Cafe **www.miramax.com** Graphics; celebrity information.

Moby Disc Records **www.mobydisc.com** Updated soundtrack listings.

Movie Clichés List
www.like.it/vertigo/cliches.html Hollywood clichés.

Movie Music UK
www.shef.ac.uk/~cm1jwb/mmuk.htm Reviews; audio clips; composer information.

Movie Wave
www.moviewave.freeserve.co.uk Fan review site.

Moviefinder.com **www.moviefinder.com** Find movies.

MovieFone **www.moviefone.com** or **www.777film.com** Movie listing guide and ticketing service; local movie show times; tickets; trailers; film reviews; photos; celebrity and more.

MovieLink **www.movielink.com** What's playing?

Movies with Classical Music
www.classicaliscool.com/filmnote.htm Information on classical music in films sorted by movie title; posted online at Film Notes.

MovieSounds **www.moviesounds.com** Film industry.

MovieTunes
www.sites.hollywood.com/movietunes Hollywood online; audio clips.

MovieWeb **www.movieWeb.com** Film industry; previews.

Moving Pictures Experts Group
drogo.cselt.stet.it/mpeg Home of MPEG; develop standards for compression, decompression, processing, and coded representation of moving pictures, and audio; technical information; FAQ; press releases.

Mr. Showbiz **Web3.starwave.com/showbiz** Information on current films.

Music Box Theatre's Home Page
www.musicboxtheatre.com Web site.

Musician's Workshop **www.musicians-workshop.com** Video and audio music instruction since 1973.

National Film Board of Canada **www.nfb.ca** Canadian films.

NetNoir-The Black Network **www.netnoir.com** Black culture, entertainment, black music, television, black news, politics; African American love and romance.

NFB-ONF **www.nfb.ca** Public agency that produces and distributes films, audiovisual and multimedia works which reflect Canada to Canadians and the rest of the world.

Paramount Pictures **www.paramount.com** Movies and TV.

Partners in Rhyme **www.partnersinrhyme.com** Provides sounds and music for films, TV, and multimedia; information; files and utilities for Macintosh and PC; book list.

Popcorn **www.popcorn.co.uk** UK film site.

Program Power Entertainment **www.programpower.com** DVD company; family entertainment; DVD-ROMs.

Prometheus Records **www.soundtrackmag.com** Specialty score releases; online home exists at the *Soundtrack! Magazine* site.

Reel Country **www.reelcountry.com** Home page.

Score! Soundtrack Reviews **www.scorereviews.com** Current review site.

ScoreLand Soundtrack Reviews **pages.prodigy.com/WizardX** Current biweekly reviews.

ScoreLogue Web Magazine **www.scorelogue.com** Composer interviews; composer chats; CD reviews; European scores; European film music; score sessions; film music industry news; composer tributes; film music information.

Scoretracks Soundtrack Reviews **www.scoretracks.com** Review site.

Screen Actors Guild **www.sag.com** Home Page.

Screen Archives Entertainment **www.screenarchives.com** Catalog of regular and rare scores; occasional auctions of collectibles.

Screen It! **www.screenit.com** Source of entertainment reviews for parents.

Silva Screen Records America **www.silvascreen.com** Releases re-recording compilations of soundtracks performed in Europe.

SMPTE.org **www.smpte.org** Home page.

Sonic Images Records **www.sonicimages.com** Wide variety of releases.

SonicNet Streamland-Music Videos On Demand **www.streamland.com** Full-length music videos on demand; access to hundreds of music videos from alternative, rock, electronic, hip-hop, and punk artists in RealVideo.

Sony Pictures Online **www.spe.sony.com** Studio Web site.

Sony/Epic/Legacy/Sony Classical **www.sonymusic.com** Site contains all the affiliate labels.

Sound and Video **www.tdk.com/snv/current.htm** Monthly Webzine; reviews; demos; articles; pro-audio; links.

Soundtrack Cinema **www.film.com** Weekly Internet radio program devoted to presenting original music composed for film and TV; RealAudio.

Soundtrack Express **www.soundtrack-express.freeserve.co.uk** One of the original score fan review sites.

Soundtrack Review Central **www.greene.xtn.net/~ghuff/src/index. htm** Polls, movie, and television reviews.

Soundtrack! Magazine **www.soundtrackmag.com** Webzine.

SoundtrackNet **www.soundtrack.net** Art and business of film and television music; film scores to pop music that show up on soundtracks; information on composers.

Soundtracks: The Epic Sound **www.gunnlace.com/tracks/scores.htm** Audio clip library; MPG3 clips of rare and regular score cues; updated weekly; auction and score sale marketplaces.

SundanceChannel **www.sundancechannel.com** Promotes indie films.

SuperCollector **www.supercollector.com** Specializing in the cult and hard-to-find; leading source for promotional releases.

SXSW Film Home **www.sxsw.com/film/index.shtml** South by Southwest Music and Media Conference and Festival; the South by Southwest Film Conference and Festival; the South by Southwest Interactive Conference.

Sync It Up **www.sync-it-up.com** Music editing services.

Tamil Film Music Page **tfmpage.com** Comprehensive resource for Tamil Film Music; discussion forum; song lyrics; streamed live songs; master index of artists.

tdfilm.com **www.tdfilm.com** Online film resource; over 8,000 links to film-related Web sites.

Teenstation.com **www.teenstation.com** Audio and video channels; newsletter.

Tennessee Film, Entertainment & Music Commission **www.state.tn.us/film** Movie locations; music producers; cable channels; video and CD-ROM production, etc.

The Black Film Center/Archive **www.indiana.edu/~bfca/Websites.html** African Americans in film.

The Cinematrax Film and Television Music Site **www.cinematrax.com/** Organization founded by film and television composers Northam and Miller; information about Film Music Magazine and The Film Music Network.

The CISF Soundtrack Auction
  www.cisf.com/auction Automated auction system for rare, promo, or regular scores.
The Film Music Network **www.filmmusic.net**
  LA-based organization to help film composers network and learn more about the film music industry; monthly workshop meetings in LA, NYC, and San Francisco; memberships; magazine subscription; CDs.
The Film Music Network Store
  www.filmmusicstore.com CDs; publications.
The Film Music Society
  www.filmmusicsociety.org Non-profit group dedicated to the preservation of film music manuscripts; formerly the SPFM; Sedona Film Festival; film scoring workshop.
The Hollywood Music Network
  www.hollywoodnetwork.com/hn/music/ desk/deskfiles.html Opening the doors to Hollywood; Discovery Awards; What's New; HN Cybercast Program; HN Faculty/Hosts; Inner Circle; Your Page; HollyNews; Movie Store; Main Index; Interactive; Awards; Festival; Music; Producing; Screenwriting; Shopping; Hollywood Music; Opportunity; Desk File Drawers; scour Hollywood for movie memorabilia, books, and more; Hollydex.com.
The Internet Movie Database **www.imdb.com**
  Database with information about movies
The James Bond Movie Page
  members.xoom.com/BondMovies Information on 007.
The James Horner Web Site **listen.to/jhorner**
  Comprehensive site with news and a forum.
The Movie Soundtrack Web Page
  www.amfilm.com/scores Capsule and extended reviews.
The Movie Times **the-movie-times.com** Movie industry news.
The New York Underground Film Festival
  www.nyuff.com Official Web site.
The Palace **www.moderntimes.com/palace**
  Hollywood's Golden Era; B Movies.
The Score
  www.Webspawner.com/users/thescore Hosted by Mike Enright; broadcast from NYC.
The Silent Film Bookshelf
  www.cinemaWeb.com/silentfilm/ bookshelf Web site for silent films.
The Society of Composers and Lyricists
  www.filmscore.org Industry forums; technology; performing rights; intellectual rights; seminars; contracts.
The Soundtrack Auction Page
  www.concentric.net/~Fortytwo/ soundtracks.html Soundtrack and movie poster auction and sale site.

The Sundance Institute **www.sundance.org**
  Sundance Film Festival.
The WWW James Horner Shrine
  www.hornershrine.com Discussion group; reviews; articles.
The Yorkton Short Film Festival
  www.yorktonshortfilm.org Dramas; shorts; documentaries; videos; children's films; made-for-TV movies; workshops; food; music; entertainment; awards; directors; producers; celebrities.
Thomas Newman **tn-page.movie.nl** Audio clips; interviews; facts; score-by-score analysis.
TrackSounds Soundtrack Appreciation Site
  www.tracksounds.com Reviews and Soundtrack Hall of Fame.
Trimark Pictures **www.trimarkpictures.com**
  Film industry.
TV Guides Movies **www.tvguide.com/movies**
  Film information; reviews; search database.
TVGEN **www.tvgen.com** TV Guide online.
Twentieth Century Fox **www.foxhome.com**
  Information; film clips.
UCLA Film Scoring Program **www.unex.ucla.edu**
  Creative and technical challenges of film scoring; instructors are award-winning composers.
Universal Pictures **www.universalstudios.com/ universal_pictures** Production notes; film clips; photographs.
Uwe's Soundtrack Pages
  home.ifkw.de/~usperl/soundtracks Tributes to Poledouris, Broughton, Debney, and IMAX scores.
Varèse Sarabande **www.varesesarabande.com**
  Historical leader in score releases.
Variety **www.variety.com** Film; TV; music; news; features.
Vintage Hollywood
  www.geocities.com/Hollywood/Studio/ 5217 Hollywood nostalgia.
Walt Disney Records
  disney.go.com/DisneyRecords Promotional site for CDs, Sing-alongs, Read-Alongs, etc.; includes audio clips.
Warner Brothers **www.movies.warnerbros.com**
  Information; movie previews.
Welcome to The Sound of Music
  www.foxhome.com/soundofmusic/som. html Information on the 1965 film; historical background; virtual tour of the Van Trapp Estate.
Women in the Director's Chair **www.widc.org**
  Not-for-profit media arts organization dedicated to promoting visibility for women media artists.
World Class Music **www.cssmusic.com**
  Libraries on CD; themes for film and TV.
World Film **worldfilm.miningco.com** Film Web site.

World Sounds **www.clip-music.com/clip-music.html** Clip music library for multimedia and video professionals.

World's Tallest Music **www.worldstallestmusic.com** Composing and production for feature films, television, advertising, and industrial film applications, specializing in documentary series and specials.

Writer's Guild of America **www.wga.org** Home page.

Yahoo! Entertainment:Movies and Film:Film Music **dir.yahoo.com/Entertainment/ Movies_and_Film/Film_Music/** Film music; showtimes; new releases; reviews; audio archives.

Young Film Composers Competition **www.turnerclassicmovies.com/music** Information; application; mentoring; compose music to an old silent film.

Folk and Traditional Music and Instruments—Folk Dancing—Bluegrass

Acoustic Musician **www.netshop.net/-jesson** Features; interviews; reviews; workshop columns; annual buyer's guide, festival and service directory.

Acoustics Records (UK) **www.acousticsrecords.co.uk** Virtuoso recordings of celtic and classical mandolin, Irish accordion, folk songs, and children's music.

AcuTab Publications **www.acutab.com** Books of authorized tab transcriptions from the playing of top bluegrass pickers; banjo accessories and software.

American Melody **www.americanmelody.com** Award-winning recordings of folk, bluegrass, and children's music and stories; audio samples.

Banjo Web Shed **www.banjowebshed.com** Banjo music; links.

Best Cajun-Zydeco Music-Dance: ZydE-Magic Site **www.erols.com/ghayman** Leading Cajun/Zydeco music and dance Web site; national and international festival and special events information.

Bluegrass Junction **www.bluegrassjunction.com** Radio station; indie music.

Bluegrass News **bluegrassnews.com** Reviews and more.

Bluegrass Now **www.bluegrassnow.com** Magazine; festival calendar in each issue; features; reviews; tour schedules; group news.

Bluegrass Unlimited **www.bluegrassmusic.com** Magazine; annual festival directory; features; interviews; band news; tour schedules.

Bluegrass/Acoustic Music Portal **music.searchking.com** Information on bluegrass music.

Breezy Ridge Instruments Ltd. **www.jpstrings.com** Strings; hammered dulcimers; guitar products; capos; fringerpicks; vintage thumbpicks; videos; Nuage Gypsy Strings.

Cajun/Zydeco Music & Dance **www.bme.jhu.edu/~jrice/cz.html** The Grand-Daddy of the Cajun & Zydeco Music and Dance Web site; important links to other major associated Web pages throughout the country.

Canadian Bluegrass **valleygrass.ca./libby** Information on bluegrass music in Canada.

Captain Fiddle Music **www.tiac.net/users/cfiddle** Music for fiddlers.

Contradance **www.io.com/~entropy/contradance/ dance-home.html** Home page.

Country Dance and Song Society **www.cdss.org** Celebrating a living tradition of English and Anglo-American folk dance and music since 1915.

Crafters of Tennessee **www.crafterstn.com** Home page; banjos; mandolins; guitars.

Cybergrass **www.banjo.com/BG** For bluegrass music enthusiasts; over 175 pages of information; artists; concerts; events; associations; bluegrass magazines, downloadable sound files; links; articles on bluegrass musicians; history of bluegrass.

Deering Banjo Co. **www.deeringbanjos.com** Banjo manufacturer.

Desktop Banjo **www.desktopmusic.com/banjo.html** Five-string banjo learning tool; generates tabulature and chords; Windows.

Digital Tradition Folksong Database **www.mudcat.org/folksearch.html** Words and music to thousands of folk songs.

Dirty Linen **www.dirtylinen.com** Online folk music magazine; tour schedules in each issue; venues and contact information; folk, world music, roots music, Celtic; features; interviews; new release and concert reviews.

Dr. Horsehair Music Co. **www.drhorsehair.com** Banjo recordings and instruction books; modern-day clawhammer banjo or frailing style; old-time minstrel banjo stroke style.

Dusty Strings Co. **www.dusty-strings.com** Folk harps; hammered dulcimers.

efolk Music: MP3s and CDs **www.efolkmusic.com** Folk music; bluegrass; Celtic music; children's music; MP3 downloads and independent CDs.

Encyclopedia of Cajun Culture
    www.cajunculture.com Cajun music and culture.
ETSU Bluegrass and Country Music Program
    cass.etsu.edu/bluegrass Bluegrass music program at East Tennessee State University.
Fiddler Magazine Home Page **www.fiddle.com** For fiddlers.
Flea Market Music Inc. **www.flea-mkt-music.com** Jumpin' Jim's ukulele products.
Folk & Celtic
    club.ib.be/claude.calteux/folk.html Links to sites of folk and Celtic music; bands; artists.
Folk Biz **www.folkmusic.org** Folk music and musicians.
Folk Corporation **www.folkcorp.co.uk** Folk music Web site; links.
Folk Den **www.folkden.com** Home page.
Folk Image **www.folkimage.com** Home page.
Folk Music **www.folkmusic.org** Folk music Web site; venues.
Folk Music Links
    Web.ukonline.co.uk/Members/ martin.nail/commerc.htm Links to record companies, publishers, retailers, and artist agents in England.
Folk of the Wood **www.folkofthewood.com** Acoustic instruments; information; lessons; accessories.
Folk Roots Home Page
    www.froots.demon.co.uk/index.html England's leading roots, folk, and world music magazine; charts; reviews.
Folk Venues **www.folkmusic.org** Venues for folk musicians.
Folkcraft Instruments **www.folkcraft.com** Hammered dulcimers; folk harps.
Folklinks.com **www.folklinks.com** Informative folk and acoustic music Web site.
FolkWeb **www.folkWeb.com** Folk music on CD.
Gold Tone Musical Instruments
    www.nbbd.com/goldtone Gold Tone banjos; Gold Tone banjitars.
Guestlist Folk Music Pages
    www.guestlist.freeserve.co.uk Extensive directory of UK folk music performers; Folktalk Magazine.
Harmonica Books
    www.celticguitarmusic.com/harpbook. htm By Glenn Weiser; *Blues and Rock Harmonica, Irish and American Fiddle Tunes for Harmonica,* and *Masters of Blues Harp.*
Harmonica World
    www.bekkoame.or.jp/~mshige Harmonica resources.

Index of Folk **www.jg.org/folk** Folk music Web site; links.
International Bluegrass Music Association (IBMA)
    www.ibma.org Venue, presenter, media, and membership mailing lists available; membership required.
International Folk Culture Center
    www.ifccsa.org U.S., Canadian, and international folk dance and music groups, camps, festivals, institutes, parties, symposia, tours, weekend centers, college and university folk dance and folklore programs, directories, libraries, museum, organizations.
International Folk Dance Resource Guide
    www.io.com/~hbp/folkdance/fd.html People all over the world express their ethnic traditions in music and dance; ancient or relatively modern, each expresses the soul of its respective community.
John C. Campbell Folk School
    www.folkschool.com Held in Brasstown, NC.
Kerrville Music Foundation Inc. Kerrville Directory **www.kerrville-music.com** Folk festival information; listings of U.S. and foreign folk venues, folk press, radio stations, newsletters, publications, record companies, agents, managers, performers, and publicists.
Mandolin Bros. Ltd. **www.mandoWeb.com** Mandolins.
Musicmaker's Kits, Inc. **www.musikit.com** Acoustic instrument kit company; offers audio files of its instruments; catalog of early music and folk instruments.
National Storytelling Association (NSA)
    www.storynet.org Membership available; directory of organizations; storytellers; workshops; festivals; production companies; publishers of storytelling works; bimonthly magazine; National Storytelling Festival first full weekend in October annually.
Old Town School of Folk Music
    www.oldtownschool.org Held in Chicago, IL.
Old-Time Herald **www.mindspring.com/-oth** Features; reviews; interviews.
Polka Store **www.polka-store.com/sheetmusic/index.htm** For polka and band lover; all occasion dance music by all types of polka players, bands, and virtuosos; cassettes, CDs, videos, and tours available.
PrinceGeorge.Com
    www.princegeorge.com/georgemusic/ tablatur.html Bagpipe, harmonica, and tin whistle tablature.
Record Label Links-The Bluegrass Telegraph
    www.bluegrasstelegraph.com/

labellinks.htm News; reviews; trivia; Talk Bluegrass; Picture This.

Ridge Runner **www.ridgerunner.com** Music instruction mail order company; digital study recorders; instruction videos for guitar, fiddle, mandolin, dobro, banjo, and other instruments.

San Francisco Folk Music Club **www.idiom.com/~poet/harmony/ folknik.html** Home page.

Sheet Music for Harmonica **www.harmonicaspot.com/cat67.htm** List of items available.

SingOut! Magazine **www.singout.org** Folk music magazine; annual directory of folk festivals; features; reviews; regular columns.

Sisters Folk Festival **www.sistersfolkfestival.com** Oregon.

Sound to Earth Inc. **www.soundtoearth.com** Mandolins.

Southeast Celtic Music Association **www.scmatx.org** Home page.

The Bluegrass Acoustic Music Web Ring **www.blueaudio.com/ring.htm** Bluegrass and acoustic music.

The Bluegrass Telegraph **www.bluegrasstelegraph.com** Reviews and more.

The Folk Alliance **www.folk.org** Folk and traditional music; annual conferences held in different locations; membership required; mailing lists available for sale.

The Folk Times **www.wizvax.net/folktimes** Calendar of acoustic music performances in upstate New York.

The FolkBook Index **www.execpc.com/~henkle /fbindex/bluegrass.html** Bluegrass and old-time music.

The Stacy Phillips Dobro & Fiddle Page **w3.nai.net/~stacyphi** Instructional books and videos for dobro and fiddle; sample lessons.

Traditional Dance in Toronto **www.dancing.org** Information on traditional dancing in the Toronto area.

Web Shed **www.Webshed.com** Center of Web music string instruments.

Weber Mandolins **www.Webermandolin.com** Mandolin manufacturer.

Women's Studies and Women's Folk Music Resources **creativefolk.com** Resources; calendar of events nationwide and more.

World Folk Music Association **wfma.net** Home page; artists index.

Government and Music Funding Sources

Arts Grants Opportunities **www.booksatoz.com** Funding sources for the arts.

Canada Council for the Arts **www.canadacouncil.ca** Canadian.

Federal Domestic Assistance Catalog **www.gsa.gov/fdac** Home page.

Foundation Center **www.fdncenter.org** Resources; opportunities.

Fundcraft Personalized Cook Books **www.fundcraft.com** Fund raisers.

Government Agencies **galaxy.einet.net/galaxy/government. html** Home page.

Idealive **www.idealive.com/about.php3** Helps artists, supporters, and investors bypass the middleman and reach each other directly; aims to create a central place where artists have the ability of posting projects seeking financing; access to the sites registered group of investors.

Music Rewards Fundraising **www.raisemoremoney.com** CDs and cassettes from top artists; year-round, holiday, Christian family, Latin, and children's programs.

National Endowment for the Arts (NEA) **www.arts.endow.gov** Learn about work being done by artists and arts organizations across the country; section on helping nonprofit organizations link with federal arts resources.

National Endowment for the Humanities (NEH) **www.nch.fed.us**

State and Regional Arts Organizations **arts.endow.gov/guide/rao_saas.html** Listing of the fifty-six state and regional arts agencies.

Texas Music Office **www.governor.state.tx.us/music/index. htm** Regional office.

The Money Tour **www.tmn.com/artswire/www/awtour/ money** Resources; opportunities.

The Women's Independent Music Show **www.eyeqradio.com** Represents a new way to bring artists, their fans, and supporters and investors together to help artists fund and successfully complete their creative projects.

U.S. Local Arts Agencies **arts.endow.gov/Guide/ rao_SAAs.html#RAOs** Local arts agencies conducting international exchange projects and activities.

U.S. Non-Profit Gateway **www.nonprofit.gov** Directory of information about grants, regulations, taxes, and government services.

University of Washington's List of Internet Funding Resources **Weber.u.washington.edu/ ~gfis/resources.html** Home page.

Guitar and Bass—
Acoustic and Electric

12 Tone Music **www.12tonemusic.com** Guitar and bass *Fretboard Flashcards; Guitar Encyclomedia.*

Accent Guitar Studio
www.accentguitar.com/bookstore.shtml
Home of the "Registry of Guitar Tutors."

Acoustic Guitar Magazine **www.acguitar.com**
Features; interviews; reviews.

Alamo Guitars **www.alamoguitars.com**
Tonemonger.

All Jazz Guitar **www.alljazzguitar.com**
Resource and reference site for jazz guitarists.

All Parts **www.allparts.com** Strings, pedals, parts, cases, etc.

Analog Man **www.analogman.com** Strings, pedals, parts, cases, etc.

Autoplayer **www.autoplayer.com** Learn guitar, bass, mandolin, bouzouki, and ukulele; software available for download and purchase; learn chords, scales, and tunes; compose tunes; Windows.

Azola Basses **www.azola.com** Bug Bass; Mini Bass; Baby Bass; Deco Bass; Jazzman; Lightning Bug.

Bass Frontiers **www.bassfrontiers.com** Bass guitar magazine.

Bass Player **www.bassplayer.com** Bass guitar magazine.

Bass Player Magazine **www.mfpsn.com** *Bass Player; Bass Player Online; Guitar & Bass Buyer's Guide.*

Basscapes.com **www.basscapes.com** Bass guitars.

Basslines **www.basslines.com** Bass accessories.

Blue Book Inc. **www.bluebookinc.com** Prices and values of guitars.

Carvin **www.carvin.com** Amplifiers.

CFox Guitars **www.cfoxguitars.com** Guitar manufacturer.

Charanga Inc. **www.guitarcoach.com** *Guitar Coach; Electronic Guitar Coach.*

Chord Melody Guitar Music
www.chordmelody.com Chord harmonizations; guitar sheet music and tab books; videos and instructional guitar music in all styles: jazz, classical, rock, country, blues, flamenco, acoustic, religious, and Christmas.

ChordWizard **www.chordwizard.com** Software for players of guitar, banjo, mandolin, bass guitar, ukulele, bouzouki, and other stringed instruments; free music theory tutorial; Windows.

Classical Guitar Composers List
www.ele.uri.edu/faculty/sun/CGCL.
html Comprehensive list of composers who have composed at least one original score for solo classical guitar.

Classical Guitar Music on the Web
btm8x5.mat.uni-bayreuth.de/~kebekus/info_musiclist.
html Downloadable classical guitar music on the World Wide Web.

Cool Jazz Chords for Guitar
coolchords.anthill.com Learn thousands of chords by knowing a few simple ideas.

Country Guitar
www.countryguitar.com/default3.htm
Country guitar Web site.

Crate Amps **www.crateamps.com** Amplifiers.

Crate Pro Audio **www.crateproaudio.com** Home page.

Crossroads Guitar **www.crossroads-guitar.com**
Interactive online guitar courses; over 110 one-hour lessons with streaming video, soundfiles, notation, tablature, and text; free MP3 practice tracks, playing tips, introductory lessons and real-time contact with instructors.

Curbow String Instruments **www.curbow.com**
Home page; custom guitar builder presents procedures to design and develop string instruments; view photo galleries, materials, and features.

Daddario **www.daddario.com** Strings, pedals, parts, cases, etc.

Danelectro **www.danelectro.com** Guitar manufacturer; guitar accessories; amplifiers.

Dasein Guitar Tuner **www.tuner.pair.com** Hear guitar through the soundcard's microphone; program instantly tells what note was just heard and the deviation from standard tuning; Windows.

Dean Musical Instruments
www.deanguitars.com Guitars.

Desktop Guitarist
www.desktopmusic.com/guitar.html
Tabulature generator, chord dictionary, guitar tuner, accompaniment player, and MIDI file generator; Windows.

Discount Distributors **www.discount-distributors.com** Strings, pedals, parts, cases, etc.

Dream Guitars & Apparel
www.dreamguitars.com Recording King; Rick & Taylor; Roy Rogers & Dale Evans.

Dreamscape.com
www.dreamscape.com/esmith/dansm/
chords/chords.htm Guitar chords.

Electro-Harmonix **www.ehx.com** Analog effects for guitar and bass.

Elixir Guitar Strings **www.goremusic.com**
Guitar strings; polyweb coating.

eMedia Guitar Method **www.emedia.org** Series of instructional software for guitar; java chord dictionary with audio playback; Macintosh; Windows.

Emedia Music **www.emediamusic.com** Guitar and bass software.

Encyclopedia of Bass Logic **www.basslogic.com** Instructional text for the electric bass; technique, transcriptions, music theory, and rhythms.

Epiphone **www.gibson.com** Division of Gibson Guitar Corp.; acoustic and electric guitars; amplifiers; accessories.

Ernie Ball **www.ernieball.com** Guitars, basses, and strings.

Essential Music Theory for Electric Bass **www.starion.com/jewel** Includes ear-training practice CD.

EVD String Instruments **www.evd303.com** Variations on traditional acoustic guitars, banjos, and lyres; view custom designs and testimonials.

Experience Hendrix **www.jimi-hendrix.com** Information on Jimi Hendrix.

Fastfingers **www.fastfingers.co.uk** Guitar tuition courses covering all guitar styles; courses on compact disc, tape, or video.

Fender Guitars **www.fender.com** Product catalog; technical support; find date guitar was made with serial number; contests; E-zine.

Fernandes Guitars **www.fernandesguitars.com** Guitar manufactuter.

Fine Fretted Stringed Instruments-Campbell **www.flamenco.org** Specializing in fine classical and flamenco guitars.

Finger Style Guitar **www.fingerstyleguitar.com** Features; reviews; news.

Flamenco Guitar Transcriptions **www.ctv.es/guitar** Study of the flamenco guitar throughout the twentieth century; 231 soleares falsetas from the 1900s to the 1990s in standard notation and tablature.

Flamenco World **www.flamenco-world.com** Site for flamenco music; music and dance videos; CDs; online magazine; interviews and biographies of the world's greatest guitarists and singers.

Flat Pick **www.flatpick.com** Guitar magazine.

Fodera Guitars **www.fodera.com** Fodera Bass Guitars; Fodera Accessories; Fodera Electric Bass Strings.

Fresh Tabs **www.FreshTabs.com** Guitar tablature.

Fret Board Basics **www.twofooter.com/msj** Guitar instructional video; basic licks played at slow speed.

Fret Master **www.fretmaster.net** Strings, pedals, parts, cases, etc.

FretsOnly **www.fretsonly.com** Online catalog of various educational products for guitar, banjo, mandolin, and violin; by Ashley Mark Publishing Company.

Full Album Tabs **www.fullalbumtabs.com** Guitar tabulature; corresponding author's own work; represents their interpretation of the song.

Gary Talley **www.garytalley.com** Guitar instruction for songwriters; video.

Gas Pedal **www.gaspedal.com** Strings, pedals, parts, cases, etc.

Genz Benz Enclosures **www.genzbenz.com** Amplifiers.

George L's Musical Products **www.georgels.com** Strings, pedals, parts, cases, etc.

GHS Strings **www.ghsstrings.com** Guitar strings.

Gibson Guitar **www.gibson.com** Home page; guitar manufacturer based in Nashville; acoustic and electric; strings and accessories; merchandise; music news; references; free online appraisal; dealer directory; auction.

Gig Accessories **www.gig-accessories.com** Accessories.

Gig Mate **www.gigmate.com** Strings, pedals, parts, cases, etc.

Gitargrrl.com **www.gitargrrl.com** Home page.

GMW Guitarworks **www.gmwguitars.com** Empire Guitars; GMW Guitarworks.

Gretsch **www.gretsch.com** Guitar and drum manufacturer.

Gruhn Guitars **www.gruhn.com** Nashville-based vintage guitar dealer; catalog; photo gallery.

Guild Guitars **www.guildguitars.com** Guitar Web site.

Guitar and Bass Guitar Lessons on the Web **www.visionmusic.com** Guitar education site; free online music lessons for the evolving guitarist or bassist.

Guitar Auction **www.guitarauction.com** Home page.

Guitar Base **www.gbase.com** Guitar Web site; guitar and vintage guitar inventory on the Internet; online community; locate dealers; classified ads; teachers.

Guitar Center **www.guitarcenter.com** Guitars; amps; drums; keyboards; software; recording and P.A. gear; DJ and lighting; fifty-seven locations nationwide.

Guitar Chord Calculator **www.guitarcalc.com** Program shows the correct hand position for every chord; Windows.

Guitar Chords **www.lib.virginia.edu/dmmc/Music/ GuitarChords/chord dictionary** Chord dictionary.

Guitar Clinic **www.fbass.com** Home page.

Guitar College, Inc. **www.guitarcollege.com** Home study courses for guitar.

Guitar Concept **guitarconcept.home.att.net** Guitar lessons online or by U.S. mail.

Guitar EncycloMedia **www.12tonemusic.com** Comprehensive presentation of musical thought as it is applied to the guitar; "Fretboard Flashcards," a tool for guitar and four or five string bass.

Guitar Foundation of America-Classical Guitar **www.cyberg8t.com/gfa** Home page.

Guitar Gallery Sheet **www.guitargallerymusic.com** Catalog of guitar music and instructional videos; also banjo, mandolin, fiddle, bass, dulcimer, harmonica, penny whistle, autoharp, songbooks, and more.

Guitar Geek **www.guitargeek.com** Home page.

Guitar Instruction Music Theory **www.guitarmusic.com/links/ instruction/music_theory1.s** Home page; instruction; related sites; music theory chords and scales; licks and tricks; standard and alternate tunings; guitar playing technique.

Guitar Lessons & Tabs, Co. **www.guitarlessonstabs.com** Streaming-videos, books, tabs, and MP3s; online instructor for private online lessons included free.

Guitar Lessons at Home **www.guitar-lessons-at-home.com** Home page.

Guitar Lessons at Musiclearning.Com **www.musiclearning.com** Guitar lessons with play-along MIDI files and RealAudio listening examples.

Guitar Links **www.guitarlinks.com** Guitar Web site links.

Guitar Loops **www.guitarloops.com** Home page.

Guitar Mag **www.guitarmag.com** Guitar Webzine.

Guitar Magic **www.sdgsoft.com** Guitar software for both electric and acoustic guitar players; Windows.

Guitar Net **www.guitar.net** Chord Archive features a different chord every week.

Guitar Notes **www.guitarnotes.com** Guitar links; lessons; MP3s; tabs; shopping; reviews; listings of over 600 guitar dealers; details on how to purchase amps and related accessories.

Guitar One **www.guitaronemag.com** Guitar magazine.

Guitar Online **guitaronline.notrix.de** Guitar chords and tabs page.

Guitar Online **www.guitar-online.com** Guitar courses online, via E-mail or CD-ROM; videos, scores, and tablatures; MIDI files; online tuner and metronome.

Guitar Player Magazine **www.guitarplayer.com** or **www.mfpsn.com** Guitar magazine; buyer's guide.

Guitar Playing **www.guitarplaying.com** Guitar Web site.

Guitar Pro Manual **www.booklocker.com/bookpages/ syurtsever.html** Self-instruction manual on how to play the guitar; over seventy pages of text and illustrations.

Guitar Reality-Virtual Instructor **www.guitareality.com** Guitar instructional software with downloadable demo; Windows.

Guitar Simplified **www.guitarsimplified.com** The "Guitar Barre" method; online sales of a lesson book and a play-along video; for beginners.

Guitar Sounds **www.guitarsounds.com** The Peter Pupping Quartet.

Guitar Tab Archives **www.cc.umist.ac.uk** Guitar tablature.

Guitar World **www.guitarworld.com** Electric; features; reviews.

Guitar.com **www.guitar.com** Guitar guide; chord generator; instructors; artists; MP3; tablature.

Guitar4u.com **www.guitar4u.com** Information on instruction and music theory; special lessons are provided by teachers at the Berklee College of Music.

Guitarfx.com **www.guitarfx.com** Home page.

Guitarists.net **www.guitarists.net** Guitar Web site.

GuitarLessons.net **www.guitarlessons.net** Guitar lessons taught by a professional guitarist.

Guitar-Online **www.guitar-online.co.uk** Online video guitar lessons; download tab notation with text and graphic explanations.

Guitarras Manuel Rodriguez & Sons; S.L. **www.guitars-m-r-sons.com** Classical and Flamenco; Cutaway Models; Cadete and Senorita Models.

GuitarSite.com **www.hitsquad.com/rd/gsite/?nl22** For guitarists by guitarists.

GuitarTab.com **www.musictheory.com** Online guitar tab archive; links to OLGA, a database of tablatures and song transcriptions and other tab sites.

GuitarTrainer **www.artios.co.za/gtrainerWeb** Sight-reading instructor for guitar and bass guitar; teaches the association between a note on a sheet and the fretboard position; Windows.

Guitropolis **www.guitropolis.com** Interactive game software; ten chapters; over sixty songs; Macintosh; Windows.

G-Vox Interactive Music **www.gvox.com** *Guitar 101* and *Guitar System* software.

Hammertone **www.guitarclinic.com** Octave Twelve guitars.

Harmon **www.harmon.com** Amplifiers.

Highly Strung **www.highlystrung.co.uk** Strings, pedals, parts, cases, etc.

Hot Licks Productions **www.hotlicks.com** Home page; instructional media.

Ibanez **www.ibanez.com** Guitar manufacturer.

International Guitar Seminar **www.guitarseminars.com** Guitar Web site; seminars.

Jackson Guitars **www.jacksonguitars.com** Guitar manufacturer.

Jam Bass **www.jambass.com** Bass guitars.

Jazz Guitar **www.jazzguitar.com** Guitar magazine.

Jazz Guitar International **www.musicWeb-uk.com/eurojazz.html** European online jazz guitar CD merchandising site.

Jazz Guitar Online **www.jazzguitar.com** For jazz guitarists.

Jean Larrivee Guitars Ltd. **www.larrivec.com** Guitar manufacturer.

Jimi Hendrix **www.experience.org/jimi** Guitar techniques; songwriting; performances; trademark chords; explores Jimi's songwriting process and the *Electric Ladyland* album.

Johnson Amp **www.johnson-amp.com** Amplifiers.

Just Classical Guitar Home Page **www.ga-usa.com/jcg** Guitar archive; Web portal; music; events; schools; classical guitar in Italy and abroad; classical composers; magazines.

Just Strings **www.juststrings.com** Large selection of guitar and bass strings.

Kaman Music Corp. **www.kamanmusic.com** Ovation; Takamine; Hamer; Toca; Gibraltar; CB.

Kellar Bass **www.kellarbass.com** Bass guitars.

Ken Smith Basses Ltd. **www.kensmithbasses.com** Bass guitars.

La Bella Strings **www.labella.com** La Bella; Criterion; Electrics; Super Steps; Deep Talkin' Bass; Slappers; Pacesetter; Folksinger; Elite Series; Series 2001; Silk & Steel; Kapalua; New Yorkers.

Lakland Basses **www.lakland.com** Standard; Deluxe; Classic; Joe Osborn Signature; Bob Glaub Signature; Jerry Scheff Signature; Willie Weeks Signature.

Learn Guitar Chords **www.alberts.com/authorpages/00013892/prod_505** *Guitar Chord Buster* adds a virtual guitar to the computer screen; reference and learning tool for guitar beginners, professionals, and teachers.

Learn to Play Guitar **www.guitarcalc.com/learnguitar** Free guitar E-book to download; music software.

Legend Hammered Dulcimers **www.folkcraft.com** Hammered dulcimers.

Levy's Leathers Ltd. **www.levysleathers.com** Home page.

Marshall Amplifiers **www.marshallamps.com** Amplification systems.

Martin Guitar Company **www.martinguitar.com** Guitars; strings; pedals; parts; cases; etc.

Mesa Boogie **www.mesaboogie.com** Guitar amplifiers; photos; product information; English and German.

Metal Method **www.metalmethod.com** Video guitar lessons; weekly free lessons include tablature, WAV, and MP3 files.

MetalTabs.com **www.metaltabs.com** Heavy metal guitar tabs.

Music Theory Course for Guitar **www.guitar-jimsuttoninst.com/MT.html** International correspondence guitar school.

Musical Instrument Makers Forum **www.mimf.com** Acoustic guitar making; electric guitar building; guitar repair; violin making; online interactive course in instrument making; discussion forum; community for musicians and instrument makers.

Musikraft **www.musikraft.com** Strings, pedals, parts, cases, etc.

National Guitar Summer Workshop **www.guitarworkshop.com** Held June through August in various locations.

Net Guitar **www.netguitar.com** Stringed instrument division deals in new and vintage guitars; sales and repair company.

Net Music School **www.netmusicschool.com** Online music school offering beginner guitar lessons, music teacher search, and music resources.

Online Guitar Archive **www.olga.net** Guitar resources; tablature.

Ovation **www.kamanmusic.com/ovation** Since 1966; round back design guitars; products; pickups; electronic accessories.

PDS Music **www.pdsmusic.com** Acoustic and classical guitar lessons offered by international mail order correspondence; free sample lessons.

Peavey **www.peavey.com** Amplifiers.

Pedal Boards **www.pedalboards.com** Strings, pedals, parts, cases, etc.

Pedal Man **www.pedalman.com** Strings, pedals, parts, cases, etc.

Pedal Worlds **www.pedalworld.com** Strings, pedals, parts, cases, etc.

Phantom Guitar Works Inc.
www.phantomguitars.com Phantom Guitars; Teardrop Guitars; Mando Guitars.

Picks by the Pound **www.picksbythepound.com** Guitar picks.

Pignose Amps **www.pignoseamps.com** Amplifiers.

Play Guitar **www.nl-guitar.com** Download program to learn how to play guitar; music educational programs for schools.

Play Jazz **www.playjazz.com** Jazz guitar site.

Power-Chord.com **www.power-chord.com/gaff/mapper/fretboard map** Guitar chords.

Practice Pal **www.accentguitar.com/pp.shtml** Software package developed to prepare students for the Registry of Guitar Tutors electric guitar examination.

Pro Bass Gear/Pro Guitar Gear **www.probassgear.com** Guitars and basses.

Quick Study Creations **www.guitarnobrainer.com** Learn guitar styles, guitar chords, and transposing keys; for beginners.

RainSong Graphite Guitars **www.rainsong.com** RainSong; WS 1000; WS 2000; WS 1100; JZ 1000.

Registry Publications Examination **members.aol.com/registrypl/index2.htm** Handbooks for electric guitar, classical guitar and bass guitar; books and audiocassettes covering all aspects of guitar from beginners to advanced; performance and improvisation.

Renaissance Guitars **www.renaissanceguitars.com** Renaissance Guitars & Basses; Rick Turner Guitars; Electroline Basses; Model T Guitars.

Rifftech Guitar Lessons **www.wincom.net/~rockon** Free online lessons and more.

Rio Grande Pickups **www.riograndepickups.com** Pickups.

Sabine **www.sabineusa.com** Chromatic tuners for all stringed instruments..

Samick Music Corp. **www.samickmusicusa.com** Guitar manufacturer.

Samson Technologies Corp. **www.samsontech.com** Strings, pedals, parts, cases, amplifiers.

Santa Cruz Guitar Co. **www.santacruzguitar.com** Guitars.

Schecter Guitar Research **www.schecterguitars.com** Custom Guitars & Basses; Diamond Series Guitars; Basses & 7-String Electrics; Diamond Acoustics; CB-2000.

Self Tuning **www.selftuning.com** Strings, pedals, parts, cases, etc.

Seymour Duncan **www.seymourduncan.com** Pickups.

Sheet Music for Guitar **www.migman.com.au/aes/sheet.htm** Sources of printed music for guitar.

Sierra Steel Guitars **www.sierrasteelguitar.com** Steel guitars; lap steel; cases.

Sonic Bass **www.sonicbass.co.uk** Bass guitars.

Spector Design Ltd. **www.spectorbass.com** Bass guitars and strings.

Stefan Grossman's Guitar Workshop **www.guitarvideos.com** Comprehensive series of video and audio guitar lessons in a wide variety of styles, featuring world-renowned instructors.

Steinberger **www.gibson.com/products/steinberger** Headless guitars and basses; company information.

String Letter Publishing **www.stringletter.com** Publisher of guitar magazines, books, songbooks, and CDs.

String Tech **www.stringtech.com** Strings, pedals, parts, cases, etc.

Strings Etc. **www.stringsetc.net** Strings, pedals, parts, cases, etc.

Strings Magazine **www.stringsmagazine.com** Magazine about string instruments.

Super Guitar Chord Finder **www.ready4music.com** Learn, search for, analyze, and play guitar chords; Windows.

Tacoma Guitars USA **www.tacomaguitars.com** Tacoma USA; Olympia.

Taylor Guitars **www.taylorguitars.com** Guitar manufacturer based in El Cajon, CA; newsletter; clinics.

TCguitar.com **www.tcguitar.com** Guitar magazine.

Teaching the Folk Guitar **www.radioyur.com/yufpub.html** Learn to teach basic guitar skills to students of all ages; method for teaching guitar in a group situation; 256-page teaching manual with two cassettes.

Technics USA **www.technicsusa.com** Bass guitars.

The Blues Bible **www.onlinerock.com/services/danmc2** Learn to play blues guitar; chord diagrams; lead scale diagrams; slide guitar diagrams; audio examples; information on ordering the CD-ROM.

The Classical Guitar Home Page **www.guitarist.com/cg/cg.htm** The original Classical Guitar Home Page; created in 1994.

The Complete Fingerstyle Guitarist
www.city2000.com/learnguitar Video
series; for beginners and advanced guitar players.
The International Guitar Research Archive
www.csun.edu/-igra Research on guitars.
The Natural Approach to Guitar
www.thenaturalapproach.com
Revolutionary video guitar program; teaches
students to see and hear the neck as one unit; no
memorizing scales; improvise in any style.
The Old Pueblo Guitar Company
www.opgc.com/instruct.htm The Old
Pueblo Guitar Company offers guitars, guitar
accessories, guitar lessons, guitar music, guitar
recordings, and general information.
The Virtual Guitarist
www.thevirtualguitarist.com.au Lessons
available by online sound files, images and text,
and by E-mail; for classical and rock guitar.
Theory of Music Applied to Guitar
www.migman.com.au/aes/theory.htm
Music theory as applied to guitar.
TrueFire.com **www.truefire.com** Guitar
instruction; digital self-publishing and
distribution system for guitar instruction;
original music, literature, art, and reference
materials; available in MP3, pdf, html, and
RealAudio formats; content may be purchased for
a nominal fee, then immediately downloaded.
Tuning Fork **www.eurocool.com** Tuning
application to be used with a Palm device.
Ultra Guitar Method **www.ultraguitar.com** New
method of guitar improvisation; informative
approach to understanding and employing the
entire guitar fingerboard in any type of playing
situation.
Vguitar.com **www.vguitar.com** Guitar magazine.
W. L. Gore & Associates, Inc.
www.goremusic.com Strings, pedals, parts,
cases, etc.
W. Paul Guitars Inc. **www.wpaulguitars.com**
Timeless Timber guitars and bass guitars.
Washburn International **www.washburn.com**
Acoustic and electric guitars and basses.

Holiday Music

4Hanukkah **www.4hanukkah.com** Festival of
Lights; Online Menorah, Digital Dreidel, and
Byte of Hanukkah; traditions; recipes; gift ideas.
Andrew's Summary of Commonly Observed U.S.
Holidays **visionary2000.com/holidays**
This document summarizes the important dates
commonly observed in the United States,
including important occasions observed by major
immigrant groups.
Black History Month, Kwanzaa, and Martin Luther
King Day Resources

creativefolk.com/blackhistory.html
Provides the origins of Black History Month,
Kwanzaa, and Martin Luther King Day; links to
Internet resources including recipes, songs,
games, and speeches.
Chanukkah Celebrations at the Holiday Spot
www.theholidayspot.com/hanukkah/
index.htm Free Chanukkah wallpaper, recipes,
letterhead, music, history, and more.
Christkindlmarkt Bethlehem
secure.rnci.com/christkindlmarkt/home.
htm Annual event held in December featuring
handmade crafts, holiday music, children's
activities, specialty foods, and more.
Christmas and Hanukkah Celebrations
www.holidaywishes.net/main Christmas
Season Celebration of Lights; drive-through
holiday light show.
Christmas around the World
www.christmas.com Clickable world map
with national traditions; lots more.
Christmas Holiday Fun Page
hometown.aol.com/SantiKlaus/
KidsPartiesXmas Site for kids; unique games
and party ideas for celebrating the season at home
or in the classroom; Word Search; Word
Scramble; gift opening game and more.
Christmas Jokes
theholidayspot.com/christmas/
christmas_jokes Jokes about the holiday with
music.
Christmas Songs: Words and Music
www.homestead.com/stnick/
christmassongs.html MIDI files and lyrics
to over forty popular Christmas songs.
Do You Hear What I Hear?
www.onr.com/user/rbanks/xmas.htm
Reviews and promotions of Christmas and other
holiday music CDs.
DontBblu's Holiday Sing Along Website
www.DontBblu.com/holidayhome.html
Holiday songs; MIDI music and lyrics; 250
songs; information on Christmas, Chanukah, and
Kwanzaa.
Halloween-History and Traditions of the Holiday
wilstar.com/holidays/hallown.htm
History and customs of Halloween.
Hanukkah **www.jcn18.com/holiday/hanukkah**
Stories; music; Hanukkah today.
Happy Easter from Holiday House
www.geocities.com/Heartland/Fields/
3794/Easter Easter music; links.
Happy Thanksgiving
www.theholidayspot.com/thanksgiving/
index.htm Greetings; clip art; recipes.
Hatikvah Music **hatikvahmusic.com** Jewish
Music; Klezmer, Yiddish, Ladino, Sephardic,

Cantorial, Israeli, and children's holiday CDs, tapes, and videos.

Haunted Halloween
members.aol.com/media27/haunted.htm Interactive haunted house file with spooky 2D and 3D animations, pictures, music, and sounds.

Have Yourself a Merry Little Christmas Page
www.kate.net/holidays/christmas Large categorized list of Christmas links.

Holiday & Christmas MIDI Song Files
www.lockergnome.com/MIDI/holiday. html Over thirty-five high-quality Christmas music MIDI files.

Holiday Happenings Webring
www.webring.org/cgi-bin/webring? ring=holidays Holiday pages.

Holiday Stuff for Children
home.amaonline.com/teacherstuff/ holiday.htm Thanksgiving and Christmas sites; arts and crafts, coloring pages; holiday stories.

Holiday Year Round Ring
www.webring.org/cgi-bin/webring? ring=hyr;list Web ring of holiday-related links.

Holidays **www.suite101.com/welcome.cfm/ holidays** Information about various holidays.

Merry Christmas Happy Hanukkah—A Multilingual Songbook & CD **www.pianopress.com** Thirty-two traditional favorites; piano/vocal/guitar; lyrics in English, Hebrew, Spanish, German, French, and Latin; CD-ROM version prints scores; RealAudio files.

Merry Christmas
www.bishart.com/merry_christmas.htm Celebrate Christmas with holiday links, music and, eToys.

Musical Candles **www.musical-candles.com** Candles play CD quality music while fiber-optic wick is lit; six melodies from which to choose.

New Year's Day
www.wilstar.com/holidays/newyear.htm History, traditions, and customs of New Year's Day and how it is celebrated.

Rosh Hashanah in CyberSpace
members.xoom.com/Web_lady/ roshhashanah/index.htm Resource which includes a brief description of the holiday, links to Jewish MIDIs, graphic and design sites, history and traditions, food, online Jewish bookstores, selected holiday books, sites for kids, and much more.

Santa's Christmas Music
www.primenet.com/~kringle/carols. html Hear and see the words to Christmas music.

Sheryl's Holidays Site
www.sherylfranklin.com/holidays

Collection of pages and links related to all holidays.

Sleigh Ride **www2.acc.af.mil/music/holiday** Christmas and holiday season music; premiere of a new Hanukkah piece; in MP3 and RealAudio; Air Force band site.

Thanksgiving Day **www.0-0.com/thanksgiving** More than one hundred annotated Thanksgiving links.

The Holiday Page-History and Customs
wilstar.com/holidays Explains the customs and history of most holidays, including, but not limited to, Christmas, Easter, and New Year's Day; games, graphics, music, and poetry.

Valentines Day in CyberSpace
members.xoom.com/web_lady/ valentine/index.html Resources.

Valentines Word Searches
www.splam.com/holiday/val/word.html Holiday Macintosh and PC shareware and freeware; coloring pages; crafts; word searches; mazes; graphics and music.

WAVs for the Holidays
members.aol.com/ilovewavs/index.htm Over one hundred short Thanksgiving, Christmas, and New Years files.

Year Round Holiday Games for Families
hometown.aol.com/SAmon349/ KidsParties/HolidayFun Word searches, mazes, word scrambles, and secret code puzzles for each of the major holidays; poetry; crafts; words to songs.

International

150 International Music Links
ingeb.org/midimidi.html Links and MIDI files to countries and ethnic music.

4Arabs Music **www.4arabs.com/music** RealAudio files of Arabic music to download; Arabic tapes and CDs; online forum for discussing Arabic music.

Adria Net-Dance Hall-Night Clubs-Italy
www.adria.net/uk/discotec.htm Survey under localities.

Africa Online Music Forum
www.africaonline.com/AfricaOnline/cgi /chat.cgi?c Ongoing discussion of African music.

Africa Online: Moroccan Music
www.africaonline.com/AfricaOnline/ music/morocco Moroccan music page within the Africa Online site.

African Music and Dance Ensemble
www.cnmat.berkeley.edu/~ladzekpo/ Ensemble.html Web site for African music.

Ambient/World Music from Australia
ourworld.compuserve.com/homepages/ evolving/ambie Links to Australian eclectic artist sites.

Ancient Music of Ireland
services.worldnet.net/~pybertra/ceol/ homepage Discusses Ancient Irish music with an emphasis on the Bunting Collection of harp music (1792); MIDI files.

Arab Music
trumpet.sdsu.edu/M151/Arab_Music1. html Major influences; assimilated cultures; Medieval Europe; structure of modern-day Arabic music including maqam and iqa.

Arabic Music Info Source
members.aol.com/amisource Resource for Arabic music.

Archives of African American Music and Culture
Mission **www.indiana.edu/~aaamc** African American music Web site.

Arts, Culture, and Music in India
www.Webindia.com/india/music.htm Art forms and entertainment in India; classical music and dance, movies, theatre, photography; many links.

Australian Music CDs from Australian Artists
Online **www.musicworld.com.au** CDs of Australian music.

Australian Originals
www.australianoriginals.com Didgeridoo; Yidaki-Doo.

Belly Dance Home Page **www.bdancer.com** Local features; schedule of dancers; FAQ.

Benno **www2.passagen.se/benno** Swedish independent music.

Bhargava & Co. **www.indianmusicals.com** Natraj.

Big Sky World of Chinese Musical Instruments
www.bigskymusic.com Instruments of the classic Chinese orchestra including four sections: the bowed strings, plucked strings, winds, and percussion.

Blissco **www.blisscorporation.com** Italian electronic and dance music company.

Books on Music of India
www.vedamsbooks.com/music.htm Annotated catalogue of books on various aspects of music of India; detailed descriptions.

California Newsreel-African American Music and Cultural History
www.newsreel.org/aamusics.htm Videos on African American music.

Celtic Connection Music Page **www.celtic-connection.com/music** Interviews and reviews from the Celtic Connection; published ten times a year from Vancouver, British Columbia, Canada.

Celtic Music on the Web: Record Labels
www.wizvax.net/jcaffery/celtic/ record.html Web sites of Celtic music record labels.

Celtic Music.com **www.celticmusic.com** Celtic music Web site; MP3s.

Center for Music of the Andes
otto.cmr.fsu.edu/~cma/andes.htm Brief history and information about Andean music.

Ceolas Celtic Music Archive
www.ceolas.org/ceolas.html Celtic music Web site; notation; links.

Ceolas **www.ceolas.org/about** Celtic music on the Internet.

Chandra's-Middle Eastern Belly Dance Supplies
www.chandras.com Catalog of Belly dance and Middle Eastern dance supplies; music; costumes and more.

Charts All Over the World
www.lanet.lv/misc/charts International music charts.

Children's Choir of the Royal Danish Academy of Music **home3.inet.tele.dk/dkdmbkor/ dkdmbku1.htm** Practise choir for future conductors and teachers; well-regarded concert choir; toured all over the world.

China: Classical Music
www.medieval.org/music/world/china. html Information on Chinese music and instruments; listings of recordings.

China's MP3 Music **www.listentochina.com** Chinese MP3 music.

Chinese Music
www.surfchina.com/html/artsandculture _performing Collection of sites related to Chinese music.

Classical Music of St.Petersburg, Russia
www.classicalmusic.spb.ru All about classical music in St. Petersburg; concert halls; musical theaters; musicians; Russian composers; classical MP3; Russian musical links.

Condor Records **www.condorrecords.com** World music with free audio samples; Andean and Native American music.

Coyne Celtic Imports **www.coyneceltic.com** Celtic music Web site; bagpipe accessories.

Culturekiosque **www.culturekiosque.com** Cultural topics; articles in different languages.

Czech Library of Musical Links
www.jcu.cz/firmy/faktor/pckho.htm Index site; artists; labels; music libraries.

Djembe Online **www.djembe.dk** Scandinavian forum for cross culture and world music; African and Latin American culture debate; world music record reviews; film and book reviews.

Fair Music **www.fair-music.com** Newsletter; links; artist bios; German music chart; in German and English.

FinnDiscog **www.sci.fi/~phinnWeb/diy** Do It Yourself (DIY) Finnish self-releases.

Finnish Music Information Centre **www.fimic.fi** Finnish music; facts about composers, artists, and groups of contemporary music; folk and world.

Folk Music of England, Scotland, Ireland, Wales, and America **www.contemplator.com/folk.html** Traditional music; lyrics; tune information; historical background; MIDIs; related links.

France MP3 **www.francemp3.com** Download site; MP3.

French Music Database **www.sirius.com/~alee/fmusic.html** French artists and recordings.

Greek Songs Database **www.edu.physics.uch.gr/songs** Database of Greek music; lyrics to songs; history; Greek artists.

Hawaiian Music 101 **www.tropicaldisc.com/primer.html** Descriptions of the primary types of Hawaiian music.

Hong Kong Online Music Store **www.hkmusic.net** Music in Cantonese, Mandarin, Japanese, and English.

Hong Kong Pop Stars **huifong.hypermart.net** Popular music in Hong Kong.

IMMEDIA! **www.immedia.com.au** Australian music industry directory.

Indiamusic.com **www.indiamusic.com** Hindi, Punjabi, Pakistani, Ghazals, Pop, Filmi, and Bhangra songs in Real Audio and MP3 format; over 1,000 songs; complete Indian music and video.

Indian Classical Music and Dance Kalavant Center **www.mightyhost.com/kalavant** Works to preserve and help foster growth and innovations in Indian music and dance.

Indian Music Glossary **chandrakantha.com/tablasite/glossary.htm** Glossary of terms used in Indian music.

Indian Music **www.allindia.com/arts/musint.htm** Background on Indian music.

Inmusica-Classical Music in Italy **www.inmusica.com/inmus.htm** Classical music, musicians, and dates.

International Charts **dir.yahoo.com/Entertainment/Music/Charts/Countries** Best selling music in countries all over the world.

Internet Islamic History Sourcebook **www.fordham.edu/halsall/islam/islamsbook.html** MIDI sound samples.

Irish Music Box **www.dojo.ie/musicbox** Online resource for Irish music.

Irish Music **www.mayo-ireland.ie/irishmusic.htm** Irish music Web site.

Irish Music Magazine **mag.irish-music.net** Monthly folk and traditional Irish music magazine from Ireland; published on paper with some articles online.

Irish World Music Centre **www.ul.ie/~iwmc** University of Limerick; set up in 1994 by Dr. Mícheál Súilleabháin.

Italia Mia-Italian Music **www.italiamia.com/music.html** Italian music Web sites.

Jewish Culture and History **www.igc.apc.org/ddickerson/judaica.html** Global Jewish culture.

JewishMusic.com **www.jewishmusic.com** Jewish music books; sounds; videos.

Jungle Life **www.nst.co.jp/~jungle** Japanese independent music.

Kabuki for Everyone **www.fix.co.jp/kabuki/kabuki.html** Traditional form of Japanese theater.

Kami: Belly Dancer **members.xoom.com/kami_bdancer/Belly_Dancer** Videos and music of belly dancers around the world.

Lo'Jo **www.lojo.org** World music, concerts, and press kit; French and English.

Millennium Music: New Beats for the New Age-World African Network **www.wanonline.com/blackhistory/blackhistory6250.html** Comprehensive site covering news, sports, entertainment, lifestyle, discussions, and commentary in African and African American communities around the world.

Moroccan Music **www.moroccanmusic.com** Music of Morocco.

Music from the Faroe Islands **www.framtak.com/fo_music/spaelimen.html** CDs; ballads; original music and new arrangements of traditional Faronese tunes.

Music India OnLine **www.musicindiaonline.com** Updates; mailing list; Real Player G2 required to hear songs listed.

Music of Japan **www.jinjapan.org/today/culture/culture10.html#mu** Brief history of Japanese traditional music, from its roots to its present status.

Musica Russica **www.musicarussica.com** Russian choral music.

Musicanews **www.musicanews.com** Italian music Webzine.

Musicfinland.com **www.musicfinland.com/classical** Finnish classical music scene.

New Music Express Charts
 www.nme.com/charts Music magazine from England; cutting edge music.
PakistaniMusic Modern Age
 www.pakistanimusic.com/music/ modernage Modern Age Mirch Masala; choose songs from each artist's individual page.
PakistaniMusic Religious
 www.pakistanimusic.com/music/ religious Collection of Naats, Surahs from the Holy Quran with translation in English; miscellaneous audio related to Islam.
Playloud **www.Webcom.com/playloud** French concert directory.
Rampant Scotland Directory-Music and Dance
 www.rampantscotland.com/music.htm Scottish music and dance.
Royal Music
 www.geocities.com/Athens/Forum/ 8424/music.html Links to all types of music from around the world; the Queen's favorite bands.
Russian Independent Music
 www.gromco.com/music/rim Online guide to Russian independent bands and labels; interviews; sound files; news; Russian record reviews; discussion groups; Russian/American dictionary with translations of music terminology.
Scandinavian Indie
 www.lysator.liu.se/~chief/scan.html Internet guide to Scandinavian independent music.
Scottish Music Information
 www.music.gla.ac.uk/HTMLFolder/ Resources/SMIC Based in Glasgow; information about the Scottish music scene; concert diary; Scottish music on compact disc; the *Scottish Music Handbook.*
Simaku **www.simaku.com** Site in English and Albanian; Eastern European music.
Sounds of Scotland
 www.Webcraft.co.uk/Webcraft/music Scottish music.
Sportos.com **www.sportos.com/tusovka** History of rock in Russia; audio clips; links.
Studio Two Recording, Dublin **www.studiotwo.ie** Client list includes some of the most renowned artists of world music, including Bono and the Edge, Paul Brady and Elvis, Spice Girls and Boyzone.
Supersonic Guide
 www.freestyle.com/supersonic British music Web sites.
Swedish Music Festivals
 www.musikfestivaler.se From spring to autumn there are festivals throughout Sweden; folk music, chamber music, opera, jazz, or choral music; program folder available in Swedish, English, and German.
The Irish Traditional Music Archive
 www.itma.ie/home/itmae1.htm Reference archive and resource center for the traditional song, music, and dance of Ireland.
The Jewish Music Heritage Trust **www.jmht.org** Jewish music Web site.
The Jewish Ring **www.Webring.org/cgi- bin/Webring?ring=jewish;list** Huge Webring with over 300 sites.
The Lengthy List of Jewish Links
 www.mcs.net/~grossman/jewish.html Over 300 categorized links to pages of Jewish interest.
The Music of East Asia
 www.eyeneer.com/World/Ea/index.html Essay analyzing the development of music in this region; emphasis on Chinese music.
Traditional Cretan Music **www.sfakia- crete.com/sfakia-crete/crete-music** History, instruments, and artists of traditional Cretan music; sound samples; links.
Turkish Music Club **www.turkishmusic.com** Complete source of Turkish music.
UK-Dance **www.uk-dance.org** Mailing list for people to discuss everything to do with dance music culture in the UK.
Unsound Records Sydney
 www.unsound.com.au/htmlf/indexf. html Australian Web site; soul, reggae, dance, hip-hop, trip-hop, R&B, soundtracks, and world music CDs, vinyl, and videos.
Waltons Irish Music Inc.
 www.waltonsirishmusic.com Bodhran drums; penny whistles; instructional books; songbooks; instructional videos.

Jazz, Blues, and Swing

11th East Coast International Blues and Roots Music Festival **www.bluesfest.com.au** Australian blues festival.
420 Blues **www.420blues.com** Home page.
4Blues.com **www.4blues.com** Listen to blues MP3s; read about blues legends, blues festivals, and concert tickets; blues clubs and singers are listed.
A Passion 4 Jazz **www.apassion4jazz.net** Information; resources; links.
Acoustic Records
 home.c2i.net/acousticrecords Independent Norwegian jazz record label; artist information; reviews; MP3 samples and more.
Advance Music **www.advancemusic.com** Jazz Conception; Jazz Workshop Series.

Aebersold Jazz Online **www.jajazz.com** Producer and seller of play-along discs and educational materials.

All about Jazz **www.allaboutjazz.com** Reviews and more.

Alligator Records **www.alligator.com** Foremost authority on blues music and blues artists; view artist bios and liner notes; online catalog.

All-Jazz Clearinghouse **www.all-jazz.com** Site for professional and amateur musicians; fans; promoters; record labels; festival directors and the music industry; jazz art; photos; posters; CDs; books; discographies and more.

Any Swing Goes **www.anyswinggoes.com** Swing music Web site.

Association of British Jazz Musicians (ABJM) **dialspace.dial.pipex.com/jazz/abjm.htm** Nonprofit organization; represents the interests of UK jazz musicians; supported by the musician's union and leading UK jazz personalities; lobbying organization; regular meetings for members; newsletter.

Australian Rock, Blues, Folk MP3 Music Downloads **www.iinet.net.au/~property** Music downloads and Web entertainment.

Bird Lives! **www.birdlives.com** Weekly jazz-zine; sneak previews.

Blue Note Records **www.bluenote.com** Jazz label; reviews; news; online catalog, artist and tour information; RealAudio clips; Jukebox StreamWorks audio.

Blues Bank Collective **www.bluesbank.org** Dedicated to uniting people of all ages, races, and creeds through the distinctly soulful American music called blues.

Blues before Sunrise **www.cramer-ts.com/blues** To explore, preserve, and popularize the first fifty years of recorded blues; to present blues as America's true roots music; to profile its influence on American popular music including gospel.

Blues Blitz **www.bluesblitz.com** Home page.

Blues Boy Music **www.bluesboymusic.com** Home page.

Blues Express, Inc. **www.bluesexpress.com** Source for blues music on the Internet; blues music TV show; RealAudio and RealVideo clips of blues music.

Blues for Peace Cafe **www.bluesforpeace.com** Web radio, blues books, art, CDs, gifts, and more.

Blues Music Magazine **imp.cssc.olemiss.edu/blues.html** Living Blues.

Blues on Stage **www.mnblues.com** Comprehensive blues guide; reviews.

Blues Paradise-Classic Blues Musicians **www.bluesparadise.com** Links to national and regional blues acts; schedule for regional blues venues; festival information and more.

Blues Revue **www.bluesrevue.com** Magazine site with blues MP3s.

Blues Summit: Blues Radio Stations on Yahoo! Broadcast **www.broadcast.com/radio/blues/blues** Variety of formats.

Blues Traveler **www.bluestraveler.com** Blues Web site.

Blues Union **www.bluesunion.com** Blues Web site.

Blues World **www.bluesworld.com** Blues Web site.

BLUES! **www.overnet.com.ar/Users/fwwbt.html** Friends worldwide blues tribute; non-business organization dedicated to the blues.

Blues.com **www.blues.com** Information; resources; links.

BluesNet **www.hub.org/bluesnet** Articles, photographs, and more; traditional and historical blues artists.

Bluestar **www.bluestar.de** Blues Web site.

BluesWEB **www.island.net/~blues** Harp amplifier sound samples; custom-built harmonicas; action and sound.

Camsco Music: Traditional Folk, World, and Blues Music **www.camsco.com** Traditional blues and folk music of America and the world.

Contemporary Jazz **www.contemporaryjazz.com** Jazz Web site.

Cyberjaz.com **www.cyberjaz.com** Jazz Web site; hard-to-find and rare recordings.

DownBeat **downbeatjazz.tunes.com** Jazz articles; news; features; archives.

Dr. Jazz Operations **www.drjazz.com** Independent radio and print media record promotion firm in the U.S. specializing in jazz, blues, and world music.

Educationline.com (Music, The Universal Language) **www.educationline.com/bluesring.html** Games; lessons; monthly newsletter; jazz greats; bulletin board ideas.

Electric Blue **www.electricblue.net** Blues Web site.

Electric Blues **www.electricblues.com** Hundreds of blues CD ratings; biweekly CD reviews with RealAudio, RealAudio Blues Jukebox, and Real Audio Blues links; all artists linked to discographies/soundclips.

Fivenote Music Publishing **www.fivenotemusic.com** Publishes six music books containing jazz improvisation method, theory, and resources for learning and improving skills for beginning through advanced players of treble clef instruments.

Glenn Miller Orchestra **www.glennmillerorchestra.com** Official Web site.

Horizon Online: Indonesian Jazz Bulletin **www.vision.net.id/horizon** Information about jazz in Indonesia; musicians; groups; history; festivals; jazz clubs.

House of Blues **www.hob.com** Live concert cybercasts; music news; on demand concert archives; interviews; music reviews; Internet radio; music editorial.

InterJazzional **www.geocities.com/SoHo/Coffeehouse/ 8624** Home page; jazz across the borders.

International Association of Jazz Educators **www.iaje.org** Official Web site.

Jakarta International Jazz Festival **www.vision.net.id/jakjazz** Asian jazz festival.

JAZCLASS **www.jazclass.aust.com** Music lessons on music theory, blues, jazz, improvisation, chords, and scales on all instruments; saxophone technique.

Jazz and Blues Report **www.jazz-blues.com** Reviews of jazz, blues, fusion, and swing music from record labels like Alligator, Rounder, Blind Pig, and more.

Jazz Central Station **www.jazzcentralstation.com/newjcs/ main/splome.asp** Internet jazz resource for fans, musicians, and the music industry.

Jazz Corner **www.jazzcorner.com** Jazz Web site.

Jazz Ear 1 **www.ear1.com/cgi- bin/WebObjects/WMJazzGenre** Source for jazz music; CDs; videos; interviews; contests; tour dates; over 1,000 official artist sites.

Jazz in France **www.jazzfrance.com/en** Concerts; festivals; French Jazz record labels; magazines; forums; music reviews; audio samples.

Jazz Is **www.jazzis.com** Jazz resources.

Jazz IZ **www.jazziz.com** Features; reviews; news.

Jazz Legends **jazz_legends.vstoremusic.com** The History of Jazz Music Store.

Jazz Master **www.jazzmaster.com** Information; resources; links.

Jazz Net **www.culturekiosque.com/jazz** Jazz Web site.

Jazz Online **www.jazzonline.com** Monthly Webzine; news; features; links; artist reviews; Jazz 101; introduction to the world of jazz.

Jazz Portal-Jazz on Web **www.jazzonWeb.com** Jazz portal on the Web; organized by categories;

anything about jazz; musical instruments; scores; musicians; MP3; jazz styles; festivals and more.

Jazz Promo **www.jazzpromo.com** Jazz Web site.

Jazz Radio **www.jazzradio.org** From Lincoln Center in NYC; concert series.

Jazz Review **www.jazzreview.com** Jazz music reviews; festivals; MP3; photography, art and more; weekly source for the hottest new jazz releases.

Jazz Roots Rhythms **www.jdscomm.com/jazz1.html** Jazz, soul, blues, gospel, world music; San Francisco and the global music scene.

Jazz Scale Suggester System **www.w- link.net/~jsss/jsss.htm** Enter jazz chord chart; will suggest and explain scale possibilities for solos.

Jazz Services **www.jazzservices.org.uk/jazzsite.htm** Jazz Web site.

Jazz Solo Transcriptions Online **www.glasnet.ru/~ilia/jazzsolo** Jazz solos transcribed to the sheet notes in PDF format.

Jazz Stuff **www.jazzstuff.com** Jazz Web site.

Jazz Times Magazine Inc. **www.jazztimes.com** Club Guide in September issue; night clubs; managers; booking agents; features; reviews; news.

Jazz World **www.jazzworld.com** Information; resources; links.

Jazz, Blues, Flamenco, and World Music Posters **www.arrakis.es/~artstudiohita** Limited- edition prints.

Jazz.com **www.jazz.com** Home page; resources; links.

Jazz.ru **www.jazz.ru** Jazz Web site.

Jazzbreak **www.jazzbreak.com** Jazz guide; history; musicians; fanzine; news.

Jazzharmony.com **www.jazzharmony.com** Contemporary methods for piano, ear training, chords, and jazz voicings; jazz standard fake books; free monthly chord post; includes teaching and learning tips about chords.

JazzInternet.com **jazzinternet.com** Jazz resources worldwide; jazz radio; RealAudio sites; "Jazz Club" with message board and chat; global resource.

JazzUtopia **www.jazzutopia.com** Jazz music books, videos, and CDs for listening, practicing, and learning.

Jazzworx! **www.jazzworx.com.au** Set of learning tools; lesson by lesson on a double CD and book; three-volume series; beginning, intermediate, and advanced.

JVC Jazz Festival **www.festivalproductions.net** Held in August in Newport, RI.

Lejazzetal.com **www.lejazzetal.com** Jazz Web site.

Life Force Jazz **www.lifeforcejazz.com** Jazz Web site.

Marc Sabatella's Jazz Improvisation Primer: Other Instruments **www.chordboard.com/primer/ms-primer-6-4.html** The use of other instruments, such as brass or woodwind instruments, as accompanying instruments is usually limited to a few background riffs or repeated phrases.

Midnight Flyer
www.fatmusic.com/midnightflyer Blues music.

Montreux Sounds Records
www.montreuxsounds.ch The Montreux Jazz Festival audio-video library.

New Jazz Archives
www.eyeneer.com/Jazz/index.html Jazz Web site.

New Mexico Jazz Workshop
www.flash.net/~nmjw Dedicated to American jazz; premier jazz presenting and education organization in New Mexico.

New Orleans Music Radio: WWOZ
www.wwoz.org Listener supported jazz and heritage station for New Orleans and the surrounding region; from blues to jazz, cajun, zydeco, gospel, Brazilian, and Caribbean.

New Orleans Music Resources
www.partyhats.com New Orleans music resources; free classified listings; Web radio; mall; music history.

New York Jazz Artist Management
www.nyjam.com Representing NYC artists.

Newworldnjazz.com **www.newworldnjazz.com** Jazz Web site.

Official Website of Billie Holiday
www.cmgww.com/music/holiday/holiday.html Brief bio; photo gallery; career summary; artwork from the U.S. postal stamp.

Oscar Peterson **www.oscarpeterson.com/op** Signature CD-ROM project; music book of transcriptions with audio CD; up-to-date personal Web site.

Photographs from the Golden Age of Jazz **memory.loc.gov/ammem/wghtml/wghome.html** William P. Gottlieb Collection; over 1,600 photographs of celebrated jazz artists; documents the jazz scene from 1938 to 1948 in NYC and Washington, D.C.

Pittsburgh Blues Women
www.pghblueswomen.com Chicago and New Orleans are known for blues music; many female blues performers are from these cities.

Play Like a Pro
www.coastnet.com/~pier79.bc.ca/

plp2000/index_plp Music improvisation course in Acrobat PDF format.

Posi-Tone Jazz World **posi-tone.com** For jazz enthusiasts; links to tribute sites, legends, and other jazz-related sites.

Primavera Jazz! **www.primaverarecords.com** Independent jazz CDs.

Real Blues Magazine
www.realbluesmagazine.com Guide for blues music.

Russ Neff's Guide to Real Jazz
home.earthlink.net/~mftjazz Information about jazz music and musicians.

SaxTrax.com **www.saxtrax.com** Smooth jazz, traditional jazz, and new age CDs.

Scottyboy's Blues Page
www.geocities.com/SunsetStrip/4466 Rare blues music sounds; pictures.

Sher Music **www.shermusic.com** Publisher of jazz educational materials; *The New Real Book;* Brazilian and Latin songbooks.

SkyJazz Internet Radio **www.skyjazz.com** Jazz in four categories: Big Band, Light & Easy, Straight Ahead, and All Requests.

Smooth Sounds **www.smoothsounds.com** Contemporary jazz CDs; traditional jazz CDs; new age CDs; video and links.

Sonny Boy Lee's "Ain't nothin' but the blues!" **www.sonnyboylee.com** Blues artists pages and links to blues music sites worldwide.

Southwest Blues **www.southwestblues.com** Blues festival.

Spacejazz.com **www.spacejazz.com** Music page with RealAudio files.

Spajazzy.com **www.spajazzy.com** Jazz Web site.

Stanford Jazz Workshop **www.stanfordjazz.org** Jazz education.

Stricktly Jazz **www.stricktlyjazz.com** Jazz Web site.

Swedejazz.se **www.swedejazz.se** Web site about Swedish jazz.

Swingin' Jazz Fiddle **www.swinginjazzfiddle** For jazz fiddlers.

Texas Blues Music **www.texasbluesmusic.com** Information about the blues from Texas; blues clubs; guitar maintenance; commentary; flatted thirds and more.

The Blue Flame Café **www.blueflamecafe.com** Interactive biographical encyclopedia of great blues singers.

The Blue Highway **thebluehighway.com** History of and tribute to the blues.

The Blue Zone **bluezone.org** Blues bands.

The Blues Experience **www.bestblues.com** Blues music and blues information; RealAudio Webcasts of The Blues Experience; recommended blues CDs and books; blues quiz; monthly blues contests.

The Blues Fake Book
www.netstoreusa.com/music/002/ HL00240082.shtml Fake book of over 400 songs for all 'C' instruments; sheet music.

The Blues Foundation **www.blues.org** Organized and founded in 1980 to promote and preserve blues music around the globe.

The Jazz Age Page
www.btinternet.com/~dreklind/ Jazzhome.htm Historical view through the music and events of the twenties and thirties; music clips; biographies.

The Jazz Age: A Fusion of Music and Literature
osgood.colgate.edu/tmaikels/jazz.html Readings and more.

The Jazz Composers Collective
www.jazzcollective.com Musician-run, nonprofit organization dedicated to presenting the works of composers; concert series; newsletter.

The Jazz Store **www.thejazzstore.com** Collectible jazz albums and merchandise.

The Jazzserver **www.jazzserver.org** Interactive jazz database; jazz groups; samples; venues and festivals from all over the world

The JazzSource **www.jazzsource.com** Comprehensive international resource to the world of jazz.

The St. Louis Blues Society **www.stlblues.org** Official Web site.

TheJazzPages: Jazz in Deutschland **www.jazzpages.com** Jazz in Germany.

Thelonious Monk Institute of Jazz **monkinstitute.com** Official site for Thelonious Monk Institute of Jazz; photos and information.

Village Vanguard **www.villagevanguard.net** Famous jazz club; recording venue; schedules; information.

Warner Bros. JazzSpace **www.wbjazz.com** Jazz Web site.

Yahoo! Entertainment: Music: Genres: Blues **www.yahoo.com/Entertainment/Music/ Genres/Blues** Blues music.

Yazoo Blues **www.yazoobluesmailorder.com** Deep, gritty, traditional blues; delta blues; acoustic blues; online catalog.

Latin and Carribean Music—Calypso—Reggae

About Ska/Reggae **ska.about.com** Reggae Web site; information; resources.

Afromix **www.ina.fr/Music/index.en.html** Music from Africa and the Caribbean.

All Latin Music TV **www.alllatinmusictv.com** Music videos; interviews and performances by the movers and shakers of today and yesterday in the genre.

ART-COM International Latin Music Megastore **www.artcomintl.com/music.htm** Online Hispanic/Latino resource for Latin music CDs and videos; Latin pop, Latin rap, danza, flamenco, mariachi, merengue, salsa, tango, tejano, and more.

Bajan Calypso Barn **www.iere.com/thebarn** Calypso music Web site.

Bembe Records **www.bembe.com** Cuban music record label.

Brazilian Music UpToDate **www.brmusic.com/uptodate** Music of Brazil.

Calypso Tent of the Air **www.kaiso.net** Calypso music Web site.

Caravan Music Online Catalog of Latin/Brazilian Music **www.caravanmusic.com** Online mail order CD catalog; buyers guide for music from Latin America and beyond; world music genres covering Brazil, Portugal, Spain, Cuba, Argentina, Colombia, Argentina, Puerto Rico, and more.

Caribbean Beat **www.caribbeat.com.jm** Home page.

Caribbean Festival **www.caribbeanfestival.org** Calypso music Web site.

Caribbean Music and Dance Programs **www.caribmusic.com** Educational tours with music, dance, and cultural workshops in Cuba, Brazil, Puerto Rico, Trinidad, and the Dominican Republic.

Descarga **www.descarga.com** Information about Afro-Latin music; source for tropical Latin compact discs, videos, books, instructional material, and percussion instruments.

Discover Kingston **discoverjamaica.com/gleaner/discover/ kingston.html** Reggae Web site.

DubWire **www.dubwire.com** Reggae music; ska; roots music.

Guide to Latin Music **www.caravanmusic.com/ GuideLatinMusic.htm** *Caravan Music Guide to Latin Music* by Michael Crockett.

Heartbeat Records **www.rounder.com/heartbeat** Reggae Web site.

Hispanic Online **www.hisp.com** Online home of *Hispanic* and *Moderna* magazines.

Hispano Music and Culture of the Northern Rio Grande **memory.loc.gov/ammem/rghtml/ rghome.html** Juan B. Rael Collection of religious and secular music of Spanish-speaking residents of northern New Mexico; essays in English and Spanish; RealAudio and WAV files.

International Latin Music Hall of Fame
www.latinfame.com Official home page.
Jammin Reggae Archives **niceup.com** Reggae music.
KHS Online-Latin
sps.k12.mo.us/khs/latin/latlinks.htm Latin music and culture.
LaMusica.com/Latin Music Online
www.lamusica.com or
www.latinmusiconline.com Photos and backstage interviews from the International Latin Music Hall of Fame.
LARitmo **www.laritmo.com** Latin American music Webzine; interviews; articles; charts.
Latin American Folk Institute **www.lafi.org** Guide to Latin and AfroCuban music.
Latin American Music Center
www.music.indiana.edu/som/lamc or
www.music.indiana.edu/som/lamc/lamctext.html First URL has many graphics; second URL is text only.
Latin American Music Magazine
www.laritmo.com or
www.laritmo.com/chart.html From NYC; bridge between the Latin music community and the Internet; interviews of established and up-and-coming artists; top Latin charts; music news and more.
Latin Jazz Club **www.LatinJazzClub.com** Latin jazz.
Latin Music Entertainment, Inc.
www.lmeonline.com Licenses, manufactures, markets, and distributes Latin music on compact disc and cassette.
Latin Music Express **www.latin-music-express.com** Caribbean and Latin music distributor; over 3,000 CDs in stock; articles about music.
Latin Music from Picadillo **www.picadillo.com** Latin music site; Cuban music, salsa, songo, timba, and guaguanco; complete songs in RealAudio; extensive press archive in English.
Latin Music Specialist
www.latinmusicspecialists.com Latin music library for TV, film, and commercials.
Latin Music World **www.latinmusicworld.com** Home page.
Latin Pop Music **latinpop.vstoremusic.com** Latin pop, ballad, and rock artists and groups; romantic music of Latino artists.
Latin Real Book, Latin-Jazz
www.shermusic.com/latrealb.htm Contemporary and classic salsa, Latin jazz and Brazilian music arrangements; exactly as recorded, to help bands play in authentic Latin styles.
Latin Sequences of Miami
www.latinosequences.com Cumbia,

merengue, salsa, and all Latin rhythms; free catalog; se habla español.
Latin/Jazz Reviews
www.warr.org/latinjazz.html Latin and Jazz artists.
Latin-All about Music-Music.com
www.music.com/latin Latin music.
Latin-Beat.net **latin-beat.net** Latin music, culture, recordings, and shopping; Latin dances; music samples and steps; stars, posters, magazines, leathers, instruments.
LatinMusica **www.latinmusica.com** Latin music cyberstore; music, videos, DVD, CDs and movies.
Latino Web **www.latinoweb.com** Latino culture.
LatinWorld **www.latinworld.com** Articles; travel; adventure; music.
Library of Congress/HLAS Online Home Page **lcWeb2.loc.gov/hlas** *HLAS Handbook;* bibliography on Latin America; selected and annotated by scholars.
Lord Kitchener Tribute
www.intr.net/goyewole/kitchbd.html Calypso music Web site.
Memory Lane Music
www.interlog.com/~socagm/memorylane2/index.html Calypso music Web site.
Mezcla Message Board **www.mezcla.org/bbs** Cuban music; cultural and musical happenings in Havana.
Music Imports **www.musicimports.com/music_latin.stm** Over 20,000 titles of Latin music.
Music in Latin America-LANIC
lanic.utexas.edu/la/region/music Bembe Records Afro-Latin music; Iberian and Latin American music; online mailing list; conference announcements.
MusicaPeruana.com **www.musicaperuana.com** Music of Peru.
Mybodega.com
www.mybodega.com/latin_music.htm Latin Music Superstore; rare and hard-to-find imports; rhythms and sounds from the Latin music world; Latino books and foods; Spanish videos and special gifts.
Orientation Latin America & The Caribbean **la.orientation.com** Art; literature; culture; politics; music; news; events; travel; food; business; discussions.
Puro Mariachi **www.mariachi.org** The Mexican musical genre; conferences; musicians and bands; events.
Reggae Lyrics Archive **hem.passagen.se/selahis** Reggae lyrics.

Reggae Ring **www.reggaering.org** Reggae Web
  sites; links.
Reggae Sunsplash **www.reggaesunsplash.com**
  Annual festival.
Reggae Train **www.reggaetrain.com** Reggae Web
  site; artist database.
Reggae Web **www.reggaeWeb.com/main.htm**
  Reggae resources and information; news.
Ruff Cut **www.ruffkut.com** Reggae Web site;
  streamed audio; reggae mixes.
Salsa Dance Site **www.salsadancesite.com**
  Information, services, and products.
Samba Musica **www.sambamusica.com** Samba
  music Web site.
Shm Records **www.shmrecords.com** Reggae Web
  site.
Skinheads—The Good, the Bad, and the Ugly
  www.macropolis.demon.co.uk Reggae
  Web site.
Socafusion **www.geocities.com/Hollywood/**
  Highrise/5148/SOCAFUSION.htm Soca
  music Web site.
Sony Music Latin America
  www.sonymusiclatin.com Official Web
  site.
Sounds of Brazil **www.sobs.com** NYC club;
  World and Latin music; news; calendar.
Tango Reporter **www.tangoreporter.com**
  Monthly magazine in Spanish; tango music.
Tex-Mex-Tejana-Chicana Music **www.chicana-**
  tejana-music.com/chicana.html Border
  music.
The Latin Explosion **www.latinexplosion.com**
  Web site home page.
The Mighty Sparrow **www.mightysparrow.com**
  Calypso music Web site.
The Real Jamaica Ska **www.slip.not/~skajam**
  Reggae Web site.
The Reggae Source **www.reggaesource.com**
  Links to reggae Web sites.
The Soul of Latino New York
  www.riodesoul.com NYC guide to Latino
  life; nightlife; live music; schools of Latin
  dance; restaurants; arts and culture; community
  events; gay and lesbian organizations.
Todotango.com **www.todotango.com** Original
  tango master recordings destroyed over fifty years
  ago; online tango music club featuring unique
  tango classics.
Trinidad & Tobago Instruments Ltd.
  www.steelpansttil.com Steel drums;
  Panland; TTIL.
Trinidad Guardian **www.guardian.co.tt** Calypso
  music Web site.
Tropical Hammer Steel Drum Arrangements
  www.tropicalhammer.com/smusic.html
  Single lead; eighty-five-gallon lead; double

tenors; double seconds; tenor bass; child's drum;
  covers and cases; sheet music.
Tropical Music & Pro Audio
  www.tropicalmusic.com Palmer Espana;
  Palmer Pans; Juggs; Biscayne; Starforce USA;
  Techparts; H. Hoffer; Afrosound.
Tropical Music **www.tropical-music.com**
  Newsboard; world music; Cuban music; MP3.
Women in Mariachi Music **www.mariachi-**
  publishing.com/womenmariachi Unique
  mujeres in mariachi music.
World Reggae Music
  members.primary.net/~swdrasta
  International reggae site.
WRTO—Latin Music **www.wrto.com** Latin music
  from Miami; live music; chat.

Music Education

Acoustic Systems **www.acousticsystems.com**
  Practice rooms; instrument storage cabinets.
After School Catalog **www.schoolagenotes.com**
  Access to over one hundred resources for projects
  and themes, activities, arts and crafts,
  multicultural ideas, games, science, music and
  movement, self esteem, and more.
All Things Musical **www.allthingsmusical.com**
  National music education resource guide and Web
  site.
American Music Conference **www.amc.org**
  Information; resources; links.
American Orff-Schulwerk Association
  www.aosa.org Official Web site.
Aria **www.globalthinking.com/aria** Series of
  summer institutes where academics, teachers, and
  students will learn about the music industry and
  its operation from both philosophical and
  practical perspectives; objective is to explore the
  forces, trends, practices, and products of the
  music entertainment industry in order to
  incorporate this information into contemporary
  music education; participants and faculty alike
  will investigate various cultural, technological,
  and market factors influencing music, society,
  and business throughout the world.
Association for Technology in Music Instruction
  www.music.org/atmi Home page.
Berklee College of Music Home Page
  www.berklee.edu Pragmatic educational
  approach to jazz, pop, rock, world music, and
  classical music; Boston, MA.
Blair School of Music
  www.vanderbilt.edu/Blair/htdocs/
  Blairhome.html Vanderbilt University,
  Nashville, TN.
Cassette & Video Learning Systems
  www.cvls.com Watch & Learn Video Primer.

Clarus Music, Ltd. **www.clarusmusic.com**
Worldwide K-12 catalog mail order dealer; sell to
music and nonmusic educators.

Classical Music Resource
www.nhptv.org/kn/vs/musla6.sht
Classical music resources for K-12 instruction.

Coalition for Music Education in B.C.
www.bcmusiccoalition.org Music
education advocacy information for parents,
educational decision makers, and teachers.

College Music Society
www.collegemusicsociety.org or
www.music.org Annual convention; mailing
lists; publications; Music Vacancy List (MVL)
weekly E-mail listings.

Crown Trophy **www.crowntrophy.com** Medals
and awards for music students.

DCI Music Videos **www.wbpdealers.com**
Interworld Music; Bamo Instructional Music
Programs; Music Source International; REH
Music Videos; Ultimate Series; Manhattan
Music Publications.

Eastman School of Music
www.rochester.edu/Eastman The Eastman
education prepares students artistically,
intellectually, and professionally for the rapidly
changing world in which musicians now live;
ranked No. 1 in the *U.S. News and World Report*
survey of the nations best graduate schools.

Educational Activities **www.edact.com** Publishes
educational software, children's music,
educational videos; early childhood recordings;
adult ed and K-12 software.

Educational Programs Publications
www.educationalprograms.com Home
page.

Educational Software Cooperative (ESC) Links
www.edu-soft.org/escother.shtml Links
to instructional software Web sites.

Educator's Music Annex
www.educatorsmusic.com Educational
supplier.

Exploding Art Music Productions
www.explodingart.com Committed to
research, promotion, and development of music
education; specializing in contemporary music
practices including music technology and rock
music.

Expression Center for New Media
www.xnewmedia.com Digital visual media
and sound arts education.

Full Tilt Music **www.fulltiltmusic.com** Live
Internet music lessons for everyone; access to
music lesson resources.

Gateway 2000 Music Education
**www.gw2k.com/majoract/educate/
tchrtool/music.html**

*Global Access to Educational Sources-Art and
Music*
**www.geocities.com/Athens/Academy/
6617/arts.html** A middle-school cybrary of
sites in art and music.

Happy Note!
www.happynote.com/music/learn.html
Computer game; allows people to learn how to
read music while playing; Windows.

Homeschool Fun Units
**www.53.cyberhost.net/homescho/
unit.html** Study units.

Homespun Tapes Online
www.homespuntapes.com Wide selection
of music instruction on videos, CDs, and
audiocassettes for all instruments and styles.

*Influence of Rock Music and Videos on Young
People*
**www.vicnet.net.au:80/vicnet/health/
Rockmusicfact** Make sophisticated judgments
about what is real on television; Center for
Adolescent Health.

Innovative Learning Designs
www.musicreading.com Home page.

Instrumental Classmates
www.instrumentalclassmates.com Meet
the Instruments.

International Schools Service **www.iss.edu** Home
page.

International Workshops
www.internationalworkshops.org General
music; conducting; piano; strings; jazz
improvisation.

Internet Resources for Teachers
www.gbonline.com/~dignan Annotated and
frequently updated resources for incorporating the
Internet into teaching.

Introduction to Music
omnidisc.com/MUSIC/index.html Web-
based course.

Jam Track **www.jamtrack.com** Music practice
jam tapes and CDs; full band backup for
jamming riffs and licks in many styles; for
beginning to intermediate musicians on guitar,
piano, keyboard, or solo instruments.

K-12 Resources for Music Educators
**www.isd77.k12.mn.us/resources/
staffpages/shirk** Home page.

Learn About Music **www.learnaboutmusic.com**
Music education.

Lessons4you.com **www.lessons4you.com**
Online music lessons; instructors.

LessonTime **www.LessonTime.com** Internet
service to help students find music teachers;
national marketing service for teachers; personal
profile; free membership.

Marcia's Lesson Links
members.aol.com/MGoudie/index.html

Educational bookmarks and lesson links for elementary teachers.

McGraw-Hill School Division
www.mhschool.com Home page.

Mediascope: National Television Violence Study
cii2.cochran.com/mnet/eng/med/home/ resource/ntvs The first of three segments studying media violence; Media Awareness Network.

Mike Mangini's Rhythm Knowledge Online
www.rhythmknowledge.com Rhythm instruction materials for all instruments.

Modern Music Methods
www.choicemall.com/playfullmusik Home page.

Mollard Conducting Batons Inc.
www.mollard.com Mollard & Brite Stixs.

Mr. Holland's Opus Foundation
www.mhopus.org In support of music education.

Multicultural Workshops
www.uidaho.edu/LS/Music/sombios/ A-L.html#nkreutzer Multicultural resources for educators.

Murphy Cap and Gown **www.murphyrobes.com** Robes.

Music & Entertainment Industry Educators Association (MEIEA)
www.wiu.edu/users/mimusba/meiea The Music & Entertainment Industry Educators Association was organized in 1979 to bring together educators and the leaders of the music and entertainment industry.

Music Curriculum **www.athena.athenet.net/- wslow/resources.html** Home page.

Music Education and Student Self-Concept
arts.usf.edu/music/rpme/rpmereyn.htm A review of literature concerning music education and student self-concept.

Music Education Online
www.geocities.com/Athens/2405 Links; bulletin board.

Music Education Resource Links
www.cs.uop.edu/~cpiper/musiced.html Links to curriculum resources for each of the nine national content standards as established by the Music Educators National Conference (MENC).

Music Education Software
www.musicmall.com/cmp/educatin.htm A variety of music software for learning piano, guitar, ear training, and music theory.

Music Educators Market Place
www.musicedmarket.com Online retailer.

Music Educators National Conference (MENC)
www.menc.org/index2.html Official Web site; online help for teachers and parents.

Music Instruction Software
cctr.umkc.edu/userx/bhugh/musicold. html Educational software of interest to music teachers and students; main focus is freely available software on the Internet that will help students master the basics.

Music Lessons on Video **www.musicvideo.com** Country, bluegrass, blues, jazz, rock, and gospel instructional music videos.

Music Minus One **www.musicminusone.com** or **www.pocketsongs.com** *Music Minus One; Pocket Songs; Just Tracks;* participatory recordings; accompaniment music; play-along and sing-along for all musicians and vocalists; popular, classical, jazz, rock, and country.

Music Notes **www.musicnotes.net** Publishes *Music You Can Read;* music curriculum for elementary music teachers, home schoolers, or persons interested in learning to read music.

Music Simply Music
www.musicsimplymusic.com Helping teachers, parents, and students share the gift of music.

Music Staff
www.musicstaff.com/customsearch1.asp Find a music teacher.

Music Teacher Find
www.musicteacherfind.com Bringing teachers and students together.

Music Teachers National Association (MTNA)
www.mtna.org Member and program benefits; convention information; publications; resources; links.

Music Technology Learning Center
www.mtlc.net Music technology in the schools and at home.

Musica **www.musica.uci.edu** Music and science information; computer archive; research notes and abstracts on the effects of music on the brain; collected by the Center for Neurobiology at UC Irvine.

Musicianship Basics
www.dragnet.com.au/~donovan/mb Music education software for schools and piano teachers; graded ear training and theory activities for all music students; demos for Macintosh and Windows.

MusickEd.com **musicked.com** Study guides and learning tools for all instruments; membership includes free access to chat rooms and other musical services; online lessons for beginners to professional musicians.

Musicline Publications **www.musicline-ltd.com** Stage musicals and shows for schools, youth theatres, and amateur groups.

Musicnet **library.thinkquest.org** Online guide to music education; encyclopedia; collection of educational contests and games; discussion about music professions.

MusicNet: The Online Guide to Music Education **tqd.advanced.org/3306** Internet site dedicated to the spread of music education; interactive encyclopedia.

Nada Brahma Productions **www.clark.net/pub/nadaprod/index.html** Promotes multicultural education through live presentations and interactive programs of world music, children's music, and dance; programs also available for adults.

National Standards for Music **www.dnh.mv.net/ipusers/orol/district/ issues** Music curriculum for grades K-12.

National Teachers Clearinghouse **www.teachersclearinghouse.com** Nationwide vacancies; teacher and principal jobs.

Net Music School **www.netmusicschool.com** Online music school offering beginning guitar lessons; music teacher search; music resources.

New World School of the Arts **www.mdcc.edu/nwsa/music/music.html** Music Division located in Miami, FL.

Online Music Academy **www.harvestmusic.net** Interactive CDs for Win95/98/NT or online lessons.

Peery **www.PeeryProducts.com** Risers and skirting for performances.

Performance Plus **www.educationalprograms.com** Music education.

Pieces of Music Games **www.alberts.com/authorpages/ 00001919/prod_666** Three educational games: Music Matching, Music Bingo, and Music Missing; teach the names of music symbols; for Windows.

Position Statement on Early Childhood Education **www.menc.org/information/prek12/ echild.html** Argues for the inclusion of music as part of the early childhood curriculum; includes benefits of early music instruction and curriculum recommendations.

Private Lessons **www.privatelessons.com** Locate a private local music teacher; add teachers' names to the searchable database.

PureGold Teaching Tools **www.puregoldteachingtools.com** Teaching aids for classroom teachers, private teachers, parents, students, homeschoolers, and music therapists.

Rhythm without the Blues! **www.islandnet.com/~soundmus** Rhythm training course designed for step-by-step learning.

ScholarStuff **www.scholarstuff.com** Directory of education sites; colleges and universities; educational software; financial aid.

School Music **www.schoolmusic.com** Music education products; music software; printed music; instruments and accessories.

School Music Master **www.cmp.net/smm** For managing school music program; Windows.

Schools of Music in the United States **www.music.indiana.edu./ music_resources/som.html#usa** Directory of U.S. music schools.

SmarterKids.com **www.smarterkids.com/ prod_list.asp?searchtype=ais** Educational books, audio materials, and software for music teaching.

SoundTree **www.soundtree.com** Resource guide for music educators.

St. John's College **www.sjcsf.edu** Founded in 1696; two campuses: Annapolis, Maryland, and Santa Fe, New Mexico; awards Bachelor and Master of Arts degrees; coeducational, four-year liberal arts college; distinctive "great books" curriculum, including music.

Suzuki Association of the Americas, Inc. **www.suzukiassociation.org** Official Web site.

Suzuki Music Academy **www.suzukimusicacademy.com** Suzuki Method classical music study; for children age two and up.

Suzuki Musical Instruments **www.suzukimusic.com** Educational musical instruments.

Tapestry **www.tapestrymusic.com** Music for educators.

Teachers.Net **www.teachers.net/careers** Teacher jobs; employment information.

Teaching and Learning on the WWW **www.mcli.dist.maricopa.edu/tl** Database of educational sites.

Teaching Tools **www2.netcom.com/~crcjct/ teachingtools.html** Series of educational tools for parents, teachers, child care professionals, and counselors; books on parents, preteens, preschoolers, and vegetarianism.

Technology in Music Education **www.ti-me.org** Information; resources; links.

The Complete Guide to Running a Private Music Studio **lightning.prohosting.com/~butler** Guide book for the music teacher.

The Computer Teacher's Resource Page **nimbus.temple.edu/~jallis00** Links to educational sites, project ideas, lesson plans, and tools for using computers in the K-8 curriculum.

The Grove/Rasch School without Walls **www.dickgrove.com** College-level music courses based on the Grove School of Music in Los Angeles, CA; videos, books, CDs, cassettes; correspondence courses.

The Land of Music **www.landofmusic.com**
Tapes and materials for teaching music to young
children.

The Learning Toolbox
**www.edumart.com/sui/edumart/ecat.cgi/
learningtoo** Videos, cassettes, CDs, and
musical instruments for the music teacher.

The Online Conservatory
www.onlineconservatory.com Online
music school offering live, one-on-one and
interactive piano lessons over the Internet.

The WholeARTs Internet Music Conservatory
www.wholarts.com/music/ed Online
courses in music.

Understanding Music
www.understandingmusic.com Interactive
music school.

Virtual Music Classroom
www.cnet.unb.ca/achn/kodaly/koteach
Music activities and resources.

Wenger **www.wengercorp.com** Instrument
storage; lockers.

World In Tune Music Education
**members.aol.com/worldntune/
index.html** Integrated curriculum for K-12
music classes in the arts, humanities, history,
math.

Music and Health—
Healing Music

Alexander Center
www.alexandercenter.com/pa/index.html
Alexander Technique for musicians; articles;
links.

Alexander Technique
www.alexandertechnique.com Systematic
guide to information and resources on and off the
Internet.

American Music Therapy Association
www.musictherapy.org Find a music
therapist; career options.

Animated American Sign Language Dictionary
www.bconnex.net/~randys Animated
dictionary of the language.

Ask Dr. Weil **cgi.pathfinder.com/drweil** Q & A
with Dr. Andrew Weil.

Canadian Network for Health in the Arts (CNHA)
Web.idirect.com/~cnha/index.html
Official Web site.

Center for Voice Disorders
www.wfubmc.edu/voice Information about
the causes and treatments of voice disorders;
singer's problems.

Crystal Singing Bowls Relaxation Massage Music
www.crystalmusic.com Massage relaxation
music played on thirty-five pure quartz crystal
bowls; for deep relaxation, insomnia, and stress
reduction.

Dalcroze Society of America
www.msu.edu/user/thomasna Home page;
training programs; biography; articles about
Dalcroze Eurhythmics.

Donna Michael **www.donnamichael.com**
Healing music; performances; CDs; workshops.

Ear, Nose, and Throat Information Center
www.sinuscarecenter.com Public
information brochures; symptoms; self-help;
hearing loss.

Exercises for Carpal Tunnel Syndrome
**www.aaos.org/wordhtml/press/exerci.
htm** Preventative exercises.

H. E. A. R. **www.hearnet.com** Hearing protection;
earplugs; referral for hearing help.

Hand Health **www.handhealth.com** *Finger
Fitness* program; help for hands.

Hands On! **www.lunnflutes.com/ho.htm**
Online newsletter about performance health for
flutists; list of performance health clinics; links.

HealingMusic.Net **www.healingmusic.net** *Love
Is a Sound* CDs and books; MidiVox Voice to
MIDI products; singing courses; composing and
songwriting services; sound healing and music
healing techniques and resources.

Healthwindows.com **www.healthwindows.com**
Home page; articles on music and health.

House Ear Research Institute-Hearing Conservation
www.hei.org Sound Partner Program; HIP-
Hearing is Priceless.

International Arts Medicine Association (IAMA)
member.aol.com/iamaorg/index.html
Home page; links to therapy sites.

Internet Resources on the Alexander Technique
www.life.uiuc.edu/jeff/alextech.html
Collection of links; articles.

Journal Articles
**www.sailor.lib.md.us/topics/music/
music.txt.** Bibliography of articles focusing on
musician health problems; alternative therapies.

Keys to Health **www.keystohealth.com**
Relaxation music, new age music, romantic
music, and meditation music.

KidMusicMed **www.kidmusicmed.org** A
program to provide emotional, physical, and
psychosocial support for kids with cancer and
other serious illnesses through songwriting;
Music Mentors work with kids as cowriters.

Medical and Sports Music
**www.iuma.com/IUMA/Bands/Medical__
Sports_Music_In** Free MP3 downloads; tour
dates; lyrics; compact disks.

Medical Issues in Music
www.lib.washington.edu/music/

medicine.html Performance anxiety; beta
blockers; injuries; medical clinics for performers;
links.
Men's Health
   www.menshealth.com/index.html Online
   edition of the magazine.
Mental Health Net www.mentalhelp.net
   Directory of online mental-health resources.
Mighty Special Music Makers
   www.erols.com/centers/msmm/
   textpage.htm Asks for volunteers to organize
   bands for people with mental and physical
   disabilities; explains mission; gives background.
Music Maker Relief Foundation
   www.musicmaker.org Charity honors and
   aids traditional Southern musicians over the age
   of fifty-five who earn less than $18,000 a year.
Music Medicine www.rvik.ismennt.is/-
jssen/musmed.html Experiences of a pianist
dealing with repetitive stress injury linked to
playing; emphasis on the importance of proper
technique to avoid long-term injury.
Music Relaxation www.7net.net/music
   Relaxation music, new age music, romantic
   music, and meditation music.
Music Therapy falcon.cc.ukans.edu/-
   memt/mt.html Music therapy Web site.
Musician's Health www.musicianshealth.com
   Health information for musicians.
Musicians and Injuries
   www.engr.unl.edu/ee/eeshop/music.
   html Information for musicians with injuries.
Musicians On Call www.musiciansoncall.org
   Visit hospitals in NYC on a weekly basis; go
   from room to room singing for people who are
   too sick to leave their beds.
Performing Arts Medicine
   www.ithaca.edu/hshp/pt/pt1/index.html
   Newsletter; information for the performer and
   health practitioner; links to resources.
Performing Arts Psychophysiology
   www.performingartspsych.com Formerly
   Musician's Stress Management; seminars;
   workshops; for teachers and performers.
Quantic Music Productions
   www.quantikmusic.com/index-a.html
   The Quantic New Age music series for
   relaxation, meditation, and self-healing sessions.
RelaxedMusic Main Page
   www.xoommemberstores.com/site/
   209259 Hypnosis reports; pure relaxation CD.
Road Recovery
   www.roadrecovery.com/clear.gif For
   musicians who have over-indulged.
Special Music by Special People
   www.specialmusic.org Compact discs;
   MP3 and Quicktime music projects; music

composed by people with developmental
disabilities and other challenges.
The Hand www.med.und.nodak.edu/users/
   jwhiting/hand.html Four major medical
   conditions affecting the hand; development;
   symptoms; treatment.
WellnessWeb wellweb.com Preventative
   medicine.
Wired Seniors Home Page
   www.seniorsmusic.com The Internet's
   largest source of information exclusively for the
   over fifty age group.
Women's Health www.nytimes.com/women
   New York Times Web site on women's health
   issues.

Music History

A Short Bibliography of Early Music
   www.pbm.com/~lindahl/articles/music_
   bibliography Information on early music.
American Music through 1880
   www.andrew.cmu.edu/user/rrollett/
   AmericanMusic Brief articles on many
   aspects of religious music; Psalters; singing
   techniques; denominations; notable musicians.
American Recordings american.recordings.com
   American artists and history.
Baroque Music for the New Age
   www.islandnet.com/~arton/baroque.
   html Baroque music; definitions; history;
   performance; CDs; links.
Baroque Music
   www.sesk.org/Aesthetics/Music/
   Baroque.htm Humorous introduction; styles;
   dates; musicians.
*Basic Music: Your Guide to Music of the Western
   World* www.basicmusic.net Biographies,
   compositions, and recommended recordings of
   composers of all genres and styles of music; This
   Day in Music; musical glossary; musical forms;
   music and entertainment news.
Canadian Music Encyclopedia www.canoe.ca/
   JamMusicPopEncycloPages/home.html
   Chronicles by artist the history of Canadian
   contemporary music from the 1950s to the
   present.
ClassicalNet: Medieval Music Links
   classicalmus.interspeed.net/medieval.
   html Includes Gregorian Chant.
Early Music America www.cwru.edu/orgs/ema
   Music in early America.
Early Music and Score Archive
   www.ace.acadiau.ca/dat.ftp/music Scores
   and more.
Early Music FAQ www.medieval.org/emfaq
   Comprehensive information on Medieval,

Renaissance, and Baroque music; repertory overview; CDs; links.

Early Music WWW
www.virtual.com/jr/earlym.html Resources; links.

Essentials of Music
www.essentialsofmusic.com From Sony Classical and W.W. Norton; basic information about classical music; eras; terms; composers; audio.

Feminist Theory and Music 4
wsrv.clas.virginia.edu/~smp8a/ftm. program.html Bringing feminism into music studies; musicology and gender studies.

Genders OnLine Journal www.genders.org Peer-reviewed academic journal publishing essays about gender and sexuality in relation to social, political, artistic, and economic concerns.

General Music 101
www.talkcity.com/atmusic.GM101/ Gmindex.shrml History of music and music theory; includes every style period; musical examples.

Great Moments in Music History
www.dakota.net/ -pwinn/humor/musichist.shtml Historical events in music.

Gregorian Chant Home Page
www.music.princeton.edu/chant_html The Nassau Edition of Gregorian Chant; Princeton University course materials.

Hellenic Music Resources
www.Webexpert.net/vasilios/ GRMUSIC.htm Collection of links to resources on Hellenic music; ancient to modern.

History Happens www.ushistory.com History Web site on the Internet.

History Net www.TheHistoryNet.com History on the Internet.

History of Ancient Greek Music
w4u.eexi.gr/~gymfil/brown A history of Ancient Greek music from the beginnings of Greek music to 330 B.C.

Journal of Seventeenth-Century Music
www.sscm.harvard.edu/jscm/Welcome. html Information on music of the seventeenth century; Baroque music.

Library of Congress American Memory Site
memory.loc.gov/ammem/amhome.html Collection Finder/Sound Recordings; thousands of historical public domain MP3 files; photos.

Medieval Music & Arts Foundation
www.medieval.org Information and resources for medieval music, including both Western and non-Western; recording suggestions, discussion, and analysis for various styles; database and links.

MIDI Connection File Library: Renaissance Period
mail.dtx-bbs.com/-raborn.renaissa.html Renaissance music MIDI files.

Museum of Music History
www.zti.hu/museum.htm Located in Budapest.

Music History 102
www.ipl.org/exhibit.mushist Separates Western classical music into nine periods; RealAudio files illustrate examples; survey of Western classical music; landmark works of the great composers; stylistic trends in music from the Middle Ages to the present.

Music History 102: The Baroque Age
www.ipl.org/exhibit/mushist/bar/index. htm Information on Baroque music.

Music History
library.advanced.org/15413/history/ music-history.htm or hyperion.advanced.org/15413/history/ music-history.htm Music from the Medieval times to the twentieth century.

Music History Resources
members.tripod.com/~papandr/ musicology.html Collection of outlines on various music history topics.

Music History Resources
www.nerdworld.com/nw1240.html Information on music history; links.

Music History Suite101.com
www.suite101.com/welcome.cfm/ music_history Home page; arts and humanities; history; articles; links; discussions.

Music History Titles from CD-ROM Access
www.cdaccess.com/html/pc/63mhis.htm Directory of music history-related CD-ROM titles, including composers.

Music in the Ancient World
albums.photopoint.com/j/ AlbumIndex?u=49275 Over forty graphics; ancient images; reconstructed scores; scanned text related to ancient Greek, Egyptian, and Hebrew music.

Orpheon www.orpheon.org Museum of historical musical instruments.

Poetry and Music of the War between the States
www.erols.com/kfraser U.S. Civil War music history.

Renaissance Dance
www.ucs.mun.ca/~andrew/rendance.html Central resource for information on European dance from the fifteenth to early seventeenth centuries.

Renaissance Instruments www.hike.te.chiba-u.ac.jp/cons1 Musical instruments of the Renaissance.

Sixteenth-Century Printed Tablatures for the Lute, Vihuela, Guitar, and Cittern
www.lib.duke.edu/music/lute/home. html Sixteenth-century tablature.

Smithsonian Institution **www.si.edu** History of the Smithsonian and the United States.

Society for Seventeenth-Century Music
rism.harvard.edu/sscm Information on music of the seventeenth century.

Stamp on Black History Index
library.advanced.org/10320 or **tqd.advanced.org/2667** Inventions and discoveries; works of art; excellence in science, music, medicine, sports; important roles in history.

The Galpin Society for the Study of Musical Instruments
www.music.ed.ac.uk/euchmi/galpin/ index.html#gw Home page.

The History of Experimental Music in Northern California **tesla.csuhayward.edu/history** New images section; John Cage.

The History of Today **www.on-this-day.com** Daily historical facts and events; famous birthdays; world and music history.

The Lute Society of America
www.cs.dartmouth.edu/ -wbc/lsa/lsa.html History of the lute; links.

The Music History Webring
www.angelfire.com/mt/fragianni Internet sites which feature information on music history, ancient or modern.

The Sonneck Society for American Music
www.asin.org/sonneck Home page.

The Use of Music and Dance in Teaching U.S. History
pw2.netcom.com/~wandaron/history. html One of the most successful techniques in teaching history has been the use of music and dance.

This Day in Music History **datadragon.com/day** or **www.gspyo.com/day** Daily listing of what happened on this day in music history; search engine and calendar information.

Those Were the Days, Today in History
www.440.com/twtd/today.html or **www.440int.com/twtd/today.html** Daily summary of news events, famous birthdays, and hit music that happened on this day in history.

Today in All Kinds of History
www.geocities.com/SunsetStrip/4656/ indexhis.htm Today in history, music history, sports history, celebrity birthdays, TV and movie history; related links to other sites and more.

Today in Classical Music History
www.npr.org/programs/pt/news/history/ classhist.html What happened on this date in classical music history.

Today in History **coach.indiana.net** What happened on this date in history.

Vatican Exhibit: Early Manuscripts
www.ncsa.uiuc.edu/SDG/Experimental/ vatican.exhibit.exhibit.emusic/Music. html Early music manuscripts.

Yahoo! Arts:Humanities:History:Today in History
www.yahoo.com/Arts/Humanities/ History/Today_in_History Find out significant events for any given day.

Yahoo! Entertainment:Music:History
www.yahoo.com/Entertainment/Music/ History Music history.

Music Libraries

Berklee School of Music Library
library.berklee.edu Cross-referenced recordings.

BLAISE: The British Library's Automated Information Service
portico.bl.uk/nbs/blaise/overview.html Home page.

COPAC **www.curlopac.ac.uk/curlinfo** Access to the library catalogs of Cambridge, Edinburgh, Glasgow, Leeds, and Oxford.

Harvard University
www.rism.harvard.edu/MusicLibrary/ Welcome.html Loeb Music Library; U.S. home of RISM.

Hytelnet Library Catalogues
library.usask.ca/hytelnet/sites1.htm Telnet locations with log-in or password instructions for each location.

Indiana University Library
www.music.indiana.edu/muslib.html William and Gayle Cook Music Library; access to important library catalogs for music in the United States and abroad; one of ten members of the Associated Music Libraries Group; includes direct links to the Library of Congress and BLAISE.

Infobahn Librarian **www.ualberta.ca/-nfriesen** Sources of interest to librarians; lists of libraries on the Internet.

International Federation of Library Associations and Institutions
www.nic.bnc.ca/ifla/II/libdoc.htm Home page.

IRCAM **www.ircam.fr/index-e.html** Advanced new music center.

IRCAM Library
www.ircam.fr/biblio/query.html Home page.

Italian Music Libraries
IC:382.CILEA.IT/music/mussigle.htm Comprehensive list in alphabetical order.

Journals and Magazines
> www.indiana.edu/music_resources/
> journals.html_ Journals and magazines listed.

Libraries around the World
> www.lib.utexas.edu/Libs/
> World_Libraries.html Libraries listed.

Library of Congress
> www.lcWeb.loc.gov/homepage/
> lchp.html Largest music library in the United
> States.

LIBWEB: Library WWW Services
> sunsite.Berkeley.edu/libweb
> Comprehensive resource for finding links to
> libraries with Web pages.

Links to Music Information Projects (European Union)
> www.echo.lu/libraries/en/music.html
> Links to current European music projects,
> international music associations, and information
> sources by country.

Massachusetts Institute of Technology
> nimrod.mit.edu/depts/music/
> music-top.html Music library.

Music Librarianship www.depaul.edu Home
> page.

Music Libraries www.ruf.rice.edu/-
> brownlib/music/music.html#hplibs
> Music libraries listed.

Music Library Association
> www.musiclibraryassoc.org Placement
> service for music librarians and more.

Music Library www.library.cornell.edu/music
> The Music Library contains a collection of
> printed music, sound and visual recordings, and
> writings about music and dance consisting
> primarily of Western art music and dance; also
> includes a representative body of non-Western,
> folk, and popular musics.

RISM Series A/II Music Manuscripts
> www.rism.harvard.edu.rism.
> Welcome.html#InternetProject Music
> manuscripts.

RISM-US
> www.sscm.harvard.edu/RISM/Welcome.
> html Home page.

Special Libraries of the United States and Canada
> www.cftech.com/BrainBank/
> OTHERREFERENCE/LIBRARIE
> Directory of major libraries of the United States
> and Canada; special collections; categorized by
> state.

*The International Association of Music Information
Centres IAMIC*
> www.ingress.com/amc/iamic.htm Home
> page.

Thesaurus Musicarum Italicarum candl.let.ruu.nl
> Home page.

UCLA Music Library
> www.library.ucla.edu/libraries/music
> University of California at Los Angeles music
> library.

UCSB Music Library
> www.library.ucsb.edu/subj/music.html
> The music collection is located on the second
> floor of the Arts Library, situated at the western
> end of the Music Building complex; over 70,000
> books, musical scores, and more.

Yale University Library
> www.library.yale.edu/guide1.htm Home
> page.

Music Magazines, E-Zines, Webzines, and Newspapers

Addicted to Noise www.addict.com/ATN or
> www.addictedtonoise.com Webzine; one of
> the first; album reviews; daily news; articles.

All Star Magazine www.allstarmag.com
> Webzine.

Allmusic Zine
> allmusic.com/zine/world_set.html
> Covers all genres of music; reviews; articles;
> interviews; updated daily.

Alternative Music Magazines
> www.prospernet.com/newsmagazines/
> music/alternative.html List of magazines
> including description of contents.

Alternative Press Magazine www.altpress.com
> or www.ap.com or
> www.alternativepress.com News; reviews;
> features; interviews; sound clips.

Apogee Photo Magazine www.apogeephoto.com
> Articles on all aspects of photography.

ARJ NewsLink ajr.newslink.org Publication
> search engine.

Ask Magpie Magazines www.askmagpie.com
> Magazine subscriptions; buy direct from the
> publishers Web sites; links to 6,500 magazine
> and journal Web sites; compare titles, contents,
> and subscription prices.

Audities www.audities.com/audities Popular
> music Webzine; tour updates; reviews; links.

Band Index www.bandindex.com Webzine;
> message board; music news; bands; contests;
> links.

Bards Crier www.bardscrier.com Weekly
> guerrilla music marketing and promotion E-zine
> for the working musician.

Beats E-zine beatsezine.com Music industry
> resource.

BerkleePress www.berkleepress.com Online
> magazine; publisher.

BestEzines.com **www.bestezines.com** Reviews E-zines in twenty categories and announces weekly winners.

Bestmusiczines.com **www.bestmusiczines.com** Music zines; magazines; artists; indie music.

Billboard **www.billboard.com** Industry news; interviews; features; reviews; Radio Charts: Hot 100 Singles, Billboard Top 200 Albums, Pop, Country, Hits of the World, Contemporary Christian, Gospel, R & B, Rap, Dance Music, Latin, Blues, Reggae, World Music, Internet and Indie Charts and more; Top Videos; Fun and Games; The Power Book guide to radio and record promotion; online store.

Black Hole **www.yourblackhole.com** Online magazine.

Blah 3.com **www.rantuk.com** UK music news; alternative bands.

BMI Music World **www.bmi.com/MusicWorld** U.S. performing rights organization; text and photos from the offline quarterly magazine.

British Music Page **easyWeb.easynet.co.uk/~snc/british.htm** Twentieth-century British classical music; online magazine; articles; features; recommended listening list; composers; concert information; links; sound clip of the month.

B-Side **www.ifnet.com/bside/index.html** Music Webzine; articles; interviews; reviews; RealAudio.

Bunnyhop **www.bunnyhop.com** Monthly magazine; interviews; alternative.

Burrelle's Media Directories **www.burrelles.Internet.net** Information available for U.S., Canada, and Mexico; Daily Newspapers, Newspapers, and Related Media; Non-Daily Newspapers, Magazines, and Newsletters; Broadcast Media: Television and Cable, Radio; available in print, on CD-ROM, and on the Internet.

Business Newswire **www.businessnewswire.com** Free service for event announcements.

Canadian Magazine Publishers Association **www.cmpa.ca** Official Web site.

Canadian Musician **www.canadianmusician.com** Music of Canada; news; articles; reviews; industry information.

Cash Box **www.cashbox.com** No longer in publication; information available.

CCM **www.ccmcom.com** American lifestyle and music magazine.

Charts All Over the World **www.lanet.lv/misc/charts** Updated weekly; all countries.

Chicago Tribune **www.chicagotribune.com** Newspaper.

Circus **www.circusmagazine.com** Heavy metal.

Citi:Zen **www.citizenmag.com** Webzine; Shockwave graphics; RealAudio sound; reviews.

CMJ Online **www.cmjmusic.com** Charts of college and commercial radio; reviews of new releases.

CNN Interactive **www.cnn.com/SHOWBIZ/Music** Music information; celebrities.

College Newspapers **www.cpnet.com** Publication search engine.

Collegiate Presswire **www.cpwire.com** Press release and newswire service.

Crawdaddy **www.cdaddy.com** U.S. classic rock magazine; interviews; features.

Cybervibe **www.cybervibe.com** Webzine.

Dazed and Confused **www.confused.com** UK fashion and music magazine.

Details **www.swoon.com/mag_rack/details.html** Entertainment and lifestyle magazine.

Dog Days Mediation **www.musicmediation.com/newsletter.htm** Newsletter.

Dotmusic **www.dotmusic.co.uk** Guide to music; news.

Editor & Publisher **www.mediainfo.com** *International Year Book:* U.S. Dailies, U.S. Weeklies, and Special Newspapers, Canadian Newspapers, Foreign Newspapers, News, Picture and Syndicated Services; database available on disk or labels.

Entertainment Weekly Online **www.pathfinder.com/ew** Online version of the entertainment magazine.

Eworldwire **www.eworldwire.com** Press release and newswire service.

Excite's News Tracker **nt.excite.com** Archive resource; tool for searching offline publications.

Ezine Adsource **www.ezineadsource.com/d6pages/div6main.htm** E-zine directory.

Ezine Seek **www.ezineseek.com** E-zine search engine.

Ezine Universe **www.ezine-universe.com** Directory organized by category and searchable by keyword.

EZines Database **www.infojump.com** Magazine database; E-zines arranged by category; sample and review.

E-zines Today **www.ezinestoday.com** Promotion list; announces free subscription E-zines.

E-zineZ.com **www.E-zinez.com** Searchable directory.

Fast Forward **www.discmakers.com/ffwd**
Interviews; articles.

Feed **www.feedmag.com** NYC E-zine; digital and
popular culture.

Fix Magazine **www.fix.com** Interviews; articles;
photos.

Gajoob **www.gajoob.com** Webzine; articles;
links; reviews.

Gale Directory of Publication and Broadcast Media
www.gale.com Annual Guide listing
newspapers, magazines, journals, radio stations,
television stations, and cable systems; sold as a
three-volume set: *Newsletters in Print,
Encyclopedia of Associations, International
Associations.*

Gavin **www.gavin.com** News; new releases; artist
features; radio charts for all genres; links.

Gebbie Press **www.gebbieinc.com** Publication
search engine.

Groove Planet **www.grooveplanet.com**
Reviews; interviews; audio clips; Top 40;
articles.

Hot Bot: News Channel **www.newsbot.com**
Search news archives.

HotWired **www.hotwired.com** RealAudio;
interviews.

iMusic News Agent
imusic.interserv.com/newsagent Music
headlines and news.

Ink Blot Magazine **www.inkblotmagazine.com**
Rock magazine; pop culture.

Insomniazine **www.insomniazine.co.uk**
London-based; events; dates listings.

Intermixx **www.intermixx.com** Webzine.

International Index to Music Periodicals
iimpft.chadwyck.com IIMP Full Text;
technical support; subscription options; free
trials.

International Media Guides, Inc. (IMG)
www.internationalmedia.com Five
directories with media data on 17,000
publications worldwide.

Internet Media Fax **www.imediafax.com** Press
release and newswire service.

Internet Professional Publishers Association
www.ippa.org Association of over 10,500
professionals involved in New Media and the
Internet.

Jam! **www.canoe.ca/Jam** Offbeat entertainment
and cultural news.

Jelly **www.jellyroll.com** The "Real Music
Newsletter"; American roots.

John Labovitz's Ezine List
www.meer.net/~johnl/E-zine-list E-zine
directory.

Level:11 **www.level11mag.com** Webzine;
publishing; recording; NAMM; MIDI;
RealAudio.

Life **www.pathfinder.com/Life** Photographs;
past features.

Live Magazine **www.livemagazine.com** Online
magazine.

Live Sound! International Magazine
www.livesoundint.com Webzine.

Live Update **www.liveupdate.com** Webzine.

Los Angeles Times Entertainment Section
www.calendarlive.com Entertainment
journalism.

Making Music **www.makingmusic.co.uk** UK
music magazine online.

MediaFinder **www.mediafinder.com** Publication
search engine.

MediaINFO Links **www.mediainfo.com/emedia**
Publication search engine.

MediaMagnet **www.mediamagnetpro.com**
Press release utility.

Metrozine **www.metrozine.com** Interactive
magazine; new musicians; bands.

Mixmag/Mixmag Update
www.techno.de/mixmag UK DJ magazine;
news.

Mix Magazine **www.mixmag.com** Music
industry resources.

MP Music **www.mpmusic.com** Music Previews
Network; Billboard 200; Hot 100 Singles and
more.

Mr. Showbiz **www.mrshowbiz.com** News;
photos.

MTV Online **www.mtv.com** Industry news; bands;
local music.

Music 365 **www.music365.co.uk** Online
magazine; information; news; reviews; events;
chat.

Music Alive Magazine **www.musicalive.com**
Webzine.

Music Industry News Network - Music Dish
www.Mi2n.com Webzine; industry
newsletter; links; newswire service for music
professionals featuring band and record label
annoucements, tour and event dates, digital music
news and new releases.

Music Magazines
www.palatka.net/music/mmag.html
Links to music magazines.

Music Magazines Online
**www.bib.lu.se/elbibl/projekt5/
homepage.html** Detailed list of online
magazines in all genres; lists of other sites which
list music magazines.

Music Maker Publications Inc.
www.recordingmag.com *Recording;
Musico Pro; Playback Platinum.*

Music Maniac **www.music.maniac.com**
Webzine.

Music Newswire **www.musicnewswire.com**
Music industry.

Music Universe **www.musicuniverse.com**
Webzine; reviews; articles.

Musician **www.musicianmag.com** Artist
interviews; business features; working musician
and record reviews.

Musicsearch Magazine Listings
www.musicsearch.com/NewsRoom/
Magazines.html Music magazines are listed
alphabetically; brief descriptions of content and
subject matter.

Muzine **www.nmsu.edu/muzine/index.htm**
Online music magazine; articles about
instruments and activities.

Nando Entertainment
www.nandotimes.com/entertainment
Online entertainment newspaper.

National Geographic
www.nationalgeographic.com/media/
ngm Wild animals; primitive tribes;
explorations.

NetPOST **www.netpost.com** Press release and
newswire service.

New Media Music **www.newmediamusic.com**
Industry newsletter; subscriptions.

New Musical Express **www.nme.com** Music news
and gossip.

NeWo News **newo.com/news** Publication search
engine.

News Bureau **www.newsbureau.com** Online
press release service.

News Hunt **www.newshunt.com** Search news
archives.

News Paper Association of America
www.newspaperlinks.com Publication
search engine.

News Resource **newo.com/news** E-zine search
engine.

News365 **www.news365.com** Publication search
engine.

NewsDirectory.com **www.newsd.com**
Publication search engine.

Newshub **www.newshub.com** Search news
archives.

NME **www.nme.com** UK Webzine; indie news;
reviews; rock quotes; directory.

Northern Light
www.northernlight.com/news.html
Archive resource; tool for searching offline
publications.

Old Farmer's Almanac **www.almanac.com**
Trivia; folk wisdom.

Online Newspapers
digistar.mb.ca/newspaper.htm or

newspapers.com List of dailies; weeklies;
specialty; college papers.

Parrot Media Network **www.parrotmedia.com**
U.S. TV Station Directory: printed quarterly;
U.S. Cable TV Directory: printed semiannually;
Newspaper Directory: printed semiannually;
Radio Directory: printed semiannually; directories
priced per issue or per year; subscriptions
available for online use; directories updated daily.

Pause and Play **www.pauseandplay.com**
Webzine.

People Online **www.people.com** or
www.pathfinder.com/people Entertainment
news; profiles.

Pig Publications **www.pigpublications.com**
Reviews; news; sounds; list of modern rock
bands.

Pitchfork **www.live-wire.com** Alternative music
Webzine.

Planet Noise **www.planet-noise.com** Webzine.

Poets & Writers Magazine **www.pw.org** Webzine.

Pollstar **www.pollstar.com** Industry news; tour
schedules; box office reports; albums sales; radio
plays.

Popwire Mag **www.popwire.com** International
music site.

Preview Tunes **www.previewtunes.com** New
releases; albums; songs; videos.

PR News Wire **www.prnewswire.com** Press
release and newswire service.

Pro Audio Review **www.imaspub.com** *Pro Audio
Review; Radio World.*

Publishers Weekly
www.publishersweekly.com Online
version of the industry magazine.

PubList **www.publist.com** Publication search
engine.

Q **www.qonline.co.uk** Pop music culture in
England; archives.

Radio & Records Online **www.rronline.com**
Industry newspaper; information; facts and
figures; links to a wide range of sources
including record labels and industry sites;
industry news; radio news; reviews; radio charts.

Relix **www.relix.com** San Francisco acid rock.

Renegade Newsletter
renegadereviews.homepage.com/intro.
html Newsletter.

Rockrgrl **www.rockrgrl.com** or
www.indieWeb.com/rockrgrl Webzine for
women musicians; interviews; reviews.

Rolling Stone **www.rollingstone.com** Features;
CD reviews; music news; E-mail newsletter;
MP3 and music video Pick of the Day; message
board and more.

Salon **www.salon.com** Music news.

Sonic State **www.sonicstate.com** Music industry news.

Spacejam Musicpage **www.spacejam.de** E-zine with music and art.

Spin **www.spin.com** Music news and information.

Stereophile **www.stereophile.com** Online magazine.

Strobe **www.iuma.com/Strobe** Monthly Webzine; alternative; unsigned bands; reviews.

Talk Music **www.talkmusic.com** Webzine; *Music Business Daily.*

The American Spectator **www.spectator.org** Politics and entertainment news.

The Celebrity Café **www.thecelebritycafe.com** Publishes celebrity interviews.

The GPI Group—A Division of Miller Freeman PSN Inc. **www.mfi.com** *Guitar Player; Keyboard; Bass Player; Guitar & Bass Buyer's Guide; Music Technology Buyer's Guide; Music Gear Online; Guitar Player Online; Keyboard Online; Bass Player Online.*

The Island Ear **www.islandear.com** Webzine.

The iZine **www.thei.aust.com** Entertainment news from Australia.

The Music Tank **www.themusictank.com** Webzine.

The New York Times **www.nytimes.com** Newspaper.

The New York Times – Online Music **www.nytimes.com/library/tech/ reference/index-music.html** Online music.

The Noise Box **www.thenoisebox.com** Webzine.

The Ultimate Band List **www.ubl.com/magazines** E-zine directory.

The World's Greatest Music Magazine Online **www.qonline.co.uk** From the UK's biggest selling music magazine; latest music news and reviews; Gig Guide; quizzes; competitions; chat; database of 17,000 Q reviews.

Time **time.com** News coverage.

Time – MP3 Central **www.time.com/time/digital/reports/ mp3/index.html** MP3 coverage.

Top **www.totp.beeb.com** Current charts; news; links; competitions.

TotalNEWS **www.totalnews.com** Search news archives.

U.S. News & World Report Online **www.usnews.com** News magazine.

UK Music Magazines **www.ukdirectory.co.uk/ent/mag.htm** Directory of UK-based magazines; wide range of interests.

UK Piano Page **www.airtime.co.uk/forte/mag.htm** List of UK-based online music magazines; classical to underground dance music.

URL Wire **www.urlwire.com** Press release and newswire service.

USA Today Hot Site **www.usatoday.com/life/cyber/ch.htm** Awards Web site.

USA Today **www.usatoday.com** Newspaper.

USA Today Life **www.usatoday.com/life/lfront.htm** Entertainment section.

Virgin.Net **www.virgin.net** News; reviews.

Viva Music **www.vivamusic.com** Free music business reports.

Wall of Sound **www.wallofsound.com** News and reviews; interviews; artist pages; tours; ABC's Go Network.

WebNoize **www.webnoize.com** Webzine; news; reviews; streaming audio; guide to special events; digital music updates.

Weekly Wire **www.weeklywire.com/ww/current/ ww_contents.html** Culture coverage; music; movies; books.

West Coast Music Review **wcmr.com** U.S. Webzine for West Coast music; reviews; interviews; articles; links.

Wired **www.wired.com** Webzine.

Working Press of The Nations **www.reedref.com** *Newspaper Directory:* weekly, daily, college, features syndicates, news and photo service, wire services; *TV & Radio Directory:* 13,000 TV and radio stations, 5,700 local programs by subject; *Magazines:* 5,400 magazines grouped by subject area.

World Press and Media Finder **www.escapeartist.com/media/media.htm** Publication search engine.

World Wide News Sources on the Internet **www.discover.co.uk/NET/NEWS/news. html** Guide to international news sources.

Writers Digest Zine Awards **www.writers-digest.com/zineawards** E-zine awards.

Yahoo Media Services **dir.yahoo.com/Business_and_Economy/ Companies/Communications_and_Media _Services** Press release and newswire service.

Yahoo! Entertainment Summary **www.yahoo.com/headlines/ entertainment** Entertainment industry headlines.

Yahoo! Music UK & Ireland **uk.news.yahoo.com/m/music.html** Music news and links.

ZDNet Music News **music.zdnet.com** Music news service.

Music on the Internet—
MP3 Sites, Software, and
Hardware—Streaming Audio and Video

@soft **www.atsoft.net/welcome.htm** Web design and more.

101 CD **www.101cd.com** Download site; MP3.

2Look4 **www.2look4.com** MP3 search site.

303Tek Screensaver **www.internal.co.jp/e/toolbox/index.html** Screensaver that plays MP3s; Direct-X3 and MMX processor required to run.

507Music **507music.com** Sell music on the Internet; all styles.

52ndStreamMedia **www.52media.com** All styles music on the Internet.

A Guide to Legal MP3 Sites **www.narcopop.com** MP3 reference site.

A2B **www.a2bmusic.com** or **www.a-to-b.com** Proprietary music format; requires A2B Player; does not play MP3 or WAV files.

Aggressive Music **www.aggressivemusic.com** MP3 site; guitar tabs; lyrics.

Air Tunes **www.airtunes.com** Download site; MP3.

Airmp3.com **www.airmp3.com** Lists of meta-searches, archives, and top-ranked songs.

All Napster MP3 Webfront **www.searchlord.com/info/file_search/napster** Napster MP3 Webfront for Napster registered users and various networks which permit the Napster protocol and Napster servers.

Alta Vista **www.altavista.com** MP3/Audio tab at top of home page.

AltoMP3 Maker **www.yuansoft.com** CD to MP3 converter or CD ripper; works as a CDDB2-Enabled (TM) CD player; for Windows 9X/NT/2000.

Amplified.com **www.amplified.com** Digital media technology; database and DRM solutions; services for entertainment companies and retailers selling through the Internet; fulfillment of CDs; DVDs; digital downloads; custom CDs; song samples; artist and content data; licensing; links.

Aneon Software **aneon.bizland.com** MP3 player with built-in help files and Internet link for artist look up; drag-and-drop play list.

Asia Mix **www.asiamix.com** Download site; MP3.

Atomic Pop **www.atomicpop.com** New mix of music and interactive entertainment featuring audio and video streams, digital downloads, CDs, games, and more.

Audible.com **www.audible.com/mp3** Spoken-word MP3s.

Audio Galaxy **www.audiogalaxy.com** Download site; MP3; free Web site hosting; indie artists; MP3 search engine; chat.

Audio Hub **www.sounds-online.com** MP3s; hardware; software; radio; music hosting; Webcasting; chat; links.

Audio Net CD Jukebox **www.audionet.com/jukebox** Submit music; plays tracks; sell music.

Audio Places **www.audioplaces.com** MP3 search engines; find MP3 music and other audio files.

Audioactive **www.audioactive.com/download/dnl_ovw.html** Windows MP3 player; supports M3U playlists and ID3 tags.

AudioActive Player for Windows **www.audioactive.com/player** MP3 player and encoder software.

AudioCatalyst Encoder for Mac and Windows **www.audiocatalyst.com** MP3 player and encoder software.

Audiofind **www.audiofind.com** MP3 search engine.

Audion **www.panic.com** For Macintosh; MP3s; audio CDs; streaming Web audio.

Audiopia.com **www.audiopia.com** Download site; MP3.

AudioPix **www.audiopix.com** For creating multimedia slide show presentations; merges together two Internet technologies - JPEG and MP3.

AudioRequest Home MP3 Player **www.audiorequest.com** MP3 hardware player manufacturers.

Audiosoft **europe.audiosoft.com/virtuosa** *Virtuosa Gold* MP3 jukebox; ripper, encoder, downloader, player, organizer, and CD burner all in one.

Audiosoft **www.audiosoft.f2s.com** Freeware programs to download.

AudioSoftware.com **www.audiosoftware.com** Audio compression software shop; directory; downloads for MP3 players, encoders, rippers, and utilities; links to programs used to play, record, make, copy, and edit audio; MP3 related programs.

AudioTools.co.uk **www.audiotools.co.uk** Audio tools and utilities for audio conversion, playback, DJ mixing, CD audio extraction, sound editing, and more.

Audiovalley.Com **www.audiovalley.com** All-in-one MP3 search engine and legal music downloads.

Auto PC **www.autopc.com** Windows system for cars; CDs; CD-ROMs; MP3s next.

Award Sites **www.awardsites.com** Awards Web site.

Axialis AX-CDPlayer
www.axialis.com/axcdplayer CDDB compatible CD player for Windows 95; automatically get disc and track titles accessing CDDB worldwide database through the Internet.

Band Tools **www.bandtools.com** Internet music Web site; all styles.

Beatnik **www.beatnik.com** or **www.headspace.com** Software synthesizer plug-in and library of sounds for interactive music playback on the Internet; for Netscape Navigator and Microsoft Internet Explorer; converts MIDI sequence files to RMF (Rich Music Format).

Benway Doktor **www.benway.doktor.co.uk** Download site; MP3.

Berkeley Multimedia Research Center **bmrc.berkeley.edu/projects/mpeg** MPEG information.

Beta Lounge **www.betalounge.com** Weekly new music forum in MP3.

Black Diamond Sound Systems **www.blackdiamondsound.com** Turn computer into a virtual recording studio with music software including the audio file editing and MP3 encoding program *TsunamiPro*.

Blocks Anonymous **etcwww.kripto.org/blocks** File-sharing designed for those with permanent "always on" Internet connections like DSL.

Box Tunnel AVS Presets **boxtunnel.tripod.com** AVS audio visualization presets for Winamp; submitted by readers and judged by site administrators.

Buymp3.com **www.buymp3.com** Virtual retailer; hundreds of categories; search by artist name or title.

Byte Audio **www.byteaudio.com** Global resource for digital audio and video.

Card Services International **www.cardservices.com** Credit card processing service.

CCNow **www.ccnow.com** Internet billing service.

CD Baby **www.cdbaby.com** Online store; download site; MP3; drop shipper.

CD Debut **www.cddebut.com** Download site; MP3; indie submissions.

CD Hit List **www.cdhitlist.com** Download site; MP3.

CD Mama **www.cdmama.com** Download site; MP3.

CD Nature **www.cdnature.com** Download site; MP3.

CD Now **www.cdnow.com** Online store; download site; MP3; drop shipper; Cosmic Music Network for new artists.

CD Street **www.cdstreet.com** Download site; MP3.

Cductive **www.cductive.com** Make custom CDs; sample new music; has licensing agreements with over 200 record labels.

Cherokee Electronics I-Jam Portable Player **www.mp3ijam.com** MP3 hardware player manufacturers.

City Music **www.citymusic.com** The Virtual Music Store; download MP3s; browse.

CL-Amp **www4.tripnet.se/~slarti/ f_cl-amp_uk.htm** MP3 player for BeOS; makes use of Winamp skins; many formats supported including MP3 VBR.

Cleveland-Metal **www.cleveland-metal.com** Download site; MP3.

ClickBank **www.clickbank.com** Internet billing service.

Cloning Napster **music.gamespot.com/features/ napsterclone** ZDNet article discussing the five best alternatives to Napster; explanation of file sharing and how it works.

CompactFlash Cards **www.compactflash.org** Store digital information; half the size of a floppy disk.

ComTry MP3 **www.mp3downloader.com** Software application that helps user find MP3 files on the Internet.

CoolPlayer **www.daansystems.com/coolplayer** Windows MP3 player with a simple user interface.

Cornerband.com **www.cornerband.com** Legal access to RIAA licensed music; Dallas based.

Creative Labs Nomad Portable Player **www.nomadworld.com** MP3 hardware player manufacturers; portable digital audio players; free MP3 music downloads; featured artists; digital audio news; pick a country; information on the next-generation portable digital audio player.

CustomDisc.com **www.customdisc.com** Interface for CD compilation; custom CDs.

Customize.org **www.customize.org** MP3 software accessories; skins; plug-ins.

CuteFTP **www.cuteftp.com** Popular FTP program for transferring MP3 files.

Cyber Musicians **www.CyberMusician.com** Home page.

Daily MP3 **www.dailymp3.com/main.html** Updated daily; MP3 news; player software; song files; downloads; links.

DAMP **www.damp-mp3.co.uk** Full-featured MP3 player for DOS; contains support of PLS and M3U playlists; has a special visualization option similar to Winamp's plug-ins.

DC Software **fon.fon.bg.ac.yu/~dcolak** *Party DJ* MP3 software program.

Degy Shop **www.degyshop.com** Download site; MP3.

Destiny Media Player
www.radiodestiny.com/listen Plays MP3 compressed audio and Destiny's proprietary Web-based radio broadcasting technology; Macintosh; Windows.

DFX **www.fxsound.com** Plug-in for Winamp; audio enhancing; hi-fi features.

Diamond Multimedia **www.diamondmm.com** Portable digital audio players.

Digital Club Festival
www.digitalclubnetwork.com Online music event.

Digital Music Australia
www.digitalmusic.com.au MP3s; RealAudio; downloads; links.

DigMP3.com **www.digmp3.com** Resource providing file archives for programs and utilities, a news archive, a history of MPEG3, and an MP3 file search engine.

Dimension Music **www.dimensionmusic.com** MP3 Web site; artist information; industry news; links; free MP3 information; forums; chat.

Direct Audio **www.directaudio.com** Downloadable music.

Direct Music
www.microsoft.com/directx/pavilion/ dmusic/dmusic.htm Electronic music technology; MIDI.

Discomobile **perso.club-internet.fr/ jgibart/discomobile/disco** Small MP3 player which creates effective cross fades between songs; uses Beatlock technology to adjust the songs' tempo.

Discosoft **www.discosoft.com** Player and mixer software intended for consumer and professional use; plays, MP3, WMA, MP2, PCM, and MIDI; working demo available.

DJ2000 **www.215tech.com/dj2000/index.asp** Library management system to help collect, organize, and search an MP3 collection; built-in player.

D-Lusion **www.d-lusion.com/products/index.html** Unique MP3 and soft synthesizer software.

Downloads Direct
content.ubl.com/downloadsdirect Major label and indie artists.

DreamWeaver
www.macromedia.com/dreamweaver Web page editor.

Drive Entertainment
www.driveentertainment.com Download site; MP3.

Earstein **www.earstein.com** Download site; MP3.

Easily **www.easily.co.uk** Register domain name in the UK.

Empeg Car Player **www.empeg.com** MP3 hardware player manufacturers.

EMusic **www.emusic.com** Downloadable music site; listen to song samples before purchasing; buy only certain songs instead of entire album; MP3s by known artists for sale; large catalog.

Epitaph **www.epitaph.com** Download site; MP3.

Epitonic **www.epitonic.com** Source for MP3 recordings; reviewed and selected indie MP3 music; download site.

Ether Stream **www.etherstream.com** Download site; MP3.

Experience Music Project **www.emplive.com** Internet music.

Extreme Tracking **www.extreme-dm.com/tracking** Internet resource.

EZ CD **www.ezcd.com** Download site; MP3; custom CDs.

EZ-Mixer **www.ez-mixer.com** IK Multimedia; multifunctional MP3 player/encoder; live remixing tool which emulates a two-track DJ mixer with all necessary features to produce compilation or live remix; like a DJ in a club; supports the import/export of other audio formats including Wav, Aiff, QDesign, QuickTime; direct song ripping from audio CDs.

Fairtunes Winamp Plugin
mi2n.com/press.php3?press_nb=13226 Legal downloads.

FAQ Archives **www.faqs.org** Frequently asked questions.

File Quest **www.filequest.com** Audio and video images; RealMedia; RealAudio; MP3; VQF; WAV; MIDI; Quicktime; MPEG; Schockwave and more; search for Web sites with files.

FileSwap **www.fileswap.com** Program that allows users to share music and various kinds of files by searching over other computers around the Internet.

Findsongs.com **www.findsongs.com** Access to audio search engines; artist profiles; song lyrics; CD cover artwork.

FireWorks2 **www.macromedia.com/fireworks** Graphic utility.

First Look **www.firstlook.com** Review tracks before they are released; audio samples.

Flash **www.houseofsloth.com/flash.html** Produce and deliver music, sound effects, and animation on the Internet.

Fraunhofer, Developer of the MP3 Format
www.iis.fhg.de/amm/techinf MP3 reference site; audio and multimedia technology; licensing; industry news.

FreeAmp Player for Windows and Linux
www.freeamp.org MP3 player and encoder software.

Geiss **www.geisswerks.com** Winamp plug-in; MP3 light show; visual display to music.

Get Right **www.getright.com** FTP client.

GetHits.com **www.GetHits.com** Web site promotion service.

GiantDisc MP3 Player Project
www.giantdisc.com Contains a selection of free software programs used to run a home jukebox system through a computer controlled by a PalmPilot; explanation on how to set up the system is explained on the site.

Globalstage **www.gobalstage.com** Sell music and merchandise online; Web sites.

Gnutella **www.gnutella.wego.com** Download site.

GoldWave **www.goldwave.com** Sound utility; MP3 recording and editing.

Graphic Artists Guild **www.gag.org** Graphic design for album art; weekly newsletter by subscription; free ads for those seeking artists.

Green Café **www.greencafe.com** MP3 search engines.

Harmonia Mundi **www.harmoniamundi.com** Download site; MP3.

High Criteria **www.highcriteria.com** *Total Recorder* Mp3 recording and sound editing software.

High Five **www.highfive.com** Web design tips.

HitDisc.com **www.hitdisc.com** Developer of "click and mortar" digital music distribution technologies in a stand-alone unit.

Homestead.com **www.homestead.com** Free Web sites.

Host Index **www.hostindex.com** Web site hosting.

Hotmail **www.hotmail.com** Free E-mail accounts.

HP.com **www.hp.com** Digital music.

HTML Editors
builder.cnet.com/Authoring/Htmleditors Web page editors.

HTML for the Rest of Us
www.geocities.com/SiliconValley/Lakes/3933/frame.htm HTML help.

HTML Goodies **www.htmlgoodies.com** Beginning HTML.

HTML Headquarters **Webhelp.org** Introductory HTML help.

HTML Stuff **htmlstuff.tucows.com** Internet resource.

HTML Tutorials in Web Page Design
www.bfree.on.ca/HTML Resource.

HTTP Streaming
www.real.com/devzone/library/stream/httpstream.html Resource.

I Hear You **www.ihearyou.com** Free MP3 site

i2go.com **www.i2go.com** Download site; MP3.

iBill **www.ibill.com** Internet billing service.

ID3.org **www.id3.org** ID3 tag standard.

I-Jam **www.ijamworld.com** Portable MP3 player.

Ijamworld.com **www.ijamworld.com** Download site; MP3.

Impy3 Car Player **www.impy3.com/impy3** MP3 hardware player manufacturers.

iMusic **www.imusic.com** Alternative music; chat rooms; daily news; tours; reviews; information; music community; Web sites.

InfoLink Link Checker **www.biggbyte.com** Tools necessary to maintain Web site; locate and correct problem links and pages; utilize statistic reports to keep a log of site's integrity.

Internet Album Charts **www.worldcharts.nl** For music performed on the Internet.

Java Clone **www.perham.net/mike/jnap** Java clone for MP3 file sharing.

Java Goodies **www.javagoodies.com** JavaScript repository.

Java Script Source **www.javascriptsource.com** Forms, chat, guest books, scripts for Web sites.

JazPiper **www.jazpiper.nl** Portable MP3 player.

Jean Nicolle **www.jps.net/kyunghi** *MP3 Trim; MP3 Trim Pro; Wave Trim; Wave Trim Pro;* MP3 utilities.

JukeBytes 1.0 **www.jukebytes.00go.com** JukeBytes; have .m3u and .pls playlist inside a jukebox simulator.

Junkbusters.com **www.junkbusters.com** Cookie management tools.

Juno **www.juno.com** Free E-mail accounts.

Kanoodle **www.kanoodle.com/mp3** Free Web pages; unlimited MP3 uploads; 100 percent of selling price paid to artist.

Kermit **www.oth.net** MP3 search engine; downloads.

Kick.com **www.kick.com** Music companion; personalized content delivery.

Killer Sites **www.killersites.com** Web site utility.

K-jofol **kjofol.org** MP3 player with an intuitive interface.

K-Jöfol **www.kjofol.org** Freeware multimedia/MP3 player for Windows 95/98/NT.

Laser Trax **www.lasertrax.com** Download site; MP3; artist information.

Launch.com **www.launch.com** Download site; MP3; over 4,500 music videos; news; chat; downloadable songs; LAUNCHcast enables members to design streaming audio and video music stations.

Lava **www.lava.com** MP3 listening software; graphic displays.

Layer 3 Recordings **www.layer3recordings.com** MP3 site.

Link Exchange **www.linkexchange.com** Free counter to track site access.

Liquid Audio **www.liquidaudio.com** Streaming audio format; encoded Liquid Audio files or "Liquified" files; supports all leading digital audio formats; CD quality music; downloads.

Liquid Music Network or *Liquid Platinum* **www.liquidmusicnetwork.com** Supports MP3 and all leading file formats; song distribution resource; Liquid Audio Technology; music goes to 350+ affiliates; built-in security to prevent piracy; verifiable accounting.

Listen Smart **www.listensmart.com** Download site; MP3.

Listen.com **www.listen.com** Links to online music; guide to legal MP3s; streaming video; free tracks; over 60,000 artists; all genres; reviews; newsletter.

LiveConcerts.com **www.liveconcerts.com** Live concerts cybercasted every week; archive of original music recordings.

Looksmart's Beseen **www.beseen.com** Internet resource.

Lycos MP3 Search **www.music.lycos.com/mp3** or **www.mp3.lycos.com** Search engine for MP3s; catalogs over half a million files.

Lyra **www.lyrazone.com** Portable MP3 player; audible track scanning; EQ.

MacAmp Player for Mac **www.macamp.com** MP3 player and encoder software.

Macast **www.at-soft.net** Descendent of Macamp; plays MP3s, audio CDs, and streaming content.

MacAST **www.macamp.net** Audio player formally known as MacAMP; supports MP3, MP2, CD audio, and Internet streaming audio.

Macast Lite **www.at-soft.net** MP3 only player; variety of skin choices.

Madison Project **www.madisonproject.org** IBM digital ownloads.

Mammoth **www.mammoth.com** Indie label with free MP3 samples.

Maplay **www-inst.eecs.berkeley.edu/~ctsay/mp2win32.html** Unix MP3 player; also runs on Windows.

Marcus Kuenzel **members.xoom.com/kunzel/MPEGTapeDeck** MPEG Tape Deck.

Matt's Script Archive **www.worldwidemart.com/scripts** Forms, chat, guest books, scripts for Web sites.

MAYAH Communications **www.mayah.com/english/index.html** *Edit Pro 2.04*; recording, editing, and transmission software package; allows editing of MP3 files directly.

MCY.com **www.MCY.com** Digital entertainment company offering songs and music events for audiences worldwide; download site; MP3; all genres.

Media House Software **www.mediahouse.com** Statistics server; enterprise monitor; software developer.

Media Jukebox **www.musicex.xom** For PC; MP3 creator; specially formatted MusicEx files ensure copyright protection.

Media Wizard **www.cdhnow.com/mw.html** Powerful and complete multimedia solution supporting all popular audio and video formats.

Megatunes **www.megatunes.com** Download site; MP3.

MemTurbo **www.memturbo.com** Recover and defragment RAM.

Metal Reviews **www.metal-reviews.com** Download site; MP3.

Metrotama.com **www.metrotama.com** Download site; MP3.

Microsoft Media Player **www.microsoft.com/windows/mediaplayer** Microsoft audio/video; handles MP3 files and many other audio and streaming formats.

Microsoft Media Technologies **www.microsoft.com/windows/windowsmedia/default.asp** For authoring, streaming, and securely delivering audio and video.

Microsoft Music Central **www.musiccentral.msn.com/Home.htm** All genres; Top 100 charts by city; new releases; industry news; interviews; columns; reviews; database of past reviews; concert listings.

Microsoft Public Music Products **www.microsoft.public.music.products** Newsgroup; Windows-based players.

MIDI Search Engine **www.musicrobot.com/midi search engine** Search for MIDI files.

MidiRunner **www.midirunner.com** Integrated Play Center for MIDI, MP3, Wave, CD-Audio files, and all others WindowsMedia supported sound files; can also be used to create, edit, and load playlists.

Midnight Mayhem **www.seizethenight.net** Live computer broadcast; rock music.

Midwest Underground **www.midwestunderground.com** Download site; MP3.

Mjuice.com **www.mjuice.com** Legal MP3s for sale; specially formatted; register for free.

MP123 **www.mp123.com** Download site; MP3.

MP3 2000 **www.mp3-2000.com** MP3 information; downloads; player software; news.

MP3 and Wav Converter **hammer.prohosting.com/~poweryfy** Directly converts audio between MP3 and Wav; converts audio digitally, not through the sound card for perfect copies of the originals.

MP3 Audio Player **www.yukudr.com/mp3player** EasyPEG3; simple freeware application which allows user to play MP3 audio.

MP3 Boss **homepages.msn.com/WindowsWay/ mccaffjt/index.html** Features WinAmp support; automatic scanning of MP3 tags; utility to help user manage and play collection of MP3 files; sorting; searching, filtering; file rename and move; file clean-up.

MP3 Easy Search **www.mp3easy.co.uk** Software competitive with Napster.

MP3 Explorer **ourworld.compuserve.com/homepages/ pierre_levy** MP3 utility.

MP3 FAQ **help.mp3.com/help/?hpgs1** Frequently asked MP3 questions.

MP3 File Editor **www.mp3fe.sk** Edit tags with track number; create playlists in HTML, TXT, or DBF format; rename files by tags; play MP3; multilanguage support.

MP3 Handbook.com **www.MP3handbook.com** Information on encoding, ripping, editing, and playing MP3s; MP3 and digital music links.

MP3 Hits **www.mp3hits.co.uk** Free music download search.

MP3 Illusion **www.mp3illusion.com** MP3 search engines.

MP3 Mag-Net **www.filemagnet.com/mp3/index.html** Freeware utility; queries top MP3 search engines to help find and download MP3 files.

MP3 Media **broadcast.go.com/mp3** MP3 search engine.

MP3 Music 4 Free **www.mp3-music-4-free.com**

MP3 Music Player **www.mp3musicplayer.com** MP3 search engine list; find MP3s, songs, and MIDI files; links to download sites.

MP3 Music Scene **www.mp3musicscene.com/mic/ musicindustryconnections** MP3 information Web site.

MP3 Newswire **www.mp3newswire.net** MP3 news.

MP3 Now **www.mp3now.com** MP3 reference site; links; tutorials; reviews; chat.

MP3 Park **www.mp3park.com** MP3 wares.

MP3 Place **www.mp3place.com** Tutorials and help; links to MP3 software, hardware, and downloads; digital music news.

MP3 Prepare **aryhma.pspt.fi/download/mp3prepare. html** MP3 utility.

MP3 Production Studio Encoder for Windows **www.audioactive.com/mp3** MP3 player and encoder software.

MP3 Search **www.mp3search.freeserve.co.uk** MP3 search engines on the Internet.

MP3 Search.nu **www.mp3search.nu** MP3 site search engine; gateway to the MP3 community.

MP3 Shopping **www.mp3shopping.com** MP3 players; news; software; site map; products; links; music; search.

MP3 Songs **www.mp3.songs.com** Source for MP3 recordings; new bands screened for recording quality.

MP3 Util **mp3util.cjb.net** Free resource for MP3 software including Winamp skins, plug-ins, encoders, decoders, CD rippers, and players; history of MP3; guide for beginners and advanced users.

MP3 World **www.worldkey.com/mp3world** MP3 downloads.

MP3.com Help **help.mp3.com/help/faqs/setup.html** Making MP3 files and more.

MP3.com **www.mp3.com** Discover new music; download songs; buy CDs; Winamp players; CD rippers; plug-ins; utilities; software downloads; news and information on artists; hardware and portable players; free service; industry news; bulletin boards; tutorials.

MP3.com Software Guide **www.mp3.com/software** Comprehensive list of MP3 players; playlist makers; plug-ins and encoders for a variety of operating systems; reviews and ratings.

MP3.com.au **www.mp3.com.au** Australian MP3 Web site; downloads; news; reviews; chat.

MP3.dk **www.mp3.dk** MP3 information; Internet news.

MP3Board.com **www.mp3board.com** MP3 search engine.

MP3Detective **cheqsoft.com/mp3detective/index.html** Program to search for MP3 music on PC, then play results on default jukebox; makes text and HTML file lists.

MP3Inc.com **www.mp3inc.com** MP3 portable car players; MP3 search engine.

MP3Lit.com **www.mp3lit.com** Download site; MP3.

MP3Machine.com
www.mp3machine.com/database MP3
technology.

MP3now.com **www.mp3now.com** MP3 site;
news; artist bios.

MP3now.com Software Section
www.mp3now.com/html/software.html
List of questions relating to software and links to
different programs available for download;
extensive reviews, ratings, and some screenshots.

MP3-Related Newsgroups
www.alt.binaries.sounds.mp3.indie
Newsgroups broken down into specific areas of
interest.

MP3Site **www.MP3site.com** MP3 songs from
new bands; industry news; software downloads;
links.

MP3Tech **www.mp3tech.org** MP3 technology
resource; MPEG; glossary.

MP3Yes.com **www.mp3yes.com** Offers MP3
downloads, software, hardware, news, and
newsgroups; audio search, screen savers, and
games.

MP4 Music **www.mp4music.com** Techno, jazz,
and swing.

Mpecker Encoder
www.anime.net/~go/mpeckers.html
Macintosh encoder; free program.

MPEG FAQ
www.mpeg1.de/mpegfaq/mpe632.html
MPEG information.

MPEG **www.mpeg.org** MPEG and MP3 reference
site; FAQs; links.

MPEG Official Web Site
drogo.cselt.stet.it/mpeg Home page;
official committee site.

MPEGX.com **www.mpegx.com** Large guide to
MP3 software programs and other related
material; listing of various MP3 programs with
ratings.

Mpg123 **www.mpg123.de** Fast, free MP3 audio
player for Linux, FreeBSD, Solaris, Hpux, and
near all other UNIX systems; decodes MP1 and
MP2 files.

Mplayer3 **www.mplayer3.com** Portable MP3
player; adjust bass and treble.

MPMan F20 **www.mpman.com** MP3 player.

MPMan Portable Players **www.eigerlabs.com**
MP3 hardware player manufacturers.

Mpxplay **www.geocities.com/mpxplay** 32-bit
DOS-based audio player; CD-ripper; playlist
manager; cross fading; volume correct; speed
control; long filename support.

mpXreview **www.mpXreview.com** Reviews of
MP3 music only; submit songs.

Music Boulevard **www.musicblvd.com** Liquid
Audio files; RealAudio; MPEG files; music
news.

Music Choice **www.musicchoice.com**
Commercial-free, professionally programmed
music channels and digital downloads available
on one site.

Music Choice UK **www.musicchoice.co.uk** Up
to fifty CD quality genre specific audio channels;
no ads or DJs; available twenty-four hours a day.

Music Exchange **www.musicex.com** Safe sales
and licensing of music on the Internet.

Music Grab **www.musicgrab.com** MP3 site;
links.

Music Maker **www.musicmaker.com/freecds**
Digital download Internet shop; make custom
CDs; buy tracks; Music Maker Relief
Foundation.

Music Match Jukebox **www.musicmatch.com**
MP3 player and encoder software; download
MP3s and demos; for Windows; Shoutcast
Internet radio feeds; audio CDs; ten-band graphic
equalizer; sort MP3s; auto DJ feature.

Music Seek **www.musicseek.net** Computer audio
formats like MP3, vqf, real audio, and more;
comprehensive search utility aims to find files.

Musician Assist
**www.musicianassist.com/archive/
contract** Standard contract language for booking
gigs, publishing songs, etc.

Musicworks **www.musicworks-mag.com**
Creative sound exploration.

MuzicMan **www.muzicman.com** MP3 player
and organizer; designed for converting a large CD
collection to a PC-based stereo system.

MVP **www.mvpsite.com** Free MP3, MP2, and
QDesign Music audio encoder and player; Mac
and Windows versions; converts one format to
another, plays digital music and videos, and
supports playlists.

MXMPlay: Open Cubic Player
www.cubic.org/player Open source MP3
player for DOS and Windows.

My Play **www.myplay.com** Download site; MP3.

Napamp **napamp.sourceforge.net** Download
from Napster servers directly from Winamp.

Napster **www.napster.com** Infamous MP3
download site.

NCSA: A Beginners Guide to HTML
**www.ncsa.uiuc.edu/General/Internet/
WWW/HtmlPrimer.html** HTML resource.

Net 4 Music **www.net4music.com** Download
site; MP3; digitized sheet music; MIDI files;
education; information.

Net Burner **www.net-burner.com** MP3s with a
program to burn a CD; put on Web site for
others to burn; fully automatic.

NetGuide Internet Site of the Day
www.netguide.com Awards Web site.

Netscape Composer **www.home.netscape.com** Web page editor.

Netshow **www.windowsmedia.com** WindowsMedia.

Network Solutions **www.networksolutions.com** Domain name registration.

Newbie-U **www.newbie-u.com** Information on the Internet; basic concepts of networks; Web browsers; E-mail; news reader programs; file utilities.

NEX **www.frontierlabs.com** Portable MP3 player.

Nice MC **nicemc.webhostme.com** Winamp plug-in; player becomes a video player.

Noizy Land **www.noizyland.com** Download site; MP3.

Nomad II **www.nomadworld.com** Portable MP3 player; belt clip.

Nordic DMS **www.nordicdms.com** Download site; MP3; liquid tracks; online radio; indie labels; online directories; links; only sells downloadable digital copies of songs.

Noten **www.noten.com** Download site; MP3.

Ogg Vorbis **www.vorbis.com** Open, patent-free, professional audio encoding and streaming technology.

OpenNap **opennap.sourceforge.net** Open source Napster server.

Opticom **www.opticom.de** *MP3 Producer Professional* encoder software.

Orbit Music **www.orbitmusic.com** Custom CDs.

Oth **www.oth.net** MP3 search site.

Paint Shop Pro **www.jasc.com** Graphic utility.

Pair Networks **pair.com** Site hosting.

Palavista **www.palavista.com** Digital music metacrawler.

Pandamonium **www.pandamonium.com.au** Download site; MP3.

PCDJ **www.visiosonic.com** MP3 DJ program.

PCDJ PHAT
www.visiosonic.com/products/pcdjphat.htm PC entertainment center for playing and mixing MP3 and other audio files; dual deck, manual or automatic cross fading, CD ripper, and free updates for life.

Peoplesound.com **www.peoplesound.com** MP3 download site.

Personal Jukebox PJB-100 **www.pjbox.com** Portable MP3 player.

PictureQuest **www.publishersdepot.com** Stock photography; royalty free; digital media and online images for use in Web sites.

Piranha **www.piranha.de** Download site; MP3.

Planet CD **www.planetcd.com** Download site; MP3.

Platform **www.platform.net** Download site; MP3.

PlayHear.com **www.playhear.com** Downloadable music.

PN4U **www.pn4u.com** Download site; MP3.

PNC-UK **www.pnc-uk.co.uk** Download site; MP3.

Prime Linx Inc. **www.primelinx.com** Sell chrome plates for automobile with Web site URL.

Project Cool **www.projectcool.com/sightings** Awards Web site.

Projekt **www.projekt.com** Download site; MP3.

Prolist 2000
mageos.ifrance.com/prolist2000/index.html Windows freeware MP3 player; all the basic functions.

QSound Labs, Inc. **www.qsound.com/products** Leading audio technology company; software products for 3D audio, virtual surround sound, MP3, and Internet audio.

QuickTime **www.quicktime.com** or **quicktime.apple.com** or **apple.com/quicktime/download** Streaming audio and video format; free download.

RaveMP **www.ravemp.com** Portable MP3 player; text memos; voice recording.

Raveworld.net
www.raveworld.net/portal/Record_Labels/ Live and on-demand audio and video streams; MP3 downloads; live DJ performances from top DJs; online record store; DJ equipment; community area; event calendars.

Razor & Tie
www.razorandtie.com/liquid.html Sample titles in Liquid Audio.

RB Page **www.rbpage.com** Download site; MP3.

RealAudio Player
www.idp.net/freesoft/raudio.asp The RealPlayer enables user to experience RealMedia files over the Internet or over a local area network in real time, without downloading the clip to a hard drive.

RealAudio Tutorial
www2.ncsu.edu/ncsu/cc/pub/multimed/realaudio/tutorial/create.html From NC State University.

RealJukebox Player/Encoder for Windows
www.realjukebox.com MP3 player and encoder software; download the beta version.

RealNetworks **www.real.com** The Web's first streaming media introduced in April 1995; first to stream audio to the masses; huge installed base of regular users; RealAudio; RealSystem MP; RealJukebox; RealPlayer G2; RealPlayer

Plus G2; RealProducer Plus G2; RealProducer Pro G2; RealVideo; RealFlash.

RealNetworks UK **www.real.co.uk** Delivers streamed data from Web to computer in real time; information about the technology; samples; free plug-ins download.

Resort Records **www.resortrecords.com** Label supported free MP3s.

Rhythm Net **www.rhythmnet.com** Gain exposure and industry recognition; sell songs; international distribution; sell recordings.

RIMPS MP3 Server and Playlist Manager **rimps.sourceforge.net** Web-based front end; written in PHP to make Apache a streaming MP3 server; facilities for searching; individual song playing; playlist creation.

Rioport **www.rioport.com** RioPort Audio Manager CD encoder; Diamond Multimedia Pro portable MP3 player; Rio PMP500; online catalog of MP3 hardware and accessories; free downloads.

Rollingstone.tunes.com **www.rollingstone.tunes.com** Song distribution resource; download site; MP3.

Round Tower **www.roundtower.com** Download site; MP3.

Rykodisc **www.rykodisc.com** Download site; MP3.

Samsung Yepp Portable Players **yepp.co.kr/eng** MP3 hardware player manufacturers.

Sandoras **www.sandoras.com** Download site; MP3.

SayWhat Lyrics Displayer **welcome.to/saywhat** Displays lyrics of song Winamp is playing from either MP3 or CD Track; download lyrics to 371+ songs or add them.

Search.com **hem2.passagen.se/novel** Links to many programs used to play, record, make, copy, and edit audio; MP3-related programs.

Searchlord **www.searchlord.com/info/file_search/ gnutella** Web-based front end to Gnutella that searches for any type of file, including MP3 files.

Searchterms.com **www.searchterms.com** List of frequently used Web search terms.

Sexy Analyzer **www.geocities.com/SiliconValley/ Peaks/9546/** Winamp plug-in; visual display of song's frequency.

Shanachie **www.shanachie.com** Download site; MP3.

Sharp Spider **www.sharpspider.com** Automates submissions to over 900 search and free links sites.

Sheer Dance **www.sheerdance.co.za** Download site; MP3.

Shockwave **www.shockwave.com** Streaming audio format; Macromedia.

Shoutcast **www.shoutcast.com** Streaming audio system; broadcast own station; requires Winamp; tutorials.

ShoutClub **players.shoutclub.net** Help and reviews for MP3 players; player comparisons; news; legal issues; listening stations.

Sight Sound **www.sightsound.com** Download site; MP3.

Silk City CD **www.silkcitycd.com** Download site; MP3.

Sizzling HTML Jalfrezi **www.woodhill.co.uk/html/html.htm** Resource.

SmartMedia Cards **www.simpletech.com/flash/smartmed. htm** Storage disk for MP3s.

Software.mp3.com **software.mp3.com** MP3 information; how to make MP3s.

Sonic Net **www.sonicnet.com** News; reviews; events; downloads; videos; music directory; contests; radio; artist database.

Sonicle Audio **www.sonicle.com** WebSynth audio product line; freeware version; new audio file format; support for scalable quality; pluggable decoders; G723, MPeg, AU, WAV.

Sonicrec.com **www.sonicrec.com** Download site; MP3.

Sonique Player for Windows **www.sonique.com** MP3 and audio CD player and encoder software; playlist editor.

Soritong **www.sorinara.com/soritong/english** CD audio and MP3, VQF, WAV, WMA, SH file player with organization features.

Sound Byting **www.soundbyting.com** MP3 reference site; the stances of RIAA.

Sound Click **www.soundclick.com** Download site; MP3.

Sound Jam **www.soundjam.com** *Sound Jam MP Plus*; MP3 player and encoder for Macintosh.

Sounds Big **www.soundsbig.com** Download site; MP3.

Sounds Online **www.sounds-online.com** Download site; MP3.

SoundThinking **www.redrival.com/soundthinking** Put sound on Web site without plug-ins, error messages, etc.

Spyro **www.spyro.com** Internet billing service.

Start Up Music **www.StartUpMusic.com** Selected by The Music Company for Web Development Music technology in the news; dedicated to sharpening the blur of the converging music and technology industries.

StompinGround.com **www.stompinground.com** Song distribution resource; download site; MP3; unsigned band promotion.

Stream Box **www.streambox.com** Rich media search engine/portal; over one million free audio and video streams.

Streamland **www.streamland.com** Streaming music video.

Submit It **www.submit-it.com/subopt.htm** Tips on how to submit URL to search engines.

Super Sampler **www.supersampler.com** Download site; MP3.

Symantec.com **shop.symantec.com/trialware** Web page editors.

Tactile 12000 **www.tactile12000.com** MP3 DJ program.

TagMaster **www.tagmaster.com** Web site utility.

Tagyerit **www.tagyerit.com** Music and Web culture.

TC Record Rack **www.tcrecordrack.com** Download site; MP3.

TextAloud MP3 **www.nextuptech.com/TextAloud** Converts any text into voice and to MP3; listen to text, E-mail and Web pages on computer or portable MP3 player.

The Authoritative Guide to HTML **www.iwaynet.net/~rtyler/htmltutorial/html.html** Resource.

The Best Sounding Site on the World Wide Web **www.srswowcast.com** Artist colony; share music; original programming; all genres; live chat; store; showcases.

The Canadian Online Musician's Association (COMA) **www.cpreal.com/coma** Canadian music online.

The CD Spot **www.cdspot.com** Sell CDs on consignment.

The HTML Guru **members.aol.com/htmlguru/index.html** Resource.

The Informant **informant.dartmouth.edu** Free automated search service for tracking online exposure.

The Internet Music Review Service **www.monsterbit.com/IMRS** Reviews; all genres.

The List **thelist.internet.com** or **www.thelist.com** Where to find Internet Service Providers (ISPs).

The MP3 MetaGuide **www.mp3meta.com/guide/Styles/Techno/Record_Labels** Comprehensive and up-to-date source for music and MP3 information on the Internet.

The MP3 Place **www.mp3place.com** Free downloads; information on software and hardware; links to other MP3 sites; newsletter.

The MPEG Organization **drogo.cselt.stet.it/mpeg** MP3 reference site.

The Museum of Nad New **www.glop.org/nad** MP3 player available with various looks and styles.

The Music Dish Genome Project **www.musicdish.com/genome** Plan to identify and map the components which make up the online music industry; submit site.

The Music Review **www.musicreview.com** Lists promoters; agents; managers; radio stations; TV and other music resources.

The Orbit **www.theorbit.net** Download site; MP3.

The Unsigned **www.theunsigned.com** Download site; MP3.

The Web Reference **www.webreference.com** Do-it-yourself HTML programming; Web design.

TheCounter.com **www.thecounter.com** Free Web counter-tracker.

Top 200 **www.top200.net** Top 200 MP3 sites.

Top Hosts **www.tophosts.com** The top Web host providers.

TrackerLock **www.peacefire.org/trackerlock** Free automated search service for tracking online exposure.

Tree Top **www.tree-top.com** Download site; MP3.

Tripod **www.tripod.com** Free Web sites.

Tropia **www.tropia.com** Download site; MP3.

TrueFire.com **www.truefire.com** Digital self-publishing and distribution system for guitar instruction, original music, literature, art, and reference materials; cross-platform digital formats including MP3, PDF, HTML, RealAudio, etc.

Tucows **music.tucows.com** Music Web sites; domain name register.

Tuned In **www.tunedin-hv.com** Download site; MP3.

Tunes.com **www.tunes.com** Download site; MP3; over a million song clips; music videos; artist profiles; concert photos; music news; reviews; Webcasts; archives.

Turbo MP3 **www.turbomp3.com** Portable MP3 player.

UK2 **uk2net.co.uk** Register domain name in the UK.

UltraPlayer **www.ultraplayer.com** Free Windows audio tool; plays MP3s, WAVs, and CDs; features playing and recording of streaming MP3 broadcasts; assortment of visual plug-ins and skins.

Unreal Player
> **www.internal.co.jp/e/up/index.html**
> MP3 player with separate builds for Intel and
> Cyrix/AMD chip based PCs.

Unreal Player MAX
> **www.303tek.com/e/index.html** Plays
> MP3, MIDI, .WAV, MOD, S3M, IT, XM, CD
> audio, and AVI movies; supports plug-ins.

URL-Minder **www.netmind.com/html/**
url-minder.html Free automated search
service for tracking online exposure.

Useful Links
> **www.ummusic.com/UsefulLinks.htm**
> Links for Web page designers.

Utopiasoft **www.utopiasoft.com** *Hum* MP3
Player for Windows CE.

ValidCheck.com **www.validcheck.com** Internet
billing service.

Videos.music-e.net **www.videos.music-e.net**
MP3, music videos.

Virtual DJ Studio **www.vdj.net** Player with cross
fading functionality for MP3s while playing.

Virtual Radio **www.vradio.com/vr.html** Submit
CD; nonstop net broadcaster with RealAudio.

Virtual Records **www.virtualrecords.com**
Record company open to submissions; promote
music on and off the Internet.

Virtual Turntables
> **http//www.carrotinnovations.com** or
> **carrot.prohosting.com/vtt_overview.**
> **shtml** Play and mix MP3s; options, effects and
> tools to aid in mixing of music; DJ software.

Virtual Volume **www.virtual-volume.com**
Download site; MP3.

Virtuosa Gold Player/Encoder for Windows
> **www.audiosoft.com/virtuosa** MP3 player
> and encoder software.

VisioSonic **www.visiosonic.com** Download site;
MP3; *Digital 1000 SL; Digital 1200 SL; PCDJ
Mixmaster;* DJ software.

Visual Page **shop.symantec.com/trialware** Web
page editor.

Vitaminic **www.vitaminic.co.uk** European MP3
site.

Vortex Technology **www.vortex.com/av.html**
Streaming audio and video clips.

Web Cards **www.webcards.com** Print color
postcards with Web site URL.

Web Developers Virtual Library **www.wdvl.com**
Web resource.

Web Host List **webhostlist.com** Web host
providers.

Web Monkey **www.webmonkey.com** Web site
utility.

Web Review **www.webreview.com** Web site
utility.

Web Site Awards **websiteawards.xe.net** Awards
Web site.

Web Site Garage **www.websitegarage.com** Web
site utility.

Web Sticker **www.websticker.com** Print custom
stickers, bumper stickers, decals, and labels with
Web site URL.

Web Tunes **www.webtunes.com** Download site;
MP3.

Webopedia **www.webopedia.com** Look up Web
terms.

WebResource.net **www.webresource.net** Forms,
chat, guest books, scripts for Web sites.

Winamp Player for Windows **www.winamp.com**
MP3 player and encoder software; from Nullsoft;
high-fidelity music player for Windows
95/98/NT; supports MP3, CD, and other audio
formats; has more than 5,000 skins and 150
audio visualization and effects plug-ins;
shareware; free download; the original Windows
MP3 player.

Windows Media **www.windowsmedia.com** or
windowsmedia.microsoft.com Streaming
audio format.

Windows Media Player
> **www.microsoft.com/windows/**
> **mediaplayer** Free downloads.

WinMP3Locator **www.winmp3locator.com**
Finds any MP3; verifies if files are
downloadable; defines server access conditions;
integrates with download software.

WinZip **www.winzip.com** For compressing and
decompressing zip files.

Wired Planet **www.wiredplanet.com**
Shockwave-powered music site; independent
music; downloads; artist interviews; buy CDs;
listening stations; MP3; free Wired Planet
Player.

Worldwide Bands **www.worldwidebands.com**
Source for MP3 recordings; unsigned bands.

Worldwide Music **www.wwmusic.com/-music**
Home page.

Xaudio **www.xaudio.com** Cross-platform MP3
players; Xaudio Player for Linux.

Xaudio Player **www.xaudio.com/products** MP3
audio player; supported operating systems include
Windows, WinCE, Linux, Unix, MacOS, and
others.

Xing Technology Corporation
> **www.xingtech.com** Software company that
> develops MP3 players, encoders, and rippers;
> *Xing AudioCatalyst.*

XingMp3 Player for Windows
> **www.xingtech.com/mp3/player** MP3
> player and encoder software.

XMMS **www.xmms.org** X Multimedia System; open-source MP3 player for Linux and UNIX; MP3 player and encoder software.

Yahoo! Digital **www.digital.broadcast.com** Audio link; browse many music categories.

Yahoo! Full Coverage-MP3 and Digital Music **fullcoverage.yahoo.com/Full_Coverage/ Tech/Online_Music** News and information; online digital music.

Yahoo! Geocities **www.geocities.com/join_info.html** Inexpensive Web sites.

Yahoo! Internet Life **www.zdnet.com/yil** Internet navigation; lifestyle; Web culture.

Yahoo! What's New **www.yahoo.com/picks** Awards Web site.

Yawho.com **www.yawho.com** MP3 downloads.

Yellownews MP3 Software **www.freeyellow.com/members/ flopresti/ymp3softw** Collection of MP3 software links and blurbs.

Yepp **www.yepp.co.kr** MP3 player; voice recording; phone book.

ZDNet's Ultimate CuteMX Guide **music.zdnet.com/features/cutemx** Swap files.

Zebox.xom **www.zebox.com** Free Web sites.

Zorilla **www.zorilla.com** Download site; MP3.

ZY2000 **www.zy2000.com** MP3 CD Maker; burn MP3 files into normal audio CDs; supports many popular CD recorders.

Music, Print Music, and Music Book Publishers

A. D.G. Productions **www.adgproductions.com** Publisher of music education products; songbooks, cassettes, CDs, MIDI disks, videos, and software.

Alafia Publishing and Music Sales **www.alafia.com** Publishers of instrumental music for students, teachers, and professional performers; band, jazz, religious.

Alfred Publishing Company **www.alfredpub.com** Print publisher of music education materials, including software, CDs, cassettes, videos; piano methods.

AMA USA **www.ama-verlag.com** Music publishers.

AMCOS **www.apra.com.au/AmcosWeb/PRINT/ Auspub.htm** Print music publishers and distributors in Australia.

Archives Music Writing Paper **www.daddario.com** Music writing paper; guitar tabulature; stitched books; perforated books; double folded sheets; loose-leaf sheets; spiral-bound books; manuscript pads; and archives correcting tape.

Arsis Press **www.instantWeb.com/~arsis** Publisher of concert and sacred music by women composers.

Association of American Publishers **www.publishers.org** Home page; copyright information for books and text.

Audio Publishers Association (APA) **www.audiopub.org** Nonprofit trade association representing audio publishers, audiobooks, and spoken audio.

Belmont Music Publishers **www.schoenberg.org** The legacy of Arnold Schoenberg; his music; Schoenberg Institute.

Billboard Books **www.billboard.com/books** Books on songwriting, the music business, and other music-related topics.

Boosey & Hawkes, Inc. **www.boosey.com** or **www.ny.boosey.com** International music publisher; manufacturer of acoustic instruments; twentieth-century music; international commitment to performance and music education.

Bosworth Music Publishers **www.demon.co.uk/bosworth** Founded in 1889; pedagogical music publications; Viennese operetta.

Canadian Publishers' Council **www.pubcouncil.ca** Guide to Canadian publishers; index to Canadian publishing.

C. F. Peters **www.cfpeters-ny.com** Print music publisher; classical editions.

Carl Fischer **www.carlfischer.com** New publications; retail stores; information for submitting a manuscript.

Cherry Lane Music Group **www.cherrylane.com** Publisher of songs; songbooks.

Classical Sheet Music Publishers & Distributors Catalogs **www.Webcom.com/musics/catalogs. html** Catalogs.

Cormorant Press Music Publishers **www.cormorantpress.com** Music in attached catalog is copyrighted; offered as shareware; permission to play, teach, or copy.

Creative Concepts **www.creativeconcepts.com** Print music publisher.

Directory of Music Publishers **www.mpa.org/publist.html** Large list of music publishers; links.

EMI **www.emimusicpub.com** Music publisher.

Encore Music Publishers **www.encoremupub.com** Publishers of music for brass, woodwind, and strings ensembles; publisher of music for the tuba.

European American Music Distributors
www.eamdc.com European American Music Distributors Corp. based in Miami, FL.

Frederick Harris Music
www.frederickharrismusic.com Print publisher of pedagogical materials.

G. Henle USA Inc. **www.henleusa.com** Urtext Editions; Musicological Editions; classical music.

G. Schirmer, Inc. **www.schirmer.com** Print publisher of classical music; famous yellow/gold covers; member of the Music Sales Group; details about composers; catalogue listings; premiers; links.

GIA Publications **www.giamusic.com** Major publisher of sacred choral music, hymnals, sacred music recordings, and music education materials.

Global Music Group
www.globalmusicgroup.de International publisher; Germany; UK; US.

GWP Music Publishing **gwpmusic.com** Original and arranged music for student and community instrumental and vocal ensembles.

Hal Leonard Corporation **www.halleonard.com** Print publisher of popular and educational music; software; MIDI disks; books; new music; links; contact information; company history; search by title, artist, or category.

Jane Peterer Music Corporation
www.jpmc.com/Merchant/ merchant.mv?Screen=SFNT&am New York-based music publisher; songbooks, method books, and sheet music in general.

Kjos **www.kjos.com** Piano instruction materials; band literature.

Koala Publications
www.koalapublications.com or **www.learntoplaymusic.com** *Progressive; Introducing; 10 Easy Lessons*; Australian.

Ladyslipper Music by Women
www.ladyslipper.org Publishes a comprehensive catalog of music by women featuring over 1,500 titles; indie record label.

Liben Music Publishers **www.liben.com** Contemporary orchestral and chamber music; Double Bass music and recordings.

Lumina Music **www.luminamusic.com** Sacred and secular music.

MediaNews **www.poynter.org/medianews** Web site for publishers.

Mel Bay Publications, Inc. **www.melbay.com** Print music for all instruments; CDs, cassettes, videos; method books, especially for guitar and folk instruments.

Miller Freeman Books **www.books.mfi.com** Books on contemporary music topics.

Music Publisher Sales Agency List
www.mpa.org/agency/pal.html Current directory of music publishers; index of publishers' imprints; hypertext links to entries in the directory.

Music Publishers and Vendors: The AcqWeb Directory
www.library.vanderbilt.edu/law/acqs/ pubr/music.html Directory of music publishers and vendors; related links.

Music Publishers' Association **www.mpa.org** Resources; information; links.

Music Publishers' Catalogues
www.musicpublications.com Complete searchable database and online ordering site for major music publishers.

Music Sales Corporation **www.musicsales.com** AMSCO; Omnibus Press; Jam Trax; Yorktown Music Press; Oak Publications; Passantino Manuscript Papers; Ashley Music; Ossian Publications.

Music Sales Corporation UK
www.musicsales.co.uk Popular titles for guitar, piano, keyboard, and organ; online Internet Music Shop.

Myklos Music Press **www.myklas.com** Print publisher of pedagogical materials.

National Music Publishers' Association (NMPA)
www.nmpa.org Information about music publishing, licensing requirements, copyright laws, editorial standards, and the correct use of printed music; links.

Norton **www.nortonmusic.com** Publisher of scholarly music books.

Oxford University Press **www1.oup.co.uk** Catalogue of over 4,000 titles; education, scholarly, and performance fields.

Peachpit Press **www.peachpit.com/index.html** Publisher of books on computer music technology.

Peermusic **www.peermusic.com** Music publisher.

Pensacola Publications **www.pensacolapub.com** Features the Jefferson's *How to Play Black Gospel Music* books.

Piano Press **www.pianopress.com** Songbooks for piano/vocal/guitar, CDs, CD-ROMs, and music education materials; seasonal items; workshops; poetry; annual writing contest.

Publishers & Distributors of Printed Music
www.musicyellowpages.com/popmg. htm Online yellow pages.

Publishers' Catalogue
www.lights.com/publisher Home page.

Publishers **www.sai- national.org/resource/publish.html** List of sheet music publishers and distributors on the Internet.

Publishers Marketing Association (PMA)
www.pma-online.org Largest non-profit trade association representing independent publishers of books, audio, video, and CDs; monthly newsletter; resource directory; promotional campaigns.

Publishers Weekly
www.publishersweekly.com Online version of the international news magazine for book publishing and bookselling news.

Retail Print Music Dealers Association
www.printmusic.org Publishers, retailers, and distributors of print music; membership information.

Royalty-Free Music, Inc.
members.aol.com/Katzmarek Supplier of public domain music; encyclopedia; directory; music books.

Scarecrow Press **www.scarecrowpress.com** Since 1950; large catalog of scholarly music titles; music reference books; academic trade books.

Schirmer Books/MacMillan Library Reference
www.mlr.com Scholarly music titles.

Schott Music **www.schott-music.com** Publisher of modern classical pieces; composer pages; concert diary; news; sound clips.

Second Light Music Publishing
www.secondlightmusic.com Specializes in high school/collegiate jazz band and church choir music; sound clips, score previews.

Shawnee Press **www.shawneepress.com** Music print publisher.

Six Strings Music Publishing
www.sixstringsmusicpub.com Music instruction books and videos; guitar chords, fingerstyle, bass, playing tips, diagrams, links.

Southern Music Company
www.southernmusic.com Established in 1937; distributor of sheet music, music books, and more for over 500 publishers; has published over 5,000 educational works.

Swedish Music Publishers Association
www.smff.se Swedish; live music.

The FJH Music Co. Inc. **www.fjhmusic.com** Ft. Lauderdale-based educational print music publisher; Faber & Faber methods for piano.

The World Wide Web Virtual Library: Publishers
www.comlab.ox.ac.uk/archive/publishers.html List of publishers.

Theodore Presser Company **www.presser.com** Music publisher serving musicians, music educators, and music dealers since 1783; classical editions.

Universal Editions **www.uemusic.co.at** Publishers of contemporary music; information.

Useful Addresses: Music Publishers
www.cmc.ie/addresses/publishers.html Listing of music publisher addresses.

Voice of the Rockies
www.voiceoftherockies.com Piano music catalog; sample pages.

Warner Bros. Publications
www.wbpdealers.com Warner Bros.; CPP/Belwin; Summy-Birchard; DCI Music Videos; REH & SongXpress Videos; Kalmus; Bowmar; Suzuki; Lawson-Gould; Studio P/R; Interworld; Master Teacher Series; Instrumental Classmates; Ultimate Beginner Series; Beyond Basics; Getting the Sounds.

Warner Chappell **www.warnerchappell.com** International publisher.

Washington Music Publishers and Dealers List
www.lib.washington.edu/libinfo/libunits/soc-hum/music/publishers.html Music publishers and dealers.

Willis Music Co. **www.willis-music.com** Sheet music; racks; statuettes; piano methods.

Worldwide Internet Music Resources: Music Publishers **www.music.indiana.edu/music_resources/publ.html** William and Gayle Cook Music Library, Indiana University School of Music; links to many publisher Web sites.

Writer's Digest Books **www.writersdigest.com** Books on songwriting; general writing books.

Yeah Solutions **www.yeahsolutions.com** Makers of *Music Publisher Pro* software for managing copyrights, royalties, and payments; for artists as well as publishing companies.

Music Resources, References, and Research—Music Links—Directories—Portals

181.4 Music Database **www.181-4.com/database** Music information.

1st SPOT Music **1st-spot.net/topic_music.html** Resources on music; classical, popular, country, rock, and blues; music business; orchestras; instruments.

4Trivia.com **www.4trivia.com** Trivia contests on television, movies, music, etc.

Aardvarks Best of the Web **www.stl-music.com/hub.html** Links; events; classical and popular music.

About.com Music
home.about.com/entertainment Directory of music categories; links.

AltaVista Music
dir.altavista.com/Arts/Music.shtml Music search engine.

Amazing Discographies **ad.techno.org**
Discographies; links.

Amazon **www.amazon.com/music** or
www.amazon.co.uk/music Retail site;
reference database.

America's Shrine to Music Museum
www.usd.edu/smm Home page; index;
musical instrument museum and research center
located in South Dakota.

AMG All Music Guide **www.allmusic.com**
Database of all recorded music; search by album,
artist, or song name; key artists; key albums;
music styles; music glossary; music maps; new
releases; featured albums.

Art Smart **www.art-smart.com** Database of art
searchable by over fifteen unique categories;
multiple simultaneous searches; artworks.

ArtNet **www.artnet.com** Samples of art
exhibitions around the world.

Audio Architect Links
www.audioarchitect.com/links.htm
Music resources; music magazines; synthesizer
sites; online music shops.

Audioworks List of Links
www.audioworks.com/links/linkindx.
htm Links in many categories; hardware;
instruments; music software; publications;
organizations; bands list, MIDI resources; MIDI
archives; guitar resources; records; CDs;
networking.

AustralAsia Music Industry Directory
www.immedia.comau Online directory.

Basic Music **www.basicmusic.net** Recommended
search engines.

Bibliophile **www.bibliophile.net** Over one
million books for sale by independent
booksellers worldwide; rare, used, and new
books; search by title, author, keyword, subject,
language, recent additions, and other criteria; also
lists maps, piano rolls, stereoscopic views, and
almost very kind of printed material.

BigBook **www.bigbook.com** Yellow Pages on the
Internet of every city in the country.

Bigmouth **wwwbigmouth.co.uk** Music
information in the UK; news; tour dates.

Billboard Directories **www.billboard.com**
Directories: *International Talent & Touring
Directory:* artists and their management,
performance venues, hotels, and services;
Country Music Sourcebook: labels, publishers,
recording studios, venues, clubs, concert
promoters, country artists and managers, radio
stations in U.S. and Canada; *International Latin
Music Buyer's Guide:* "Yellow Pages" of Latin
Music contacts in U.S., Mexico, Central, and
South America.

Biography **www.biography.com** Based on the
popular A&E television series; includes profiles
of composers and musicians.

Britannica Online **www.eb.com** Online version of
the Encyclopedia Britannica; articles on music
topics.

Canadian Music Website **www.canmusic.com**
Information; resources; links.

CDDB **www.cddb.com** CD Database; links to
retail sites.

Click Music **www.clickmusic.co.uk** Search
portal specializing in music; links; news;
celebrities; Internet issues; games.

Coda Music Links **www.codamusic.com/coda/**
links_db.asp#MusicSites Extensive list.

Compulink **www.compulink.co.uk/~route66**
Information for the musician; news; gigs; bands;
composers; producers; magazines; record labels;
publishers; links.

CultureFinder
www.culturefinder.com/index.htm
Calendar of musical events across the U.S.;
music information; news; interviews; online
store; purchase tickets online.

Cyber Alert **www.cyberalert.com** Clipping
service for hire; compile information daily on
topics of interest; use search engines, forums,
and online databases.

Discography **www.pcmagic.net/markw/pizzi5/**
discography/index Extensive discography
covering albums, singles, TV appearances,
books, commercials, compilations, solo work,
guest appearances, videos, MIDIs, and EPs.

*DMAs Music Links to Instrument and Vocal
Resources* **www.dmamusic.org/**
instrumentvoicelinks.html Collection of
links.

Encarta Online **www.encarta.msn.com** Online
encyclopedia.

Entertainment Network News **www.enn2.com**
Directory of entertainment Web sites.

Entertainment-Music
www.ntgi.net/ntg/mall/music.htm Over
500 links on all kinds of music.

Excite! Music **nt.excite.com/142/music** Music
search engine.

Faculty of Music: Instrument Collections
www.music.ed.ac.uk/collect The
Edinburgh University Collection of Historic
Musical Instruments; two of the most important
collections of historic instruments in Europe.

Find.com **www.biblio.find.com** Find any book;
search engine.

Fostex Links **www.fostex.com/links.html**
Links; broadcast media; concerts; events;
magazines; music manufacturers; music retailers;
musician's resources; nightclubs; publicity;

record labels; sound industry; studios and production.

Getmusic.com **www.getmusic.com** Links to all genres.

Harmony Central **www.harmony-central.com** Information on many musical topics; major collection of resources for the musician; news; communities; software; MIDI; computer music.

Hyperreal Music Machines **www.hyperreal.org/music/machines/ links** General music; MIDI and equipment sites; manufacturer sites; publications; retailers; dealers.

Infojump **www.infojump.com** Five million articles from over 4,000 publishers.

Infoseek Music **infoseek.go.com/Topic/Music?tid=242** Music portal listing sites with icons.

International Directory of Music Organizations **www.music.org/pubs/interdir/listing. html** Locate worldwide music organizations on this alphabetically cataloged site.

Internet Music Resource Guide **www.teleport.com/~celinec/music. shtml** Guide to music on the Internet; search sites.

Internet Resources for Music Scholars **www.rism.harvard.edu/MusicLibrary/ InternetResources.html** Home page.

Internet Road Map to Books **199.165.129.36/index.html** Web directory to book sites.

Letsfindout.com **www.letsfindout.com** Interactive encyclopedia.

Matra Productions **www.matraproductions.com** Music services search and resource center.

MHN Instrument Encyclopedia **www.si.umich.edu/CHICO/MHN/ enclpdia.html** Encyclopedia of musical instruments.

Music and Audio **www.musicandaudio.com/artistal.shtml** Guide to music on the Internet; links.

Music Business Solutions **www.mbsolutions.com** Resource directory; consulting; articles; books; links.

Music Clipart Gallery **www.geocities.com/Nashville/Opry/ 1809** Clip art for musicians.

Music Database **www.roadkill.com** Search by album title and artist; listeners' reviews and links.

Music Directory of Canada **www.nor.com/mbp** Listings of artists, agents, managers, labels, festivals, presenters, and other music-related resources.

Music FTP Sites **gps.leeds.ac.uk/music/Netinfo/ MusicFTP/ftp_sites.html** Home page; resources; links.

Music Guild **musicguild.org** Directories of record labels; instrument manufacturers; sound equipment; music software publishers; MIDI sites; music-related directories; links.

Music **www.aol.com/Webcenters/ entertainment/music.adp** Music downloads; news; links to music Web sites.

Music Industries Association of Canada **www.musicanada.com/miac** Canadian music industry.

Music Interactive **www.musicinteractive.com** Information; resources; links.

Music Jackpot **www.musicjackpot.com** Online connection to online music stores; CDs, tapes, music videos, laser discs, video games, sheet music, and more.

Music Links **www.yahoo.com/entertainment/music** Links to music sites on the Internet.

Music Locus **www.memphislocal.com/locus/lohist. html** News; music reports; music information; audio information; arts; music business references; gateway and guide to other networks.

Music Net Encyclopedia **www.tqd.advanced.org/3306/ cgi-bin/encyclopedia/index/html** Database of more than one hundred music terms; click on the "add" button to contribute to the database.

Music Resources **www.siba.fi/Kulttuuripalvelut/music. html** Musical Web links from the Sibelius Academy of Finland.

Music Resources on the Internet **www.music.indiana.edu/misc/ music_resources.htm** Home page; resources; links.

Music Station **www.musicstation.com/musicnewswire** or **www.musicnewswire.com** Global music information network; news; lists; guide; industry features and reviews; links to sources; MP3 links.

Music Yellow Pages **www.musicyellowpages.com** Phone numbers for virtually any music-related company.

Music.com **www.music.com** Online destination for music lovers; E-mail; weekly E-zine; music.com radio; music news; new releases; music history; birthdays; horoscopes; staff picks; free downloads; custom CDs; free MP3s; 1970s music; 1980s music; all genres; indie music; contests and more.

Musical Heritage Network Instrument Encyclopedia
**www.si.umich.edu/CHICO/MHN/
enclpdia.html** More than 140 artifacts from
the Stearns Collection at the University of
Michigan; searchable resource; musical
instruments from around the world.
Musical Quotes
**www.cybernation.com/victory/
quotations/subjects/quotes_music.html**
Famous quotations on music.
Musical Web Connections
**www.columbia.edu/~hauben/music/
Web-music.html** Large list of music links.
Musician's Links
www.xensei.com/users/the8thnote
Noncommercial listing of musician's links;
sorted by category.
MusicLink **toltec.lib.utk.edu/
-music/www.html** Extensive guide to finding
music information online.
MusicSearch.com **www.musicsearch.com**
Search engine for music only; links to artists,
events, industry news, reviews, radio stations,
and music publishers; 15,000+ links.
Music-Sites.net **music-sites.net** Music links
directory; music community.
Musreview **www.musreview.com** Music charts;
radio stations; artists; labels; country artists;
country music links; record labels; disc jockeys;
booking and talent; jazz; links and directories;
rock artists; bands; blues; music publishers;
Christian and gospel music; recording studios;
managers; rap; R&B bands; music stores;
musical instruments; music promotion; music
news; radio stations; music charts; graphic
design; production; MP3/MIDI; classical;
songwriters; reviews.
Muze.com **www.muze.com** All genres.
National Sound Archive
www.bl.uk/collections/sound-archive
Large sound archive.
NetCentral **www.netcentral.net** Central source
for music, books, contests, free chat services, and
more.
New Media Music **www.newmediamusic.com**
Resources for artists and labels; interviews; new
products and services; events; music industry
press releases.
Noize Links **www.terzoid.com/nzlinks.html**
Musical instrument company sites; software
sites; MIDI sites; manufacturer contacts; price
lists; newsgroups.
Open Directory-Arts: Music
www.dmoz.org/Arts/Music/Awards
Business; charts; comedians; computers;
education; history; instruments; karaoke;
marching.

Passport Links
206.15.71.82/map/links_f.html
Computer music; hardware and software; pro
audio gear; interfaces; sound cards; digital audio
tools; artist resources; copyright information;
songwriting; lyrics; online publishing; legal
assistance; agents; musician services;
newsgroups; music styles.
PC Webopaedia **www.pcwebopaedia.com**
Encyclopedia of computer and Internet
information.
Play Music **www.playmusic.org** Lists of
different orchestral instruments and how they are
played; music games.
Quadratic Links
www.cycling74.com/support/links.html
Links to Macintosh related sites; not music-
specific; software archives; E-zines; magazines;
shareware.
Radio Free Entertainment **www.radiofree.com**
Resource for the world of entertainment; concert
tickets; movie reviews; box office grosses; music
clips; entertainment merchandise; celebrity
picture archives.
Scottie's Music World
www.scottiesmusicworld.com Directory of
links to artists on the Web; all genres.
SearchIQ-Music
www.searchiq.com/subjects/music.htm
Directory of music search engines and directories
covering artists, albums, CDs, digital audio,
MP3, MIDI, and songs.
Selected Web Resources for Music and Musicology
**www.princeton.edu:80/
-stmoore/musiclinks.html** Information;
resources; links.
Showbiz Data **www.showbizdata.com/
3d industry** The entertainment search engine.
Sibelius Academy Music Resources
**www.siba.fi/Kulttuuripalvelut/music.
html** Complete link lists, including popular and
folk music, classical, early music, etc.
Sites and Sound Links
www.servtech.com/public/koberlan
Links to music-related material; distributors;
music magazines; record labels; music-related
newsgroups; Web directory for musicians.
Supersonic Guide
**www.nets.or.jp/supersonic/supersonic.
html** Directory of UK music sites on the
Internet.
The 8th Note
**www.xensei.com/users/the8thnote/
bystyle.html** Links by musical style include
African; Afro-Caribbean; reggae; bluegrass;
blues; Celtic/Irish; classical; orchestral; country;
electronic/ambient/techno; folk; old time; funk;

gospel; hip-hop; acid jazz; jazz; Latin; opera; punk; ragtime; rock.

The American Music Center **www.amc.net** Resource for musicians and producers; grant information; music directories; artist information and publications.

The Collections of Musical Instruments **www.loc.gov** Library of Congress; illustrated guide.

The Free Music Archive **free-music.com** Supports free music and artists; alphabetized links to CD sales, E-mail, Web sites, and free music; downloads.

The Globe **www.theglobe.com** Clubs and homepages by people with similar interests; lists 3,024 music clubs under Arts and Books Community.

The Instrument Encyclopedia **www.si.umich.edu/CHICO/MHN/ enclpdia1.html** More than 140 artifacts from the Stearns Collection at the University of Michigan; features musical instruments from around the world.

The International Association of Music Information Centres (IAMIC) **www.iamic.ie** International network of organizations promoting new music.

The Mammoth Music Meta-List **www.vibe.com/mmm** Music resources on the Internet; all genres; Webzines; festivals; FAQ; music schools and more.

The Music Makers Net Directory **magenta.com/~sms/mumaned** Links to music newsgroups; Webzines; MIDI sites; samples; equipment manufacturers; used gear price lists; CD pressers; record labels.

The Music Resource **www.themusicresource.com** Home page; resources; links.

The Music Review **www.musicreview.com** Search engine for music-related resources, record labels, agencies.

The Music TOP 10 Sites **music.top10sites.net** Top ten categories.

The Musician's Homepage **www.enteract.com/~digialex** Links; radio stations; record labels; legal information; manufacturers; list URL.

The Musician's Resource **www.themusiciansresource.com** Information for musicians.

The Names of Instruments and Voices in Foreign Languages **www-ccrma.stanford.edu/~unjung/ins.html** or **www.library.yale.edu/cataloging/music/ instname.htm** English, French, German, Italian, Russian, and Spanish.

The Sound Machine Sound Music Makers Net Directory **alpha.science.unitn.it/~oss/sourcese. html** Documents; instruments; software samples; manufacturers; record companies; retailers; CD pressers.

Tripod Music Links **members.tripod.com/~hoiyuen/MUSIC. html** Charts; awards; karaoke; lyrics; MIDI; RealAudio; record companies.

Virtual Museums **www.icom.org/vlmp** Links to hundreds of museum exhibits around the world; Smithsonian, Louvre, and more.

Virtual Tunes Music **virtualtunes.com/index.shtml** Searchable directory of music and music resources.

Voice of the Shuttle **vos.ucsb.edu** Home page.

Webring.org **www.Webring.org** Hundreds of music Webrings listed under Arts and Humanities.

Web Sites for Music Research **www.unc.edu/depts/music/research.html** Compiled by the University of North Carolina; links.

World Art Treasures **Sgwww.epfl.ch/berger** Art.

World of Mechanical Music Museum **www.mechanicalmusic.co.uk** Self-playing musical instruments; antique musical boxes.

World Talent Record's Music Resources **members.aol.com/PR4WTR/wtr1.html** Extensive collection of links for musicians and fans.

World Wide Arts Resources **www.wwar.com** Comprehensive directory of the arts on the Internet.

Worldwide Internet Music Resources **www.music.indiana.edu/ music_resources** Links divided by category; individual musicians in all genres; popular groups; ensembles; sites related to performance; composers and composition; genres and types of music; research and study; the commercial world of music; journals and magazines; bands; resources.

Y2k-Music Co.UK **www.y2k-music.co.uk** Bands; artists; audio samples; free classifieds; CDs.

Yahoo! **uk.news.yahoo.com/m/music.html** or **rock.yahoo.com** Music portal; reviews; features; news; search engine.

Yahoo! Regional Directories **dir.yahoo.com/Regional/ Web_Directories/Yahoo_Regional/ World_Yahoo_s** Collection of regional Web directories.

YAV's Music Links **www.yav.com/docs/MusicLinks.html**

Computer music; MIDI; computer music studios; algorithmic computer music; classical music; opera; music education; composers; music resources.

Music Retailers Online

123Posters **www.123posters.com** Buy music-related posters online.

1-800-MusicNow **www.1800musicnow.com** RealAudio samples; large catalog.

Accordion Store **www.accordion-store.com/sheetmusic/index.htm** For accordion players, bands, and virtuosos; cassettes; CDs; videos; tours.

Acoustic Musical Instruments **www.acousticforum.co.uk** Classified sales; musicians' community pages.

Alabama Music Inc. **www.alabamamusic.com/Main/Software.htm** Music software for learning, producing, writing, recording, printing, and scanning music.

Alexander Publishing **www.alexanderpublishing.com** Self-paced problem/solution instruction; Alexander University Campus Music Store.

Allegro Music **www.allegro-music.com** Classical, jazz, world, pop, blues, etc.

Amazingcds.com **www.amazingcds.com** Independent music artists' CDs from around the world; online music store that is listening to original music and accepting all styles of music; see Submission Information page.

Amazon **www.amazon.com** Music; books; software; reviews; links; Advantage Program for independent publishers and artists.

American Musical Supply **www.americanmusical.com** Online retailer.

Artist Direct Superstore **www.ubl.com** Online retailer.

Audiostreet **www.audiostreet.co.uk** Online music store; RealAudio samples.

Backtrack Records **www.backtrackrecords.com** Hard-to-find music; independent; imports.

Barnes and Noble **www.bn.com** Music; books; software; reviews; links.

Bass Tickets **www.basstickets.com** Concert tickets.

Beatmaker.Com **www.beatmaker.com** The Sound Store; karaoke music CDs, DVD movies, games, educational software, and more.

Blockbuster Online **www.blockbuster.com** Movie music and video shopping.

BMG Music Service **www.bmgmusicservice.com** Music club; membership.

Books and Music **www.bookandmusic.net** Home page.

Borders **www.borders.com** Online books and music retailer.

Borrow or Rob **www.borroworrob.com** U.S./UK shop; search by artist.

Buy.com **www.buy.com** Online electronics retailer.

Camelot Music **www.camelotmusic.com** Music retailer.

Carvin **www.carvin.com** Factory-direct music store.

CD Access **www.cdaccess.com** CD-ROM titles; educational.

CD Now **www.cdnow.com** CDs; Billboard charts; imports; wide selection.

CD Palace **www.cdpalace.com** Online retailer.

CD Paradise **www.cdparadise.com** Online music store; wide selection.

CD Universe **www.cduniverse.com** Online music retailer.

CD Warehouse **www.cdwarehouse.com** Online music retailer.

CD World **www.cdworld.com** Online store; imports.

Cob Records **www.elfyn.ndirect.co.net** Independent record dealer; new and used; links to UK independent record stores online.

Collector.com **www.collect.com/index.html** Directory of collectibles retailers.

Columbia House **www.columbiahouse.com** Record club online Web site.

Compact Discovery **www.compactdiscovery.com** New and used CDs for sale online.

Compare It All Music **www.compareitall.com** Guide to finding the best deals on the Internet; search.

Consortium Book Sales and Distribution **www.cbsd.com/books** Independent book publisher distributor.

Crotchet Web Store **www.crotchet.co.uk** Ten departments dedicated to classical music, jazz, film soundtracks, and world music; browse latest releases; online database.

Custom Disc **www.customdisc.com** Customized CD maker.

CyberMusic Surplus **discount-cds.m9b.com** Thousands of CDs; discounts available; virtual outlet store for classical, jazz, pop, world, new age, and blues.

Digibid.com **www.digibid.com** Online auction network; gear.

Dr. Wax **www.drwax.com** Rare items; vinyl; new indie releases.

DVD Express **www.dvdexpress.com** DVDs; concert videos.

EBopp **www.ebopp.com** Instruments and equipment.

Emusic **www.emusic.com** Customized CD maker.

Encore Music Company, Inc. **www.encoremusic.com** Sheet music; music books; accessories; gifts.

Entertainment Express **www.entexpress.com** Online retailer.

EveryCD.com **www.everycd.com** Music, DVDs, videos, and software for sale online.

Everything English **www.everythingenglish.com** New and used CDs; English paraphanalia.

Forced Exposure **www.forcedexposure.com** Online store; reviews of new releases.

Forever Vinyl **www.forevervinyl.com** Buy and sell vinyl; large inventory.

Friendship House **www.friendshiphouse.com** Music teaching aids; gifts; novelties; trophies; software; books; CDs.

German Music Express **www.musicexpress.com** Online CD store; back catalog; singles.

Getmusic.com **www.getmusic.com** New releases from BMG and Universal.

Global Audiophile **www.globalaudiophile.com** Specialist store; for collector of rare recordings.

Global Electronic Music Marketplace (GEMM) **www.gemm.com** Large catalog of music; combines catalogs of 2,000 discounters, importers, collectors, labels and artists; new, used, hard-to-find, and out-of-print albums.

HMV **www.hmv.com** Canadian retailer.

Horizon Records **www.horizonrecords.net** Folk, jazz, blues, world beat, classical, regional, Jewish, Celtic, vintage vinyl.

In Sound **www.insound.com** Not Top 40 music; chat; photos; audio samples.

Independent Distribution Network **www.idnmusic.com/index.html** Rare items.

Internet Music Shop **www.musicsales.co.uk** or **www.internetmusicshop.com** Order music products online.

K-TEL **www.ktel.com** Compilations; online retailer; digital downloads.

La Jolla Music **www.lajollamusic.com** La Jolla, CA; lessons; sheet music; band instruments.

Landphil Records **www.novia.net/landphil/indies.html** State-by-state list of independent record stores.

Liquid Music **www.liquidmusic.net** New and used CDs for sale.

Mars Music **www.marsmusic.com** Online retailer; equipment; software and more.

MGVC **www.imvs.com** Online retailer; back catalog.

Mix Bookshelf **www.mixbookshelf.com** Distributor of books on music.

Music & Arts Center **www.musicarts.com** Online music retailer.

Music and Arts Online CD Catalog **www.musicandarts.com** Contemporary and historic classical, jazz, and world music recordings.

Music Books Plus **www.vaxxine.com/mbp** Online bookstore for musicians.

Music Box World **www.musicboxworld.com** Specializes in custom music boxes, carousels, fine Italian inlaids, dolls, ballerinas, and children's boxes; choose a tune from alphabetical list of hundreds; virtual museum.

Music File **www.musicfile.com** Collectible music store; millions of used CDs, vinyl records, imports, etc.

Music for a Song **www.musicforasong.com** Over 15,000 selections including out-of-print, cut-out, hard-to-find CDs and cassettes; Gold Discs and imports.

Music Gear OnLine **musicgearonline.com** Large guide to musical equipment including music software, soundware, MIDI, MIDI controllers, effects, signal processors, synthesizers, samplers, recorders, accessories, and more.

Music in Motion **www.musicinmotion.com** Music education and gift catalog for all ages; music books, videos, audios, awards, teaching aids, posters, bulletin board aids, gifts, software, creative dramatics, multicultural resources, and more.

Music Lovers Shoppe **www.musicloversshoppe.com** Shop for music lovers.

Music Market Place **www.musicmarketplace.com** Online music retailer.

Music Mart **www.musicmart.com** Online music retailer.

Music Mongers Music & Gifts **www.musicmongers.com** Sheet music; CDs; songbooks; music instruction; music-themed gifts.

Music Previews Network **www.mpmusic.com** Listen before buying.

Music.com **www.music.com** Retailer.

Music123 **www.music123.com** Online musical instrument store.

Musical Instruments Suppliers **www.briscdisc.co.za/newinstruments/**

ownstuff.html Musical instrument importers and dealers; suppliers of music and educational software.

MusicFile **www.musicfile.com** Rare and hard-to-find items; LPs and tapes.

Musichotbid.com **www.musichotbid.com** Online music auction site.

Musician Store **www.musicianstore.com** Sheet music; software; musician's gear.

Musicians Friend **www.musiciansfriend.com** Order all types of music equipment online; music software; Effects Glossary describing various effects; streaming audio demos in RealAudio format.

MusicMaker **www.musicmaker.com** Customized CD maker.

Musicspot **www.musicspot.com** Reviews; CD information; rock music.

MusicYo.com **www.MusicYo.com** Online music store.

Muzic Depot **www.muzicdepot.com** Online music store; preview music before buying.

Net Instruments **www.netinstruments.com** Musical instruments for sale.

Norwalk Music **www.norwalkmusic.com** Online musical instrument store; links to manufacturer's Web sites; index for every instrument.

Off the Record **www.otrvinyl.com** Rare and collectible records.

Online Music Stores Index **www.cs.clemson.edu/~junderw/music/onlinestores.html** Directory of online retailers.

Other Music **www.othermusic.com** Independent record store; NYC.

P.J. Ballantine Music **www.pjballantine.com** Instructional music books, music videos, and music software for guitar, piano, keyboard, drums, bass, and vocal.

Parasol **www.parasol.com** or **www.indies.com** Indie CDs and vinyl; new and used; catalog; own labels.

Past Perfect **www.pastperfect.com** Remastered songs from the 1920s to 1940s.

Pro Audio **www.proaudiomusic.com** Equipment retailer; links.

Pro Music Find **www.promusicfind.com** Worldwide marketplace for musicians; instruments; music; downloadable sheet music and files.

Pulse Music **www.pulseonline.com** Equipment and instruments.

Quickmusic.com **www.quickmusic.com** Online retailer; search; track listings; RealAudio.

Razorcuts Custom CD **www.razorcuts.com/default1.asp** Compile a custom CD; wide range of tracks.

RBP Musician Supply **rbpgroup.vstoremusic.com** Guitars; woodwind; brass; percussion; instruments for children; large variety of international instruments.

Recycler **www.music.recycler.com** Used music equipment for sale.

Rockabilia **www.rockabilia.com** Purchase rock music collectibles online.

Rough Trade Shop **www.roughtrade.com** Alternative music; used CDs; vinyl; concert listings; tickets; search engine.

Sam Ash Music **www.SamAshMusic.com** or **www.samash.com** Online music retailer; equipment.

Seaford Music **www.seaford-music.co.uk** Classical music retailers; violin repairs and sales; international classical compact disc; sheet music and musical instrumental store based in Sussex, England.

Second Spin **www.secondspin.com** Buy and sell used CDs.

Sold Out **www.soldout.com** Purchase tickets online.

Stagepass.com **www.stagepass.com** Instructional books, videos, software, and MIDI files collections.

Stereo Liquidators **www.stereoliquidators.com** Stereo equipment.

Tempest Music **www.violin-world.com/sheetmusic** Sheet music; print music; online store and catalogue; music; stringed; bowed; woodwind; brass; piano; percussion instruments; vocal music; novelty; accessories; strings; reeds.

The CD Club Web Server **www.cd-clubs.com** CD clubs.

The DJ Store **www.thedjstore.com** Online retailer; DJ and dance party wares.

The Federal Trade Commission **www.ftc.gov** Information on consumer e-commerce protection.

The Juilliard Bookstore **www.bookstore.juilliard.edu** Resource for books and discs on or about music.

The Music House **www.themusichouse.com** Online music retailer.

The Music Market **www.themusicmarket.com** Online music retailer.

The Music Stand **www.musicstand.com** Gifts and novelties for musicians.

The Penoka Collection **www.penoka.com/d_teach.htm** Instruction books, videos.

The Sound Professionals **www.soundpros.com**
Stereo equipment.

Ticket Web **www.ticketweb.com** Purchase
tickets online.

Ticketmaster Online **www.ticketmaster.com**
Buy tickets to events online.

Ticketmaster UK **www.ticketmaster.co.uk** UK
tickets online.

Tickets.com **www.tickets.com** Purchase tickets
online.

TotalE.com **www.TotalE.com** Music; video;
CDs; DVDs.

Tower **www.tower.com** Online music retailer;
track listings; RealAudio samples.

Tower Records **www.towerrecords.com** CDs;
videos; books; records; tapes; sample tracks;
Pulse! magazine; reviews.

Tunes.com **www.tunes.com** Online music store;
track listings; sample sounds; videos; broadcasts;
news; links.

Vintage Vinyl **www.vvinyl.com** 100,000 item
inventory; all genres; 1950s, 1960s; imports.

Vinyl 4Ever **www.vinyl4ever.com** Guitar tab,
bass, woodwind, and brass music books; vinyl
records; sheet music; scores.

Virgin Megastore **www.virginmega.com** Online
music retailer.

Visual Vinyl **www.visualvinyl.co.uk** Used vinyl
and CDs.

Wax City **www.waxcity.com** Online retailer;
dance music; new releases; audio clips.

Web Tix **www.Webtix.com** Want ads for tickets.

West L.A. Music **www.westlamusic.com** Pro
gear.

West Music **www.westmusic.com** Online music
retailer.

Wherehouse Music
www.wherehousemusic.com Home page.

World Music Store **www.worldmusicstore.com**
CDs from around the world.

World Music Web **www.worldmusicweb.com**
Directory of music retailers; classified ads;
musician's forum.

World of Music Boxes
www.worldofmusicboxes.com Music box
designs and mechanical movements imported
from Switzerland, Italy, Germany, and the
Orient; classic and childrens' collectibles; jewelry
boxes; handcrafted gifts.

World Party Music **www.wpmusic.com** New and
used CDs.

World Wide Music **www.worldwidemusic.com**
CDs, cassettes, and more; cover art and sound
bites from selected CDs.

Yestermusic **www.yestermusic.com** Oldies; all
genres and decades.

Zzounds **www.zzounds.com** Online music gear
and accessories retailer.

Music Theory and Composition—Notation—Ear Training

194 Documents about 'Music Theory'
www.hcca.ohio.gov/kelleysworld/7179.htm Music theory documents.

A1 Music **www.ilovemusic.com** Music theory,
dance, and music education; compose music,
learn chords, scales, rhythm; ear training.

Adult Music Theory
www.musicarrangers.com/star-theory
Jazzy, classical.

Aesthetic Artist **www.aestheticartist.com** Web
site designed to teach beginners basic music
theory and music notation skills; free music and
art theory; philosophy of art; music
composition; lyric composition; aesthetic
philosophy and more.

AP Music Theory
www.collegeboard.org/ap/music or
www.collegeboard.com/ap/music
Teachers' corner; AP music theory credit;
placement; advanced standing policies; compact
discs.

CALMUS **rvik.ismennt.is/~kjol** Computer
program designed for music composition of
twentieth-century music; concepts used include
musical objects, polyphony, harmony, melody,
MIDI, and graphical representation.

*Center for the History of Music Theory and
Literature* **www.music.indiana.edu/chmtl**
Joint venture of Indiana University's School of
Music and the Office of Research and the
University Graduate School.

Clarion
www.sirius.com/~jalkut/RedSweater/Clarion.html Music utility; practice and be
quizzed on the intervals of the 12-tone Western
music octave division.

Comprehensive Ear Training
www.drdowningmusic.com Progressively
graded series of books, CDs, cassettes, and MIDI
discs.

Cope Media **www.cope.dk** Ear-training software
for Windows; aural training of scales, chords,
intervals, melody, rhythm, inversions,
progressions, etc.

CTHEORY **www.ctheory.com** International
journal of theory, technology, and culture;
articles, interviews, and key book reviews
published weekly.

DCU-Traditional Music Society
www.redbrick.dcu.ie/~tradsoc/theory
Music theory resources; events; recitals; message
board.

Department of Music Theory
www.oberlin.edu/con/divinfo/ musictheory/Default.html Studies in music theory are part of every program in the Oberlin Music Conservatory.

Dutch Journal of Music Theory
sca.ahk.nl/tvm/tvm.html Tijdschrift voor Muziekthoerie.

Ear Trainer **www.ilovemusic.com/ear.htm** Software program to help musical ear.

Ear Training Expedition
www.trailcreeksystems.com Ear-training software for Windows 95; helps students learn music theory and practice skills with games.

Ear Training **www.eartraining.com** Home page.

Ear Training
www.music.indiana.edu/som/courses/ t109/interval.htm Aural skills Web site.

EarMaster **www.earmaster.com** Ear training software for Windows; intervals, chords, scales, melodies, and rhythms.

EarPower **www.earpower.com/earpower.htm** Ear-training program to be used as a daily routine; compact and easy to use; many features; for anyone, from the "tone-deaf" person to the professional musician.

Eartraining
members.aol.com/LarsPeters/Info.html Practice intervals, chords, scales, and perfect pitch.

EMTfPP **www.edly.com/EMTfPPPage.html** Edly's Music Theory for Practical People makes learning theory fun.

Gary Ewer's "Easy Music Theory"
www.musictheory.halifax.ns.ca Music theory lessons on the Internet; no registration; how to write scales, chords, triads, etc.

Gordon Institute for Music Learning
www.unm.edu/~audiate/home.html Music Learning theory home page.

Hearing and Writing Music **www.rongorow.com** Professional training; self-study.

Java Music Theory
academics.hamilton.edu/music/ spellman/JavaMusic Designed to help students of music theory improve their proficiency; basic skills.

Journal of Music Theory Home Page
www.yale.edu/jmt Published twice a year, in the Spring and Fall, by Yale University.

Listen **www.edly.com/Listen.html** Music ear-training program for students and individuals wishing to strengthen their perception of melodic and harmonic material; wide variety of matching and multiple choice exercises; Macintosh.

Making Music with Algorithms
www.maths.gla.ac.uk/~km/pub/music.

htm by McAlpine, Miranda, Hoggar; Dept. of Math, Dept. of Music, Univ. of Glasgow.

Metronimo-Educational Musical Games
www.metronimo.com Music theory; classic composers; musical culture; instruments of the symphony orchestra; in English and French; Windows.

MiBAC Theory Reference
www.mibac.com/Pages/Theory/ Main_Theory.htm Online version of music theory help that is built in to the software program.

Music Composition Resource
www.und.nodak.edu/dept/mcr Sources for composers; books; articles; Web sites; recordings; FAQs.

Music Curriculum (K-12): Music Theory
www.mv.com/ipusers/orol/district/ issues/music/theory Student proficiencies in music; understand and apply principles of music theory.

Music Notation Links **www.s- line.de/homepages/gerd_castan/ compmus/musicnotation_e.html** Common music notation; shape notes; about limitations and extensions of common music notation; accordions; tablatures; diatonic accordions; konzertina notation; guitar tablatures; early Western music notation; non-Western music notation; Indian music notation; African music; Arabian music notation; Chinese music notation; Byzantine music notation; Indonesian music notation; Kinko Ryu shakuhachi notation; doumbek notation; extraterrestrial music notation; music notation and the search for extra-terrestrial intelligence.

Music of Cyberworld-Music Theory
www.philosophers.org/MusicTheory. html Music theory Web sites.

Music Research and Music Theory
www.siba.fi/Kulttuuripalvelut/theory. html Archive of Dissertation Abstracts in music.

Music Study **www.musicstudy.com** Ear-training and music theory instruction software; Macintosh; Windows.

Music Theory at Indiana University
theory.music.indiana.edu Music Theory Department at the Indiana University School of Music; nine faculty members.

Music Theory Basics at Xoom
members.xoom.com/paulbeach/2music/ default.html Website designed to teach beginners basic music theory and music notation skills; composition.

Music Theory Big Ears: The Original Online Ear Trainer **www.pageplus.com/~bigears** Web-based ear training; intervals.

Music Theory **english-
www.hss.cmu.edu/music/theory.html**
Music theory tutorial; music theory for guitar;
phrase structure analysis; glossary of terms.
Music Theory
**library.advanced.org/15413/theory/
theory.htm** or
**hyperion.advanced.org/15413/theory/
theory.htm** Basics of music theory; note
reading, intervals, scales, and more.
Music Theory Midwest **www.wmich.edu/
mus-theo/mtmw.html** Links to other music
theory societies; School of Music, Western
Michigan University.
Music Theory Online
**boethius.music.ucsb.edu/mto/mtohome.
html** Online resource for music theory.
Music Theory Software Product Type
www.lentine.com/so/mts.stm Supplier of
musical instruments, pro audio, music software,
and accessories.
Music Theory Spectrum **www-
ucpress.berkeley.edu/journals/mts** or
www.ucpress.edu/journals/mts Official
print journal of the Society for Music Theory;
articles and book reviews on topics in music
theory and analysis, including aesthetics.
Musical Definitions
**www.merton.ox.ac.uk/fun/music/
musical-definitions.html** Definitions of
musical terms.
Musicianship Basics
www.dragnet.com.au/~donovan/mb
Music education software for schools and piano
teachers; graded ear training and theory activities
for all music students; demos available;
Macintosh; Windows.
MusicTheoryCourses
**www.music.columbia.edu/
UnderGradProgram/MusicTheoryCo.**
Undergraduate theory courses seek to develop
students' abilities to hear and understand music
through the writing of harmony and counterpoint
exercises.
MuTeX-Archive's Tail
**www.gmd.de/Mail/mutex-archive-
tail/0011.html** Music typesetting theory.
Note Chaser **www.soundidea.co.uk** Music
transcription assistant; transcribe a CD track; for
the learning musician to the professional
transcriber.
Paul Renard's Music Dynamics
www.sightreading.com Sight-Reading
software.
Perfect Pitch on the Internet **www.provide.net/
~bfield/abs_pitch.html** Absolute pitch and
how it is used in music.

*Practical Music Theory-Teoría práctica de la
música* **www.teoria.com** or
home.coqui.net/alvira Web site dedicated to
the study of musical theory.
RhythmTutor
**members.aol.com/CopperSoft/rhythm.
html** Music instruction software for PC and
Macintosh; learn to sight-read musical rhythm
notation.
Richard Daniels Music **www.ncp.net/rdm**
Theory for the Serious Musician; seven books
on jazz music theory for intermediate to advanced
musicians.
Rocky Mountain Society for Music Theory
jan.ucc.nau.edu/~tas3/rmsmt.html Home
page; associated with the Society for Music
Theory; regional organization.
Sacred Harp Singing
**www.mcsr.olemiss.edu/~mudws/harp.
html** Information and resources; links.
Shape Note Singing **www.fasola.org** Home page;
information and links; print and audio examples.
SMT Server: Boethius
boethius.music.ucsb.edu/boethius.htm
Site for the Society for Music Theory; music at
UC Santa Barbara; Music Theory Online Home
Page.
SMT-Committee on the Status of Women
www.wmich.edu/mus-theo/csw.html
Society for Music Theory's Committee on the
Status of Women Web pages.
Solfege **solfege.n3.net** or
sourceforge.net/project/?group_id=1465
Ear-training software for Linux; requires *Gnome.*
Solomon's Music Theory & Composition Resources
www.azstarnet.com/~solo Resources for
composers; music theory; researchers of music;
sound files; analysis; composers and
compositions; resources in Musicology, Music
Theory, Music Instruction, Music research,
notation, recordings, and more.
Teoria **www.teoria.com/tour/program.htm**
Music theory and ear-training skills; Windows.
Texas Institute of Theory
ccwf.cc.utexas.edu/~bogo/tit/home.html
Recognized as one of the premier institutions in
the world devoted to music theory.
The Big Site of Music Notation and Engraving
**www.ColoradoCollege.edu/Dept/MU/
musicpress/engraving.html** Engraving
conventions; related links; important
bibliography.
The Chart Guy **www.thechartguy.com**
Professional chord charts and lead sheets.
The Harmonic Metronome
www.wholarts.com/music/hm Produces
scales and arpeggios, perfectly tuned and perfectly
timed.

The Oxymoron Humor Archive
  www.paul.erton.ox.ac.uk/music
  Humorous musical definitions.
The Perfect Pitch-Ear Training Super Course
  www.eartraining.com Ear-training
  instruction series for musicians of all
  instruments; on cassette or CD.
The Society for Music Theory
  boethius.music.ucsb.edu/
  smt-list/smthome.html Established in 1977
  to promote music theory as both a scholarly and
  a pedagogical discipline; about 750 members
  from around the world; about 300 institutions
  subscribe to the semiannual journal *Music
  Theory Spectrum*.
The Teacher's Apprentice for Music Theory
  www.creativeware.com/ta.htm Simplifies
  administrative tasks for the teacher; testing and
  learning tool.
THEMA **www.uga.edu/~thema** THEMA stands
  for (Music) Theory of the Middle Ages; hypertext
  transcriptions of eighteen manuscript copies of
  fourteen Latin theoretical treatises on music
  theory.
Theory **www.united-**
  trackers.org/resources/theory/index.htm
  Serial composition technique; evolved in the
  twentieth century as the final stage of tonality.
Theory of Music Examination Syllabus
  www.abrsm.ac.uk/theory.html Theory of
  Music Examination Syllabuses, Grades 1 - 8;
  The Associated Board of the Royal Schools of
  Music; setting the standards in music
  examination.
Theory Time **www.theorytime.com**
  Comprehensive music theory course; believes
  that an exceptional music theory course is
  essential for any music student.
Three Rivers **www.threeriversmusic.com**
  Music accessories; music stands.
Tonality Systems **www.xs4all.nl/~psto**
  Developer of *Symbolic Composer*.
TrackStar: Beginning Music Theory
  www.scrtec.org/track/tracks/s09756.
  html Lesson created ideally for the youngest of
  beginners.
UCLA Department of Music
  www.music.ucla.edu Home page;
  information is available on admissions, courses,
  faculty, and facilities.
University Press of New England-Popular Music in
  Theory **www.dartmouth.edu/acad-**
  inst/upne/s9719a.html Contribution to the
  debates that are central to popular music studies.
Worldwide Internet Music Resources: Music
  Theory **www.music.indiana.edu/**

music_resources/mtheory.html William
and Gayle Cook Music Library; Indiana
University School of Music.
Yahoo! Entertainment:Music:Theory
  www.yahoo.com/Entertainment/Music/
  Theory Music theory site.

Musical E-Greetings and Singing Telegrams

1 2 All 4 You Electronic Postcards
  12all4you.com/index.html Over fifty free
  card categories and options including animation,
  music, poetry, java, and send later.
1001 Postcards **www.postcards.org** Large
  collection of free virtual postcards; cartoons;
  special occasions; scenic; comedy.
All-Yours Free Christmas Greeting Cards
  www.all-
  yours.net/postcard/pictures/xmas.html
  Free season's greetings; animated holiday
  postcard with music and special effects.
American Greetings
  www.americangreetings.com Personalized
  greeting cards, printed and electronic.
Animated Christmas Holiday Greetings
  paledreams.virtualave.net/FunPages/
  christmas-2 Santa and his friends groove on.
Animated Greeting Cards with Music
  members.aol.com/media27/holiday.htm
  Christmas holiday cards with animation and
  music.
Applemania Singing Telegrams and Balloons
  www.tutuguy.com Singing telegrams in
  Seattle; for parties, birthdays, corporate events,
  Valentine's day, any occasion.
Blue Mountain **www.bluemountain.com** Variety
  of E-greetings with music.
CanWebCards **www.canwebcards.com**
  Personalized musical electronic greeting cards by
  E-mail.
Care-mail Hanukkah Cards **www.care-**
  mail.com/send/cathanukkah1.html Free
  animated and musical greetings that help save
  wildlife.
Egreetings.com **www.egreetings.com** Hosts free
  E-cards.
Hallmark **www.hallmark.com** Electronic
  greetings for E-mail friends.
Happy Birthday to You
  www.happybirthdaytoyou.com Singing
  birthday cards; personalized, professionally
  recorded versions; all styles.
International Singing Telegrams
  www.intsing.qpg.com Singing telegrams,
  balloon delivery, gift baskets, worldwide flower
  delivery and more.

P.S. I Love You!
> **www.personal-ads-network.com/PersonalSongs.shtml**
> Personalized songs on CD or cassette.

Romantic Cards
> **members.aol.com/media27/love.htm**
> Free E-mail greeting cards with animation and music; all occasions.

Santa Claus Online **www.santaclausonline.com**
> E-mail a letter to Santa Claus and he will respond personally; fun and games; holiday music; free clip art; free Christmas cards; toys and much more; listen to Santa read *Twas the Night before Christmas.*

Shopping Center
> **shop001.hypermart.net/cards.htm** Online personalized, animated, musical greeting cards; electronic cards; E-mail greetings.

Singing Phonegrams
> **www.singingphonegrams.com** Sent anywhere in the world with ten-second recorded greeting included.

Singing Telegrams Inc.
> **www.singingtelegrams.com.au** Delivering gifts, poems, balloons, and breakfasts; Sydney, Australia.

Singing Valentines
> **www.singingvalentines.com** Saying "I love you" with a song; available in all regions.

Uncle Debi's Holidays
> **home.wnm.net/~debi/holidays.htm** Links to all holidays; message mates; holiday clip art; virtual greeting cards; historical and holiday calendar; holiday histories.

Musical Theatre

Aisle Say
> **www.escape.com/~theanet/AisleSay.html** Online theatre magazine.

American Association of Community Theater
> **www.aact.org** Community theater.

American Musical Theatre **www.amtsj.org**
> Home page.

Applause Tickets **www.applause-tickets.com**
> Theatre and entertainment service; Broadway, Off Broadway, concert and ballet tickets; sightseeing and more in NYC.

Arts and Entertainment at Musical Theatre West
> **www.musical.org** News and information; southern California's oldest professional musical theatre companies; current and past productions; tickets; auditions.

Broadway Theatre **www.broadwaytheater.com**
> Theater industry.

Circle in the Square Theatre School
> **www.circlesquare.org** Professional acting and musical theatre training at the heart of Broadway.

Classic Movie and Musical Theatre Ring
> **www.geocities.com/Broadway/Stage/4020/ring.html** Submit site.

Concert Tickets
> **www.musicalchairstickets.com** Ticket agency specializing in all types of tickets including concert tickets, theatre tickets.

Eldridge Plays and Musicals **www.histage.com**
> Theatre plays and musicals for all occasions; full-length plays; one-act plays; melodramas; holiday themes; children's and full-length musicals; skits and theater collections.

Gilbert and Sullivan Archive
> **www.idbsu.edu/gas/GaS.html** Tribute to the composers.

Goodspeed Musicals: Goodspeed Library of Musical Theatre
> **www.goodspeed.org/library/library.htm** One of the most extensive musical theatre research facilities in the U.S.

Invisible Sound Design
> **invisible.freeservers.com** Custom software solutions for the entertainment industry; sound design services for musical theatre.

Jill Hobgood's Musical Sites List
> **www.saintmarys.edu/~jhobgood/Jill/theatre.html** Theatricopia; collection of musicals sites; general theatre.

London Theatre Guide
> **www.londontheatre.co.uk** Guide.

LTI Music Theatre Education
> **www.takeiteasy.org** Home page.

Music Theater International
> **www.mtishows.com** Official Web site.

Music Theatre of Southern California
> **www.musictheatre.org** Broadway at its best.

Musical Stages Online
> **www.musicalstages.co.uk** Guide to musical theatre.

Musical Theatre
> **www.arts.state.tx.us/tca/catalogs/tourcat/musictheatre** Company and artist roster; musical theatre.

Musical Theatre in Europe
> **www.eur.com/theatre** Almanac; pictures; singers; repertoire; links for 120+ theatres; search by artist or by work title; database includes 500+ titles and 5,000+ singers.

Musical Theatre Lovers United Home Page
> **www.enchanting.com/mtlu.htm** Club for Broadway and Hollywood musical buffs.

Musical Theatre Performers Web Ring
> **www.geocities.com/Broadway/3751/Webring.htm** Has 150 members; ranked #7 out of the top one hundred Web rings in the Arts.

Musical Youth Artists Repertory Theatre
www.myart.org Musical theater for children youth artists performers; repertory theater offers live stage performances using kids and young people in legitimate Broadway plays.

Musical, Opera, Theatre, & Music Station
www.insurance-finance.com/musical.htm Links regarding musicals, opera, ballet, and theatres; links to top twenty Broadway official and unofficial sites; performing arts links.

Musicals.Net **www.musicals.net** Index to many Broadway musicals; song lists; synopses; lyrics; discussion forums.

Next! Auditioning for the Musical Theatre
www.bway.net/~alper/NextHome.html Home page; what actor's resume should look like.

On Broadway WWW Information Page
artsnet.heinz.cmu.edu/OnBroadway Web site.

Performing & Writing Musical Theatre-Suite101.com
www.suite101.com/welcome.cfm/musical_theatre Articles; links; discussions.

Playbill Online **www.playbill.com** Source of theatre information; published by the same company that has printed *Playbill Magazine* on Broadway for 114 years; international theater news.

Selected Sources for Musical Theatre and Film Music **library.nevada.edu/music/rsrce/theatre.html** Home page.

Stage Directions **www.stage-directions.com** Theater industry.

Stage Kids: Scripts for School Musicals
www.stagekids.com/why.html Educational and entertaining scripts for school musicals; original plays for youth theatre shows; teacher's study guides and theater performance kits.

Starbound
www.geocities.com/Broadway/4131 Singing, dancing, and acting tips; sheet music and monologue references.

The Circus, Theatre, and Music Hall Families Page
www.users.globalnet.co.uk/~paulln/circus.htm Research resources for genealogy of circus, theatre, musical hall, and similar families.

The Definitive Musical Theatre Web Site
www.geocities.com/musicaltheatreuk Gateway to West End and Broadway musicals on the Internet.

The Lion King WWW Archive: The Broadway Musical **www.lionking.org/musical** Brief overview of the Broadway musical; reviews; current Broadway cast list; RealVideo & WAV files.

The Musical Theatre Database
www.mtdbase.com Database of American musical theatre shows, people, and songs.

The National Alliance for Musical Theatre's Web Site
www.bway.net/namt Service organization for professional theatre, light opera, and opera companies.

The Really Useful Company Presents Andrew Lloyd Webber **www.reallyuseful.com** Site devoted to promoting the musicals and other productions created by Sir Andrew Lloyd Webber.

The Sofa **www.thesofa.com** Theater industry.

Theater Express **www.theater-express.com** Theater industry.

Theatre Central **www.playbill.com/cgi-bin/plb/central?cmd=start** Theater information.

Theatre Development Fund **www.tdf.org** Nonprofit theater organization.

Theatre Net **www.theatrenet.co.uk** Theater industry.

Theatre.com **www.buybroadway.com** Web site for Broadway theater; official theatre information for the majority of Broadway shows.

University Musical Society **www.ums.org** Home page.

Whatsonstage.com **www.whatsonstage.com** UK guide to theatre, classical music, opera, and dance productions; news; seating plans; online shop.

Young People's Teen Musical Theatre Company
www.sinasohn.com/yptmtc Provides San Francisco Youth with an opportunity to receive an introduction to the world of musical theatre.

Networking—Newsgroups— Mailing Lists—Chat— Career Information— Indie Music Promotion

1212.com-Internet Music Production Guide
www.1212.com Search Engine for music sites dedicated to professional musicians, singers, recording studios, sound engineer, and composers around the world.

20hz.com **www.20hz.com** Web clearinghouse for independent record stores.

3d Industry Contacts
www.3dartist.com/3dah/contacts.htm Two-page list of hundreds of software and model/texture publishers and distributors, hardware manufacturers, and book and video publishers.

40below **40below.cjb.net** Band promotion; news; tablature; interviews.

411 Music **www.411-music.com** Stringed instruments; search for artists and bands concert schedules; DJ services; duplicating; music business bookstore.

A&R Bandit **www.wightweb.demon.co.uk/bandit** A&R services for a fee.

A&R Connection **musiccontacts.com** Get in touch with A&R reps, music producers, and record labels.

A&R Online **www.aandronline.com** Connect with A&R reps.

A&R Registry **www.musicregistry.com** A&R Web site.

Acid Planet **www.acidplanet.com** For users of Sonic Foundry's *Acid* software; self-publish music online.

AFIM (Association for Independent Music) **www.afim.org** Information; resources; links; membership; formerly NAIRD.

Agent **www.forteinc.com/getfa.htm** Newsgroup guide.

AIMusic **www.aimusic.org** Advancing independent music.

Allindie.com **www.allindie.com** Indie artists and labels.

Almost Cool **www.almostcool.org** UK indie music reviewer.

America's Job Bank **www.ajb.dni.us** Job listings by category and state.

AMP3.com **www.amp3.com** Indie music company; information and guides; hundreds of free files in all musical genres; list of MP3s by independent artists; links to software downloads and music industry news; MP3 site for independent artists; artists are paid for MP3 downloads; upload music.

Ampcast **www.ampcast.com** Highest royalty payment to artists who upload their music on the Internet; introduces new musicians and bands; downloadable MP3s; search the cross-referenced musical archives.

Amplified Amp University **www.amplifiedpromo.com/ampu.html** Indie music resource.

Applause Music Production and Performance Careers **www.cnvi.com/applause** Tips, tricks, and secrets for a show business, performance, or production career; links.

Ariel Publicity **www.arielpublicity.com** Publicity at the grassroots level.

Artist Development **www.artistdevelopment.com** Duplication; design services; promotion.

Artist Direct **www.artistdirect.com** Artist Web sites; links; search site; superstore; music downloads; music community.

Artist Forum **www.artistforum.com** Free Web sites; sell CDs.

Artist Launch **www.artistlaunch.com** Sell indie music; all styles.

Artistpro.Com **www.artistpro.com** Online community offering free education, training, and information for entire spectrum of audio recording and music production.

Association of Independent Music **www.musicindie.com** Find a manager.

Astrojams **www.astrojams.com** Bands supporting free music on the Internet; digital music technology news.

Audio Grab **www.audiograb.com** Independent music by genre; packaged players; rippers; encoders for downloading; creating MP3 files; news.

Audio Highway **www.audiohighway.com** Online indie music distribution venue.

Azevo **www.azevo.com** Promotion and distribution on the Internet.

AZRocks **www.azrocks.com** Indie music company.

B & H **www.bhphotovideo.com** Photo; video; pro-audio.

Band Name **www.bandname.com** Indie music company.

Band O Matic **www.joescafe.com/bands** Create band names; humor.

Band Radio **www.bandradio.com** Indie music company; business sense; resource for labels, radio, and bands.

Band Store **www.bandstore.com** Indie music company.

Band Things **www.bandthings.com** Web site for bands.

Band Utopia **www.bandutopia.com** Indie music resources.

Band Wagon **www.bandwagon.com** Indie music company.

Band Wear **www.bandwear.com** Indie music company.

Bandit A&R Newsletter **www.banditnewsletter.com** New music companies seeking acts, songs, and masters every month; available in U.S. and worldwide editions; sample current issue; success stories file; introductory subscriptions.

Bands on the Web **www.bandsontheweb.com** Indie music company.

Bandweb.com **www.bandweb.com** Web site solutions for bands and musicians.

BBC World of Careers **www.bbc.co.uk/jobs/bbc_woc.shtml** The British Broadcasting Corporation; jobs; careers; training opportunities.

Become a Rock Star **www.tt.net/ultramodern/vinnie** A&R online.

Best Jobs in the USA **www.bestjobsusa.com** Job listings with detailed descriptions.

Big Mama Music **www.bigmamamusic.com** Indie music promotion.

Big Meteor Publishing **www.bigmeteor.com** Free exposure for music-related site or service; indie link exchange; indie resourceland; submit site.

BigBook **www.bigbook.com** Interactive Yellow Pages.

Bigfoot **www.bigfoot.com** E-mail lookup service.

BigYellow **www.bigyellow.com** Yellow Pages; E-mail directory.

Billboard Talent Net **www.billboardtalentnet.com** Online showcase for new and developing artists; all genres; membership fee.

Bip **wwwbipbipbip.com** Indie music for sale.

Blind Frog **www.blindfrog.com** New bands.

British Unsigned Rock Bands **www.burbs.org.uk** Free resource for bands; lists artists.

Broad Band Talent **www.broadbandtalent.com/ indexhome.html** Artist promotion service.

Business Plan Software **www.palo-alto.com/contacts/contacts.cfm** Business plan and marketing plan software; reviews; download demos; read samples.

Business@Home **www.gohome.com** For individuals who operate a business from their homes.

Buzz Emporium **www.buzzemporium.com** Home page.

Buzzine **www.buzzine.com/indibuzz** Indie submissions.

California Bands **www.cabands.com** Indie music company.

Canadian Independent Record Production Association **www.cirpa.ca** Canadian indies; resources; links.

Career Opportunities in Music **plato.acadiau.ca/courses/musi/callon/ careers.htm** While many music students seek careers in the fields of teaching or performance, many other possibilities may be considered.

CareerPath.com **www.careerpath.com** Classifieds from newspapers around the U.S.

Careers in Music **spider.georgetowncollege.edu/music/ Careers/careers.html** Professional areas representing a number of career possibilities in music.

Careers in Music **www.berklee.edu/html/ca_comp.html** Careers in contemporary writing and production; jazz composition; composition arranger.

Careers in Music **www.berklee.edu/html/ca_main.html**

Careers in performance; vocal/instrumental soloist; session musician; general business musician; performing artist; orchestra/group member; background vocalist; floor show band.

Careers in Music **www.berklee.edu/html/ca_mbm.html** Careers in professional music and music business/management; careers in music business advertising.

Careers in Music **www.berklee.edu/html/ca_mpe.html** Careers in music production and engineering producer; recording studio; film; TV; radio.

Careers in Music **www.berklee.edu/html/ca_mued.html** Careers in music education; choir director; a choir director provides direction and guidance to a vocal group or choir in a school, church, or elsewhere in the community.

Careers in Music **www.berklee.edu/html/ca_musy.html** Careers in music synthesis; computer music researcher; acoustician; composer/arranger; consultant; digital audio editor; educator; film/video; sound designer; interactive multimedia; specialist; jingle writer and more.

Careers in Music **www.berklee.edu/html/ca_muth.html** Music therapy careers.

Careers in Music **www.menc.org/industry/job/carbroch. html** MENC Careers in Music brochure; resource center; careers; jobs; employment; education.

Careers in Music **www.uwrf.edu/music/careers.html** Music major graduates; professional fields open; careers that recent graduates have entered or that are available.

Careers.org **www.careers.org** The Internet's Directory of Career Directories; access to over 7,500 links sorted by topic and region.

Casino Careers Online **www.casinocareers.com** Online resume database; resumes in open access or confidential format; employment and career opportunities.

CD Labs **www.cdlabs.com** CD duplication and distribution.

CD Limits **www.cdlimits.com** Showcasing indie and unsigned bands and artists.

CD Manufacturing **www.cdmanufacturing.com** CD and cassette manufacturing.

CD Reviewers **www.cdreviews.com** Reviews CDs.

CD Shakedown **www.cdshakedown.com** CD reviews old and new; indie music.

CD Sonic **www.cdsonic.com** CD-Audio and CD-ROM duplication.

CDFront **www.cdfront.com** Independent artist music Web site.

CDIY **www.cdiy.com** MP3 site; new talent; CDs.

Center of Web **www.centerofweb.com** Home page.

Change Music.com **www.changemusic.com** Free Web sites; "revolutionary" mission; CMJ associated; search for labels, artists, and music-related companies; industry tool for U.S. bands.

CMJ **www.cmj.com** *College Music Journal;* indie music culture; links.

CMN Online **www.cmnonline.org** Home page.

Coalition of Independent Music Stores **www.cimsmusic.com/index.html** Indie music stores.

College Board Online **www.collegeboard.org** Help with exams.

CollegeNET **www.collegenet.com** Search for colleges using different criteria.

Community Musician **www.CommunityMusician.com** Organization; newsletter.

Comp.music.misc **www.comp.music.misc** Newsgroup; questions about music and computers.

Computerworld Careers **www.computerworld.com/car** Computer jobs.

Cool Site of the Day **www.coolsiteoftheday.com** Cool picks are archived; links.

Cosmic Music Network **www.cosmic.cdnow.com** Online community for unsigned artists; free posting of digital music files; contact data; chat; major labels scout for new talent.

Creative Musicians Coalition **www.aimcmc.com** International organization representing independent artists and independent record labels; albums and videos available for purchase; ongoing dialogue with artists; showcases; reviews.

Cross Over **www.CrossOver.com** Non-commercial network for youth culture and music resources.

Cybergrrl.com **www.cybergrrl.com** Entertainment and informational site to celebrate and inspire women; technology, music, travel, and books; focus on profiles of women and women's personal essays; started by Aliza Sherman who wrote the book *Cybergrrl: A Woman's Guide to the World Wide Web.*

Deja.com **www.deja.com** Find music newsgroups online.

DejaNews **www.dejanews.com** Newsgroup search engine.

DemoRama **www.demorama.com** Reviews CDs.

Dmusic.com **www.dmusic.com** Online indie distribution venue.

Do It Yourself Rock Star **www.doityourselfrockstar.com** Advice.

Duck Music **www.duckmusic.com** Musicians get online tools.

Earbuzz.com **www.earbuzz.com** Online indie store; 100 percent of profits to the artist.

Educational Finance Group **www.schoolfunds.com** How to get government education loans.

EGroups **www.egroups.com** Mail lists and discussion groups.

Entertainers Net **www.entertainersnet.com** Indie music company.

E-Press Kit **go.to/epresskit** Electronic press kits; simple, easy, and effective way to promote music.

Excite People and Chat: Music **www.excite.com/communities/ entertainment/music** Music; chat.

Faculty of Music-Careers for Music Graduates **www.unimelb.edu.au/HB/facs/MUSIC-S11740.html** Guide to courses; employment possibilities for music graduates.

Fat Cat Productions **www.fatcatprod.com** CD and DVD replication.

FemaleMusician.com **www.femalemusician.com** Music industry education for young women; indie music company.

Femina.com **www.femina.com** Searchable directory of exclusively sites for, by, and about women with a special section of sites for girls.

FezGuys.com **www.fezguys.com** Home page.

FinAid **www.finaid.org** How to borrow money for education.

Finding Fans and Selling CDs **www.discmakers.com/findingfans** How to write a press release and more.

Free International Musicians Connection **www.cpeq.com/~mplanet/muscon/ muscon.html** Free classified ads for musicians.

Free Music Classifieds **www.freemusicclassifieds.com** Home page.

Freeality Music Infomation **www.freeality.com** Home page.

Fresh Act **www.freshact.com** Career strategy.

Full Concept **www.fullconcept.com** Indie music Web site; artist promotion.

Garage Band **www.garageband.com** Indie music company; online community created by musicians for musicians.

GearSearch.com **www.gearsearch.com** New, used, or vintage gear; search by state, instrument, or country; free catalogs available from many of the companies represented.

Get Indie **www.getindie.com** Indie band distribution.

Getmusic.com **www.getmusic.com** Home page.

GetSigned.com **www.getsigned.com** Music biz advice from leading experts in the industry; indie tools; artist interviews; books; tour booking; interviews; home recording tips; gear reviews; music law; legal issues; press kits; management tips; playing live; promotion.

Girlmedia.com **www.girlmedia.com** To help female musicians and girl bands of all styles gain recognition; interviews; contests; live radio broadcast; submissions from new musicians.

Girlmusician.com **www.girlmusician.com** Designed with the female singer/songwriter in mind; emphasis on the independent recording artist.

Global Music **www.globalmusic.com** Home page.

Globalb2b.com **www.globalb2b.com** For the music industry; concentrates on effective communication services to better facilitate music-related business.

Go Music Message Boards **boards.go.com/cgi/entertainment/ request.dll?LIST&room= Music&topics=1** Chat; music.

GoGirlsMusic.com **www.gogirlsmusic.com/gogirls/index. html** Indie music; information on women-fronted and all-girl bands; all genres; music festivals.

Good Noise **www.goodnoise.com** Online indie music distribution venue.

GuitarGirls.com **www.guitargirls.com** Resource and support site for female artists who write, sing, and play guitar; features MIDI, MP3, and Real Audio files; GuitarGirls contest which showcases and promotes independent female talent.

Head Space **www.head- space.com/iworld/supersonic/lists** Mailing lists related to British music business.

Heavy Metal Bands **www.heavymetalbands.com** Indie music company.

Honky Tonkin **www.HonkyTonkin.com** No charge to be added to online site; catalog of titles goes out worldwide to wholesale and retail account base; pay per transaction; no returns; no contracts.

How to Survive as an Independent Band **technet.gtcc.cc.nc.us/pages/students/ parkerj/index.htm** Advice on topics for indie musicians.

Hungry Bands **www.hungrybands.com** Indie music company; taking submissions.

I Seek You (ICQ) **www.icq.com** or **www.icq.com/networks/Music** Chat in real time; free program download.

IChat **www.ichat.com** Software for customized chat rooms.

ICN Music Contacts **www.icn.co.uk/music.html** Aims to provide access to the music industry for the individual or small company; music contact categories; A & R contacts; CD manufacturers.

Immedia.com **www.immedia.com.au/books** Music business books catalogue; titles dealing with recording, publishing, deals, touring, legalities, business realities, making CDs, setting up a label, songwriting, publishing, performance, and production information relating to a career in the music industry.

Impact Entertainment Group **www.impactentertainmentgrp.com** Indie music company.

Incredible Useful Site of the Day **www.zdnet.com/yil/content/depts/ useful/useful.html** Useful Web sites compiled by Yahoo.

Independent Artists' Services **www.idiom.com/~upend/ias/index.html** Submit URL for a link; plan a tour; links to record labels; online radio stations; list shows on concert calendar.

Independent Bands **www.independentbands.com** Indie band listings.

Independent Distribution Network **www.idnmusic.com/index.html** Global indie network; CD catalog.

Independent Music Portal **inde4u.com** Independent and unsigned artists.

Indie Atlas **www.indieatlas.com** Indie music Web site.

Indie Band Search **www.indiebandsearch.com** Run by ModMusic, Long Island City, NY; national contest giving independent musicians, artists, songwriters, and bands a chance to be heard by entertainment professionals and compete for prizes; music of all genres will be accepted.

Indie Biz **www.indiebiz.com** Indie music Web site; band promotion.

Indie CD Shop **www.indiecdshop.com** Indie CDs.

Indie Centre **www.indiecentre.com** or **www.csd.net/~muji/indiecenre.html** Independent label information; creating a label; recording; manufacturing; sales; distribution; promotion; advertising; booking.

Indie Corner **www.IndieCorner.com** Seven-part series on *The Seven Habits of Highly Successful Musicians.*

Indie Group **www.indiegroup.com** Indie music company.

Indie Music Forum **www.IndieMusicForum.com** Annual conferences held around the United States for independent artists and musicians; workshops; seminars.

Indie Music **www.indymusic.com** Submit music.

Indie Music Resources **kathoderay.org/music** Radio promotion company; compilation CDs of new artists; co-op marketing; bands; labels; Webzines; articles; links.

Indie Pool **www.indiepool.com** Indie music company.

Indie Pro **www.indiepro.com** Indie music company.

Indie Space **www.indiespace.com** Indie music company.

Indie Tracker Magazine **www.indietrackermagazine.com** Indie music company.

Indie Unite **www.indieunite.com** Indie music site.

Indie World—The Supersonic Guide **www.headspace.org/iworld/supersonic** Search for indies.

IndieFront **charlemagne.uwaterloo.ca** Information on independent bands; articles; networking.

IndieGate **www.indiegate.com** Indie music Web site.

IndieGirl **www.indiegrrl.com** Forum for information, networking, and conversation in the realm of independent music from a female perspective; welcomes all female musicians, singers, songwriters, and others in indie music; men supportive of women in music are welcome to join.

IndieGroup **www.indiegroup.com** Artist directory.

Indie-Music.com **www.indie-music.com** Musician's resources; links; Internet primer; bands; education; labels; radio; reviews; studios; tour guide; venues; add URL; mailing list; CDs; mailing list; E-mail; ads; shop; journal; tips; local scenes.

IndieMuzic.com **www.indiemuzic.com** Community for indie musicians.

IndiePromo.com **IndiePromo.com** Information for independent musicians; resources; links; networking; E-zines; Internet radio; promotion; Web site design; tutorials; reviews; publications.

Indierec.com **www.indierec.com** Indie music company.

IndieWeb **www.indieweb.com** Independent labels and bands; D.I.Y. section; links.

IndiSonic **www.indisonic.com** Indie music site.

Infraworks.com **www.infraworks.com** Home page.

International Alliance for Women in Music **music.acu.edu/www/iawm/home.html** Home page.

International Managers Forum **www.imf-uk.org** Find a manager.

Internet @ddress.finder **www.iaf.net** Look up E-mail addresses.

Internet FAQ Consortium **www.faqs.org** Comprehensive lists of newsgroups.

Internet Relay Chat **www.ircle.com** (Macintosh) or **www.mirc.com** (Windows); IRC channels.

IRC Channels **www.liszt.com/chat** Find IRC channels for music sites.

Isyndicate.com **www.isyndicate.com** Home page.

IUMA **www.iuma.com** Independent Underground Music Archive; artists, independent bands, local talent Web pages; publishing and promotion; free MP3 and RealPlayer music track downloads for listening.

J-Bird Records **www.j-birdrecords.com** Indie artists downloads; many genres; hear samples; artists news.

Jesus Freak **www.jesusfreak.com** Indie music company.

Jimmy and Doug's Farm Club **farmclub.com** Digital jukebox; video vault; musician directory; sourcebook; snippets; free downloads; featured artists; listening room; artist pages; live Web broadcast; classifieds; chat; message board.

JobStar-Specific Career Information **www.jobsmart.org/tools/career/spec-car.htm** Public library sponsored guide to information for the job search; 1,000 job hotlines; calendar of job and career events; career centers; libraries and more.

Kathode Ray Music **www.kathoderaymusic.com** Indie music resources; promotion.

KindWeb.com **www.kindweb.com** Music resources; band links.

Kspace Music Kiosk **kspace.com/KM/music.sys/musiclist.html** Musicians; professional services and related resources; each musician supplies RealAudio samples; secure online ordering.

Kweevak.com **www.kweevak.com** Music promotion services; classic rock MP3 downloads.

LA Live **www.lalive.com** LA alternative rock.

La Costa Music Business Consultants
www.lacostamusic.com Music business advice; songwriting; publishing; artist management; publicity; production; record promotion.

LA Music Awards **www.lamusicawards.com** LA area awards.

LAMN (Los Angeles Music Network) **www.lamn.com** Official Web site.

List of Music Mailing Lists **http:www.shadow.net/~mwaas/lomml. html** International Music Mailing Lists (IMML) covers all musical genres; music composition; instruments; electronic instruments.

Listen to This **www.listentothis.com** Home page.

ListServ **scout.cs.wisc.edu** Mailing lists and discussion groups.

Liszt **www.liszt.com** or **www.liszt.com/select/Music** Mail lists and discussion groups; comprehensive lists of newsgroups.

Liszt Newsgroups UK Music **www.liszt.com/news/uk/music** List of newsgroups divided by musical genre.

Local Music **www.localmusic.com** Regional music scene information.

Local Songs **www.localsongs.com** Music and songs.

Local Sound **www.localsound.com** Indie music company.

Loud Tunes **www.loudtunes.com** Home page.

LPRecords.com **www.LPrecords.com** Internet hosting service.

Master Merchant Systems **www.mmscom.net** Point of Sale; Barcoding.

Media Omaha **www.mediaomaha.com** CD duplication.

Meet the Musicians **www.meetthemusicians.com** Home page.

Meet New Players **www.meetnewplayers.com** Indie music company.

Metro-World **www.metro-world.com** Indie music company.

Midi.net **www.midi.net/ns/index.html** Music-related resources; free listings; directories; list URL.

Miow **www.miow.com** MP3s; industry tips; chat; links; London based.

Modern Postcard **www.modernpostcard.com** Postcard printing.

Monster.com **www.monsterboard.com** Search jobs; resume builder.

MP3 Critic **www.mp3critic.com** Reviews new music from indie artists; links.

MP3 Place **www.mp3place.net** Online indie music distribution venue.

MP3 Vault **www.mp3vault.com** Online distribution.

Mr. Producer **www.mrproducer.com** Music industry; music-related business.

MultiAudio.net **www.multiaudio.net** MP3 and VQF song files; album libraries; search engines; news; top 20 playlists; tools; utilities.

Musebid.com **www.musebid.com** Auction Web site.

Musebiz.com **www.musebiz.com** Music business education.

Music and Audio Connection **www.musicandaudio.com** Discussion forums; classified ads; links; music books.

Music Bargain **www.musicbargain.com** Free classified music-related ads.

Music Biz Academy **www.musicbizacademy.com** Resources and books for indie musicians.

Music Biz Guide **home.earthlink.net/~lamusic** Information on the music industry.

Music Builder **www.MusicBuilder.com** Upload music; statistics.

Music Business Software **www.musicbusinessstore.com** Professional Music Business Contracts: 100 music industry contracts; Record Company in a Box: complete record company management software; Tour Manager: manage gigs and complete tours, financial reports, and itineraries; Macintosh; Windows.

Music Careers with Robert Rosenblatt, Esq. **www.soloperformer.com/careers** Music business and legal issues about songwriting, managers, agents, contracts, and performing.

Music Connection **www.musicconnection.com** Magazine for musicians; music marketplace; free classifieds; find pro players; exclusive directories; detailed industry reference guide in every issue.

Music Contact International **www.Music-Contact.com** Home page.

Music Contacts **www.MusicContacts.com** Get music into the hands of top music producers and A&R reps; launch a successful music career as a recording artist or songwriter.

Music Countdown **www.netmusiccountdown.com** Home page.

Music Dish **www.musicdish.com** Indie music resource; informative music industry E-newsletter; links; career tips; OMI (Online Music Industry Showcase) Award; Music Industry Survey.

Music Distribution **www.musicdistribution.com** Home page.

Music Dude **www.musicdude.com** Local music from everywhere; indie music.

Music Equipment Classifieds
www.musicequipment.com/T Free listings of equipment and instruments for sale to musicians; including guitars, keyboards, strings, and other instruments.

Music Exchange **www.musicexchange.net** Free artist listings in directory; articles; resource center.

Music for a Song **www.musicforasong.com** Home page.

Music for People **www.MusicForPeople.org** Home page.

Music Global Network **www.musicglobalnetwork.com** Digital music news; links to MP3 software and hardware; downloads.

Music in the Parks **www.musicintheparks.com** Home page.

Music Industry Career Center **www.music-careers.com** Sponsored by Sweetwater Sound; music industry companies list position openings; potential employees post resumes; free service.

Music Island **www.musicisland.com/home.htm** Contact information for record labels, legal resources, promoters, booking agents, radio stations, publishers, places to play, and more.

Music Map **www.musicmap.com** Home page.

Music Media **www.music-media.co.uk** UK bands; networking; players needed.

Music Media Interactive **www.cazmedia.com/mmi/mmimain.shtml** Main page; indie submissions.

Music Network USA **www.mnusa.com** Resources for musicians and bands; musicians seeking bands; bands seeking musicians; recording artists; songwriters; music publishers; recording studios; talent agencies; producers and more.

Music Newsgroups and Listservs **www.music.fsu.edu/news.html** Home page.

Music Players Network **www.musicplayersnetwork.com** Web site for musicians.

Music Pro Insurance **www.musicproinsurance.com** Insurance for the musician; instruments; equipment; vehicle; life.

Music Professionals **www.rocketentertainment.com/musicpro** Music contacts for music professionals; click on a yellow link to access companies; submit company before making a record.

Music Room **www.musicroom.com** To launch online catalogue.

Music Spotlight **www.musicspotlight.com** Promote music and bands on the Internet.

Music Unsigned **www.musicunsigned.com** Global launch of Songlocation; set to revolutionize the way writers and artists work.

Music Vision **www.musicvision.com** Provides publishers with technology solutions to enhance Web sites; provides services to major artists; matches Web sites with advertisers; media technologies; eleven channels.

Music Wizard **www.music-wizard.com** Music Collection Manager for Windows; manage, edit, and sort records; print professional CD covers with user defined background pictures.

Music123.com **www.music123.com** Home page.

Music2u **music2u.com** Industry online promotion services; Web design.

Musicdex.net **www.musicdex.net** Offers an extensive list of bands with WAV files; fan pages with multimedia files; MP3 and software resources; broadcast streams.

Musician Best Unsigned Band Contest **www.musicianmag.com/bub** Open to unsigned bands of all genres; sponsored by *Musician Magazine.*

Musician **www.musician.com** Resources for musicians; find a musician; musician database; gear support; free downloads.

Musician Review **www.musicianreview.com** Read and write reviews of music gear; discuss music topics; buy or sell gear; current music scene.

Musician's Phone Book **www.musiciansphonebook.com** Thousands of listings in over sixty categories; recording studios; record companies; management; purchasing; distribution; FAQ; links.

Musicians Atlas **www.musiciansatlas.com** Resource for musicians including clubs, venues, and more.

Musicians Contact Service **www.musicianscontact.com** Contact other musicians.

Musicians Hotline **www.musicianshotline.com** Networking.

Musicians Institute **www.mi.edu** Career development center for musicians located in Hollywood, CA; classes; workshops; private lessons; 500-seat concert hall.

Musicians National Referral **www.musicianreferral.com/mnr** Large referral service for pro musicians and bands; lifetime memberships available.

Musicians Online **www.musiciansonline.com** Community of musicians, recording professionals, musical instrument and equipment manufacturers, and record company A&R representatives; artist's showcases; musicians resource and publicity engine; forum for musicians to publicize themselves and their work.

Musicianswalk
www.musicianswalk.com/page2.html
Acoustic news; lessons; resources.

Musicians Web **www.musiciansWeb.net**
Resource links; showcase material.

MusiciansJunction.com
www.musiciansjunction.com/junction/tax/contact.html Meet musicians.

MusiciansPage.com **www.musicianspage.com**
Home page; resources.

Musicplayer.com **www.musicplayer.com**
Resources; networking opportunities; lessons; forums; biz; reviews.

Musicpromotion.net **musicpromotion.net**
Resources for independent musicians; publications; tutorials; articles; links; newsletter; Web site design; online ordering.

Music's New Artist Review
www.newartistreview.com Indie artists and bands; new CDs; write-ups on music and gigs.

Musinc **www.ilist.net/musinc** Music industry insider mailing list.

Mutual Music **www.mutual-music.com** Free interactive music industry resource directory; supportive services.

National Academy of Recording Arts and Sciences (NARAS) **www.grammy.com** Organization of recording professionals; presents the Grammy Awards; organizes educational programs; member services and benefits; forum; MusiCares; LARAS; Master Track; Media Center; features; daily news; Grammy winners; Grammy store; Grammy Foundation; chapter updates.

National Band Register **www.bandreg.com**
Database of names and band information; find out if a band name is in use; if not, register it to prevent other bands from using it; free; legal advice for bands; information about CDs by unsigned bands; site's magazine, *GIG*, features music industry news and reviews of unsigned bands.

Neonflame Store/Kevan Patten
www.neonflame.com/musicbiz Music business software; contracts.

Net Press Agent **www.netpressagent.com**
Electronic distribution of music over the Internet; media releases; copyright protection, directory listings and more.

NetCentral **www.netcentral.net** Music; books; contests; free chat services and more.

NetJobs **www.netjobs.com** Employment guide for Canada and America; technology positions.

New-List **www.new-list.com** Mail lists and discussion groups.

Newsgroups
www.iqsoft.com/Links/NEWSGRPS.htm Newsgroups in film and video production; music-related groups; radio; computers and animation.

Newswatcher **www.best.com/~smfr/mtnw**
Newsgroup guide.

NewTechMusic **www.newtechmusic.com**
Online music distribution company; Web sites.

Next Big Star **www.nextbigstar.com** Career strategy.

NME **www.nme.com** Pop music magazine; A&R section for demos.

NuSounds **www.nusounds.com** MP3s; photos; bios; song descriptions; contact info.

Nu-Tyme Entertainment
www.angelfire.com/biz/nutyme/index.html All area's of the business from A-Z.

Okay Music **www.okaymusic.com** Free listing of over 16,000 contacts in the music industry.

Omnibus **www.rock.n.roll.com/Omnibus**
Information on local music scenes; reviews; interviews.

OneList **www.onelist.com** Mail lists and discussion groups.

Outer Sound **www.outersound.com** Over 3,000 pages of material for those in the independent music world; music magazine; reference source; 100 articles offering practical advice to independent musicians and industry personnel; online community for the independent music world; geared to musicians, fans, and the industry.

Overseas Jobs Express **www.overseasjobs.com**
International job openings and links.

Parasol **www.cu-online.com/~parasol** Online independent music distributor; new and used; independent releases.

Peoplesound **www.peoplesound.com** A&R involvement for emerging bands.

Petersons.com **www.petersons.com** Online college and career guides.

Planet People Music
www.planetpeoplemusic.com Home page.

PlanetCD **www.PlanetCD.com** Online store for independent music; all genres; audio samples; free newsletter; indie distribution; featured artists.

PlanetJam **www.planetjam.com** Community of new music from emerging artists.

PlayHear.com **www.playhear.com** Indie submissions.

Pop Star Net **www.popstar.net** Alternative; indie Web site.

Postcard Press **www.postcardpress.com**
Bizcards; postcards.

Primordial Shmooze
elbombo.shmooze.net/pwcasual Links to

music sites; band pages; E-zines; recording studios; record labels; radio stations.

Professional Musicians **www.promusic47.org** Radio promotion; recording studio; CD manufacturing; practice rooms; instrument insurance; job referral service; gig assistance; CD mastering.

Professional PR Distribution for Indies Mi2N **www1.internetwire.com/MI2n.htm** In collaboration with Internet Wire; offering new outlet specifically created to the needs of artists, labels, and indie music dot-coms; reaches over 5,000 music reviewers and more than 150,000 industry insiders and music fans; gets artists in front of people that write reviews, sign artists, and buy CDs.

Promote Yourself **www.promote yourself.com** Musician's guide to the Zen of hype.

Public Access Usenet Sites **dir.yahoo.com/Computers_and_Internet/ Internet/Usenet/Public_Access_Usenet_ Sites** Where to find public news servers.

Publicly Accessible Mailing Lists **www.neosoft.com/internet/paml** Mail lists and discussion groups.

Punk Bands **www.punkbands.com** Indie music company.

Rainbo Records and Cassettes **www.rainborecords.com** Custom CDs, cassettes, and vinyl.

Rainmaker Publicity **www.rainmakerpublicity.com** Indie music company.

Reach for the Sky **www.sky.co.uk/RFTS/index2.htm** Advice for teenagers.

REAL Talent Directories **www.angelfire.com/biz/RealPub** Publish and showcase talent, Web site, gig, etc.

Reel Tour **www.reel-tour.com** TV series dedicated to the promotion of independent musicians, bands, and solo artists.

RemarQ **www.remarq.com** Newsgroup search engine.

Remote Music **www.remotemusic.com** A&R online.

Revolution **www.riot.co.uk** Alternative; indie Web site.

Rock Band.com **www.rockband.com** Unsigned indie music.

Rocket Fuel Online **www.rocket-fuel.com** Alternative; indie Web site.

Rocket Network **www.rocketnetwork.com** RocketPower online collaboration system; log into a virtual studio and work on a piece together; supports MP3 and MIDI.

Rock-Web.com **www.rock-Web.com/rock- music.shtml** Search engine; music industry resource; musicians directory; industry contacts; reviews; free E-mail.

Search-It-All **www.search-it- all.com/peoplefinder.asp** Reverse search engine; provide a phone number, E-mail address, or street address.

Sell Your Music Online **www.sellyourmusiconline.com** Handbook listing indie vendor and distribution sites; reviews about eighty vendor/distributor sites, twenty Web-focused promotional companies, fifteen payment-processing services, and over fifty high-grade resource sites; all sites have been critically selected; updates handbook; comprehensive guide available to musicians who rely on the Web.

Shake It Up **www3.sympatico.ca/ cms.cas** Alternative; indie Web site.

Spannet **www.spannet.org** Resource for book- selling ideas and money-making strategies for independent presses and self-publishers.

Spin Street **www.spinstreet.com** Home page.

Stargig **www.stargig.com** A&R online.

StartTheMusic.Com **www.startthemusic.com/services/ services_labels.htm** For artists, studios, producers, managers, record labels, distributors, clubs, teachers, writers, composers, retail stores, entertainment lawyers, support crews, and creators of videos.

Stolen Instrument List **www.gspyo.com/stolen** Organized by instrument type and location; list missing equipment; browse other people's stolen gear.

Streamline Music **www.streamlinemusic.com** Online indie distribution network.

Studentreel.com **www.studentreel.com** Talent search.

Taco Truffles Media **www.tacotruffles.com** Indie music promotion by John Dawes, author of *The Complete Guide to Internet Promotion for Musicians, Artists, and Songwriters*; Web site design; resources; tutorials; links.

Takeout Music **www.takeoutmusic.com** Home page.

Talkway **www.talkway.com** Newsgroups.

Telephone Directories on the Web **www.teldir.com** Links to Yellow Pages, White Pages, business directories, E-mail address directories, and fax numbers throughout the world.

The 4-Track Site **www.inch.com/~jfount/4track.html** Indie music reviewer.

The All Music Network
www.geocities.com/Nashville/3150
Information; resources; links.

The Aria Web Site
www.globalthinking.com/aria Home
page.

The Berkeley List of Musical Mailing Lists
**server.berkeley.edu/~ayukawa/lomml.
html** Index of music-related mailing lists;
subscriptions.

The Buzz Factor **www.thebuzzfactor.com** Music
marketing tip sheet by Bob Baker; indie music
marketing resources; tips and tools to help indie
musicians market their music on a budget.

The Global Muse **www.theglobalmuse.com**
Reviews and interviews; network.

The Indie Contact Bible
www.indiecontactbible.com or
www.bigmeteor.com/icb Resources for
indie musicians; large international list organized
by genre and location; links; sell CDs; available
on disk; lists publications that review CDs and
radio stations that play indie music; all genres.

The Jukebox
www.thejukebox.org/songring.htm
Home page.

The Last Resort
www.verdis.co.uk/TLR/resort.htm
Alternative; indie Web site.

The Local Scene **www.thelocalscene.com**
Alternative; indie Web site.

The Muse **www.muse.ie** Alternative; indie Web
site.

The Music Dish Genome Project
musicdish.com/genome Over 1,750 music
sites listed in twenty different categories.

The Music Zone **www.themusiczone.com** Home
page.

The Musician's Assistant
www.musicianasist.com Information
packed site for musicians; links to sites on
touring, promotion, and recording;
manufacturing, pressing, and printing; record
labels; listing of books for musicians.

The Musician's Swapmeet
www.musicansswapmeet.com Guitars,
basses, amplifiers, musical instruments, and
supplies.

The National Centre for Popular Music
www.ncpm.co.uk Learn about the music
business.

The New 2000 Music Industry Directory CD-ROM
www.musodata.com The A&R Bible; offers
the performing or recording artist A&R contacts
within agency, management, publishing, and
recording companies in the U.S., UK and
Europe.

The Official Indie List
www.bloofga.org/il/IL_FAQ.html
Alternative; indie Web site.

The Orchard **www.theorchard.com** Major online
distributor for independent artist CDs; artists
Web pages; audio samples; track listings;
photos; links.

The Palace **www.thepalace.com** Virtual chat
site.

The Small Business Corner
**www.irs.gov/bus_info/sm_bus/
index.html** Information; resources.

The Texas Music Office
**link.tsl.state.tx.us/.www/tmo.dir/tmo.
html** Texas music industry; links; newsgroups;
contacts; books; articles.

The Tip Sheet **www.tipsheet.co.uk** Industry
magazine; audio clips.

The UK Indie Band Index
**www.ee.surrey.ac.uk/Personal/
S.Procter/UK-Indie/Links** Alternative;
indie Web site.

The Velvet Rope **www.velvetrope.com** Music
industry information.

The Virtual Music Vault-Artists Search
www.tvmv.com/labels_indie.html Music
industry and technology news; record labels;
search for indie artists.

The Wonderwall
www.beat.co.uk/wonderwall.html
Alternative; indie Web site.

Tile.Net **www.tile.net** Mail lists and discussion
groups; comprehensive lists of newsgroups.

Tim Sweeney & Associates **www.tsamusic.com**
Independent artist development company;
promotion; publicity; retail marketing;
distribution network; Internet promotion;
workshops; author of *Tim Sweeney's Guide to
Releasing Independent Records; The Living
Room Sessions; The Complete Guide to Internet
Promotion for Musicians, Artists, and
Songwriters; Tim Sweeney's Guide to
Successfully Playing Live; Tim Sweeney's
Guide to Succeeding at Music Conventions.*

Tonos **www.tonos.com** Music insider's network;
tips and insight into the publishing and
songwriting industry; Mentor; Insider;
Challenges.

Topica **www.topica.com** Mail lists and discussion
groups.

*Track Star Entertainment-Creative Careers in
Music* **www.creativecareersinmusic.com**
Information on music careers.

Tune Trade **www.TuneTrade.com** Online site of
The Musician's Trade Journal, a national non-
genre-specific publication designed to provide

information and resources to independent musicians and songwriters.

Twomp Pop **www.twomp.com/pop** Alternative; indie Web site.

U.S. News.com/edu **www.usnews.com/usnews/edu/home.htm** Find a college or community college; compare colleges; college personality quiz; parents guide.

Ultimate Band List (UBL) **www.ubl.com** Artist directory; band Web sites and CDs; resources; information; music industry-related links.

Unwrapped **www.unrapped.com** Online indie distribution venue.

USCA Music **www.usca.sc.edu/Music/Website/muscareers.html** Coursework in music; provides a firm foundation for the many music careers.

Used Gear by Mail **www.ugbm.com** More than 10,000 used musical instruments for sale; FAQ; browse inventory; request monthly catalog; sell and trade used equipment.

Usenet Info Center **metalab.unc.edu/usenet-i** Comprehensive lists of newsgroups.

Village Buzz **www.Village-Buzz.com** Indie music Web site.

Virtual Promote **www.virtualpromote.com** E-commerce marketing; Web site promotion.

Vivian Neou's List of Lists **catalog.com/vivian** Mail lists and discussion groups.

Webgrrls.com **www.webgrrls.com** Hub for nearly one hundred Web sites for Webgrrls chapters around the world; local chapters have gatherings where women meet face to face to talk about the Internet and new media.

WhoWhere? **www.whowhere.com** Track down people.

Women in Music **www.womeninmusic.com** Nonprofit membership organization dedicated to promoting the advancement and recognition of women in the music industry; mentoring program.

World Records **www.worldrecords.com** Music search engine; add URL; artists; broadcast mail; classifieds; free homepages; music news by the minute; music newsgroup server; video releases; A & R service; download brochure; mainstream artist domains; artist domains; audio companies; download sites and stores; homepages; indie resources; instrument related sites; music magazines and Webzines; music style domains; miscellaneous; record labels; recording studios; radio stations; shopping basket.

World Replication Group **www.worldreplication.com** CD replication;

fulfillment; graphics; packaging; video duplication; digital audiocassettes.

World Wide Bands **worldwidebands.com** Indie music company.

World Wired Productions **www.wwpro.com** Promotion and positive representation of artists, bands, labels, agencies, and management on every level.

WorldPages **www.worldpages.com** International phone book; all the phone books in the world combined into one linked site.

Worldwide Online Music Competition **www.hitsquad.com/smm/millenium** Over $10,000 in prizes with a first prize of over $5,000; professional software, hardware, music equipment, and sheet music that anyone can win.

Writers Net **www.writers.net** Resources for writers, editors, publishers, and agents.

Writers Online Workshops **www.writersonlineworkshops.com** Introductory, intermediate, and advanced workshops in a variety of genres; writing tips.

XFM **www.xfm.co.uk** Alternative; indie Web site.

Y2K Music **www.y2k-music.co.uk** Online indie music distribution venue.

Yahoo! Clubs **clubs.yahoo.com/music** Find music-related communities.

Yahoo! Digital **digital.broadcast.com/digital/audio** Upload one song; picture; bio.

Yahoo! Newsgroup Listings **dir.yahoo.com/Computers_and_Internet/Internet/Usenet/Newsgroup_Listings** Comprehensive lists of newsgroups.

Yahoo! People Search **people.yahoo.com** Find people in Cyberspace.

Zebra Music **www.zebramusic.com** Music career development; information; tips; links; free monthly E-newsletter.

New Age and Ambient Music

4NewAgeMusic.com **www.4newagemusic.com** MP3; songs; musicians; labels; retailers.

Amazing Sounds **www.amazings.com** New age and ambient music Webzine.

Ambience for the Masses **www.sleepbot.com/ambience** Search by label, artist, or type of music.

AstroStar Astrology and New Age Resources **www.astrostar.com** Eclectic array of astrology and New Age resources; conferences; chat room; astrology; books; Atlantean crystals; romance; twin soul and more.

Backroads Music **www.backroadsmusic.com** *Heartbeats Catalog*; ambient, world, space, new age, massage, tribal, electronic, Celtic, and vocal music.

Borders.com Recommendation Center Music: New Age **www.borders.com/recommend/ music_new_age.html** Books and music; new age music was born from various philosophies which dealt in physical healing of the mind and spiritual transcendence.

Directory of New Age Music **www.newagemusic.com** Information; resources; links.

Discography of New Age, Electronic, and Ambient Music **www.slip.net/~scaruffi/newage** or **www.scaruffi.com/newage** List of albums by over 600 new age and electronic music artists.

East West Spiritual and New Age Books and Tapes **www.eastwest.com** Spiritual and new age books and tapes on the Internet; alternative health and healing; personal growth; self-help; world religions and teachers; mythology; psychology.

Encyclopedia of New Age, Electronic, and Ambient Music **www.slip.net/~scaruffi/avant/index. html** Information; resources; links.

Epsilon **www.hyperreal.org/music/epsilon** Ambient music information Web site; links.

Global Stone Music **www.globalstonemusic.com** Chakras CD; recording studio; artist Kris Stone.

GroupWeb.com **www.groupWeb.com/entertainment/ muzic/top_new_age.htm** Top chart music and soundtracks.

Higher Octave Music **www.higheroctave.com** Record label; contemporary instrumental music; smooth jazz, new age, ambient, world, and flamenco music.

IDN Catalog of Indie Music: New Age **www.idnmusic.com/catalog/new_age. html** Music catalog.

Makoche-Native American and New Age Music **www.makoche.com** Makoche Native American Indian music; label and sound studio; online catalog; ordering; free CD giveaways; RealAudio sampling; concert information.

MP3.com New Age **genres.mp3.com/music/easy_listening/ new_age** MP3 music; downloads.

Music for a New Age **www.his.com/~fjp/music.html** Organized list of links for artists, companies, record labels, radio stations, and more.

Narada Productions **www.narada.com** Record label; new instrumental, jazz and world music; influenced by jazz, world, folk, rock, pop, and classical music.

New Age **music-12.hypermart.net** Browse by subject; general; ambient; Celtic; environmental;

independents; lists the seventy-five bestsellers in each category.

New Age Music **www.astral-music.com** New Age music based on astrology, astronomy, mathematics, Middle Eastern religions, and color.

New Age Music **www.geocities.com/Yosemite/Gorge/ 7220** New Age music and related genres; ambient; space; neoclassical; electronic; progressive; acoustic.

New Age Music **www.newage-music.com** Home page.

New Age Music Links **www.newagemusic.com/link.html** Links; reviews and music excerpts in RealAudio.

New Age Music Web Ring **www.geocities.com/Vienna/Choir/3886/ Webring.htm** A way in which to develop communities on the Internet.

New Age Voice **www.newagevoice.com** Official music trade magazine.

New World Music **www.newworldmusic.com** Relaxation, world, Celtic, Native American, and uplifting music.

North Star Music **www.northstarmusic.com** Music for living.

Obsolete **www.obsolete.com** Ambient and techno links.

One World Music **www.oneworldmusic.com** Through hands-on music making, this company fosters teamwork, leadership, and innovation in the workplace, promoting cultural change and organizational development.

PlanetEarthMusic **www.planet-earth- music.com** New age music store.

Quarterlight Productions **www.donnamichael.com** New Thought keyboard/vocal artist Donna Michael; CDs; bookings; workshops.

Serenity **www.serenitymusic.com** New age record label; music for massage, reiki, relaxation, and guided imagery.

The New Age Wholesale Directory **www.clever.net/lifequest/dir.html** Listing of over 1,000 distributors and publishers; books; videos; music; tarot decks; crystals; incense.

Trillenium Music Company & Tunbridge Music **www.trillmusic.com** Serious music in many styles; to help musicians learn, grow, and work professionally.

Windham Hill **www.windham.com** Record label; artists on tour; discography.

Wings of Love New Age Guide **www.wingsoflove.net** Books; music; aromatherapy; tarot cards; art; items to stimulate the senses.

Patriotic Music, Marches, and Marching Bands

1492: An Ongoing Voyage
**sunsite.unc.edu/expo/1492.exhibit/into.
html** Commemoration of the discovery of
America.
American History in Patrotic Music
**members.xoom.com/WaveThemes/
usa.html** American patrotic music.
Ceremonial Music Online
www2.acc.af.mil/music/ceremonial
Ceremonial music in MP3 and RealAudio for all
branches of the U.S. military, veterans, and civic
organizations, police and fire departments,
scouting, and schools; *National Anthem, Taps,
Amazing Grace,* honors, service songs, marches,
bugle calls.
Erols.com **www.erols.com** Poetry and music of
the Civil War; authoritative collection of
Confederate and Union poetry; indexed by title,
first lines, and authors.
Flags of the Native Peoples of the United States
**users.aol.com/Donh523/navapage/index.
html** Photos and histories of Native American
flags.
March Music Online
www2.acc.af.mil/music/march Forty-two
MP3 and RealAudio marches by John Philip
Sousa, Karl L. King, Henry Fillmore, and
others; U.S. Air Force band site.
MasterLocke's Patriotic Links
**www.members.aol.com/MastrLocke/
patriot.htm** That Ragged Old Flag; American
Flag; Old Glory; The Pledge; State Flags.
Military Women on Sheet Music
**userpages.aug.com/captbarb/
sheetmusic.html** History of women in the
military from the revolutionary war to the
present day.
*Music for the Nation: American Sheet Music, 1870-
1885* **memory.loc.gov/ammem/smhtml/
smhome.html** or
**lcWeb2.loc.gov/ammem/smhtml/
smhome** Tens of thousands of songs and
instrumental pieces registered for copyright in the
post-Civil War era.
Patriotic Greatest Marches **www.erc-
inc.com/newp.htm** *Stars and Stripes
Forever; El Capitan March; The Gladiator
March; The Washington Post March; The
Liberty March.*
Patriotic Greeting Cards
**www.prairiefrontier.com/pfcards/
patriotic.html** Patriotic multimedia greeting
cards by Prairie Frontier.
Patriotic Music Online
www2.acc.af.mil/music/patriotic User-

requested service; *God Bless America, Battle
Hymn of the Republic, America the Beautiful,
Armed Services Medley,* and more; MP3 and
RealAudio; service of the USAF Heritage of
America Band.
Patriotic Songs List
**www.fifties web.com/lyrics/ustunes.
htm** Patriotic music from the Fifties.
Patriotic Themes
**www.schirmer.com/repertoire/
programming_patriotic.html** Home;
repertoire; patriotic themes; programming ideas.
Political Sheet Music
**www.cyberbee.com/campaign/music.
html** Political music was written to stir the
emotions, generate candidate support, and cast
doubt on the opposition; many of the lyrics in
the 1800s were set to popular tunes of the day.
*Sheet Music about Lincoln, Emancipation, and the
Civil War*
**memory.loc.gov/ammem/scsmhtml/
scsmhome.html** From the Alfred Whital Stern
Collection at the Library of Congress.
Sheryl's Holiday Site: Flag Day
**www.sherylfranklin.com/holidays/
flag_day.html** Brief history of the Pledge of
Allegiance; links to other sites related to the
U.S. flag.
*Student Travel and Tours for Marching Bands and
Choirs* **www.travelgroups.com** Student
travel and tour packages for marching bands,
choirs, sport teams, and class trips; includes
festivals and competitions.
The 4th of July Page-Patriotic Fantasy
www.wilstar.com/holidays/july4.htm
Uncle Sam's dream; contains many historic
American documents; listen to patriotic MIDI
music.
The Flag of the United States: Patriotic Writings
www.icss.com/usflag/toc.writings.html
The voice of patriotism in writing; songs and
hymns; essays; speeches; poetry; letters.
USA Patriotic Tunes
**www.discoverynet.com/~ajsnead/
patriotic/usasongs.html** USA patriotic
songs; MIDI.
USAF Heritage of America Band
www.af.mil/accband Calendar, openings, and
audition information; unit/group pages; MP3 and
RealAudio features; songs of the Air Force with
lyrics and history; space themes in classical
music.

Piano—Keyboards—Organ

A Musical Tutorial
www.datacom.ca/~ron/mtwin.htm

Tutorials, games, and lessons to help beginners learn to play piano; Windows.

Always Pianos
www.pages.prodigy.net/bufordromans Free piano-dating service; send piano's manufacturer and serial number; will E-mail back information.

American Guild of Organists **www.agohq.org** Home page.

American School of Piano Tuning **www.piano-tuning.com** Tools; diploma.

Anybody Can Play the Piano
www.anybodycanplay.com/ ACPPIANOHOMEPAGE.htm Books and videos for beginners as young as three years; information for parents, piano teachers, and caregivers about different piano methods.

Baldwin Pianos and Organs
www.baldwinpiano.com Pianos; products and accessories; Baldwin; Chickering; Wurlitzer; Pianovelle; ConcertMaster.

Boogie Woogie Press
www.colindavey.com/BoogieWoogie Boogie woogie piano music.

Capital Net Pipe Organ Links
www.capitalnet.com/~rjewell/links. html American Guild of Organists; local chapters; other pipe organ sites.

Casio Inc. **www.casio.com** Maker of electronic keyboards.

Charles Moss Piano Studio **www.sumter.net/ -ckmoss/index.html** Links to style periods: Renaissance, Baroque, Classical, Romantic, and twentieth-century.

Chopin Foundation of the United States
www.chopin.org Chopin competitions; publications and concerts.

Church Organ Systems
www.churchorgansystems.com Digital and pipe combination organs.

Classical MIDI Organ Stop
theatreorgans.com/cmos/index.html Organs; MIDI.

Estonia Piano Factory **www.estoniapiano.com** Estonia Pianos.

German Piano Imports LLC
www.bluthnerpiano.com Bluthner; Haessler.

Göteborg Organ Art Center
www.hum.gu.se/goart Study and research into all aspects of the organ; art and the organ instrument; interpretation of the music of different periods; improvisation; research into preindustrial organ building; studies of sources.

Harpsichord Clearing House
www.harpsichord.com Comprehensive resource for early keyboard instruments including the harpsichord, virginal, spinet, clavichord, fortepiano, or continuo organ in North America.

International Piano Supply
www.pianosupply.com/ips Pianos for sale.

Kawai America **www.kawaius.com** Descriptions of products; technical information; download page has free patch libraries, operating system updates and sound demos; lists company's pianos, digital keyboards, home keyboards, and synths; links to sites containing patches, librarians, and other information.

Kawai Japan
www.kawai.co.jp/english/index.html Japanese headquarters; only the home page is in English.

Keyboard Central
angelfire.com/in2/KeyboardCentral/ index.html Learn to play the keyboard, piano, or organ at home; online lessons and E-books.

Keyboard Concepts
www.keyboardconcepts.com Music for keyboards.

Keyboard Education **keyboardedu.com** Music site for keyboard players; jazz piano instruction material; teaching professional melody and harmonic ideas; fills, run, licks.

Keyboard Player **www.keyboardplayer.com** Longest running keyboard magazine in the UK; sample reviews.

Korg **www.korg.com** Leading musical instrument manufacturer of keyboards and synthesizers; product archive; downloads.

Kurzweil **www.youngchang.com/kurzweil** Company has been acquired by Young Chang; can access FTP site to download files for Kurzweil instruments; online catalog; discussion forums; technical support; links.

Kurzweil Piano DiscoKnabe Piano, Mason and Hamlin **www.pianodisc.com** Information about acoustic, digital, and player pianos.

L. Bosendorfer Klavierfabrik GMBH
www.bosendorfer.com L. Bosendorfer pianos.

Letsplaymusic.com **www.letsplaymusic.com** Learn to play music through E-mail; piano and keyboard lessons with an instructor ranging from beginner to advanced students using MIDI files.

Liszt's Lists **www.liszt.com** Music mailing lists and newsgroups listed in a single directory by topic, including "piano."

Louis Renner GMBH & Co. **www.rennerusa.com** Renner Upright; Grand Piano Actions; Hammerheads; and Piano Tools.

Lowrey Organ Co. **www.lowrey.com** Lowrey home organs.

Luciano's Piano Bar **www.piano-bar.com**
Popular music in MIDI format played at the piano; easy listening.

Mason & Hamlin **www.masonhamlin.com**
Mason & Hamlin pianos.

Mr. C's Revolutionary Chord Voicings
ourworld.cs.com/chordvoicing
Comprehensive method for the aspiring pop and jazz pianist.

Music and You **www.musicandyou.com** Online piano lessons; beginners to advanced players; jazz, blues, classical, theory, arranging, and more; free demo lessons available.

Music for Pianos
digiserve.co.uk/musicforpianos 140+ self-sequenced files; includes music by women composers.

My Piano Lessons **www.mypianolessons.com** Online piano lessons.

Ohs Catalog **www.ohscatalog.org** Catalog sales division of the organ historical society; sells pipe organ related books, CDs, videos, and sheet music.

Online Piano Lessons
www.medford.net/djsprmain/ MusicUnlimitedHomepage Play piano by ear using rhythmic patterns.

Organ Stop **www.organstop.com** Keyboards for the home and church organist; customer support materials and activities; large sheet music department.

Organ Web Ring **209.235.102.9/~org20050** 100+ Web sites; organs; organists; organ music; organ builders; organ service; pipe organs; electric organs; organ playing.

Organ1st **www.organ.co.uk** Worldwide mail order shop; organs; sheet music.

OrganTutor Organ 101 **www.organtutor.byu.edu** CD-ROM and workbook with sixty-two lessons teaching organ registration, technique, and hymn playing in classical and traditional sacred organ style.

Orgel **www.orgel.com** Pipe organs; extensive information on pipe organs and organ music; listen to classical as well as modern organ music; RealAudio; virtual photo gallery.

Patti Music **www.pattimusic.com** Piano sheet music, methods, and classical repetoire; for piano and organ teachers, classical pianists, and organ players.

Perfectly Grand Piano Accessories, Inc.
www.perfectlygrand.com For pianists.

Piano Lab Online Store **www.pianolabs.com** Piano parts and supplies.

Piano Lessons Online
www.pianolessonsonline.com Interactive

piano/keyboard lessons using the Internet and video; for all ages.

Piano on the Net
www.artdsm.com/piano/index.html Online courses using QuickTime movies to teach piano lessons and pop music theory, including some jazz and blues; beginning to advanced levels; free public educational service.

Piano Pal **www.piano-pal.com** Store and reference for piano books and single sheet music scores; popular, classical, sacred, and educational material.

Piano Power **www.pianopower.com** Endorsed by musicians and medical professionals; book series takes student to new levels of technical and musical proficiency while optimizing time and avoiding injury.

Piano Press Studio **www.pianopress.com** Piano, keyboard, theory, and voice lessons; recitals; festivals; competitions; MTNA member; original music; publications; newsletter.

Piano Productions **www.piano-productions.com/eng/index.htm** Piano-related materials.

Piano Professor **www.pianoprofessor.com** Interactive tutorial for learning basic music theory; includes a "Note Tutor" to teach how to read music and identify the corresponding keys on the piano keyboard; Windows; by SofTech Multimedia, Inc.

Piano Quest **www.pianoquest.com** Used upright and grand pianos.

Piano Spot **www.pianospot.com** Piano sheet music and accessories.

Piano Supplies **www.pianosupplies.com** Supplies for the pianist.

Piano Teams **www.pianoteams.com** Ensemble project.

Piano Technicians Guild Inc.
www.ptg.org Official Web site.

Piano Tuition **www.pianotuition.co.uk** Piano and/or keyboard lessons by a professional piano teacher conducted via E-mail or by post.

Piano Wholesalers International Inc.
www.pianowholesalers.com Kingsburg Pianos.

Piano World (formerly *All About Pianos*)
www.pianoworld.com Pianos; keyboards; digital pianos; resource for information about the piano; free sheet music; locate a piano tuner, teacher, dealer; E-newsletter; interesting facts about the piano; list of piano movers and pianos for sale; trivia quiz; competitions; links.

Piano **www.cantos.org/Piano/Piano.html** Piano tuning, repair, and regulation; piano history; piano care; piano selection.

Piano-By-Ear Institute **www.piano-by-ear.com/learn/default.htm** Multimedia, home-study, church-oriented courses teach how to use chords, rhythm, and progressions to accompany singers/musicians as they provide the melody.

Pianodisc **www.pianodisc.com** Pianodisc; PDS-128Plus; Quiettime GT-360; Knabe; Mason & Hamlin; George Steck Pianos.

Pianomate Co. **www.pianomate.com** Pianomate.

Pianomouse.com **www.pianomouse.com** Instructional software.

Pianosoft Express **www.pianosoftexpress.com** Internet source for Yamaha Disklavier and Clavinova software products.

Pipedreams **pipedreams.mpr.org/index.html** Minnesota Public Radio presents live broadcasts of organ music; recordings of show segments online; links to background information; listening tips; organ-related articles; musician profiles and more.

Piporg-l **www.albany.edu/piporg-l** Electronic mailing list devoted to pipe and electronic organs, organists, and organ music.

Play Piano by Ear **pianomusic.hypermart.net/index.html** Learn to play the piano and keyboard by ear, without relying on sheet music.

QRS Music Inc. **www.qrsmusic.com** QRS Pianomation; Story & Clark.

Rarefind Piano Showcase **www.rarefind.com** Database of used and new pianos for purchase throughout the U.S. and the world; browse through categories; search.

Rhodes Pianos **www.badrat.com/rhodes** Information; FAQ; downloadable manual.

Roland Contemporary Keyboards **www.rolandus.com** Roland Corporation; musical instrument manufacturer; product and upgrade information; downloads; includes a section on the history of General MIDI.

Scarlatti Keyboard Works **www.win.tue.nl/scarlatti** About the composer's keyboard pieces.

Schimmel Piano Corp. **www.schimmel-piano.de** Schimmel pianos.

School of Music, University of Canterbury **www.music.canterbury.ac.nz** Christ Church Town Hall pipe organ; follow progress on video clips as the 3,372 pipes were gradually pieced together; learn more about how the instrument works.

Sheet Music for Electronic Keyboard **www.pianospot.com/cat20.htm** List of items available.

Sing Along Piano Bar **www.singalongpianobar.com** Sing along piano bar.

Smithsonian's National Museum of American History "PIANO 300: Celebrating Three Centuries of People and Pianos" **www.piano300.org** Exhibition celebrating the 300th anniversary of the invention of the piano; composers' manuscripts, tools, photographs, play bills, sheet music, and other memorabilia; highlights museum's internationally distinguished collection of 250 pianos and keyboards.

Solo Piano CD Sampler Showroom **www.rainmusic.com/pianomusic/dnevue/sampler.htm** Piano CDs.

Speed Weights **www.speedweights.com** Finger weights for speed, dexterity, endurance, and control; exercise finger muscles.

Steinway and Sons **www.steinway.com** Factory tour; send a virtual postcard; learn about Steinway and Boston Piano products.

Street Organ **www.streetorgan.com** Street organ facts; history; makers; music; restoration tips; dedicated to the mechanical organ and its music.

Studiologic **www.musicindustries.com** Computer-assisted piano learning systems.

Super Sight-Reading Secrets **www.soundfeelings.com/products/music_instruction** Step-by-step program for musical keyboard players or singers.

Suzuki Corporation **www.suzukipianos.com** Digital pianos; portable keyboards; QChord; harmonicas.

Swedish Pipe Organs **www.ecs.se/organ/index-e.htm** Information about pipe organs, organ music, and organists; resources.

Technics **www.technics.co.uk** Technics pianos, organs, and keyboards.

The Herschell Carousel Factory Museum **www.carousels.com/hmusem.htm** Located in North Tonawonda, NY; area of major significance to the previous carousel and band organ manufacturing business in America.

The Keyboard Store **www.thekeyboardstore.com** New and used Korg, Yamaha, Roland, Kurzweil, and Alesis keyboards at discount prices.

The Keyboard Studio **www.keyboardstudio.com** Source for everything in music or computers.

The Online Conservatory **www.onlineconservatory.com** Online music school offering live, one-on-one, and interactive piano lessons over the Internet.

The Organ Web Ring **www.organwebring.com** For organists and organ lovers.

The Piano Book **www.tiac.net/users/pianobk**
Consumer information about buying, selling, and owning a piano.

The Piano Education Page **www.unm.edu/~loritaf/pnoedmn.html** Resource for piano teachers, students, and enthusiasts; over 600 links.

The Piano Place **www.pianoplace.com** Online catalog; piano books; CDs; videos; software; transcriptions.

The Piano Players Guide to the Internet **www.rainmusic.com/pianomusic/piano.htm** Complete guide to piano-related Web sites on the Internet; recommendations include free sheet music, online piano lessons, piano books, and pianos for sale.

The Piano Teacher's Forum **www.members.tripod.com/the_buzzard/classical/forum.html** Information on everything from motivating students to maintaining a successful studio.

UK Piano Page **www.airtime.co.uk/forte/mag.htm** List of UK-based online music magazines covering all styles of music.

Used Keyboards **www.usedkeyboards.com** Find a used keyboard online.

Van Cliburn International Piano Competition-Van Cliburn Foundation **www.cliburn.org** Information on the piano competition and foundation.

Weber Piano Co. **www.weberpiano.com** Weber Piano; Rieger-Kloss Piano; Ridgewood Piano; Sagenhaft Piano.

WM Knabe & Co. **www.pianodisc.com** Knabe Pianodisc Pianos; Quiet Time Pianos; Knabe Pianos; PianoDigital Pianos.

World Pedagogy Conference **www.pianopedagogy.com** Annual conference held in October.

Yamaha Corporation of America **www.yamaha.com** Yamaha music products and more; daily visitation of almost 10,000 people.

Young Chang Worldwide **www.youngchang.com** Information about products and services; technical help; piano education resources.

Popular Music and Culture—Fashion—Dance Music—Techno—Electronica—Rock'n'Roll—Oldies—Punk—Heavy Metal

4ClassicRock.com **www.4classicrock.com** Classic rock bands and artists; listen to music; reviews about the history of classic rock.

70s Traveler Real Audio Music Page **www.70traveler.com** Streaming RealAudio of the music from 1970 to 1980.

9fingers **www.9fingers.com** Heavy metal Web site.

A Biased History of Glam Rock **www.doremi.co.uk/glam** Links and more.

A Brief History of Banned Music in the United States **www.ericnuzum.com/banned** Selected online chronicle of music that has been banned or censored in the United States.

A Psychedelic Sixties Music Page **www.lib.virginia.eduexhibits/sixties/rock.html** Album covers; bios.

A Smaller Footprint **asmallerfootprint.com** Punk Web site.

About Heavy Metal **heavymetal.about.com/entertainment/heavymetal/mbody.htm** Hard rock and heavy metal Web site.

Absolute Authority on Rock Music **www.absoluteauthority.com/Rock_Music** Central hub for exploring the world of Rock Music on the Web; most complete collection of content, community, and tools available on the subject of Rock Music.

Access Place Music **www.accessplace.com/music.htm** Music news; reviews; online audio; MP3 files; genres; artists; songs; lyrics; concerts; tickets; CD stores; instruments; references; acoustics; electronics.

Agents of Steel **www.agents.heavy.net** German heavy metal Web site.

Alan's Celebrity Addresses **www.geocities.com/Hollywood/Hills/9842** Fan's address list.

All Time Favorites **www.alltimefavorites.com** Complete entertainment resources.

Anger Funk **www.angerfunk.com** Webzine.

Anti MTV **www.antimtv.com** Hard rock and heavy metal Web site.

Armani Exchange **www.armaniexchange.com** Fashion industry.

Art Rock **www.artrock.com** Rock music Web site.

Atlanta Groove City **www.atlantagroovecity.com** Groove music Web site.

Band Jokes **www.geocities.com/Vienna/9044** Funny stuff.

Bazaar **www.bazaar411.com** Fashion industry.

BBC Pop **www.bbc.co.uk/entertainment/popmusic** News; features; links.

Beat Boy **www.beatboy.com** Beat music Web site.

Beat Maker **www.beatmaker.com** Beat music
     Web site.
Beatflow.com **www.beatflow.com** Electronica
     music.
Beatlefest **www.beatlefest.com** The Beatles.
Beatles **www.getback.org/beatles.html** The
     Internet Beatles album.
Beatles
     **www.rockmine.music.co.uk/beatwho.ht
     m l** A Beatles who's who.
Beatles Encyclopedia
     radiowavenet.com/beatles/beatles.htm
     The Beatles.
Beatles Fans Index
     **beatles.about.com/entertainment/beatles
     /blalbums.htm** The Beatles.
Beatles Lyrics
     **members.home.net/sherlockh/beatles/
     beatles.html** The Beatles' lyrics; click on the
     album cover.
Beatles Sheet Music
     **www.netins.net/showcase/reading/beats
     heet.html** Currently available sheet music
     collections; links to find on the Internet.
Beatles Sheet Music
     **www.rarebeatles.com/sheetmu/sheetmu.
     htm** Collecting Beatles sheet music.
Beatles Web
     www.beatlesWeb.co.uk/beatlemain.htm
     The Beatles.
Beatseek **www.beatseek.com** Electronica.
Beatsezine.com **www.beatsezine.com** Beat
     music Web site.
Big Rock Farms **www.bigrockfarms.com** Rock
     music Web site.
Black Rock Coalition
     users.aol.com/brcny/home.html Home
     page.
Black Velvet **www.blackvelvet.demon.co.uk**
     Hard rock and heavy metal Web site.
Blue Eyes.com **www.blue-eyes.com** Easy
     listening music Web site.
British Pop Culture **www.sixtiespop.com** Music
     and more.
Bugle Boy **www.bugleboy.com** Fashion industry.
Canadian Musician
     www.canadianmusician.com Pop music
     magazine.
Celebmix **www.celebmix.z.com** Web sites of
     celebrities.
Celebrity Addresses
     **www3.islandnet.com/~luree/fanmail.
     html** Celebrity Web sites; actors, comedians,
     athletes, musicians, and authors.
Celebrity Connection
     members.tripod.com/~jonnykat/

celebrity.html Celebrities; musicians,
     politicians, athletes.
Celebrity Corner **www.premrad.com** Audio
     interview clips.
Celebrity Site of the Day **www.net-v.com/csotd**
     Links to celebrity sites.
CelebSite **www.celebsite.com** Celebrity profiles.
Chronology of San Francisco Rock Music 1965-1969
     www.sfmuseum.org/hist1/rock.html
     Museum of City of San Francisco.
Classic Rock Daily **www.classicrockdaily.com**
     Hard rock and heavy metal Web site.
Club Velvet **www.tamboo.com** Easy listening
     music Web site.
CNN Style **www.cnn.com/STYLE** Fashion
     journalism.
Comic Book Continuum
     www.detnews.com/metro/hobbies/comix
     Comics news.
Comics.com **www.comics.com** United Media.
Concert in the Sky Diskology **www.great-
     music.net/diskog.html** History of pop
     music; RealAudio samples.
Cover Heaven **freespace.virgin.net/love.day/
     coverheaven** Record cover artwork.
Covers **covers.virtualave.net** Album cover
     database.
Cross Rock **www.crossrock.com** Rock music
     Web site.
Dance Music Authority Magazine
     www.dmadance.com Club information.
Dance Music Home Page
     **dancemusic.about.com/musicperform/
     dancemusic/mbody.htm** Starting place for
     exploring dance music on the Internet; dance
     clubs; artists; contests; interviews; RealAudio;
     MP3; reviews; links.
Dance Music of the Eighties
     www.andwedanced.com Home page.
Dancesite **www.dancesite.com** Tracks available
     to audio-stream; reviews; news.
Delicious Vinyl **www.dvinyl.com** Record label;
     hip-hop; urban.
Designer City **www.designercity.com** Fashion
     industry.
Disco 1999 **www.disco1999.com** Disco music
     Web site.
Disco Inferno
     **hem.passagen.se/discoguy/artists/
     artists.html** Guide to disco.
Disco Music **www.discomusic.com** Disco music
     Web site.
Disquiet **www.disquiet.com** Interviews;
     electronica.
DJ Bernie **www.djbernie.com** DJ music Web
     site.
DJ Bigant **www.djbigant.com** DJ music Web site.

DJ Rhythms **www.djrhythms.com** Electronica.

DJ Union **www.djunion.com** DJ music Web site.

DJ.net **www.dj.net** DJ music Web site.

Do the Dance **www.dothedance.com** LA based DJ service; all occasions; CDs; videos.

Donna Karan **www.donnakaran.com** Fashion industry.

Driveways of the Rich & Famous **www.driveways.com** Self-mocking celebrity interviews.

Drum and Bass Arena **www.breakbeat.co.uk** News; reviews; interviews; dance E-zine.

Elle **www.ellemag.com** French fashion; photos.

ERock **www.erock.net** Rock music Web site.

Etnopop.com **www.etnopop.com** Pop music Web site.

Eurodance Hits **www.eurodancehits.com** Information on artists; releases in European dance music; Annual Cyberspace Euro-Energy Awards.

Extreme Music News **www.nestor.minsk.by/emn** Hard rock and heavy metal Web site.

Faith Groove **www.faithgroove.com** Groove music Web site.

Fansites Database **www.fansites.com** Database of fan Web sites; all genres.

Fashion Angel **www.fashionangel.com** Fashion industry.

Fashion Live **www.worldmedia.fr/fashion** Parisian fashion scene.

Fashion.net **www.fashion.net** Guide to Internet fashion sites.

FirstView **www.firstview.com** The latest fashions displayed online.

Flash Rock **www.flashrock.com** Rock music Web site.

Forever Metal **www.thats-metal.de** German heavy metal Web site.

Free Online Music Game **music.jdlh.com** Play against people from all over the world on '60s, '70s, '80s, and '90s music trivia.

French Kiss Rocks **www.frenchkissrocks.com** Rock music Web site.

Funk Logic **www.funklogic.com** Funk music Web site.

George Starostin's Classic Rock Album Reviews **starling.rinet.ru/music/index.htm** Detailed reviews of 1960s and '70s rock and pop music; ratings; best-of lists; etc.

Gianni Versace **www.versace.com** Tribute to Versace's life and work.

Glamour **www.swoon.com/mag_rack/glamour.html** Interactive fashion and lifestyle. Online edition of *Glamour*.

Global Beat **www.globalbeat.com** Beat music Web site.

Golden Age of Rock and Roll **www.geocities.com/sunset/4001/stome/the_golden_age.htm** Hard rock and heavy metal Web site.

Goldmine **www.krause.com/records/gm** Magazine site for collectors.

Goldmine Online **www.krause.com/goldmine** Site for record collectors; appraise values of records; photos; articles; columns; ads.

Good Times Mag **www.goodtimesmag.com** Pop music magazine.

Great Modern Pictures **greatmodernpictures.com** Photography Web site.

Groove House **www.groovehouse.com** Groove music Web site.

Groove Kitchen **www.groovekitchen.net** Groove music Web site.

Guess **www.guess.com** Fashion Web site.

Hard Rock Cafe **hardrock.com** Hard rock and heavy metal Web site.

Hard Rock Hotel **www.hardrockhotel.com** Las Vegas hotel and casino.

Hard Rock Live **www.hardrocklive.com** Live versions of hits previously unreleased.

Hard Rock Universe **homes.acmecity.com/music/metal/399** Hard rock and heavy metal Web site.

Heavy Harmonies **www.heavyharmonies.com** Metal and hard rock bands.

History of Banned Music **www.pathfinder.com/ew/siteoftheweek/0,2028,503,00.html** Everything you ever wanted to know about dirty lyrics.

Hits Under the Hammer **www.icollector.com/live/hits.htm** Online auction of music memorabilia.

Hugh's Lounge in Foggy London **www.users.dircon.co.uk** Easy listening music Web site.

Hyper Real **www.hyperreal.org** Dance culture Web site.

Hypermode **www.hypermode.com/cover/jsindex.** Underground fashions.

Hyperreal **www.hyperreal.org** Electronica music; techno commune; music; culture; lifestyle.

In the 80s.com **www.inthe80s.com/bands** Index.

Indigenous Rocks **www.indigenousrocks.com** Rock music Web site.

KNAC Online **www.knac.com/servlet/index** Hard rock and heavy metal Web site.

Levi's **www.levi.com** Fashion Web site.

Lilith Fair **www.lilithfair.com** Official Web site.

Look Online **www.lookonline.com** Fashion industry.

Losing Today **www.losingtoday.com** Pop music magazine.

Lumiere **www.lumiere.com** Slow pages look dazzling.

Made in Italy **www.made-in-italy.com/fashion/fm.htm** Fashion industry.

Marvel Online **www.marvelonline.com** Online site for the comic book company.

Media Rocks **www.mediarocks.com** Rock music Web site.

Melissa's Punk/Alternative World of Music **www.geocities.com/sunsetstrip/concert/ 5943** Links; information; bands.

Metal Edge Online **www.mtledge.com** Hard rock and heavy metal Web site.

Metal Hammer **www.metalhammer.co.uk** Hard rock and heavy metal Web site; magazine.

Metal Head Music **www.metalheadmusic.com** Metal magazine.

Metal Is **www.metal-is.com** Metal magazine.

Metal Links **www.metallinks.com** Hard rock and heavy metal Web site.

Metal Maniacs **www.metalmaniacs.com** Metal magazine.

Metal Thai **www.metalthai.net** Metal magazine.

Mishatzar **www.mishatzar.com** Fashion industry.

Mixology **www.mixology.co.uk/mix/mixology. htm** Site for DJs; producers; dance music industry.

Modern Rock **www.modernrock.com** Rock music Web site.

Moondog's This Week in Music History **Webhome.idirect.com/~moondog/ thisweek.html** Trivia; past events; new releases; birthdays; tragedies; the latest in rock and roll.

Moonshine Music **www.moonshine.com** Techno; dance; house; trance; acid jazz; jungle; hardcore; breakbeat; triphop; electronic listening music.

Motion **motion.state51.co.uk** Search resource for dance record shops.

MP3 Music World **www.rapping.com/musicworld** Pop, rock, and dance music.

Mr. Blackwell's Wit & Wisdom **www.mrblackwell.com** Fashion victims.

Music and Dance Productions **www.musicanddance.com** DJ Services; overview.

Music Fan Clubs **www.musicfanclubs.org** Links to fan club Web sites.

Music Soup **www.music-soup.com** Music news, reviews, and charts of various genres including pop, rock, R&B, rap, hip-hop, and country.

Music Styles by AMG **allmusic.com/mus_Styles.html** Descriptions of all popular music styles of the twentieth century by professional music journalists.

Music.com **www.music.com** Affiliate partner of DreamWorks label; free downloads of major stars.

Musician and Instrument Jokes **www.mit.edu/people/job/jokes** Lots of jokes.

Mutha Funkas **www.muthafunkas.com** Funk music Web site.

Net Beat **www.netbeat.com** Beat music Web site.

Night Wing Rocks **www.nightwingrocks.com** Rock music Web site.

NJ Rocks **www.njrocks.com** Rock music Web site.

Northern UK's Metal Page **www.shipley.ac.uk/north** Hard rock and heavy metal Web site.

NY Style **www.nystyle.com** Fashion magazine and store.

Oldies Music **www.oldiesmusic.com** History, trivia and charts of the '50s, '60s, and '70s.

Online Rock **www.onlinerock.com** Rock music Web site.

Pathfinder **www.pathfinder.com/altculture/aentries/ o/oldhamxt.html** Fashion industry.

PC DJ **www.pcdj.com** DJ music Web site.

Peace Rock **www.peacerock.com** Collectibles.

Peaceville **www.peaceville.com** Hard rock and heavy metal Web site.

Pop History Now! **www.pophistorynow.com** Features a random year in pop history every weekday; covers music, television, movies, news, and politics.

Pop Music Directory **www.pop-music.com** Pop; rock; dance; indie.

Pop Star Net **www.popstar.net** Pop music.

Pop.com **www.pop.com** Pop music Web site.

Punk Rock Women **www.connect.ca/~rina/index.html** Punk and new wave Web site.

Raga Rock **www.ragarock.com** Rock music Web site.

Rave-Club Info and Electronic Music Links around the World **spraci.cia.com.au/ravew.htm** Easy-to-use links page.

Recollections **www.recollections.co.uk** Memorabilia; listed by artists A-Z.

Remix Live **www.remixlive.com** Dance music Web site.

Rhythm Net **www.rhythmnet.com** Home page.

Rock 108 from Key J **www.keyj.com** Hard rock and heavy metal Web site; information; news; radio service.

Rock and Heavy Metal Page **www.rockworld.ndirect.co.uk** Hard rock and heavy metal Web site.

Rock and Roll Hall of Fame **www.rockhall.com** Hard rock and heavy metal Web site.

Rock Around the World **www.ratw.com** Photo library; radio show archive; 1970s.

Rock Auction **www.rockauction.com** Rock music Web site.

Rock Bottom **www.rock-bottom.com** Rock music Web site.

Rock Daily **www.rockdaily.com** Rock music Web site.

Rock Mall Trivia Challenge **www.rockmall.com/arcade.shtml** Music, entertainment, and culture.

Rock Music **www.suite101.com/welcome.cfm/rock_music** Rock music Web site.

Rock Music Music Network **www.rock.com** Guide; streaming audio; online store.

Rock News **www.rocknews.com** Rock music.

Rock Online **www.rockonline.com** Rock 'n' roll Web site.

Rock Round the World Rockabilly **www.geocities.com/SunsetStrip/Backstage/6273** World club for rockabilly fans; meet others on mailing list; visit their Web sites; submit a venue to the database; send rockabilly link and get listed.

Rock Universe **www.rockuniverse.com** Webzine.

Rock.com **www.rock.com** Rock music Web site.

Rock.theShoppe.com **www.rock.theshoppe.com** Rock music Web site.

Rocka.com **www.rocka.com** Rock music Web site.

Rockabilly **www.rockabilly.nl** Rockabilly music Web site.

Rockabillyhall.com **www.rockabillyhall.com** Rockabilly music Web site.

Rockete.com **www.rockete.com** Rock music Web site.

Rockfest **www.rockfest.org** Rock music Web site.

Rockhall.com **www.rockhall.com** Official Web site of the Rock and Roll Hall of Fame Museum located in Cleveland, OH, and now in cyberspace; popular music used in interdisciplinary teaching.

Rockhouse **www.rockhouse.de** Rock music Web site.

RockinRoll.com **www.rockinroll.com** Rock music Web site.

RocknRoots.com **www.rocknroots.com** Rock music Web site.

Rockperry.fi **www.rockperry.fi** Rock music Web site.

Rusmetal.ru **www.rusmetal.ru** Rock music Web site.

Russian Darkside **www.darkside.ekort.ou** Russian hard rock and heavy metal Web site.

Saturday Night Fever **room34.com/snf** Movie Web site.

Seventh on Sixth **www.7thonsixth.com** Fashion from many designers; the runway scene and designers; links to designers including Calvin Klein, Hugo Boss, John Bartlett, Perry Ellis, Ralph Lauren, Tommy Hilfiger, and many others.

Seventies Dance Music **izan.simplenet.com/70.html** Disco Music of the '70s; images; information; lyrics; MIDI; RealAudio clips; links and more.

Show Biz Expo **www.showbizexpo.com** Fashion industry.

Simplenet.com **ews.simplenet.com/designer** Fashion industry.

Slitzine **www.geocities.com/sunsetstrip/palms/4001/index.htm** California glam punk.

Speed Garage **www.speedgarage.com** Dance music; audio files; links.

Spring Groove **www.springgroove.com** Groove music Web site.

Stone Rock **www.stonerrock.com** Rock music Web site.

Street Sound **ssound.pseudo.com** House music and electronica.

Style 365 **www.style365.com** Directory of fashion Web sites.

Super Model **www.supermodel.com/newswire/index.html** Fashion industry.

Super Seventies Rock Site **www.geocities.com/SunsetStrip/8678** Top hits; photos; links.

Swank-o-Rama **www.mindspring.com/~jpmckay/sound.html** Easy listening music Web site.

Teddy Rocks **www.teddyrocks.com** Rock music Web site.

The '80s Server **www.80s.com/Entertainment/music** Dedicated to pop culture of the 1980s.

The Album Covers Page **www.knl.com/albums** Artwork.

The Best Game Music in the World **gamemusic.siliconcircus.co.uk** Popular music from computer and video games.

The Center for Popular Music
popmusic.mtsu.edu Popular music
information and resources.

The Church of Saturday Night Live
dan.elwood.net Fan clubs for SNL current
players and alumni.

The Dance Music Resource Pages
www.juno.co.uk Complete weekly listing of
new UK dance releases, including catalog
numbers and distributor information; future
releases; UK dance radio listings; over 500 dance-
related links.

The Dark Site of Metal **metal.de** Hard rock and
heavy metal Web site.

The Fillmore **www.thefillmore.com** In San
Francisco; famous for booking big names in the
'60s; Joplin; Hendrix; Grateful Dead; Jefferson
Airplane and more.

The Gap **www.gap.com** Fashion site.

The Lounge Scene
www.geocities.com/Tokyo/3076 Easy
listening music Web site.

The Mod Sixties Web Ring
**www.realcrazy.freeserve.co.uk/mod-
sixties-Webring.htm** Sixties music Web
sites; links.

The Musical World of Rocky Horror
www.rockymusic.org Audio and more;
largest Rocky Horror sounds collection on the
Internet; images; lyrics; reviews.

The Official George Carlin Web Site
www.georgecarlin.com Living comedy
legend.

The Official Oldies Music Ring
**www.Webring.org/cgi-
bin/Webring?ring=tdm;list** Collection of
official sites dedicated to the people that created
"oldies music."

The Progressive Rock Website
www.progrock.net Newsletter.

The Punk Rock Academy
www.ieway.com/yeast/punk.htm To
educate, inform, and share with the world the
music, culture, and philosophy of Punk.

The Rock 'n' Roll Vault -This Week in Rock 'n' Roll
www.rocknrollvault.com/thisweek.htm
The best of rock 'n' roll from the last fifty years;
weekly updates; historical events; music of the
past; The Beatles; birthdays; tragedies and more.

The Sixties
www.slip.net/~scmetro/sixties.htm
Music and more.

The Space Age Pop Page
home.earthlink.net/~spaceagepop
Encyclopedia of space age pop, exotica, and
lounge music and musicians.

The Wanderer **www.wanderers.com/wanderer**
Oldies Web site.

This Day in Music from Billboard Online
www.billboard.com/thisday/thisday.asp
Popular music history.

Tombstone **www.tombstone.gr** Hard rock and
heavy metal Web site.

Tommy Hilfiger **www.tommy.com** Designer Web
site.

Top 10 Music from Top10city.com
**www.top10city.com/entertainment/
music/music.html** Chart pages.

Trouser Press **www.trouserpress.com** Rock
magazine; archives online.

UExpress Comics
www.uexpress.com/ups/comics Archives
of United Press Syndicate.

UK Metal Underground
**www.geocities.com/sunsetstrip/
palladium/9133/main.htm** Hard rock and
heavy metal Web site.

Ultra Groove **www.ultragroove.com** Groove
music Web site.

Upbeat **www.upbeat.co.uk** Beat music.

Videogame Music Archive **www.vgmusic.com**
11,000+ game music MIDI files.

Vintage Classic Rock
**www.geocities.com/SunsetStrip/
Theater/5441/music.html** Links.

Welcome to Vik's Lounge **www.chaoskitty.com**
Easy listening music Web site.

Woman Rock **www.womanrock.com** Home;
features; interviews; reviews; events; radio;
message board; links; shop; membership; music
resources.

World of Twist **www.music-
network.com/flotsam/world_of_twist** Do
the twist!

World Style **www.worldstyle.com** Fashion
industry.

X-Network **www.x-network.co.uk** For DJs and
clubbers.

R&B, Rap, Hip-Hop, and Soul

360 Degreez of Hip Hop
www.5.50megs.com/hiphop RealAudio;
reviews; store; release dates.

88HipHop.com **www.88hiphop.com** Current
events; reviews; music; videos; links; indie
artists.

Aka.com **www.aka.com** Network of over 125 hip-
hop related sites; links; reviews; digital audio
files.

Altrap.com **www.altrap.com** Hip-hop culture and
perspective.

Atomic Pop
**www.atomicpop.com/aboutatomicpop/
index.html** Hip-hop Web site.

Basically Hip-Hop **www.basically-hiphop.com** RealAudio on the Internet.

Beatbreaks **www.beatbreaks.com** Hip-hop Web site.

Boomshaka Music **www.boomshakamusic.com** Hip-hop Web site.

CJ's House of Soul **www.flavourtown.com** R&B and modern soul Web site.

Davey D's Hip-Hop Corner **www.daveyd.com** Radio shows; visitor polls; boards; newsletters; news.

DJ Rap **www.dj-rap.com** DJ rap music Web site.

E-Jams **www.ejams.com** R&B music site; interactive music survey; contests; chat rooms; trivia; music charts; bulletin boards; links and music information.

Gargantua Soul **www.gargantuasoul.com** Soul music Web site.

GunshotUK **www.gunshotuk.com** UK hip-hop site.

Hip-Hop Spot **www.hiphophotspot.com** Interactive Web site; dedicated to helping indie artists achieve their goals; free resources.

Hip-Hop Bot **www.hiphopbot.com** DJs; turntables; clubbing; bars; nightclubs; urban culture; artists; groups; events; online events; tours; audio; lyrics; new artists; fashion; labels; online labels; links; link exchanges; magazines; online magazines; MP3s; downloads; utilities; new school artists; news; Internet broadcasts; old school artists; soul artists; groups.

Hip-Hop Directory **www.hiphopdirectory.com** Hip-hop music; links.

Hip-Hop Elements **www.hiphop-elements.com** Free subscription to The Elements Newsletter; news; charts; playlists; album reviews; free CD drawing every week.

Hip-Hop Forever **www.hiphopforever.hypermart.net** Hip-hop Web site.

Hip-Hop **www.dacrossroadz.cjb.net** Hip-hop Web site.

Hip-Hop Music & Cult **www.suite101.com/welcome.cfm/ hip_hop_music** Hip-hop music; links.

Hip-Hop Music UK **www.hiphopmusic.co.uk** Underground hip-hop music and culture in the UK and the U.S.; news; reviews; interviews.

Hip-Hop Zone **www.hip-hopzone.com** Hip-hop music Web site.

HipHopCity.com **www.hiphopcity.com** Hip-hop directory; top 100; add a site; search.

HipHopMusic.co.uk **www.hiphopmusic.co.uk** UK hip-hop Web site.

HipHopSite.com **www.hiphopsite.com** Hip-hop music Web site.

Miami Hip-Hop **www.miamihiphop.com** Hip-hop Web site.

My Soul Sings **www.mysoulsings.com** Soul music Web site.

Original Hip-Hop Lyrics Archive **www.ohhla.com** Large database.

Rap Sheet **www.rapsheet.com** Rap music Web site.

Rap Station **www.rapstation.com** Rap music Web site.

Rapco.com **www.rapco.com** Rap music Web site.

Rhythm & Blues Foundation **www.rhythm-n-blues.org** Home page.

Rhythm and Blues Music Primer **www.theprimer.org** R&B and modern soul Web site.

Rock Rap **www.rockrap.com** Rap music Web site.

Roland Groove **www.rolandgroove.com** Groove music Web site.

RRC: Archives **members.labridge.com/rockrap/archive/ index.html** The hidden history of rock and rap music.

Soul A Go-Go **www.soul-a-go-go.demon.co.uk** Soul Web site.

Soul Festival **www.soulfestival.com** Soul music Web site.

Soul Flow **www.soulflow.net** Soul music Web site.

Soul on the Net **www.personal.cet.aci.il/yonin** Soul Web site.

Soul Watch **www.soulwatch.com** Soul music Web site.

Soulful Sound **www.soulfulsound.com** Soul music Web site.

Street Jamz **www.streetjamz.com** Showcasing local and independent unsigned black music.

Street Zone **www.steetzone.com** Swedish hip-hop Web site.

StreetSounds from Pseudo **www.ssound.pseudo.com** R&B and modern soul Web site.

Support Online Hip-Hop **www.sohh.com** News section; bulletin boards; music and culture.

The Booty Bone **www.freeserve.com** R&B and modern soul Web site.

The Primer **www.theprimer.org.uk** Soul Web site.

The R&B Page **www.rbpage.com** R&B and modern soul Web site.

The R&B Primer Introductory Page **www.zoo.co.uk/~primer** Dedicated to the world of blues and soul music.

The Source **thesource.tunes.com/sections/home** or

www.thesource.com Hip-hop; rap; features; reviews.

The Stax Site **perso.wanadoo.fr/stax.site** Soul Web site.

Underground Hip-Hop
www.undergroundhiphop.com Streaming audio of singles; emerging artists.

Vibe **www.vibe.com** Hip-hop and urban music and culture.

Whoopass **www.btinternet.com/~labid.malik** R&B and modern soul Web site.

Wodie **www.wodie.com** Hip-hop Web site; World Wide Wodie Forum.

Radio, Internet Radio, and Television

1groove.com **www.1groove.com** Internet radio station.

2000 **www.cazmedia.com/mmi/ wcaz2000.shtml** Internet radio site.

2kool4radio **www.2kool4radio.com** Radio station that plays indie music.

369shoutcaster
www.thirdroad.com/369shoutcasters Radio station that plays indie music.

4QIR-Quantum Radio **4qir.quantum-radio.net.au** AFVN Archives of music from around the world.

A&E **www.aetv.com** or **www.AandE.com** Arts and Entertainment; program listings and previews.

ABC **www.abc.com** American Broadcasting Company.

Academy of Television Arts & Sciences
www.emmys.org Information on the Emmy awards.

Action Radio **www.chez.com/actionradio** International Internet radio.

Adventures in Good Music
www.wclv.com/aigm.htm Listing of future radio programs and other interesting information.

All India Internet Radio **www.aiir.com** Entertainment and news programs.

Alternative Entertainment Network
www.cummingsvideo.com Entertainment and documentary programming.

Ambrosia's Music Channel
www.nightowl.net/~amber/index.htm Constantly changing bands lineup; streaming video and audio; information.

American Movie Classics **www.amctv.com** Classic films.

American Music Channel
www.americanmusicchannel.com Internet broadcast network devoted exclusively to country music.

AminoRadio **www.aminoradio.com/dyn/MRN** Twenty-four hour station; electronic music; techno; house.

Amp Radio **www.subband.com/ampr** For Macintosh Internet radio.

Anti-Elitist Audio **subrealsongs.com/antielitist** Internet radio site for independent bands and artists.

Audiences Unlimited
www.audiencesunlimited.com Free tickets to TV show tapings.

AudioNet **www.audionet.com** Internet radio site that accepts submissions.

Austin City Limits **www.klru.org** Program featuring original music.

Barrcode **www.barrcode.com** BCX and BRIAN editing and playout software for radio stations.

Bayou Boogie Radio Show **www.bayoubeat.com** World music radio.

BBC Music Live **www.bbc.co.uk/musiclive** UK's biggest broadcast live music festival; six-day celebration of musical diversity taking place in Glasgow in May.

Beatlock Technology
djmixpro.com/beatlock.html DJ *Mix Pro* DJ mixing program for parties and nightclubs or background music; design mixes on headphones while music is playing on speakers.

Beat-Mix Wizard **www.beat-mix.com** MP3 player designed for professional DJs; digital pitch-shift, pitch bend, automatic or manual cross fading and beat mixing, point-click playlist maker, and an automatic database generator; demo available.

BET **www.betnetworks.com** Black Entertainment Television.

Beta Lounge **www.betalounge.com** Techno music.

Big Wooden Radio **www.bigwoodenradio.com** Radio station.

Black Channel **www.blackchannel.de** Radio station.

Bravo Cable Network **www.bravotv.com** Bravo cable television network.

Bring the Noise! **bringthenoise.com** Radio Web site; hip-hop.

Broadcast Science **www.broadcastscience.nl** Advanced software for the broadcast industry; automation systems, cart replacement software, and transmission line protection software.

Broadcast.com **www.broadcast.com/radio** Live Web performances; hosts hundreds of radio stations including offline and Internet radio stations; browse; streaming media programming; Web TV; audio books.

BroadcastMusic.com
www.broadcastmusic.com Internet radio Web site.

BRS Web-Radio www.web-radio.com Find offline radio stations that simulcast their shows on the Internet.

Burli Software Inc. www.burli.com *Newsroom System* integrates newswires, audio feeds, faxes, E-mail, Web access, and more in an intuitive drag-and-drop editing interface.

C-500.com www.c500.com For low-power and college radio stations across the country; consult music charts; join mailing list; view message board.

Cart Selector Broadcast Software
www.cklpradio.com/cart_selector.html Manages cart and source numbers for radio traffic systems; tracks numbers by client and advertiser, run dates, activity expiry; purges; generates detailed reporting.

CBC Television and Radio www.cbc.ca Television and radio Web site.

CBS www.cbs.com Central Broadcasting System.

Cherry Moon www.cherrymoon.com Radio station.

Choice Radio www.choiceradio.com Radio Web site.

CleanAirwaves.com
www.homestead.com/cleanairwaves/ tv.html Directory of addresses of major media and television sources.

College Broadcast www.collegebroadcast.com Radio station.

College Music www.collegemusic.com Internet radio.

College Radio List
www.jett.com/collegeradio.clgradio. html State-by-state list of college radio stations.

Comedy Central www.comcentral.com Humor.

Cosmic Radio www.cosmicradio.com or www.Worldwide-Radio.com Internet-based radio station offering music to over a million listeners per week; for musicians, offers a free opportunity to get music heard; music submitted to the station gets airplay and some promotion through biweekly newsletter and radio playlist; online record store; fee includes benefits.

Country Music Television (CMT)
www.country.com Country music videos.

Cyber Radio www.cyberradio.2000.com Internet radio; new releases.

Dbotv.com www.dbotv.com Set to break new ground in interactive TV.

Destiny Media Player www.radiodestiny.com For listening to MP3s and Internet radio; easy installation; links; access to hundreds of Internet radio stations.

DigAS www.david-gmbh.de Digital audio system for broadcast professionals; system modules are a complete package of programs for working with audio material in radio stations.

Disney Channel
www.disney.com/disneychannel Family entertainment; Disney movies.

DJ Jukebox
www.gammadyne.com/jukebox.htm Playlist generator and MP3 organizer; supports remote control through a LAN; rate each song to ensure favorites are played often.

DJ Mac www.mixthisdjs.com/djsonly.html Software for DJs; allows tracking of shows, income, employees, and clients; free download.

DJ Mix Pro
djmixpro.com/djmixpro/djmixpro.html MP3 player and mixer; performs fully automatic quality DJ mixes, including cross fading and beat matching between songs; screenshots.

DJ Solutions New!
www.teleport.com/~sundholm Business management software for mobile disc jockeys, karaoke, or rentals; free demo available.

DJjmixed.com www.djmixed.com Home page.

DMX Music www.dmxmusic.com Digital Music Express (DMX) provides digital music by subscription to businesses and consumers via cable, satellite, and disc.

Dot Music www.dotmusic.com Mainstream music heard on the radio; music news; downloads; online CD store.

DRS-DigiTrax Services www.drs-digitrax.com Producers of video software; teleprompter, video, and video broadcast software.

E! Entertainment Television www.eonline.com Entertainment news.

Express.com www.express.com Entertainment commerce channel.

EyeQRadio.com www.eyeqradio.com Dedicated to showcasing women in music, specifically the independent female artist/musician.

FOLK DJ-L www.folkradio.org Lists folk stations; shows; DJs and playlists.

FOX fox.com FOX Television Network.

Fox.com www.foxnetwork.com Fox online site.

GAYBC Radio Network www.gaybc.com Webcasting service for the global gay, lesbian, bisexual, and transgender community; news, talk shows, music, and special events.

GIST www.thegist.com Listings and articles.

Globalmedia.com www.globalmedia.com Creates E-commerce sites and audio streams for over 100 radio and TV stations; rankings; music videos.

GLR www.bbc.co.uk/england/glr Radio Web site; London station.

GoGaGa **www.gogaga.com** Unusual music programming.

Grand Royal **www.grandroyal.com/grRadio/ index.html** Beastie Boys Internet radio station; twenty-four hours; online store.

Greenwitch **www.greenwitch.com** Internet radio site that accepts submissions; San Francisco based; production company; twenty-four hours; commercial-free.

Hamfests **www.arrl.org/hamfests.html** Calendar of events run by ham radio operators.

Hard Radio **www.hardradio.com** Internet radio Web site; hard rock.

HBO **www.hbo.com** HBO Web site.

History of TV Advertising **adage.com/news_and_features/ special_reports/tv** Television history from the advertising perspective.

House of Blues **www.hob.com** Internet radio site that accepts submissions.

Imagine Radio **www.imagineradio.com** Build own Internet radio station; link to main site; stations; chat.

IndiePromo.com IR List **www.indiepromo.com/ir** Radio directory.

Industrial-Radio **www.industrial-radio.com** Radio station.

Intercollegiate Broadcasting System (IBS) **www.ibsradio.org** College radio.

International Radio Station List **wmbr.mit.edu/stations/list.html** Lists U.S., Canadian, European, and other international stations; list of stations that broadcast on the Internet.

Internet Radio at MusicPromotion.net **musicpromotion.net/music/promotion/ ir.html** Resources; links to Internet radio stations and radio stations around the world; DJs; station managers; software.

Internet Radio **www.cmj.com/Musiclinks/ir.html** Radio on the Internet.

InterneTV **www.internetv.com** Internet television in its early stages.

Jam Television **www.canoe.ca/Television** News about TV and other entertainment in U.S. and Canada.

Jam TV **www.jamtv.com** Television Web site.

Jazz 88 Radio **www.jazz88.org** Radio; world music; jazz.

KCRW **www.kcrw.org** Eclectic music.

Kill Pop Radio **www.killpopradio.com** Radio Web site.

Knitting Factory **www.knittingfactory.com/live/index. html** Eclectic; from NYC.

Launch **www.launch.com** Online radio channel; recommend new music; videos; search engine; store; Webzine.

LesBiGay Radio Chicago **www.lesbigayradio.com** AM 1240 and 1470; daily show aimed at the gay, lesbian, transgender, and bisexual population; RealAudio.

Like Television **www.liketelevision.commusicv** TV Web site.

Live Broadband Radio and Television Broadcasts **broadcast-live.com/broadband.html** High speed television broadcasts around the world.

Live Radio and Television from Asia **broadcast-live.com/asia.html** Live television and radio broadcasts from China, India, Japan, Korea, Singapore, Thailand, and elsewhere in Asia; music, news, and sports.

Live Radio and Television from Europe **broadcast-live.com/europe.html** Watch television and listen to radio broadcasts; music; news and sports.

Live Television from around the World **broadcast-live.com/television** Live television broadcasts are available from a number of countries including Belgium, Croatia, Canada, France, Germany, United States, and the UK from this site.

Live365 **www.live365.com** Create an Internet radio station for free.

LiveConcerts **www.liveconcerts.com** Internet radio site that accepts submissions; live netcasts of rock concerts.

Loop Recorder **www.config.de/LoopRecorder** Designed for capturing songs from the radio; loop mode infinitely records up to a specified number of minutes in a continuous loop while scrolling the data.

Loud Factory **www.loudfactory.com** Radio Web site; twenty-four hours; MP3 format; artists information.

M4Radio **www.m4radio.com** Radio Web site.

MediaBureau.com **www.mediabureau.com** Live and direct Web casts and original content.

Mic Check Radio **www.miccheckradio.com** Radio Web site.

MIT Internet Radio Directory **wmbr.mit.edu/stations** Worldwide Internet radio directory.

Mix III **www.gi-ad.com/GIADsw/MixIII.html** Program to play music like a DJ; users can program music styles, rhythms, melodies, and mix a range of audio files.

MP3Spy **www.mp3spy.com** Search for Internet radio sites using Shoutcast MP3 streaming technology; find specific genres and programming; Game Spy Industries.

Much Music **www.muchmusic.com** Streaming audio and video.

Music Choice **www.musicchoice.com** Commercial-free professionally programmed music channels and digital downloads.

Music Radio **www.Webzone.net/willhoite/music/ music.html** College stations; commercial stations; links to international stations; music search engine; charts.

Music Television (MTV) **www.mtv.com** Music videos; features.

Music Video Detail **www.qrsmusic.com/music/videos/ qrs5mus16.htm** Assortment of sing-along videos.

National Association of College Broadcasters (NACB) **www.hofstra.edu/nacb** Official Web site.

National Public Radio **www.npr.org** Home page of NPR.

NBC **www.nbc.com** National Broadcast Network.

Net Broadcaster **www.netbroadcaster.com** Source for streaming entertainment; celebrities.

Net Radio **www.netradio.com** Radio Web site; listen or purchase; over 120 music channels; downloads.

Net Radio Showcase **www.netradioshowcase.com** Radio Web site.

NetRadio Network **www.netradio.net** All kinds of music programming.

NetRadio.com **www.netradio.net** Over 120 channels of music playing continuously; purchase CDs online; requires RealMedia Player or Windows Media Player; all genres.

New Era Radio **www.neweraradio.com** Radio Web site.

New Releases Video **www.newreleasesvideo.com** New video releases.

Next **www.nextDJ.com** DJ gear.

Nick at Nite & TV Land **nick-at-nite.com** Games; vintage TV.

Nickelodeon **www.nick.com** Entertainment for young people.

Nordic.com Radio Listings **www.nordicdms.com** All genres; links to over one hundred radio stations; downloads.

On Air **www.onair.com** Home page.

ON-AIR Pro **www.on-airpro.com** Workflow system for on-air promotion in television; tracks and coordinates spot creation process from inception to broadcast; Macintosh and Windows.

ON-AIR.com **www.on-air.com** Three genres of music; Internet-only radio station.

Onradio.com **www.onradio.com** Internet radio.

PBS **www.pbs.org** Public Broadcasting Station.

Prairie Home Companion **phc.npr.org** Online site of the public radio program.

Pseudo.com **www.pseudo.com** Internet radio; audio; video; chat; message boards.

Queer FM **www.lesbigay.com/queerfm** News, information, and music for the lesbian, gay, bisexual, and transgender communities.

Radio 1 **www.bbc.co.uk/radio1** Radio Web site; RealAudio streams.

Radio 2 **www.bbc.co.uk/radio2** Radio Web site; jazz; folk; country.

Radio 3 **www.bbc.co.uk/radio3** Radio Web site; classical.

Radio 4 All **www.radio4all.org** Links to microbroadcasters.

Radio Airplay **www.radioairplay.com** Radio charts and playlists.

Radio Connection **www.radioconnection.com** Train for a career in the music industry; on-the-job training in local major recording studios, radio, and TV stations.

Radio Destiny **www.radiodestiny.com** Radio Web site.

Radio Directory **www.radiodirectory.com/Stations** Radio directory organized by geographical location.

Radio Etc. **www.radioetc.com** Radio Web site.

Radio Free Tokyo **www.radiofreetokyo.com** Radio Web site.

Radio Freedom **www.radiofreedom.com** Radio Web site.

Radio HK **www.radiohk.com/radio** Submit CD; full-time Internet broadcasting site.

Radio Margaritaville **www.margaritaville.com** Jimmy Buffet's Internet radio Web site.

Radio Moi **www.radiomoi.com** or **www.musicmusicmusic.com** Radio Web site; MP3 format; create own station; stations; music library; facts.

Radio Net **www.radionet.com** Internet radio site.

Radio Promo **www.radiopromo.com** Radio Web site.

Radio Show Prep **www.freeyellow.com/members6/ bestprep/MusLabel.html** 5,900 links to radio show prep sites; free online show prep material.

Radio Spy **www.radiospy.com** Shareware program; organize audio feeds; daily Internet radio news; chat tools.

Radio Tower **www.radiotower.com** Radio Web site.

Radio Viva **www.radiovivapr.com** Radio Web site.

Radio Wave **www.radiowave.com** Radio Web site; list of radio stations; streaming requires RadioWave.com player.

Radio X **www.radiox.com** Information about Internet radio shows.

Radio.Netscape **www.radio.netscape.com** Radio Web site.

Radiojock.com **www.radiojock.com/labels.html** Web site for professional broadcasters; production and equipment sources; music; charts; show prep; mix jocks; links to related Web sites.

RadioTV **www.radiotv.com** Internet radio site that accepts submissions.

Real Net Radio **www.RealNetRadio.com** Independent radio station on the Internet; provides unsigned artists with a means of getting their music heard; upload music; maintain custom playlist of music.

RealGuide **www.realguide.real.com** Comprehensive directory of RealAudio and RealVideo broadcast sites.

Relax Online College Radio Directory **www.relaxonline.com/radio** State-by-state listing of college radio stations.

Rip-Off Radio **thebigripoff.com** Plays all music genres twenty-four hours.

Rock'n'Roots **www.rocknroots.com** Weekly one-hour eclectic music public radio program.

Rolling Stone Radio **www.rsradio.com** Internet radio site; stations; list of artists.

Rough Guide to Rock **www.roughguides.com/rock** Rock A-Z online.

Sci-Fi Channel: Dominion **www.scifi.com** Science fiction.

Ska Radio **www.skaradio.com** Radio Web site.

SonicNet Radio **www.radio.sonicnet.com** Custom radio section.

Spank Radio **www.spanlradio.com** Underground music twenty-four hours.

Special TV Resources **www.specialWeb.com/tv** Directory of television Web sites.

Spike Radio **www.spikeradio.com** Global Web radio network.

Spinner **www.spinner.com** Internet radio site; channels in all genres; free Spinner player; over one hundred stations; artist information.

Spot Taxi **www.spottaxi.com** Streamline and integrate Internet radio advertising systems.

Sunday Morning Klezmer & Other Jewish Music **www.angelfire.com/nj/ WBZCFMsndymrnngklzmr** An Internet and radio exploration of Jewish music, art, and culture.

Tactile12000 MP3 DJ **www.tactile12000.com** 3D interactive simulation of a DJ setup; allows users to cross fade, backspin, and change the speed of full-length WAV and MP3 files; Macintosh; Windows.

Talk Radio News **www.talkradionews.com** Radio Web site; online version; news from Washington, D.C.

Television Schedules of the World **www.buttle.com/tv/schedule.htm** Global TV listings.

Texas Internet Radio **www.texasinternetradio.com** Internet radio Web site.

The Box **www.thebox.com** Music videos.

The Cyberdog Music Industry Databases **www.radzone.org/threeminutedog/ cyberdog.html** Directory of college radio stations organized by state.

The DJ **www.thedj.com/home/page** Radio Web site; accepts submissions.

The Groove Box **www.groove-box.com** Low bandwidth background music; searching; news and more.

The History Channel **www.HistoryChannel.com** History channel.

The Home of Television Theme Lyrics **www.geocities.com/Hollywood/ Academy/4760** TV song lyrics.

The Music Review **www.musicreview.com** Radio station search engine; access to radio charts; lists by format; AM and FM stations.

The Nashville Network & CMT **www.country.com** Country Music Television; music videos; Grand Ol' Opry and more.

The Womb **www.thewomb.com** Electronica Internet radio Web site.

Tuneto.com **www.tuneto.com** Radio Web site.

Turner Classic Movies **turner.com/tcm/index.htm** Classic movies.

TV Guide Online **www.tvguide.com** Online version of TV Guide.

TV Guide Soaps **www.tvguide.com/soaps** Soap opera plot updates.

Ultimate TV **www.ultimatetv.com** Schedules and articles; online magazine covering television.

V Tuner **www.vtuner.com** Information about Internet radio shows.

VH1 **www.vh1.com** Online version of the cable channel; video hits; popular music; original movies.

Vidnet **www.vidnetusa.com** Music videos.

Virgin Radio **www.virginradio.com** Radio Web site.

Virtually Canadian **www.virtuallycanadian.com** Radio Web site; 24-hour station; archive section replay live broadcasts; event listings; artist interviews.

Virtue TV **www.virtuetv.com** Live Internet video broadcasts.

Vision TV Net **www.visiontvnet.com** Internet television.

Visual Radio **www.visualradio.com** Online multimedia service.

vTunner **www.vTunner.com** Program for finding radio stations and TV programming around the world.

Web Radio **www.Webradio.com** Internet radio site.

Women on Air **www.womenonair.com** Weekly one-hour radio series; eclectic mix of female artists from around the world.

Woofur **www.woofur.com** Internet radio; independent music of all genres.

World Classical Radio **www.u.arizona.edu/-rcampbel/worldclassicalradio.html** Listing of full-time classical music radio stations worldwide.

World Music Radio **www.worldmusicradio.org** Internet radio site that accepts submissions; member driven, noncommercial Internet radio station; world and traditional music.

World Radio Network **www.wrn.org** Live international newscasts.

World Wide Broadcast Network **www.wwbc.net** Streaming media portal for over 8,000 live concert events; Internet radio stations, music more.

World Wide Web Virtual Library **www.comlab.ox.ac.uk.archive/publishers/boradcast.html** International lists by country; TV, radio, and satellite.

Worldbeat Center **oneworldradiotv.com** Twenty-four hour world and reggae music; Internet radio; live shows Monday through Saturday from 1-5 PM.

Worldwide-Radio **www.worldwide-radio.com** Radio Web site; original Web radio station.

x-radio.com: DJ Music and Culture **www.x-radio.com/** X-Radio.com Electronic music; Internet Radio; online store; specialize in house, techno, trance, jungle, hip-hop, reggae, ambient, breakbeat, drum and bass, and more.

Yesterday USA **www.yesterdayusa.com** Radio Web site; radio shows from 1920s to 1950s.

Zero24-7 Details **www.zero24-7.org/main.html** Internet radio.

Ragtime

20 Ragtime Jazz Classics for Piano **www.netstoreusa.com/music/004/**

HL00490247.shtml Ragtime classics; sheet music.

After Hours Ragtime Café **www.stormi.com/music.html** The charm of yesteryear.

Colin D. MacDonald's Ragtime-March-Waltz Website Welcome Page **www.ragtimemusic.com** Ragtime, march, and waltz MIDI files.

Doc Wilson's Ragtime MIDI Files **www.geocities.com/BourbonStreet/Delta/5253/midis.html** MIDI files.

John Roache's Ragtime **members.aol.com/ragtimers** Ragtime, jazz, and stride piano MIDI sequences; online catalog for ragtime, stride, and novelty piano music.

Kansas City Ragtime Revelry **www.sound.net/~garyr/revelry/raghome2.shtml** Nonprofit corporation dedicated to the promotion and preservation of Kansas City's legacy of ragtime music.

Mary Haley's Ragtime Home Page **www.ragtimers.org/~ragtimers** Information on ragtime concerts, festivals, societies, and clubs; list of ragtime CD recordings and sheet music; pointer to MIDI files; where to order ragtime merchandise; FAQ.

Music Links **www.rtpress.com/links.htm** Links to music sites; ragtime, oldtime, and stride; American variety stage; vaudeville; entertainment 1870-1920.

Northern Virginia Ragtime Society (NVRS) **www.nvrs.org** Official Web site.

Oleg Mezjuev's Home Page **www.geocities.com/Paris/1790** Ragtime Press MIDI Music Archive; over one hundred live recorded MIDI files.

Paragon Ragtime Orchestra **www.paragonragtime.com** Professional organization performing ragtime-era music; vaudeville hits; silent movie accompaniments; dance-hall favorites.

'Perfessor' Bill Edwards Ragtime Sheet Music Covers and MIDI Files **www.perfessorbill.com** Restored sheet music covers and MIDI files.

Player Piano **www.ragtimewest.com** Close to one hundred pages; WAV files; MIDI files.

Rag and Then Some from the Performance Series **www.qrsmusic.com/music/performance/q5mp_8.htm** CDs and floppy disks; Nostalgic Series; Performance Series; Concert Series; George Gershwin.

Ragtime Alphbetic Index **www.rtpress.com/titles.htm** Alphabetic listing of song titles and authors available; live MIDI performances.

Ragtime and Early Jazz: 1900-1935
**www.netstoreusa.com/music/
002/HL00240074.shtml** Fake book.
Ragtime for Guitar
**village.infoWeb.ne.jp/~ragtime/
english.htm** Arrangements for guitar.
*Ragtime Jazz Vaudeville 1920s Vintage Recordings
on Cassette and CD*
www.vintage-recordings.com Large
selection; online catalog; samples.
Ragtime MIDI by Walt E. Smith
**members.aol.com/waltesmith/ragtime.
htm** For noncommercial use only.
Ragtime MIDI Files by Warren Trachtman
www.trachtman.org/ragtime Ragtime
MIDI files of piano pieces by Scott Joplin,
James Scott, Joseph Lamb, Jelly Roll Morton,
Eubie Blake, and others; Piano Soundfonts.
Ragtime Press MIDI Music Archive
www.rtpress.com Ragtime, blues, stride, and
boogie piano played live by Sue Keller.
Ragtime Rendevous-Ragtime by Mail
www.jazzbymail.com/ragtime.html
Online music store specializing in classic jazz
and ragtime; traditional jazz and Dixieland.
Ragtime Sheet Music and Books
**www.trachtman.org/ragtime/
musicbooks.htm** Links to ragtime audio CDs
and tapes, collections of ragtime sheet music, and
books about ragtime.
Ragtime Solos and Duets
**www.netstoreusa.com/music/
504/HL50462620.shtml** For C instruments;
flute; guitar; piano; keyboard; percussion; solo
instrumental; woodwind.
Ragtime Tunes
**www.discoverynet.com/~ajsnead/
ragtime/ragtime.html** MIDI files.
Ragtime-Blues-Hot Piano
www.doctorjazz.freeserve.co.uk Ragtime
piano music; MIDI files of some of the great
ragtime artists; photographs; document archives.
Rocky Mountain Ragtime Festival
www.ragtimers.org/rmrf Annual event at
Boulder's Unity Church.
SC Music
**www.unc.edu/depts/csas/socult/music/
ragtime.htm** Ragtime piano music, created
almost entirely by black Southerners, has roots
in minstrel show cakewalks, most of them
composed by Northern white men.
Scott Joplin International Ragtime Foundation
www.scottjoplin.org Located in Sedalia,
Missouri, the Cradle of Ragtime.
Scott Joplin Ragtime Guitar Sheet Music
**www.netstoreusa.com/music/025/
HL02506923.shtml** Ragtime for guitar.

Sourcing Ragtime and Old-Time Piano Music
perfessorbill.tripod.com/links1.htm
Links for ragtime and old-time piano music.
Stomp Off Records
www.stompoffrecords.com/ragtime.html
Search by genre.
Swedish Ragtime Home Page **www.ragtime.nu**
Ragtime MIDI files; rags written by Swedish,
international, classic, and contemporary ragtime
composers.
The Ragtime Centennial Show
www.rrragtimer.com Online show takes
audience back one hundred years to the
beginnings of Ragtime.
Vaudeville and Ragtime Show
www.bestwebs.com/vaudeville Early
ragtime and vaudeville performers; songs and
routines.
Vintage Music-Ragtime Jazz Vaudeville
www.vintage-music.com/ragtime Antique
ragtime; jazz; vaudeville; links.
West Coast Ragtime Society
www.ragtimemusic.com/WCRS Official
Web site.

Record Labels

A&M Records **www.amrecords.com** Links to
A&M artist sites; news; tours; A&M
merchandise; information including how to
submit a demo; jobs at A&M; tracking down old
records.
Almo **www.almosounds.com** Label Web site.
American Recordings **american.recordings.com**
Labels; RealAudio; band information; tour dates.
Arioso.com-Classical Music Record Companies
**www.arioso.com/noframes/records/
record1.htm** Complete contact information for
classical and contemporary concert music.
Ari's Simple List of Record Labels
guxx.com/recordlabels/index.html Record
labels.
Arista Records **www.aristarec.com** Hi and low
bandwidth access; graphics oriented; information
on artists; weekly word section; listen to new
items in RealAudio; audio and video clips; chat
area.
Association of Independent Record Labels
www.air.org.au National Association of
Australian Owned Independent Record Labels.
Atlantic Records **www.atlantic-records.com**
Label Web site; artists; news; events; tours.
Authentic Performance Recording Labels
www.intr.net/bleissa/lists/labels.html
Period instrument; authentic performance
recording labels or sublabels.
Band Radio Directory: Record Companies
www.bandradio.com/dir/

Record_Companies Record labels.
Blue Note Records **www.bluenote.com** Jazz; information; artists; catalogue; shopping; new releases; FAQ; history of the company.
BMG Entertainment **www.bmg.com** Browse music by genre; own over 200 record labels; music club site; order CDs online.
Canadian Music Labels **www.canehdian.com/industry/labels. html** Canadian record labels.
Capitol Records **www.hollywoodandvine.com** Current releases; tours; chances to win; listen to album extracts; join the monthly newsletter; information about Capitol Studios and gear.
CCM World-Record Labels **members.aol.com/ccmlinks/ record_labels.html** Christian record label marketing hierarchy; up-to-date listing of links to Christian record labels, distribution groups, and marketing entities.
Classical Music Record Companies on the Web **www.search-beat.com/labels.htm** The Classical Music Beat; classical music history Internet links; classical music history time lines; composer history resources.
CollegeMusic.com-Record Label Search **www.collegemusic.com/content/labels** Record labels.
Columbia Records **www.columbiarecords.com** Record label; video channel; artist biographies and schedules; reviews; links.
Cooking Vinyl **www.cookingvinyl.com** Eclectic roster.
Country Music Record Labels **www.faroc.com.au/~srenfrey/labels. html** Home page.
Curb Records **www.curb.com** Record label; artist information; new releases.
Decca **www.decca-nashville.com** Home page; win free stuff; browse the site; for country fans; information; news; sound bites.
Del-FI Records **www.del-fi.com** Rock 'n' roll legends; blues.
Deutsche Grammophon **www.dgclassics.com** Classical music record label; new releases; tour dates; new studio.
Dirty Linen-Record Company Addresses **www.futuris.net/linen/special/label. html** Record company addresses; links to sites.
Dreamworks Records **www.dreamworksrecords.com** Record label; artist information; new releases.
Early Music Record Labels **www.concerto.demon.co.uk** Details of record labels that issue recordings of early music and their Web sites.
Edel **www.edel.co.uk** German company; indie labels.

Electro Groove-Electronica Guide for the Internet-Record Labels **www.electrogroove.com/labels.htm** Guide to electronica and techno on the Internet; Internet radio broadcasting; groups and DJs with audio/visual sites; mega resources.
Elektra **www.elektra.com** Individual artists; search music topics; browse archives; check tour dates; store; download audio and video clips.
EMI-Chrysalis **www.emirecords.co.uk** Label Web site.
EMI Music **www.emimusic.ca** Record label; artist information; new releases.
Epic Records **www.epicrecords.com** Record label; artist information; new releases.
Fast Track for Record Labels and DVD Publishers **www.infront.co.uk/ fasttrackrecordlabels.jhtml** Designed to increase sales.
Geffen Records **www.geffen.com** Record label; tours; new releases; artist links.
Groovenet Music Resource: Record Labels **www.groovenet.com/recordlabels** Record labels.
HandiLinks to Music Labels **ahandyguide.com/cat1/m/m354.htm** Links to over 500 record labels.
Headz Magazine Online-Labels **www.headzmagazine.com/labels.html** Record labels.
Hightone Records **www.hightone.com/index.html** Independent record label; American roots music.
Hollywood Records **www.hollywoodrec.com** Artists; soundtracks; pictures; tracks; videos; tours.
Hyperion **www.hyperion-records.co.uk** British classical music label.
In Heaven . . . Record Labels **www.thecompany.net/jason/muslabels. html** Record labels.
Independent Record Labels **www.shef.ac.uk/misc/rec/ps/efi/elabels. html** Outline details and contact information; catalogues of releases; links.
Independent Record Labels, Links, and Info **members.tripod.com/Hz_dB/labels.html** Record labels.
Info for Artists and Labels **www.racerrecords.com/ArtistsAndLabels .html** Believe in sharing information and in supporting other folks who are trying to make music available, whether those people are artists or other labels.
Instrumental Music-Record Labels **www.instrumentalmusic.com/labels/**

index.html Instrumental music record labels; thirty-six new age labels; four guitar instrumental labels; world music record labels.

Interscope Records
www.interscoperecords.com Record labels; tracks; videos.

Island Def Jam **www.islanddefjam.com** Label Web site.

Island Records **www.island.co.uk** Catalogue; noticeboard; chat room; staff room; what's new; tour dates; history of Island Records; RealAudio extracts.

Jazz Links: Labels
www.pk.edu.pl/~pmj/jazzlinks/labels. html Home Page.

Jive **www.peeps.com/jiverecords/index.html** Label Web site.

Matador Records **www.matador.recs.com** Indie label in NYC; online catalogs; newsletter.

Maverick **www.maverickrc.com** Information; artists; forums; owned by Madonna.

MCA Nashville **www.mca-nashville.com** Record label Web site.

MCA Records America **www.mcarecords.com** Label Web site; country artists.

MCA-Universal Music **www.mcamei.com** or **www.universalmusic.co.uk** UK site uses Shockwave; features; artists; club information; tour dates; new releases and interviews.

MDVD Network **www.mdvdnetwork.com** Record label Web site.

Mercury Records **www.mercuryrecords.com** Record label; artist information; links.

Metal Index: Record Labels
www.metalindex.com/recordlabels.html Record labels.

Metal Labels: Death Metal/Black Metal Record Labels
www.evilmusic.com/db/labels.html Metal labels.

Motown **www.motown.com** Information; music; featured artists; games and trivia.

MPEG3 Music Archive: Record Labels
www.nordicdms.com/indielabels or **www.nordicrecords.com/indielabels** MPEG3 and MPEG2 music; Indie bands; free MPEG audio players; MP3 and MP2 search engine; photo gallery; vinyl database; music links; Web rings; over 1,100 MPGs with samples.

Music Base **www.musicbase.co.uk** British record labels.

Music Guild Directory
www.musicguild.org/directory/record. htm List of links; information about the record companies.

Naxos **www.naxosusa.com** Classical.

Nettwerk **www.nettwerk.com** Nettwerk Records.

Nimbus **www.nimbus.ltd.uk/nrl/index.html** Classical label.

Open Directory-Arts: Music: Record Labels
www.dmoz.org/Arts/Music/Business/ Record_Labels Record Labels (822); Ambient (32); Bluegrass (15); Christian (43).

P.A.W.S.: Scandinavian Record Labels and Distributors **home.swipnet.se/~w-53855/labels.html** or **home5.swipnet.se/~w-53855/labels.html** Record labels and distributors.

Parlophone **www.lookon.net** Audio streams; upcoming releases.

Phillips Classics **www.philclas.polygram.nl** List of artists and composers; information and recording details.

POLLSTAR-The Concert Hotwire
www.pollstar.com/therecordlabels.html Record labels.

Polydor **www.polydor.co.uk** Label Web site.

Polygram **www.polygram.com/polygram** Record label.

Polygram Records
www.polygram.com/polygram Search site by artist, label, country, film, and video title or by company.

RCA US
www.peeps.com/artists/frames/rca.html Index of the label roster.

RCA Victor **www.rcavictor.com** Information; artists.

Record Company Addresses
www.dirtynelson.com/linen/special/ label.html Updated about every two months; send corrections to office@dirtylinen.com.

Record Label Music
www.recordlabelmusic.com Home page.

Record Labels (A-Z)
www.ummusic.com/Labels/index.htm List of links to record labels.

Record Labels @ BandLink.Net
www.bandlink.net/labels.html Alphabetical and comprehensive list of major and independent record labels on the Internet.

Record Labels @ Indie-Music.com
www.indie-music.com/labels.htm Large list of record labels; listed alphabetically, starting with numbers and symbols first.

Record Labels @ World Records
www.worldrecords.com Complete alphabetical listing of independent record labels; search under Record Label Sites.

Record Labels
ion.apana.org.au/~mdagn/labels.html or **spraci.cia.com.au/labels/labels.htm** Record Labels in Australia.

Record Labels
members.aol.com/LEGION59/labels.
html Record labels.
Record Labels **www.geld.com/tweenet/labels**
Record labels A-Z.
Record Labels
www.geocities.com/SunsetStrip/Bistro/
5480/labels.html For record labels and
companies; submit link; posts messages from
record labels.
Record Labels
www.oilfactory.com/labels/index.html
List of links to record labels on the Internet.
Record Labels
www.rhythmnet.com/l/default.html
Rhythm Net record labels.
Record Labels **www.tweekitten.com/Labels**
Record labels index.
Record Labels
www.zebramusic.com/labels.html Record
labels; musicians tip sheet; instructional videos;
gig sharing network; special reports and services;
articles and interviews.
Record Labels on the Web
www.arancidamoeba.com/labels.html or
www-kzsu.stanford.edu/~music/
label-www.html Database of record label Web
site links searchable by location and genre; labels
perpetually added; dead links regularly removed.
Record Labels Webring
www.bigfoot.com/~songringmall/label.
htm Webring for record labels.
Recording Labels **www.babylon.gr/lrec.htm**
Links record labels; E-mail URL and will add to
links section.
Reprise Records **www.RepriseRec.com** Record
label; artists; audio files.
Rhino **www.rhino.com** U.S. reissue label.
Rounder Records **www.rounder.com** Independent
record label; Massachusetts based; folk; roots;
ethnic; children's.
Ruffhouse **www.ruffhouse.com** Urban label.
Rykodisc **www.rykodisc.com/3** Independent
record label; rereleases; new releases; catalog;
articles; tours; message board.
Scandinavian Indie-Record Labels
www.lysator.liu.se/~chief/reclabel.html
Lists for Sweden, Norway, Finland, Denmark,
and Iceland.
Scandinavian Indie-Swedish Record Labels
www.lysator.liu.se/~chief/swlabels.
html or
sf.www.lysator.liu.se/~chief/swlabels.
html Swedish record labels and companies;
information regarding address, phone, fax,
Internet links, and E-mail.
Snowboarding-Online.com
www.solsnowboarding.com/directories/

recordlabels.html Photos; record labels
directory.
Sony Music **www.sonymusic.com** or
www.music.sony.com/Music or
www.musiceurope.com or
www.sonymusic.co.uk Information; artists;
tours; new releases; back catalogue; news; live
Web broadcasts; multimedia; interviews; music
and video clips.
SpinSpin Indie Record Labels
www.alphalink.com.au/~snf/spinspin/
labels/index.html "Independent recording
labels have a knack of starting up, releasing a
few 7"s and an ep, and then folding; other indie's
go on for years and years."
Sun Records **www.sunrecco.com** or
www.sunstudio.com Where rock and roll
began; label for Elvis Presley, Jerry Lee Lewis,
Johnny Cash, B.B. King, Roy Orbison, and
others from the Golden Age; history of Sun's
development; information on major artists.
TAXI: Major Record Labels
www.taxi.com/members/links-
labels.html Independent A&R Vehicle that
connects unsigned artists, bands, and songwriters
with major record labels, publishers, and film and
TV music supervisors.
The Knowledge **www.theknowledge.com** Indie
and mainstream labels.
The MP3meta Guide
www.mp3meta.com/guide/Business/
Record_Labels Comprehensive and up-to-date
source for music and MP3 information on the
Internet.
The Music Review: Record Labels
user.aol.com/selfnet/labels.htm Music
industry data.
The Musician's Homepage-Record Labels
www.thechairlift.com/~digialex/
bandlabl.html or
www.enteract.com/~digialex/bandlabl.
html A-Z record label lists.
The Partial Guide to Independent Record Labels
www3.sympatico.ca/partialguide/indie.
html Indie labels.
ThePunkPage.com-Labels
www.thepunkpage.com/labels.html Punk
record labels.
TT Net **www.tt.net** Record label sites; band
information.
TVT Records **www.tvtrecords.com** Record label.
UBL.COM **www.ubl.com/label** Links to
Hollywood Records; Maverick Records;
Dreamworks Records; record label listings;
alphabetical label listings.
Universal Classics **www.universalclassics.com**
Rosters of classical labels; artist bios.

Universal Music **www.universalmusic.com**
Label Web site; news; links.

Verve Records
**www.vervemusicgroup.com/verve/
index.html** Great jazz artists.

Vinyl Network : Drum & Bass Online **www.vinyl-net.com** Online mail order record store; drum &
bass/jungle specialist; back catalogue coverage of
over 200 labels with comprehensive review
sections.

Virgin Records **www.virginrecords.com** or
www.vmg.co.uk or
www.virginmusiccanada.com Music
information; technical questions; who to send
demo tapes to; artists.

Walt Disney Records **www.disney.com** or
**www.disney.com/DisneyRecords/index.
html** Information; pictures; new releases; audio
and video downloads.

Warner Bros. Records **www.wbr.com** or
www.warnermusic.ca or
www.music.warnerbros.com Feature
artists; company's artists; new releases; job
opportunities; Newswire; artists' message board;
tour dates and information; FAQ; subscribe to
the mailing list; audio and video clips.

World Wide Punk: Punk Labels
www.worldwidepunk.com/labels.html
Directory of punk, hardcore, ska, Oi, and other
record labels; hundreds of record labels,
distributors, stores, mail orders, etc.

*Worldwide Internet Music Resources: Record
Labels, Record Producers*
**www.music.indiana.edu/
music_resources/recind.html** William and
Gayle Cook Music Library, Indiana University
School of Music.

Worldwide List of Record Labels
spraci.cia.com.au/labels/labelsw.htm or
ion.apana.org.au/~mdagn/labelsw.html
Alphabetical list of links to information about
record labels around the world.

WWP-Record Labels
www.wwpro.com/labels.asp Search for
record labels around the world.

Recording

4-Track Recording Tips
**members.tripod.com/~PROPAC/4track.
htm** Tutorial; tips on recording; EQ; links to
recording equipment manufacturers.

A Dictionary of Record Producers
**www.officialsmithereens.com/
dikenwriting.html** Record producers.

Abbey Road Studios
www.abbeyroad.co.uk/indexpm.html
Famous recording studio.

Absolute Sound **www.theabsolutesound.com**
Journal of Audio and Music; articles.

Ampex Parts Sources
recordist.com/ampex/ampexpts.html
Sources for Ampex parts.

Analog Tape Recorders
**arts.ucsc.edu/ems/music/equipment/
analog_recorders/Analog_Recorders.
html** FAQ.

*Association of Professional Recording Services
(APRS)* **www.aprs.co.uk** UK-based
professional audio organization; traditional music
studios; project studios; postproduction;
broadcast; live sound; film soundtracks;
duplication; training; leading force within the
British music industry; concerned with standards,
training, technical, and legal issues; Board of
Directors are elected by members; studios can
become members; list of associated studios.

Audio Amateur Publications
www.audioexpress.com/index1.htm
Resources for building and repairing equipment.

Audio Amigo **www.audioamigo.com** Audio
recording; digital home studio equipment; digital;
resources; multitrack digital recording software;
articles on promotion, home recording, and audio
mastering.

Audio Arts **www.AudioArts.com** Recording Web
site.

Audio Café **www.audiocafe.com** Reference for
audio equipment manufacturers and products;
monthly quizzes; reviews; directories of
manufacturers; classified ads.

Audio Engineering
www.audioengineering.pagina.nl Home
page.

Audio Engineering Society (AES) **www.aes.org**
Professional society devoted exclusively to audio
technology; membership includes leading
engineers, scientists, and other authorities;
membership information; members in forty-
seven concentrated geographic areas throughout
the world; conferences; links to other audio-
related links including audio education and
research; audio equipment; audio-related usenet
newsgroups; computers and audio; electronic
music and MIDI; magazines and publications;
music; musical instruments; professional audio
companies; professional organizations; radio and
broadcast; search the WWW; test and
measurement; submit an audio related URL.

Audio Forums **www.AudioForums.com** Audio-
related forums.

Audio Home Recording Act of 1992
**www4.law.cornell.edu/uscode/17/
ch10.text.html** Information and details.

Audio Institute of America
www.audioinstitute.com Train to be a
recording engineer.
Audio Revolution **www.audiorevolution.com**
Reviews; Audio Video Marketplace.
Audio Seminars **www.audioseminars.com** Live
sound training; system engineering.
Audio Web **www.audioweb.com** Auction and
classified Web site; reviews.
Audio Web Sites @ World Records
www.worldrecords.com Audio companies;
recording; amps; synthesizers; mixers; FX;
microphones; software; ADAT; audio magazines;
cables; gear; speakers; hardware; tapes/CDs;
MIDI; consoles; MP3; CD-ROM; audio
production accessories; suppliers; online audio
stores; audio consultants.
Audio World **www.audioworld.com** Digital
music news; articles; industry news.
Audio-Related Internet World Wide Web and FTP
Sites **www.wssh.net/~wattsup/arsl.html**
Large collection of links.
Classic and Vintage Audio Circuits
w3.one.net/~robgrow/circuits/circuits.
html Schematics.
Consumer Electronics Manufacturers Association
www.cemacity.com Industry legislation
related to electronics manufacturers; trade show
information.
Cops **www.cops.co.uk/cops** UK music and
software manufacturing.
Daw-mac.com **www.daw-mac.com** For
Macintosh users in the studio.
Digital Domain **www.digido.com** Site to help
audio engineers and musicians make compact
discs and CD-ROMs; CD and CD-ROM
mastering.
Disc Makers **www.discmakers.com** Audio
duplication company; tutorials; CD promotion;
pocket guides; newsletter.
Disctronics **www.disctronics.co.uk**
Manufacturing; U.S., UK, and Europe.
Doctor Audio **www.DoctorAudio.com** Recording
Web site.
Electronic Musician **www.emusician.com**
Recording magazine; product reviews; articles;
features; resource for musicians interested in
personal music production; direct access to music
industry and article databases; download past
features and reviews.
EQ **www.eqmag.com** Recording magazine.
Global Express Media
www.globalexpressmedia.com CD
reproduction and related services.
Home Recording **www.homerecording.com**
Equipment reviews; MP3; digital music
recording on CDs or hard disks; tutorial for

beginners; mailing list; articles on recording and
mixing; FAQs on how to get started; active
forum; detailed glossary; numerous tutorials.
Home Recording Rights Coalition **www.hrrc.org**
or **www.yearbooknews.com/html/**
HomeRRC.html or
www.access.digex.net/~hrrc Coalition to
preserve the rights of those who use home audio
and video recording products; legislative issues;
digital copyright law; links.
Keyboard Magazine **www.keyboardmag.com**
Recording information; product reviews; articles;
columns.
Keyboard Online **www.keyboardonline.com**
Webzine.
Live-Audio.com **www.Live-Audio.com** Home
page.
Magnetic Tape Recorder Alignment
www.Webcom.com/~hurleyj/service/
bilver-align.html Tutorial.
Mix Online **www.mixonline.com/index.html**
Commercial and project studio recording; concert
sound; audio for film; video; news, features;
opinions; tests; links.
Mixed **www.Mixed.net** Recording Web site.
Music Maker Publications **recordingmag.com**
Recording Magazine; Music Pro Magazine;
database of back issues; catalog of books and
CDs for recording musicians.
Music Producers Guild **mpg.org.uk** Information;
for professionals.
Music Producers Guild of America
www.mpga.org Producers.
Musician's Tech Central
www.musicianstechcentral.com/library.
html Technical information; links.
Muzique.com **www.muzique.com** Bibliography
of books on musical electronics.
National Association of Recording Merchandisers
(NARM) **www.narm.com** Official Web site.
Nimbus Manufacturing **www.nimbused.com**
Audio duplication company.
Oasis CD & Cassette Duplication
www.oasisCD.com Audio duplication
company.
Octave.com **www.octave.com/en/library.htm**
Articles on recordable CDs.
Online Antique Phonograph Gallery
www.inkyfingers.com/~inky/Record.
html History; photographs.
Pro Audio Music **www.ProAudioMusic.com**
Recording Web site.
Pro Audio.net **www.soundwave.com** News;
information; discussion groups.
Pro Studio Edition **www.discmakers.com/pse**
Studio newsletter; interviews with engineers;
recording tips.

Prorec.com **www.prorec.com** Introductory and advanced technology; online music magazine; site index which can be viewed by title, company, product, author, or topic; bookstore; classified ads; active discussion board.

Random Access **www.pixelite.com/windaw** Information on recording software and hardware; discussion forums.

Re-Pro International **www.aprs.co.uk** Resource for producers and engineers.

Real Engineers **www.RealEngineers.com** Audio engineer database.

Rec.audio.pro **rec.audio.pro** Recording and live sound newsgroup; FAQ.

Rec.audio.tech **rec.audio.tech** Audio technology newsgroup.

Rec.audio.tubes **rec.audio.tubes** Audio technology newsgroup.

Recording Engineer Training **www.sna.com/musicbiz** On-the-job training in local major recording studios.

Recording **dir.yahoo.com/Entertainment/Music/ Recording** Information on recording.

Recording **www.recordingmag.com** Recording magazine; TAXI newsletter included.

Recording Connection **www.recordingconnection.com** Training for engineers.

Recording Industry Association of America (RIAA) **www.riaa.com** Current copyright infringement and piracy issues; censorship; information; resources; links.

Recording Studios @ World Records **www.worldrecords.com** List of recording studio Web sites.

Recording Technology History **ac.acusd.edu/History/recording/notes. html** History of sound recording; digital technologies and MP3.

Recording Workshop **www.recordingworkshop.com** Learn the art of recording.

Recordingeq.com **recordingeq.com** Recording Web site.

Remix Connection **www.RemixConnection.com** Recording Web site.

Re-Pro Guild of Recording Producers, Directors, and Engineers **www.aprs.co.uk/repro/index.html** International association for studio and music producers, sound directors, recording and mixing engineers, programmers, and remixers; forum.

Sound on Sound **www.sospubs.co.uk** UK high-tech recording magazine; articles and reviews; online forum.

Studio Finder **www.studiofinder.com** Database of over 5,000 studios by location, equipment, and experience.

Studio Menu **www.studiomenu.com** Recording Web site.

Studio Online **www.tcanet.com/s_o** Webzine on working in the recording studio; netcasting; concerts; articles; reviews; links.

Studio Sound **www.prostudio.com/studiosound** Features from current and past issues are available to read and download.

Studio Tips **www.studiotips.com** Acoustics; studio design; wiring.

Studiobase **www.demon.co.uk/studiobase** Lists of UK recording studios; recording engineers; mixers; hire companies; studio design and construction; record companies; mastering; manufacturers; distributors; software; management; rehearsal facilities.

Studiobase Record Producers List A-Z **www.demon.co.uk/studiobase/producer** Record producers.

Sun Studio **www.sunstudio.com** Virtual tour of the legendary studio; artist bios of those who recorded there.

The Encyclopedia of Record Producers **www.mojavemusic.com** Database of producers.

The Mastering Board **webbd.nls.net/webboard/wbpx.dll/ ~mastering** Audio topics; bulletin board; acoustics.

The Recording Studio Design Page **www.mcs.net/~malcolm** Acoustics and sound proofing.

The Recording Website **www.recordingwebsite.com** or **recording.hostway.com** Audio recording advice and tips; pro audio.

The Stereo Shop **www.thestereoshop.com/links.htm** Large collection of links to manufacturer sites.

Total Recording **www.kiqproductions.com** Book; Golden Ears Audio Eartraining course for musicians, engineers, and producers.

World Wide Pro Audio Directory **www.audiodirectory.nl** Over 10,000 manufacturers and dealers listed; search by subject.

Religious and Gospel Music—Inspirational

1Christian.net **www.1christian.net** Christian music network.

A Little Religion and Romance Music **www.greaterthings.com/Music** Online

MIDI albums and singles; originals and arrangements of spiritual, romantic, and patriotic songs, hymns, anthems, medleys; CD available.

All Gospel Music Network
www.allgospel.net/shop/start.asp Instructional videos for the beginning piano player to the advanced organ player.

Bible Gateway **www.bible.gospelcom.net** Bible-search resource.

Black Gospel Music Clef
www.blackgospel.com/tools/ sheetmusic.htm Dedicated to providing resources and information for participants and supporters of black gospel music.

Black Gospel Music Marketplace
www.blackgospel.com/marketplace/ sheet Products related to black gospel music; CDs; videos; books; publications; sheet music; equipment and more.

Cathedral Classical **www.ndirect.co.uk/~amen** Organ and sacred music.

CCM Online **www.ccmcom.com** Christian Music magazine; radio charts; countdown; Christian stations reporting.

Ceremony Music Resource Page
www.castle.net/~energize/CMRP/index. html Selection lists; online sound files; CD retailers; articles and books, etc.

Choir and Organ **www.orphpl.com/choir.htm** Music magazine; religious, secular, choral, reviews, news, and events.

Christian Answers.Net
www.christiananswers.net/midimenu. html Christian background music; TM page; 100+ MIDI files; floating music menu.

Christian Artists
tlem.netcentral.net/cmr/database.html Database.

Christian Artists Music Festival and Competition
www.Christian-artists.com Christian music festival.

Christian Books, Music, and Movies
www.powernet.net/~scrnplay/page102. html Online resource for religious products.

Christian Media, Music and Worship
www.connect.ab.ca/~kwalden/music. htm Contemporary, traditional, and alternative praise and worship music links.

Christian Music Central Radio
www.cmcentral.net/radio Web radio station playing popular Christian music.

Christian Music Place
www.placetobe.org/cmp/central.htm Resources for writers of Christian music.

Christian Songwriters Group
www.christiansongwriters.com Christian music songwriters.

Coalition of Internet Church Music Publishers
www.redshift.com/~bowms1/cicmp Dedicated Christians who compose and publish music for Christian worship; independent publishers.

Contemporary Christian Music
www.ccmusic.org Directories of Christian music and artists sites; concert dates.

Cornerstone Festival
www.cornerstone.jesusfreak.com Christian music festival.

Country Gospel Guild
www.countrygospelguild.com Home page.

Country Gospel News Magazine **www.paradise- serve.com/users/cgnm** Gospel music publication.

Creation Festival
www.gospelcom.net/creation Christian music festival.

Education Secretary's Statement on Religious Expression **www.ed.gov/Speeches/08- 1995/religion.html** Guidelines set forth by the U.S. Department of Education to clarify the First Amendment rights and responsibilities of students, parents, and schools.

Family-Styled Records **www.tgn.net/~fjones** Religious and family-oriented music.

FindGrace.com **www.findgrace.com** Christian news; free Christian MP3 music; free Bible software; commentary from respected Bible teachers; online Bible study.

Get Christian Music
www.getchristianmusic.com Christian music Web site.

GNMS.COM **www.gnms.com** Church music, worship, and drama materials from all publishers/suppliers; large inventory.

Godspell-The Musical
www.netpuppy.com/godspell/ themusical.htm Brief summary of the musical; cast/crew list and production diary.

Gospel Flava **www.gospelflava.com** Gospel music Web site.

Gospel Music Association (GMA)
www.gospelmusic.org Membership; gospel music links; resources for writers of Christian music.

Gospel Music Lessons
www.sensationalgospelmusic.com Gospel music books and audiocassette tapes for both adults and children.

Gospel Record Club
www.gospelrecordclub.com Gospel music.

Gospelcom.net **www.gospelcom.net/preview** Film preview Web site.

Heart Songs **www.heartsongs.org** Christian music.

Holy Land Arts **www.holylandarts.com**
Download site; MP3.

Hymn Site **www.HymnSite.com** MIDI hymns
and psalm tunes from The United Methodist
Hymnal.

John's Christian Music World
www.jps.net/watling Links; news; reviews
for all types of Christian music.

K-LOVE Radio **KLOVE.com** Contemporary
Christian music heard around the world; listener-
supported; noncommercial.

KXCD **www.kxcd.org** Commercial-free and
uninterrupted Christian alternative rock;
streaming MP3 station.

Lammas Records **www.lammas.co.uk** Solo,
choral, and organ music from Britain's cathedrals.

Liturgical Studies and Liturgical Music
**www.csbsju.edu/library/internet/
theoltgy.html** Annotated directory; historical;
scholarly; links encompass many different rites
of the Catholic Church including the Eastern
rites; links to some Protestant music and liturgy
links.

Music Ministry Webring
**www.Webring.org/cgi-
bin/Webring?ring=musministry** A
Webring for church music ministries; where to
list your church's choir or music department, or
any other pages related to music ministry; pages
for independent Christian musicians, recording
artists, dealers, etc.

Music Workshops: The Messiah
www.cstones.com/TheMessiah.html
Class materials for children or choirs; musical,
historical, and religious aspects.

Praise Charts
www.praisecharts.com/catalog.htm
Worship resource center; sheet music to popular
worship songs; supplied by a growing network
of arrangers.

Reflection Christian Music Resources
**www.users.zetnet.co.uk/mlehr/reflec/
reflec.htm** Original Christian worship music;
MIDIs and sheet music available for downloading
and use.

Religious Education Tolerance Association
**www.Webring.org/cgi-
bin/Webring?ring=relednetrin** Dedicated to
religious education and debunking information
about religions; any site that has information
concerning their (or other) religions may join;
will not be added to this ring if into bashing other
religions.

Religious Information Source-BELIEVE **www.mb-
soft.com/believe/index.html** Hundreds of
informative articles on important words,
subjects, and terms in Christianity and other
major world religions; source of information for
deeper understanding of religious subjects.

Religious Resources on the Net
www.aphids.com/relres Religious
Resources on the Net is a comprehensive,
searchable database of religious and Christian
Web sites on the Internet. Visitors to the Web
site can browse through over one hundred topics
or use our search engine to generate a listing of
religious resources containing selected words or
phrases.

Religious Science
www.religiousscience.org/firstrs1.htm
Ernest Holmes.

Religious Society of Friends **www.quaker.org** The
official Quaker home page; large listing of
Quaker links on the Web; hosting for a number
of Quaker groups.

Religious Songs and Hymns
www.bol.net/overseer5/hymns.html
Lyrics and MIDI files of hymns; picture
songbook format.

Religious Worship MIDI Sites
**www.valkhorn.com/directory/
midi_files/religious_** Listing of Web sites
with religious worship MIDI files.

Sacred Harp and Shape-Note Music Resources
**www.mcsr.olemiss.edu/~mudws/
resource** Describes printed music, literature,
recordings, and other related resources.

Sacred Music
**toltec.lib.utk.edu/~music/guides/sacred.
html** Bibliography of library holdings; relevant
card catalog numbers; links.

Sacred Music **www.sacredmusic.com** Religious
music Web site.

Sacred Music News and Review
www.tempomusic.com/smnr Religious
music.

Stravinsky's Religious Works
www.cco.caltech.edu/~tan/Stravinsky
Includes *Symphony of Psalms, Mass*, and
Requiem Canticles; illustrated biography of
Stravinsky's life; listening guide and
commentary.

Syndicated Contemporary Christian Music
www.GospelTrack.com GospelTrack;
syndicated radio program; Contemporary
Christian music; ministry messages between
tracks; RealAudio.

The Alive Christian Music Festival
www.place2be.org/cmp/alive Christian
music festival.

*The Almost Definitive Contemporary Christian
Music Hot-Page*
www.afn.org/~mrblue/ccm/ccm.html
Artist and band links; brief history.

The California Mission Site
 www.californiamissions.com Histories for each of the twenty-one California Missions; music; color and black-and-white photographs.

The Cyber Hymnal **tch.simplenet.com** Over 2,100 Christian hymns and gospel songs; lyrics; scores; MIDI files; pictures; history and more; free downloads.

The Holy Bible
 www.cybercomm.net/~dcon/drbible. html Translated from the Latin; first published by the English College at Douay, A.D. 1609.

The Music of Angels
 home.att.net/~shakercrafts/docs/ bell.html Musical notation.

The Musical Reforms of Martin Luther
 classicalmus.interspeed.net/articles/ luther.html Article tracing the musical reforms of Dr. Martin Luther; role as a compiler and composer of music.

The Singing News **www.singingnews.com** Southern gospel music; features; charts.

The World of Christian Music
 www.worldofcm.com Online magazine of Contemporary Christian music charts; top artists, albums, reviews, etc.

Today's Christian Music.com
 www.todayschristianmusic.com Contemporary Christian; live RealAudio feed.

Top Christian Music Titles
 www.emmanuel.kiev.ua/music_groupE. html Music hit parade of Christian musicians; MP3 songs available for free download.

Vatican Exhibit
 metalab.unc.edu/expo/vatican.exhibit/ exhibit/e-m Virtual exhibition from the Vatican; from Gregorian Chant to opera's origins; music hall.

Voice of the Shuttle: Religious Studies Page
 vos.ucsb.edu/shuttle/religion.html Resources; links to religious sites, journals, sociologists, papers, and sacred texts.

Voices from the Past
 www.watchmanmag.com/0112/011203. htm Origins of instrumental music in Christian worship.

WAGG 1320 AM **www.bham.net/wagg** Traditional and contemporary gospel music; special church and religious programs; news and community service.

Warrior Music Magazine
 www.warriormusicmagazine.com Streaming MP3 radio; music reviews; quote; links and more; Christian music for GenXers.

Wedding Chapel
 www.music.com/weddingchapel Wedding music.

WeddingMusic2Dance.com
 www.weddingmusic2dance.com Home page.

Worship Music **www.worshipmusic.com** Christian worship music; praise music media.

Xcess Christian Rock Music Festival
 www.xcess.org Christian music festival.

Search Engines

100 Hottest Sites **www.100hot.com** Directory of popular sites in ten categories.

About.com **www.about.com** Human driven search engine.

All the Web **www.alltheweb.com** Search engine.

All-in-One **www.albany.net/allinone** Compilation of search tools available.

AltaVista **www.altavista.digital.com** One of the top search engines; large database.

AOL.com **www.aol.com** Web guide; sites for many subjects and interests.

Argus Clearinghouse **www.clearinghouse.net** Specialty search engine; find music-related search engines.

Ask Jeeves **www.askjeeves.com** Ask questions; replies with a list of answers about where to find related material.

Beaucoup **www.beaucoup.com** Specialty search engine; find music-related search engines.

Bigfoot **www.bigfoot.com** Search for E-mail and Web addresses; Yellow Pages.

Brittanica Internet Guide **www.ebig.com** Directory; topics and search facilities.

CNet **cnet.com/Content/Features/Dlife/ Search** Information about search engines.

Copernic for Windows 95
 www.download.com/PC/Result/ TitleDetail/0,4,203-27560- g,501000.html Search major search engines simultaneously; duplicates automatically removed; results stored in folders; program ranks results; refine search; look for specific words in results; open Web pages; searches are stored.

CUSI-Configurable Unified Search Engine
 www.nexor.com/public/cusi Customized searches; World Wide Web indexes; robot-generated indexes; software searches; people searches and dictionaries.

Data Grabber for the PC
 www.wildcowpublishing.com/datagrab. html Utility in task bar; type in a search query, select a search engine from the drop-down menu and click on Go; results presented in browser window; list of search engines and URLs from text file; edit to add favorites; update outdated links.

Directory Guide **directoryguide/com** Catalogue and directory of over 400 sites.

Disinformation **www.disinfo.com** Alternative, subculture search engine.

Dogpile **www.dogpile.com** Multisearch engine; lists up to twenty-four search engines; specify order in which to search.

Euroseek **www.euroseek.net** European-based search engine; can search in any country, in any language.

Excite **www.excite.com** Concept-based searches narrow search to relevant sites.

Excite UK **excite.co.uk** Searches UK and European sites.

FinderSeeker **www.finderseeker.com** Specialty search engine; find music-related search engines.

GOD (Global Online Directory) **god.co.uk** Based in UK; search globally.

Go-Get-It for Windows 95
www.jla.com/htms/gogetit/ourdwnld. htm Search up to ten search engines with keywords and phrases; store in folders for easy reference; results are displayed when found; can view in program or transfer to browser; can download Web pages and complete Web sites for offline viewing; personal information service.

Google **www.google.com** Search engine; fast and effective.

GoTo **www.goto.com** Search engine.

Grab-a-Site **www.bluesquirrel.com** Offline browser; download entire Web site.

HotBot **www.hotbot.com** Popular search engine; many categories.

Husky Search
www.huskysearch.cs.washington.edu Specify how long engines perform search; search options include by region, target site, or category.

Inference Find **www.inference.com/infind** Brings up best search engines; merges results; deletes redundancies; organizes hits into understandable groupings; returns quickly; lists results by subject and site.

Infoseek **www.infoseek.com** Comprehensive search engine with large database; Web guides; searches newsgroups and other Internet sources; also has a UK site.

Infospace **www.infospace.com** Many categories including Yellow Pages, White Pages, business listings, personal E-mail addresses; business finder and people finder on UK site.

LookSmart **www.looksmart.com** Search topics in over 17,000 categories.

LookSmart UK **www.looksmart.co.uk** Search UK or international sites.

Lycos **www.lycos.com** Long-established search engine; large, fast, and effective.

Lycos UK **www.lycosuk.co.uk** Search the UK and Ireland.

Magellen **mckinley.com** Directory; list of topics; Yellow Pages; People Finder.

Mamma.com **www.mamma.com** "The mother" of all search engines.

MetaCrawler **www.metacrawler.com** Meta search engine; search multiple engines.

MetaFind **www.metafind.com** Meta search engine; search multiple engines.

MetaSearch **metasearch.com** Goes to six search engines.

NearSite for the PC **www.nearsite.com** Collects and stores Web pages for offline browsing; set up any number of pages or sites; program automatically downloads; schedule facility automatically updates sites.

NetAttache Lite for Windows 95 and 3.1
www.tympani.com/ftp/download/ NetAttache/na32v25e.exe Retrieves Web pages for offline reading; organizes Web entries; stores text and images; read pages offline; interactive linking online.

News from Yahoo
www.yahoo.com/headlines/international World headlines.

Northern Light **www.northernlight.com** Search folders organize results to narrow search; information from over 2,900 journals, books, magazines, and databases.

Open Text **opentext.com** Search site with a lot of graphics.

People Search **www.yahoo.four11.com/cgi-bin/Four11Main?yahoo&template= yahoo.t** Search engine for people.

PlanetSearch **www.planetsearch.com** News, finance, and wealth; color-coded bar system indicates rating of sites by each word.

Savvy Search **www.savvysearch.com** or **guaraldi.cs.colostate.edu:2000** Meta search engine; search multiple engines; queries multiple search engines at the same time; indicate number of results wanted; Search Plan ranks nineteen search engines; divides groups by usefulness.

Search Engine Guide
www.searchengineguide.com Guide to general and subject-specific search engines, portals, and directories; search the resources by keyword or browse by category.

Search Engine Watch **searchenginewatch.com** Information about search engines; links to major search engines and others; how to use search engines.

Search Engines Galore
www.searchenginesgalore.com All in one search engine directory.

Search.Com **www.search.com** Search in a range of categories and topics; over one hundred specialty searches listed alphabetically; music entries.

Searching the Web **www.hypernews.org/HyperNews/get/www/searching.html** Information about search engines, services, directories, software, and articles.

SearchWolf **www.msw.com.au/search** Search several engines; Web page crawler; compiles lists of files, FTP sites and links; MP3 Wolf scans the Internet for MP3, MIDI, Wave, and other music files and links.

SuperSeek **www.superseek.com** Meta search engine; search multiple engines.

TechSeeker **www.bluesquirrel.com** Combines results of over ninety online technical resources; drivers, software, technical solutions, and product information.

The Big Hub **www.thebighub.com** Specialty search engine; find music-related search engines.

The Free Encyclopedia **www.encyclopedia.com** Over 17,000 articles from *The Concise Columbia Electronic Encyclopedia.*

The Informant **informant.dartmouth.edu** Automated service that monitors URL search engine placement.

The Internet Sleuth **www.isleuth.com** Select up to six databases such as news, business, software, Web directories; list of twenty-one categories; subcategories.

The Mining Company **home.miningco.com** List of categories; over 500 topics.

The Open Directory **www.dmoz.org** Human-driven search engine.

The Spider's Apprentice **www.monash.com/spidap.htm** Search engines how-to.

The Web Robots Page **info.Webcrawler.com/mak/projects/robots/robots.html** About the software search engines use to gather information.

Tierra Highlights 2 for Windows 95 **www.tierra.com/products2/highlights2.html** Select sites; monitors for changes; toolbar; task tray icon; works with Netscape and Internet Explorer.

TrackerLock **www.peacefire.org/tracerlock** Automated service that monitors URL search engine placement.

UK Index **www.ukindex.co.uk** List of UK sites; search by category.

Ultra Infoseek **ultra.infoseek.com** Searches the Internet, news, companies, and Usenet data.

URL-Minder **www.netmind.com/html/url-minder.html** Automated service that monitors URL search engine placement.

W3 Search Engines **cuiwww.unige.ch/meta-index.html** Lists some of the most useful search engines on the Web; search in list-based catalogues, spider-based catalogues, people databases, and many other search engines.

Web Compass **www.quarterdeck.com** Commercial program; demo available; queries up to thirty-five search engines at once; ranks for relevancy on a scale of 1 to 100; builds summaries from results; automatically organizes results by topic.

WebCrawler **www.webcrawler.com** Search by topic; create personalized search pages; UK site link goes to *Excite UK.*

WebSeeker **www.bluesquirrel.com** Uses up to 120 search engines.

Webtaxi **webtaxi.com** Select from a large list of directories and search engines.

WebTurbo for PC, Java Version for Mac **www.webturbo.com** Icon on header bar of browser for quick access; on-screen video tutorial; queries many search engines; can search on multiple topics; Web Preview creates summaries of pages.

WebWhacker for Windows and the Mac **www.bluesquirrel.com** Commercial program; demo versions for Windows 3.1, Windows 95, and the Mac; download entire sites for offline viewing.

Wired Cybrarian **www.wired.com/cybrarian** Nine categories: Reference, Technology, Current Affairs, Business, Recreation, Investing and Finance, Media, Culture, and Health and Science; each has several subcategories; links to sites with freeware and shareware.

Yahoo **www.yahoo.com** First and most well-known search engine and directory on the Internet; list of categories; several search methods.

Yahoo UK **www.yahoo.co.uk** Search UK and Ireland sites.

Sheet Music — Historical Collections

About Sheet Music **odyssey.lib.duke.edu/sheetmusic/about.html** or **scriptorium.lib.duke.edu/sheetmusic/about.html** Historic American sheet music; what is sheet music?

African-American Sheet Music **memory.loc.gov/ammem/award97/rpbhtml** From Brown University.

Alley Kat Sheet Music Center
> **www.alleykatsheetmusic.com** Discounted sheet music; Broadway; movies; classical; secular; sacred; country; pop; reference; personality; music for fretted instruments; piano; organ; keyboard; instrumental; vocal scores; fake books and more.

Amazing Music World
> **www.amazingmusicworld.com** Downloadable sheet music; requires ActiveX.

Antiques Unique - Sheet Music
> **www.cjnetworks.com/~dkinion/ topantique/sheet/sheet.html** or **www.sunnetworks.net/~dkinion/ topantique/sheet/sheet.html** Over 2,000 listings by title, subject, and date; click on pictures to see a larger image.

A-Z Music **www.a-zmusic.com** Printed music and sheet music for most music styles and instruments in both notation and tablature forms; catalog; order online.

Best Music Books **www.bestmusicbooks.com** Books on music.

Best Sheet Music **www.bestsheetmusic.com** Guide to sheet music and tab sites available on the Internet.

Blackdots Online Sheet Music
> **www.blackdots.com** Sheet music catalog for serious musicians and educators; includes 100,000 titles in classical, band, choral, solo, jazz, piano, and pop categories.

Burt's Music in Print **www.burtsmusic.com** Large sheet music distributor.

CD Sheet Music **www.cdsheetmusic.com** Complete collections of printable piano works on CD-ROM; the cure for "overflowing piano bench syndrome."

Charles Dumont & Son Inc.
> **www.dumontmusic.com** Alfred; Mel Bay; Cherry Lane; CPP/Belwin; International; Kjos; Hal Leonard; Koala; Music Sales; Warner Music; The Ultimate Display Rack System.

Classical Sheet Music Publishers and Distributors Catalogs
> **www.Webcom.com/musics/catalogs. html** Sheet music publishers and distributors catalogs.

Creative Music **www.creativemusic.com** Online sheet music store; in-stock inventory.

Demiq Music **www.demiq.com** Sheet music publisher of choral, instrumental, opera, orchestral classics, and unique new works.

Discount Sheet Music
> **www.netstoreusa.com/music/ welcome.shtml** Detailed listing of 250,000 songs.

Free Sheet Music **www.freesheetmusic.net** Sheet music search; downloads.

Free Sheet Music Guide
> **www.freesheetmusicguide.com** Free online sheet music.

Free Sheet Music on the Internet
> **www.rainmusic.com/pianomusic/ free.htm** Reviews of sites that feature free sheet music.

GMD Music Archive: Sheet Music
> **www.gmd.de/misc/music/scores/ welcome.html** Sheet music.

Graphire Music Notation Connection
> **www.sover.net/~graphire** Professional music typesetting software; information about printed music.

Historic American Sheet Music
> **memory.loc.gov/ammem/award97/ ncdhtml/hasmhome.html** Includes 3042 pieces of sheet music published in America between 1850 and 1920; selected from the collections at Duke University.

International Print Edition **www.ipe-music.com** Masters Collection; IPE Scores.

J. W. Pepper Music Network
> **www.jwpepper.com/indexb.html** Sheet music and music books; music software products; music teaching tools; music distributor specializing in music performance materials for schools, churches, community musical organizations, and home music enjoyment; online ordering.

Jump! Music-Sheet Music Store
> **www.jumpmusic.com** Songbooks; software.

Koala Publications
> **www.learntoplaymusic.com** Home page; Australian company.

Maestronet
> **www.maestronet.com/samples.html** Sheet music download samples; requires Adobe Acrobat Reader version 2.0 or higher; MIDI files.

Music Books Plus **www.musicbooksplus.com** or **www.vaxxine.com/mbp** Online music bookstore.

Music, Music, Music **www.music-music-music.com/sheet music** Vintage sheet music that is hard to find or out of print.

Music Notes **www.musicnotes.com** Digital sheet music; download and print; music books; classical, piano, guitar, and instrumental.

Music Room **www.musicroom.com** Sheet music available online.

Music Students **www.musicstudents.com** Sheet music online.

Musica Viva
> **www.musicaviva.com/links.html** Free sheet music on the Internet; extensive list of Web sites.

Musicscores.com **www.music-scores.com** Free classical sheet music; book and CD recommendations; free music scores and MIDI files; free classical sheet music downloads.

My Sheet Music **www.dalymusic.com** Free and "pay and play" music.

New York Sheet Music Society **www.johnnymercer.com/nysms.htm** Johnny Mercer Web site; the New York Sheet Music Society; established in 1980; began with a small, dedicated group of collectors.

Notation Machine **notationmachine.com** Convert files recorded directly from CDs and tapes into sheet music.

Old and Gold **www.oldandgold.com/plus.html** Sheet music; songbooks; guitar tabs; records; over a quarter million titles; order online.

Paradise Music **paradise-music.hypermart.net** Quality guitar tablature; sheet music from a database of over 260,000 titles.

Piano Press **www.pianopress.com** Sheet music for piano/vocal/guitar; world music repertoire guide; seasonal music; CDs; CD-ROMs.

Print Music Online **www.printmusiconline.com** Print music; sheet music; band methods; instructional videos.

Printed Music Worldwide **www.printed-music.com** Subscription directory for producers of printed classical music.

Score Online **www.score-on-line.com** Sheet music online.

Sheet Music Service **www.sheetmusicservice.com** Sheet music that is hard to find or out of print.

Sheet Music **www.4pianos.com.au/sheetmusic.html** Sheet music direct sales, service, and product support; supply sheet music to teachers, students, schools, churches, and musicians.

Sheet Music Cabinets **www.bondypiano.com/cabinets.htm** Piano sales and services, large selection of pianos, uprights, grand pianos, and sheet music cabinets.

Sheet Music Cataloging Guidelines **www.lib.duke.edu/music/sheetmusic/ sheetmusic.html** Experimental page to test World Wide Web access to the draft guidelines.

Sheet Music Center for Collector's of Vintage Popular Sheet Music **www.sheetmusiccenter.com** Buy, sell, and trade old sheet music.

Sheet Music Collections **www.lib.duke.edu/music/sheetmusic/ collections.html** Collections of sheet music with public access either through a Web page or online catalog.

Sheet Music Direct America **www.smdamerica.com** Sheet music delivered to computer within minutes.

Sheet Music Direct **www.sheetmusicdirect.com** Browse sheet music titles; download and print out for a fee; thousands of titles in many notation styles.

Sheet Music for Piano, Vocal, and Guitar **www.biznest.com/music/sheet** Publications in book form; singles for piano, keyboard, vocal, guitar, and more; every music style; old hits and artists; today's top performers.

Sheet Music Information **www.lib.duke.edu/music/sheetmusic** Produced under the auspices of the Music Library Association; maintained as part of the Duke University Library Web pages as a courtesy to patrons and to promote the use of sheet music.

Sheet Music on CD-ROM **www.celestin.com/sheetmusic** Over one hundred arrangements; copyright free.

Sheet Music Online **www.sheetmusic1.com** Free downloads of public domain piano music; emphasis on music education resources.

Sheet Music Online **www.sheetmusiconline.net** Free sheet music; sheet music search; downloads.

Sheet Music Plus **www.sheetmusicplus.com** or **www.printedmusic.com** Sheet music super store.

Sheet Music Search Service **www.sheetmusicsearch.com** Find any sheet music by title, author, instrumentation, and style; get any recorded music transcribed; transpose music for singers to their key.

Sheet Music, Etc. **www.sheetmusicetc.com/musicshop** Sheet music online.

Sheet-Music **www.sheet-music.com** Sheet music online.

Sunhawk **www.sunhawk.com** Sheet music in digital and print formats; Solero format; view, print, and listen over the Internet.

The Collectics **www.collectics.com/bookstore_music. html** Reference books and price guides on vintage records and sheet music.

The Free Sheet Music Directory **home.sol.no/~fnordber/MV/links.html** Directory of Web sites offering free sheet music.

The Historic American Sheet Music Project **scriptorium.lib.duke.edu/sheetmusic** Provides access to digital images of 3,042 pieces of sheet music published in America between 1850 and 1920.

The Lester S. Levy Collection of Sheet Music **levysheetmusic.mse.jhu.edu** Part of Special Collections at the Milton S. Eisenhower

Library of The Johns Hopkins University; comprised of popular American music spanning the period 1780 to 1960; over 26,000 pieces of music are indexed; images of the cover and music are available for pieces of music more than seventy-five years old.

The Notation Machine
www.notationmachine.com Make sheet music by importing CDs and tapes into the computer.

The Sheet Music Addict
www.sheetmusicaddict.com Sheet music for the avid collector.

Transcribe Custom Sheet Music **www.transcribe.com** Transcription services.

UNC-Chapel Hill Music Library
www.lib.unc.edu/music/eam.html Nineteenth-century American sheet music.

Vintage Sheet Music Storefront
members.aol.com/vinsheets Vintage sheet music.

Virtual Sheet Music
www.virtualsheetmusic.com Classical sheet music downloads.

World Wide Music Online Sheet-Music Catalog
www.world-wide-music.com Specialty vendor of classical sheet music and recordings; a virtual store; promotes and sells the scores and recordings of self-published musicians on consignment; caters to avid musicians.

Songwriting—Songwriting Contests and Camps

650 WSM (Grand Ole Opry) **www.650wsm.com** The Grand Ole Opry's very own and first radio station, WSM-am 650, is now live on the Internet; "Opry Star Spotlight" show with host Matthew Gillian offers songwriters an opportunity to play their songs on the air.

A Rhyming Dictionary for Poetry and Songwriting
www.writeexpress.com/online.html WriteExpress Online Rhyming Dictionary; word rhyme; end rhymes; last syllable rhymes; double rhymes; beginning rhymes and more.

Alaska Midnight Sun Songwriters Camp
www.songcamp.com Held in June in Anchorage.

American Songwriter
www.americansongwriter.com Magazine for songwriters; features; interviews; reviews; events listings; Nashville based; lyric writing competition; links.

American Songwriter Network (ASN)
www.tiac.net/users/asn/index.htm Home page.

Angel Fire Lyric Contest
www.angelfire.com/co2/contempo

Contemporary Songwriter Magazine lyric contest.

Artist Survival Manual **www.angelfire.com/tn/capitolmanagement/survivalmanual.html** Free 100+ page book; answers questions about recording in Nashville.

Arts Midwest **www.artsmidwest.org** Minnesota songwriters organization.

Austin Songwriters Group
www.austinsongwriter.org Regional songwriters organization.

Baltimore Songwriters Association
www.electrobus.com/bsa Regional songwriters organization.

Bands, Songwriting, and Lyrics
www.musiclyne.homepage.com Home page.

Bermuda Songwriters Association
www.bsabermuda.com Songwriting organization.

Best Lyrics **www.bestlyrics.com** Recent songs updated daily.

Beth Nielsen Chapman
www.bethnielsenchapman.net Prolific Nashville-based songwriter; career; upcoming performances.

Big Index
www.myths.com/pub/lyrics/bigindex.html Lyrics Web site.

Billboard Song Contest
www.billboard.com/songcontest Presented by *Billboard* and the Oklahoma City University School of Music and Performing Arts, Music, and Entertainment Business Program. Songs may be submitted in thirteen different genres; deadlines, rules.

British Academy of Composers and Songwriters
www.britishacademy.co.uk UK songwriters organization.

California Coast Music Camp **musiccamp.org** Held in July.

Camp Summer Songs **www.summersongs.com** Weeklong summer camp for songwriters; workshops; seminars; critiques; performances; networking.

Carolina Association of Songwriters
www.caos.org South Carolina organization.

Central Carolina Songwriters Association (CCSA)
www.ncneighbors.com/147.com North Carolina organization.

Central Oregon Songwriters Association
cosa4u.tripod.com Regional songwriters organization.

Chris Austin Songwriting Contest
www.merlefest.org/songwritingcontest.htm Annual songwriting contest.

Clichés and Rhymes
www.eccentricsoftware.com/zkdemo.

html Search a word; find its cliches and rhymes.

Club Nashville **www.clubnashville.com** Radio; artists; songwriting and publishing; record companies; recording and studios; charts; public relations; bluegrass; Americana; Christian and gospel; organizations; publications; equipment; life in Nashville; archives; The Blue Chip Radio Report; members; search.

Colorado Music Association
www.coloradomusic.org Home page.

Connecticut Songwriters Association
www.ctsongs.com Home page.

Cool Songwriting and Songwriting Links
pw2.netcom.com/~coolsong/ coolsonglinks.html Links for songwriters.

Country Songwriters Resources
www.maxpages.com/musiccontacts Music contacts; names/addresses; information for country music songwriters and musicians seeking direct contact with Nashville record label insiders, A&R, producers, and country music industry contacts.

Craft of Songwriting
www.craftofsongwriting.com Web site hosted by Danny Arena and Sara Light; resources for songwriters; information; chat; links.

Daily Inspirations for Songwriters
www.egroups.com/group/ DIforSongwriters Daily E-newsletter dedicated to songwriters; helpful hints; links.

Dallas Songwriters Association
www.dallassongwriters.org Regional songwriters organization.

Dave Kennedy's Songwriting and Recording Webpage
www.wserv.com/~dkennedy/page10. html Information for songwriters; recording tips.

Diane Warren **www.realsongs.com** Prolific songwriter of popular music.

District of Columbia Songwriters Association of Washington **www.saw.org** Home page.

Education Planet-Songwriting Resources
www.educationplanet.com/search/ Art_and_M...ic/Songwriting K-12 education Web guide helps teachers, students, and parents find quality educational resources.

EGroups Songcraft
www.egroups.com/community/songcraft List for songwriters, publishers, pluggers, labels, and industry professionals.

ElectricEarl.com
www.electricearl.com/mlinks09.html Songwriting and publishing music links.

Elements of Style
www.columbia.edu/acis/bartleby/strunk Online edition of the book that is a landmark book of good writing habits.

Enormous Records Songwriting Contest
www.enormousrecords.com/Contest.htm Outlet for singers and songwriters to promote original pop, rock, jazz, country, bluegrass, rhythm and blues, urban, alternative, and more.

Exit In **www.exit-in.com** Nashville club in Vanderbilt University area; Billy Block's Western Beat; Roots Revival; writer's night.

Fiction Songs **www.fictionsongs.com** Home page.

Fort Bend Songwriters Association **www.fbsa.org** Regional songwriters organization.

Fort Worth Songwriter's Association
www.fwsa.com Regional songwriters organization.

Georgia Music Industry Association, Inc.
www.gmia.org Home page.

Get Lyrics **www.getlyrics.com** Full album song lyrics.

Glade's Songwriter Page
www.zapcom.net/~glade For songwriters.

Great American Song Contest
www.songpro.com Annual song contest.

Grendel's Lyric Archive
www.seas.upenn.edu/~avernon/lyrics. html Arranged by artist.

Guild of International Songwriters and Composers
www.songwriters-guild.com Member services; copyright assistance; song critiques; demos; publishing.

Harlan Howard **www.harlanhoward.com** Country music songwriter; hundreds of hits; publishing company in Nashville, TN; Harlan Howard Songs, Inc.

Harriet Schock **www.harrietschock.com** Hit singer songwriter based in LA; correspondence courses; workshops; performances; author of *Becoming Remarkable;* CDs; links.

Hitlist Music Lyrics
www.hitlist.com/music/lyrics.php3 Music entertainment and information content online; full archive searchable by artists with any piece of music information in the world, including full-length songs and lyrics.

Hitquarters **www.hitquarters.com** Source of information for songwriters, artists, musicians, and producers; online directory of record company A & Rs, managers, publishers, and producers.

Hugh Prestwood **www.hughprestwood.com** Prolific country singer/songwriter; NY-based; song camp instructor.

Independent Songwriter
www.independentsongwriter.com Online magazine for songwriters.

Indianapolis Songwriters Association, Inc.
listen.to/indysongwriter Regional songwriters organization.

International Songwriters Association (ISA)
www.songwriter.co.uk Songs and
songwriting; *The Songwriter* founded in 1967;
published by the ISA.

Irene Jackson's Songwriting Workshop
www.irenejackson.com/workshp.html
Tips; links to relevant sites; post lyrics or
discuss songwriting on the songwriting board;
tools.

Jeff Mallet's Songwriter Site **www.lyricist.com**
Large collection of useful links and resources for
songwriters; FAQ; updates.

John Braheny **www.johnbraheny.com** LA-based
songwriting coach; author of *The Craft and
Business of Songwriting;* musician; songwriter;
performer; recording artist.

Just Plain Folks **www.jpfolks.com** Created by
Brian Austin Whitney; online group of over
8,000 songwriters, recording artists, music
publishers, record labels, performing arts
societies, educational institutions, recording
studios and engineers, producers, legal
professionals, publicists and journalists,
publications, music manufacturers and retailers;
helpful resources including mentor program,
chat, bulletin board, E-newsletter; regional and
national tours.

*Kerrville Newfolk Songwriting Contest for Emerging
Songwriters* **www.kerrville-
music.com/index.html** Prestigious folk
award; information; deadline and rules for current
year.

Kerrville Song School **www.kerrville-
music.com** Kerrville Music Foundation,
Kerrville, TX.

Kiss This Guy **www.kissthisguy.com** Archive of
misheard lyrics.

Lamb's Retreat for Songwriters **www.jdlamb.com**
Held in Michigan.

Let's Sing It **www.letssingit.com** Thousands of
lyrics to all styles of music.

Li'l Hanks Guide for Songwriters
www.halsguide.com Resources for
songwriters; newsgroups; links.

Live on the Net **www.liveonthenet.com** Venue
in Nashville broadcasts nightly show called *Live
from the Spoke in Nashville;* over the Internet
nightly from 8-9PM CST.

Louisianna Songwriters Association
www.lasongwriters.org Regional
songwriters organization.

Lyric Crawler **www.lyriccrawler.com** Lyrics
search engine; more than 120,000 songs.

Lyric Find **www.lyricfind.com** Search database
of over 11,000 lyrics.

Lyric Hound **www.lyrichound.com** Over 13,000
lyrics; new and old songs; full text search.

Lyric Writers
www.egroups.com/group/LyricWriters
Home page for lyricists to share ideas and
experiences.

Lyric X **www.lyricX.com** Lyrics Web site.

Lyricalline Songwriting Resource Forum
**www.lyricalline.com/theforum/index.
html** Resources for songwriters; free E-
newsletter; forum; radio show; Q&A; interviews;
articles; services.

Lyricist Software
www.virtualstudiosystems.com Word
processor designed for musicians, songwriters and
poets; includes rhyming dictionary, spell checker,
thesaurus, album categorization, and more;
download.

LyricPro **www.lyricpro.com** Software for
songwriters; archive song titles and ideas; edit
lyrics with a rhyming dictionary; track publishers
and submissions; create charts.

Lyrics HQ **www.lyricsHQ.com** Post lyric
requests; trade lyrics.

Lyrics **www.lyrics.com/index.htm** Words to
songs.

Lyrics Kingdom **www.poplyrics.net** Top 50
Billboard singles and albums; hundreds of artists.

Lyrics Post **www.lyricspost.com** Large lyrics
database.

Lyrics Review **www.lyricsreview.com** Submit
lyrics to be reviewed.

Lyrics Ring
tinpan.fortunecity.com/tripper/811 Song
lyrics for pop, rock, and hip-hop.

Lyrics World **www.lyricsworld.com** Index; links
to all of the lyrics available at Lyrics World;
songs found in *Top 40 Hits of 1930-1999, #1
Songs of 1930-1999, Top Singles by Decade*, and
Artist Collections.

LyricsSearch.net **www.LyricsSearch.net** Search
over 100,000 songs.

Memphis Songwriters' Association
www.memphissongwriters.com Regional
songwriters organization.

Merriam-Webster Dictionary **www.m-
w.com/home.htm** Online dictionary.

Mid-Atlantic Song Contest
www.saw.org/index.html Annual
songwriting competition.

Minnesota Association of Songwriters
www.isc.net/mas Regional songwriters
organization.

MIT Songwriting Club Index
**web.mit.edu/songwriting/www/index.
html** List of songwriting clubs.

Muse's Muse **www.musesmuse.com**
Songwriting resources and services; tips and

tools; chat; articles; free E-newsletter; reviews; links.

Music and Audio Connection Songwriting Forum
www.musicandaudio.com/forumdx.htm
Online discussion group.

Music and Lyrics **www.music-and-lyrics.co.uk**
Tips for songwriters.

Music Links for Songwriters
electricearl.com/mlinks09.html Home page.

Music Orlando Songwriters' Bulletin Board Virginia Organization of Composers and Lyricists
members.aol.com/vocal10 Regional songwriters organization.

Music Row **www.musicrow.com** Information for songwriters; industry news and articles; *Row Fax* tip sheet subscriptions; current listings.

Music Theory for Songwriters
members.aol.com/chordmaps Questions about chords; music theory.

Napa Valley Music Festival Emerging Songwriter's Showcase **www.napafest.com** Showcase for songwriters.

NashCamp Songwriting School
www.nashcamp.com Songwriter summer camp in Nashville with pro-writers and music industry professionals; week long session of songwriting workshops; networking; performances.

Nashville Music Link Collections
www.nashville.net/~troppo/collect.htm
Add URL; directory of Web sites relating to or of interest to the Nashville Music Industry.

Nashville Number System
www.telalink.net/~troppo/nns.htm Book *The Nashville Number System* by Chas Williams; charts; endorsements; ordering information.

Nashville Pop Songwriter's Association International **www.npsai.com** For songwriters of popular music.

Nashville Publishers Network
www.songnet.com/npn Dedicated to networking in the Nashville music community.

Nashville Redbook
www.nol.com/redbookform.html
Complete directory of Nashville's music and entertainment industry.

Nashville Scene **www.nashscene.com**
Entertainment newspaper; back issues; classifieds.

Nashville Songs **www.nashvillesongs.com**
Home page.

Nashville Songwriters Association International (NSAI) **www.nashvillesongwriters.com**
Nonprofit service organization for songwriters of all levels and genres; based in Nashville, TN; annual Spring Symposium; Song Camps;

weekly and regional workshops; free song critique service for members; insurance plans; Songwriter Achievement Awards.

Nashville Songwriting Page
www.cupitmusic.com/songwriting
Resources for songwriters.

Nashville's Music Underground
www.geocities.com/Nashville/Opry/4174 RealAudio; classifieds; links; artists; clubs; departments.

NashvilleSongService.com
www.NashvilleSongService.com Work with lyric writers worldwide to help them accompolish their songwriting goals.

NashvilleSound.com **www.nashvillesound.com**
Directory of resources of interest to Nashville music industry professionals.

New Song Check List
www.wserv.com/~dkennedy/page2.html
Site for songwriters.

North Carolina Songwriters Co-op
www.ncsongwriters.interspeed.net
Regional songwriters organization.

Northern California Songwriters Association
www.ncsasong.org Nonprofit; annual conference in September; networking and performance opportunities; workshops; resources; annual songwriting contest.

Ohio Songwriters & Poets Critique
www.freeyellow.com:8080/members2/spcmusic Regional organization.

Oklahoma Songwriters & Composers Association
www.oksongwriters.org Regional songwriters organization; annual songwriting contest.

OneLook Dictionaries **www.onelook.com**
Definitions searched by keyword.

Online Rhyming Dictionary
www.link.cs.cmu.edu/dougb/rhyme-doc.html By Noel Gallagher.

Orbison
www.egroups.com/group/orbison_list
Place for country songwriters to interact online.

Pacific Song Contest
www.pacificsongcontest.com Annual songwriting contest.

Paramount: The Nashville Songwriting Connection
www.paramountsong.com Nashville songwriting resource.

Pat and Pete Luboff **www.writesongs.com**
Songwriting coaches; authors of *88 Songwriting Wrongs and How to Write Them;* consultation; instruction; workshops.

Pat Pattison
members.aol.com/ptpattison/lyricpages
or **www.patpattison.com** Lyric writing instructor; author of several books on writing lyrics; links.

Performing Songwriter

www.performingsongwriter.com
Magazine; current issue; resource center;
festivals; competitions; contact information; DIY
product reviews.

Phil Swann

**www.countrymusical.com/philswann.
htm** Songwriter; songwriting coach; LA based.

Philadelphia Songwriters Association

members.aol.com/philasong Informal
group; meetings are free; guest speakers and song
critiques.

Phrase Finder **www.shu.ac.uk/Webj-
admin/phrases** Find phrases using keywords.

Pinewoods Camp **www.cdss.org** Country Song
and Dance Society of America; Haydenville, MA.

PitchSheet.com **www.pitchsheet.com** Interactive
tip sheet for the professional songwriting
community.

Pittsburgh Songwriters Association

trfn.clpgh.org/psa Regional songwriters
organization.

Pop Songwriters **www.egroups.com/group/
popsongwriters** Newsgroup; subscribe.

Portland Songwriters Association

www.teleport.com/~psa Regional
songwriters organization; annual songwriting
contest.

PublishSongs.com **www.PublishSongs.com**
Pitch songs; create an account; add songs;
songwriter profile; FAQ; traffic stats.

Ralph Murphy

www.ascap.com/nashville/murphy.html
Hit songwriter; ASCAP Nashville.

Rhyme Dictionaries

**www.writeexpress.com/cgi-
bin/rhymer.cgi** or
**www.link.cs.cmu.edu/dougb/rhyme-
doc.html** Use rhyme dictionaries to gather
potential words for songs.

RhymeWIZARD **www.rhymewizard.com**
Software for Macintosh and Windows.

Rhymezone.com **www.rhymezone.com** Online
rhyming dictionary; find phrases.

Rhyming Dictionary

**www.link.cs.cmu.edu/dougb/rhyme-
doc.html** Rhyming dictionary.

Rhyming Dictionary

www.togethersoftware.com/search.asp
Rhyme online.

Rocky Mountain Folks Song School

www.bluegrass.com Held in August in
Lyons, CO; Planet Bluegrass.

Roget's Thesaurus **www.thesaurus.com** or
**humanities.uchicago.edu/forms_unrest/
roget.html** Online version of the thesaurus.

Ryman Auditorium **www.ryman.com** Nashville
venue; original home of *The Grand Ol' Opry*.

San Diego NSAI Regional Workshop

**hometown.aol.com/sdnsai/myhomepage/
index.html** Regional workshop focusing on
the craft and business of songwriting; monthly
meetings; special events with pro-writers,
authors, and industry guests; song critiques; open
mic; networking.

San Diego Songwriters Guild (SDSG)

www.sdsongwriters.org Monday night
meetings; pitch sessions; guest speakers; annual
songwriting contest; newsletter; open mic;
networking.

Semantic Rhyming Dictionary

**www.link.cs.cmu.edu/dougb/rhyme-
doc.html** Online rhyming resource.

Seth Jackson's Songwriting and Music Business Info

www.mindspring.com/~hitmeister Web
site for songwriters; Los Angeles NSAI regional
workshop; links.

Singers Looking for Songs

**www.songmd.com/html/listings/songs.
html** All genres; contact information.

Singer-Songwriter Directory

singer-songwriter.com Information and
links for songwriters; list of music publishers.

Sisters Folk Festival

**www.informat.com/bz/folkfest/
songwriting.html** Songwriting contest.

Software for Songwriters

www.musicbusinessstore.com Music
contracts; record company software; tour
management.

Song Explorer **www.songexplorer.com**
Comprehensive music recommendation system
on the Internet.

Song Lyrics Online **www.song.lyrics.online**
Song lyrics.

Song Rights **www.songrights.com** Song rights;
legal aspects of songwriting; topics; summary;
reviews; ninety-six-page soft bound primer on
legal issues facing songwriters.

Song Ring Mall **www.songringmall.com**
Songwriter Web ring.

Song Writing Tools

**www.wserv.com/~dkennedy/
page11.html** Information for songwriters.

Songbook.net **www.songbook.net** Information
and resources for songwriters; links.

SongBoy.com **www.songboy.com** Home page.

SongCraft **www.songcraft.com** Kerrville New
Folk winner Mike Brandon; SW Missouri NSA
(NSAI) Workshop; links.

SongCritique.com **songcritique.com** A place for
songwriter's to critique each other's work.

SongExplorer.com **www.SongExplorer.com**
Music recommendation source.

Songfile.com **www.songfile.com** or
www.lyrics.ch/index.htm Database of over
two million songs.
SongLink International **www.songlink.com** Tip
sheet publication; international listings for all
types of music and artists; listings include the
artist, label, style of music needed, and contact
information for each pitch; pitch instructions;
links.
SongNet.com **www.songnet.com** Where
professionals find songs.
SongPitch.com **www.songpitch.com** Nashville-
based online song pitch service; song audio
samples posted by writers; accessed by publishers
and producers.
Songplayer **www.songplayer.com** Learn guitar
and keyboards for songwiters.
Songs Alive **www.songsalive.org** How to get
started in the music business; nonprofit
organization dedicated to the nurturing, support,
and promotion of songwriters and composers
worldwide.
Songs for Sale **www.songsforsale.co.uk** Online
music publisher.
SongScope.com **www.songscope.com** Online
independent songwriter song shopping catalog;
open to all songwriters; list individual songs or
catalogs; critiques.
Songshark **www.songshark.com** Rip-offs and
scams in the music industry; lists known scams
and shady companies; links.
Songshopscoop.com **www.songshopscoop.com**
Holiday weekend retreats in the Northeast with
pro-songwriters; workshops; critique sessions;
networking.
Songsite **expage.com/page/tuneman** Questions
and comments about the craft of songwriting.
Songs-R-Us **home.earthlink.net/~songsrus**
Songwriter Web ring.
Songster Software **www.songstersoftware.com**
Keep track of pitch list; song profile; lyrics;
contacts; track sheet; import sound files;
schedules; royalty statement; copyright forms and
more.
Songwriter and Music Copyright Resources
www.copyright.net/resource.htm Includes
copyright resources, performance rights
organizations, mechanical rights organizations,
international organizations, publishers,
songwriter resources, other music organizations,
general music resources, online resources, books,
trades, magazines, and publications.
Songwriter **www.songwriter.co.uk** Home page.
Songwriter Universe
www.songwriteruniverse.com Founded by
Dale Kawashima; information; links; services for
songwriters.

Songwriters & Poets Critique
www.freeyellow.com/members2/
spcmusic Critiques.
Songwriter's Circle
www.insidetheWeb.com/mbs.cgi/
mb989094 Home page.
Songwriters Directory
www.songwritersdirectory.com Share
talent and market songs; comprehensive reference
tool and songwriter database; opportunities for
recording artists to find songs, producers to find
new music for movies and television and record
labels to find new artists.
Songwriter's Guide
astro.caltech.edu/~mjk/songwriting.
html Information for songwriters.
Songwriters Haven
www.freeyellow.com/members5/
jamielc/index.html Web site for songwriters.
Songwriters on Songwriting
home.earthlink.net/~zollo/song.htm
Book by Paul Zollo; Da Capo Press; 656 pages.
Songwriters Q & A **www.songwritersq-a.com**
Questions and answers for songwriters.
Songwriters Resource at Writers Write
www.writerswrite.com/songwriting For
songwriters.
Songwriters Resource Network
www.songpro.com News and information for
songwriters; current articles on the craft of
songwriting and the music business; Great
American Song Contest; meet other songwriters,
music collaborators, recording artists, publishers,
producers, and music industry contacts; in-depth
evaluations of songs and lyrics; books and
publications; fun page; test musical IQ on
legendary songwriters and songwriting; links for
songwriters and musicians.
Songwriters, Composers, and Lyricists Association
(SCALA)
www.senet.com.au/~scala/perspex1.htm
Perspectives on songwriting.
Songwriting @ Suite101.com
www.suite101.com/welcome.cfm/songw
riting Home page; articles; links; discussions.
Songwriting Articles
mattressemporium.com/dave/
songwriting.htm Songwriting and lyric
writing; articles; links; songwriters toolbox;
newsletters; tips and more.
Songwriting Books-Music Business Bookstore @
TuneTrade.com
www.tunetrade.com/song.html Books on
songwriting.
Songwriting Contest by Song Spree and Spree
Productions
home.earthlink.net/~spree/index.html
Record and seriously promote winners; offer

publishing; pay royalties for CDs; winners have been signed with publishers.

Songwriting
www.lib.ox.ac.uk/internet/news/faq/ archive/songwriting Information.

Songwriting Tip Sheet
members.wbs.net/homepages/b/e/r/ bernancountry/tips.html Information for songwriters.

Songwriting Tips
www.immortalbeloved.com/pages/ songtips.htm Hints for songwriters.

Songwriting Tips
www.wserv.com/~dkennedy/page30. html Help for songwriters.

Songwriting Tips and Hints
griffin.multimedia.edu/~psa/tips.htm Information for songwriters.

Songwriting Tools
www.wserv.com/~dkennedy/page11. html Help for songwriters.

Songwriting with Jason Blume
www.jasonblume.com Tips for songwriters; workshops and seminars; critique service; author of *Six Steps to Songwriting Success: The Comprehensive Guide to Writing and Marketing Hit Songs* (Billboard Books); CD information; one of the nation's most successful songwriters and respected songwriting teachers; one of few songwriters to have singles on the Country, Pop, and R&B charts at the same time; songs recorded by *The Backstreet Boys, Britney Spears, Colin Raye, John Berry,* and more.

Southern Utah Songwriting School & Acoustic Concerts of Southern Utah
www.songschool.8m.com or **www.acousticconcerts.com** Trish Gale Productions; St. George, UT.

Summer Songwriting Workshop **www.berklee.edu** Held in August at the Berklee College of Music, Boston, MA.

TAXI **www.taxi.com** Independent A&R Vehicle; connects unsigned artists, bands, and songwriters with major record labels, publishers, and film and TV music supervisors; biweekly listings in all genres; song critiques; related links; free annual TAXI Road Rally convention in Los Angeles, CA, in November.

Tennessee Songwriters Association International
www.clubnashville.com/tsai.htm Pitch a publisher night; pro rap night; critique night; legend series; awards banquet.

The Bluebird Café **www.bluebirdcafe.com** Famous Nashville venue for songwriters; writer's nights; open mic; guest performers.

The Boston Songwriters Workshop
www.laverty.org/bsw Regional songwriters organization.

The Chicago Songwriters Collective
www.chicagosongwriters.com Regional songwriters organization.

The Female Singer/Songwriter Web Ring
www.geocities.com/sunsetstrip/ backstage/9036 For female musicians.

The Freedom Exchange **www.grays.net/discus** Online workshop for songwriters.

The Guild of International Songwriters & Composers **www.icn.co.uk/gisc.html** International songwriting organization based in England.

The International Lyrics Server **www.lyrics.ch** Lyrics to more than 100,000 songs.

The John Lennon Songwriting Contest
www.jlsc.com Check for updates on the current year's contest; winners; prizes; print contest application.

The Lyrics Library
tinpan.fortunecity.com/blondie/313 Links to many different lyric Web sites.

The Original Songwriters Showcase
www.showcaselondon.co.uk London songwriter showcase; weekly.

The Princeton Songwriters / NSAI Regional Workshop **community.nj.com/cc/ princetonsongwriters** Educational activities to promote learning the art, craft, and business of songwriting.

The Semantic Rhyming Dictionary
www.cs.cmu.edu/~dougb/rhyme.html Dictionary of rhyming words.

The Song Site **www.thesongsite.com** Home page.

The Song Workshop **www.worktape.com** Resources for songwriters; *When a Work Tape is Enough* CD by Steven Dale Jones; links.

The Songworks **www.thesongworks.com** Online song recording service; links to song contests.

The Songwriters Association of Washington
www.saw.org Regional songwriters organization.

The Songwriters Collaboration Network
www.songmd.com/html/network.html Hosted by Molly-Ann Leikin; monthly contest; consultation; correspondence course; Molly's column; books and tapes; Molly's credits; links.

The Songwriter's Connection
www.journeypublishing.com Resources for songwriters; information; newsletter; books.

The Songwriters Guild of America (SGA)
www.songwriters.org Membership; SGA songwriter's contract; educational workshops; regional offices.

The Tao of Songwriting
www.navpoint.com/~lastending/tao.htm Online resource for songwriters around the world.

The Top 20 Lyrics Sites
www.notwo.com/lyrics/index.html
Lyrics online.
The Ultimate Country Music Contacts Directory
www.maxpages.com/musiccontacts
Songwriter resources; links to Nashville music
contacts.
The USA Songwriting Competition
www.songwriting.net Annual competition;
deadline May 31; fifteen categories, including
lyrics only; see Web site for updates, contest
rules, prizes, winners, and more.
Thesaurus **www.link.cs.cmu.edu/lexfn** Find
the right word(s).
Tucson Folk Festival Songwriting Competition
www.rtd.com/-dsimpson/con_song.htm
Annual songwriting contest.
Unisong: Passport for a Musical Planet
www.unisong.com Created by songwriters,
for songwriters; to unite a world community
bonded by the creation of music; international
songwriter resource links; annual international
song contest.
Washington Area Music Association
www.wamadc.com Regional organization.
Webster's Dictionary **www.m-**
w.com/dictionary.htm Look up words
online.
Wisconsin Songwriters
www.geocities.com/Nashville/Rodeo/
2907/page6.htm Song contest.
Word Together Online Rhyming Dictionary for
Poetry and Songwriting
www.togethersoftware.com/search.asp
Find rhymes online; professional rhyming
dictionary; integrated pronunciation, definition,
and thesaurus; reference tool.
Write Hit Songs **www.writehitsongs.com** Web
site for songwriters.
WritingSongs.com **www.writingsongs.com**
Writing music; songs; lyrics; information; links.

Stringed Instruments — Violin — Viola — Cello — Bass — Harp

Berg Bows **www.bergbows.com** Bows.
Bernard Ellis **www.ellisium.cwc.net** Handmade
early string instruments; supply worldwide to
professional and amateur musicians, museums,
cultural foundations, and university departments.
Clarenbridge Harps **www.folkcraft.com**
Amergin; Amergin II; Erin; McClain; Adare.
Dogal String **www.dogalstrings.com** Classical
and modern instruments; strings.
Harpress of California **www.harpress.com** Harp
sheet music, instructional books, recordings, and
videos.

Heftone Musical Instruments **www.msen.com**
Upright string basses.
Ithaca Stringed Instruments
www.ithacastring.com Home-builder of
custom guitars, violins, violas, and cellos;
product catalog; articles; reviews; contact
information.
Johnson String Instruments **www.johnson-**
inst.com Violins, violas, cellos, and their
bows; new and antique violins, violas, bows, and
cellos; online catalog; repairs and rentals.
Jordan Electric Violins **www.jordanmusic.com**
Electric violins; electric violas; electric cellos;
electric basses.
Lamoureux Violins **www.lviolins.com** Discount
supplier to classical musicians, music educators,
and students; resources for both traditional and
Suzuki methods of teaching violin, viola, cello,
bass, piano, flute, harp, guitar, and recorder;
music books and sheet music in all genres.
Lashof Violins.com **www.lashofviolins.com**
Care and maintenance of string instruments.
Meisel Stringed Instruments
www.meiselmusic.com Meisel; Mittenwald;
Mozart; Spitfire; Skyinbow; GIG Stands;
Innovation Strings; Pyramid Syntha-Core.
Otto Musica U.S.A. Inc. **www.ottomusica.com**
Violin bows; violin cases; cello cases; violin
strings; violin shoulder rests; violin rosin;
violins; cellos; recorders.
Perfekt Noten Fingerboard Labels for Violin
www.perfektnoten.com Labels to help
reinforce correct finger positions on the
fingerboard.
Rugeri Music Teaching Methods
www.rugeri.com Teaching literature for
strings.
Shar Music **www.sharmusic.com** Online violin
shop; sheet music for stringed instruments.
Southwest Strings **www.swstrings.com** Music
products; strings; sheet music.
String Instruments **www.nwu.edu** Violin; viola;
cello; harp.
String Works **www.stringworks.com** Violin sales
and rentals.
Stringnet **www.stringnet.com** String
instruments; violin; viola; cello; bass; bows and
accessories.
Super-Sensitive Musical String Company
www.supersensitive.com Strings and
accessories for bowed instruments.
Tempest Music **www.violin-**
world.com/sheetmusic Classical specialist;
music and accessories for stringed instruments.
The Cello Page **www.cello.org** Information;
resources; links.

The Harp Column **www.harpcolumn.com**
Webzine; CD reviews; interviews.

The Harp Page
www.tns.lcs.mit.edu/harp/harp.html
Harp information; links to harp publications and
events; harps in the news and on the Web.

The Internet Cello Society **www.cello.org** Links
to home pages of amateur and professional
cellists; cello news groups, articles, auditions,
and job openings.

The String Pedagogy Notebook
**www.personal.umich.edu/~
mhopkins/string.html** Database of graded
orchestra literature; for teachers and performers of
string music.

Thomastik-Infeld Vienna **www.thomastik-
infeld.com** Dominant perlon violin strings.

Tuner & Metronome **www.cresco-
consulting.com** Software tuner; allows
student to tune his or her violin using the
computer microphone; plays notes to allow
learning how to tune by ear; Windows.

VioLink-The World of Violins **www.violink.com**
Wide collection of links and data about
instruments, schools, organizations, performers,
events, publications, images, sounds, business,
stolen instruments, technique, research, historical
resources, etc.

Violin-World **www.violin-world.com** Stringed
instruments; violin; viola; cello; double bass;
strings; bows; cases; sheet music; online store
and catalogue; announcements; classifieds;
teachers directory; sound advice; articles; music
jokes.

V-I-P String Series
www.choicemall.com/playfullmusik
Beginning level string program.

Wood Violins **www.markwoodmusic.com**
Fretted or fretless vipers; electric violins.

World of Violins **library.usask.ca** Catgut
Acoustical Society; Internet Viola Society;
Internet Cello Society; International Society of
Bassists; string instruments.

Zeta Music Systems **www.zetamusic.com**
Violins; basses; cellos; violas; amps.

Vocal Music—Choral and Opera—Singing

4Singing **www.4singing.com/staying.shtml**
Instructors; advice; information on singers; how
to maintain and protect the voice.

Academic Choir Apparel
www.academicapparel.com Choir robes.

A-Cappella **www.a-cappella.com** Order online;
RealAudio.

Alfred Publishing's Choral, Vocal, & Handbell Site
**www.alfredpub.com/vocal/chorhome.
html** Complete listing of school choral releases;
top sellers; staging suggestions.

America Sings **www.americasings.org** Home
page.

American Choral Directors Association (ACDA)
www.ACDAonline.org or
www.choralnet.org/acda1.htm News;
about ACDA; officers; staff; chapters: divisions,
states, students; *Choral Journal;* national
convention; division conventions; repertoire and
standards; membership form; member services;
online store.

Anyone Can Sing **www.singtome.com** Articles
and tips; links; advice column; monthly
newsletter.

Aria Database **www.aria-database.com** Quick
search; arias; operas; composers; roles; diverse
collection of information on over 1,000 operatic
arias; for singers and non-singers; includes
translations and aria texts of most arias;
collection of MIDI files of operatic arias and
ensembles.

Audio-Technica **www.audio-technica.com**
Microphones.

Barbershop Harmony **www.spebsqsa.org** Locate
a barbershop quartet or barbershop chorus; find
arrangements and songbooks; purchase CDs and
videos.

Choir and Organ Classical Music Magazine
www.orphpl.com/choir.htm Religious;
secular; choral; reviews; news; events.

Choral Clewes Vocal Music Instruction Series
www.choralclewes.com For teachers, choral
directors, home schoolers, and professional
singers.

Choral Music **home.att.net/~langburn**
Information on over one hundred published
compositions and arrangements; accompanied and
a cappella; mixed and treble; sacred and secular;
reviews; performances; repertoire suggestions;
ordering tips.

ChoralNet **www.choralnet.org** Internet launching
point for all choral music; collection of links
including reference and research resources;
database for choral repertoire, events and
performances; news; Web message boards;
worldwide directory of choirs on the Web;
archives; E-mail lists; support.

ChoralWeb **www.choralweb.com** Publisher of
vocal music and more.

Choristers Guild **www.choristersguild.org**
Home page.

Classical Singer **www.classicalsinger.com** For
singers of classical music.

Classical Vocal Rep
www.classicalvocalrep.com Vocal music books.

Cybersing: Information for Singers
www.cybersing.com Information for beginning and advanced singers; basics of singing.

DigiTech **www.digitech.com** Vocal harmony and effects processors.

Early Music Vocal Ensembles
www.intr.net/bleissa/lists/choral.html Organized into sections: mixed vocal ensembles; may include instrumental accompaniment.

EatSleepMusic **www.eatsleepmusic.com** Online Karaoke; contests; free downloads; player; links; children's sing-along music.

EON **www.european-opera-network.org/en** European opera network.

Gilded Age Opera Tours **www.go2opera.com** Opera, music, and travel.

Great Singers
www.greatsingers.co.uk/index.html Over 300 biographies; singers; groups.

Handlo Music **www.handlo.com/choral** Choral sheet music delivered via E-mail for output from a computer printer.

Healthy Voice **www.healthwindows.com/ healthwindows/mtnl0627_music.asp** Tips on developing and maintaining a healthy voice.

International Vocalist **www.vocalist.org** Resource and database for singers.

ISong.com **www.isong.com** Accompaniment tracks.

Karaoke Plus **www.megastarusa.com** Megastar singing systems.

Karaoke Singer Magazine
www.karaokesingermagazine.com Home page.

KJPro Karaoke Software **www.kjpro.com** *KJ Pro* Windows program for creating karaoke songbooks.

La Scala **lascala.milano.it** World's most famous opera house.

Learn to Sing! **www.inachord.to** Voice lessons with Dave and Shalee; eight simple lessons in a four-CD set for men and women.

Lisa Popeil-The Total Singer **www.popeil.com** Video course for all styles and levels.

MacroMusic's Online Vocal Music Store
www.macromusic.com/store/ searchengines/Vocal Vocal music titles.

Medicine in the Vocal Arts
www.bgsm.edu/voice/ medicine_vocal_arts.html Vocal training.

Metropolitan Opera Broadcasts
www.metopera.org/broadcast International radio broadcasts; telecast series.

Metropolitan Opera
www.metopera.org/home.html Schedules of upcoming presentations and performer bios; online version of the opera quiz.

Music Curriculum (K-12): Singing and Choral Performance
www.mv.com/ipusers/orol/district/ issues/music/sing.html Student proficiencies in singing and choral performance; sing different kinds of music accurately, expressively, and in a healthy manner.

National Association of Teachers of Singing
www.nats.org Home page; membership; resources; links.

Neumann **www.neumann.com** Microphones.

New York City Opera **www.nycopera.com** Opera company.

Opera America **www.operaam.org** Information about opera in the United States.

Opera Composers
lucia.stanford.edu/opera/composers. html For composers listed in the main index there are either complete opera lists, with date and place of premiere or time of composition if known, or links to individual pages providing additional information.

Opera News **www.operanews.com** News on opera-related features and events.

Opera Related Links on the WWW
users.lia.net/dlever/Links.htm Includes links to the following: Atlanta Opera's "Opera 101" glossary of terms A-L and M-Z; Basic Recorded Opera; Classical Music in Italy; Classics World's Opera/Vocal Area; Cologne Opera (German); Current Opera Digest; Current Opera Home Page; Data on the History of Opera; Folkoperan Online; Gilbert & Sullivan Archive; Great Performances Schedule; Great Readings and Opera; International Opera Locations; Internet Movie Database; Los Angeles Music Center Opera Page; Mr. Opera's Classical Music and Opera Page; New York City Opera Online Site; New York Foundation for the Arts: Directory of Services; NPR's Performance Today Page; Opera and Music Page; Opera Companies on World Wide Web; Opera Factory; Opera Glass; Opera in the Muse; Opera Libretti Page; Opera Schedule Server; Opera-L Home Page; Origins of Opera; Richard Repp's Vocal Resources Page; Richard Wagner Archive Page; Royal Swedish Opera House Page; Salzburg Information Center; San Diego Opera; San Francisco Opera; Santa Fe Opera; Sarasota Opera Home Page; Seattle Opera Home Page; Sydney Opera House Page; Teatro alla Scala of Milano, Italy; Texaco -

Metropolitan Opera International Radio Network Page; Verdi Opera; Wagner's Ring Home Page; Washington Opera Home Page; West Bay Opera; William Schende's Wide World of Opera; Yahoo's Opera Page and more.

Operabase **www.operabase.com** Schedules; venues; festivals; reviews; links.

Optimal Breathing for Singing **www.breathing.com** Manual with exercises for the singing voice.

Pocket Songs **www.pocketsongs.com** Instrumental track sing-along CDs and cassettes of popular music and standards; large catalog.

Practice Choral Parts on the Web **www.channel1.com/users/gsilvis** Collection of MIDI files and tools to help singers learn their notes.

Primarily A Cappella Catalog **www.singers.com** Specializing in a cappella recordings, videos, and vocal arrangements in all styles including vocal jazz, gospel, choral, doo-wop, folk, barbershop, and contemporary.

ProSing **www.prosing.com** *Top & Country Hits Today; Legends; Monster Hits; Star Disk; Baseline; Sound Choice Pioneer; Music Maestro; Sun Fly; Dick; Vocopro; Gemini; RSQ; JVC; Venturer; Audio 2000.*

Public Domain Opera Libretti and Other Vocal Texts **php.indiana.edu/~lneff/libretti.html** Libretti and vocal text Web site.

Real Tracks **www.RealTracks.com** Karaoke backing tracks for singers.

Royal Opera House **www.royalopera.org** Opera Web site.

Santa Fe Opera **www.walpole.com/walpole/ Santa_Fe_Opera** International opera house located outside of Santa Fe, NM; summer season.

Schoolmusic.com **www.schoolmusic.com/printedmusic/ choral.asp** Featured choral products in selected categories.

Secrets of Singing by Jeffrey Allen **www.vocalsuccess.com** Vocal method; books; videos; tips; links; order online.

Shaker Microphone **www.bluenight.com** Microphones.

Showoffs Studio **www.nefsky.com** For performers; singing classes; workshops; talent showcase.

Shure **www.shure.com** Leading manufacturer of microphones.

Sing Your Life **www.singyourlife.com** Self-teaching manual emphasizing vocal strength and endurance.

Singers Online **www.singersonline.com** NYC-based organization focusing on Broadway style; workshops and classes.

Singing Championship **www.singingchampionship.com** National Karaoke singing contest.

Singing for Money **members.aol.com/ifsnet/sfmhome.html** Singer's resource.

Singing for the Soul **www.singingforthesoul.com** Singing lessons on tape.

Singing Store **www.singingstore.com** Everything for the singer; tracks.

Singing: The New Grove **www.geocities.com/Vienna/Strasse/ 2200** Singing and opera history from *The New Grove Dictionary of Music and Musicians;* reprinted with permission.

SongXpress **www.songxpress.com** Classic Blues; Classic Rock; Modern Rock.

Sound Choice **www.soundchoice.com** Accompaniment tracks for singers.

Susan's Room: Vocal Workout **www.songwriter.com/susan/workout. html** Song-based method for developing the singing voice; for all contemporary singers, beginners to advanced.

The Gregorian Chant Home Page **silvertone.princeton.edu/chant_html** Links to other chant research sites on the Web; Medieval music theory sites; resources for chant performance; ecclesiastical, historical, humanistic, and information sciences.

The Lied and Song Texts Page **www.recmusic.org/lieder** Introduction; what's new; search composers (1,520); poets (1,985); languages (23); first lines; titles; random art songs in English or in English translation (5,921); guest book.

The Metropolitan Chorus **www.metchorus.org** The 100-voice Metropolitan Chorus presents concerts featuring music of great variety, spanning time from the Renaissance to the twentieth century; strong emphasis on American composers.

The Singer's Workshop **www.thesingersworkshop.com** Professional singing coach Lis Lewis; background singing; session singing; The Charisma Factor; tips for the aspiring singer; breath control; articles on preparing for the stage; finding the right voice teacher; LA based.

The Voices Studio **www.thevoicestudio.com** For the vocalist.

Timbo's Barbershop Web Server **www.timc.pop.upenn.edu** What's happening in the world of barbershop quartets throughout the U.S.

UTK Song Index **toltec.lib.utk.edu/~music/songindex**

Publicly available database providing access to citations for about 50,000 songs in more than 1,400 published song anthologies; owned by the George F. DeVine Music Library at the University of Tennessee, Knoxville; searches by title, large work (operas, song cycles, etc.), or call number of the anthology.

Vocal Instruction **www.vocalinstruction.com** Extend the range of your voice.

Vocal Music-Choral and Opera **library.usask.ca/subjects/music/vocal. html** Index; excellent resource page for choirs and choir conductors; links to American Choral Directors Association; The Aria Database; CHORALNET homepage; Classical MIDI with words; Digital Tradition Folksong (texts of folksongs); Gregorian Chant; International Lyrics Server; Good for folk-song lyrics; Libretto Homepage; Lied and Song Texts page; Metropolitan Opera Broadcasts; Opera Links; Opera Navigation Center; Song Index.

Vocal Power Seminars & Master Classes **www.music-world.com/vpi-smnr.htm** Vocal Power Method; vocal training; proper breathing techniques; singing lessons.

Voice Database **www.voicedatabase.com** Resource for voice-over artists; vocalists.

Voice Instructors Directory **www.music-world.com/instruct.htm** Vocal instructors.

Voice Teachers **www.voiceteachers.com** Find a teacher; add a new teacher; listed by state.

Voice-Craft Electronics Co.; Ltd. **www.voice-craft.com.tw** Voice-Craft; Dynasonic.

Workshop on Church Music **coned.byu.edu/cw/cwchmusi/classdes. htm** Accompanying a choir at the organ; applying registration and dynamics.

Worldwide Internet Music Resources: Opera, Opera Companies **www.music.indiana.edu/ music_resources/opera.html** Aria database; arias; librettos; translations; composers and more.

Yahoo! Entertainment:Music:Vocal **www.yahoo.com/Entertainment/Music/ Vocal** Daily news, reviews, charts, artist and album information for rock, jazz, urban, country, and more.

Yodeling Instructional Video **www.yodelers.com** Intended to help find natural yodel voice break.

You Can Sing with Impact! **www.singwithimpact.com** Daily warm-up workout.

World Music

Africa1.com **www.africa1.com** World music radio.

African-American Mosaic **lcWeb.loc.gov/exhibits/african/intro. html** African American history and culture.

Afrojazz **www.afrojazz.com** World music Web site; Cuban musicians.

All Nations Cultural Festival **www.northernnet.com/leepfrog** Ethnic festival and booking agency.

Alterations Garden **www.alterationsgarden.com** World and ethnic music; CDs; store.

Ancient-Future.Com: World Music Online **www.ancient-future.com** World music movement; traditional world music education; global music and dance forums.

Asian American Resources **www.mit.edu/afs/athena.mit.edu/ user/i/r/irie/www/aar.html** Asian American Web sites.

BBC World Service **www.bbc.co.uk/worldservice/pop** World music Web site.

Best of Most Worlds—Streaming MP3 Station **zoope.com/b/bestworlds** Traditional, modern, and world-influenced music from around the globe.

Blue Gum Designs **www.bluegumdesigns.com** Didgeridoos; Blue Gum Designs Didgeridoos.

Center for World Music **www.centerforworldmusic.org/ dance.html** World music center based in San Diego, CA.

Charlie Gillett **www.roughguides.com/charlie** World music Web site.

Chico World Music Festival **www.chicomusicfestival.com/ ChicoIndex.html** Two days of music in Bidwell Park in September.

Corazong **www.corazong.com** Roots, world music, singer songwriter, punk, alternative, and blues music.

Cultural Bridge Productions **www.culturalbridge.com** Essays on world cultures.

Eclectic Music Reviews **www.nua-tech.com/paddy/music.shtml** Reviews of world music, techno, blues, classical, gospel, rock, and more.

Global Fusion Catalogue **www.global.fusion.ndirect.co.uk** Traditional world music, classical world music, and world fusion music ranging from acoustic English folk, to Latin jazz, to cutting edge dance remixes.

Global Oasis: World Music **www.globaloasis.iinet.net.au/music. html** Articles on world music and percussion.

Groovesite **www.groovesite.com** World music
Web site.

*Grooveworks-Art for the Sake of Music-World
Music Shirts*
www.grooveworks.com/shirts.htm
Combines music and T-shirt art; African
American, Native American, and
cultural/political themes on shirts.

Index of Native American Resources on the Internet
**hanksville.phast.umass.edu/misc/
NAresources.html** Native American culture
Web sites.

International Music Archives
www.eyeneer.com/World/index.html
Music and musical instruments of the world;
articles and pictures; categorized geographically.

M.E.L.T. 2000 **www.melt2000.com** World
music and jazz.

Mondomix-Musiques du Monde-World Music
www.mondomix.org Un regard actuel et
federateur sur les musiques du monde; retrouvez
tous les artistes, les labels, les medias, les
concerts, et les festivals de world music.

Music of the World **www.musicoftheworld.com**
Independent record label that produces high
quality recordings of traditional and contemporary
world music.

Musical Instruments of the World
**www.eyeneer.com/World/Instruments/
index.html** Brief articles and pictures of
various primitive instruments.

NativeWeb **www.nativeWeb.org** Information of
interest to indigenous peoples; seeks to represent
all indigenous peoples of the planet.

New Native **www.wcpworld.com** World music
Web site.

RootsWorld **www.rootsworld.com** Magazine of
world music; roots music; music that defies easy
classification.

Shakuhachi Flute Sheet Music
www.shakuhachi.com/toc-sm.html
Listing of shakuhachi scores.

Sheet Music for the Native American Flute
**www.teleport.com/~wjstroud/sheetmus.
html** Native American flutes and music; sound
samples; music tapes and CDs; artists/musicians;
authentic Native American flutes and flute-
making kits; books on how to play and make
flutes; stories.

Sonika Records **www.sonika.com** World Music
recording company; music styles ranging from
Afro-Beat to Latin.

The Afro-American Web Ring
www.halcon.com/halcon/1ring.html
Sites of interest to African Americans.

The Ultimate Ethnic Musical Instruments Source
josh.bakehorn.net/store.html Ethnic
instruments.

The Web of Culture **www.webofculture.com**
World cultures; check local currency for most
countries; find an embassy or consulate in the
U.S.; see schedules of holidays in different
countries.

Warrior Caste **www.musiq.com/warcaste** An
international collaborative ambient project
integrating world music performances with
electronic treatments and electroacoustics; audio
samples; complete discography.

Womad **womadusa.org** World music.

World Fusion Music Links **www.ancient-
future.com/links/index.html** Links page
for the world music and dance movements;
traditional and world fusion music.

World Music Charts
www.lanet.lv/misc/charts/#us or
www.worldmusiccharts.com 900 pages
online; charts in over seventy-six countries;
updated weekly.

World Music Charts
wwweltmusk.de/charts/main.htm World
music Web site.

World Music Homepage **w3.to/worldmusic**
World music Web site.

World Music
worldmusic.miningco.com/index.htm
World music information.

World Music **www.music.indiana.edu/
music_resources/ethnic.html** Information;
resources; links.

World Music **www.worldmusic.org** Concerts
from around the world.

World Music Portal
www.worldmusicportal.com Home page;
links.

World Music Press **www.worldmusicpress.com**
Home page.

World of Music
**saxland.freeservers.com/worldofmusic.
html** WAV and MIDI pages; ska and general
links.

5

Tech Talk: Internet Terms A-Z

Following is a list of Internet-related terms not previously defined in this book.

A2B AT&T's music distribution system.

AAC Advanced Audio Coding; part of MPEG-2; audio compression system with better compression rates than MP3.

AARC Alliance of Artists and Recording Companies.

Access Provider Organization that provides access to the Internet via a dial-up account; fee depends on the amount of usage or other individual contract specifications.

Access Speed The speed of an online connection; measured in bits per second (bps); determined by the speed of the modem and the maximum speed allowed by the ISP.

ActiveX Microsoft standard for computer program building blocks known as *objects.*

Ad Banner Graphics that link to an advertiser's Web site; advertisement in the form of a graphic image on the Internet; most banner ads are animated GIF files.

Ad Click The click on an advertisement on a Web site that takes the user to another Web site.

Ad View A Web page that presents an ad or several ads; user may click on after viewing.

ADC Analog-to-digital converter.

ADPCM Adaptive Differential Pulse Code Modulation; a type of digital audio compression that predicts the values of upcoming samples.

ADSL Asymmetric Digital Subscriber Line; technology that transmits data over phone lines faster in one direction than in the other; a type of DSL that sacrifices upload speed for increased download speed.

AFAIK E-mail acronym meaning "as far as I know."

AIFF Audio Interchange File Format; a type of sound file; a common audio format for the Macintosh; normally uncompressed.

ALT Alternative hierarchy of Usenet newsgroups.

Analog Audio Audio represented by a signal that continuously varies; sound that has not been turned into numbers; an analog sound wave can be infinitely variable; digitized sound is limited to discrete values.

Anonymous FTP A way of using the FTP program to log on to another computer to copy files without an account on the other computer; enter "anonymous" as the username and E-mail address as the password.

Applet Small computer program written in the Java programming language embedded in an HTML page; when the page is accessed, the browser downloads the applet and runs it on the computer; applets cannot read or write data onto a computer; applets can only be used if the browser supports Java.

Archive A single file containing a group of files that have been compressed together for efficient storage; must use a program such as PKZIP or Stuffit to get the original files back out.

ARPANET U.S. Department of Defense original ancestor of the Internet.

Article Message someone sends to a newsgroup to be read by those in the newsgroup.

ASCII American Standard Code for Information Interchange; widely used text set that describes up to 255 characters and code points.

ASFS Encoded compressed music file format supported by Virtuosa Gold.

Aspect Ratio Proportional image sizing during enlargement or reduction; expressed as a width-to-height ratio.

ASPI A method of accessing a CD-ROM drive; originally developed for SCSI; works well with IDE drives via the ATAPI protocol.

Asynchronous Communication that does not depend on two parties talking simultaneously.

ATAPI Protocol used to communicate with non-hard drive IDE devices such as CD-ROMs.

ATM Asynchronous Transfer Mode; high bandwidth technology enabling rapid transmission of large files.

Attachment Computer file attached or "electronically stapled" to an E-mail message and sent with it.

AU Audio format found on Sun and NeXT computers.

Authentication Technique whereby access to the Internet or Intranet resources requires the user to identify self by entering a username and password; also called "logging in."

Auxiliary Refers to the socket on a sound card that connects with other audio playing devices; also called "line in."

AVI Audio Visual Interface; Microsoft graphics standard for compressed movie clips.

Bandwidth The measure of a medium's data transfer capability; the transmission capacity of a network or other communications medium.

Baud The number of electrical symbols per second that a modem sends down a phone line; often used as a synonym for bps (bits per second).

BBS Bulletin Board System; electronic message system dialed up directly to read and post messages.

BCC Blind Carbon Copy; BCC addresses get a copy of an E-mail without other recipients knowing about it; usually used for long mailing lists.

Binary File File that contains information consisting of more than text such as a picture, sounds, a spreadsheet, an archive, or a word-processing document.

BinHex File-encoding system popular among Macintosh users.

Bit Depth Number of bits in a pixel; used to describe a monitor's graphic resolution.

Bit Rate Measured in *kilobits per second* or *Kbps*; number of bits used each second to represent a digital signal; binary digit (either a 1 or a 0); smallest unit of measure for computer data; bits can be *on* or *off* (symbolized by 1 or 0) and are used in various combinations to represent different types of information; amount of data used to hold a given length of music.

Bitmap Description of images or fonts within a grid of pixels; small dots put together to make a black-and-white or color picture.

BITNET Older network of large computers connected to the Internet.

Bookmark Browser feature allowing user to save a link to a Web page; the bookmark is used to return to that page.

Bounce When an E-mail is returned because it could not be delivered to the specified address; returned as "undeliverable" to a bad address.

bps or **bits per second** Measure of how fast data is transmitted; used to describe modem speed.

Bridge Page Page created to connect a Web site's content and an advertiser's Web site; tracks click-throughs from ad banners.

Broadband Term describing advanced networks that deliver high-speed data access of up to 1,000 times faster than ISDN; used in conjunction with cable modems.

Broadcasting Method of transmitting information; sends the same information to all systems.

Browser or **Web Browser** Software program used to locate and view HTML documents on the Internet; e.g., Netscape, Microsoft Explorer.

BTW E-mail acronym meaning "by the way."

Byte A set of eight bits that represent a number from 0 to 255; computer memory is measured in bytes; place for temporary storage of data.

Cable Modem Modem technology that uses standard television cable to deliver increased access speed without a phone dial-up connection.

Cache Hardware or software that speeds up the flow of data.

CAV Constant Angular Velocity.

CBR Constant Bit-Rate; describes MP3 files where each second of music is compressed to the same size.

CC Carbon Copy. CC addressees get a copy of an E-mail, and the other recipients are informed of this; to send somebody a copy of an E-mail message.

CCIR Center for Communications Research.

CCITT Former name for ITU-T, the committee that sets worldwide communication standards.

CD-R Compact Disc-Recordable; a CD that can be recorded only once; drives and media that allow one to make CD-ROMs and audio CDs with a computer.

CD-ROM Compact Disc-Read Only Memory; refers to a prerecorded data CD.

CD-RW Compact Disc-Rewritable; a CD that can be recorded and erased multiple times; drives and reusable media that allow one to store data in a CD-like format; cannot be read by normal CD players or CD-ROM drives; most CD-RW drives can also write to CD-R media.

CD Compact Disc.

CDA Compact Disc Audio; refers to the uncompressed encoding method used to store audio on a standard CD.

CGI Common Gateway Interface; interface that allows scripts or programs to run on a Web server; CGI-scripts are used to put the content of a form into an E-mail message, to perform a database query, to generate HTML; most popular languages for CGI-scripts are Perl and C.

CGI-BIN Most common name of a directory on a Web server in which CGI-scripts are stored.

Channel In IRC, a group of people chatting together; a major interest area on a service provider one can easily access.

Chanop Channel Operator; in charge of keeping order in a channel in IRC.

Chat Online interactive communication on the Web; "talk" in real time with others in the "chat room"; words are typed instead of spoken; talk (or type) live to other network users from all parts of the world; on the Internet, use Internet Relay Chat (IRC).

Checksum Unique number generated by applying a formula to the contents of a data file; used to determine if a file has been modified or if two files are identical, without directly comparing the files.

Click-Through Rate Percentage of users who click on a viewed advertisement; indicates the effectiveness of the ad.

Client Errors Error occurring due to an invalid request by the visitor's browser.

Client/Server Model A division of labor between computers; computers that provide a service other computers can use are called *servers*; the users are called *clients*.

Client The browser used by a visitor to a Web site; a computer that uses the services of another computer, or *server*.

Clipping The flattening of a waveform peak when it reaches the maximum level.

CLV Constant Linear Velocity.

CODEC Compressor/Decompressor; algorithm for encoding and decoding digital information; system to store data in less space.

Commercial Online Service Computer network that offers its members access to its own chat rooms, bulletin boards, and other online features for a monthly fee; e.g., America Online, CompuServe, and The Microsoft Network.

Communications Program A program run on a personal computer that enables user to call up and communicate with other computers; a.k.a. terminal programs or terminal emulators.

CompactFlash Small solid-state memory card with an onboard controller; emulates a hard disk.

Compress Store a set of data using less space while retaining necessary information.

Compression Method of encoding data to optimize space; technology that reduces the size of a file to save bandwidth.

Constant Bit Rate See CBR.

Cookie Files containing information about visitors to a Web site including user name and preferences; this information is provided by the user during the first visit to a server; the server records this information in a text file and stores the file on the visitor's hard drive; when the visitor accesses the same Web site again, the server looks for the cookie and configures itself based on the information provided.

Country Code The last part of a geographic address, which indicates in which country the host computer is located.

Crossfade A way of using a mixer to overlap the start of one song with the end of another and adjust the levels, creating a smooth transition.

CUL E-mail acronym meaning "see you later."

Cyberspace The virtual environment of communication created by phone, E-mail, and fax.

DAC Digital-to-Analog Converter.

DAE Digital Audio Extraction; ability of a CD-ROM drive to transfer the digital audio information from an audio CD to the computer.

DAT Digital Audio Tape.

Data Encryption Key String of characters used to encode a message; can only be read by someone with another related key.

Data Transfer Rate The rate that data can be transferred to computers or networks.

DB-25 The style of data plug on most modems and serial ports; shaped like a two-inch-high, thin letter *D* with twenty-five pins; Macs use a smaller, round plug.

DB Decibel; a relative unit measurement for sound.

Decode To convert a compressed audio file into uncompressed, unencoded digital audio information.

Decompress To convert a compressed audio file into an uncompressed one.

Decompression The process of restoring a compressed file to its original form.

Dedicated Line Leased phone line used exclusively for computer communications.

Delivery Platform End-user platform that plays multimedia or other software.

Delphi Online service that supports text-oriented Internet tools; good for users of older computers and the visually impaired.

Dial-Up Networking Windows 95 built-in TCP/IP program for connecting to PPP or SLIP accounts.

Dial-Up Temporary connection over a phone line to the ISP computer in order to establish a connection to the Internet; the availability of a phone line for voice or data transmission.

Digest Compilation of messages that have been posted to a mailing list during the past few days or the past week.

Digital Audio Recording of sound stored as a series of numbers; audio represented by numbers, usually in binary format (1s and 0s).

Digital Audio Extraction (DAE) The process of copying audio data directly from a CD; also referred to as ripping.

Digitize To convert analog audio into digital audio by repeatedly measuring or sampling the sound wave.

Discography A musician's full catalog of works or recordings in chronological order.

Distributor Agency that carries and supplies a product to retailers and end-users.

Dithering Method of adding random noise to a digital audio signal to minimize the effect of distortion from quantization.

DNS Domain Name Server or Domain Name System; maps IP numbers to a more easily remembered name; a computer on the Internet that translates between Internet domain names and Internet numerical addresses; also called "name server."

Docking Station Holder used to store a portable MP3 player; is connected to the PC and is used to transfer data to the player from the PC; some recharge the player's batteries.

Domain Name The part of a URL that is user-specific; the specific name that identifies an Internet site; most domain names are assigned by Network Solutions and are purchased on a first come first served basis.

Download Transfer of data from a server to a computer's hard disk; to copy a file from a remote computer to another computer.

DSL Digital Subscriber Line; technology that increases the capacity of telephone lines.

Duplex Ability to send information in both directions.

DVD Digital Versatile Disc; a high-density media, similar to a CD, with a capacity of up to 18.8 GB.

Dynamic Range The range of signal levels an audio system or piece of audio equipment is able to handle.

E-zine A magazine that exists in cyberspace.

Elm Full-screen UNIX mail reader.

E-mail Electronic Mail; message transmitted and sent over the Internet from one person to another, or to a large number of E-mail addresses on a mailing list.

E-mail Acronyms Letter abbreviations of common expressions.

E-mail Address Electronic mail address in the form of user@domain.

EMF Electro-Magnetic Frequency.

Encode To convert data into a specific file format.

Encoder Software or hardware that encodes information.

Encoding The process of converting uncompressed audio into a compressed format.

Encrypted Data files that are stored such that they can't be read without a password or key; process used to create audio files that will only run on the user's player and nowhere else.

Encryption Procedure that scrambles the contents of a file prior to sending it over the Internet; the recipient must have the appropriate software to decrypt the file; security practice of scrambling a file's contents so the information is not able to be read without a software key.

Engine A multimedia software program that displays content and directs interaction.

Enqueue Queue, or place, in a list of items to be processed.

EOT E-mail acronym meaning "end of thread."

EPAC Perceptual audio encoding scheme based on PAC.

Equalization Adjusting the relative levels of bands of frequencies to modify or make smoother the frequency response of an audio signal or file.

Eudora Mail-handling program that runs on Macintosh and Windows.

FAQ Frequently Asked Questions; document or article that contains the most common questions and answers on a particular subject; E-mail acronym meaning "frequently asked questions."

FIDONET Worldwide network of bulletin-board systems with E-mail access.

Filters A way to narrow the scope of a report or view by specifying ranges or types of data to include or exclude.

Finger A program that displays information about someone on the Internet; the act of getting information about someone on the Internet by using the finger program.

Firewall Specially programmed computer that connects a local network to the Internet and, for security reasons, lets only certain kinds of messages in and out; security architecture between the Internet and a private network that protects the private network from unauthorized access.

Firmware Computer programs that are stored on a piece of hardware.

Flame War Two or more individuals engaged in flaming.

Flame An E-mail message relaying a nasty or personal attack; to post angry, inflammatory, or insulting messages.

Flaming Rude, scolding, or nasty E-mail and newsgroup replies.

Flash Memory Computer memory that does not lose stored data when the power is shut off.

Flash Animation software from Macromedia used to develop Web graphics.

Font Comprehensive set of characters in one design or style.

Forms HTML page which passes variables back to the server; used to gather information from users; a.k.a. scripts.

Frame A small chunk of data; specifically on audio CDs.

Freenet Free online system offering local communities information and limited access to the Internet.

Freeware Software that is free.

Front End End-user's operational interface to an information system.

FTP File Transfer Protocol; Method of transferring files from one computer to another over the Internet; standard method of sending files between computers over the Internet; a protocol used to transfer files across the Internet.

FTP Server A computer on the Internet that stores files for transmission by FTP.

Fulfillment Service provided by a CD printer, duplicator, or manufacturer that includes warehousing inventory, processing, and shipping orders to customers.

FWIW E-mail acronym meaning "for what it's worth."

FYI E-mail acronym meaning "for your information."

GAL E-mail acronym meaning "get a life."

Gateway Device that allows data from one network to access another; a computer that connects one network with another, where the two networks use different protocols.

GB Gigabyte. 2 to the 30th power (1,073,741,824) bytes.

Genre A category of music such as country, blues, jazz, rock, etc.

gHz One billion cycles per second.

GIF Graphics Interchange Format; patented type of graphics file; files in this format end in .gif and are called GIF files or GIFs; common graphics file format on the Internet; can display 256 colors at the maximum (8 bits); mostly used to show clip-art images; photographic images are usually in the JPEG format; GIF 89a standard allows multiple images in one file and can be used to show some animation on a Web site; developed by CompuServe.

Gigabyte One billion bytes or characters of data; 1 Kb = 1,024 bytes; 1 Mb = 1,024 Kb (=1,048,576 bytes); 1 Gb = 1,024 Mb (= 1,073,741,824 bytes).

GKA Government Key Access; U.S. government proposal to require that encryption software include a way for the government to break the code.

Gopher Internet system allowing user to find information by using menus.

Gopherspace The world of Gopher menus.

Handle User's nickname or screen name.

Hardware Actual physical parts of computer equipment, as opposed to *software* programs, files, etc.

Header The beginning of an E-mail message; To and From addresses, subject and date.

Hertz (Hz) Cycles per second; used as a measurement of frequency.

Hierarchy In Usenet, the major group to which a newsgroup belongs; seven major hierarchies are "comp," "rec," "soc," "sci," "news," "misc," and "talk."

Hit Single request from a browser to a server; access of a file on a Web page.

Home Page The main page of a Web site; provides an overview; links to rest of site; may contain a table of contents for the site; Web page about a person or organization.

Host The server on which a Web site is stored; a computer on the Internet.

Hostname The name of a computer on the Internet.

Hot Spots Areas of a multimedia display screen that accept user interaction.

HTML Hypertext Markup Language; the standard tool or coding language for creating Web pages; language used to write pages for the World Wide Web; text includes codes that define fonts, layout, embedded graphics, and hypertext links; a way to format text by placing marks or tags around the text.

HTTP Hypertext Transfer Protocol; the way in which Web pages are transferred over the Net; World Wide Web protocol for moving hypertext (HTML) files across the Internet.

HTTPS Variant form of HTTP that encrypts messages for security.

Huffman Encoding Method of data compression that uses shorter codes to represent patterns that are more common.

Hyperlink Place on a Web page that, when accessed or "clicked," will send the user to a different Web page; often underlined and/or blue.

Hypermedia Method of accessing different media elements (text, graphics, etc.) in an interactive, navigable form.

Hypertext Text that includes hyperlinks to other Web pages; the cross-linking of media, especially texts, for reference purposes; system of writing and displaying text that enables the text to be linked in multiple ways, available at different levels of detail, and with links to related documents; World Wide Web uses both hypertext and hypermedia.

ID3 Tag Method for storing data within an MP3 file.

ID3 Format for including informational tags in an MP3 file, allowing multiple players to display information about the song.

IDE Integrated Drive Electronics.

IETF Internet Engineering Task Force; group that develops new technical standards for the Intenet.

IICS International Interactive Communications Society; organization of multimedia and interface designers.

IKWYM or **IKWUM** E-mail acronym meaning "I know what you mean."

IMA International Multimedia Association; consortium of companies that fosters multimedia and interface designers, multimedia standards, and business.

Image Map Graphic that includes embedded spots that link to related files.

IMCO E-mail acronym meaning "in my considered opinion."

IME E-mail acronym meaning "in my experience."

IMHO E-mail acronym meaning "in my humble opinion."

Impression A page view; every time an HTML document is retrieved; request for a Web page on a server; most server log files count impressions, not "hits" to measure the popularity of a Web site.

Indie Independent; unsigned musician, artist, or band.

Instant Relay Chat (IRC) System enabling Internet users to talk to each other in real time.

Interactive Media presentation to a user where user navigates content.

Interface Integrated design of a presentation; the ability to operate technology.

Internet Explorer Popular Web browser from Microsoft; Windows and Macintosh versions.

Internet Phone Program that enables user to use the Internet to talk to others by using a microphone and speakers, instead of long-distance telephone calls.

Internet Radio Streaming digital audio transmissions over the Internet; can be listened to by those with the compatible receiving program.

Internet Society Organization dedicated to supporting the growth and evolution of the Internet.

Internet Network system that allows global communication; system by which all the computers in the world communicate.

InterNIC Internet Network Information Center; keeps track of domain names; a.k.a. Network Solutions; central repository of information about the Internet.

Interrupt Character A key or combination of keys to stop what is happening on a computer.

Intranet Private business network; secure environment to share information within a business and over the Internet; private version of the Internet allowing people within an organization to exchange data using Internet tools.

IOW E-mail acronym meaning "in other words."

IP Address Internet Protocol Address; identifies a computer connected to the Internet; numeric URL; every Internet site has two addresses, the IP address and the URL or domain name.

IRC Chat Real-time text-based chat over the Internet.

ISA Industry Standard Architecture; older type of PC interface (bus) for plug-in cards.

ISDN Integrated Services Digital Network; digital network that permits simultaneous digital voice and data transmission; a type of digital telephone line capable of transmitting combinations of voice and data at up to 128 kbps.

ISO International Standards Organization; group that sets standards for engineering and design concerns.

Isochronous Providing consistent bandwidth to time-sensitive applications.

ISP Internet Service Provider; provides Internet access to its members.

ITU-T International Telecommunications Union; sets worldwide communication standards.

IYSWIM E-mail acronym meaning "if you see what I mean."

Jack A connector that receives another connector into it; a.k.a. a socket; generic term for plug-in connectors on audio equipment.

Java Computer language invented by Sun Microsystems; Java programs can run on any modern computer; ideal for delivering application programs over the Internet; platform-independent programming language; Java-enabled Web pages can include animations, scrolling text, sound effects, and games; many people surf the Web with a Java disabled browser as they don't want to wait for the applet to download; specific programming language that supports enhanced features.

JavaScript Scripting language unrelated to Java; designed by Netscape; embedded into HTML documents.

Jitter Correction Method of reading overlapping blocks of data from CD-ROMs to eliminate jitter.

Jitter Errors introduced into a digital signal because of the seeking inaccuracy of some CD-ROM drives.

JPEG Joint Photographic Experts Group; image compression standard; optimized for full-color digital images; can choose the amount of compression; the higher the compression rate, the lesser the quality of the image has; nearly all full-color photographs on the Web are JPG files; GIFs are used to display clip-art images; type of still-image file found all over the Interet; files in this format end in .jpg or .jpeg and are called JPEG (pronounced "JAY-peg") files.

K 1,000.

Kb Kilobyte 2 to the 10th power (1,024 bytes).

Kbps or **Kb/sec** Kilobits per second; Kilobytes (bytes x 1,024) per second; measurement of the amount of data it takes to make a second of music in an MP3 file.

KHz Thousands of cycles per second.

Kill File File that tells newsreader which newsgroup articles user wishes to skip.

Kilobit or **Kilobyte (Kb)** Rounded a thousand bytes; actually, 1,024 (2 to the 10th power) bytes; 1,000 bytes or characters of data; the smallest unit of computer data storage.

Line-In Jack Designed to accept the output from a line-level output.

Line-Level Range of levels found on inputs and outputs of audio equipment.

Line-Out Jack Bypasses the amplifier of a piece of audio equipment.

Link Marked text or picture within a hypertext document, usually underlined or highlighted; one mouse click brings user to another Web page or to another place on the same page; essential in hypertext documents.

Linux Public-domain version of the UNIX operating system; runs on personal computers; supported by enthusiasts on the Internet.

Listproc Like LISTSERV; program that handles mailing lists.

LISTSERV Programs that automatically manages mailing lists; distribute messages posted to the list; add and delete members so list owner does not have to do it manually; names of mailing lists maintained by LISTSERV often end with "-L."

LMK E-mail acronym meaning "let me know."

Location Internet address as displayed on browser; by typing in the URL of a Web site into the location bar of a browser, the browser will take the user to the Web page.

Log File Audit file of hits to a Web server; file that contains recorded events of a computer system, including server access log files, error log files, etc.

Login To enter into a computer system; the account name or user ID that must be entered before user is allowed access to the computer system.

LOL E-mail acronym meaning "laugh out loud."

Lossless Compression Compression methods in which the compressed file can be decompressed into an exact replica of the original uncompressed file; reproduction methods in which the copy is an exact match of the original data; a compression algorithm in which a compressed image's quality is maintained after decompression.

Lossy Compression Compression method that removes redundant or irrelevant information; can not reproduce an exact copy of the original data; reproduction methods in which the copy is not an exact match of the original.

Lurk To read a newsgroup, mailing list, or chat group without posting any messages; a person who lurks is a "lurker."

Lynx Fast, character-based Web browser with no pictures.

MacBinary File-encoding system popular among Macintosh users.

MacTCP Computer on the Internet that provides mail services.

Mail Server Server of ISP that handles incoming and outgoing E-mail.

Mailing List E-mail-based discussion group on a specific topic; list servers maintain a list of E-mail addresses of subscribers; when an E-mail message is sent to the group, it is copied and sent to all subscribers.

Majordomo Like LISTSERV; program that handles mailing lists.

MB Megabyte 2 to the 20th power (1,048,576) bytes.

Mbone Multicast Backbone; Internet subnetwork supporting live video and multimedia.

Megabyte About one million bytes; exactly 1,048,576 bytes (2 to the 20th power), or 1,024 Kb; one million bytes or characters of data.

Memory Card Nonvolatile, solid-state memory; Compact Flash; SmartMedia.

MHz One million cycles per second.

Mic In Socket on a sound card designed to have a microphone connected to it.

Microdrive Small hard drive that can be used in place of flash memory in some instances; miniature hard disk made by IBM; about the size of a matchbook.

Microsoft Network, The (MSN) Commercial online service; provides many Internet services, including E-mail, Usenet newsgroups, and access to the World Wide Web.

MIDI Musical Instrument Digital Interface; a way to transmit music as actual notes rather than as digitized sounds; many electronic instruments have a MIDI output; a standard for connecting electronic instruments and computers; file format used to store the computer equivalent of sheet music, including a list of which notes are played and what instruments are playing.

Mil When these letters appear as the last part of the Internet address or URL, it indicates that the host computer is run by the U.S. military.

MIME Multipurpose Internet Mail Extensions; used to send pictures, word-processing files, and other nontext information via E-mail.

MiniDisc Small, rewritable optical disc designed by Sony Corporation for recording and playing audio; similar to a CD.

MiniPlug Plug used on the end of headphones for portable tape or CD players.

Mirror FTP or Web server that provides copies of the same files as another server; spreads out the load for more popular FTP and Web sites.

Modem MOdulator-DEModulator. Allows computers to transmit information to each other via telephone lines; communications device that converts analog signals to or from digital data for processing by a computer.

Moderated Mailing List Mailing list run by a moderator.

Moderated Newsgroup Newsgroup run by a moderator.

Moderator Someone who reviews the messages posted to a mailing list or newsgroup before releasing them to the public; moderator may eliminate messages that are inappropriate.

Mosaic Older Web browser.

MP2 MPEG Audio Layer-II.

MP3 Compression standard for music; almost no loss of quality; popular file format.

MPEG3 MPEG Audio Layer-III; standard of audio compression originally designed for inclusion with compressed video.

MP4 Various audio compression schemes considered to be better than MP3, including AAC.

MPC Multimedia PC; Microsoft trademark specifying a standard of an Intel-based CPU with a CD-ROM player, soundboard, speakers, and pointing device.

MPEG Moving Pictures Expert Group. Compression standard for video in a format similar to JPEG; type of video file found on the Internet; files in this format end in ".mpg"; graphics standard for compressed movie clips; MPEGs are smaller than QT or AVI files, but require a powerful processor for playback; standards are labeled MPEG-1, MPEG-2, etc.

MPMan Series of portable MP3 players.

MUD Multi-User Dungeon; started as a Dungeons and Dragons type game for many players; now an Internet subculture.

Multicasting Method of transmitting information allowing multiple users or systems to subscribe to the same stream or channel.

Multimedia Combined use of several forms of media (e.g., text, graphics, and audio) into a product or presentation.

Multiplexing Technique of combining multiple communications channels at the same time.

Navigator Web browser from Netscape.

NBC Not backwards compatible.

Net Surfing Browsing the Internet.

Net Short for Internet.

Netiquette Network Etiquette; code of good manners on the Internet.

Netizen Responsible Internet citizen.

Netlag Condition that occurs on the Internet when heavy "traffic" slows down the server response time.

Netscape Navigator Web Browser for Windows, Macintosh, and UNIX.

Network Computer Computer that lacks a hard disk and receives all data over a computer network such as the Internet.

Network Wire that allows a group of computers to communicate and share resources; computers that are connected together; local area networks; wide area networks; interconnected networks all over the world form the Internet.

Newbie A newcomer to the Internet.

News Server A computer on the Internet that receives Usenet newsgroups.

News Type of Usenet newsgroup that has discussions about newsgroups.

Newsgroup Discussion group on USENET among those who share a common interest; thousands of newsgroups, covering all topics of interest.

Newsreader Program that lets user read and respond to the messages in Usenet newsgroups.

NIC Network Information Center; responsible for coordinating a set of networks so that the names, network numbers, and other technical details are consistent from one network to another.

Niche A dedicated submarket.

Nickname In IRC, the name by which a user identifies him- or herself while chatting.

NNTP Network News Transport Protocol; protocol to transport USENET postings over a TCP/IP network.

Node Computer on the Internet, also called a "host."

Normalization Process of adjusting the level of a digital audio file so that all songs play at the same volume.

Nyquiest Theorem Theory stating that the sampling rate of a signal must be at least twice the highest frequency that needs to be produced.

Objects Data and the computer programs that work with the data.

Offline Not connected to a computer network.

Online Services Online commercial companies, such as America Online (AOL) and Compuserve, that offer Internet and Web access as well as exclusive membership options; connected to a computer network.

OS Operating System.

OTOH E-mail acronym meaning "on the other hand."

Packet A chunk of information sent over a network; each packet includes the addresses sent to and from.

Page Views Page Impressions; hits to HTML pages only; access to non-HTML documents is not counted.

Page Short for "Web page" or one single file on the Web; document available by way of the Internet; pages may include text, graphics files, sound files, and/or video clips.

Parity System for checking for errors when data is transmitted from one computer to another.

Password Secret code that must be entered after user ID or login name in order to log on to a computer; secret code used to keep things private.

Patch Small program used to change or update another program; file that updates a program by modifying or replacing only the parts of the program that have changed.

PCI Peripheral Component Interface; newer type of PC interface (bus) for plug-in cards.

PCM Pulse Code Modulation.

PCMCIA Card or PC Cards Personal Computer Memory Card Industry Association; small plug-in card used on notebook computers or laptops to add features such as a modem, network interfaces, and external drives; look like thick credit cards.

PDF File Method for distributing formatted documents over the Internet; requires Acrobat Reader.

PERL Practical Extraction and Report Language; powerful computer language; used for writing CGI scripts which handle input/output actions on Web pages.

PICS Platform for Internet Content Selection; a way of marking pages with ratings about what they contain.

Pine Popular UNIX-based mail program.

Ping Program that checks to see whether user can communicate with another computer on the Internet; sends a short message to which the other computer automatically responds

PITA E-mail acronym meaning "pain in the ass."

PKZIP File-compression program that runs on PCs; creates a ZIP file that contains compressed versions of one or more files; to restore files to former size and shape, use PKUNZIP or WinZip.

Platform Set of operating system hardware and software standards that dictate functionality; the operating system.

Player Computer or device that plays a multimedia program; device or program that decodes and plays digital audio files.

Playlist File with a list of songs for a player to play or select from; list of songs that can be played in succession, automatically.

Plug-in Small program that another program can run, adding functions to the larger program; small piece of software, usually from a third-party developer, that adds new features to another larger software application; computer program added to a browser to help it handle a special type of file; software module that adds functions to a program.

Plug Connector that gets inserted into a socket.

POP Post Office Protocol; system by which a mail server on the Internet lets user pick up E-mail and download it to PC or Mac; Internet protocol used by ISP to handle E-mail for its subscribers; synonym for an E-mail account.

Port Number Identifying number assigned to each program that is chatting on the Internet.

Posting Single message posted to a newsgroup, bulletin board, or mailing list; article published on or submitted to a Usenet newsgroup or mailing list.

POV E-mail acronym meaning "point of view."

PPP Point-to-Point Protocol; scheme for connecting a computer to the Internet over a telephone line.

Preamp Device that sets the level of an audio signal before it is sent to the main amplifier.

Protocol Set of rules that specifies how data is exchanged; established method of exchanging data over a network or the Internet.

Provider Individual or company that supplies content, supplies, or services.

Psycho-Acoustic Encoding Lossy digital audio compression based on the properties of human hearing.

Public Key Cryptography Method for sending secret messages whereby user gets two keys: a *public key* given out freely so that people can send coded messages and a *private key* that decodes them.

Pulse Code Modulation (PCM) Common format for uncompressed digital audio that uses fixed length pulses to represent binary data.

Qualified Hits Hits to a Web site that deliver information to the end user.

Quantization Rounding of voltage sample values to the nearest integer.

Query String User input to a server on the Internet.

QuickTime Video file format invented by Apple Computer; widely used on the Internet; audio and video encoding and streaming media system; file format for compressing video clips.

RAM Random Access Memory.

RCA Plug Standard connector used for connecting audio and video components.

Real Audio Program that allows the user to immediately hear an online audio file; popular standard for streaming audio.

Red Book Audio Standard format for audio CDs.

Referrer URL of an HTML page that refers to another Web site; link.

Resolution The number of bits used to represent each sample in an uncompressed digital audio signal (e.g., 4.8, 16, or 20 bits).

Return Code The return status of a request which specifies whether the transfer was successful or not and why; 200 = success OK; 201 = success created; 202 = success accepted; 203 = success partial information; 204 = success no response; 300 = success redirected; 301 = success moved; 302 = success found; 303 = success new method; 304 = success not modified; 400 = failed bad request; 401 = failed unauthorized; 402 = failed payment required; 403 = failed forbidden; 404 = failed not found; 500 = failed internal error; 501 = failed not implemented; 502 = failed overloaded temporarily; 503 = failed gateway timeout.

RFC Request for Comment; numbered series of documents that specify how different parts of the Internet work.

Rip To copy the digital audio information from an audio CD onto a computer.

Ripping Digital audio extraction.

ROFL E-mail acronym meaning "rolls on the floor laughing."

Router Sends data packets back and forth between networks; computer that connects two or more networks.

RSA Patented public key encryption system.

RSN E-mail acronym meaning "real soon now."

RTFM E-mail acronym meaning "read the !#%@$ manual"; suggestion made by people who feel their time has been wasted by asking a question the user could have found the answer to by looking it up.

Sample Single digital measurement of a sound wave; a series of samples is used to make a digital audio recording; segments of existing recorded works being included in a new work.

SanDisc Compact brand of flash memory storage.

SCMS Serial Copy Management System.

SCSI Small Computer System Interface.

SDMI Secure Digital Music Initiative; an attempt to create a digital audio file format that will be acceptable to the RIAA by eliminating concerns about uncontrolled digital copying.

Search Engine Web tool site that helps user locate information on the Internet; Web site that allows users to search for keywords on Web pages.

Sector Pie-shaped section of a disc that holds a fixed amount of data; sectors on CDs are often referred to as frames.

Secure Server Server that uses security measures to prevent access by an unauthorized party.

Secured Transaction Online transaction, often involving a credit card number, that uses security measures to prevent access by an unauthorized party.

Serial Port Place on the back of a computer where a modem is plugged in; a.k.a. "communications port."

Server Error Error occurring at the server.

Server Computer that has a permanent connection to the Internet; purpose is to supply information to clients; provides Web site housing and access; designated network computer that stores and manages specific data files; computer that provides a service to other computers known as "clients" on a network.

SGML Standardized General Markup Language; formatting language from which HTML was developed.

Shareware Programs that are distributed at no charge by the publisher, but with the expectation that the user will try them and then pay for them if they find the program useful; computer programs that are easily available to try with the understanding that the user will send the requested payment to the shareware provider specified in the program; an honor system; software that can be freely distributed and evaluated but must be purchased if used beyond a certain time period.

Shockwave Standard for viewing interactive multimedia on the Internet; advanced multimedia authoring and viewing system.

SHOUTcast Streaming MP3 system developed by Nullsoft; popular streaming audio solution supported by Winamp; often used for Internet radio stations.

Signature File Small ASCII text file, up to five lines, automatically attached to the end of an E-mail message; often includes additional information about the author and a hyperlink.

SIG E-mail acronym meaning "special interest group."

Site A place on the Internet; a home page or a collection of Web pages.

Skin File or group of files that creates a different look for a program without changing its function; file that controls the appearance of a program's user interface.

SLIP Serial Line Internet Protocol; software for connecting a computer to the Internet over a serial line.

Smart Agent Web monitoring software that alerts users to changes or updates.

SmartMedia Popular standard for flash memory cards; used by MP3 players, digital cameras, and other portable devices; type of memory card with no onboard controller.

Smiley Combination of special characters that portray emotions; hundreds have been invented, but only a few are in active use; a.k.a. emoticons or "emotion icons"; examples follow:

:-)	with a nose
:)	without a nose
:->	another smile
:-D	said with a smile
;-)	wink
:-(	sad face with a nose
(:-(	full sad face
(:-)	full face
[ ]	hug, usually put around

someone's name, for example [Jason]

[[[[ ]]]]	big hug

SMTP Simple Mail Transfer Protocol; method by which Internet mail is delivered from one computer to another; protocol to send and receive E-mail between servers on the Internet.

Snail Mail Mail delivered by the U.S. Postal Service; refers to its slowness in relation to electronic mail.

SO E-mail acronym meaning "significant other."

Soc Type of newsgroup that discusses social topics.

Socket Connector that one inserts another connector into; a jack; logical "port" a program uses to connect to another program running on another computer on the Internet.

Software Programs and information that a computer uses; in contrast to hardware, which are the actual physical parts of a computer.

Sound Card Internal computer device used to turn computer data into output for speakers, and to digitize audio from outside the computer.

Sound Recording Term that encompasses streaming audio, video, and text.

Spam Junk E-mail; a serious breach of netiquette; the act of posting inappropriate commercial messages to a large number of unrelated, uninterested Usenet newsgroups or mailing lists.

Spider Small piece of software used by search engines for indexing key information.

SSL Secure Socket Layer; Web-based technology that lets one computer verify another's identity and allow secure connections; protocol that allows sending encrypted messages across the Internet; uses public key encryption to pass data between a browser and a given server.

Streaming Audio/Video Technology that allows digital audio or video to play while it is still downloading; system for sending sound files over the Internet that begins playing the sound before the file finishes downloading; RealAudio is the most popular.

Streaming Continuous data transport in the order it was sent without duplication.

StuffIt File-compression program that runs on Macintosh; creates an SIT file that contains compressed versions of one or more files; to restore one of those files to its former size and shape, one uses UnStuffIt.

Suffix The three-digit suffix of a domain can be used to identify the type of organization; .com = commercial; .edu = educational; .gov = government; .int = international; .mil = military; .net = network; .org = organization.

Surf or **Surfing** Browsing the Internet.

Synchronization Process of synchronizing overlapping blocks of sectors to eliminate jitter.

Synchronous Communications between two devices at the same time.

T1 Telecommunications standard that carries twenty-four voice calls or data at 1.44 million bps over a pair of telephone lines.

Tag Piece of descriptive text embedded into an MP3 system.

TCP/IP Transmission Control Protocol/Internet Protocol; the system networks use to communicate with each other on the Internet; the language of the Internet.

Telnet Program that lets user log in to other computers on the Internet; Internet protocol that lets user connect machine as a remote terminal to a host computer somewhere on the Internet.

Terminal Previously consisted of a screen, a keyboard, and a cable that connected it to a computer; can now use a terminal emulator, terminal program, or communications program.

Tethered System Hardware MP3 playing device designed to stay connected to a computer.

Text File File that contains only textual characters, with no special formatting, graphical information, sound clips, or video; a.k.a. ASCII text files.

THD Total Harmonic Distortion.

Theme Different design for a program's appearance, like a "skin."

Thread Article posted to a Usenet newsgroup, along with follow-up articles, etc.

TIA E-mail acronym meaning "thanks in advance."

Time Out When a Web page is requested and the server that hosts the Web page does not respond in a certain amount of time, the user may get the message "connection timed out."

Track An entire song.

Transfer Rate The speed at which data can be transferred.

Triple-Dub Short way to say "www" when giving a URL.

Trumpet Widely used newsreader program that runs on Windows.

TTFN E-mail acronym meaning "ta-ta for now."

TwinVQ Transform-domain Weighted Interleave Vector Quantization; audioencoding scheme developed by the NTT Human Interface lab.

UDP User Datagram Protocol; system used for applications to send quick messages.

Unicasting Method of transmitting information that uses independent streams or channels to send the same information to multiple users.

Unicode Extension of ASCII that attempts to include the characters of all written languages.

UNIX Operating system developed by AT&T.

Upload Sending files from one computer to another computer through the Internet.

URL Uniform Resource Locator; standardized way of naming network resources; used for linking pages together on the World Wide Web; a Web address; URL typed into a browser will access a specific site; means of identifying an exact location on the Internet.

URN Uniform Resource Name; Web page name that doesn't change when the page is moved to a different computer; solution to the broken-link problem.

USB Universal Serial Bus; high-speed interface for personal computers; supports multiple devices.

Usenet System of online message boards available through the Internet; thousands of newsgroups; messages read by using a newsreader.

User Agent Fields in an extended Web server log file indicating the browser and the platform used by a visitor.

User ID Identifier user enters each time a particular service on the Internet is accessed; always accompanied by a password.

User Session Worldwide decentralized distribution system of newsgroups; at least 30,000 newsgroups are available through the Internet.

Uucp UNIX-to-UNIX Copy; old mail system used by UNIX systems.

UUENCODE/UUDECODE Method of encoding files to make them suitable for sending as E-mail.

Variable Bit Rate (VBR) System of MP3 encoding that does not record every segment of the music at the same bit rate.

Viewer Used by Internet client programs to show files other than text.

Virtual Reality 3D visual computer simulation that responds to inputs.

Virtuosa Gold Player/encoder program for MP3s; encoding that does not record every segment of the music at the same bit rate.

Visit User Session; all activity for one user of a Web site; terminated when a user is inactive for more than thirty minutes; to access a Web page. A visit usually includes several hits.

VQF File extension for Twin VQ.

VRML Virtual Reality Modeling Language; Virtual Reality Markup Language; method for creating 3D environments on the Internet; requires a VRML plug-in for browser; standard for designing virtual reality pages.

VT100 Model number of a terminal made in the early 1980s by Digital Equipment Corporation.

Watermarking Method of transparently embedding data in a file to identify the copyright holder.

WAV File Popular Windows format for sound files (.wav files) found on the Internet; common type of audio file, usually uncompressed; pronounced "wave."

Web Page Document available on the World Wide Web.

Web Server Computer that stores and delivers all files for a Web site.

Webmaster The person who is responsible for the Web server.

Winamp Popular player program for MP3s and other digital audio formats.

Winsock Windows Sockets; standard way for Windows programs to work with TCP/IP; application programming interface by which Windows-based Internet-access programs access the Internet.

WinZip File-compression program that runs under Windows; reads and creates a ZIP file that contains compressed versions of one or more files.

WMA Proprietary audio encoding scheme developed by Microsoft.

World Wide Web Hypermedia system that lets user browse through information; central repository of information; Internet client-server system to distribute information, based upon the hypertext transfer protocol (HTTP); a.k.a. WWW, W3, or the Web; created at CERN in Geneva, Switzerland, in 1991 by Dr. Tim Berners-Lee.

WYSIWYG E-mail acronym meaning "what you see is what you get"; phrase used to explain that what you see on the screen is what you will get on a printout.

X.400 Mail standard that competes with the Internet SMTP mail standard.

X.500 Standard for white-pages E-mail directory services.

Xmodem Protocol for sending files between computers; second choice after Zmodem.

XON/XOFF Computer's response when data is coming in too fast; hardware flow control.

YABA E-mail acronym meaning "yet another bloody acronym."

ZIP File File that has been compressed using PKZIP, WinZip, or a compatible program.

Zmodem Protocol for sending files between computers.

Zone The last part of an Internet host name; two letters long indicates the country code in which the organization that owns the computer is located; three letters long indicates a code indicating the type of organization that owns the computer.

Bibliography

Althouse, Jay. *Copyright: The Complete Guide for Music Educators.* Van Nuys, CA: Alfred Publishing Co, Inc., 1997.

Bates, Jefferson D. *Writing with Precision.* New York: Penguin Books, 2000.

Besenjak, Cheryl. *Copyright Plain and Simple.* Franklin Lakes, NJ: Career Press, 1997.

Blesh, Rudi. "Scott Joplin: Black American Classicist" in *Scott Joplin Collected Piano Works.* Miami, FL: Warner Bros. Publications, 1971.

Bloom, Jason. *Six Steps to Songwriting Success—The Comprehensive Guide to Writing and Marketing Hit Songs.* New York: Billboard Books, 1999.

Bond, Sherry. *The Songwriter's and Musician's Guide to Nashville.* Cincinnati, OH: Writers Digest Books, 1991.

Bradney, Gail, and Lowell Miller. *Wholesale by Mail and Online 2000.* New York: Harper Collins, 1999.

Buchmam, Dian Dincin, and Seli Groves. *The Writers Digest Guide to Manuscript Formats.* Cincinnati, OH: Writers Digest Books, 1987.

Burt, George. *The Art of Film Music.* Boston: Northeastern University Press, 1994.

Bye, Dean. *You Can Teach Yourself about Music.* Pacific, MO: Mel Bay Publications, 1989.

Churchill, Sharal. *The Indie Guide Book to Music Supervision for Films.* Los Angeles: Filmic Press, LLC, 2000.

Cool, Lisa Collier. *How to Write Irresistible Query Letters.* Cincinnati, OH: Writers Digest Books, 1987.

Cooper, Helen. *The Basic Guide to How to Read Music.* New York: AMSCO Publications, 1986.

Cupit, Jerry. *Nashville Songwriting.* Nashville, TN: Cupit Music, 1995.

Curtis, Richard. *How to Be Your Own Literary Agent.* Boston: Houghton Mifflin Company, 1984.

Davis, Sheila. *The Craft of Lyric Writing.* Cincinnati, OH: Writers Digest Books, 1985.

Dawes, John, and Tim Sweeney. *The Complete Guide to Internet Promotion for Artists, Musicians, and Songwriters.* Temecula, CA: Tim Sweeney and Associates, 2000.

Dearing, James W. *Making Money Making Music (No Matter Where You Live).* Cincinnati, OH: Writers Digest Books, 1982.

Delton, Judy. *The Twenty-Nine Most Common Writing Mistakes and How to Avoid Them.* Cincinnati, OH: Writers Digest Books, 1985.

Downing, Douglas, and Michael Covington. *Dictionary of Computer Terms.* Hauppauge, NY: Barron's Educational Series, Inc., 1992.

Editors of *Songwriter's Market.* *The Songwriter's Market Guide to Song and Demo Submission Formats.* Cincinnati, OH: Writers Digest Books, 1994.

Eiche, Jon. *What's MIDI?—Making Musical Instruments Work Together.* Milwaukee, WI: Hal Leonard Publishing Corporation, 1990.

Fries, Bruce, with Marty Fries. *The MP3 and Internet Audio Handbook—Your Guide to the Digital Music Revolution.* Burtonsville, MD: TeamCom Books, 2000.

Gerou, Tom, and Linda Lusk. *Essential Dictionary of Music Notation.* Van Nuys, CA: Alfred Publishing Company, Inc., 1996.

Gibson, James. *How You Can Make $30,000 a Year As a Musician without a Record Contract.* Cincinnati, OH: Writers Digest Books, 1986.

Goldberg, Natalie. *Writing Down the Bones.* New York: Quality Paperback Book Club, 1990.

Goldstein, Jeri. *How to Be Your Own Booking Agent.* Charlottesville, VA: The New Music Times, Inc., 1998.

Guiheen, Annamarie, and Marie-Reine A. Pafik. *The Sheet Music Reference and Price Guide.* Paducah, KY: Collector Books, 1995.

Hamm, Charles. *Music in the New World.* New York: W. W. Norton and Company, 1983.

Harnsberger, Lindsey C. *Essential Dictionary of Music.* Van Nuys, CA: Alfred Publishing Company, Inc., 1976.

Harris, James F. *Philosophy at 33-1/3 RPM—Themes of Classic Rock Music.* Chicago, IL: Open Court, 1993.

Higgins, William R. *A Resource Guide to Computer Applications in Music Education.* Grantham, PA: Messiah College, 1994.

Hill, Brad. *Internet Directory for Dummies.* Foster City, CA: IDG Books Worldwide, 1999.

Hill, Dave. *Designer Boys and Material Girls.* New York: Landford Press, 1986.

Hustwit, Gary. *The Musician's Guide to the Internet.* San Diego, CA: Rockpress Publishing, 1997.

———. *Websites for Musicians.* San Diego, CA: Rockpress Publishing, 2000.

Irvine, Demar. *Writing about Music.* Seattle: University of Washington Press, 1979.

Jamsa, Kris. *Welcome to Personal Computers.* New York: MIS Press, 1992.

Josefs, Jai. *Writing Music for Hit Songs.* New York: Schirmer Books, 1996.

Kasha, Al, and Joel Hirschorn. *If They Ask You, You Can Write a Song.* New York: Simon & Schuster, 1989.

Kimple, Dan. *Networking in the Music Business.* Cincinnati, OH: Writers Digest Books, 1993.

Klavens, Kent J. *Protecting Your Songs and Yourself.* Cincinnati, OH: Writers Digest Books, 1989.

Krasilovsky, M. William, and Sidney Shemel. *This Business of Music.* New York: Billboard Books, 2000.

Kushner, David. *Music Online for Dummies.* Foster City, CA: IDG Books Worldwide, 2000.

Larsen, Michael. *How to Write a Book Proposal.* Cincinnati, OH: Writers Digest Books, 1985.

Levine, John R., Carol Baroudi, and Margaret Levine Young. *The Internet for Dummies.* Foster City, CA: IDG Books Worldwide, 1997.

Levine, Michael. *The Music Business Address Book.* New York: Harper and Row, 1989.

Levitin, Dan. *From Demo Tape to Record Deal.* Van Nuys, CA: Alfred Publishing Company, Inc., 1992.

Linderman, Hank. *Hot Tips for the Home Recording Studio.* Cincinnati, OH: Writer's Digest Books, 1994.

Livingston, Robert Allen. *Music Business Reference.* Cardiff-by-the-Sea, CA: La Costa Music Business Consultants, 1988.

Luboff, Pat, and Pete Luboff. *Eighty-Eight Songwriting Wrongs and How to Right Them.* Cincinnati, OH: Writers Digest Books, 1992.

Maran, Richard. *Creating Web Pages Simplified.* Foster City, CA: IDG Books Worldwide, Inc., 1996.

———. *Internet and World Wide Web Simplified.* Foster City, CA: IDG Books Worldwide, Inc., 1997.

Mash, David S. *Computers and the Music Educator.* Melville, NY: SoundTree, 1996.

———. *Musicians and Computers.* Miami, FL: Warner Bros. Publications, 1998.

———. *Musicians and Multimedia.* Miami, FL: Warner Bros. Publications, 1998.

———. *Musicians and the Internet.* Miami, FL: Warner Bros. Publications, 1998.

McCormick, Scott. *The Musician's Guide to the Web.* Pennsauken, NJ: Disc Makers, 2000.

MENC. *Growing Up Complete—The Imperative for Music Education.* Reston, VA: MENC, 1991.

———. *National Standards for Arts Education.* Reston, VA: MENC, 1994.

———. *The School Music Program: Description and Standards.* Reston, VA: MENC, 1986.

Metter, Ellen. *Facts in a Flash—A Resource Guide for Writers from Cruising the Stacks to Surfing the Net.* Cincinnati, OH: Writers Digest Books, 1999.

Monaco, Bob, and James Riordan. *Platinum Rainbow.* Sherman Oaks, CA: Swordsman Press, 1980.

Muench, Teri, and Susan Pomerantz. *Attention A & R.* Van Nuys, CA: Alfred Publishing Company, 1988.

Murrow, Don. *Sequencing Basics.* Miami, FL: Warner Bros. Publications, 1998.

Nackid, Terri, ed. *The MTNA Guide to Music Instruction Software.* Cincinnati: OH: Music Teachers National Association, 1996.

NAMM. *NAMM 2000, 2001 International Music Market Show Directory.* Carlsbad, CA: NAMM, 2000, 2001.

Newer, Hank. *How to Write Like an Expert about Anything.* Cincinnati, OH: Writers Digest Books, 1995.

Noad, Frederick. *The Virtual Guitarist—Hardware, Software, and Web Sites for the Guitar.* New York: Schirmer Books, 1998.

Northam, Mark, and Lisa Anne Miller. *Film and Television Composer's Resource Guide.* Los Angeles: CinemaTrax, 1997.

NSAI. *The Essential Songwriter's Contract Handbook.* Nashville, TN: NSAI, 1994.

Oland, Pamela Phillips. *You Can Write Great Lyrics*. Cincinnati, OH: Writers Digest Books, 1989.

Patterson, Jeff, and Ryan Melcher. *Audio on the Web—the Official IUMA Guide*. Berkeley, CA: Peachpit Press, 1998.

Pattison, Pat. *Writing Better Lyrics*. Cincinnati, OH: Writers Digest Books, 1995.

Pickow, Peter, and Amy Appleby. *The Billboard Book of Songwriting*. New York: Billboard Publications, 1988.

Poe, Randy. *Music Publishing*. Cincinnati, OH: Writers Digest Books, 1997.

Prendergast, Roy M. *Film Music—A Neglected Art*. New York: W. W. Norton Company, Inc., 1977.

Rabin, Carol Price. *The Complete Guide to Music Festivals in America*. Great Barrington, MA: Berkshire House, 1990.

Rachlin, Harvey. *The Songwriter's and Musician's Guide to Making Great Demos*. Cincinnati, OH: Writers Digest Books, 1988.

———. *The Songwriter's Handbook*. New York: Funk and Wagnells, 1977.

Randall, Robin, and Janice Peterson. *Lead Sheet Bible*. Milwaukee, WI: Hal Leonard Publishing Company, 1997.

Randel, Don. *The New Harvard Dictionary of Music*. Cambridge, MA: Belknap Press of Harvard University Press, 1986.

Rapaport, Diane S. *How to Make and Sell Your Own Recording*. Englewood Cliffs, NJ: Prentice Hall, 1992.

Rudolph, Thomas E. *Teaching Music with Technology*. Chicago, IL: GIA Publications, Inc., 1996.

Rudolph, Thomas, Floyd Richmond, David Mash, and David Williams. *Technology Strategies for Music Education*. Wyncote, PA: Technology Institute for Music Educators, 1997.

Russell, William. "Notes on Boogie Woogie" in *Frontiers of Jazz*, ed. by Ralph de Toledano. New York: Ungar Pub., 1962.

Schock, Harriet. *Becoming Remarkable for Songwriters and Those Who Love Songs*. Nevada City, CA: Blue Dolphin Publishing, Inc., 1998.

Schuller, Gunther. "The Future of Form in Jazz" in *Saturday Review*, January 12, 1957, 62.

Sharp, J. D. *Home Recording Techniques*. Van Nuys, CA: Alfred Publishing, Inc., 1992.

Skolnik, Peter L. *Fads*. New York: Thomas Y. Crowell Company, 1978.

Stanfield, Jana. *The Musicians Guide to Making and Selling Your Own CDs and Cassettes*. Cincinnati, OH: Writers Digest Books, 1997.

Stangl, Jean. *How to Get Your Teaching Ideas Published*. New York: Walker and Company, 1994.

Starr, Greg R. *What's a Sequencer?—A Basic Guide to Their Features and Use*. Milwaukee, WI: Hal Leonard Publishing Corporation, 1990.

Stern, Jane, and Michael Stern. *Encyclopedia of Pop Culture*. New York: Harper Perennial, 1992.

Stewart, Dave. *The Musician's Guide to Reading and Writing Music*. San Francisco: Miller Freeman Books, 1999.

Trubitt, David. *Managing MIDI*. Van Nuys, CA: Alfred Publishing Company, Inc., 1992.

Tucker, Susan, and Linda Lee Strother. *The Soul of a Writer*. Nashville, TN: Journey Publishing Company, 1996.

Underhill, Rod, and Nat Gertler. *The Complete Idiot's Guide to MP3: Music on the Internet*. Indianapolis, IN: Que Corporation, 2000.

Uscher, Nancy. *Your Own Way in Music—A Career and Resource Guide*. New York: St. Martin's Press, 1990.

Waterman, Guy. "Ragtime" in *Jazz*, ed. by Nat Hentoff and Albert McCarthy. New York: Rinehart & Co., Inc., 1959.

Waugh, Ian. *Music on the Internet (and Where to Find It)*. Kent, U.K.: PC Publishing, 1998.

Webb, Jimmy. *Tunesmith—Inside the Art of Songwriting*. New York: Hyperion, 1998.

Westin, Helen. *Introducing the Song Sheet*. Nashville, TN: Thomas Nelson, Inc., 1976.

Whitmore, Lee. *MIDI Basics*. Miami, FL: Warner Bros. Publications, 1998.

Williams, David Brian, and Peter Richard Webster. *Experiencing Music Technology—Software, Data, and Hardware*. New York: Schirmer Books, 1996.

Williams, Robin. *The Little Mac Book*. Berkeley, CA: Peachpit Press, 1993.

Wills, Dominic, and Ben Wardle. *The Virgin Internet Music Guide Version 1.0*. London: Virgin Publishing Ltd., 2000.

Zollo, Paul. *Beginning Songwriter's Answer Book*. Cincinnati, OH: Writers Digest Books, 1993.

About the Author

Elizabeth C. Axford (B.A., Music, University of Illinois, Urbana-Champaign; M.A., Musicology, San Diego State University) is an independent piano instructor and freelance writer living in Del Mar, California. She is an active member of the California Association of Professional Music Teachers (CAPMT), an affiliate of the Music Teachers National Association (MTNA). She is also an active member of the Nashville Songwriters Association International (NSAI), serving as regional workshop coordinator in both Miami, FL (1990-1992) and San Diego, CA (1992-present).

Ms. Axford has been teaching piano, keyboard, music theory, and voice to students of all ages, levels, and backgrounds since 1984.

She has attended or produced over one hundred songwriting, music industry, and piano pedagogy seminars and conferences in San Diego, Miami, Los Angeles, and Nashville. Ms. Axford is a published songwriter and arranger of piano music, as well as a published poet. Her song *Personal Touch* has been licensed by MDVD Network to be recorded by the new boy band *Fresh*. She is the online keyboard columnist for Indie-Music.com. Other publications by Ms. Axford include *Traditional World Music Influences in Contemporary Solo Piano Literature* (Scarecrow Press, 1997), *Merry Christmas Happy Hanukkah—A Multilingual Songbook and CD* (Piano Press, 1999), and *Shadows from the Clouds—A Collection of Poems and Vignettes* (Piano Press, 2001).

Born in Van Nuys, California in 1958, Ms. Axford has lived in six different states, including California, Texas, Illinois, New Mexico, Kansas and Florida.

NORTHERN ILLINOIS UNIVERSITY

3 1211 01252881 2